eading Key

)eep, Short, and Compound.
:s *sound* is shown in **bold** typ

so	sure	**ch**ur**ch**	**y**ea	hu**ng**
zoo	mea**S**ure	**j**ud**ge**	**w**oe	**h**a-**h**a
ado	**o**n	w**oo**l	**ou**t	**ah**
up	**oa**k	**oo**ze	**oi**l	**aw**e
rray	**ear**	**I**an	**yew**

y single letters : **the** ϱ, **of** ſ, **and** ι, **to** ʼ.
receding ' Namer ' dot : e.g. ·ƆOſ, Rome.
ιe alphabet *in pairs*, as listed for Writers overleaf.

Bernard Shaw
VOLUMES IV & V

Bernard Shaw

MICHAEL HOLROYD

Volumes IV & V
The Shaw Companion

Chatto & Windus

LONDON

Published in 1992 by
Chatto & Windus Ltd
20 Vauxhall Bridge Road
London SW1V 2SA

A CIP catalogue record for this book
is available from
the British Library.

ISBN 0 7011 3755 X

Photoset and printed by Redwood Press Limited
Melksham, Wiltshire

Designed by Ron Costley
Index by Vicki Robinson

CONTENTS

PREFACE

Money is the most important thing in the world.
Preface to *Major Barbara*

'I wish that there could also come later the posthumous life of Shaw,' wrote Anthony Burgess when reviewing my apparently final volume on G.B.S. in *The Observer*. He wanted 'the saga of the estate, the failure of the alphabetic project, the success of *My Fair Lady* which, we've been told, ravaged Shaw's financial afterlife with fantastic and ruinous imposts'. *The Last Laugh*, following the tributaries of two Last Wills and Testaments, attempts to trace that sequel. It is a biography of Shaw's afterlife: a non-fiction, Anglo-Irish comedy of novella length showing how a writer's aspirations and those of his wife were ingeniously diverted in the crosscurrents of modern market economies.

'You would certainly think anyone mad if he claimed to own the air or the sunlight of the sea,' Shaw wrote in the 1920s. Sixty years later it is perhaps G.B.S. who looks rather mad after a decade of privatization. The very frontiers of privacy have moved. There is greater secrecy now surrounding people's financial commitments than their personal relationships. When I began this biography in the mid-1970s I believed that I was writing a work of cultural history. As 'Victorian values' were partially re-introduced, however, many of the social issues over which Shaw had campaigned began to be refought. Latterly he achieved the Shavian position of being simultaneously successful and discredited. He remains controversial. By current standards you cannot ignore a writer whose estate makes almost half-a-million pounds a year more than forty years after his death.

In some respects this epilogue is a peculiarly English narrative. Set amid the persisting legal fogs that fill *Bleak House*, it points parenthetically to the financial adjustments and social conceits of a country in historical decline, plots some awkward connections between yesterday's patronage and today's sponsorship, and follows the mysterious wanderings of individual quixotry through a dense world of business ethics.

Finally it reminds us of the brevity of our collective memory.

To my twenty chapters of biography spread over four volumes I have now added some nine thousand reference notes. From academic readers in particular I have received plenty of encouragement with this task, and I thank them kindly. The method I have used for these notes was pioneered by Janet Adam-Smith in her biography of John Buchan (1965) and developed independently by myself and by Alan Bell in his *Life of Sydney Smith* (1980) – we discovered accidentally that we were using the same system. The reasons for their appearance at the end of the biography and not with each volume have been set out in the bibliographical notes printed in *The Search for Love* and *The Lure of Fantasy*. I have worked often from manuscript sources or photocopies of manuscripts, diaries and letters especially, that have later been published in scholarly volumes. Wherever possible I have listed these volumes retrospectively as my sources and by doing so hope to make these notes more easily usable and up-to-date. The labour of revising my abridged references and matching them to the exigencies of a grander house style has been gallantly shared by Vivian Elliot. Her industry and good nature in cleansing what she calls my 'foul copy' and making it fair cannot be exaggerated.

This volume also contains a new appendix covering Shaw's films, an addition to my Postscript, and a cumulative index prepared by Vicki Robinson from her four previous indexes which should provide a shield against the critic who volunteered to shoot me on my doorstep if such a valuable device were lacking.

'How often I have said, in my life ... It is the end, and it was not the end, and yet the end cannot be far off now,' wrote Samuel Beckett in *From An Abandoned Work*.

This is the end.

THE LAST LAUGH

1950–1992

Concerning the dead
Nothing ill should be said
So of Shaw let us say:-

> To an age in decay
> He was prophet and priest,
> Providing the yeast
> For the dough of our doubt;
> So puffing it out
> It *appeared* to make bread
> And we *seemed* to be fed.
> His dream was that we
> Could be equal and free
> By dictator's decree
> G.B.S. ... R.I.P.

Colin Hurry, November 1950

'Well, now as to practical matters. You may have an idea that Ive flung my money about; but I havnt: I'm richer today than when I first came into the property. Ive used my knowledge of the world to invest my money in ways that other men have overlooked; and whatever else I may be, I'm a safe man from the money point of view.'

Mrs Warren's Profession, Act III

THE LAST LAUGH

I

All mercantile transactions were accompanied with music, so that they were called Musical Banks . . .
Samuel Butler, *Erewhon*

Shaw's will, when it was published in March 1951, turned out to be a most unpopular document. 'Had he deliberately set out to ensure that the least possible profit should accrue to future generations from his wealth,' commented *The Economist*, 'it is hard to see how he could have done better.' Several newspapers carried the same incredulous headline: 'Left a fortune for reform of alphabet.' It seemed as prodigiously silly as anything since Labiche's statistician set out to enumerate the widows crossing the Pont Neuf.

The gross value of his estate amounted to £367,233 (equivalent to £5,000,000 in 1990). It was an extraordinary sum for a writer: Thomas Hardy had left £91,000 in 1928; G. K. Chesterton £28,000 in 1936; J. M. Barrie £173,500 in 1937; H. G. Wells £60,000 in 1946. In due course an assessment of his copyrights would have to be added to Shaw's estate, and since G.B.S. himself had calculated that these copyrights 'may run into six figures', the total fortune had every chance of rising to a glittering £500,000. What was to become of this spectacular wealth, largely accumulated over the years from money spent by the public on books and theatre tickets? Apparently it had been fool's gold, an old fool's gold, and was posthumously reverting to base metal. People felt the same sense of loss as if they had been tricked out of a lawful prize. Such squandering struck them as unpardonable in the early 1950s.

The British public had been living through more than a decade of austerity which only now was coming to an end with the final lifting of food rationing and the long-awaited opening of the Festival of Britain. Six million people paid five shillings to step from a past world of grey skies and khaki clothing, export rejects, bomb sites, into the bright new architecture of coloured festival pavilions with dazzling murals and futuristic shapes topped by a filigree 'Skylon' tower taller than any

3

building in London and prevented from taking off into the heavens, it appeared, by its almost invisible cables. At the centre of the festival, like a science fiction vision, stood the miraculous Dome of Discovery. Aeronautical technology developed in the war was suddenly being put to domestic and industrial use. People wondered whether this was a mirage of Modernism or the blueprint for a new world.

To recover from post-war 'hunger, poverty, desperation and chaos', Britain had borrowed over $2,500,000,000 in Marshall aid from the United States, more than any other European country. By the beginning of 1951 her overseas trade enabled her to dispense with further borrowing, yet she appeared to have traded away part of her sovereignty. The cultural, educational and intellectual practices in which Shaw had sought to invest his posthumous copyright income were to be eroded by the need to make Britain's academies, galleries and museums part of an expanding entertainment industry. With its thirty acres of pleasure gardens and fun fairs in Battersea, the Festival of Britain would retrospectively look more like a theme park for tourists than a commemoration of the Great Exhibition that in 1851 had converted its profits into funds for scholarships.

It was the worst of times for financing scholarship in the arts and humanities. Many Americans felt they had already sent over more than they could afford, while everyone in Britain needed to spend money on themselves. Nevertheless a Shaw Memorial Fund was set up in 1951, its objects being to subsidize young authors, dramatists and musicians, encourage the 'worthy presentation' of Shaw's own plays at festivals, and maintain the fabric of Shaw's Corner which he had given to the National Trust without an endowment. Though these aims were more acceptable than reforming the alphabet, the public did not see why it should have to pay for them when there was so much of Shaw's own money apparently going to waste. 'I regret that the public should be asked, at this time, to subscribe a quarter of a million pounds to undertake three enterprises, one of which is unnecessary, the second of which is unimportant, and the third of which is dangerous,' wrote Rebecca West. '. . . I do not know why such a fund . . . should be associated with the name of Bernard Shaw, who preferred to help literature in another way and had a right to do so if he chose.' The fact that Clement Attlee, the Prime Minister, was associating himself with the campaign, together with a rumour that it was to have the support of the Labour Government, made the venture all the more untimely. Following some hesitation, its opening was delayed until after the general election which that October swept Attlee from office and returned the Conservatives to power. Within a few days all the Festival of Britain structures except the Concert Hall were dismantled, leaving people wondering whether this new architecture had been built to last like 'proper' buildings in the past, or even the tower blocks and symmetrical housing estates that were spreading round them; or alternatively whether it had merely been a collection of adult toys.

On 23 November, the new Chancellor of the Exchequer R. A. Butler (who that year was elected President of the Royal Society of Literature and later created Baron Butler of Saffron Walden) launched the appeal as 'a world tribute to Shaw's memory'. He looked forward to some 'spectacular donations', for 'if there was to be a tribute to Shaw it must be on a worthy scale'.

'A passable Shavian comedy could be worked up out of the meeting held this afternoon to open the Shaw memorial appeal,' reported the *Manchester Guardian*. Almost at once the proceedings were splattered with confusion. Lady Astor got to her feet and described how she had implored G.B.S. on his deathbed to renounce his alfabet trusts. She appealed to the Chancellor of the Exchequer 'to break that ridiculous will', adding darkly that the money would be better spent in establishing a society to save Shaw 'from his so-called friends'. Her outburst appeared in all the national newspapers. The actor Sir Lewis Casson also took the floor, accusing the National Trust of making 'a great mistake' in accepting Shaw's 'dreadful house'. Lewis had been Drama Director of the Council for the Encouragement of Music and the Arts (CEMA, the precursor of the Arts Council) and, until recently, President of British Actors' Equity. His opinions were also widely reported. Finally Marie Stopes pleaded for the money to be used instead for a life-size statue of G.B.S. in Adelphi Gardens, and the meeting broke up discordantly leaving Shaw's biographer St John Ervine 'full of doubts and disapproval'.

'I do not know of any precedent for such a tribute to the memory of any man of letters,' cautioned T. S. Eliot. '... The work of Mr Shaw is not likely to be forgotten. Several of his plays should certainly be included in the repertory of a National Theatre; they will, in any case, be performed so long as England retains any pride in its theatre. I cannot see why the plays of Mr Shaw, simply for their dramatic merit, should enjoy an advantage over the plays of Shakespeare, Jonson, Congreve, Yeats and Synge, among which some of them already have an assured place.' The target was £250,000 (equivalent to more than £3,000,000 in 1990) and the total eventually reached £416 (£6,000 in 1990). It was 'a complete failure and a disastrous flop', lamented Archibald Henderson.

Yet Shaw's finances were not quite what the public perceived them to be. The net value of his estate was £301,585 of which £180,571 became immediately due in death duties. Nor was this all. Once the copyrights had been valued, 70 per cent of this notional amount would have to be paid in additional death duties. Besides this, there were more than a dozen annuities in Shaw's will, mostly bequests to those who had worked for him at Ayot and in London, which had to be met each year. Since his royalties were bringing in less than £50,000 a year, and might soon decrease (his earliest plays shortly coming out of copyright in the United States), there seemed a likelihood that the alfabet trusts, which were confined to twenty-one years from his death so as to avoid the legal taint of perpetuity, would be largely washed out. No one could tell what would happen. Towards the end of 1951 public attention turned to what the *Star* called 'The "Tangled Will" of Mrs Shaw'.

*

Charlotte Shaw had bequeathed £94,000 to Ireland for educational purposes. The main provisions in her will resemble clauses from the five wills Shaw himself made between 1901 and 1937. She wanted the money to be used for three objects: bringing masterpieces of fine art, including music and painting, within the reach of all classes of Irish people; teaching Irish people the secrets of self-control, elocution, oratory and deportment; and the endowment of a Chair or Readership at an Irish University for instruction in these matters of fine art and social intercourse. Her wishes were considered so unusual that the National Provincial Bank, as trustee of her estate, brought the matter before the Chancery Division of the High Court in London to determine whether under English law they constituted a valid charitable trust.

The last day of November 1951 was dubbed 'Irish Day' by the English newspapers. Solicitors and barristers from all the interested parties gathered in the courtroom of Mr Justice Vaisey. The English bank questioned the will, and an Irish bank defended it. The Attorney-General supported it and was himself supported by the Public Trustee on behalf of Bernard Shaw's estate. But lawyers representing Charlotte's next of kin challenged the trusts as being void by reason of remoteness and uncertainty.

Everyone thoroughly agreed on Charlotte's highmindedness. She had made her will in 1937 and after a pause, a pause of fourteen years, it had come for mature examination to Chancery. A murmur of approval went round the court when the judge described it as 'a very interesting document revealing a mind of a very high quality and a lady with every wish to do right'. It was at Chancery because 'the lady seems to have got tangled up in a web of her own verbosity and it makes it very difficult to untangle her'. No one recognized the unconscious pun relating to Sidney Webb who had helped to draft Charlotte's will. They were relishing what they conceived to be the fanciful Shavian circumlocutions of the case. There was laughter in court when his lordship said he detected 'an inspiration which derives from another source, but I must not say where'.

Charlotte's will seemed oddly lacking in the good manners she sought to promote. 'It is not very complimentary to those people she hoped to benefit, is it?' the judge inquired.

'It does occur to me that if a person of Irish domicile were to promote a trust for curing the awkward manners, vulgarities of speech and social impossibilities of English people, then it would be regarded as not very well calculated to add to the friendliness of the nations.'

There was more laughter when Sir Charles Russell, a King's Counsel instructed by the National City Bank (an Irish bank appointed as the ultimate trustee under Charlotte's will), replied: 'quite frankly, my lord, we are prepared to accept these insults.'

The case was to be decided less by legal argument than by the self-control and deportment of contending counsel. Charlotte had bequeathed her niece Cecily Colthurst £20,000 which was paid to her in 1944. But if the court declared a partial intestacy and Charlotte's wishes were blocked, then Mrs Colthurst would inherit the extra £94,000. Here was a case that needed to be presented with delicacy if it were not to appear grasping. But Pascoe Hayward KC, representing Mrs Colthurst, was not delicate. While Sir Charles Russell politely referred to Charlotte as a 'serious-minded lady dealing with a serious subject', Mr Pascoe Hayward called her a 'cranky' person whose large fortune was in danger of being lamentably 'frittered away' by a lot of other 'cranky people'. It would be open to her trustees, he protested, to encourage social intercourse by giving 'a series of cocktail parties'. Were he himself a trustee, he persisted, he would instil self-control by building plenty of good strong nourishing prisons and seeing 'that people who do not control themselves go there'. These trusts were 'doomed to failure', he concluded, for the very proper legal reason that there was no precedent for them. So how could the public benefit? 'There is no evidence that anyone in Ireland – and they do the maddest things in Ireland – has ever tried to instruct anyone in social intercourse.'

'"Finishing School" for the Irish People', announced the *Manchester Guardian* on 4 December. 'Disposal of Mrs Shaw's Money Settled.' Refusing to test the validity of the trusts by presupposing perverse ways of applying them, Mr Justice Vaisey (otherwise Sir Harry Vaisey) decided that under English law Charlotte had kept herself within the necessary limits 'by a rather narrow margin'.

So the money passed out of England into Ireland. 'How the people of Ireland will react to such intensive treatment as Mrs Shaw appears to envisage', Mr Justice Vaisey remarked, 'I ought not to speculate.' But a ripple of delirious speculation was already passing over the twenty-six counties of the Republic. 'Ireland Seeks Shaw Culture', announced the newspapers. '£94,000 Rush For Grants By Mrs G.B.S.' Before long almost a hundred applications had been prepared by universities, cultural groups, local authorities and some enterprising individuals demanding art galleries, gramophone records, endowments for lectures, subsidies for theatres. '£94,000 sounds a lot of money,' parried an official at the National City Bank in Dublin, 'and many of the applicants seem to have dreams of building palaces.' £94,000 *was* a lot of money in the early 1950s, equivalent to a little over £1,000,000 in the early 1990s. People were impatient to show off the flicker and dazzle of their new deportment. But the bands got no new instruments, and no foundations for new libraries were laid. After a year, cultural life in Ireland seemed unchanged; and after two years it was still further unchanged. The National and Municipal Art Galleries in Dublin did not know what was going on, neither did the Royal Academy of Music nor the Dublin School of Art, and their cumulative lack of knowledge was comprehensively shared by the Abbey and Gate theatres. 'Where is the £94,000?' the *News Chronicle* demanded.

There were excellent banking reasons for this inactivity. For until the £94,000 had accrued sufficient interest to make possible grants of 'some £3,000 a year', positively nothing could be done.

The first results of Charlotte's bequest were witnessed in the summer of 1954 at a hostel in Termonfeckin, County Louth, where forty students assembled for a week of instruction by artists, linguists, and the director of a mannequin agency. The successful applicant had been Forás Éireann, an *omnium gatherum* of native 'sons of the soil' formed in 1949 to plant village halls in rural communities. 'The students will be available later to conduct other similar courses throughout the country,' reported the *Irish Independent*. Forás Éireann 'hopes to be able to lend itself further to the purposes of the bequest'. So it was to be...

...and so it still is. Under the Trustees Act of 1893 the National City Bank retired and appointed the Bank of Ireland in its place. But Forás Éireann continues to distribute Charlotte's money as part of its policy for developing rural Ireland in accordance with 'Christian and national ways of life'. No Chair or Readership has been established at any Irish university. After forty years of capitalist expansion and inflation the value of Charlotte's money would have risen to almost £1,250,000 if it had kept level with the cost-of-living index. In fact the size of annual donations suggests that it has fallen dramatically. 'Each year we spend, roughly, about £2,500 to £3,000 under the heading of Art,' writes the Trust organizer at Forás Éireann, 'and this is used to support smaller ventures throughout the twenty-six counties.'

'It is the policy of the Bank,' writes the Bank of Ireland, 'for confidentiality reasons, not to reveal any details about the financial aspect of the Trust.'

Charlotte's grand pretensions, with all the hopes once circling them, had in any case fallen behind a constellation of events that began to cluster and pulse round G.B.S.'s will in the centenary year of his birth.

*

On 15 March 1956 a spectacular musical adaptation of Shaw's phonetic romance *Pygmalion* opened at the Mark Hellinger Theater on Broadway. *My Fair Lady* contained fifteen numbers composed by Frederick Loewe with lyrics by Alan J. Lerner, and it was directed by Moss Hart. Yet the production was in many ways a very English affair. With his irrepressible leer and roguish eye, his stentorian roar, Stanley Holloway played the undeserving dustman Doolittle in a broad style that derived from the old music hall tradition ('With a Little Bit of Luck', 'Get me to the Church on Time'). He incorporated the same ironic cheerfulness he had earlier brought to the gravedigger in *Hamlet*. Stella Campbell's part as the flower girl was taken by the twenty-one-year-old Julie Andrews. Known mostly as a pantomime performer in Britain, she had recently won a devoted American following in *The Boy Friend* and was to complete her conquest of New York by singing and dancing Eliza's new role ('Wouldn't it be Loverly', 'I Could Have Danced All Night') with charming expressiveness. Rex Harrison brought off a histrionic triumph by turning his lack of singing voice into the half-rasping, half-caressing baritone patter of Henry Higgins's 'I'm an Ordinary Man', 'A Hymn to Him' and 'Why Can't the English'. Cecil Beaton's rich costumes, which ranged from a street crowd of raffish cockney buskers to the wheel hats and feathered parasols of Mrs Higgins's fashionable tea-party and the mock-stately black, white and grey pageant of the 'Ascot Gavotte', were to be taken up by New York *couturiers* and judged to be more attractive than all the posters of the British Tourist Board. *My Fair Lady* seemed one of those rare theatrical collaborations in which everyone, working on top form, came harmoniously together. Like the comic operas of Gilbert and Sullivan, like *The Merry Widow*, *Oklahoma!*, *Annie Get Your Gun* and *Me and My Girl* (which also derives from *Pygmalion*), this new musical exerted a lasting attraction. Moss Hart's production was to run on Broadway for 2,717 performances over six and a half years, by which time $55,000,000 had already been made from performances round the world, plus another $10,000,000 from recordings and film rights, breaking all financial records.

Even at the previews in New Haven it was obvious that *My Fair Lady* was destined to be a popular success. This prospect, together with a rise in the number of international performances of Shaw's plays, suddenly brought his six-year-old will into new focus.

*

The Official Trustee Act introduced by the Liberal Government in 1906 had created an official whose advantage over private and commercial trustees was to lie in the certainty that trust funds which he administered would never be embezzled, lost in speculation, or misdirected. Shaw had appointed the Public Trustee as his executrix in a will he made in 1913 and in all subsequent wills. 'I was a strong advocate of a Public Trustee long before 1906,' he wrote.

Referring to Shaw's last will, the Public Trustee Wyndham Hirst (later Sir Wyndham Hirst) had stated in 1951 that his 'primary duty' was to satisfy all legatees and annuitants. Research into the proposed new alfabet was to remain 'a secondary matter' and could be considered 'only if anything is left over'. Owing to the 'very material increases in death duties', there did not appear much danger of serious money being left over. So the alfabet could safely be laid to one side. 'It may be several months, or even years, before we can submit all the valuations necessary for a final assessment,' an official in his department hazarded. For five and a half years, while lodging a 'corrective affidavit' to show additions to the estate, the Public Trustee sat negotiating with the Estate Duty Office. Then, in the spring of 1956, they hit on the figure of £433,500. It was a handsome amount, indeed unprecedented, bringing the net value of Shaw's estate nicely beyond £700,000 (equivalent to £6,250,000 in 1990) and raising the final death duties to a magnificent pinnacle of £524,000 (£4,750,000 in 1990). More than half this sum was due at once and might possibly be swelled by a further generous accretion of interest. Nevertheless, it would still not be a substantial enough obstacle to keep the fearful alfabet long entombed. As the alfabet's custodian, there was only one judicious course of action open to the Public Trustee, and that was to bring the whole matter to Chancery, where it would be placed under the scrutiny of the High Court. On 26 March 1956, eleven days after the successful opening of *My Fair Lady* on Broadway, *The Times* announced in London that the British Museum was to challenge the validity of these alfabet trusts. When a question about Shaw's will was asked in the House of Commons the following month, the Chancellor of the Exchequer, Harold Macmillan (later Lord Stockton), was able to reply that 'the matter is *sub judice* and I can make no statement...'

It was not easy for interested members of the public to find their way to the case when it opened in January 1957. On the Warned List it had appeared somewhat eccentrically as 'Public Trustee v. Day and Others', Fred Day being Shaw's gardener, whose annuity (with that of his wife) was to be reviewed during the first morning. Several wandering Shavians were gathered up and mistakenly conducted to the more glamorous business of Diana Dors, the 'blonde bombshell' who was petitioning for a divorce in another court nearby. Extricating themselves from the crowd, they finally settled into the more reposeful atmosphere of the Lord Chancellor's Court and, during the long implacable afternoon, heard the legal distinction between 'benevolent' and 'philanthropic' begin to drift backwards and forwards over the network of Shaw's Last Will and Testament.

'The Lord Chancellor's Court is Gothic in more than architecture,' observed the *Manchester Guardian*. 'Mr Justice Harman's face in repose

– elongated and narrow-eyed, with the light falling on it from above –
might at times have been that of a medieval king in effigy. The lethargy
that sometimes overtook the spectators as precedents were unrolled
might have put them in mind of something very old and long lasting – the
case of Jarndyce v. Jarndyce, say – rather than the quick by-play of the
court scenes in "The Devil's Disciple".'

Shaw had believed that the need for alphabetical reform arose from
the fact that there were more sounds in the English language than there
were letters in its Latin alphabet. Some letters were therefore used to
signify more than one sound and the language was choked with illogical
two-letter combinations, such as *sh*, *th* and *ng*. This notorious orthography, perverting the natural logic of children's minds, was partly responsible for the high proportion of semi-literates in Britain and had slowed
down the spread of English as an international language. English usage
was overloaded with unnecessary grammar and tedious penwork. These
convictions sprang perhaps from Shaw's own backward years at school
and his need to escape deprivation in Ireland.

All this Shaw had argued in his lifetime. But believing his main
contribution to the cause of alphabet reform to be that of propaganda,
supported by money, he advanced the economic case for reform in his
will. 'Write up in letters of gold round your office,' he had instructed
James Pitman in 1947, '*England Knows Nothing of Phonetics, Hates Education, But Will Do Anything For Money*.' Having found no public department or learned society to nominate as the executant of his easy alfabet,
he had been obliged to create two private trusts. The first was designed
to find out, by means of statistical inquiry, how much time could be saved
by people who spoke the English language and wrote it using the
proposed alfabet, thereby showing the extent of time and labour wasted
by the use of the present alphabet, and then, if possible, to make a
calculation of this waste in terms of loss of money. The second trust was
to transliterate *Androcles and the Lion* into the phonetic alfabet, assuming
a given pronunciation of English, to publish and advertise this transliteration in a special bi-alphabetic edition with the existing alphabet on
one side and the proposed alfabet on the other, and so by the dissemi-
nation of copies in public libraries and by the general debate this would
give rise to, persuade the Government or public or English-speaking
world to adopt it.

The legal machinery used by the Chancery Division of the High
Court of Justice to test the validity of Shaw's trusts was the Preamble to

the Statute of Queen Elizabeth I. Of the five categories of charity there enumerated, two appeared *prima facie* applicable to this case: the third category which was education, and the fourth category which was public utility.

There were four parties represented in court. The Attorney-General was in it *parens patriae*, as the official protector of charities. His counsel, Mr E. Milner Holland QC (later Sir Edward Milner Holland) contended that the trusts were legal charities and could not be invalidated for unenforceability or uncertainty since the Charity Commissioners might modify them if necessary to see that the testator's wishes were carried out in spirit even if they could not be carried out to the letter. The Public Trustee was in it as Shaw's executor. Though unable to conceal his personal opinion that these alfabetical matters were a lot of poppycock, he argued through his counsel, Mr Robert Lazarus, that even if the trusts were not charitable, he should be allowed to carry out the provisions of Shaw's bequest. The British Museum and the Royal Academy of Dramatic Art were in it as ultimate residuary legatees and had instructed Sir Charles Russell QC – the same Charles Russell who had so successfully fought for Charlotte's Irish trust over five years earlier – to contest the validity of these alfabetical trusts. The third residuary legatee, the National Gallery of Ireland, had engaged Mr K. E. Elphinstone *not* to contest the validity of the trusts. 'Is that in order to put the court in a greater difficulty by having no help from you, or what?' inquired Mr Justice Harman. To which Mr Elphinstone replied that the Governor and Guardians of the National Gallery of Ireland 'did not want to put forward any argument to defeat the intention of a very distinguished fellow-Irishman in a matter very dear to his heart'. He did not explain that, Irish charity laws being stricter than English, his participation might imperil the contestants' claim.

The residuary legatees were in a very favourable position, for even if they lost the case, all Shaw's royalties after 1971 would still automatically become theirs. But if they won it, the royalties would go to them immediately in three equal portions. 'They may be likened to a schoolboy who has a half-share in a bottle of pop, half of which gets spilt when the bottle is opened, and who proceeds to drink all that is left because *his* half-share was at the bottom,' wrote Barbara Smoker, a founder member of the Phonetic Alphabet Association. 'Not content with having the comparatively safe bottom half of the Shaw residue, the British Museum and the Royal Academy of Dramatic Art have also been claiming in the Chancery Court whatever can be salvaged of the top half – which will be so much more now than seemed likely a year ago.'

There were seldom more than thirty members of the public in court – mainly a scattering of intellectual-looking old gentlemen, some middle-aged women in astrakhan collars and brown hats, a few young Indian and Scandinavian students of British justice. There was also the thirty-three-year-old Barbara Smoker.

Barbara Smoker occupied two attic rooms without inside sanitation on Catford Hill. She was a freethinker, ate very little meat, and bought her clothes mainly at jumble sales. Barbara Smoker had no job, but made a meagre living by winning competitions – literary competitions and competitions on the backs of tins and packets for slogans, jingles, ditties – with a little journalism besides.

Barbara Smoker had no job but she was always busy. On Thursdays, for example, she could be heard on her soap box at Tower Hill contradicting what the Methodist minister Donald Soper (later Baron Soper) had been saying on Wednesdays. She was a passionate campaigner, coherent, courageous, iconoclastic, unconquerable in her crusade against the Big Lie of religion. For forty years she was to persist, without a job, working round the clock as Chairman of the Voluntary Euthanasia Society, President of the National Secular Society, a champion of the Family Squatting Movement, a force within the Radical Alternatives to Prison Committee.

She had come to the Chancery Court in her dual role as secretary of the Phonetic Alphabet Association and assistant secretary of the Shaw Society. It had not been easy. When Shaw's solicitors informed her they were allowed to divulge no information whatever, not even the date of the hearing, she took to telephoning the Public Trustee; and when she found he was never in his office, she wrote him letters which though acknowledged were never answered. Finally she had gone to the court itself, made friends with an official there, and arranged to speak to him each day until the case opened.

The setting and proceedings promised 'little scope for cut-and-thrust comedy', regretted the *Manchester Guardian*. '. . . Shaw and the Gothic do not mix.' But amid their blue bags and pink ribbons, their interminable briefs, learned counsel essayed quite a few comic recitatives. They questioned whether Shaw's name should begin with a *P*. When Charles Russell cited a precedent involving a man who left a legacy to a horse and a dog which the court found was not charitable, Mr Justice Harman objected that there was no horse or dog in Shaw's will. 'No, My Lord, but I submit there is some analogy between a pet animal and a pet hobby.' To which his Lordship conceded: 'I suppose they might both be called hobby-horses.'

Sir Charles Russell was an impressive advocate on behalf of the British Museum and the Royal Academy of Dramatic Art, and his speeches, enriched with many gnarled precedents and crackling Latin tags, made very pretty hearing. Listening to him from the public gallery, it took Barbara Smoker several minutes to realize that no one without prior knowledge of phonetics, and the allied subjects of typography and shorthand, could possibly understand that most of his mellifluous statements were rubbish. It appeared that she was the one person in court who had this purifying knowledge – indeed she was bursting with it. It was crucial that she educate learned counsel. Except for an affidavit from Daniel Jones, the Professor Emeritus of Phonetics at the University of London, and despite some expert advice from Shaw's old colleague James Pitman (whose heart quite frankly was in simplified spelling rather than alphabet reform), the Attorney-General's case sounded pitifully unprepared. Incredible as it seemed, he knew nothing of Jesperson and Zamenhof, or even the difference between inflected and agglutinated language! When Barbara Smoker heard Charles Russell claim that the alfabet trusts would require a change of law because they were analogous to political trusts, when she saw this contention go unchallenged, knowing herself that nothing more would be involved than had been needed for the teaching of shorthand as a supplementary means of writing or the invention of Morse Code, she could bear it no longer. *My Lord!*

But 'there was nothing I could do there and then unless I wanted to risk being sent out of the court.' When the case was adjourned for the day, however, and before it was resumed next morning, she was on to the Attorney-General's counsel, and he could not throw her off. Though she was in her own words 'a mere nobody', Mr E. Milner Holland QC had little option but to receive her evidence.

He had no sense of the avalanche he had set in motion. From the public gallery she descended to the body of the court and into the thick of the fight. Each day with her pens and papers she would set about demolishing the British Museum and the Royal Academy of Dramatic Art. At the end of each day she had amassed thousands of potent words ready to slip into Mr E. Milner Holland's briefcase. She filled his bag with facts – facts about David's *Neuhand*, Kunowski's *Sprechspur*, the Ridge-Beedle design system, the Erhard Roman Augmented and Dewey's work on the relative frequency of English speech sounds. She gave him evidence to study in the evenings on the educational use of phonetic lettering in more than sixty West German schools, and explained why the word 'though' in two letters supported his case while the word 'enough' in four did not. Sometimes, quite often in fact, when especially horrified by the court's ignorance, she could not restrain herself from sending over sheaves of writings to him in court. She was disappointed to find that it was considered bad form for barristers to refer to notes, let alone read out well-prepared arguments. It seemed that everything must appear to flow in a spontaneous stream of inspiration. When some of her points, involving delicate phonetic technicalities, came out strangely garbled, she also discovered that it was impossible for any self-respecting barrister to correct himself. But she wrote on and was pleased to see that by the end of the week, when Mr E. Milner Holland QC opened his tremendously bulging briefcase and she looked into its jaws, over half the material to be digested there was her own.

'Public Trustee v. Day and Others' spread itself over nine days with a three-day adjournment. This was Barbara Smoker's first experience of Chancery. Visiting Mr E. Milner Holland QC in his chambers she was horrified to find him catching up with his other cases. Each night she had been typing out her notes, while he had been merely using his train journeys for the Shaw case. He reassured her somewhat, however, by explaining that he had omitted much of her scholarly advice because it referred to legally irrelevant issues. The fact that these issues were being introduced by opposing counsel was, he added, a sign that the opposition was worried.

The hearing ended with Sir Charles Russell quoting a line from *Androcles and the Lion* – 'Did um get an awful thorn into um's tootsum wootsum?' – and querying whether a phonetic transliteration of this speech would really be charitable. Mr Justice Harman reserved his judgment for four weeks.

*

When making his will Shaw had discovered that his solicitor, unable to credit the alfabet trusts, had drafted the clauses as if they were ingenious devices for tax avoidance. He was therefore obliged to take up the pen and redraft some of these passages himself. What he wrote, though clear enough to the man or woman on the Clapham Omnibus, baffled the lawyers, while the legal repetitions and prolixities of the skilled equity draughtsman looked in their baroque magnificence like gibberish to the ordinary reader. It was an awkward mixture of styles, 'a marriage of incompatibles', admitted Mr Justice Harman when delivering his reserved judgment on 20 February 1957. The 'delicate testamentary machinery devised by the conveyancer could but suffer when subjected to the *cacœthes scribendi* [urge to write] of the author', he regretted, 'even though the latter's language if it stood alone, might be a literary masterpiece'. The long and complicated document had been made when Shaw was in his ninety-fourth year but it 'was rather youthful exuberance than the hesitations of old age that marred its symmetry', his lordship remarked.

Mr Justice Harman did not sound hostile to G.B.S. He described him as 'an indefatigable reformer' who had acted as 'a kind of "itching powder" to the British public, to the English-speaking peoples and indeed to an even wider audience', bombarding them all with 'such a combination of paradox and wit that he became before his death a kind of oracle – the Shavian oracle'.

English orthography and pronunciation, he continued, were obvious targets for the reformer.

'It was as difficult for the native to defend the one as it was for the foreigner to compass the other. The evidence showed that for many years Shaw had been interested in the subject. Perhaps his best known excursion in the field is *Pygmalion* ... It was indeed a curious reflection that this same work, tagged with versicles which I suppose Shaw would have detested, and tricked out with music, which he would have eschewed ... was now charming huge audiences on the other side of the Atlantic and had given birth to the present proceedings ... receipts from this source had enabled the executor at length to get on terms with the enormous death duties payable on the estate, thus bringing the interpretation of the will into the realm of practical politics.'

Mr Justice Harman took more than an hour to read his judgment. 'Who was to say whether this project was beneficial?' he asked. The answer, of course, was that Mr Justice Harman was to say. He confessed to some reluctance in preventing a man disposing of his own money as he thought fit. Nevertheless this was what he was going to do. He was 'not at liberty' to confer a halo of charity on the trusts because they appeared merely 'to tend to the increase of public knowledge'. In the end it was excruciatingly simple. The trusts were for an object rather than a person and an object could not complain to Chancery which therefore was not able to control the trust and so would not allow it to continue. Consequently the will created neither a valid charitable trust, his lordship concluded, nor a valid unenforceable trust. Both trusts therefore being void, the three residuary legatees were entitled to come into their inheritance at once – as soon as all legal expenses had been settled.

This summing-up pleased the lawyers. Mr Justice Harman, they reminded themselves, was himself an Irishman. They congratulated him on blending law and literature in a brilliant pastiche of Shaw's lucid style that 'will hold its place in any company in any age', stated Lord Birkett. Two years later Mr Justice Harman was created Lord Justice Harman, and in 1961 his judgment found a place in *The Law as Literature: An Anthology of Great Writing in and about the Law* published by The Bodley Head, which not long afterwards took over from Constable as the publishers of Shaw's own work.

It was a setback, Shavians agreed, but hardly a defeat. In the 1940s, having read of a Chancery judge who ruled as invalid a bequest leaving the testator's property to community centres and handed the money instead to the next of kin, Shaw had accepted that he must run a similar risk. 'If nothing happens, or the bequest fails through any cause', he wrote to James Pitman in the summer of 1944, 'I have provided alternative destinations for the money which will prevent its being "left in the air" in any case.'

'I cannot guard against litigation over my definition of a British alphabet; but as I attach much more importance to advertisement of the need for the alphabet than to the success of my attempt to provide it my ghost will be perfectly satisfied if the lawyers and litigants keep the subject in the headlines for the twenty years' perpetuity limit.'

The two stalwarts in this business of keeping Shaw's alfabet in the headlines were Barbara Smoker and the half-Irish Old Etonian publisher and educationist James Pitman. One in Catford, the other in Chelsea, they formed an odd but admirable team. Pitman, then in his young fifties, was an engagingly eclectic character who had been an international athlete, director of the Bank of England and for the last dozen years Conservative Member of Parliament for Bath. 'He was not very quick on the uptake,' Barbara Smoker severely noted, and he wrote 'in the most appalling Pitman shorthand I had ever seen'. He would end each day in chaos, but all was smoothed back into order next morning by his perfect secretary, Miss Blisset. Spelling reform circulated in Pitman's blood: it was his love, and eventually his infatuation.

It was amazing to Pitman that the judge had found his way to such a consummate misinterpretation of Shaw's clearly expressed intentions. It was equally amazing that the Attorney-General had no wish to appeal. As soon as the judgment had been given, Pitman called a press conference under his own name and that of his fellow dare-devil Barbara Smoker. The costs of the Chancery case were estimated at between £6,000 and £10,000 and an appeal would require over £3,000 more. Apparently undeterred by the fate of the Shaw Memorial Fund six years earlier, Pitman suggested opening a public subscription, to be managed by the Shaw Society, which would facilitate the appeal or alternatively assist the implementation of Shaw's wishes privately. In confidence Pitman told the Shaw Society that if the subscription failed he would put up the money himself.

The press conference was well attended and became front-page news when journalists later reported that Pitman had been rebuked for holding it by the Attorney-General Sir Reginald Manningham-Buller (then nicknamed Sir Reginald Bullying-Manner, and later created Viscount Dilhorne). This vexing business was beginning to plague the Attorney-General. He wished it would go away. Instead he was obliged to issue a statement reminding the press that James Pitman was not a party to the case. They had spoken 'casually' in the Division Lobby at Westminster, and the Attorney-General felt distressed that their conversation, being 'of an informal, confidential, and private character', should have been made public. It was breaching club rules. Naturally he would appeal if there were grounds for doing so. But, of course, there weren't. On 7 May the two of them clashed again, this time in public on the floor of the House of Commons, and their irritated exchanges occupied twelve columns of Hansard's official report, further appeasing Shaw's ghost.

James Pitman and Barbara Smoker disagreed on many things. They disagreed on the conduct of the case in Chancery, on the legitimate grounds for an appeal, and on the conflicting merits of simplified spelling versus phonetic reform. But they campaigned together in confident Shavian style. While he kept matters boiling in the House of

Commons, bending some ears and boxing others, she composed press statements from her lair in the Shaw Society which were quoted in news bulletins and reproduced in *The Times*. She did more: throwing out many thousands of words, loaded with research findings, in lectures, articles, and unanswered correspondence to the Attorney-General. 'But I do not kid myself that it does very much good,' she admitted.

By the summer they had attracted some unexpected support from the United States. A New York attorney, Mrs Clara Richter, flew into London 'hell bent with a mission from God' to set the English law right. Following a late *levée* at the Dorchester Hotel, *The Times* reported that she would be representing the American Theater Council and had obtained an 'encouraging' legal opinion in London. 'She plainly let it be known what kind of woman the various authorities concerned would be up against,' commented *The Shavian*, 'and quite frankly we think they deserve it.'

The difficulty facing these campaigners was that the public cared nothing for alphabet reform. Fumes of sanctity shrouded the conventions of established language. If shamed and goaded, the public would probably have applauded the anonymous defender of English orthography who, a few days after Shaw's death, had paid the statutory shilling to file a protest against his will on the ground that it would 'gravely affect the majesty of the English language and would have serious repercussions on English literature'.

Barbara Smoker and James Pitman could not reach the Attorney-General but, by somehow keeping it all in the newspapers and by obtaining a counsel's opinion that was not utterly unfavourable, they did force some action out of the Public Trustee who, on the last day allowed, lodged an appeal. His case was the same as it had been in the Chancery Court, namely that the trusts might be valid even if not charitable, and that he should therefore be allowed to carry out Shaw's wishes. Knowing by now that this was an impossible position in law (and influenced perhaps by his Dickensian name of Mr Baulkwill), many Shavians believed that the Public Trustee had secretly been supporting the British Museum. On appeal this case had become a pretence behind which negotiations for an out-of-court settlement could take place. 'Efforts are being made to reach agreement, I understand, between certain beneficiaries under the will and the Public Trustee, who is Shaw's executor, and the Attorney-General,' reported *The Daily Telegraph* on 29 October 1957.

When 'Public Trustee v. Day and Others' came up before the Court of Appeal on 19 December, the court approved the terms of this agreement. 'My only regret,' said the Master of the Rolls, Baron Evershed (who was assisted by Lords Justice Romer and Ormerod) 'is that we are deprived of hearing what might have been very interesting arguments.' Counsel for the Public Trustee agreed: 'From a lawyer's point of view it is rather a pity.' Counsel for the Attorney-General, for the Trustees of the British Museum and the Royal Academy of Dramatic Art, for the Governors and Guardians of the National Gallery of Ireland all joined in the laughter.

*

The terms of this compromise were made public by Mr Baulkwill immediately the appeals had been dismissed. A sum of £8,300 (equivalent to £70,000 in 1990) had been entrusted to him by the residuary legatees, and he was allocating £500 of this amount as the prize in a competition for the new phonetic alfabet. The closing date was to be 1 January 1959, and he had appointed a committee of assessors to help him with the task of finding a winner: Peter MacCarthy, Head of the Department of Phonetics at the University of Leeds, Alan Dodson, chief typographer at the Stationery Office (who later resigned on going to live in South Africa), and James Pitman. The copyright of the new alfabet would be vested in the Public Trustee who would try to persuade the English-speaking world to use it. 'It will take any intelligent person only twenty-four hours to learn it with slow progress,' James Pitman predicted.

With an army of 50,000 transliterated copies of *Androcles*, Pitman believed the new model alfabet would prove invincible. But to Barbara Smoker's mind £8,300 was a 'paltry sum' which might possibly fund a bi-alphabetic *Androcles* but could never promote the vital statistical survey into phonetic economy. In seizing the shadow of Shaw's idea, might they not be losing something of substance? 'The three residuary legatees may confidently expect to share more than a hundred times the alphabet allocation,' she complained; 'so they have hardly strained the quality of mercy in favour of a cause which their benefactor had at heart.'

She too had this cause at heart. But she could not carry her complaints too far without appearing churlish to James Pitman. It was he who had negotiated the £8,300 and without him the poor alfabet might have received nothing at all. Alternatively it might have been awarded

£15,000 or won the appeal. Once more they disagreed, once again they sank these disagreements in their adjoining passion. They wanted to free the association between ideas and signs from common conventions. For the subject held a compelling beauty for them. They knew the public was deaf to these harmonious symbols and their reverberating possibilities. They knew that they might be classed with idiots who 'scribbled obscene pencillings in public lavatories'. Nevertheless, like the person who invented zero in the numerical system and gave rise to dreams of riches, they shared a common purpose of lifting this alphabetic burden, carved in stone in the dim ages, from the human mind. In their differing styles, they dreamed of replacing man's antiquated utensils and unearthing the clue to a mystery: why was it that spoken communication had always been comparatively rapid, easy and delightful, and written communication cumbrous and wearisome? Was there a deficiency in the optic nerve, a superiority in the aural nerve? This was a fundamental question on which the continuation of our literary tradition might depend. 'Why do we use a long series of arbitrary marks to represent what the voice utters at a single effort?' Sir Isaac Pitman had asked in his *Introduction to Phonography*. 'Why, in short, are not our *written signs* as simple as *spoken sounds*?' Shaw had reminded James Pitman of his grandfather's words when inviting him to keep a friendly eye on the progress of his will. To carry through the alphabetical clauses in this will, 'which generously and ingeniously sought to achieve for the language he so greatly loved the dearly cherished hopes of an exceptional man', was now James Pitman's sacramental mission.

My Fair Lady began its record-breaking run at London's Drury Lane Theatre in the spring of 1958. By the autumn James Pitman had inserted a two-page advertisement of the proposed alfabet into the programme sponsored by the silversmiths Mappin & Webb. Many of Shaw's ideas 'were so novel and penetrating that they were rejected by his contemporaries', he wrote, '– and this particular idea was so novel, and so demanding in its need to think freshly, that very few people have yet understood it'. He requested members of the audience to 'keep a space in your bookshelf' for the bi-alphabetic *Androcles*. Designs for the new alfabet were coming in from all parts of the world, and when eventually it was established we could look forward to savings in paper, ink, machine-time, storage and transport 'of £3,000,000 or $10,000,000 *a day*'.

By the end of 1958, four hundred and sixty-seven valid entries for the contest had been received by the Public Trustee. More than half of them came from the United Kingdom, but there were sixty from the United States, forty from Canada, eleven from India, ten from Germany, six from Ireland and several from Africa, South America and Eastern Europe. 'We were astonished by the merit and quantity of the work produced,' remarked James Pitman a year later. It had taken him and Peter MacCarthy the whole of 1959 to find a winner and even then they had failed to do so, coming up instead with four 'semi-winners'. Dr S. L. Pugmire, a psychiatrist working with mentally handicapped children at the Whittingham Hospital near Preston, had produced a geometric design; Mr Kingsley Read, the author of *Quickscript*, who had designed everything from pavilions for trade fairs to suits of armour for pageants and had corresponded with G.B.S. in the 1940s, submitted a cursive system; and there were script or 'current' alfabets from Mrs Pauline Bassett from Nova Scotia and Mr J. F. Magrath, an insurance broker, who had worked out his design on daily train journeys between London and Kent. All of them received cheques for £125 and the Public Trustee announced that the four winning alphabets would be co-ordinated to produce a final design for use in implementing Shaw's wishes. 'We are launching a ship,' declared Mr Baulkwill, 'and we don't know where it's going.'

It did not look to Barbara Smoker as if this vessel would get far. She regretted Shaw's failure to tie up his trusts with infant literacy. Had he nominated Enid Blyton's *Noddy* instead of his own *Androcles* the Chancery Court decision would have 'undoubtedly gone the other way'. She also deplored the absence of any expert calligrapher or educational psychologist among the assessors, and pointed out that any fusion between the four winning designs was impossible. James Pitman however felt exuberant. The final alfabet was an improved version of Kingsley Read's aesthetically pleasing forty-eight letter 'sound-writing' system. It contained little reference to the other three versions but was 'better than most other alphabets', conceded Barbara Smoker who was to be employed as specialist editor on the new *Androcles*.

In February 1961 *The Times* announced that this special edition of *Androcles* 'is likely to be on the bookstalls by early autumn'. By December the Public Trustee, who had now been knighted, forecast publication early in the New Year. On 26 February the *Daily Mail* unveiled a scoop:

'The secret publishers of the weird, phonetic version of *Androcles and the Lion* which George Bernard Shaw provided for in his will, have been unmasked.

'And it turns out that this is another scoop for Sir Allen Lane and his Penguins, who published *Lady Chatterley's Lover*, the money-spinner of 1961.'

The delay had been largely caused by contradictory instructions from Pitman, Penguin, the expert Phonetician and the Public Trustee, Sir Reginald Baulkwill. Eventually Barbara Smoker 'walked out in a huff' leaving Hans Schmoller, the publisher's renowned master of typography, floundering among the hieroglyphics of 'the world's strangest typeface'.

Androcles and the Lion, An Old Fable Renovated by Bernard Shaw with a Parallel Text in Shaw's Alphabet to be Read in Conjunction Showing its Economies in Writing and Reading was finally published on 22 November 1962. The Public Trustee's issue comprised 13,000 copies of which 12,680 were presented free to libraries: 1,900 within the United Kingdom, 1,230 around the Commonwealth, 8,690 to the United States, 710 to Canada and throughout South America and 150 to 'National Libraries of the World'. Approximately 34,000 copies of an ordinary issue costing 3s 6d were on sale to the public, an indeterminate number being exported to the United States from the second English impression. Within each copy a white Guide Card was inserted on which two keys to the alphabet (one arranged phonetically for writers, the other graphically for readers) were duplicated from the last pages of the book. There were also some 'Suggestions for Writing' supplied by Kingsley Read, some 'Notes on the Spelling' from Peter MacCarthy and a Foreword by the new Public Trustee, C. R. Sopwith (Sir Reginald Baulkwill having retired to Devon). The book was dedicated to James Pitman, now Sir James Pitman KBE, 'in grateful acknowledgement of his unstinted co-operation and continuous support over a period of nine years in carrying out Bernard Shaw's wishes'.

It was a kind of triumph. The poetry lay in its algebra and arithmetic, and in the mysterious dream encoded by these symbols and ciphers. In a disarming Introduction James Pitman sought to advise readers on the choreography of its use. 'Open the book and hold it upside down in front of a mirror,' he counselled. '. . . Keep the back of the book pressed against your lips, and advance towards the mirror until you are able to see individual characters clearly enough to be able to copy them.' Before long, he promised, users would be able to speed up such exercises and for those who attained gymnastic facility 'reading may be 50–75 per cent, and writing 80–100 per cent faster, and even 200–300 per cent, by using simple abbreviations'. He urged owners of this wonderful book to make their friends buy copies so that they could all correspond with one another in the new script. The following year he offered to form circles of five or six of these correspondents who, 'drawn together in a friendship by Shaw's alphabet, will all circulate their own letters to which each in turn will add'. But the success was more experimental than popular, and Pitman remained puzzled as to why these dancing circles never joined and multiplied as he hoped. He was disappointed too by the conservatism of the Ministry of Education which was offered Shaw's alfabet in principle, in draft and upon completion, and turned it down at all three stages. But Shaw's trusts did assist in the temporary success of Pitman's Initial Teaching Alphabet for children, and encouraged him to go on and on battering at the walls of prejudice until his death in 1985.

Barbara Smoker still campaigns. From time to time, when not producing strings of verse with which to tie up the deity, conducting gay and lesbian weddings, speaking from the public gallery of the House of Commons against the Vietnam War or, an elderly lady now, being knocked to the ground with her Free Speech banner by crowds of Muslims calling for the death of Salman Rushdie, she has returned to her alphabetic high ground to see if the walls have yet come tumbling down. 'History is certainly on the side of a new alphabet,' she believes. '... It is absurd that in the twentieth century we should still be using what is basically the ancient Phoenician alphabet, with its cumbersome letters and its bad phonetics ... If Shaw's dream comes true – a dream shared by men of vision for nearly five centuries – who knows what miracles of human progress it may bring in its wake?'

The interest in Shaw's alfabet rose with the renovated *Androcles* and then waned. There were few funds left for the clinical survey. Peter MacCarthy handed this over to one of his students, Gordon Walsh, who went off to conduct his investigations from the University of Ife in Nigeria. The first part of his paper was completed in September 1967. But since 'Shavian is not available in Nigeria', Gordon Walsh concluded, it was 'necessary for tests to be conducted in Britain'. A year later *The Times* announced that the report was finished and that there would 'shortly be an exploratory meeting' to discuss whether it should be published. In January 1970 *The Scotsman* revealed that the results would soon be made known. 'If my report had been dramatic or epoch-making,' volunteered Peter MacCarthy, 'it would have been doubtless published before.' When questioned about the findings in March 1970, the Public Trustee, Mr Brian Davies (Sir Charles Sopwith having gone to the Inland Revenue), replied: 'It's not very urgent, and I'm very busy.' Though he had forecast early publication, he privately believed that publication was impossible. There was no more money (equivalent to nothing in 1990) for tests to be conducted in Britain. The impression of a full report was conveyed, and an appearance of publication presented sometime in the 1970s. The conclusions 'hardly caused a ripple of public interest', Barabara Smoker vaguely recalled. In any event, as Peter MacCarthy made plain, all that had been attempted was the technical discharge of the Public Trustee's obligations. Sometimes he wondered if it had all been a Shavian joke.

2

Why not a Financial Symphony?
Shaw to Elgar (29 June 1932)

In the spirit of the new age, public interest quickly veered off from the letters to the figures, following the trail of money to the three residuary legatees. There had been rumours that Shaw's bequest to the British Museum was enabling the government to cut back its normal subsidy. 'I impress upon the Financial Secretary that the last thing Bernard Shaw would have wished was to relieve the Treasury,' said the Labour Member of Parliament Emrys Hughes. Sir Edward Boyle, Financial Secretary to the Treasury, assured the House that G.B.S.'s literary work had not been financing an armaments programme. When reminded by James Pitman that Shaw's bequest to the trustees of the British Museum had been 'in acknowledgment of the incalculable value to me of my daily resort to the Reading Room of that Institution', Sir Edward Boyle revealed that over the two years money had been coming in from Shaw's royalties, £163,924 had been received by the museum, and up to £85,000 was owing to it in repayments of tax levied on the income of the estate prior to the settlement of the court action (the total equivalent to £2,000,000 in 1990). The terms of the bequest were legally 'unrestricted' in the sense that the trustees of the museum were free to do what they liked with this money and all further income over the next forty years. But since the income would virtually cease after the year 2000, when the main copyrights lapsed, a capital fund had been set up. And so that 'no act of discourtesy was done to the dead', explained Sir Edward Boyle, the trustees of the British Museum had decided that income from this capital sum 'should in due course be used primarily for the benefit of the library'.

Two years later the museum's assistant secretary reported that most of the money received had been invested by a firm of merchant bankers 'on the best terms the market will offer'. In answer to a question from the Fabian Member of Parliament John Parker, a Vice President of the Shaw Society, the Under-Secretary of State at the Department of Education and Science, Jennie Lee (later Baroness Lee of Asheridge), stated that £646,417-4s-3d (equivalent to £4,000,000 in 1990) had come to the British Museum as its share in Bernard Shaw's estate by the end of 1965.

'Sir David Wilson and the trustees are to be congratulated on the funds they have raised to improve the display of the collections,' wrote Lord Annan in 1991. During the previous fifteen years the royalty income of the Shaw Estate had settled down to between £275,000 and £500,000 a year. 'I conclude that in the fullness of time the whole library department of the Museum will benefit,' a *Sunday Times* journalist had predicted. But when the library department separated from the museum in 1973, no reference was officially made to a Shaw capital fund to be used 'primarily for the benefit of the library'.

Donations from the Shaw Fund towards heritage purchases by the British Museum Manuscripts Department and the British Library between 1960 and 1990 amounted to approximately £400,000 – or a little over £13,000 a year on average. Such donations were given as 'a matter of grace' on the part of the British Museum Trustees, and since the British Library executive was never shown the accounts of the Trust it could not know how small a proportion of the Shaw Fund's expenditure it received – less than one tenth of its growing income. So the very 'act of discourtesy . . . to the dead' that Sir Edward Boyle assured the House of Commons in 1959 would not be committed actually was committed. In an attempt to clarify matters, the Shadow Minister for the Arts, Mark Fisher, asked some questions similar to those put by James Pitman and John Parker in the House of Commons in 1959 and 1965: what in effect was the total sum that had accrued to the British Museum by the end of 1990 and what was properly due to the British Library? But the Minister with responsibility for Arts and Libraries, Tim Renton, answered that this was 'not a subject on which I have any specific responsibility'. On the advice of the Director of the British Museum, Sir David Wilson, the Trustees had decided not to disclose the figure to anyone because they were 'the Trustees' private monies' and public disclosure would enable Treasury officials to take the Shaw income into account when determining the British Museum's annual grant. The annual amounts from the Shaw bequest were audited by the Comptroller and Auditor-General, but expenditure was not scrutinized by the Public Accounts Committee or the Treasury.

It was open for Sir David Wilson and his trustees to transfer this problem on to the shoulders of the British Library, along with the money Shaw had plainly intended to be used for library purposes. But short of such an act of integrity, the British Museum's secrecy seemed pragmatic in view of what happened to another of Shaw's residuary legatees, the Royal Academy of Dramatic Art.

*

Shaw had been fond of RADA. He gave lectures to its students, campaigned for the introduction of women to its governing body, served as a member of its council from 1911 to 1941 (coming to 102 of its 141 meetings in that period), and contributed £5,000 towards its new building in Gower Street in the 1920s (equivalent to £100,000 in 1990). His bequest, which was to change the status of the Academy, brought about a crisis in the summer of 1965. 'Is My Fair Lady behind the real-life drama at RADA?' queried *The Sunday Times*. On 30 May that year the Academy's Principal, John Fernald, suddenly resigned. Fernald had been on the teaching staff at RADA before the war, then in the late 1940s became director of the Liverpool Playhouse before being appointed Principal of RADA in 1955. As a director he possessed a controlled lightness of touch and a quality of lyricism that worked especially well with Chekhov. He was well liked by the RADA students, the more impecunious of whom he would help out with gifts of money for travel, lodging and food. He soon raised the standards of teaching by weeding out frivolous applications from rich débutantes, arranging student tours round the country and overseas, and widening the experience of his young trainees by bringing back talented ex-students to act with them. A few big decisions, such as the building of an expensive new rehearsal room, were taken in Council. But for the most part he and his bursar, Sybil Topham, liked to settle everything between them. After all, most things were fundamentally simple. He regarded the Shaw money 'as a means of helping his students, whom he adored,' remembered his daughter Karin Fernald.

By the mid-1960s the Academy had accumulated a capital of £750,000 (equivalent to more than £5,000,000 in 1990) and the Shaw bequest was producing a yearly income exceeding £30,000 (over £200,000 in 1990). This fortune, which transformed RADA from an orphan to an heiress, awakened interest among the governing body, in particular the film producer Sir Michael Balcon. At that time the administration as well as the artistic direction was vested in the Principal. But Fernald took little interest in administration. He kept no proper accounting system and had failed to maximize the benefits of Shaw's royalties with a professional investment policy. To the rising financial men he appeared guileless, and they questioned the validity of his costly tours for students.

This was a watershed in the Academy's affairs as it moved from the gentle ebb and flow of the amateur world towards the boom and crash of modern marketing. At an extraordinary general meeting held on the morning of Tuesday 13 July 1965 and crowded with famous actors, what some newspapers called 'the Battle of Gower Street' was fought out between Fernald's loyal supporters led by Richard Briers and Peter O'Toole and the governing body led by Sir Felix Aylmer. Both Fernald and Aylmer were Vice-Presidents of the Shaw Society, a stage-direction which gave Shavian piquancy to the contest.

This backstage drama erupted into the newspapers after RADA turned down an offer from John Fernald to withdraw his resignation. An army of actors paraded through the streets calling on the governing body itself to resign. Then the Privy Council met to investigate technical misdemeanours and, following changes to the Academy's charter, new elections were held. There was a fresh splash of discord and further ripples of publicity: then an Administrator-Registrar was appointed and a Finance Office created 'to allow the Principal to concentrate on training and the educational side of things'. But this did not impress John Fernald who believed that 'the constraints imposed by a non-artistic administrator have usually been found to be at the best un-acceptable, and at the worst, unworkable'. He left England to run another drama school and theatre in Michigan in the United States, and during the 1970s took a professorial post in the Department of Theater at New York State University.

Over the years, while RADA's accounts continued to show a deficit, the springs of Shaw's bequest revived a three-year Acting Diploma course as well as two-year Stage Management and Specialist Technical courses. The money was also used to buy new equipment and top up the maintenance of students relying on a declining system of discretionary awards.

Then, early in 1990, though still based in Gower Street (which it leased from the University of London), the Academy purchased the freehold of a building nearby at 18 Chenies Street. The cost was £5,250,000. It was financed by a government grant of £500,000, a donation of £1,000,000 from British Telecom, and the sale of shares worth £3,750,000 from the RADA portfolio largely made up from Shaw's invested royalties. This was supplemented late in 1991 by a grant of £500,000 from the Foundation for Sport and the Arts for conversion costs. In 1962 the Academy had become an independent charity and the acquisition of these new premises was intended as a further step towards the ideal of self-sufficiency when Shaw's royalties cease after the year 2000.

Would the Academy have been able to achieve more, become self-supporting, with more government aid? Or would it have subsided into aid-dependency? Would it have survived at all without Shaw's money? The chairman, Sir Richard Attenborough, believes it must have closed. During the Thatcher decade there was no choice for arts organizations but to expel the dilettante and measure efficiency by profit. But some of the dangers of implementing arts-marketing without the introduction of new tax laws had been spelt out a quarter of a century earlier when James Pitman argued in Parliament in favour of special arrangements for legacies to public and charitable institutions wholly or partly supported by government funds. If the Exchequer contribution to such institutions was consequently reduced, he explained, the purpose of the testator would be rendered void to the detriment of the public's future interests.

In the case of Shaw's estate, the Exchequer had already imposed death duties of more than £500,000 in the 1950s. Shaw's intention was not to benefit to any greater extent the generality of taxpayers but to favour two special sections of the public: those who would be using 'the Reading Room of the British Museum and those would-be actors, actresses and producers who would be thus receiving better training themselves for a part in the dramatic arts'. The Financial Secretary to the Treasury, Sir Edward Boyle (later Baron Boyle of Handsworth), had assured the House of Commons in December 1959 that the Treasury objected strongly to the principle that trustees should use trust funds 'in a way which would merely reduce their demand on public funds, either to maintain an existing service or to start a new one'.

'The Treasury even in times of great stringency in our national and economic affairs has never sought to argue that the cost of a service should be reduced by a contribution from other resources available to the Trustees, or that public funds should not be provided to improve a service merely because the Trustees could afford to do it themselves ... I do not think there has been a convenient occasion for stating the principle, which I think is an important one, that in deciding the expenditure on Vote-borne departments we do not say that the Treasury contribution should be automatically reduced simply because some other source may become available.'

Between principle and practice, private and public money, swirled many confusing cross-currents. In 1967, less than two years after John Fernald's resignation and the fall-out of publicity over Shaw's bequest, the Treasury cancelled its grant to RADA. This lesson was not lost on its co-residuary legatee, the British Museum. Until the mid-1960s the trustees had been happy to make known what money was accruing to the museum from Shaw's royalties and to explain how it was primarily to be used. But over the next twenty-five years, as the cumulative under-funding of national arts institutions grew worse, secrecy and guile seemed to be forced upon those trying to represent the best interests of these institutions. Every one of them was in competition with every other one for sponsorship and grants, even complementary bodies such as the British Museum and British Library. It was not difficult in such embattled circumstances to overlook the wishes of the dead.

What were Shaw's wishes? When he referred to the British Museum in his letters, the context shows that he had in mind the library or manuscripts department of the museum (later the British Library Reference Division). 'Why do you not get a reader's ticket at the British Museum,' he asks his Polish translator Floryan Sobieniowski. 'I spent every day of my life there for several years.' His debt to that great institution 'contracted in the early days when I read and worked for many years in its Reading Room,' he explained to Edy Craig, 'is inestimable, and gives it a right to anything of mine that is of sufficient public interest to be worthy of its acceptance.' What he described in his will as 'such letters and documents as might be worth preserving in a public collection such as that of the British Museum,' including the drafts of eighteen plays, were handed to the Manuscripts Department by the Public Trustee and now form the centre of its large Shaw Collection.

'There are people in this country who are watching very closely the interests of Bernard Shaw ... to see that the purpose for which [he] left his money will be fulfilled,' Emrys Hughes had told Parliament at the end of the 1950s. But as such people died, the knowledge of these interests and that purpose faded. This was what James Pitman had warned the House of Commons might happen. 'Let it not be said in the world of literature and throughout the whole English-speaking world,' he exhorted his fellow Members of Parliament, 'that a great Irishman and genius of the English language who sought to help English literature and English drama found honourable respect for the terms of his will only in Ireland.'

*

Compared with its English counterparts the National Gallery of Ireland had what *The Sunday Times* described in the early 1960s as a 'delightful' policy 'which is to invest not in shares but in pictures'. No tablets were then placed under pictures bought by the gallery showing the source of the purchase money, and there was no list of the works bought from the Shaw Fund. Gradually rumours began circulating in Dublin pubs that Shaw's money had been spent on a number of marvellous fakes and forgeries. Barbara Smoker, arriving from London in the 1960s and asking to see some pictures bought from the Shaw bequest, was shown a couple of religious works by Murillo and a Crucifix by Giovanni di Paolo (a rare and highly valued work) which considerably offended her. Twenty years later, when challenged to put on an exhibition of selected works bought from the Shaw Fund over a quarter of a century so as to celebrate the old patronage and invite new business sponsorship, the director of the gallery regretfully declined because 'it will not be within our resources to mount the Shaw show'. The gallery's resources were shortly afterwards reported in the *Sunday Press*. According to figures supplied to the Comptroller and Auditor-General, £164,714 had been received by the gallery from the Shaw bequest in the twelve months ending on 31 March 1990, and the total in investments and at the bank was £751,173. This sum attracted the notice of the Shaw Birthplace Trust which, with a £60,000 overdraft, had bought 33 Synge Street the previous year for £111,000 and was endeavouring to create a Shaw museum in the near-derelict building. Threatened with an appeal from this Trust, the director of the National Gallery, Raymond Keaveney, replied that 'We have had our own contingencies since then and the sum in the Shaw bequest is very much smaller.'

The 'delightful policy' of simply buying pictures had long been modified by the Governors and Guardians of the gallery. Increasingly money from the Shaw Fund was spent on the insurance of paintings and, in the 1980s, on the conversion and refurbishment of an extension to the gallery at 90 Merrion Square, as well as on the purchase of other sites in Clare Street and Clare Lane. The last work bought by the gallery was a modest, rather indifferent picture by William Ashford called *A bowl of flowers* in 1985.

The gallery's stewardship of the Shaw bequest during much of the thirty-three years it has been receiving Shaw's royalties has been set out by one of the Keepers, Dr Michael Wynne.

'As monies come in from the royalties we endeavour to allow the substantial sum to be accumulated, and from this we buy significant works of art and designate that they have been purchased from the George Bernard Shaw Fund. Occasionally some of the works bought from the fund are relatively minor. This situation arises when towards the end of the financial year we have spent all the government grant for acquisitions and are anxious to seize the opportunity of acquiring something that is important for the collection.'

What was important for the collection was the strengthening of various schools of painting. This has meant that the Shaw Fund purchases were not artistically integral and could not be made to 'form an exhibition of a worthiness due to our great benefactor', Dr Wynne explains (though a very interesting exhibition of this sort was shown in 1987 from purchases made by Sir Michael Levey on his retirement as Director of the National Gallery in London). Nearer the year 2000, Dr Wynne believes, it may be appropriate to publish a brochure with illustrations in colour and a comprehensive list of Shaw acquisitions. 'In the meantime the best tribute which we can pay is to make sure that the purchases made through the Shaw Fund are correctly labelled, and have the descriptions of them published through books like your own.' In 1991 Dr Wynne compiled a list of these purchases from the gallery records (see Appendix C).

The outstanding features of the gallery's collection have been a small but spectacularly good choice of seventeenth-century French paintings (among which are an excellent Claude and Poussin), special attention to religious art which has resulted in a fine holding of Italian Baroque pictures, and some creditable examples of Irish art. The list of works bought from the Shaw Fund shows how the gallery has complemented these areas with a number of art-historically interesting pictures. To the Claude and Poussin, for example, it has added a composition by a comparatively rare painter Louis Le Nain, a late and beautiful Vouet (whose reputation following an exhibition in Paris early in 1991 has been rapidly rising) and a fascinating work (*The Image of Saint Alexis*) showing the extraordinary effects of light by Etienne de la Tour, son of the more famous Georges de la Tour. Additions to the eighteenth-century collection include a rather dull Nattier, but also an excellent portrait by the Swedish painter (of the French school) Roslin and, merging into the nineteenth century, an early and uncommon Baroque studio work, David's *Funeral of Patroclus*. A more characteristic example of David's school is represented by the portrait of Marie-Julie Bonaparte by his pupil Baron Gérard.

The Italian Baroque section at the gallery, which has works by artists such as Castiglione, Lorenzo Lippi, Felice Ficherelli and Carlo Dolci who are little represented in the United Kingdom and were bought cheap earlier in the century when religious pictures were not greatly valued elsewhere, has been enriched by a unique battle scene from Tasso by Cigoli, a major seventeenth-century Florentine painter. The two Murillos (one characteristic, the other untypical) were presumably bought to add to the Roman Catholic content of the collection. Unable to afford a Simone Martini, the gallery bought instead *The Annunciation* painted in 1410 by Jacques Iverny. It cost £250,000 in 1965 and is valued at considerably more than ten times that sum twenty-five years later. The gallery also picked up a wrongly attributed painting of a sleeping girl, a subtle exploration of virtually one colour, later confirmed as a Goya.

The plan appears to have been to buy Renaissance and Baroque sculpture in the 1960s and 1970s when, as compared with Old Master paintings, this sculpture was inexpensive. The two works by Richier, the sixteenth-century French Renaissance sculptor, are remarkable purchases, Duquesnoy's *Cardinal Guido Bentivoglio* is the bust of a distinguished art patron (who discovered Claude Lorrain) by a comparatively unknown yet impressive sculptor.

The Irish school has been reinforced with some eighteenth- and early nineteenth-century landscapes, notably two beautiful paintings by Nathaniel Grogan, three pictures by the idiosyncratic Jack Yeats and Nathaniel Hone's satire on Reynolds as an eclectic artist, a masterpiece which provides a commentary on eighteenth-century art theory and, possibly better than any other single work, conveys the spirit of these Shaw Fund purchases.

Perhaps there is the odd picture from which Shaw himself would have recoiled (though his art criticism does not reveal him as being irredeemably hostile to religious paintings). He would see, however, that the collection he had got to know as a boy as he wandered through the gallery rooms, catching sight of a larger imaginative world and dreaming of being an artist himself, has been greatly enhanced through his bequest.

*

Two further threads appear in the financial tapestry of Shaw's estate. When his seagoing uncle, the Rabelaisian doctor Walter John Gurly, had died at the end of the nineteenth century, G.B.S. found himself the owner of 'his cursed property and debts' in Carlow. He had little power to control or direct the management of these Irish properties, and instead of title deeds had received a bundle of mortgages and a packet of worthless pawn tickets. 'A horrible misfortune has happened to me – a money trouble,' he notified Ellen Terry a few days after coming into his inheritance.

'I have succeeded through the death of my uncle to a family estate in Ireland – a miserable relic of former country splendour, all mortgages and poor relations ... My blessed uncle had not paid even his servant's wages for ten years, and had borrowed every farthing he could. I shall have to pay his debts because I am inheriting the privileges of paying the interest on half a dozen Carlow mortgages.'

The principal site was known as the Old Assembly Rooms in the centre of Carlow. It was a fair-sized building, measuring some ninety feet in depth and commanding a fifty-foot frontage described by the *Carlow Nationalist* as being 'inspiringly designed in the style of the classic revival of the eighteenth century, characteristic of Irish Public buildings of that date'. For many years it functioned as some class of a country club and was used for public entertainments, though according to Shaw's uncle it would have made a better observatory as you 'could watch the movements of the heavenly bodies through the holes in the roof'.

In 1915 Shaw received a petition inviting him to present this property to the town of Carlow for use as a technical school. 'At present,' he was told, 'the classes in Technical Instruction are being held in makeshift premises. Consequently instruction is very much restricted.' As the consideration for this deal he was promised that his 'honoured name will be revered in perpetuity'.

These Assembly Rooms had long been a bad bargain for G.B.S., costing him over the years almost three hundred pounds. He had hesitated between allowing himself to be evicted by stopping payment of the head rents and inventing a sale of the imposing façade to an American millionaire for re-erection in the United States. On the whole it seemed better to have his name 'revered in perpetuity'. Besides, from the public point of view, there was a good deal to be said for complying with this request. 'Unfortunately the place is leased and subleased,' he replied. '... Lately I had all but succeeded in buying out the lessor when he fell into the Barrow and was drowned; and I have not yet succeeded in discovering who his successor is.' It took Shaw until the autumn of 1919 finally to disencumber the Assembly Rooms and sign the deed transferring them to Carlow 'in consideration of the place being used for public purposes and (if possible) the old front of the building being retained for the sake of its decorative effect'. The property was later turned into a Vocational School and after Shaw's death, its façade still intact, has become the County Library Headquarters.

The remaining seventeen parcels of Gurly property (including a burial ground called 'The Graves') Shaw retained for another twenty-five years. 'I am myself a landlord, and, what is worse, an absentee landlord,' he wrote in *Everybody's Political What's What?* 'Since I inherited my property ... I once spent a few hours in its neighborhood without entering or identifying a single house on it.' To assist matters he employed a local man, Major Fitzmaurice, as his business agent. 'Many people who dont know me (and perhaps some who do),' he told Fitzmaurice, 'imagine that I am a difficult man to deal with because my writings rub them up the wrong way.' Actually most of his tenants soon came to realize that he was peculiarly soft-hearted. Sometimes he would receive bills from Carlow shopkeepers due from his tenants who had pledged his credit by guaranteeing payment from him in London. 'I wonder would Mrs Aylward take £50 to leave the country and settle in China,' he wrote of one tenant who regularly calculated at the end of each quarter that he owed her money. His correspondence with Major Fitzmaurice shows him to have been forever making the roofs good, guarding against vandalism, replacing cisterns, clearing gutters. 'My attempts to repair houses on my estate have generally begun by the collapse of the whole edifice,' he admitted. By his eighty-eighth year he decided that 'if I could live another 88 years I would knock down every house on the property and replace it with a new one, with a garage and a modern kitchen, with all the latest labor saving contrivances and con-ditioned air, to teach the Carlovians to want such things'.

In his published writings G.B.S. represented himself as a conven-tional absentee landlord in order to show up the legal impropriety of the property market. 'I pocket a modest income from it, earned by the labor of its inhabitants, who have never seen me nor received any service from me,' he confessed. 'A grosser malversation can hardly be imagined; but it is not my fault: I have to accept it as the law of the land; for there is no alternative open to me. I am strongly in favor of this little estate of mine being municipalized.'

With this in mind he wrote asking the Taoiseach Éamon de Valera in May 1945 to introduce into the Dáil a new law enabling local authorities to accept, hold and administer gifts of property provided they adopt a 'Civic Improvement Scheme'. To his delight, this Local Authorities (Acceptance of Gifts) Bill was quickly drafted and passed that summer. 'Splendid!' Shaw congratulated de Valera. 'It would have taken thirty years in this unhappy country.' On 13 August 1945 all Shaw's Carlow property was passed to the Urban District Council. According to the Act, civic improvement included anything that tended to 'improve the amenities' of the area or was 'conducive to the welfare of the inhabi-tants'. A condition of all gifts, and their income, was that they could not be absorbed into general assets for the relief of rates since, drawing on his experience on the St Pancras Vestry, Shaw believed that a reduction in rates merely assisted landlords 'on whom the rates finally fell, without benefiting the country or improving the town'.

'I am far too good a Socialist to believe that Socialism can be estab-lished by private enterprise,' Shaw had written to Major Fitzmaurice. Yet by his own private enterprise he had established a modest instalment of socialism in Ireland. For nearly twenty-five years the Carlow Urban

District Council made financial help available from its Shaw Fund for cultural and artistic purposes. But subsequent legislation in Ireland, including the Local Government (Planning and Development) Act 1963, the Housing Act 1966, and the Arts Act 1973, all of which enabled local councils to subsidize a widening range of endeavours out of the rates, brought about a Gilbertian situation in which the Shaw Fund could not be used for any identifiable civic improvement without being in breach of its rates relief condition. For another twenty-five years, while lawyers brooded on this predicament, the funds were frozen at the bank except for one strange payment each December to erect a Christmas Crib at the Courthouse. Tiring of this stalemate, the Carlovians eventually came up with a brainwave, and invited the British ambassador to open their own Shaw-funded Shaw Festival in 1991 with its programme of lectures, workshops in the Old Assembly Rooms, school prizes, musical events (including a selection from *My Fair Lady*), the renaming of the Town Park after G.B.S. and a spirited production of *How He Lied to Her Husband*.

The last financial thread was spun from Shaw's Nobel Prize for Literature. 'I cannot persuade myself to accept the money,' he had written in November 1926 to the Royal Swedish Academy. Four months later, on 27 March 1927, he signed a Trust Deed creating an Anglo-Swedish Literary Foundation for the translation into English of classical Swedish literature. To this he donated all his prize money, which amounted to 118,165 Swedish Kronor then worth approximately £6,500 (equivalent to £130,000 in 1990).

The objects of the Anglo-Swedish Literary Foundation were defined in the Trust Deed as 'the encouragement of cultural intercourse between Sweden and the British Islands through the promotion and diffusion of knowledge and appreciation of the literature and art of Sweden in the British Islands'. The first patron of the Foundation was the King of Sweden and its trustees still include the Swedish ambassador. Though some grants were made to facilitate productions of Strindberg's plays and to support Swedish music in Britain, most of the money has been spent on the translation of Swedish books. There were translations of Swedish Nobel Prize winners Pär Lagerkvist, Eyvind Johnson and Harry Martinson, novels by Hjalmar Bergman (considered by many critics to be the greatest Swedish prose writer of the twentieth century), Strindberg's plays, anthologies of Swedish poetry and short stories, and some non-fiction including a vivid description of nineteenth-century

England by Erik Gustaf Geijer, Ingvar Andersson's history of Sweden (for many years the only history of Sweden available in English), and biographies of Carl Linnaeus by Knut Hagberg and of the Swedish composer Franz Berwald by Robert Layton.

After the Second World War the Foundation reconstructed the Swedish section in the library of University College, London, enabling it to become a centre for lending Swedish books, and made donations of books to libraries round Britain that had been depleted in the war. 'The Foundation's funds are not advertised,' wrote the Swedish cultural attaché. 'Possibly its funds are exhausted,' Shaw had written to his bibliographer Loewenstein in 1950. By 1974 its unadvertised balance at the bank appears to have dwindled alarmingly to £1,157 plus a few pence. But with a deft redefinition of its objects (replacing 'the literature and art of Sweden' with the words 'Swedish culture') the trustees were able to replenish the capital with money from the sale of the Swedish Institute's office in London.

From the early 1980s the Foundation has widened its ancillary activities by supporting the newly formed Swedish English Literary Translators' Association and its journal, *Swedish Book Review*; by assisting a translator-in-residence scheme; and enabling Swedish writers to visit Britain, English translators to visit Sweden. In 1991 this contribution to Anglo-Swedish relations from the man who was 'dead against prizes' was recognized by the creation of a three-yearly Bernard Shaw Prize. The first prize was presented at the Swedish Embassy in London to Tom Geddes for his translation of Torgny Lindgren's novel, *The Way of a Serpent*.

*

'Please do not ask Mr Bernard Shaw for money,' reads a blue-green stereotyped postcard G.B.S. had drafted in 1935. 'He has not enough to help the large number of his readers who are in urgent need of it. He can write for you: he cannot finance you.' During the last fifteen years of his life he fended off an increasing number of appellants with variously coloured cards. But though gaining a reputation for thrift, he still received a mass of appeals from 'charitable institutions, religious sects and churches, inventors, Utopian writers desirous of establishing international millennial leagues, parents unable to afford secondary education for their children: in short, everybody and every enterprise in financial straits of any sort'.

Such appeals were founded on the notion that he was a multi-millionaire whereas, he would explain, all his income 'except enough to meet his permanent engagements is confiscated by the Exchequer and redistributed to those with smaller tax-free incomes or applied to general purposes from which everyone benefits'. He did not complain of this system, 'having advocated it for half a century, and nationalized all his landed property,' but his correspondents could not have his income in cash from himself as well as in services from their country. 'It is useless to ask him for money: he has none to spare,' reads a rose-coloured card drafted in 1949. Then, having demonstrated that 'No other reply to appeals is possible,' he would secrete a cheque into his envelopes for the Actors' Orphanage, Royal Literary Fund, the Society for the Protection of Birds, the Lord Mayor's National Flood Distress Fund, the King Edward Memorial Hospital, Travellers' Aid Society, Chaim Weizmann's Zionist Appeal, the Shakespeare Memorial Theatre at Stratford-upon-Avon, the National Theatre in London and, as bail money or pension money, for eyeglasses or boots, to an always-lengthening list of individuals. 'On your life, don't tell anybody,' he warned the actor Esmé Percy, one of the most regular performer-producers of his plays, to whom he had made a gift of £100 (equivalent to £2,000 in 1990). Had he permitted such things to become public, 'his name and Charlotte's would have headed most subscription lists, for their contribution was invariably the largest'.

In his biography published in 1956, St John Ervine described Shaw's testament as being 'one of the most public-spirited documents in the whole history of bequests'. The author of *Socialism for Millionaires* (1901) became the posthumous multi-millionaire supplicants had so optimistically cherished in his lifetime. Forty years after his death his own birthplace in Synge Street lay derelict, but G.B.S. was at last becoming recognized, in the words of Dan H. Laurence, as probably 'the most charitable professional man of his generation'.

Great men do not, as a rule, endow their own memorials. That is for posterity...
Ivor Brown, *Time and Tide* (29 December 1951)

On the afternoon of 17 March 1951 Dame Edith Evans declared 'Shaw's Corner' open to the public. In persistent rain, like the rain that had fallen while Shaw's ashes were being scattered in the garden less than four months earlier, 200 people gathered for the ceremony at Ayot St Lawrence. Television cameras and radio microphones were there to observe and record them as they overflowed from the heated marquees on to the lawn. Invitations had been sent to everyone who knew G.B.S., from the village postmistress Jisbella Lyth to the Fabian Saint Joan Mary Hankinson. 'I knew him well and loved him, and so did my wife,' replied Sean O'Casey who was too ill to travel. 'A man of most excellent fancy. May we become more worthy of his greatness.' 'Will be in spirit with you,' Gabriel Pascal cabled from California a few days later.

Never before had the National Trust possessed a house with 'the imprint of genius still warm upon it'. Edith Evans recalled the gaiety and charm of G.B.S., his eighteenth-century manners and provocative methods of directing his own plays. 'At rehearsals he would always tell us what we did wrong,' the *News of the World* reported her as saying, 'and then act a bit to show us how to do it. I used to think his acting was terrible.'

'At one rehearsal, suddenly without any warning he bent and very swiftly kissed me. I didn't get very much pleasure out of it because I was so surprised. We all looked a bit staggered.'

The house was to be open four afternoons a week and all day on Sundays, and visitors were to be charged two shillings for admission. On Sunday 18 March some 600 of them arrived in the village and on Easter Monday there were more than 1,000. They came from all over Britain and around Europe, from Canada, South America, the United States, India, China...

'Trouble has come to Ayot,' announced the *Evening News*. Before the end of the month pandemonium was sweeping through the village. A few of the 150 inhabitants, such as the landlord of the Brocket Arms, believed they should face up to the rigours of prosperity and welcome tourists during Festival year. But most villagers were already 'fed up with being famous'. They foresaw a catastrophic future: their fields reduced to car parks, their cottages converted into cafés, their shops crammed with hideous Shavian mugs and ashtrays. Did they really want to be outnumbered ten to one by invading sightseers trampling on the flower-beds and have their way impeded by erupting litter-bins, snack-bars-on-wheels, Italianate ice-cream men in white coats? Did they want to be pointed at by screaming advertisements and deafened by the perpetual hooting of unending traffic? In short: must they live like a cursed tribe longing for the comforts of summer rain and winter snow?

These were some of the chilling questions put to villagers at an emergency meeting in the parish church. A one-armed captain stood up and ringingly declared that he would 'move heaven & earth' to get Shaw's Corner closed; a surveyor cried out that he would bring a case against the National Trust under the Town and Country Planning Act; and several younger villagers, forming themselves into guerrilla groups, set out on raiding parties and uprooted more than thirty Automobile Association signposts.

Then suddenly the trouble lifted. Fifteen thousand people came to Shaw's Corner during the first five months, but by September the figure had settled down to fewer than 2,000 a month. The police withdrew, the special bus service was discontinued, and a gentler convoy of cars and charabancs parked comfortably in what had once been Shaw's kitchen garden.

Many Shavians expected Shaw's 'friend and factotum' Dr Fritz Loewenstein to be appointed as first curator of the house. He expected it himself and had been assiduously campaigning for this appointment ever since Shaw gave his house to the National Trust in 1944. 'I beg to offer you my services,' he had written that year. ' . . . Once the National Trust has taken over the property and has come to a decision with regard to the intended Shaw Museum, you might find it desirable to have the help of somebody who is not wholly uninformed with regard to Mr Shaw's works etc., and who at the same time is an ardent admirer of the G.O.M. and all he stands for.'

While assuring him that it would be 'only too glad to enlist your help and guidance', the National Trust cautioned Loewenstein against giving Shaw the impression 'that we were discussing any future plans about his house behind his back'. This agreed, discussions continued and by the end of 1944 Loewenstein persuaded James Lees-Milne at the Trust to try out a new plan on G.B.S. This was to plant his seedling Shaw Society at Ayot St Lawrence once Shaw himself had made room for it by dying. Under Loewenstein's care the Society could then flower and Shaw's Corner come into its own as 'a meeting place for Shavians from all parts of the world, a centre for Shavian thought, a place for recreation (open air performances in the grounds) and of study' where scholars could browse on Loewenstein's rich pasture of 'old rubbish' as G.B.S. had called it. In his enthusiasm Loewenstein believed they could start making an inventory of the contents in Shaw's Corner right away. From the National Trust's offices in London he hurried down to Ayot St Lawrence and arrived in time to see G.B.S. opening this letter. 'He read it attentively but made no comment,' Loewenstein reported back. 'You will probably hear from him shortly. Kindly keep me posted.'

Shaw's letter five days later reminded the National Trust that he was also leaving it the contents of his home. He could not make an inventory of these contents because he wished to transfer 'a lot of things from London, and get rid of some superfluities'. If anything went wrong, the Trust could let the house furnished 'for £300 a year or thereabouts'. As for the Shaw Societies, they 'will all die of old age in four years at most', he added.

G.B.S. was then in his eighty-ninth year. His letter stirred some feelings of compunction in James Lees-Milne. 'I have been rather a nuisance to you, I am afraid,' he wrote. By the same post he also told Loewenstein: 'I do not feel inclined to write to him any further on the matter, as I am sure you will agree.'

Loewenstein declared himself 'delighted with Shaw's answer'. All the same, he could not altogether let the matter go no further, and over the next five years occasionally pressed the National Trust for some legal assurance over the housing of his Shaw Society. To top up the goodwill he also sent in bulletins on Shaw's health, and notes about precious objects in the house (the Rodin bust, the Augustus John portrait) for the proposed inventory. Finally, in the morning of 2 November 1950, he telephoned the National Trust's head office with news of Shaw's death and asked for a draft contract on the house.

Legally Shaw's Corner could not be 'vested' with the National Trust until probate had been granted. This gave the Trust some two and a half months in which to sort out an embarrassing financial problem. For as

Shaw's vigilant secretary Blanche Patch assured everyone, 'owing to its inaccessibility, visitors' fees would not pay for its upkeep'.

Shaw himself had originally considered his neighbours, Stephen and Clare Winsten, biographer and artist, as paying custodians. 'I have in mind a gentleman who will probably be my acting literary executor,' he had informed the Trust. 'He and his wife are very anxious to reside in the house and shew it off to visitors. They are ardent Shavians and can afford the tenancy ...' But the Winstens had grown impatient, quarrelled with Shaw, and moved to Oxford from where they now wrote to the Trust claiming several items in the house as their own. They did not appear likely candidates for the new tenancy – besides, it 'would raise a local outcry,' Blanche Patch volunteered, 'as when they lived nearby these people never paid their bills'.

Blanche Patch was a loquacious source of information to the National Trust. For years she had been waiting to pour out her scandal into the right ears. Now she poured with a vengeance. She was especially eager to damage Loewenstein's reputation. After all, he had been nothing more than an office boy, she said, and was certainly never invited to dinner at the house. Indeed, the housekeeper Mrs Laden would not even let him sit down there for fear he would 'dirty her chairs'. Charlotte Shaw, she remembered, had also 'detested' him. It was bad enough to hear that the Public Trustee was allowing him to carry on work five days a week using Charlotte's old bedroom as his study. To give him the whole house would be sacrilege.

The National Trust's secretary Jack Rathbone could see that Miss Patch was 'plainly very jealous' of Loewenstein. But she was so full of amusing stories he could not help liking her. When he asked her whom she would recommend as curator, however, she came up with an ex-policeman from the village – a strange choice as National Trust custodian of literature.

Despite all that Blanche Patch could bring against him, Loewenstein retained strong claims on Shaw's Corner. For although the National Trust never gave him a binding undertaking, he had been led to understand that 'it would be a very satisfactory and appropriate solution for the Trust to let the building to the Shavian Society, provided we could come to terms on a financial basis particularly ...' To meet such terms, Loewenstein now introduced a colleague who was prepared to pay the Trust £500 a year (equivalent to more than £6,000 in 1990) for a full repairing lease on the house. He proposed that the two of them occupy the top floors (part of which would also be used as an office for the Shaw Society) and maintain the three main reception rooms and the garden as a 'Shavian Shrine' for National Trust visitors. 'With due diffidence,' he wrote, 'I submit that no person or group of persons can present a better claim to tenant Shaw's lease or give a better guarantee that the property and its contents will be preserved for the benefit of the Nation as a worthy memorial.'

It was hardly surprising if Loewenstein took it for granted that he would be offered a joint tenancy. He had done everything asked of him – indeed he had done rather more, collecting extravagant messages from Shaw Societies round the world applauding the prospect of this glorious installation. But there were rumours that Lady Astor had opposed him. 'I thought for a moment of asking Lady Astor what she thought of Loewenstein,' Harold Nicolson, a National Trust vice-chairman (later Sir Harold Nicolson), wrote to the Trust's Secretary Jack Rathbone, 'but no sooner had the thought raised its little head than it popped down again. Nancy's opinion on any matter is really of little value to anybody.'

What was of value were the opinions of the arbiters and aesthetes of the National Trust itself – and these opinions were unanimous. 'We disliked Loewenstein ... intensely.' By the end of 1951 the Trust had decided that 'the Shaw Society and Dr Loewenstein should not be made responsible for the maintenance of the house unless absolutely necessary'.

It was never made clear what was so peculiarly odious about Loewenstein that he 'would be a discredit to the Trust'. Perhaps it was the fact that he was never to be seen, even for a cup of tea, without his solicitor. Or that he had, according to a fellow bibliographer, 'a servility and unction that Uriah Heep might have envied'. The fact that he was Jewish counted against him not at all, or hardly at all, not greatly anyway. It was simply that a German Jew with a foreign doctorate on Japanese prints was unlikely to understand the sophisticated operations of English life with its nuances of social elevation, its protected areas of financial accumulation. Sensing that things might not after all be going his way, he summoned the Past-Presidents and Vice-Presidents, officers and founder-members of the Shaw Society to do battle for him, men like Gabriel Pascal and Shaw's German translator Siegfried Trebitsch, the Marxist-Leninist lawyer D. N. Pritt, the American mathematician and biographer Archibald Henderson. The Trust sifted through such names and found two, the Labour Member of Parliament David Hardman and the playwright Benn Levy, whom it thought possible to approach, but neither of them would give references testifying to Loewenstein's financial respectability. 'If we could afford it,' Jack Rathbone informed Lord Crawford (alias Lord Bathniel, Baron Wigan and the eleventh Earl of Balcarres), 'I would like to keep on Mrs Laden and I think she would keep the house beautifully, and shew it well.'

Alice Laden had been Shaw's housekeeper since Charlotte's death in 1943. She dazzled everyone. 'She is an interesting-looking and obviously very efficient woman,' Jack Rathbone enthused, 'scarlet-nailed and heavily made up.' To him and Harold Nicolson and the Trust's adviser on historic buildings, James Lees-Milne, she handed several cups of good strong tea, then proudly led them round the rooms and told them that she would like to go on living there as their employee. By the time she packed them off home she had enchanted these connoisseurs and *cognoscenti* of the Trust. It was as if they had fallen under the spell of their school matron. Mrs Laden was quite authoritarian in her way, yet she knew her place and unlike Loewenstein would be in every way a credit to them. In every way except one. For as Loewenstein reminded them, the Trust would have to pay her a salary whereas he would be paying a yearly rent. Here was the plot of a Trollope novel. 'This is going to be a very difficult problem,' concluded Jack Rathbone.

G.B.S. had often emphasized the power of money in his cautionary tales of capitalism, his treatises and treasure hunts for the stage. The story of his posthumous affairs was also largely directed by money motives. Money was granite and rainbow, the practical means to an end and a fabulous end in itself. By the beginning of 1951 the National Trust thought it saw a way of reconciling ends and means by paying the £1,500 costs of the Shaw Memorial Fund Appeal (equivalent to £20,000 in 1990) in exchange for being given first call on the fund when the donations came in. 'I am sure a national appeal, possibly even an international one, is the answer to the difficult financial problem,' wrote Jack Rathbone.

Having invested its hopes in this appeal the Trust was free to appoint Mrs Laden as first custodian of Shaw's Corner. Though 'much appreciative' of Loewenstein's vicarious offer of £500 a year, they 'could not see their way to accepting it,' Jack Rathbone wrote, 'at any rate for the time being'.

All the protagonists were at the house for the opening garden party in March 1951 – Stephen and Clare Winsten, Blanche Patch, Mrs Laden, the officers and gentlemen of the National Trust, and Dr Loewenstein with a squadron from the Shaw Society. So Shaw's Corner took its place with the houses of Carlyle, Kipling and Wordsworth, with Coleridge's, Hardy's and Meredith's cottages, in a special category of properties preserved not for their architectural merit but for their association with great writers. Here was Shaw's workshop, wrote the drama critic Ivor Brown, and 'the workshop of a great man has its vivid associations and abiding interest'.

*

'Mrs Laden is doing wonderfully,' a National Trust memorandum noted soon afterwards. Yet she could not get accustomed to the place without Mr Shaw. It was no longer 'Shaw's Corner', she used to say, but 'Everybody's Corner'. At the same time G.B.S.'s presence grew intensifyingly real to her. She kept on expecting to see him sitting at the dining-room table or appearing at the kitchen hatch to ask her for something – indeed she almost felt 'I was seeing his ghost at times'. When she considered how he would have disliked all these strangers messing up the floors with their muddy boots and dropping tickets everywhere, she could not help getting depressed. Before the end of the year she resigned as custodian and went home to Scotland. 'She plans to add to the recent spate of Shaviana with a book on the years she spent with Shaw,' reported the *Birmingham Post*. Twenty-two years later she served up her intelligent man's guide to the kitchen, *The George Bernard Shaw Vegetarian Cook Book*.

In the first twelve months after Shaw's death almost 20,000 people had come to see the house, producing a surplus of nearly £3,000 (equivalent to £40,000 in 1990), and in the following year over 10,000 visitors arrived raising another £1,000 (equivalent to £12,000). After paying all expenses the National Trust would have been solidly in profit had it not spent its resources hunting that crock of gold at the end of the Memorial Appeal. 'A full report on the failure, with no bones made about who was responsible, could make good reading,' suggested the *Manchester Guardian*. Did this failure simply mark the decline of a writer's reputation after death? Was it particularly steep after such a long public career? 'Shaw's greatest publicity agent died with him,' commented the *Evening Standard*. Or did the start of thirteen years of Conservative government in Britain make these times peculiarly hostile to G.B.S.? Some believed that the death of George VI early in

February 1952, so soon after the official launch (already delayed until after the general election of 1951), was fatal to its chances. Others thought that the medley of squabbling and indifferent members of the Shaw Memorial National Committee was chiefly to blame. Then there were those who blamed the house itself. 'I cannot help wondering whether there are not other houses in England, falling or likely to fall into decay, of historic interest and of beauty without and within, which have a greater claim upon our generosity and self-denial,' mused T. S. Eliot.

From letters sent to the National Trust it is clear that the public misunderstood Shaw's reason for providing the Trust with 'not a single penny' to endow the upkeep of his gift. They believed this proved his fundamental meanness. They did not recognize the paradox of a secretly generous man. Shaw wanted his money to go as far as possible, reaching a considerable number of individuals and institutions. He had given valuable possessions to the National Theatre, National Portrait Gallery, London School of Economics, Fitzwilliam Museum, Tate Gallery, the Metropolitan Museum in New York, the National Library and Municipal Gallery in Dublin. He feared that there might not be enough funds left in his estate for all the annuitants among his employees and family, as well as for the Royal Academy of Dramatic Art, the National Gallery of Ireland, the library department of the British Museum – and his pet alfabet.

The National Trust's deficit had risen in 1950 from £31,000 to £56,000 (equivalent in 1990 to about £800,000). This followed the government's failure to implement a recommendation of the Gowers Report that direct relief from taxation should be granted to owners of historic country houses in return for an undertaking to open them to the public. 'We cannot afford to run this property at a loss,' stated a National Trust memorandum on Ayot St Lawrence. To offset possible loss the Trust sold at auction some of Shaw's silver for £547 (equivalent to £6,500 in 1990), then some furniture for £145-13s-6d, and then again more furniture (including Shaw's pianola for £1-12s-6d) and photographic equipment. It was also given the £416 raised by the appeal. 'Considerable competition' allegedly existed for Mrs Laden's post. Eventually, the second custodian of Shaw's Corner was appointed: a retired police officer then serving as steward to the Conservative Club in Sevenoaks.

This bizarre choice, bringing to mind Miss Patch's odd proposal less than eighteen months earlier, once more passed over the claims of Loewenstein who was never again considered as a National Trust curator. 'Shaw expresses no wish in his will that Loewenstein should live at Shaw's Corner,' Jack Rathbone had written, 'and we have a free hand, except for finance.'

Financially Shaw's Corner continued to be so famously difficult that the Shaw Society ran an ironic advertisement soliciting offers (in the spirit of Act II of *The Apple Cart*) for its complete removal to New England. Attendance fell to fewer than 7,000 visitors a year. Then, following its temporary closure, the house was leased to a private American tenant, C. J. Casserley, and reopened in 1957 by Blanche Patch. Casserley had offered to take this 'millstone round your neck' on condition he need open it to the public no more than once a week and keep a percentage of the admission fees. In lieu of rent he developed the habit of making sensational discoveries of priceless Shavian items that everyone already knew were there. After a year, the National Trust instituted proceedings against him for rent arrears of £250, and he surrendered the lease, throwing in some garden tools as part payment but leaving without settling the rates. The ex-policeman was quickly reinstated, but after his death Clare Winsten's statue of Saint Joan was stolen from the garden in April 1968 and later found damaged beyond repair. It was a nadir in the fortunes of Ayot.

Since no one seemed eager to live among Shaw's possessions and open the place to visitors, maintain the garden and pay rent, a separate flat was made for private tenants incorporating the housekeeper's second-floor quarters, while the property continued to be administered by custodians who occupied the first floor and used the kitchen on the ground floor. This dual arrangement persisted precariously until the 1970s when an apartment was created on the first and second floors for new tenants. In the 1980s these rooms were redesigned as the custodians' quarters, while some of the first-floor rooms, the kitchen and scullery were made open to the public.

The fortunes of the house revived. Over thirty items belonging to G.B.S. discovered in the basement of the Public Trustee's Office – including steel spectacles, silver whistle, gold fountain pen, green penknife – were moved to Ayot, and a room was opened for exhibitions of his books and plays. By 1990 Shaw's Corner was open seven months a year and attracting 17,000 visitors at an admission price of £2 for those who were not members of the National Trust. The problem was how to keep the numbers down.

*

Among those who signed the visitors' book in the 1980s were Loewenstein's family. Loewenstein's own fortunes had sunk rapidly in the 1950s. It was all very different from what he expected. Shaw had expressed a wish in his will that 'my Bibliographer Fritz Erwin Loewenstein Doctor of Philosophy and Founder of the London Shaw Society (now residing at Torca Cottage in Saint Albans) whose knowledge of my literary affairs and interest in my reputation qualify him exceptionally for such employment shall be consulted and employed by my Executor and Trustee' whenever his assistance 'may be desirable and available'. Loewenstein's skills were continuously available, and he was naturally disappointed that they were never desired. A rumour also arose that the Public Trustee had denied him 'a small sum (about £100) that he claimed Shaw had promised to him,' the source of this probably being an uncashed cheque for £100 (equivalent to £1,400 in 1990) still among Loewenstein's private papers.

In fact Shaw made three agreements with Loewenstein during the last eighteen months of his life. On 28 June 1949 and again on 17 February 1950 he guaranteed to pay him sums of £1,500 with the proviso that no more than £500 should be paid in any one year 'to ensure the maintenance of the said Fritz Erwin Loewenstein during the said years and also enable him to complete the bibliography of my works and writings on which he is engaged'. The first of these payments in the June 1949 agreement was to be made in 1951, while the February 1950 agreement covered the years 1954, 1955 and 1956. Both agreements were to pass on from Shaw himself to his 'successors in title and assigns'.

Then, on 4 September 1950, six days before he was to fall in his garden, Shaw signed a third agreement guaranteeing Loewenstein yet another £500 a year for three unspecified years. This third document is similar to the first two, neither of which is referred to or revoked, giving rise to a suspicion that one of the previous agreements had passed from Shaw's memory. All three agreements were witnessed by Mrs Laden and the few variations that appear in the last one seem to have arisen from the making of Shaw's will which was completed on 12 June 1950. He uses the words 'my Executors Administrators assignees and successors' in place of 'myself my successors in title and assigns', and the document ends:

'I charge my estate with the said payments to ensure the maintenance of the said Fritz Erwin Loewenstein and thus enable him to complete his bibliography of my works and writings upon which he is professionally and independently engaged.'

With a total of £4,500 to be paid between 1949 and 1959 (equivalent to £8,000 a year or over £60,000 altogether in the 1990s), Loewenstein's maintenance seemed reasonably secure, especially if he were living at Shaw's Corner. But he was never to receive this money. That Shaw intended to provide for Loewenstein's needs over at least six and possibly nine years is plain to the ordinary reader of these documents. Yet deep obscurities began to unravel themselves before the eyes of trained experts. For Shaw had drafted these agreements, in all their bewildering clarity, without benefit of lawyers. Although they looked and sounded legal, thoroughly legal, it was within the powers of experienced counsel, men who had eaten their dinners and taken silk, to fish up profound uncertainties as to whether they actually formed binding contracts. Indeed it was impossible, they eventually agreed, to decide the matter one way or the other.

Behind this dilemma was the fact that the Public Trustee did not want to pay Loewenstein. It was obvious that his bibliography was of no pecuniary interest to Shaw's estate. In other ways too he was becoming an irritating financial liability. For example, Shaw had given his bank a guarantee for £3,000 in the late 1940s so as to enable Loewenstein to take the tenancy of Torca Cottage in St Albans. In the summer of 1951 the Public Trustee found himself obliged to pay £2,775-0s-4d (equivalent to almost £40,000 in 1990) in settlement of the bank's claim.

Perhaps it was this disagreeable transaction that stiffened the Public Trustee's determination not to pay out the £500 a year stipend during the 1950s. He contended that since Loewenstein was doing little to fulfil his side of the commitment there was an absence of valid consideration, and consequently no legal contracts existed. Loewenstein, who had a shopping bag bursting with bibliographic cards, challenged this contention. He then started litigation proceedings, though somewhat undermining his case by making it known at a meeting of the Shaw Society on 23 November 1952 that he had 'forsaken his bibliographic commitment'. While lawyers analysed the agreements, he sold his large assemblage of Shaviana and his wife opened 'Ann's Pantry' selling continental cakes and coffee in St Albans. Then with some bitterness he took his family in 1955 back to Germany where, as a refugee from the Hitler regime, he was entitled to approximately £2,000 compensation. Finally, on 17 June 1956, while living in Frankfurt, he accepted in full settlement of his claim on Shaw's estate a Court Order for £600 (equivalent to £6,000 in 1990).

*

For almost half a lifetime Fritz Loewenstein, Doctor of Philosophy, had rejoiced in the title of Shaw's 'official Bibliographer & Remembrancer'. But it was for the creation of the Shaw Society that he was himself chiefly to be remembered. Shaw had given this Society four years of life at most and 'it has been the great pleasure of the members to prove him wrong,' wrote T. F. Evans in the twenty-fifth anniversary of the Society's journal *The Shavian*.

Loewenstein's place in the Shaw Society had been filled by a vivacious actor-librarian called Eric Batson who gradually built up the membership until the thousandth member was enrolled in 1963. Though it was never the 'centre for Shavian Thought' Loewenstein visualized, the Shaw Society became for a period the custodian of Shaw's reputation. Batson seemed to know everybody and was immensely popular. He organized meetings that often ended in uproar, inaugurated full-dress play performances in the garden at Ayot on Shaw's birthday each year and made *The Shavian* a journal of peculiar intelligence. In its pages readers could inquire as to their proper response to *My Fair Lady* which was so delighting the public everywhere and would so have exasperated G.B.S. An ingenious solution was proposed by Eric Bentley who recommended Shavians to go and enjoy the first act but then leave at the interval – so missing the descent into conventional romance – and sell their tickets to the non-Shavians still queuing outside the theatre.

It was Batson who 'taught me how to campaign', remembered Barbara Smoker, 'and how to be effective in all sorts of ways'. He marshalled his most spectacular campaign against the Public Trustee whom he suspected of conniving with the Society of Authors (which acts as literary agent for the Shaw Estate) to restrict performances of *Pygmalion* on stage, film, radio and television for up to ten years so that *My Fair Lady* might have a clear run. In Clause 7 of his will, Shaw had written that the Public Trustee should not 'be bound by commercial considerations exclusively it being my desire that he shall give due weight to artistic and public and human considerations...' It was plain to Batson that the Public Trustee had taken absolutely no notice of Shaw's wishes, and was imposing a new type of commercial dictatorship. So he briefed the Member of Parliament for St Pancras South, Lena Jeger (later Baroness Jeger of St Pancras), who brought the matter up before the Attorney-General. Here was further irritation for Sir Reginald Manningham-Buller. He was always having to make sense of Shaw's contentious will. He rose to his feet in the House of Commons and explained that the Public Trustee 'is required by law to administer trusts to the best advantage of the beneficiaries'. Obviously this must mean the best financial advantage. What else? In any case, since the rules of the Public Trustee's Office 'require him to observe strict secrecy,' Manningham-Buller concluded, no inquiry could be made into his administration.

Such secrecy was all Batson required. On behalf of the Shaw Society he formed a 'Not Bloody Likely' committee to prevent the powers of the new Copyright Act from being used as an instrument for censorship. Recognizing that the Public Trustee was too deeply bunkered for attack, he bombarded the Society of Authors. The Society of Authors had denied imposing a ban on *Pygmalion*, admitting merely to 'some form of traffic control ... if congestion and collisions are to be avoided'. But letters of protest from T. S. Eliot, E. M. Forster, Allen Lane, Stephen Spender and many others were soon stacking the correspondence of *The Times*. Was Shakespeare's *Othello* restricted to allow Verdi's *Otello* a clear run? Then Graham Greene announced his resignation from the Society of Authors and urged others to follow him. 'Otherwise we become accomplices in the affair.' Under this threat the Society of Authors made an unacknowledged retreat by allowing several productions of *Pygmalion* to go ahead. The Shaw Society announced a victory and declared a truce.

These were the golden years of the Shaw Society: a period well-furnished with publications by Shaw's surviving friends, beginning with Hesketh Pearson's *G.B.S. A Postscript* and Blanche Patch's *Thirty Years with G.B.S.* in 1951, reaching its pinnacle five years later, the *annus mirabilis* of his centenary, and declining in the 1960s as his remaining friends died and the centre of Shaw studies, growing more academic, moved to the United States and Canada.

4

*I take a Shavian to be one who takes nothing on authority, even when the
authority is Bernard Shaw.*
Brigid Brophy, 'I Never Eat Dead' (1966)

Death appeared to have put little check on Shaw's own literary output.
His career hurried on with newly published fiction and criticism, works
on music and politics, Shakespearean commentaries, Irish essays, autobiographies and plays (*Buoyant Billions, Farfetched Fables, & Shakes versus
Shav* came out in 1951 as the thirty-seventh volume in his Standard
Edition). To the serene flow of what are catalogued as 'books and
ephemeral publications' were to be added contributions to periodicals
and to other authors' volumes, recordings of his broadcasts, his correspondence with Mrs Patrick Campbell, Granville-Barker, Molly Tompkins, Dame Laurentia McLachlan and others. There were additional
manifestations and outpourings not to be found in the orthodox canon of
his life and works, including eighteen misattributed love poems he never
composed for Ellen Terry (according to a graphologist in the 1980s they
were written by a woman), some highly original dramas dictated through
the ether to sensitively psychic men and women, the appearance of
babies attributed to his miraculous interventions at night, simultaneous
glimpses of his revisitings from distant parts of the world, all enriching
the Shavian apocrypha. To some people it felt as if he were not dead at
all. Far from it. 'Shaw has been to my house more than a dozen times
since his death,' Frances Day revealed to the *Sunday Graphic* in 1953.
'... The first time I thought it was a mouse.'

The Public Trustee had recognized Gabriel Pascal's film rights to a
number of Shaw's plays and the newspapers announced his immediate
filming of half a dozen masterpieces such as *Man and Superman* in Spain
and *Candida* starring Gracie Fields. In 1951 Pascal made a deal for
Androcles and the Lion in collaboration with the elusive billionaire
Howard Hughes who had taken over RKO Studios in 1948. It was to be
his first film in Hollywood. Howard Hughes 'has gambled approximately
$2,000,000 [over £10,000,000 in 1990] on Mr Pascal's reputation,'
announced the *New York Times*. Pascal wanted Chaplin to play Androcles, but this was the McCarthy era and Chaplin, discredited as a
communist sympathizer, was unemployable in the United States. The

production was to begin with the silent Marx brother Harpo as Androcles and Rex Harrison cast as the Emperor, but these parts were taken over by a young comedian in the Danny Kaye style called Alan Young (following a failed screen test by Frank Sinatra) and the Shavian theatre actor Maurice Evans. Jean Simmons played Lavinia. 'I didn't know what was happening,' she said later. '... [I] didn't know what I was getting into.' The supporting players included a comically miscast Victor Mature as the Captain, a somewhat drunken Robert Newton as Ferrovius, and a lion called Jackie.

It was unlikely material for a Hollywood epic, this story of a Greek tailor who pulls a thorn from the paw of a wounded beast which later refuses to eat him in the Roman Colosseum. Shaw had created a fabulous pantomime and Pascal's ponderous treatment changed his work into the very type of banal melodrama G.B.S. had been satirizing.

Camera work was completed on 17 November 1951 after ten weeks of shooting. Pascal and Hughes 'have yet to meet', the *New York Times* revealed the following day. In their single telephone conversation Pascal had convinced Hughes that G.B.S. would bring 'class' to his lacklustre studio. But Hughes sensed something missing from *Androcles* and, to Pascal's indignation, inserted several scenes of vestal virgins romping round a steam bath.

Before the première, Pascal went out of his way to praise the superiority of Hollywood's technical equipment and the co-operation of the production crew. 'Everybody was anxious for the success of the picture,' he said. Their anxiety was natural. 'As the film went on,' remembered Pascal's wife, 'I began to perspire and shiver at the same time. I had no doubt that it would be ill-received and was going to be a disastrous flop.'

The New York critics were unamused by *Androcles* when it opened at the Capital Theatre in January 1953 and accused Pascal of having 'thrown Shaw to the lions of R.K.O.' 'This is the prelude to my end,' Pascal remarked at the rather grim celebration party in New York. But he put a brave face on it. 'The hell with Shaw and his plays. I want life.' Eighteen months later he was dead. Pursued by mysteriously contending women, haunted by Shaw's spirit, he struggled to keep up his option payments on the musical rights of *Pygmalion* which would miraculously raise him from posthumous bankruptcy. At the Broadway première of *My Fair Lady* in 1956, his widow Valerie Pascal opened her programme and stared at the acknowledgement. 'Adapted from George Bernard Shaw's *Pygmalion*, produced on the screen by Gabriel Pascal.' These lines in small print 'entwining the two names' read like an epitaph on a tombstone, she thought, 'a small memorial to a strange friendship of two dead men'. Shaw, she believed, would have been mischievously delighted.

But Shaw would not have been delighted. Those who named him 'George' usually traduced him. Years earlier a well-known composer and librettist had proposed making a musical of *Captain Brassbound's Conversion* featuring 'a chorus of scallywags, a chorus of Moorish brigands, a chorus for the relieving party ... a chorus for the United States marines ... a chorus of oriental damsels who appeared mysteriously in the garden of the Scottish missionary, and ... a Moorish maiden, who sang an amorous ditty to Captain Brassbound and left the impression that she shared his hours of dalliance.' Altogether, Shaw concluded, 'the play was not as I conceived it, and I declined the honour [and] told the authors that if the thing was produced I'd have the law on them'. As for *Pygmalion*, it had 'its own verbal music' like *Arms and the Man*. 'I have no intention of allowing the history of the Chocolate Soldier to be repeated,' he had insisted. He had got into difficulties over the unauthorized musical of *Arms and the Man* after Siegfried Trebitsch accepted £40 in 1907 (equivalent to £1,500 in 1990) for the right to adapt his German translation of the play into an operetta-libretto for Oscar Straus. Though Shaw sent Trebitsch the £40 with which to repay the librettists, the damage was done. He would not accept royalties from Straus's popular *Der tapfere Soldat*, but he did not have the heart to issue a veto. After that everyone wanted to make a film of it, but 'I will not license the Chocolate Soldier under any circumstances.' In 1941 Trebitsch received an offer of $30,000 from Metro-Goldwyn-Mayer to translate a film scenario if he could get Shaw's authorization. But 'there is no present help nor much future promise in this,' Shaw warned Trebitsch. '... I was pledged to Pascal not to allow such a filming, and anyhow it would not have been a decent transaction.' So Ferenc Molnar, the Hungarian playwright, adapted his comedy *The Guardsman* to fit Straus's score for the film version called *Soldier*.

Shaw believed *The Chocolate Soldier* to have been a sentimental travesty of *Arms and the Man* and when Franz Lehár, creator of *The Merry Widow*, proposed making a musical version of *Pygmalion*, he was adamant that such a travesty should not happen again. To all composers he made the same reply and for the rest of his life rejected all appeals to 'downgrade' *Pygmalion* into a musical. 'I absolutely forbid any such outrage,' he wrote in his ninety-second year. This was one battle he believed he had won.

Like the characters in *Widowers' Houses*, Trebitsch and Pascal were caught in the cash nexus. 'I have not the intention to sell Shaw's letters during my lifetime,' Trebitsch wrote to Archibald Henderson in 1953. He had deposited more than 600 of these letters, postcards and telegrams from Shaw in his Austrian bank. They were, he reckoned, worth $100,000. 'I may be *forced* one day to sell, not to let my wife pennyless,' he conceded. Two years after Tina Trebitsch's death, when Trebitsch himself was in his eighty-eighth year, he finally agreed to let the Berg Collection at the New York Public Library purchase his long-held treasure. The end was sad. He 'went to his bank, retrieved the heavy bundle of correspondence, and suffered a heart attack'.

Pascal had briefly been President of the Shaw Society and Trebitsch, who came to London to treat the Society to a special reading of *Jitta's Atonement*, was a Vice-President. *The Shavian* recorded both their deaths: Pascal's in New York on 6 July 1954, Trebitsch's on 3 June 1956 in Vienna. During the 1960s there were regular listings of these deaths of old associates: Barry Jackson in 1961, Sydney Cockerell and Lawrence Langner in 1962, Nancy Astor, Hesketh Pearson and Sean O'Casey in 1964 and, supported by Shaw's annuity at the Onslow Court Hotel, Blanche Patch in 1966. There was also the Secretary of the Shaw Society, Eric Batson. When very young Batson had been epileptic and because of this he was later refused entry into the United States. As he progressed into his late forties he grew strangely volatile. He would incessantly telephone Barbara Smoker and, somehow identifying himself with Shaw, complain about Charlotte's refusal to be a wife to him in the fullest sense while preventing him from having any sexual liaison elsewhere. Another sign of instability was his obsessive hatred of fast cars. At the age of fifty he was confined to a mental hospital for his own protection. But this was in 1965, when wards were being opened up and staff cut down. He had no difficulty in slipping out unseen. Then he threw himself in front of a speeding car and died of multiple injuries.

And so to Loewenstein. While developing his mastery of Mediterranean gardening and an infatuation with the German laws of reparation (which, according to family legend, were improved with his advice) he still maintained connections with the Shaw Society from his homes on the Continent. In 1959 he moved with his wife from Frankfurt to San Remo because it was cheaper and nearer France, and then in 1966 to

Merano in the Dolomites because it was German-speaking and he could live near a synagogue. He remained comparatively poor. During Shaw's lifetime he had written (and G.B.S. rewritten) several articles, published some notes on *An Unsocial Socialist* as well as an eccentric pamphlet on Shaw's rehearsal copies, and seasoned the Shavian legend with *Bernard Shaw through the Camera*. Following Shaw's death, some of his scratchings on the copyrighting of the earlier plays appeared as a supplement to the Shaw Society's *Bulletin*. But after leaving England he published nothing. By the time he died in 1969 a new era of Shavian scholarship was flourishing across the Atlantic.

*

It had begun in November 1952 when, at the Shaw Society, Loewenstein relinquished his bibliography. In the audience that day was a young graduate, a junior colleague of Henry James's biographer and bibliographer Leon Edel, who, having been encouraged by Eric Batson to transfer his interests from Henry James to G.B.S., had recently joined the Shaw Society. Hearing Loewenstein's recantation, he suddenly stood up and affirmed that he would undertake the massive bibliography himself. This young man was Dan H. Laurence who for more than a quarter of a century was to tower over Shaw studies, producing between 1965 and 1988 four scrupulously edited volumes of Shaw's *Collected Letters* and in 1983 a meticulous and comprehensive two-volume Shaw bibliography. These works, together with *The Annual of Bernard Shaw Studies* (an indispensable sign of Shaw's status in the American academies), which is published at Pennsylvania State University State Press under the energetic editorship of Stanley Weintraub, are cornerstones of modern Shaw scholarship.

Shaw had handed over the management of his literary and theatre business to the Society of Authors in 1946. So huge had this business grown, and so complex its scholarly ramifications throughout the world, that in 1973 the Society of Authors issued a press release announcing the formation of an Academic Advisory Committee to help avoid the duplication of projects, and the appointment of Dan H. Laurence as Literary Adviser to vet the use of unpublished material, supervise authentic texts, and guide the publication policy. For half a lifetime Laurence was to work as editorial supervisor on *The Bodley Head Bernard Shaw Collected Plays and their Prefaces* (7 volumes, 1970–74), as general editor of *Bernard Shaw Early Texts: Play Manuscripts in Facsimile* (12 volumes, 1981), and editor of the complete musical criticism, *Shaw's Music* (3 volumes, 1981). He also acted as adviser for some major collectors of Shaw's manuscripts in the United States and in the 1980s as literary adviser to the Shaw Festival at Niagara-on-the-Lake in Canada. From 1970 onwards the quality of editorial work on Shaw prospered with such publications as Stanley Weintraub's two-volume *Shaw: An Autobiography* (1969–70), E. Dean Bevan's ten-volume *A Concordance of the plays and prefaces of Bernard Shaw* (1972), T. F. Evans's *Shaw: The Critical Heritage* (1976), Bernard F. Dukore's *The Collected Screenplays of Bernard Shaw* (1980), the two-volume edition of *The Diaries* annotated by Stanley Weintraub, and A. M. Gibbs's *Shaw: Interviews and Recollections* (1990).

The quantity of academic work also proliferated. By the twenty-fifth anniversary of Shaw's death in 1975 *The Shaw Review* in the United States estimated that in excess of 1,000 articles, more than 100 dissertations and 110 full-length books in six languages had been written on Shaw. There were to be continual additions, among them some amazing curiosities. Items Shaw had excluded from his Standard Edition were added posthumously to this scholarly impedimenta. His ghosted writings for Vandeleur Lee, the 'Practical System of Moral Education for Females' called *My Dear Dorothea* which he composed at the age of twenty-one, his unfinished *Passion Play*, incomplete sixth novel and abandoned work on Soviet Russia, even his Last Will and Testament, were brought to printers and bound into books and pamphlets. All sorts of errant and discarded fragments were rounded up. The evidence on censorship he had given before the Select Committee on the Stage in 1909 was extracted from the minutes and granted separate publication, his marginalia and rehearsal notes reset on centre pages, his uncollected pieces collected, his verses viewed and old reviews re-viewed.

In the 1980s the number of works about Shaw rose to over 300. There were also by this time fifty Study Guides and Notes to his plays issued for students. 'Blast all schools and schoolbooks! They are making literature loathed,' Shaw had written to his publisher in the 1920s when refusing permission to include part of *Saint Joan* in a textbook for the Middle Forms of secondary schools. ' . . . I lay my eternal curse on whomsoever shall now or at any time hereafter make schoolbooks of my works, and make me hated as Shakespear is hated.' This curse was printed as an epigraph to one of the series of revision aids for school examinations.

During Shaw's lifetime the polemical attacks had eventually given way to adulation and anecdotage. The best criticism of his work had been written about his plays-in-performance by contemporary reviewers such as William Archer, Max Beerbohm and Desmond MacCarthy. Already by the late 1930s and increasingly in the period of reaction following Shaw's death, the work of these reviewer-critics had given place to more distant academic assessments. The most influential of these was Raymond Williams's *Drama from Ibsen to Eliot* (1952). Raymond Williams found it difficult to believe that Shaw's 'dynamic as a dramatist can survive its period'. In a revised edition published in 1968 under the title *Drama from Ibsen to Brecht*, he amended 'can' to 'ought to'. The new criticism had little interest in the theatre. Most favourable verdicts on G.B.S. in the 1940s and 1950s had been the work of 'plodding and laborious minds'. In 1947 Eric Bentley described the job of reading books on Shaw as 'a gruelling experience'. Ten years later Kenneth Muir complained that 'there is hardly any serious critical study of his work with the exception of Eric Bentley'.

Eric Bentley brought the fresh intellect of a younger generation to Shaw's work. By the 1960s a new wave of critics, chiefly in the United States and Canada, were turning their attention to the plays and, beginning with Martin Meisel's comprehensive *Shaw and the Nineteenth Century Theater* (1963), producing work of far deeper perception.

Despite the enormous monument raised to him, Shaw's reputation was still insecure and he remained an isolated figure. 'Like Humpty Dumpty he has been fragmented,' wrote the Shavian scholar Margery Morgan, 'and it is almost as hard to put him together again.' One of the few books in which he appeared alongside his contemporaries had been J. I. M. Stewart's *Eight Modern Writers* (1963), the twelfth volume of *The Oxford History of English Literature*. The unusual format covering a period from 1880 to 1940 and containing independent studies of three Irish writers (Yeats and Joyce besides Shaw), an American (Henry James), a Pole (Conrad), a man who escaped England (D. H. Lawrence), the Indian-born Kipling, but no women, drew attention to Shaw's critical awkwardness – the awkwardness of legitimately excluding him or convincingly integrating him into any literary survey.

Shaw belonged equally to the Victorian age and the twentieth century, was part of Irish as well as English culture, and gave forth plays whose prodigality of speech was for a time drowned in the desolate pauses, racked silence, of Beckett and Pinter. Many writers are exiles, as J. I. M.

Stewart implies, but in his posthumous life G.B.S. seemed an exile who had never found another country. He was like a teacher of truants, a collectivist with brilliant individuals for disciples such as Brigid Brophy, Benny Green and Colin Wilson whose work had nothing in common except the leavening influence of Shaw.

In politics too he seemed to be without a constituency, having aligned himself, albeit eccentrically, with the rise of communism that subsequently fell and was by 1991 apparently at an end. What had maddened Shaw was that many of those who supported the Versailles Treaty, who advocated hostility to the Soviet revolution from its earliest days and thereby assisted the rise of nationalist and military dictatorships in the 1920s were later promoted as the champion opponents of Hitler and Stalin. Truly we loved our enemies and felt lost without them. There was in Shaw an immature leaning towards strong men deriving perhaps from the absence of a strong father, and he made frequent stupid and insensitive statements particularly about Stalin in the last twenty years of his life. Like his own surgeon, Cutler Walpole in *The Doctor's Dilemma*, he went on repeating one monotonous and fantastic solution for the blood poisoning of capitalism. Like Shotover in *Heartbreak House* he appeared to batten down the hatches while others were deserting the ship. But his ideal of democratic communism arising from a passionate desire for a more just society based on co-operation rather than competition for profit, was worlds away from the squalid party political regimes of Brezhnev, Andropov and Chernenko that arose after his death. He would inevitably have rejoiced in the dismantling of the Soviet empire and eagerly looked forward to the release and reseeding of all the hopes made sterile in that empire. Whatever happened, he believed that history did not end but was everlasting. He had written optimistically of collapsing systems, inadequate ideologies and the vanishing statues that mark the failing of our dreams in *The Simpleton of the Unexpected Isles*. 'We are not here to fulfil prophecies and fit ourselves into puzzles, but to wrestle with life as it comes. And it never comes as we expect it to come ... Let it come.'

Two remarkable biographies of Shaw appeared within fifteen years of his death. St John Ervine's *Bernard Shaw: His Life, Work and Friends* (1956) had been started a decade before Shaw's death and for almost thirty years this book rather than Archibald Henderson's *George Bernard Shaw: Man of the Century* (1956) was to share with the enlarged edition of Hesketh Pearson's *Bernard Shaw: His Life and Personality* (1961) the function of a standard Life. The other biography was an extraordinary work, *Shaw of Dublin: The Formative Years* (1964) by B. C. Rosset. Rosset was an American in the tradition of Demetrius O'Bolger, that unfortunate 'son of an Irish inspector of police'. He was no writer. His book was a compendium of research and speculation along the network originally threaded by O'Bolger fifty years earlier. But since there was now no disabling help from G.B.S., Rosset was able to do something O'Bolger could not do. He went to Dublin, rented a room in the Synge Street house where Shaw was born, and married the caterer at Trinity College Dublin (who later received an honorary degree for her culinary services). From here he plunged into his investigations round Shaw's home surroundings and came up with some of the discoveries for which O'Bolger had been looking. For example, Shaw wrote that Vandeleur Lee 'had to make his position in London before he could provide the musical setting for my mother and sister'. It was not 'an elopement,' he cautioned O'Bolger, but 'a practical necessity'. Some months, he implied, perhaps a year or two, had separated Lee's departure from his mother's. 'I forget the precise date of the débâcle . . . ' But from the list of departures for Holyhead printed in *The Irish Times* Rosset found the precise dates and the fact that Mrs Shaw had followed Lee to London only a few days after his departure, on her twenty-first wedding anniversary. But the hand of G.B.S. stretched back to shut this book almost as decisively as it had O'Bolger's. Rosset had quoted from Shaw without the permission of the Shaw Estate, and the Society of Authors stepped in to withdraw the book from publication. Not long afterwards, when Rosset died, the repeated history of O'Bolger seemed complete.

*

Seeking equilibrium within contending cultures, the Shaw Estate appeared to have made an alliance between rarefied scholarship and rampant commercialism. In 1963 the profit on *My Fair Lady* was extended when Warner Brothers paid $5,500,000 to the composer-writer team for screen rights. For twenty-four weeks' work while her singing voice was being dubbed, the new Eliza, Audrey Hepburn, was given a salary of $1,000,000. She took the place of Julie Andrews, the star of the stage version (thought by Jack Warner to be unknown by the general public), and, though not nominated herself, was chosen that year (1964) to present Julie Andrews with an Oscar for her performance in *Mary Poppins*.

'Filming *My Fair Lady* was not at all a piece of cake,' Rex Harrison recalled. Under the direction of George Cukor, 'the most famous director of women in the business', an atmosphere of conflict, chagrin and catastrophe quietly filled the studio. But from these rifts and squabbles emerged a well-mannered, slightly pale replica of the theatre musical. This result was partly due to the number of old stagers (Stanley Holloway, Cecil Beaton and Rex Harrison himself) transferred from the Broadway production, and partly attributed to the Shaw Estate which, growing apprehensive after the onslaughts from T. S. Eliot, E. M. Forster, Graham Greene and others, was reported to have 'refused any further excisions in what had once been "Pygmalion"'. Oscars were presented to André Previn for his musical adaptation, to Rex Harrison, George Cukor and Cecil Beaton among others, and fifteen years later, justifying the Shaw Estate's careful policy, the film had earned CBS more than $33,000,000.

The Society of Authors struggled to give respectability to the outpouring of Shavian productions during the 1950s and 1960s. When Otto Preminger proposed making a film of *Saint Joan* for United Artists in 1956, the Society very happily accepted his choice of scriptwriter, its recent excommunicant Graham Greene. But though both were sincere enemies of Western capitalism, Greene and Shaw seemed incompatible. The seedy population of Greeneland with their painful uncertainties and sinister injustices had no bright quarter for G.B.S. whose cheerful unfamiliarity with the allures of evil eventually made him, to Greene's mind, one of its public agents. Greene had responded to the most anguished of Shaw's plays, *Heartbreak House*, and also loved *Saint Joan* which, 'with a blur of happiness', he associated with his wife Vivien during the months of their engagement. But thirty years later it was no longer sacred to him. So 'I didn't mind adapting his work'.

Preminger wanted someone 'new and fresh' to play Joan, an actress whom audiences could not identify with previous roles. He advertised for a discovery. Eighteen thousand applications arrived and, gathering his bandwagon of publicity, Preminger set off on a crusade round twenty-one cities of the world holding open auditions for this 'Role of the Century'. His search led to a seventeen-year-old chemist's daughter from Marshalltown in Iowa, called Jean Seberg. 'She has the looks, intelligence, feeling and just the right innocence,' Preminger announced. Though she had played a few roles in the local stock company, Jean Seberg was without any professional experience. 'I became very fond of her,' remembered John Gielgud, 'realizing from that first reading what an impossible task must await her.'

Well before shooting started in the new year, Preminger had fixed the date of the première for the second week of May 1957 in Paris and Orléans (with New York and London premières following in June). He preferred to work to schedule, he said, rather than by inspiration. Graham Greene was given six weeks to write his script and, despite crises in the production, including the last-minute withdrawal of Richard Burton as Warwick (replaced by John Gielgud) and of Paul Scofield as Ladvenu (replaced by Kenneth Haigh) as well as the accidental singeing of Jean Seberg at Shepperton studios (witnessed by Barbara Smoker), Preminger faithfully held to his schedule. His *Saint Joan* was a rather glumly assembled 110-minute version of the three and a half hour play, reported *The Times* correspondent in Paris. 'The adapter, Mr Graham Greene, has been at pains to telescope Shaw's argument as faithfully as possible, and the main themes of the trial scene are preserved without fear of offending either theologians or believers in Joan's superhuman freedom from mortal frailty.'

The critics in New York generally treated Greene and Preminger with respect, but were disappointed by the film's lack of spiritual excitement and the failure of its dramatic moments to move them. It seemed a tepid affair, the play's argumentative wit replaced by waves of celestial cinema music. 'I alone am to blame,' declared Preminger. Shaw's *Saint Joan* was 'an intellectual thing,' he regretted, 'it is not a very dramatic play and I found out later . . .'

There were good performances from Gielgud as the coldly impeccable Warwick, Felix Aylmer in the role of the impassive Inquisitor and Harry Andrews as the robustly dogmatic Stogumber. But Preminger was blamed for the miscasting of 'the screen's favourite giggling killer' Richard Widmark playing the sensitive Dauphin, and for the shortcomings of Jean Seberg. The critics described her as 'acting like a ham sandwich' and looking like 'Peter Pan flashing his sword at the pirates'. 'I don't think I ever completely recovered my confidence,' she wrote. Later, through her performance in Godard's *A Bout de Souffle* and her marriage to Romain Gary, she recreated herself as part of the *nouvelle vague* in France. Then she was caught up by the Black Panther Party in the United States. She committed suicide at the end of the 1970s.

The Society of Authors had granted Preminger a licence on condition that changes in the film script did not exceed 24 per cent of the original play. He assured astonished reporters that Graham Greene's version had 'less than 5 per cent deviation, and that is mainly structural not verbal'.

In his Preface to *Saint Joan* Shaw had issued 'Some well-meant Proposals for the Improvement of the Play'. By excising all references to such tedious matters as the Church, he pointed out, to the feudal system, the theory of heresy and so on and so forth, the work could be wonderfully shortened.

'The experienced knights of the blue pencil, having saved an hour and a half by disembowelling the play, would at once proceed to waste two hours in building elaborate scenery, having real water in the river Loire and a real bridge across it, and ... Joan on a real horse. The coronation would eclipse all previous theatrical displays, shewing, first, the procession through the streets of Rheims, and then the service in the cathedral, with special music written for both. Joan would be burnt on stage ... on the principle that it does not matter in the least why a woman is burnt provided she is burnt, and people can pay to see it done.'

This passage, written in 1924, appeared over thirty years later to be an uncannily accurate summary of the Preminger–Greene film. 'The play of course had to be cut for film purposes,' Greene explained in the *New Statesman*, 'but these cuts were mainly drawn from the long discussions on the growth of nationality and the decay of feudalism which would hardly have been understood by film audiences.' But, by taking away the intelligent core of the play, the film blurred its outlines and diminished Joan, the critic Penelope Houston observed, 'into a figure altogether less commanding and fanatical, less formidable and less interesting'.

Graham Greene had been prepared for some salvoes of critical hostility. 'The critics will say another deplorable adaptation,' he wrote, 'though I would defend my script for retaining, however rearranged, Shaw's epilogue and for keeping a sense of responsibility to the author.' He also defended himself strongly against the charge of being brought in to de-Protestantize Shaw's heroine. 'Such a role was never proposed to me nor would I have accepted it,' he wrote. '... There is nothing in Shaw's play offensive to Catholics ... No line was altered for the purpose of watering down Shaw's Protestantism or instilling a Catholic tone.' Evidently Greene did not know of Catholic Action's threat to veto Shaw's own screenplay of *Saint Joan* in the 1930s. What had been objectionable to Catholics then was the depiction of Joan's trial as legally fair and his portrayal of the judges as true representatives of the Church. Greene's additional dialogue appears to get round these difficulties. For he shows Stogumber telling Warwick that particular French priests rather than the Church were responsible for the trial, and he makes Warwick say to Stogumber that Joan will be safely burnt before the Pope hears anything of the matter.

'Anyway I got a few laughs that were not in Bernard Shaw,' Greene later remarked: 'at least I can claim that.'

Some jokes (notably Dubedat's assertion: 'I dont believe in morality. I'm a disciple of Bernard Shaw') were missing from the next Shaw play to be adapted on to film, Metro-Goldwyn-Mayer's *The Doctor's Dilemma* which opened in New York at the end of 1958. Though its screen treatment appeared rather too glossy for some astringent Shavians ('worth seeing for the delphiniums alone,' commented *The Times Educational Supplement*), 'by normal standards of film adaptation, it is remarkably faithful,' *The Shavian* had advised its readers.

With the prospect of bringing Shaw's work before a younger audience, the Society of Authors had made a rather uncommercial contract with MGM, but still reserved rights of approval over the adaptation, choice of director and casting of parts. The screenplay was written by Anatole de Grunwald, 'a very erudite and cultured gentleman', remembered Dirk Bogarde who took the role of Louis Dubedat. ' . . . I never had another script-writer as brilliant until I met Harold Pinter.' Grunwald encouraged the cast to immerse themselves in the original play. But he cut the character of Dr Schutzmacher, the handsome middle-aged Jew who had made his money as a 'sixpenny doctor in a Midlands town', and changed the emphasis of the drama from reflections on the unchanging ethics of Harley Street even after the creation of the Welfare State and its National Health Service to a love story about a scoundrel who was adored by women.

For its director Anthony Asquith *The Doctor's Dilemma* was to be something of an experimental art movie. Converting the female lead from a Cornishwoman into a Breton, he chose the beautiful twenty-six-year-old Leslie Caron, adored as the *ingénue* in *Gigi*, to play opposite Dirk Bogarde (who had recently starred romantically as Sydney Carton in *A Tale of Two Cities*) and, as a further development in the 'Beatonization' of Shaw, persuaded Cecil Beaton to work free of charge designing aesthetic loose-flowing garments for her. These dresses suggested a Pre-Raphaelite atmosphere while concealing Leslie Caron's pregnancy (her daughter was to be called Jennifer after the good-looking Jennifer Dubedat). 'She had to have three sets of each costume because she blew-up and blew-down almost daily.'

Asquith wanted to frame this glamorous young couple with a collection of the very best classical actors then in Britain. 'Shaw's doctors survive the Health Service,' ran an enthusiastic headline in the *Evening Standard*. Critics relished the accomplished performances of Robert Morley fruitily booming away as Sir Ralph Bloomfield Bonington, Alastair Sim, wicked of eye and rolling of tongue as Cutler Walpole, and Felix Aylmer presiding over them with Olympian detachment as Sir Patrick Cullen. The film received good notices. But it was less popular with a cinema public looking forward to seeing Dirk Bogarde in yet another slapstick sequel to Richard Gordon's *Doctor in the House*, and unaware that *The Doctor's Dilemma* was to be a turning-point in his career.

Anthony Asquith, who had directed at least eight films in collaboration with Terence Rattigan and many others deriving from plays (including most famously *The Importance of Being Earnest*), was a director committed to filmed theatre. But he had few visual gifts, little enthusiasm for the drama of ideas, and did not share Shaw's political passions. The question raised by his refined and attenuated version of *The Doctor's Dilemma* was to what extent stage plays were translatable to the screen and whether film makers were at their best directing other people's dramas. 'The subsequent story of Shaw on the screen is generally not a happy one,' noted the critic Donald P. Costello. 'When Shaw films flop, they do it big.' Of the five other films made from Shaw's plays between 1958 and 1968, two never had the chance to 'flop big'. *Helden* was a German version of *Arms and the Man* directed by Franz Peter Wirth in 1958; and *Frau Warrens Gewerbe*, starring Lilli Palmer, was a German adaptation of an original screenplay by Anatole de Grunwald based on *Mrs Warren's Profession* and directed by Akos von Rathony the following year. Neither was shown in Britain or the United States where storms were soon breaking out among accredited Shavians as to which of the last three English-speaking Shaw films really was the worst horror of all.

'*The Devil's Disciple* could have been much better,' admitted Kirk Douglas who played devilish Dick Dudgeon in the Hecht–Hill–Lancaster film of Shaw's melodrama. But the question that troubled many who saw it was: *could it have been worse?* The film was a long-cherished project of Burt Lancaster. He had been trying to make it for over ten years. First he was held up by the arbitrary business habits of Gabriel Pascal, then delayed by the caution of the Society of Authors. But he had put some $800,000 of his own money into it, believing Shaw's play for puritans to be so saturated with off-stage romantic action that it cried out for film treatment. Concentrating on these opportunities for action, the script grew so at odds with the Society of Authors' regulations over limited changes to Shaw's dialogue that its revelation of extreme circumstances bringing out a man's unexpected character vanished.

Immense trouble was taken over this accomplishment. A brilliant British director, Alexander Mackendrick, who had recently made a key film of the 1950s, *Sweet Smell of Success*, revealing the tawdry glamour of the Times Square newspaper world, was hired to replace Anthony Asquith – and then sacked after two weeks because of 'differences of opinion with the producers on how the story should be screened'. Mackendrick, a lifelong admirer of Shaw, had got the point of *The Devil's Disciple* whereas Kirk Douglas and Burt Lancaster, who feared he would 'lose money by making it too highbrow', saw it as a swashbuckling follow-up to *Gunfight at the OK Corral*. Mackendrick's career 'never fully recovered from this dismissal'. He was replaced by Guy Hamilton who amiably gave way to Burt Lancaster. The co-producer Harold Hecht, fresh from having meticulously re-created the English seaside in Hollywood for his film of Terence Rattigan's *Separate Tables*, now went to infinite pains simulating eighteenth-century New England west of London. Colonial buildings designed in Hollywood and then prefabricated in Elstree Studios were hauled along winding Wiltshire roads by 60-foot conveyors and assembled on some acres of muddy gravel-strewn grass at Dyrham Park which was then occupied by a Los Angeles businessman. Here an assortment of actor-dragoons were assisted daily in the authentic complexities of drill and musketry by a young lecturer from Hull University who had been technical adviser on Kirk Douglas's *The Vikings*, while back at Elstree a dialogue director schooled the English cast in correct American parlance.

There was much to make *The Devil's Disciple* a serious candidate for Shaw's worst film. It suffered, wrote a critic in the *Guardian*, from 'the sort of vestigial respectfulness which damages a play without creating an honest-to-goodness film'. The nineteen-year-old Janette Scott, who had been appearing in films since the age of two, was obviously uncomfortable as the ladylike Judith Anderson, while the first sight of Burt Lancaster as her parson husband (generally agreed at the time to be an extreme example of his talent for taking on unsuitable roles) was irrecoverably comic. But the film was partly saved by a *tour de force* from Laurence Olivier as General Burgoyne. He had enormously irritated Burt Lancaster by repeatedly calling him Kirk. But 'in my opinion this Burgoyne is going to run away with the picture,' Burt Lancaster predicted after Olivier completed his part. Kirk Douglas agreed after seeing the première in New York on 20 August 1959. 'Larry Olivier was so brilliant, he stole the picture completely.'

'The cinematic vogue for Shaw continues,' reported *The Times* the following year announcing Shaw's next film. This was the inspiration of an untried producer called Pierre Rouve who wanted Anthony Asquith to direct *The Millionairess* for Twentieth Century-Fox. The Society of Authors agreed on condition that a reliable scriptwriter was chosen to adapt the play. This turned out to be Wolf Mankowitz, a specialist in musicals, who had adapted his own stories 'Make Me an Offer' and 'A Kid for Two Farthings' into films, and whose *Expresso Bongo* had recently featured the nineteen-year-old Cliff Richard as an exploited pop-singer. Mankowitz seemed to offer Shaw's work another opportunity of reaching a young audience. He saw his job as one of making the film into a vehicle for its two stars, Peter Sellers and Sophia Loren.

Peter Sellers was best known for his role as the militant shop steward Fred Kite in *I'm All Right Jack*, and as one of the Goons on radio. Until now he had regarded himself only as 'an ugly-looking comic'. The prospect of playing opposite a sex-goddess who looked 'a lot different from Harry Secombe'·dizzied him. Most of the drama took place beyond range of the cameras. Sophia Loren's 'black emeralds' worth £750,000 were stolen; and Peter Sellers, who fainted at the news, went on to break up his marriage under the delusion that Sophia Loren had fallen in love with him – 'I always try to establish a friendly relation with my leading men,' she explained. Realizing that his Indianization of Shaw's serious looking Egyptian doctor could be the opportunity for making an international reputation (the film was actually banned in Egypt but did well in the States), Sellers persistently tried to change the scenes and Anthony Asquith, now at the crumbling end of his career, could not stand up to him. Asquith's technical skill 'has never been in doubt', wrote one critic after the première in London on 20 October 1960. 'The flatness, the slapdash craftsmanship, above all the sheer vulgarity of *The Millionairess* is consequently all the more baffling.' Prolonged superimpositions, frantic cross-cutting and a battery of technical tricks were used to change Shaw's story into an adolescent romp, full of juvenile pranks and haphazard effects but without dramatic cohesion. In the play it is the athletic Alastair Fitzfassenden who 'strips well'; in the film it is Sophia Loren as the Amazonian heroine Epifania who extravagantly undresses. 'This lark,' wrote C. A. Lejeune in the *Observer*, ' ... can in no way be considered GBS's work.' A few non-Shavian critics rejoiced. You cannot displease everyone all the time. 'As I watched I nearly imitated Mr Khrushchev and began thumping my seat,' wrote Alexander Walker in the *Evening Standard*. 'But not in anger. In delight. Delight at the best film of a Bernard Shaw play since *Pygmalion* – a play that has been refurbished inside and out by Anthony Asquith and now fizzes with effrontery and dances a jig with absurdity.' But according to *The Shaw Review*, Shavians who had been 'so ill-advised or morbidly curious' as to see it could only feel relief that 'the credit line which says "Based on a play by George Bernard Shaw" slips by so fast that if you aren't watching closely you won't see it. It might better say "Based on a title by George Bernard Shaw".'

For most Shavians this was the worst travesty of all. Or so it seemed. But the Irish playwright Hugh Leonard, who scripted *Great Catherine* for Peter O'Toole in 1968, profoundly disagrees. Originally he was commissioned to write two fifty-five-minute screenplays, *Great Catherine* and *The Shewing-up of Blanco Posnet* which were to be shown back-to-back and entitled *The Shavians*. But *Blanco Posnet* soon vanished and Peter O'Toole asked instead for a hundred-minute version of Shaw's Byronic skit with the Battle of Bunker Hill refought on a gigantic set, and much wild Cossack dancing, frenzied chases and general slapstick added for the team of Zero Mostel, Akim Tamiroff, Jack Hawkins, Kenneth Griffith, Jeanne Moreau, Marie Lohr and himself. Gordon Flemyng, whose chief credit was for *Doctor Who* on television, directed the film and the chaos was wonderful. 'Interviewing Jeanne Moreau during the shooting of *Great Catherine*,' wrote a critic from *Sight and Sound*, 'I might just as well have been in the middle of the elephant house at the zoo.' Many of Shaw's bravura jokes still worked well, but Hugh Leonard is adamant: '*Great Catherine* was probably the worst film ever made.'

In all these adaptations, as well as in Pascal's *Pygmalion*, *Major Barbara* and *Caesar and Cleopatra* made during Shaw's lifetime, there are 'actors looking for sizeable roles, directors seizing upon carefully crafted texts, and producers trying to combine the search for prestige and box office success,' writes the film critic Philip French. '... What none of these pictures has is a director in control of the project who combines visual flair and a genuine interest in ideas.'

'One would like to have seen an Orson Welles film of *Heartbreak House*, with himself as Captain Shotover; Peter O'Toole as Tanner in a film of *Man and Superman* rather than in *Great Catherine*; Stanley Kubrick make a film of *Caesar and Cleopatra* or indeed one of half-a-dozen other plays. The younger contemporary director who could be the right adaptor of Shaw is Peter Greenaway.'

None of Shaw's films, nor the musicals made from his plays, repeated the box office success of *My Fair Lady*, though that success lured many librettists and song writers into prolonged negotiations over *The Devil's Disciple, Major Barbara, Man and Superman*. An American musical of *Caesar and Cleopatra* called *Her First Roman* opened and closed at Boston in the late 1960s, and in the early 1970s Richard Rodgers's charming small-scale adaptation of *Androcles and the Lion*, starring Noël Coward and Norman Wisdom, did not reach Broadway though Norman Wisdom records that 'it was undoubtedly the most exhilarating and excitingly happy experience of my career'. In Britain in the early 1980s a musical version of *The Admirable Bashville* failed to escape from Regent's Park, but dreams were rekindled at Chichester in 1991 and summer aspirations rose on the carnival airs of *Valentine's Day*, Benny Green and Denis King's new musical of *You Never Can Tell*...

*

Though G.B.S. posthumously appeared in several one-man productions and many stage impersonations in concert with Wittgenstein, Wilde, Wells, Yeats, Joyce, Ibsen, Shakespeare and Augustus John, with Isadora Duncan, Marie Stopes and Madame Blavatsky; though he could be seen dancing in a Sadler's Wells ballet, heard singing in a musical by Stephen Sondheim and a musical biography by Johnny Dankworth and Benny Green; though there have been performances of his non-dramatic works such as a theatre version of *The Black Girl* by Christopher Isherwood and the filming of his novel *Love Among the Artists* for television, as well as the dramatic parcelling up of his letters to Janet Achurch, Stella Campbell, Ellen Terry, Kathleen Scott, Margaret Wheeler, Gilbert Murray, Dame Laurentia McLachlan and Sydney

Cockerell, the staple of the Shaw Estate remains the publication and production of his plays.

Every year, for over thirty posthumous years, the number of Shaw plays produced was remarkably consistent. On average the Society of Authors issued twenty-five licences for stock performances in the United States and fifty repertory licences in the United Kingdom. Each year too the number of amateur performances in the United States, as well as those in the United Kingdom, worked out at approximately 1,000. On the European continent and in South America, Shaw's reputation was long tied down by the complex arrangements he had made with his translators (including Trebitsch in Germany, Castelli in Italy, and the Hamons in France). Not until the late 1960s did his work struggle free from these dated versions. Germany, with new translations by Heinrich and Marie Böll, Wolfgang Hildesheimer and Martin Walser all published by Suhrkamp Verlag, produced the largest number of Shaw plays on radio, television and the stage. France, where his plays were brought out by L'Arch Editeur, and Italy, where they were reissued by Arnoldo Mondadori, followed Germany. There was also a marked increase in new Spanish translations and at the beginning of the 1990s a complete edition of his work in Japan.

In Britain, Shaw's plays came and went like sunspots in periodic bursts. Fifteen of them had been put on in London as a public valediction in 1951, and for the centenary of his birth five years later there was a further ten presentations round the country. Between 1964 and 1974 the Society of Authors licensed twenty major productions (excluding repertory performances) of full-length plays and seven of one-act plays. Then in 1975 came another burst of activity with John Schlesinger's staging of *Heartbreak House* at the Old Vic, Simon Callow in *The Doctor's Dilemma* and Stephen Murray in *On the Rocks* at the Mermaid, and Clifford Williams's *Too True to be Good* starring Judi Dench and Ian McKellen at the Globe. The early 1980s, with productions of *Major Barbara* and the full-length *Man and Superman* at the National Theatre, as well as London presentations of *Captain Brassbound's Conversion* with Penelope Keith, *Arms and the Man* with Richard Briers, and *Village Wooing* with Judi Dench, marked another surge of Shavian activity in the London theatre.

There was need for an interlude. Shavian productions had fitted mainly into one of three categories. Often they were used as vehicles for star performers. This practice started in 1951 when Laurence Olivier and Vivien Leigh played *Caesar and Cleopatra* on alternate nights with *Antony and Cleopatra* in London and New York, and it was to end in the early 1980s with Peter O'Toole's 'theatre of comedy' series *Man and Superman, Pygmalion* and *The Apple Cart*. 'Many, no doubt, were drawn to this revival of an early Shaw play by the name of Mr Tyrone Power,' commented *The Times* critic reviewing *The Devil's Disciple* in 1956. '... it was the play itself that appeared to take everybody by surprise.' Though there were glorious exceptions including Ralph Richardson's hilarious waiter in *You Never Can Tell* (1966) and Eileen Atkins's formidable St Joan (1977), too many of these star performances – Kay Hammond in *Man and Superman* (1951), Charles Laughton's *Major Barbara* (1956), John Gielgud's infantile Caesar in *Caesar and Cleopatra* (1971), Ingrid Bergman's uncadenced Lady Cicely Waynflete in *Captain Brassbound's Conversion* (1971–2) – were plainly miscast and threw a shadow over Shaw's reputation in the theatre. 'Given his cavalier confrontationalism as dramatist, his fervour as egalitarian moralist,' wrote Susan Todd in the *New Statesman* in 1984, 'it seems unpleasantly ironic that he should have been, for so long now, appropriated by the richest, glossiest, most commercial production companies for what is called "revival." The term suggests the dead, but Shaw's work didn't die. It just got gobbled up, assimilated in the treacly repertoire of plays considered suitable as "star vehicles".'

Yet Shaw's gentility, and the making over of himself as a deliberate wooing of audiences after his 'unpleasant' plays, was partly to blame for such middle-class glossiness. This glossy patina spread over more run-of-the-mill productions. The London theatres filled with a second category of work, the pastime of venerable actors and directors presenting Shaw as a matinée author whose plays could never have shocked and stimulated audiences at the Royal Court Theatre as John Osborne shocked and stimulated them there fifty years later. Few people noticed the family resemblance between Jimmy Porter and John Tanner.

Apart from two or three plays, Shaw's work had never conquered London's West End during his lifetime, nor had it conquered Broadway. The transfer of his early drama from the Royal Court to the Savoy Theatre petered out, and between the wars his place was established in Birmingham and Malvern rather than in London. He grew popular too with touring companies such as the Macdona Players led by Esmé Percy and with provincial repertory theatres at Edinburgh and Glasgow, Chichester and Oxford (where Frank Hauser staged a series of Shaw dramas at the Playhouse). In London he found various homes beyond the West End: in the little 'Q' Theatre built by Jack and Beatrice Leon at the foot of Kew Bridge and the small Everyman Theatre on the hill in Hampstead, at the Lyric Theatre in Hammersmith, Alec Clunes's miniature Arts Theatre in Great Newport Street, and Bernard Miles's Mermaid Theatre at Puddle Dock.

Outstanding productions of his plays nevertheless occasionally appeared in the West End: among them, after many years given over to *My Fair Lady*, a wonderful rediscovery in 1974 of *Pygmalion* at the Albery Theatre directed by John Dexter, with Diana Rigg and Alec McCowen as a dramatically poised, psychologically observed Eliza and Higgins; and two years later, as the Royal Shakespeare Company's celebration of the American bicentennial at the Aldwych Theatre, Jack Gold's tongue-in-cheek exploitation of *The Devil's Disciple* featuring John Wood as the debonair Burgoyne and Tom Conti riding the part of Richard Dudgeon 'like it's a bronco in a rodeo'.

But what original thought went into directing Shaw's work was un-sustained. It had promised better. 'The Shaw revival in Britain began on 15 March 1965 with Ronald Eyre's production of *Widowers' Houses*,' Irving Wardle wrote. ' . . . the work itself was quite enough to demolish a whole swathe of Shavian preconceptions and reveal an alarmingly human face under the grinning mask.' But when Ronald Eyre came to direct Shaw's companion piece, *Mrs Warren's Profession*, at the Old Vic at the end of 1970, Irving Wardle conceded: 'lightning does not strike twice in the same place, least of all theatrical lightning; and there are no grand illuminations to be found in this revival'. Again, reviewing Frank Dunlop's vivid production of *Too True to be Good* a few months after *Widowers' Houses*, Irving Wardle predicted in *The Times* that it would be seen as 'a well-calculated act of revaluation designed to open up his neglected last phase'. But despite some promisingly surreal versions of *Heartbreak House* and a heroic experiment with *Back to Methuselah* (1984) conducted by nine actors under the direction of Bill Pryde, Shaw's last phase was never convincingly opened up. Nor, despite a few brilliant individual performances – Ian McKellen in *O'Flaherty, V.C.* (1966) at the Mermaid or in *Too True to be Good* (1975) for the Royal Shakespeare Company – did the London theatre move far into this third category of production and away from the standard Shavian comedies and chron-icles. By 1973, after the death of Peter Bridge, a young commercial manager with a flair for bringing Shaw productions to the West End, Irving Wardle concluded that 'the Shavian revival is on the ebb'.

This reflected in part the prevailing post-Brechtian theatre at the Royal Court and a shift in the training methods of actors following Joan Littlewood's revolution at Stratford East. The abandonment, outside Shakespeare, of stylized speech training (with actors practising like singers) in favour of improvisation and realism, and the rise of the actor-director which seemed to clash with Shaw's theatrical ideology of power to the playwright, lay at the root of a growing embarrassment at the National Theatre over its attitude to Shaw. Meanwhile, desperate economies in the commercial theatre increasingly handicapped the productions of plays demanding full casts and changes of sets, and led the way to sparse two-voice texts, the transfer of television material and the more lavish appeal of West End musicals.

But a bolder revival was already taking place in Canada where Shaw's drama had been made popular by Maurice Colbourne and Barry Jones's tours, the expert presentations by the Canadian Broadcasting Corporation, and performances up and down the leading Little Theatres (as the non-professional centres were known). The plays had survived their reputation for being iconoclastic and even revolutionary, and the Anglo-Irish G.B.S. became a favourite entertainer with Anglo-Canadian audiences untroubled by his political convictions.

In 1962 a modest Shaw Festival started in Ontario. Its founder was a Toronto lawyer, Brian Doherty, who (rather in the manner of Barry Jackson at Birmingham) had lost money through his passion for the theatre. Retiring to the small nineteenth-century town Niagara-on-the-Lake, he launched his Shaw Festival with four amateur performances of *Don Juan in Hell* played on weekends in the cramped and suffocating Old Court House. By 1963 the Festival began staging full-length productions. After three semi-professional seasons sustained by the actors' enthusiasm and the commitment of the artistic director Andrew Allan, the venture was 'transformed for ever' in 1966 by the arrival of Barry Morse. He brought showmanship to the Festival. 'Working with Barry,' remembered Brian Doherty, 'was like going over Niagara Falls in a barrel.' There seemed nothing he could not do by way of blandishment, cajolery, the exploitation of friends and the inflammation of strangers. Television audiences saw him seated on a kitchen chair at a card table in the middle of a traffic island prompting questions on his lack of office facilities. As with Malvern during the 1930s, not everyone in Niagara was friendly. 'We encountered bloody-mindedness as well as saintly kindness,' he records, ' – but gradually the town warmed up.' He extended the season to nine weeks and staged three full-length Shaw plays, persuading the local military to fire 'a monstrous rocket from the roof of the building' at their opening performance. The result was a sell-out. 'We sold all the seats we had to sell' – 350 for each show totalling 25,000 seats throughout the season in a town with a population of little more than 5,000 inhabitants (the population of the whole district, including a large part of the north-east corner of the Peninsula, is only 12,000).

The Festival expanded again under the artistic director Paxton Whitehead. A beautiful new rose-coloured theatre designed by the Canadian architect Ron Thom holding 832 seats was opened in the summer of 1973. Seven years later, when Christopher Newton came from the Vancouver Playhouse to take over the directorship, a third theatre, the Royal George, was purchased. Originally built as a vaude-ville theatre in 1913, it had been used to entertain the troops in the First World War and subsequently functioned as a road house, a cinema, and a home for the Canadian Mime Theatre. Restoring the Edwardian décor, the Shaw Festival was to put on its most popular plays, the rediscovered musicals and lunchtime productions there.

Being close to the United States, the Festival could attract audiences from across the border with farces and musical comedies, dramas of romance and detection. It gained a reputation for lightness of heart at the expense of Shaw's darker humour, and during the 1980s made a name for itself with a number of extraordinary productions: *Cyrano de Bergerac, Camille*, Brecht's *A Respectable Wedding*, and a controversial *Saint Joan* without the Epilogue. There were unusual Shaw plays too: *The Simpleton of the Unexpected Isles* (1983), *On the Rocks* (1986), *Getting Married* (1989); a haunting *Heartbreak House* in 1985, a memorable *Man and Superman* played with *Don Juan in Hell* in 1989, a triumphant *Millionairess* starring Nicola Cavendish in 1991. 'The standard there is very high indeed,' reported the editor of *The Shavian*, T. F. Evans. *You Never Can Tell* (1988) and *Misalliance* (1990) were, he judged, 'the best all-round productions of the ten or dozen each of these plays that I have seen'. Already by 1980 the Festival had created an ensemble on European lines. Lasting eight months of the year, it now imports international directors and presents, besides Shavian drama each year, plays from Russia, France, Scandinavia, Germany, Hungary, Canada and the United States. 'In the last seven years we have scrupulously kept to our mandate of plays written during Shaw's lifetime – nothing else,'

Christopher Newton wrote in 1991. 'It gives us a unique perspective on dramatic literature ... It forces us to look at the old from a new vantage point.' What had begun at Malvern in the 1930s was accomplished in Niagara fifty years later. By the early 1990s some forty-five plays by Shaw had been presented in almost ninety productions, together with work by over a hundred and twenty other dramatists, many of which toured Canada and the United States. A fringe of seminars, special events, and projects for young people sprang up. From the days when actors banged nails into the walls to hang their clothes and dressed in the Court House kitchen or a derelict barn by the parking lot, the Shaw Festival had flowered into a centre for the performing arts and 'one of the most exciting theatrical events on the North American continent,' wrote the *Guardian* critic Michael Billington.

'In Canada, we were less liable to be spotted for cuts of the original,' explained the doyen of Canada's theatre critics, Herbert Whittaker. In Britain, and to some extent in the United States, directors were sometimes intimidated by Shaw's authoritative stage directions and the policing of texts by the Society of Authors' Academic Advisory Committee. It was not always remembered that these stage directions had been added, like the prefaces, as a narrative enabling these works to appear in published form and be read by the public almost as if they were novels. There were also many stories of Shaw's terrific refusals to cut his own plays during his lifetime, which antagonized some directors by seeming to fix a precedent.

But G.B.S. was an apostle of change, adept at bringing his facts up to date. 'If I were you I should cut the part,' he had advised Ellen Terry while she was preparing the role of Imogen for Henry Irving's production of *Cymbeline*. Shaw used Shakespeare like everyone else uses Shakespeare: as an autobiographical code. Towards the end of his life he was telling Dame Laurentia McLachlan: 'I need pruning. There's a lot of dead wood.' He knew that he overwrote and that naturally 'I shall have my period of staleness and out-of-dateness for years after my death.' This reaction was to be compounded by the advent of television with its habit of 'small acting' in front of cameras in place of the flamboyant performances demanded by the Shavian theatre.

'Do not treat my printed text with blindly superstitious reverence,' Shaw told a producer when in his nineties. 'It must always be adapted intelligently to the studio, the screen, the stage, or whatever the physical conditions of performance may be.' During his posthumous period of staleness there was far too little intelligent adaptation, too much super-stitious reverence. The première of *Geneva* with its extra act was given at the Mermaid in 1971, but seven years later the director Christopher Morahan was refused permission to add the original unperformed last act of *The Philanderer* to his imaginative production at the National Theatre in London, and the chance of seeing a substantially new play was further delayed. In the last decade of Shaw's copyright, however, the Shaw Estate has allowed a world première of the full-length *Philanderer* at the Hampstead Theatre (1991) signalling a new opportunity for Shaw on stage.

The difficulty in presenting Shaw's plays to modern audiences is not simply a matter of pruning texts and transcending acting fashions. It is also a matter of deciding what sort of plays he wrote. Borges praised him for creating superb characters on stage, Brecht for subverting character and introducing the spirit of alienation. 'As an imitator of Ibsen, Strindberg, Chekhov or Shakespeare,' wrote Margery Morgan, 'Shaw produced work that impresses us much more by its differences from his models, radical differences of tone and quality, than by the detectable similarities.' These differences have led to a confusing divergence of critical opinion.

Shaw's originality depends on a peculiar vision which has been likened to El Greco's astigmatism. In his Preface to *Plays Unpleasant*, he had written of 'having got a clue to my real condition' from an ophthal-mic physician who 'tested my eyesight one evening, and informed me that it was quite uninteresting to him because it was normal ... normal sight conferring the power of seeing things accurately, and being enjoyed by only about ten per cent of the population, the remaining ninety percent being abnormal.' Shaw uses this story to establish his credentials as a 'realist', but as his method of telling the story shows he was no more realistic or 'natural' in his way of thinking than Hamlet (to whom he sometimes likened himself), though his 'mind's eye' has something of the same ingrained theatricality.

> HAMLET: My father, methinks I see my father.
> HORATIO: O where, my lord?
> HAMLET: In my mind's eye, Horatio.

Shaw's mental vision, which 'saw things differently from other people's eyes, and saw them better,' was an example of what ophthalmic opticians would now call antimetropic sight: one eye focused short, the other long.

This is what Shaw himself was indicating when he told G. K. Chesterton that an Irishman had one eye for reality and the other for poetry. In his earlier plays he had begun by looking at his contemporary world, singling out themes of recurring topicality – feminism, disarmament, medical and marital ethics, property values versus human values, the relationship between Ireland and England, the peaceful invasion of Britain by the United States, the rise of trade union power. In sociological and political terms, 'almost all of Shaw's plays are at almost all times timely,' Sheridan Morley wrote when reviewing *Misalliance* in 1973. 'He seems to be foreseeing our future,' wrote Alan Brien commenting on *Too True to be Good* in 1975. Being a philosophical dramatist and an acute social analyst, Shaw identified basic unchanging motives and processes. In his later plays he went on to cultivate the long-range outlook that strengthened his impersonal habit of mind, training his eye for poetry into a prophetic gaze that seemed to stare 'through you or over you', Leonard Woolf noticed, 'into a distant world or universe'. This abstract view became part of his special equipment in the theatre, enabling him to use ancient theatrical forms to present contemporary themes.

Only the most flexible direction, which recognizes that Shaw sometimes worked in several genres within the same play, can bring together the various movements of his work. Drama was for him a broad spectrum that terminated at one end in opera (he considered Shakespeare's *Othello* as essentially a musical melodrama). 'My method, my system, my tradition, is founded on music,' he wrote. Seeking a rhetorical notation based on music pitch and dynamics, bringing musical ideas to acting, using operatic allusion to play up romantic sentiment and operatic conceptions to shape his scenes as overtures, arias, duets, ensembles, Shaw's theatre of ideas calls for the opera-inspired direction given by Richard Jones to the work of Corneille and Ostrovsky, and by Steven Pimlott to Molière's *The Miser* in the early 1990s.

*

'The man's life and works are either nothing or they belong to the future,' wrote Eric Bentley in 1951. Shaw's life and works were rightly challenged after his death by later generations demanding a close examination of both before accepting him as one of their representatives in history.

In 1970 the Shaw Estate decided to commission an authorized biography to complement the critical exploration of his dramaturgical techniques and the relationship between his art and politics. 'All the biographies so far have been partial,' explained Elizabeth Barber, General Secretary of the Society of Authors, in an interview for *The Times*. 'St John Ervine in 1956 was the most comprehensive, but the time has come, the estate feels, for an assessment of the man in his period.' There was some wonder, however, mixed with consternation, when scholars found that the wheel had stopped with its arrow pointing at a biographer who had no experience of politics or theatre, no academic qualifications, and no record of having worked on Shaw.

I was thirty-four and this experience was certainly new for me. I was then writing the Life of a flamboyant heterosexual, having previously published books about a notorious homosexual and an unknown impoverished writer who, following the appearance of my book, stubbornly remained unknown. People usually implored me not to write biographies of their friends and members of their family. Now I was gaining respectability, albeit controversial respectability. The feeling was not altogether comfortable. This invitation from the British Museum, the Royal Academy of Dramatic Art, and the National Gallery of Ireland was obviously a great honour, but it was also a considerable terror. To my eyes G.B.S. appeared a gigantic and incomprehensible figure with whom I felt little intimacy, yet this was a challenge I really ought to accept. Nevertheless I hesitated. I had heard that Shaw wrote ten letters a day, every day, all his adult life, and that people kept his letters. I knew that he had composed more than fifty plays, that there was a collected edition of almost forty volumes, and many library yards of books about him, as well as huge deposits of unpublished papers around the world. I began to suspect that with his shorthand and his secretaries G.B.S. could actually write in a day more words than I could read in a day. Since he lived into his mid-nineties working vigorously to the end, this was an alarming prospect. I therefore prevaricated. Having recently begun research for a life of Augustus John I was able to advance this as a proper reason for being unable to start on G.B.S. until the mid-1970s. The Shaw Estate was unmoved.

In 1975 I began my Shavian research in Dublin. Here I found there was almost no one who, even when they had no information at all, would not be prepared to volunteer something over a jar or two. For a long time I was encumbered with help. People I had never heard of came to my door to advise me sympathetically that they knew nothing. Many wrote letters to the same effect: some hopefully in verse; others more prosaically enclosing business cards. One lady wanted to know whether Shaw's biographer could obtain an introduction for her to the Royal Family. Everyone pressed in on me so warmly that I was moved to reply with such politeness that my replies elicited answers to which I felt bound to respond. One lady (whom I never met), noting the volume of our correspondence over the years, ventured to ask whether we had ever had an affair, the crucial part of which had escaped her. I was swimming in the wake of the great Shavian legend. Eventually I found myself pursuing G.B.S. to Soviet Russia, New Zealand, Italy, South Africa, and also to many places he had never been but which now held his manuscripts. There is a Shaw Collection at the British Library: there is a Shaw distribution throughout the world.

It took me some three years to get a sense of breaking Shaw's literary code, the alpha and omega of his dramatic style, and picking up subtle underlying themes which, to reach an immediate public, he had orchestrated for trumpet and big drum. Many people had come to think of G.B.S. as having only ink in his veins and having been born with a long white beard. I have tried to dismantle this bearded literary superman and replace him with a more recognizable if still uncommon human being. Behind the public phenomenon was a private individual, infrequently glimpsed, who gives G.B.S. his concealed humanity. He covered up his vulnerability with dazzling panache: I have tried to uncover it and, without losing the sparkle of this panache, show the need he had while alive for such brilliant covering. He has been an unsettling companion, stimulating, exasperating, who uses all his powers of lucidity and dark exhilarating humour, to challenge orthodoxies, subvert conventions, uproot fashion and make us see an alternative view. This is an honourable function of literature. His childhood and adolescence had been rich only in dreams, he told Ellen Terry, frightful and loveless in reality. It was the dreamer who went on to write plays and the man who wanted to make the realities of the world less frightful who played with politics. 'Live in contact with dreams and you will get something of their charm: live in contact with facts and you will get something of their brutality,' he wrote in *John Bull's Other Island*. 'I wish I could find a country to live in where the facts were not brutal and the dreams not unreal.'

There is such a country and its name is Utopia. 'A map of the world that does not include Utopia,' wrote Oscar Wilde in *The Soul of Man Under Socialism*, 'is not worth glancing at.' For some tastes there is not enough evidence of love in Shaw's Utopia. 'I implore you not to describe me as a loveable human being,' he appealed to Lawrence Langner. But he had also written: 'let those who may complain that it was all on paper remember only on paper has humanity yet achieved glory, beauty, truth, knowledge, virtue, and abiding love.' He wanted people to grow more self-sufficient rather than depend for their vital happiness on the off-chance of romance, with its partiality, favouritism, unfairness, and abiding penalties. What existed as sentimentality in others was turned within him into political idealism. He became a saint of the lonely and the fugleman of those who were out of step with their times. He gave them a heartening message. For every disadvantage, in Shavian terms, becomes a potential asset in disguise. The art of life is the art of heroic paradox. But under the play of his paradoxes, between his life and the work, moves a current of passion, often diverted and running with ironic cross-currents. It is this that I have sought to navigate.

Shaw objected to biography in his time because, by presenting 'barren scoundrels as explorers and discoverers', it glamorized the past and idealized a corrupt system. As a young man in the 1880s he had called for the revolution in biographical writing that was to be pioneered by Lytton Strachey. A little later, in 1905, Shaw wrote to Henry Irving's son: 'If you write a life of your father, don't make it a vestryman's epitaph. Let us have the truth about the artist ... The artist sacrifices everything to his art, beginning with himself.' Later, when infiltrating the work of his own biographers with concealed autobiography, he sacrificed something of his life so that these books might act as endorsements to his political commitments and avoid giving pain to living people. But he had also acknowledged that 'no man has an accurate knowledge of his own life & that when an autobiography does not agree with a biography, the biography is probably right and the autobiography wrong'.

Treating the gospels as early examples of biography Shaw noted in the Preface to *Androcles and the Lion* how St Matthew ('like most biographers') tended to 'identify the opinions and prejudices of his hero with his own', while St John used biography as a record of the 'fulfilment of ancient Jewish prophecies'. He concluded: 'When you read a biography remember that the truth is never fit for publication.' Since Shaw's death, biographical technique and subject matter have expanded so that biography now embraces the whole range of human experience, in so far as it is recoverable, and accepts it as fit for publication. I do not specifically identify my opinions and prejudices with Shaw's so far as I am aware, nor have I used his life to record the fulfilment or non-fulfilment of socialist prophecies. My deepest involvement is with biography itself and its never-ending love-affair with human nature, and my aim has been to come a little nearer a biographical ideal described by Hugh Kingsmill as 'the complete sympathy of complete detachment'.

POSTSCRIPT

I must stop, leaving much unsaid ... I have gone on as far as I am able.
Everybody's Political What's What?

The Shaw Companion commences with Shaw's death and finishes with the publisher's deadline. This short postscript follows precedents from G.B.S. himself who tied last-minute scenes into *Geneva*, his harlequinade on the rapid developments of contemporary politics; and it will end rather as he ended the Envoy to *Everybody's Political What's What?* – after which he went back and inserted an extra act into *Geneva*.

*

The first Bernard Shaw Summer School was opened in Dublin on 21 June 1991. This three-day event, putting many surprising participants (from Roy Hattersley MP to Seamus Heaney) through their paces, was crammed with seminars, suppers, film shows, music, theatre, and had been the inspiration of Cornelius Howard, a lunchtime legend at the Department of Foreign Affairs where until recently he had managed Irish cultural relations with the rest of the world.

'Money talks: money prints: money broadcasts: money reigns,' wrote Shaw in his Preface to *The Apple Cart*. The Festival Programme contained an urgent appeal for money from the chairperson of the Shaw Birthplace Trust, Nora Lever. She was a woman with two telephones. On one she indulged her Shavian passion; on the other she exercised her compassion for Dublin's stray cats. During the late summer of 1991, the stricken Irish cats were obliged to wait their turn in the streets while the professor set her trustees on to the Taoiseach, Charles Haughey. 'It could only happen in Ireland', she lamented, 'that during the year in which we celebrate our European Cultural Capital status, we have to beg for money to rescue the house of a Nobel Prizewinning writer.'

Nora Lever's begging powers were formidable, but then so was the financial plight of 33 Synge Street. With help from the American Women's Club of Dublin, one room had already been refurbished and opened by President Mary Robinson with an evening of Victorian music.

But elsewhere the ceilings sagged, walls crumbled, and there was an odour of decay. 'In fact it's a wreck,' pronounced Professor Lever when inviting journalists to 'Come in, and see the devastation.'

With an overdraft of more than £50,000 it could only be a matter of weeks before the bank foreclosed and put the property back on the market. But Nora Lever made sure that the unfortunate Taoiseach was continuously beset with questions, petitions, suggestions, appeals. 'We would like to be as generous as we can about these matters,' he pleaded. He was saddened to hear the government's indirect allocation of £10,000 through the Irish Sailors' and Soldiers' Land fund dismissed as 'derisory'. Yet it was certainly true that the amount of money needed to convert the house into a museum and international centre for students would be less than the Shaw royalties that went to the National Gallery of Ireland in one year – royalties that in recent times appeared to have been used for purposes normally financed out of central government funds.

Nora Lever spread the campaign into British and American newspapers, commandeered as trustees some of her fiercest stray-cat colleagues, obliged the bank to grant a short extension, and called a press conference. It would be 'monstrous' declared the *Evening Press*, a 'disgrace' announced the *Sunday Press*, a 'national disgrace' agreed the *Irish Press*, if Ireland failed to honour Dublin's debt to G.B.S.

On 23 October, acknowledging that he had been 'made aware' of the difficulties of the Shaw Birthplace Museum Trust, the Taoiseach promised in the Dáil to allocate 'a further grant of approximately £54,000 also from the Irish Sailors' and Soldiers' Land Trust to complete the purchase of the property'.† So the house was saved and the Taoiseach happily prepared to leave office.

*

On 14 November, almost one hundred years after its composition, the world première of a Shaw play opened at the Hampstead Theatre in London.

In 1893, when Lady Colin Campbell had persuaded him to cancel his original last act of *The Philanderer* because it was then impossibly far ahead of its time, Shaw had written another act that could be performed either as an alternative end, substituting a conventional marriage for a

---

†Following a restoration appeal, launched with a brochure from Penguin Books, the Shaw House was signed over to Dublin Tourism on 15 September 1992. It will be opened as a museum in 1993, with furniture provided by the Shaw Trust. Meanwhile the three-year-old Shaw Society of Dublin prospers and flourishes.

happy separation, or (once public opinion found his unorthodox treatment of divorce acceptable on stage) as a penultimate act which lent
extra irony to his original conclusion.

'They think this a happy ending, Julia, these men: our lords and
masters!' he makes Grace Tranfield say during the additional act. But
when publishing *The Philanderer* as one of his 'three Unpleasant Plays' in
1898, Shaw printed only this implausible 'happy ending' as his finale,
moving the comedy nearer the traditional Victorian farce. This, too, was
the version that, with a few revisions, reappeared over thirty years later in
his Collected Edition. 'I make no attempt to bring the play up to date,' he
wrote in a prefatory note of 1930. Nowhere is there any mention of the
missing act. Much of what he had intended to pour into the full-length
play he had by that time decanted into other plays. He had transformed
the philanderer Leonard Charteris into John Tanner, the Don Juan of
Man and Superman; re-examined Dr Paramour's medical ethics in *The
Doctor's Dilemma*; exposed the restrictions of conventional marriage in
Getting Married; and pursued the new disquisitory trail first attempted in
the cancelled act through *Misalliance* and *Heartbreak House*.

The Philanderer had been an unhappy work, stirring up memories
of his unfortunate affair with Jenny Patterson, forcing compromise on
him to no avail, and fitting awkwardly between *Widowers' Houses* and
Mrs Warren's Profession. He had apparently put the abandoned act
out of his mind and it was unknown to his contemporaries. After his
death, it found its way as part of the Shaw Collection into the Department of Manuscripts at the British Museum. It was first published in
facsimile in 1981, though it has never been printed and was not seen on
stage until the actor Brian Cox decided to direct it at the Hampstead
Theatre.

The question was whether the complete version would succeed as
intellectual comedy in the theatre and restore *The Philanderer* to its full
weight as one of the three 'Plays Unpleasant'. The critics were pretty
well unanimous. In *The Sunday Telegraph* John Gross described the new
material as a 'welcome addition' and the four-act play as a 'decided
success'. 'It gives a much-needed Ibsenite irony and bite,' wrote
Michael Billington in the *Guardian*, '. . . This is good hard-hitting stuff'.
In *The Times Literary Supplement* David Trotter argued that, by releasing
it from the limitations of topical comedy, 'the fourth Act makes *The
Philanderer* a much better play', and Christopher Edwards in *The Spectator* wrote that it now 'ends on a note that is worldly, humane and honest

about marriage ... the insights Shaw advances touch upon something universal in sexual relations'.

*

During the last six months of 1991 Shaw produced only one new massive book: a five-hundred-page volume bringing together his contributions between 1885 and 1888 to the *Pall Mall Gazette*, lavishly edited by Brian Tyson and entitled *Shaw's Book Reviews*. But G.B.S. has by no means slacked off. There is a substantial load of fresh works by him being conveyed via scholars to the printers, in particular a dozen additional volumes of his correspondence with William Archer, Nancy Astor, John Farleigh, Augustin Hamon, Gilbert Murray, Gabriel Pascal, H. G. Wells, Lady Gregory, Margaret Wheeler – and Charlotte's correspondence with T. E. Lawrence.

There has also been considerable activity in the manuscripts market. In November a wide-ranging collection of Shaw materials formed by an internationally known Shavian scholar, Sidney P. Albert, was acquired by Brown University in the United States; and in London, on 12 December, the *New Statesman* archive went under the hammer as part of a Sotheby auction in which the Shaw manuscripts, exceeding their estimates, fetched £18,450. The year culminated with the spectacular discovery of the original letters from Shaw to Ellen Terry. This correspondence had been bought by Elbridge Adams shortly after Ellen Terry's death and printed by his company, the Fountain Press, in 1931 edited by 'Christopher St John', the pseudonym of Christabell Marshall. Her volume contained one hundred and ninety-one letters from Ellen Terry to Shaw with one hundred and eighteen of his to her which G.B.S. revised for publication. (Dan H. Laurence made accurate transcripts of ninety-seven of these from photocopies at the Library of Congress in Washington for his *Bernard Shaw: Collected Letters*.)

The original correspondence was now valued by Bernard Quaritch Ltd for a 'willing seller, willing buyer' price of £75,000 and offered for sale to the British Library. The British Library at once applied to the British Museum for this money to be made available from the Shaw Fund which Parliament was told more than thirty years earlier would be used 'primarily for the benefit of the library'. Since the late 1950s the British Museum had been receiving from the Shaw Estate the equivalent of twice this sum each year for its capital investment fund. In ordinary circumstances it would have taken the British Museum up to five years to contribute so large a sum as £75,000 for British Library heritage purchases. But could it refuse to pay Shaw's money for Shaw's letters? The question was to come before the new Director of the British Museum, Dr Robert Anderson, in the new financial year and he had promised 'some key changes'.

The financial year was less than a week old when the British Museum decided to grant the money for this purchase. Since the British Library had long owned Ellen Terry's letters to Shaw, this fascinating correspondence was finally brought together, and a display put on exhibition in the summer of 1992.

The question remained as to whether this grant signalled a new spirit of co-operation between the Library and the Museum over the Shaw Fund or had been made in special circumstances and 'without prejudice'. Plans by Mark Fisher MP for an Adjournment Debate on the matter in the House of Commons were forestalled by the onset of the spring General Election, and instead Lord Annan inaugurated a short debate in the House of Lords on 27 February. He reminded Lord Astor, Conservative spokesman for the arts, of Edward Boyle's assurances and drew attention to the odd manner in which they had been ignored. He was supported by, among others, Baroness Birk, Lord Jenkins of Putney and Lord Eccles who had managed the Shaw Fund in the 1960s and 'greatly increased its capital'. But the eminent archaeologist, Lord Renfrew of Kaimsthorn, speaking as a trustee of the British Museum, merely stonewalled by inviting Lord Astor to confirm that the Shaw bequest had been technically 'unrestricted' and to agree that the British Library Act 1972 made no specific provision for the transfer of trust funds to the library.

The debate spilled over into the correspondence columns of *The Times*. Despite the case in Chancery against Shaw's alphabet trusts, Lord Renfrew wrote (10 April): 'I do not believe Shaw's wishes to have been ignored (and would be unhappy if they were).' He added that he would have been 'outraged to see Parliament misled'. Though more of Shaw's money had gone on refurbishing the Museum's galleries and modernizing its non-vegetarian restaurant than to the British Library, Lord Renfrew could not see that anything unusual had been dug up. But the extended debate gave the public new information, and the general view, as reported in the newspapers, was that if the Museum was not to appear unconscionably greedy and the Library extremely feeble, then some fairer arrangement must be reached. In the summer of 1992 the two institutions met to discuss the situation ...

The year 1992 had started with a vintage production of *Misalliance* by the American Repertory Theatre in Cambridge, Massachusetts, its length beneficially cut by over twenty minutes. In London there was a blitz of revivals, including Alec McCowen in a museum-like *Caesar and Cleopatra* at the Greenwich Theatre, Alan Howard and Frances Barber in a spectacularly staged 'complete representation' of *Pygmalion* (conflating the theatre and film texts) at the Olivier (while *My Fair Lady* toured the country with Edward Fox), Trevor Nunn's grand but unstable production of *Heartbreak House* starring Paul Scofield and Vanessa Redgrave; as well as an exhibition chronicling Shaw's life and work at the National Portrait Gallery.

As to the future – which promises new films of *Saint Joan* and *Mrs Warren's Profession* (scripted by Fay Weldon), the coming of *Valentine's Day* to the West End and, in the United States, an international centennial conference marking the first production of *Widowers' Houses* in December 1892 and 'the beginning of modern drama in the English language' –

(to be continued by them that can)

APPENDIX A

CHARLOTTE SHAW'S
LAST WILL AND TESTAMENT

[This Will, dated 2nd September 1937, with a Codicil dated 27th November 1940, was granted Probate on 12th February 1944.]

I Charlotte Frances Shaw of 4 Whitehall Court in the County of London Wife of George Bernard Shaw *hereby revoke* all testamentary dispositions heretofore made by me *and declare* this to be my last Will which I make this second day of September One thousand nine hundred and thirty seven.

1.   *I desire* to be cremated and that my ashes shall be taken to Ireland and scattered on Irish ground and *I also desire* that no flowers shall be sacrificed, no black clothes worn and no memorial service held at my funeral.

2.   *Inasmuch* as I have an English domicile it is my wish and intention that this my Will and any Codicil hereto shall be construed and operate as if I were now and remained until my death domiciled in England.

3.   (a) *I appoint* my Husband the said *George Bernard Shaw* and *The National Provincial Bank Limited* (hereinafter called 'the English Bank') to be the *Executors* and General *Trustees* of this my Will and I declare that the English Bank may act as such Executor and Trustee on the terms and conditions and (subject as hereinafter mentioned) with the right of remuneration set forth in the English Bank's Trustee and Executorship Regulations in force at the date hereof.

(b) As from the date of my death or the death of my said Husband whichever event shall last happen *I appoint The National City Bank Limited* of Number 10 College Green Dublin (hereinafter called 'the Irish Bank') to be the *Special Trustee* of this my Will as respects the ultimate Trust Fund hereinafter mentioned and I *declare* that the Irish Bank may act as such Trustee on the terms and conditions and (subject as hereinafter mentioned) with the right of remuneration set forth in the Irish Bank's Trustee and Executorship Regulations in force at the date hereof and

(c) *I declare also* that the expression 'my Trustees' shall mean the General Trustees or Trustee for the time being hereof whether original or substituted except where such construction is precluded by the context.

4.   *I bequeath* all my 'personal chattels' as defined by Section 55 (1) (X) of the Administration of Estates Act 1925 to my said Husband but if he shall

91

predecease me then subject to the provisions of Clause 5 hereof to my niece Cecily Charlotte Colthurst.

5.   If at my death I should be possessed of any manuscripts of published or unpublished works or writings, letters, papers or documents of whatever kind relating to or connected with my said Husband George Bernard Shaw or his work (hereinafter called 'my Husband's papers') and bequeathed by him to me under his Will should he predecease me then *I direct* the English Bank to hand over all my Husband's papers to The Public Trustee or other the Executors or Trustees of his Will to be dealt with and held by him or them *Upon the Trusts* declared in the said Will of my said Husband concerning my Husband's papers in all respects as if I had predeceased my said Husband.

6.   *I bequeath* the following legacies free of all duties namely:

   To Sidney James Baron Passfield the sum of One thousand pounds.

   To John Frederick Leman Whelen the sum of Five hundred pounds.

7.   *I bequeath* the following legacies and annuities free of duties to vest and to commence to be payable on and from the date of the death of the survivor of myself and my said Husband (hereinafter called 'the date of payment') videlicet:

(i)   (a) *To* my Gardener Harry Batchelor Higgs the sum of One hundred and fifty pounds and to his Wife Clara the sum of One hundred and fifty pounds but if either of them shall die before the date of payment the legacy of the one so dying shall be payable to the survivor.

   (b) *To* the said Harry Batchelor Higgs and Clara Higgs during their joint lives an annuity of Three hundred and twelve pounds payable to them in equal shares of One hundred and fifty six pounds each and after the death of one of them the whole of the said annuity of Three hundred and twelve pounds shall be paid to the survivor of them during his or her life.

(ii)   (a) *To* my chauffeur George Frederick Day the sum of One hundred pounds if he shall be living at the date of payment.

   (b) *To* the said George Frederick Day during his life and his present Wife after his death if she shall survive him an annuity of One hundred and fifty six pounds.

(iii)   *To* Emma Hodgman formerly in my service as housemaid an annuity of Fifty two pounds during her life.

(iv)   *To* Kate Hodgman formerly in my service as parlourmaid an annuity of Fifty two pounds during her life.

(v)   *To* Mrs Margaret Bilton of 48, Wilman Road Tunbridge Wells Kent an annuity of One hundred and fifty six pounds during her life and to Alice Bilton (daughter of the said Margaret Bilton) after the death of her Mother if the said Alice Bilton shall survive the said Margaret Bilton an annuity of One hundred and four pounds.

8.   *The* annuities bequeathed by this my Will or any Codicil hereto are to be payable as and from the date of payment by equal weekly monthly or quarterly payments whichever shall be most convenient to my Trustees and to the respective annuitants the final decision as to the method of payment of the said annuities to rest with my Trustees and the first payments to be made at the expiration of one week month or quarter from the date of payment according to whether the annuities are paid weekly monthly or quarterly.

9. (i)   *I declare* that my Trustees may provide for the said annuities by purchasing Government or Insurance Office Annuities or may appropriate and retain a sufficient part of my estate or of the investments representing the same of the nature hereinafter authorised as investments of trust moneys under this my Will as a fund for answering by the annual income thereof the annuities hereinbefore given and the expenses incidental to the payment thereof respectively with power to vary such investments. *And I declare* that if the annual income of the appropriated fund shall at the time of appropriation be sufficient to satisfy the said annuities or such of them as shall for the time being be payable under this my Will such appropriation shall be a complete satisfaction of the trust or direction hereinafter declared to provide for such annuities and that no annuitant shall have any claim against or right to resort to any part of my estate (other than the said appropriated fund) for the payment of his or her annuity and further that if the income of the appropriated fund shall at any time prove insufficient for payment in full of any of the said annuities resort may be had to the capital thereof from time to time to make good such deficiency and the surplus income (if any) of the said fund from time to time remaining after payment of the said annuities shall be applicable as income of the ultimate Trust Fund (hereinafter defined).

  (ii) As and when any of the said annuities shall cease the appropriated fund or so much thereof as shall not have been applied in payment of the said annuities or any of them and shall not be required to answer any subsisting annuity shall sink into and form part of the ultimate Trust Fund and until any such annuity shall be provided for in manner aforesaid the same shall be paid out of the income of my residuary estate.

10.   *The* foregoing annuities shall in all cases become operative only if the named annuitant shall not have done or suffered anything whereby the

bequeathed annuity or any part of it would through the annuitant's act or default or by operation or process of law or otherwise become vested in some other person or persons and shall continue only until and unless the annuitant shall assign charge or encumber or affect to assign charge or encumber the relevant annuity or any part thereof. And in the event of any of the said annuities not becoming or ceasing to become payable otherwise than by the death of the annuitant my Trustees may at their absolute discretion apply the annuity for the benefit of the annuitant or add it to the income of the ultimate Trust Fund.

11. *I devise* and *bequeath* all the real and personal property whatsoever and wheresoever of or to which I shall be seized possessed or entitled at my death or over which I shall then have a general power of appointment or disposition by Will or of which I shall then be tenant in tail in possession except property otherwise disposed of by this my Will or any Codicil hereto *Unto* my Trustees *Upon the Trusts* and with and subject to the powers and provisions hereinafter declared of and concerning the same that is to say:

12. *Upon Trust* that my Trustees shall sell call in collect and convert into money the said real and personal property at such time or times and in such manner as they shall think fit (but as to reversionary property not until it falls into possession unless it should appear to my Trustees that an earlier sale would be beneficial) with power to postpone the sale calling in or conversion of the whole or any part or parts of the said property including leaseholds or other property of a terminable hazardous or wasting nature during such period as they shall think proper and to retain the same or any part thereof in its present form of investment without being responsible for loss *And I direct* that the income of such of the same premises as for the time being shall remain unsold shall as well during the first year after my death as afterwards be applied as if the same were income arising from investments hereinafter directed to be made of the proceeds of sale thereof and that no reversionary or other property not actually producing income shall be treated as producing income for the purposes of this my Will.

13. *My* Trustees shall out of the moneys to arise from the sale calling in and conversion of or forming part of my said real and personal estate pay my funeral and testamentary expenses (including all estate duty leviable at my death in respect of my residuary estate) and debts and the legacies and annuities given by this my Will and any Codicil hereto and all death duties and other moneys which under or by virtue of any direction or bequest free of duty contained in this my Will or any Codicil hereto are payable out of my general personal estate.

14. *My* Trustees shall at their discretion invest the residue of the said moneys in the names of my Trustees in or upon any of the investments

hereby authorised with power to vary or transpose such investments for or into others of a nature hereby authorised.

15. *My* Trustees shall stand possessed of the residue of the said moneys and the investments for the time being representing the same and such part of my estate as shall for the time being remain unsold and unconverted (all of which premises are hereinafter referred to as 'the Trust Fund') *Upon the Trusts* following that is to say:

16. *Upon Trust* to pay the annual income of the Trust Fund to my said Husband if he shall survive me during his life and subject thereto.

17. *Upon Trust* to raise out of the Trust Fund a legacy of Twenty thousand pounds free of duty (thereinafter called 'Mrs Colthurst's Fund') and to hold the same *Upon Trust* to invest the said legacy in any of the investments hereby authorised and to pay the annual income thereof to my niece Cecily Charlotte Colthurst during her life and after her death my Trustees shall hold Mrs Colthurst's Fund *Upon Trust* for such of them her two daughters Mary Penelope Hamilton and Shournagh Dorothy Combe as shall survive me and if both then in equal shares absolutely but if either of my said nieces shall predecease me leaving a child or children who shall survive me and attain the age of twenty one years such child or children shall take by substitution if more than one in equal shares as tenants in common the share of and in Mrs Colthurst's Fund which such niece would have taken if she had survived me *And* subject to the trusts aforesaid Mrs Colthurst's Fund shall fall into and form part of the ultimate Trust Fund hereinafter mentioned.

18. *Subject* to the trusts aforesaid and to the powers hereby or by law conferred upon my Trustees and to any and every exercise of such respective powers my Trustees shall stand possessed of the Trust Fund or the residue thereof which premises and the property for the time being representing the same are in this my Will for brevity called 'the Ultimate Trust Fund' *Upon Trust* as soon as conveniently may be after my death or the death of my Husband whichever event shall last happen to transfer the same to and vest the same in the Irish bank.

19. (i) *Whereas:*
    (a) I am desirous of promoting and encouraging in Ireland the bringing of the masterpieces of fine art within the reach of the Irish people of all classes so that they may have increased opportunity of studying such masterpieces and of acquiring a fuller and wider knowledge thereof, and
    (b) In the course of a long life I have had many opportunities of observing the extent to which the most highly instructed and capable persons have their efficiency defeated and their influence limited for want of any organised instruction and training for the

personal contacts whether with individuals or popular audiences without which their knowledge is incommunicable (except through books) and how the authority which their abilities should give them is made derisory by their awkward manners and how their employment in positions for which they have valuable qualifications is made socially impossible by vulgarities of speech and other defects as easily corrigible by teaching and training as simple illiteracy and whereas my experience and observation have convinced me that the lack of such training produces not only much social friction but grave pathological results which seem quite unconnected with it and that social intercourse is a fine art with a technique which everybody can and should acquire.

(ii) *Now* with a view to furthering and carrying out the objects which I have at heart *I hereby declare* that the Irish Bank shall stand possessed of the Ultimate Trust Fund as and when so transferred to and vested in the Irish Bank *Upon the Trusts* and with and subject to the powers and provision following that is to say:

(a) The Irish Bank may either allow the same or any part or parts thereof respectively to remain as actually invested so long as the Irish Bank shall think fit or may at any time or times at the discretion of the Irish Bank sell call in or convert into money the same or any part thereof and at the like discretion invest the moneys produced thereby and any other capital moneys which may be received by the Irish Bank in respect of the Ultimate Trust Fund in the name of the Irish Bank in or upon any investments or investment hereby authorised with power at such discretion as aforesaid to vary or transpose any investments for or into another or others of any nature hereby authorised.

(b) The Irish Bank shall pay or apply the net income of the Ultimate Trust Fund in perpetuity to in or towards all or any one or more of the following objects and in such proportions and in such manner as the Irish Bank shall in its absolute discretion from time to time think fit that is to say:

(c) The making of grants contributions and payments to any foundation corporate body institution association or fund now existing or hereafter coming into existence within the special period hereinafter defined having for its object the bringing of the masterpieces of fine art within the reach of the people of Ireland of all classes in their own country provided that no such foundation corporate body institution association or fund shall be eligible as an object of this trust if:

(i) It is not of a public character or

96

(ii) In the case of a foundation corporate body institution or association it is at liberty to pay or distribute any profits to or among any of its members subscribers contributors or benefactors or the fund or any part thereof or any income therefrom may be so paid or applied or

(iii) Any of the members subscribers contributors or benefactors would have any right to participate in the assets or in the fund in the event of its dissolution or distribution.

(d) The teaching promotion and encouragement in Ireland of self control, elocution, oratory, deportment, the arts of personal contact, of social intercourse, and the other arts of public, private, professional and business life.

(e) The establishment and endowment within the special period either solely or jointly with any person or persons or any other corporation of any educational institution or any Chair or Readership in any University College or Educational Institution now existing or coming into existence within the special period in Ireland for the purpose of giving instruction in or promoting the study by the general public of the subjects mentioned in this Clause 19 or any of them Provided that no such College or Educational Institution has for its sole object the exclusive or complete training in any single profession or calling.

(iii) *I declare* that for the purpose of this my Will the expression 'masterpieces of fine art' means and includes works of the highest class in the fields of orchestral and classical music painting sculpture fine printing and literature produced or originating not in any one Country exclusively but in any Country in the world and by or among people in any age period or date whether ancient or modern.

20. *I declare* that the expression 'the special period' hereinbefore referred to shall mean the lives of the issue now living of his late Majesty King George the Fifth and the life of the survivor of them and twenty one years after the death of the survivor of them.

21. *Notwithstanding* anything herein contained I empower the Irish Bank for any of the foregoing purposes or objects in its absolute discretion to expend or lay out the capital of the Ultimate Trust Fund or any part thereof in paying or transferring the same to the Trustees or other Governing Body of any such foundation corporate body institution association fund educational institution (whether or not established by the Irish Bank under the power in that behalf hereinbefore contained) University or College as hereinbefore mentioned either absolutely or by way of loan and if by way of loan either at such rate of interest as the Irish Bank shall think fit or without charging any interest.

22. *Without* prejudice to the right of the Irish Bank to employ and pay any Secretary Clerk or other administrative officer or officers (whether a member or members of its Staff or not) for the purpose of administering the foregoing trusts of the Ultimate Trust Fund if the Irish Bank shall deem it necessary or desirable so to do it is my desire that the moneys directed to be paid or applied under such foregoing trusts shall be used directly for the promotion of the objects therein referred to and shall not be expended for the erection of new buildings the maintenance of buildings or for the upkeep of any establishment or the maintenance of any subordinate Staff employed in connection with the said objects or in any manner ancillary to the main objects but notwithstanding this indication of my wishes I *give* the Irish Bank uncontrolled discretion as to the manner in which such moneys shall be expended or applied for or towards any or all of the above objects.

23. *The* expression 'Ireland' wherever used in this my Will shall denote the existing Irish Free State and any other future extension of it that may take place.

24. *All* moneys liable to be invested under this my Will may be invested in or upon any Stocks funds or securities of or guaranteed by the Government of the United Kingdom of Great Britain and Northern Ireland or India or any British Colony or Dependency (including therein any Dominion Commonwealth Union or Mandated Territory forming part of the British Empire or any Province or State having a separate local legislature and forming part thereof respectively and including Ireland) or any Foreign State or in or upon the Stocks Shares Bonds Debentures Securities or Investments of any Company or of any Municipal or other Corporation Local Board or Public Body in the United Kingdom as aforesaid or British Colony or Dependency as aforesaid or in the purchase or on mortgage (whether contributory or otherwise) of any real or leasehold property in the United Kingdom as aforesaid or in Ireland.

25. (a) The aforesaid right of the English Bank to remuneration shall not include the right to any withdrawal fee in respect of the Ultimate Trust Fund or any part thereof.

    (b) The aforesaid right of the Irish Bank to remuneration shall be varied in that the Irish Bank shall in lieu of the usual income fee be entitled to an income fee at the rate of Five pounds per centum on the gross income before deduction of income tax or any other outgoings with a minimum yearly income fee of One hundred and fifty pounds in addition to such payment (if any) as it shall make to any Secretary Clerk or other administrative officer or officers in accordance with the authority hereinbefore given.

26. *I suggest* that on any occasion on which the services of a Solicitor may be

required it will be advisable to resort to the firm of Barrington & Son of Dublin for Irish business and for other than Irish business the firm of Lawrence, Graham & Company of London as these firms are conversant with my affairs but without prejudice to the right of any Bank being at the time an Executor or Trustee hereof to consult any other Solicitor in any case in which it shall think it proper so to do.

In witness whereof I have hereunto set my hand the day and year first above written

Signed by the above named Testatrix
Charlotte Frances Shaw as and for her last Will in the presence of us present at the same time who in her presence and at her request and in the presence of each other have hereunto subscribed our names as witnesses

Charlotte Frances Shaw

E. W. Wykes
  New Square
  Lincoln's Inn
Solicitor

[Signature indecipherable] MRCS LRCP
  50 York Mansions
  SW11
Medical Practitioner

I, CHARLOTTE FRANCES SHAW of 4, Whitehall Court in the County of London, wife of George Bernard Shaw DECLARE this to be a Codicil to my Will which bears date the second day of September One thousand nine hundred and thirty-seven.

1. I BEQUEATH the letters which were written to me by Colonel T.E. Lawrence and which are at present in safe custody at the British Museum to the British Museum absolutely.

2. I BEQUEATH the sum of One hundred pounds to ROBERT STUD-MAN free of duty who is employed at 4, Whitehall Court and attending to me and Fifty pounds to MAGGIE CASHIN free of duty who is in my service and I declare that the said legacies shall be paid to them whether or not he or she shall

be at 4, Whitehall Court and attending to me or in my service at the date of my death.

3. IN all other respects I confirm my said Will IN WITNESS whereof I have hereunto set my hand this twenty seventh day of November One thousand nine hundred and forty.

SIGNED by the above-named Testatrix
in our presence by us in her presence
and in that of each other

Charlotte Frances Shaw

Blanche E. Patch
   Onslow Court Hotel
   Queen's Gate
   SW7
Spinster

Clara Rebecca Higgs
   Ayot St Lawrence Welwyn Herts
Housekeeper

APPENDIX B

BERNARD SHAW'S
LAST WILL AND TESTAMENT

[This Will, dated 12th June, 1950, was granted Probate on 20th March, 1951.]

This is the Last Will and Testament of me George Bernard Shaw of 4 Whitehall Court in the County of London and of Ayot Saint Lawrence in the County of Herts   Author

1. I revoke all Wills and testamentary dispositions heretofore made by me.

2. I appoint the Public Trustee as the sole Executor and Trustee of this my Will who is hereinafter referred to as 'my Trustee.'

3. I desire that my dead body shall be cremated and its ashes inseparably mixed with those of my late wife now in the custody of the Golders Green Crematorium and in this condition inurned or scattered in the garden of the house in Ayot Saint Lawrence where we lived together for thirty five years unless some other disposal of them should be in the opinion of my Trustee more eligible. Personally I prefer the garden to the cloister.

4. As my religious convictions and scientific views cannot at present be more specifically defined than as those of a believer in Creative Evolution I desire that no public monument or work of art or inscription or sermon or ritual service commemorating me shall suggest that I accepted the tenets peculiar to any established Church or denomination [*sic*] nor take the form of a cross or any other instrument of torture or symbol of blood sacrifice.

5. I bequeath my copyrights performing rights filming rights television rights and all cognate rights now in existence or hereafter to be created with the manuscripts typescripts and other documents in which I have such rights to my Trustee Upon trust to apply the proceeds resulting from the exploitation of such rights or the sale or other lucrative use of such documents as income of my estate.

6. I bequeath all papers and documents in my possession in which I have no copyright and which belong to me as material objects only to my Trustee to be examined as soon as conveniently after my death and divided as nearly as may be into sections as follows:—
   Section A. Papers (if any) concerning my late wife's family or affairs.

Section B. Old Diaries account books Bank passbooks paid cheques and their counterfoils expired agreements box office returns and other records of my business operations and personal and domestic expenditure capable of being used by economic or legal historians or by biographers seeking documentary evidence as to prices and practices during the period covered by my lifetime.

Section C. Such letters and documents as might be worth preserving in a public collection such as that of the British Museum.

Section D. All documents needed for the administration of my estate and the carrying out of the provisions of this my Will.

Section E. Uninteresting documents of no use except as waste paper.

I bequeath the contents of these sections to my Trustee with the suggestion that the contents of Section A (if any) be presented to my late wife's niece Mrs Cecily Charlotte Colthurst or should she predecease me to such surviving relative of hers as my Trustee may select; that the contents of Section B be offered to the British Library of Political Science in Clare Market London for the purpose indicated and those of Section C to the British Museum or failing acceptance to any other suitable public collection whilst the contents of Sections D and E can be retained or destroyed by my Trustee as may be expedient. And I declare that if any doubt or disputes should arise as to which papers shall be thus dealt with the question shall be settled by my Trustee whose decision shall be final Provided Always that my Trustee shall retain all or any of the aforesaid papers and documents for such period as shall in his opinion be desirable.

7. I declare that my Trustee shall manage and deal with my author's rights with all the powers in that behalf of an absolute owner (subject as hereinafter provided) for so long as may prove necessary or expedient during a period ending at the expiration of twenty years from the day of the death of the last survivor of all the lineal descendants of His late Majesty King George the Fifth who shall be living at the time of my death (hereinafter called 'the Special period') bearing in mind that the licensing of theatrical performances and especially of cinematographic exhibitions and the like with the collection of royalties thereon will be a principal source of revenue besides continuing my practice in England of manufacturing my literary works at the cost of my estate and causing copies thereof to be sold on commission by a Publisher and shall make such other arrangements with Publishers and others as my Trustee shall think fit Provided always that my Trustee shall not sell assign or alienate such copyrights and other rights or any of them and shall not grant any licence or enter into any agreement or other arrangement in respect of the said copyrights and other rights or any of them which shall irrevocably bind or affect the same for a period

exceeding five years (unless with power of revocation) at any one time calculated from the date of the execution of such licence agreement or arrangement but with power to renew or re-grant the same for any period not exceeding the aforesaid period and so on from time to time And I further declare that my Trustee shall not in dealing with any such rights be bound by commercial considerations exclusively it being my desire that he shall give due weight to artistic and public and human considerations to the best of his judgment and counsel.

8. I desire that my Trustee shall do all things and make out of my estate all payments necessary to preserve my aforesaid copyrights or any of them and to procure any renewal of the same that can be obtained And I authorise him to make such payments accordingly And for the guidance of my Trustee I record that with regard to my copyrights in the United States of America (which are of considerable value) the same do not continue automatically for a period of fifty years from the author's death (as in England and other countries) but continue for a period of twenty eight years only from the date of first publication with a right of renewal for a further period of twenty eight years upon application being made and registered within one year prior to the expiration of the first term.

9. I direct my Trustee without charging any payment to authorise Mrs Stella Mervyn Beech now residing at 122 Sussex Gardens in the County of London W.2 daughter of the late eminent actress professionally known as Mrs Patrick Campbell to print and publish after my death all or any of the letters written by me to the said eminent actress and in the event of Mrs Beech's death before such publication to give such authority (which is a permission and not an assignment of copyright) to Mrs Patrick Campbell's grandson Patrick Beech and without imposing any trust I desire that the proceeds of such publication should be reserved as far as possible by Mrs Beech or Patrick Beech for the secondary education of Mrs Campbell's grandchildren and their children (such being her own wish) and any legacy duty payable by reason of such authority being given shall be paid out of my estate.

10. Whereas I possess a bust of myself in white marble by the eminent Hungarian sculptor Sigismund Strobl and now in the custody of the London County Council I bequeath it to the as yet unbuilt Shakespeare Memorial National Theatre in London and I direct my Trustee to leave the said bust in the said custody until the opening of the said National Theatre.

11. Whereas certain portraits of myself in painting or sculpture are at present in public galleries or institutions as for example the marble bust by Rodin in the Dublin Municipal Gallery a painting by Augustus John in the

Fitzwilliam Museum in Cambridge a bust in bronze by Paul Troubetskoy in the National Gallery of British Art at Millbank in London (known also as The Tate Gallery) and an earlier bronze by the same sculptor in the Foyer of the Theatre Guild at 245 West 52nd Street in New York City I bequeath all of them and any others that may be in the like circumstances at my death to the several institutions in whose custody they stand save that in the case of the said Theatre Guild which is not in its nature a permanent institution I direct that on the Guild's dissolution or the winding up of its business from any cause during the special period the bust shall pass to the Metropolitan Museum in New York City or failing its acceptance for immediate or future exhibition in that institution to the next most eligible (in my Trustee's opinion) American public collection willing to accept it.

12. I bequeath absolutely the Crayon drawing of the late Harley Granville-Barker by John Singer Sargent to the Trustees for the time being of the National Portrait Gallery in London in whose custody it now is.

13. I bequeath to the National Trust all that is mine of the furniture cars and other contents except my cars and their appurtenances of the house garage and garden and grounds in the village of Ayot Saint Lawrence ordnance mapped as 'Shaw's Corner' now the property of the said National Trust to be preserved as objects of memorial or artistic interest or disposed of or held in reserve for the benefit of the said premises or the said village as to the said Trust may in its judgment seem advisable.

14. Whereas it has been my custom to allow the Actors' Orphanage to receive and retain fees collected by the Collection Bureau of the Incorporated Society of Authors Playwrights and Composers for performance in the United Kingdom of my play entitled 'Passion Poison and Petrifaction' and I desire that such arrangement shall be continued Now I hereby direct my Trustee to continue such arrangement accordingly and to permit and authorise the performance (but without expense to my estate) of my aforesaid play at any time on the request of the Secretary of the aforesaid Society or of the aforesaid Orphanage and for the benefit thereof and to allow the aforesaid Society to continue to collect all fees in respect of the aforesaid play and pay the same to the aforesaid Orphanage for the benefit thereof and if any such fees as aforesaid shall come to the hands of my Trustee then my Trustee shall hold the same upon trust for such Orphanage absolutely And I declare that the receipt of the Secretary Treasurer or other officer of the aforesaid Society or of the aforesaid Orphanage for any such fees as aforesaid shall be a sufficient discharge for the same and that any legacy duty payable in respect of the same shall be borne by the said Orphanage.

15. I authorise the Fabian Society of London so long as it shall remain an avowedly Socialistic Society and after it shall have ceased so to be if and whilst such avowal shall be contrary to law to print and publish for the benefit of such Society and its Cause all writing [*sic*] of mine which are or shall be at the time of my death included or with my consent about to be included amongst its publications and I direct my Trustee if necessary to grant to such Society such license as will give effect completely or as far as possible to the provisions of this Clause which however must not be construed as giving the said Society any sole or exclusive property in the copyrights concerned and any legacy duty payable by reason of such license being given shall be borne by the said Society.

16. I empower my Trustee to procure all necessary assistance and expert advice legal artistic literary or other for the discharge of his relevant functions and to pay its cost out of my estate.

17. Provided always And I declare that as my fashion of literary composition often obliges me to make my first draft without full and final regard to temperance of expression generosity or justice to individuals accuracy of history or public propriety generally and to remedy this imperfection by later corrections it is my wish and I charge my Trustee and all others under whose eyes any of my literary works and documents may pass not to publish or quote or suffer to be published or quoted any edition or extracts from my works in which any earlier text shall be substituted either wholly or partly for the text as contained in the printed volumes finally passed by me for press except in the case of texts which I may be prevented by death or disablement from so passing And further that in any critical or biographical notes that may from good reasons make public any passages written by me but subsequently altered or discarded heed be taken both to the credit and the feelings of any surviving person alluded to therein but no suppressions need be made for the purpose of whitewashing my own character or conduct.

18. I bequeath to every indoor and outdoor servant or labourer including charwoman chauffeur and gardener (hereinafter respectively referred to as such servant) of mine (other than any such as may be entitled to an annuity or pension under the provisions of the following clauses of this my Will) who shall be in the exclusive employ or in the case of my residing in a service flat the daily service of me at the time of my death and shall then have been in such employ for a continuous or virtually continuous period (that is to say only interrupted by illness or the like or military service and not by a formal discharge) of not less than seven years a sum equal to one year's wages or periodical gratuity of such servant and to every such servant

of mine (other than as aforesaid) who shall be in the exclusive employ of me at the time of my death and shall then have been in my employ for a period of less than seven years but for a continuous or virtually continuous period of not less than three years a sum equal to six months' wages or periodical gratuity of such servant and to every such servant of mine (other than as aforesaid) who shall be in the exclusive employ of me at the time of my death and shall then have been in such employ for a period of less than three years a sum equal to three months' wages or periodical gratuity of such servant all such bequests as aforesaid to be in addition to any wages that may be or become legally due to any such servant as aforesaid Provided always And I further declare that whether the foregoing bequests shall become operative or not my Trustee shall have absolute power to act reasonably and generously in the case of any servant of mine or of my late wife who in the opinion of my Trustee is not sufficiently dealt with under the provisions hereinbefore made and accordingly to make to any such servant any such payment or additional payment out of my Estate as my Trustee shall in his discretion think desirable but without imposing any obligation upon him to make any such payment.

19. I declare that every annuity hereinafter or by any Codicil hereto bequeathed is bequeathed subject to the provisions relating to annuities hereinafter contained.

20. I declare that if at the time of my death any person or persons who shall not then be in my employ but shall have formerly been in the employ of me or of my late wife and who shall not otherwise become entitled to any benefit under this my Will and shall be in receipt of a pension or allowance from me then I bequeath to such person or persons an Annuity equal in amount to the amount of such pension or allowance of which such former servant shall be then in receipt.

21. I bequeath to my retired gardener Harry Batchelor Higgs an annuity of One hundred and fifty six pounds and I direct my Trustee to see to it that the monument I have had erected in Windlesham Cemetery to him and his late wife shall on his death at the cost of my estate have its inscription completed and thereafter be cared for by the Cemetery authorities in consideration of an appropriate capital sum.

22. I bequeath to Emma Hodgman formerly in my service as Housemaid and now or lately resident at 130 Windmill Road in Gillingham Kent an annuity of Fifty two pounds.

23. I bequeath to Mrs Margaret Bilton now or lately residing at 48 Wilmer Road Tunbridge Wells and formerly in my service as housekeeper an

annuity of One hundred and fifty six pounds to be continued after her death to her daughter Alice Bilton if surviving and on the respective deaths of the said Margaret Bilton and the said Alice Bilton I direct my Trustee to pay or apply for the benefit of the survivor of them or to such other person or persons and in such manner as he shall in his discretion think fit a sum of Twenty five pounds out of the capital of my Residuary Estate for or towards the funeral expenses incurred consequent on their respective deaths.

24. Whereas the annuities hereby bequeathed to Harry Batchelor [The surname, Higgs, was inadvertently omitted by the calligrapher.] Frederick William Day and Margaret Day Mrs Margaret Bilton and Alice Bilton and Emma Hodgman are provided for as from my death by the Will of my late wife Charlotte Frances Shaw my bequests to them herein shall be subject to such reductions and increases as may bring their benefits to the same level as if only one Will and that the most favourable to them shall come into force at my decease.

25. I bequeath to Mrs Georgina Musters the daughter of my mother's half sister Arabella Gillmore an annuity of Three hundred and sixty five pounds.

26. I bequeath to Eames Bagenal Rogers now or lately residing at 1249 Yale Street Santa Monica California the son of my mother's late half-sister Charlotte Rogers and to his wife after his death if she shall survive him an annuity of Fifty two pounds.

27. I bequeath to Georgina Meredith now residing at 34 Barrow Street in the City of Dublin daughter of my mother's late half-sister Charlotte Rogers an annuity of Fifty two pounds.

28. I bequeath to Ethel Gordon Walters at present residing at 34 Queens Gardens in the County of London w.1 daughter of my first cousin the late James Cockaigne Shaw an annuity of Two hundred and thirty four pounds.

29. I bequeath to my former housemaid Mrs Ronald Smith (born Margaret Cashin) a deferred annuity of Fifty two pounds a year should she survive or be separated from her husband Ronald Smith or a later husband if any.

30. I bequeath to my chauffeur and gardener Frederick William Day and his Wife Margaret Day jointly an annuity of One hundred and fifty six pounds to be continued in full to the survivor of them.

31. I bequeath to Eva Maria Schneider now residing at 196 Rivermead Court Hurlingham London s.w.6 an annuity of One hundred and twenty pounds in remembrance of her devoted services to my late sister Lucy.

32. I bequeath to my Secretary Blanche Patch Spinster an annuity of Five hundred pounds.

33. The following provisions shall apply to all annuities hereby or by any Codicil hereto bequeathed—
    (1) The bequest of an annuity shall become operative only if the named annuitant shall not at my death have done or suffered anything whereby the bequeathed annuity or any part of it would become vested in or payable to some other person or persons and shall continue only until the annuitant shall become bankrupt or assign or charge the said annuity or any part thereof or do or suffer anything whereby the said annuity or any part thereof would become vested in or payable to any other person and in the event of any annuity not becoming or ceasing to become payable by the effect of this subclause my Trustee may at his absolute discretion during the rest of the life of the annuitant apply out of the income of my residuary trust funds hereinafter defined any sums not exceeding in any year the amount of the relevant annuity for the benefit of the annuitant and for the purposes of sub-clause (3) of this clause any sums which my Trustee decides to apply as aforesaid in any year shall be treated as if the aggregate of the same was an annuity.
    (2) Every annuity shall be payable by equal quarterly payments payable in advance the first payment to become payable as at my death and to be paid as soon thereafter as my Trustee is in a position to pay the same.
    (3) Every annuity shall unless and until a sum shall have been appropriated to provide for the same as hereinafter authorised or until the expiration of twenty one years from my death or the previous cesser whether partial or complete of the trust of the balance of the income of my Residuary Trust Funds hereinafter contained be payable only out of the income of my Residuary Trust Funds in each year from my death available for the payment thereof and if the income of my Residuary Trust Funds shall be insufficient to pay the said annuities in full the annuitant shall be entitled to be paid any capital sum in satisfaction of his or her annuity as a legacy but the said annuity shall abate pro rata for such period and to such an extent as shall be necessary having regard to the insufficiency of such income as aforesaid but if at the end of any year from my death there should be income available (after paying the full amounts of the said annuities for the time being payable for that year) to pay the amounts or part of the amounts by which the annuities then still payable had previously abated my Trustee shall out of such income pay the said amounts or such parts of the said amounts and rateably in proportion to such last mentioned annuities as such income shall be sufficient to satisfy. Upon the expiration of twenty one years

from my death or the cesser whether partial or complete of the said trust of the balance of the said income the annuities then subsisting if not then provided for under sub-clause (4) hereof and any amounts by which such annuities had previously abated if not made good shall be a charge on the capital of my Residuary Trust Funds.

(4) My Trustee may in his discretion at any time provide for the payment of the annuities for the time being subsisting by appropriating and retaining out of my Residuary Trust Funds and investing in the name of my Trustee in any of the investments hereinafter authorised (with power for my Trustee to vary or transpose such investments for others hereby authorised) such a sum as when so invested shall at the time of investment be sufficient by means of the income thereof to pay the said annuities And I declare that such appropriation as aforesaid shall be complete provision for such annuities and that in case the income of the appropriated fund shall at any time prove insufficient for payment in full of such annuities resort may be had to the capital thereof from time to time to make good such deficiency and the surplus (if any) of the income of the said fund from time to time remaining after payment of such annuities shall form part of the income of my Residuary Trust Funds And I declare that as and when any annuity provided for by means of the appropriated fund as aforesaid shall cease to be payable so much of the appropriated fund as my Trustee shall not think it necessary to retain to answer any remaining annuities shall revert to the capital of my Residuary Trust Funds.

(5) My Trustee shall have power if in his absolute discretion he thinks fit during the lives or life of any of the annuitants out of the income of my Residuary Trust Funds in any year not required for payment of such of the annuities as shall for the time being be payable or if he thinks fit out of the capital of my Residuary Trust Funds to make such additional payment to the annuitants for the time being living as in his opinion may be required to make good to such annuitants any decrease in the values of their annuities which shall be due to an increase [sic] [this should read 'decrease'] in the purchasing power of the £ sterling after the date of this my Will.

34. I declare that all legacies (whether pecuniary or specific) and annuities bequeathed by this my Will or any Codicil shall be paid without deduction of legacy duty or any other duties payable in respect of the same and that the said duties including any duty chargeable by reason of an annuity arising on or being increased by the death of any annuitant shall be paid out of my real and personal estate hereinafter devised and bequeathed by way of residue.

35. I devise and bequeath all my real and personal estate not otherwise

specifically disposed of by this my Will or any Codicil hereto and all property over which I have general power of appointment unto my Trustee Upon trust that my Trustee shall (subject to the power of postponing the sale and conversion thereof hereinafter contained) sell my real estate and sell call in or otherwise convert into money as much as may be needed of my personal estate (other than any copyrights which as provided by Clause 7 of this my Will are not to be sold) to increase the ready monies of which I may be possessed at my death to an amount sufficient to pay my funeral and testamentary expenses and debts estate duty legacy duty and all the duties payable on my death in respect of my estate or the bequests hereby made free of duty (other than testamentary expenses) and the legacies bequeathed by this my Will or any Codicil hereto or to make such other payments or investments or change of investments as in his opinion shall be advisable in the interest of my estate and shall invest the residue of such monies in manner hereinafter authorised And shall stand possessed of the said residuary trust moneys and the investments for the time being representing the same and all other investments for the time being forming part of my residuary estate (herein called my Residuary Trust Funds) and the annual income thereof Upon the trusts hereby declared of and concerning the same.

(1) To institute and finance a series of inquiries to ascertain or estimate as far as possible the following statistics (*a*) the number of extant persons who speak the English language and write it by the established and official alphabet of 26 letters (hereinafter called Dr. Johnson's Alphabet) (*b*) how much time could be saved per individual scribe by the substitution for the said Alphabet of an Alphabet containing at least 40 letters (hereinafter called the Proposed British Alphabet) enabling the said language to be written without indicating single sounds by groups of letters or by diacritical marks instead of by one symbol for each sound (*c*) how many of these persons are engaged in writing or printing English at any and every moment in the world; (*d*) on these factors to estimate the time and labour wasted by our lack of at least 14 unequivocal single symbols; (*e*) to add where possible to the estimates of time lost or saved by the difference between Dr. Johnson's Alphabet and the Proposed British Alphabet estimates of the loss of income in British and American currency. The enquiry must be confined strictly to the statistical and mathematical problems to be solved without regard to the views of professional and amateur phoneticians, etymologists, Spelling Reformers, patentees of universal languages, inventors of shorthand codes for verbatim reporting or rival alphabets, teachers of the established orthography, disputants about pronunciation, or any of the irreconcilables whose wranglings have overlooked and confused

the single issue of labour saving and made change impossible during the last hundred years. The inquiry must not imply any approval or disapproval of the Proposed British Alphabet by the inquirers or by my Trustee.

(2) To employ a phonetic expert to transliterate my play entitled 'Androcles & the Lion' into the Proposed British Alphabet assuming the pronunciation to resemble that recorded of His Majesty our late King George V. and sometimes described as Northern English.

(3) To employ an artist-calligrapher to fair-copy the transliteration for reproduction by lithography photography or any other method that may serve in the absence of printers' types.

(4) To advertise and publish the transliteration with the original Dr. Johnson's lettering opposite the transliteration page by page and a glossary of the two alphabets at the end and to present copies to public libraries in the British Isles, the British Commonwealth, the American States North and South and to national libraries everywhere in that order.

36. I desire my Trustee to bear in mind that the Proposed British Alphabet does not pretend to be exhaustive as it contains only sixteen vowels whereas by infinitesimal movements of the tongue countless different vowels can be produced all of them in use among speakers of English who utter the same vowels no oftener than they make the same finger prints. Nevertheless they can understand one another's speech and writing sufficiently to converse and correspond: for instance, a graduate of Trinity College Dublin has no difficulty in understanding a graduate of Oxford University when one says that 'the sun rohze,' and the other 'the san raheoze' nor are either of them puzzled when a peasant calls his childhood his 'chawldid.' For a university graduate calls my native country Awlind.

37. It is possible that the Ministry of Education may institute the inquiry and adopt the Proposed British Alphabet to be taught in the schools it controls in which event subsection 1 of Clause 35 foregoing and its relevant sequels will be contraindicated as superfluous and Clause 40 come into operation accordingly but the adoption must be exact and no account taken of the numerous alternative spelling Reforms now advocated or hereafter proposed.

38. I hereby devise and bequeath the balance of the income of my Residuary Trust Funds not required during the period of twenty one years after my death to pay the annuities hereby or by any Codicil hereto bequeathed or for any other purpose upon which income of my Residuary Trust Funds may under the trusts hereinbefore contained be applicable Upon trust

during the special period but subject to cesser as hereinafter provided To apply the same as follows:—

A. To remunerate the services and defray the expenses incidental to these proceedings and generally to the launching advertising and propaganda of the said British Alphabet.

B. To acquire by employment purchase or otherwise the copyrights and patents (if any) created by or involved in the designing and manufacture of the said Alphabet or the publication of the works printed in it without exploiting the said rights or for commercial profit.

C. To wind-up the enterprise when the aforesaid steps have been taken or if and when its official adoption or general vogue shall make further recourse to my estate and action on the part of my Trustee in respect of this charitable Trust superfluous.

39. Pending the operation of the foregoing clause I direct that my Trustee shall for the said period of twenty one years from my death accumulate the said balance of the income of my Residuary Trust Funds in the way of compound interest by investing the same and the resulting income thereof from time to time in any investment in which my Residuary Trust Funds are authorised to be invested.

40. Subject to the trusts hereinbefore declared of my Residuary Trust Funds and the income thereof or if and so far as such trusts shall fail through judicial decision or any other cause beyond my Trustee's control my Trustee shall stand possessed of my Residuary Trust Funds and the income thereof but subject to a charge on the capital as well as the income thereof for payment of such of the annuities hereby bequeathed as shall be subsisting Upon trust as to one third thereof for the Trustees of the British Museum in acknowledgment of the incalculable value to me of my daily resort to the Reading Room of that Institution at the beginning of my career as to one third of the same Upon trust for the National Gallery of Ireland and as to the remaining one third of the same Upon trust for the Royal Academy of Dramatic Art at 61 Gower Street in the County of London and should any of these three institutions be permanently closed at the date when the trust to accumulate the said balance of income of my Residuary Trust Funds shall cease the others or other shall succeed to its share and if more than one equally.

41. I authorise my Trustee to postpone for such period as he shall in his discretion think fit the sale and conversion of all or any part of my real and personal estate hereinbefore devised and bequeathed in trust for sale and conversion notwithstanding the same may be of a perishable or wearing out nature (but if any part of my estate shall be of a reversionary nature the

same shall not be sold or converted into money until it falls into possession unless my Trustee shall think it probable that a loss will arise to my estate by postponing the sale and conversion thereof) and to retain any stocks shares or securities of which I may be possessed at my death whether fully paid up or not (but my real estate shall be impressed with the quality of personal estate from the time of my death) And I declare that the net income arising from any part of my real or personal estate previous to the sale or con-version thereof shall as well during the first year after my death as after-wards be applied in the same manner as if the same were income arising from such investments as are by this my Will authorised but that no reversionary or other property forming part of my estate not actually producing income shall be treated as producing income.

42. Should my Trustee have occasion to realise any of my investments in the shares and loan stocks of Friendly Societies not quoted on the Stock Exchange and therefore often sold by Executors and others at less than their value I direct my Trustee not to dispose of them without first offering them to the Directors of the said Societies they being commonly ready to liquidate such stocks at their face value.

43. I declare that my Trustee shall be at liberty to grant time or other in-dulgence to any debtor in respect of any unsecured personal loans made by me and (in particular when the loan has not in his judgment been a matter of business) to forego payment of and absolutely release all or any part of the amount of any such debts or loan without being answerable for any loss which may thereby arise and with regard to any such debts owing to me or claims I may have against any person or persons I express it to be my wish that my Trustee shall in the exercise of the aforesaid power deal kindly or leniently with all such debtors or other person or persons where a strict observation of the law would involve manifest injustice hardship or mean-ness (but no distinction in this respect is to be made in favour of my relatives as distinguished from other persons) And I also declare that certain bequests I have made in former Wills in favour of various persons I have now omitted to make not on account of any change of feeling on my part towards them but because deaths marriages and change of circumstances have rendered such bequests unnecessary and I also record my regret that my means are not sufficient to provide for material pledges of my regard for the many friends who as colleagues in the Socialistic movement or as artists co-operating with me in the performance of my plays or otherwise have not only made my career possible but hallowed it with kindly human relations.

44. I declare that all monies liable to be invested under my Will may be invested

in any investment or securities for the time being authorised by law for the investment of trust funds.

45. I authorise my Trustee to apportion as my Trustee shall think fit among the trust premises any charges deductions or outgoings whatsoever and to determine whether any money shall for the purpose of this my Will be considered annual income or not and the power of appropriation conferred by the administration of Estates Act 1925 shall be exercisable by my Trustee whether acting as personal representative or trustee and without any of the consents made requisite by that Act.

46. I declare that the Executor and Trustee for the time being of this my Will may instead of acting personally employ and pay a Solicitor Accountant Agent Literary Executor Bibliographer or any other person or persons to transact any business or do any act required to be done in connection with the administration of my estate or the trusts hereby declared including the receipt and payment of money and the keeping and preparation of books and accounts And I express it to be my wish (but without imposing any obligation) that my present English Solicitors the firm of J. N. Mason & Co of 41–44 Temple Chambers in the City of London my American Attorneys the firm of Stern & Reubens of 1 East 45th Street in New York City my Accountant Walter Smee now practising at 22 Shaftesbury Avenue West Central London, my British Publishers Messrs Constable & Co of 10 Orange Street in the County of London my Printers Messrs R. & R. Clark of Brandon Street Edinburgh, my present Secretary Blanche Patch, my Bibliographer Fritz Erwin Loewenstein Doctor of Philosophy and Founder of the London Shaw Society (now residing at Torca Cottage in Saint Albans) whose knowledge of my literary affairs and interest in my reputation qualify him exceptionally for such employment shall be consulted and employed by my Executor and Trustee whenever their assistance may be desirable and available and that the Incorporated Society of Authors Playwrights and Composers shall continue to be employed as my Theatrical Agents on the special conditions now established between us. To this I add that my country Solicitor Ivo L. Currall of 2 Gordon Chambers 1 Upper George Street Luton in the County of Bedford is also familiar with my local affairs.

47. Having been born a British subject in Ireland in 1856 subsequently registered as a citizen of Eire and finally privileged to remain a British subject by the Home Secretary's letter dated the twenty seventh day of June One thousand nine hundred and forty nine I declare that my domicile of choice is English and desire that my Will be construed and take effect according to English law.

In Witness whereof I have hereunto to set my hand to this and the thirteen preceding sheets of paper this twelfth day of June One thousand nine hundred and fifty.

Signed and acknowledged by the said George Bernard Shaw the Testator as and for his last Will and Testament in the presence of us who in his presence at his request and in the presence of each other all being present at the same time have hereunto subscribed our names as witnesses

G. Bernard Shaw

    E. Marjorie White Married woman

      22 Compton Avenue, Luton, Beds.

    Harold O. White, Master Printer,

      22 Compton Avenue, Luton, Beds.

APPENDIX C

(Artists' first names are only given to distinguish between common surnames, or to detail relatively minor artists. Figures in left column are catalogue numbers. Date purchased is given in brackets.)

Paintings, watercolours and drawings

1384 Domenico Tintoretto, *Venice, Queen of the Adriatic*, (1959)
1385 Domenico Ghirlandaio, *(?) Portrait of Clarice Orsini*, (1959)
1645 Louis Le Nain, *Adoration of the Shepherds*, (1961)
1646 Jean Nattier, *Carlotta Frederika Sparre, Countess Fersen*, (1961)
3315 Maurice Quentin De La Tour, *Louis Auguste Thibault-Dunois*, (1961)
1719 Murillo, *The Holy Family*, (1962)
1720 Murillo, *St Mary Magdalen*, (1962)
1721 El Mudo, *Abraham welcoming the three angels*, (1962)
1722 Courbet, *Dr Adolphe Marlet*, (1962)
1723 Boucher, *A young girl in a park*, (1962)
1737 Jack B. Yeats, *The double jockey act*, (1963)
1766 Jack B. Yeats, *About to write a letter*, (1964)
1768 Giovanni Di Paolo, *Crucifix*, (1964)
1769 Jack B. Yeats, *Grief*, (1965)
1760 Jacques Iverny, *The Annunciation*, (1965)
1790 Nathaniel Hone, The Elder, *The Conjurer*, (1966)
1812 Cigoli, *The Siege*, (1967)
1822 Marquet, *Porquerolles*, (1967)
1824 Roslin, *Le Marquis de Vaudreuil*, (1967)
1835–58 Various Schools, *Twenty-four icons* (The Allen Collection), (1968)
1867 La Tour, *The Image of Saint Alexis*, (1968)
1859 Walter Osborne, *Portrait of a gentleman*, (1968)
1860 Thomas Hickey, *Colonel William Kirkpatrick*, (1968)
1928 Goya, *El Sueño*, (1969)
4025 Valencian School, *Landscape with canopy and a legionary*, (1971)
4026 Valencian School, *Landscape with an angel bearing a martyr's crown*, (1971)
1982 Vouet, *The four seasons*, (1971)
4050 Eva Gonzales, *Two children playing on sand dunes*, (1972)

4052 Thomas Roberts, *A landscape*, (1972)

7515–33 Francis Place, *Twenty-three drawings*, (1972)

4055 Baron Gérard, *Marie-Julie Bonaparte, Queen of Spain, with her daughters, Zenaïde and Charlotte*, (1972)

4060 Jacques-Louis David, *The funeral of Patroclus*, (1973)

4074 Nathaniel Grogan, *A view towards Cork, on the river Lee*, (1973)

4089 Sogliani, *The Virgin and Child with St John the Baptist*, (1974)

4137 William Ashford, *A view of Dublin from Marino*, (1976)

4138 William Ashford, *A view of Dublin from Chapelizod*, (1976)

4170 French School, *Large apse*, (1976)

4171 French School, *Small apse*, (1976)

4186 Juan Fernandez, *A still life with citrons, a knife etc*, (1976)

4303 Nathaniel Grogan, *A harbour in County Cork*, (1978)

4304 Philip Hussey, *An interior with members of a family*, (1978)

4313 Fragonard, *Venus and Cupid*, (1978)

4315 Provoost, *Triptych: Virgin and Child with saints*, (1979)

4326 Reynolds, *The Right Honourable John Hely-Hutchinson*, (1979)

4339 Wheatley, *The Marquess and Marchioness of Antrim*, (1980)

4355 Van Dongen, *Stella in a flowered hat*, (1981)

4361 Signac, *Lady on a terrace, Saint-Tropez*, (1982)

4367 Henry Brooke, *The continence of Scipio*, (1982)

4468 Italian School, *A young man of the Branconio family (c. 1610)*, (1983)

4459 Camille Pissarro, *A bouquet of flowers in a vase*, (1983)

4463–66 Thomas Roberts, *Lucan House and three views in the demesne*, (1983)

4485 Soutine, *Man walking the stairs*, (1984)

4490 Nolde, *Two women in a garden*, (1984)

4508 William Ashford, *A bowl of flowers*, (1985)

Sculptures

8011 Renoir, *Pendule: hymne à la vie*, (1966)

8030 Duquesnoy, *Cardinal Guido Bentivoglio*, (1967)

8031 Attr. Juan Alonso Villabrille y Ron, *Elias overthrowing the false prophets of Baal*, (1967)

8028/29 Attr. Brustolon, *A pair of jardinières*, (1967)

8049 Ghiberti workshop, *Virgin and Child*, (1968)

8050 Courbet, *Madame Buchon*, (1968)

8051 Attr. Caffieri, *Bust of a lady*, (1968)

8052 Thomas Kirk, *Judge Charles Burton*, (1968)

8081 Dietz, *Chronos eating one of his children*, (1970)

8246 Richier, *The Virgin*, (1978)

8247 Richier, *St John the Evangelist*, (1978)

8303 Lawrence MacDonald, *Eurydice*, (1984)

APPENDIX D

FILMS MADE FROM SHAW'S PLAYS
*(Original Shaw titles are given in square brackets
below the film title, where they differ)*

Roman Boxera (Czechoslovakia)

[*Cashel Byron's Profession*]

FIRST SHOWING	1921
DIRECTOR	Vaclav Binovec
PRODUCER	Weteb Studios
SCREENPLAY	Suzanne Marwille
CAST INCLUDES	Frank: Frank Rose-Ruzicka
	Marta: Suzanne Marwille
	Theodor: V. Ch. Vladimirov

Cathedral Scene from Saint Joan (UK)

FIRST SHOWING	July/August 1927 (London)
DIRECTOR	Widgey Newman
PRODUCER	Vivian Van Dam (for the DeForest Phonofilm Company)
SCREENPLAY	Bernard Shaw
CAST INCLUDES	Saint Joan: Sybil Thorndike

How He Lied to Her Husband (UK)

FIRST SHOWING	12 January 1931 (London)
DIRECTOR	Cecil Lewis
PRODUCER	John Maxwell (for British International Pictures)
SCREENPLAY	Bernard Shaw
CAST INCLUDES	Herself: Vera Lennox
	Her Lover: Robert Harris
	Her Husband: Edmund Gwenn

Arms and the Man (UK)

FIRST SHOWINGS	4 August 1932 (Malvern Festival)
	24 September 1932 (London)
DIRECTOR	Cecil Lewis
PRODUCER	John Maxwell (for British International Pictures)
SCREENPLAY	Bernard Shaw
CAST INCLUDES	Paul Petkoff: Frederick Lloyd
	Bluntschli: Barry Jones
	Sergius Saranoff: Maurice Colbourne
	Raina: Anne Grey
	Catherine: Margaret Scudamore
	Louka: Angela Baddeley

Pygmalion (Germany)

FIRST SHOWING	2 September 1935 (Berlin)
DIRECTOR	Erich Engel
PRODUCER	Eberhard Klagemann (for Klagemann Film der Tobis-Rota)
SCREENPLAY	Heinrich Oberländer and Walter Wassermann
CAST INCLUDES	Eliza Doolittle: Jenny Jugo
	Henry Higgins: Gustaf Gründgens
	Col. Pickering: Anton Edthofer
	Alfred Doolittle: Eugen Klöpfer

Pygmalion (The Netherlands)

FIRST SHOWING	March 1937 (Amsterdam)
DIRECTOR	Ludwig Berger
PRODUCER	Rudolph Meyer (for Filmex Cinetone of Amsterdam)
SCREENPLAY	Ludwig Berger
CAST INCLUDES	Eliza Doolittle: Lily Bouwmeester
	Henry Higgins: Johan de Meester
	Col. Pickering: Eduard Verkade
	Alfred Doolittle: Matthieu van Eysden

Pygmalion (UK)

FIRST SHOWINGS	6 October 1938 (London)
	7 December 1938 (New York)

DIRECTORS	Anthony Asquith and Leslie Howard
PRODUCER	Gabriel Pascal
SCREENPLAY	Bernard Shaw (with additional dialogue by W.P. Lipscomb and Cecil Lewis)
MUSIC	Arthur Honegger
COSTUMES	Worth and Schiaparelli/Prof. Czettell
CAST INCLUDES	Eliza Doolittle: Wendy Hiller
	Henry Higgins: Leslie Howard
	Col. Pickering: Scott Sunderland
	Alfred Doolittle: Wilfrid Lawson
	Mrs Higgins: Marie Lohr

Major Barbara (UK)

FIRST SHOWINGS	7 April 1941 (London)
	13 May 1941 (New York)
DIRECTOR	Gabriel Pascal
PRODUCER	Gabriel Pascal
SCREENPLAY	Bernard Shaw
MUSIC	William Walton
COSTUMES	Cecil Beaton
CAST INCLUDES	Major Barbara: Wendy Hiller
	Adolphus Cusins: Rex Harrison
	Undershaft: Robert Morley
	Bill Walker: Robert Newton
	Snobby Price: Emlyn Williams
	The General: Sybil Thorndike
	Lady Britomart: Marie Lohr
	Jenny Hill: Deborah Kerr
	Policeman: Stanley Holloway
	James: Felix Aylmer

Caesar and Cleopatra (UK)

FIRST SHOWINGS	13 December 1945 (London)
	5 September 1946 (New York)
DIRECTOR	Gabriel Pascal
PRODUCER	Gabriel Pascal (for Rank Organisation)
SCREENPLAY	Bernard Shaw
MUSIC	Georges Auric
COSTUMES	Oliver Messel
CAST INCLUDES	Caesar: Claude Rains

Cleopatra: Vivien Leigh
Ftatateeta: Flora Robson
Pothinus: Francis L. Sullivan
Rufio: Basil Sydney
Britannus: Cecil Parker
Apollodorus: Stewart Granger
Belzanor: Stanley Holloway
Harp Girl: Jean Simmons
1st Nobleman: Felix Aylmer

Androcles and the Lion (USA)

FIRST SHOWINGS	14 January 1953 (New York)
	16 October 1953 (London)
DIRECTOR	Chester Erskine
PRODUCER	Gabriel Pascal (for RKO Pictures)
SCREENPLAY	Chester Erskine and Ken Englund
CAST INCLUDES	The Emperor: Maurice Evans
	The Captain: Victor Mature
	Androcles: Alan Young
	Lavinia: Jean Simmons
	Megaera: Elsa Lanchester
	Ferrovius: Robert Newton

Saint Joan (USA)

FIRST SHOWINGS	11 May 1957 (Paris)
	19 June 1957 (London)
	26 June 1957 (New York)
DIRECTOR	Otto Preminger
PRODUCER	Otto Preminger (for United Artists)
SCREENPLAY	Graham Greene
CAST INCLUDES	Saint Joan: Jean Seberg
	The Dauphin: Richard Widmark
	Dunois: Richard Todd
	Earl of Warwick: John Gielgud
	John de Stogumber: Harry Andrews
	De Courcelles: Barry Jones
	The Inquisitor: Felix Aylmer

The Doctor's Dilemma (UK)

FIRST SHOWINGS	17 December 1958 (New York)
	23 April 1959 (London)

DIRECTOR   Anthony Asquith
PRODUCER   Anatole de Grunwald (for Metro Goldwyn Mayer)
SCREENPLAY   Anatole de Grunwald
COSTUMES   Cecil Beaton
CAST INCLUDES   Jennifer Dubedat: Leslie Caron
                   Louis Dubedat: Dirk Bogarde
                   Sir Ralph Bloomfield Bonington: Robert Morley
                   Cutler Walpole: Alastair Sim
                   Sir Patrick Cullen: Felix Aylmer

Helden (Germany)

[*Arms and the Man*]

FIRST SHOWING   17 December 1958 (Hamburg)
DIRECTOR   Franz Peter Wirth
PRODUCERS   H. R. Sokal and P. Goldbaum (for Bavaria-
                   Filmkunst)
SCREENPLAY   Johanna Sibelius and Eberhard Keindorff
CAST INCLUDES   Paul Petkoff: Kurt Kasznar
                   Sergius Saranoff: Jan Hendricks
                   Bluntschli: O. W. Fischer
                   Nicola: Manfred Inger

Frau Warrens Gewerbe (Germany)

[*Mrs Warren's Profession*]

FIRST SHOWING   12 January 1960 (Hanover)
DIRECTOR   Akos von Rathony
PRODUCER   Heinz-Günter Sass (for Real Film GmbH)
SCREENPLAY   Johanna Sibelius and Eberhard Keindorff, from a
                   screenplay by Anatole de Grunwald
CAST INCLUDES   Frau Warren: Lilli Palmer

The Devil's Disciple (USA)

FIRST SHOWINGS   20 August 1959 (New York)
                   2 September 1959 (London)
DIRECTOR   Guy Hamilton
PRODUCER   Harold Hecht (for Brynaprod, SA, and Hecht-
                   Hill-Lancaster Films Ltd)

SCREENPLAY   John Dighton and Roland Kibbee
CAST INCLUDES   Revd Anthony Anderson: Burt Lancaster
    Dick Dudgeon: Kirk Douglas
    General Burgoyne: Laurence Olivier
    Judith Anderson: Janette Scott

The Millionairess (UK)

FIRST SHOWINGS   20 October 1960 (London)
    9 February 1961 (New York)
DIRECTOR   Anthony Asquith
PRODUCER   Pierre Rouve (for Dimitri de Grunwald)
SCREENPLAY   Wolf Mankowitz
COSTUMES   Pierre Balmain
CAST INCLUDES   Epifania: Sophia Loren
    Dr Kabir: Peter Sellers
    Sagamore: Alastair Sim

My Fair Lady (USA)
[Musical based on *Pygmalion*]

FIRST SHOWING   October 1964 (New York)
DIRECTOR   George Cukor
PRODUCER   Jack L. Warner (for CBS/Warner)
SCREENPLAY   Alan J. Lerner
MUSIC   adapted by André Previn from the original score
    by Frederick Loewe
COSTUMES   Cecil Beaton
CAST INCLUDES   Eliza Doolittle: Audrey Hepburn
    Henry Higgins: Rex Harrison
    Alfred Doolittle: Stanley Holloway
    Col. Pickering: Wilfred Hyde-White
    Mrs Higgins: Gladys Cooper

Great Catherine (UK)

FIRST SHOWING   1968 (London)
DIRECTOR   Gordon Flemyng
PRODUCER   Jules Buck (Warner/Keep Films)
SCREENPLAY   Hugh Leonard

CAST INCLUDES   Catherine the Great: Jeanne Moreau
Captain Edstaston: Peter O'Toole
Prince Patiomkin: Zero Mostel
The Sergeant: Akim Tamiroff
Sir George Gorse: Jack Hawkins

SOURCE NOTES

Bernard Shaw

VOLUMES I, II, III & IV

SOURCE NOTES

The following source notes are divided by volume and chapter. The left-hand column gives the page and line reference for the final word of the quotation; the key word is given in bold at the start of the note. Full details of publication and source are supplied at first mention in each chapter and when a reminder may be helpful. Except in certain cases, references to Shaw's plays are to the most complete edition, *Collected Plays with their Prefaces*, and for writings on music to *Shaw's Music*. For other works, issued by Shaw in the Limited or Ayot St Lawrence editions of his Collected Works, and in the Standard Edition format, reference is mainly to the Standard Edition. For further details of these publications, see Dan H. Laurence, *Bernard Shaw: A Bibliography* (1983).

Listed below are the abbreviations used in the notes for published sources and collections to which most frequent reference is made, together with full details of these publications and collections.

KEY TO ABBREVIATIONS OF MOST FREQUENTLY CITED PUBLISHED SOURCES

*CL*1–4   *Bernard Shaw: Collected Letters* (ed. Dan H. Laurence; Max Reinhardt, London).
vol. 1 (1874–1897) pub. 1965.
vol. 2 (1898–1910) pub. 1972.
vol. 3 (1911–1925) pub. 1985.
vol. 4 (1926–1950) pub. 1988.

A Correspondence   *Ellen Terry and Bernard Shaw: A Correspondence* (ed. Christopher St John; Constable, London 1931). Page references mainly from the reset edition of November 1931.

*CP*1–7   *The Bodley Head Bernard Shaw: Collected Plays with their Prefaces* (Max Reinhardt 1970–74).

Diaries 1–2   *Bernard Shaw: The Diaries: 1885–1897* (edited and annotated by Stanley Weintraub; The Pennsylvania State University Press, 1986). Two volumes.

The Diary of Beatrice Webb *The Diary of Beatrice Webb* (ed. Norman and Jeanne MacKenzie; Virago in association with the London School of Economics and Political Science, London).
vol. 1 (1873–1892) *Glitter Around and Darkness Within* pub. 1982.
vol. 2 (1892–1905) *All the Good Things of Life* pub. 1983.
vol. 3 (1905–1924) *The Power to Alter Things* pub. 1984.
vol. 4 (1924–1943) *The Wheel of Life* pub. 1985.

EPWW Bernard Shaw, *Everybody's Political What's What?* (1944). Part of *The Works of Bernard Shaw*, Standard Edition (Constable, London, 1931–51).

IWG *The Intelligent Woman's Guide to Socialism and Capitalism* (1930). Volume 20 of *The Works of Bernard Shaw*, Collected Edition (Constable, London, 1930–38). First edition of *IWG* published 1928. Shaw added two chapters on Sovietism and Communism for the Pelican two-volume edition in 1937. The Penguin edition of 1982 has an Introduction by Margaret Walters. Page references mainly to this edition.

The Letters of Sidney and Beatrice Webb *The Letters of Sidney and Beatrice Webb* (ed. Norman MacKenzie; Cambridge University Press in co-operation with the London School of Economics and Political Science, Cambridge 1978).
vol. 1 (1873–1892) *Apprenticeships*
vol. 2 (1892–1912) *Partnership*
vol. 3 (1912–1947) *Pilgrimage*

OTN 1–3 Bernard Shaw, *Our Theatres in the Nineties: Criticisms contributed Week by Week to the Saturday Review from January 1895 to May 1898*. Three volumes (1931). Volumes 23–25 of *The Works of Bernard Shaw*, Collected Edition (1930–38).

Shaw: An Exhibit *Shaw: An Exhibit*, A Catalog by Dan H. Laurence for an Exhibit Selected and Prepared with Lois B. Garcia (University of Texas at Austin, 1977).

Shaw/Barker letters *Bernard Shaw's Letters to Granville Barker* (ed. C. B. Purdom with commentary and notes. Theatre Arts Books, New York 1957).

Shaw/Trebitsch letters *Bernard Shaw's Letters to Siegfried Trebitsch* (ed. Samuel A. Weiss, Stanford University Press, Stanford, California, 1986).

SM1–3   *The Bodley Head Bernard Shaw: Shaw's Music: The complete musical criticism in three volumes* (ed. Dan H. Laurence 1981).
vol. 1 (1876–1890); vol. 2 (1890–1893); vol. 3 (1893–1950).

SSS   Bernard Shaw, *Sixteen Self Sketches* (Constable, London 1949).

Their Correspondence   *Bernard Shaw and Mrs Patrick Campbell: Their Correspondence* (ed. Alan Dent, Victor Gollancz, London 1952).

KEY TO ABBREVIATIONS OF COLLECTIONS

Alexander Turnbull Library	Alexander Turnbull Library, Wellington, New Zealand
Bancroft	Bancroft Library, University of California, Berkeley
BBC, Caversham	British Broadcasting Corporation Written Archives, Caversham
Berg	Henry W. and Albert A. Berg Collection, New York Public Library
BL	British Library Manuscript Room Collection, London
Boston	Mugar Memorial Library, Boston University
Bucknell	Ellen Clarke Bertrand Library, Bucknell University
Cambridge	Cambridge University Library
Carlow	Carlow County Council, Ireland
Colby	Colby College Library, Waterville, Maine
Columbia	Rare Book and Manuscript Library, Columbia University in the City of New York
Cornell	Bernard F. Burgunder Collection, Cornell University Library
Detroit	Rare Book Room, Detroit Public Library
Fales	De Coursey Fales Library, New York University
Folger	Folger Shakespeare Library, Washington
Glasgow	University of Glasgow Library
Hofstra	Hofstra University Library, Hempstead, New York
Houghton	Houghton Library, Harvard University
Illinois	University of Illinois Library at Urbana-Champaign

Iowa	University of Iowa Libraries
Ireland	National Library of Ireland, Dublin
LSE	London School of Economics; British Library of Political and Economic Science
Musée Rodin	Musée Rodin, Paris
NT	National Trust Head Office, London
North Carolina	Southern Historical Collection, University of North Carolina, Chapel Hill
Nuffield	Fabian Society Archive, Nuffield College Library, Oxford
Penguin Archive	Penguin Archive, University of Bristol Library
Philadelphia	Rare Book Department, Free Library of Philadelphia
Plunkett	Plunkett Foundation, Oxford
Princeton	Robert H. Taylor Collection, Rare Books & Special Collections, Princeton University Library
Reading	University of Reading Library
Scotland	National Library of Scotland, Edinburgh
Texas	Harry Ransom Humanities Research Center, University of Texas
UCL	Pearson Papers, University College Library, London
Worcester Record Office	A section of the Hereford and Worcester Record Office
Yale	Beinecke Rare Book and Manuscript Library, Yale University

CHAPTER I

page / line

3 / Ep.   **Irish:** 'Shaw Speaks to his Native City', *New York Journal-
              American*, 17 and 18 March 1946. See Bernard Shaw, *The
              Matter with Ireland* (ed. with an introduction by David H.
              Greene and Dan H. Laurence 1962) p. 294.

4 / 5   **want him:** Eric Bentley on 'Shaw Dead', *Envoy* February 1951,
              p. 15. See *Shaw: The Critical Heritage* (ed. T. F. Evans 1976)
              p. 404.

4 / 34   **cloister:** Clause 3 of Shaw's will. Vide supra p. 101, this
              volume.

5 / 3   **aspirations:** Statement for the press, 3 November 1950.

5 / 4   **country:** *The Matter with Ireland* p. ix.

5 / 9   **horse:** The Duke of Wellington. See also letter from John
              Heuston to *Manchester Guardian* 9 January 1958.

5 / 14   **illusions:** Demetrius O'Bolger questionnaire (Houghton). See
              also letter to *Hibernia* 25 October 1948 (Boston).

5 / Ep. 1   **specialities:** G.B.S. to H. H. Champion, 17 November 1912
              (Texas).

5 / Ep. 2   **humanity:** G.B.S. to Miss A. L. Shaw, 23 November 1916,
              *CL*3 p. 437.

6 / 25   **doze:** Description by Charles MacMahon Shaw, *Bernard's
              Brethren* (1939) p. 40.

6 / 27   **windows:** Preface to *Immaturity* (1931) p. ix.

6 / 34   **aristocracy:** G.B.S. addition to manuscript of Archibald
              Henderson's *Playboy and Prophet* p. 17 (North Carolina).

6 / last   **over her:** *Bernard's Brethren* facing p. 132; cf Preface to
              Immaturity pp. viii–ix.

7 / 5   **bishop:** See *Bernard's Brethren* facing p. 151; cf G.B.S. to
              Dorothy Eagle, 26 April 1946: '... the Reverend William
              George [Carroll] was a man of conspicuous character, ability
              and scholarship. My father told me he would have been a
              bishop if only he had been able to control his temper. But as
              bishops are allowed, & even expected, to have dominant
              tempers the real reason was that he was a Republican and an

Irish Protestant clergyman holding such views was then a
monstrosity never before regarded as possible, and out of the
question as a bishop.'

7/ 7   **inebriates:** G.B.S. to Lady Mary Murray, 1 September 1898,
*CL*2 p. 60.

7/ 10   **there:** Preface to *Immaturity* p. viii.

7/ 12   **drinking:** BL Add. MS 50710 B.

7/ 16   **unstable:** For a note on Henry Shaw's career see BL Add. MS
50710 A.

7/ 24   **ever:** BL Add. MS 50710 B.

7/ 32   **dotty:** *Bernard's Brethren* facing p. 134.

7/ 40   **heaven:** Preface to *Immaturity* pp. xxiv–xxv; cf *SSS* pp. 42–3
(which differs in some details from the first version, 'In the
Days of my Youth', in *Mainly About People*, 17 September
1898).

8/ 10   **cupboard:** Part of G.B.S.'s instructions ('Take this out') to
C. M. Shaw regarding a passage excised from p. 71 of the
published version of *Bernard's Brethren* (Ireland).

8/ Ep.   **long ago:** G.B.S. to Rachel Mahaffy, 6 June 1939 (Ireland MS
3229)

8/ 28   **person:** G.B.S. to Ellen Terry, 11 June 1897, *CL*1 p. 773.

9/ 16   **Gurly:** *SSS* p. 11.

9/ 18   **Gourlay:** G.B.S. undated note to F. E. Loewenstein for
I. Woodbine Morgan (Texas).

9/ 19   **Huguenots:** More likely Scottish. See R. F. Rattray, *Bernard
Shaw: A Chronicle* (1951) pp. 11–12; also *The Irish Ancestor*
no. 2, 1978, pp. 69–73.

10/ 4   **himself:** G.B.S. to Frank Harris, 5 June 1930, *The Playwright
and the Pirate: Bernard Shaw and Frank Harris: A
Correspondence* (ed. with an introduction by Stanley Weintraub
1982) p. 224; cf *EPWW* p. 51. Archibald Henderson in *George
Bernard Shaw: Man of the Century* (1956) confuses Walter
Bagnall Gurly with G.B.S.'s paternal grandfather, Bernard
Shaw.

10/ 7   **life:** Lucinda Elizabeth Shaw to G.B.S., 25 March 1894, BL
Add. MS 50513 ff. 41–2.

10/ 18   *performer:* Lucinda Elizabeth Shaw to G.B.S., 24 March
1894, BL Add. MS 50513 ff. 39–40.

10/ 21   **skill:** 'English Music', *The World* 14 March 1894, *SM*3 p. 157.

11/ 5   **house:** G.B.S. to O'Bolger, February 1916 (Texas): cf *SSS*
pp. 10–11, where Shaw alters his story from this earlier
version to assert his mother's 'innocence' and unworldliness.

11/ 24   **run:** BL Add. MS 50710 B.

11/30   **granite:** *SSS* p. 9.

12/ 3   **innocence:** Marginal comment on Demetrius O'Bolger's MS, 'The Influence of Mr Shaw's Youth on his Views and Personality' (Houghton).

12/24   **confess:** G.B.S. to Frank Harris, 5 June 1930, *The Playwright and the Pirate* p. 226; cf *SSS* pp. 11–12.

13/ 3   **Stock:** See *CL*1 p. 133; also John O'Donovan, *Shaw and the Charlatan Genius* (1965) p. 24.

13/Ep.   **very worst:** G.B.S. to Nancy Astor, 21 August 1943 (Reading).

13/28   **like:** Cf *SSS* p. 12 and *CL*3 p. 364.

13/30   **arrangements:** G.B.S. to Mr and Miss Devine, Sotheby's Catalogue, 7 July 1970, item 567.

13/last   **soon:** G.B.S. to Katharine Cornell, 30 July 1941, *CL*4 p. 608.

13/last   **calculated:** 'As I was born without a watch I cannot tell the exact hour at which I emerged; but I have been told that it was after dark.' G.B.S. note for F. E. Loewenstein, 13 March 1950 (Texas).

14/ 5   **fire:** G.B.S. to Dorothy Eagle, vide supra.

14/18   **head:** A characteristic joke by George Carr Shaw; see *SSS* pp. 3–4.

14/20   **fight:** Joe Foy, a schoolfriend of Shaw's, interviewed by Seán MacRéamoinn on Radio Éireann, 30 November 1950; see also Deena Hanson, 'George Bernard Shaw', Radio Éireann, 26 July 1956 and 'Boys at Play', *Shaw: Interviews and Recollections* (ed. A. M. Gibbs 1990) pp. 10–11.

14/30   **afterwards:** *SSS* p. 48.

14/38   **written:** Preface to *Immaturity* p. xxi.

15/ 5   **Mill:** George Carr Shaw to Lucinda Elizabeth Shaw, 14 July 1857 and 11 August 1857, BL Add. MS 50508.

15/10   **in it:** G.B.S. to Pat O'Reilly, 29 July 1950 (Ireland)

15/13   **villagers:** See G.B.S. note for W. J. Jacob, April 1949 (Bucknell).

15/19   **geniality:** G.B.S., 'George Clibborn (Snr.)', BL Add. MS 50710 A; cf Preface to *Immaturity* p. xi.

15/32   **else?:** *SSS* pp. 12 and 106; cf G.B.S. to Ellen Terry, 11 June 1897, *CL*1 p. 773.

15/34   **began:** G.B.S. to Ellen Terry, 11 June 1897, *CL*1 p. 773; cf G.B.S. to Janet Achurch, 9 December 1897, *CL*1 p. 828.

15/last   **on me:** *SSS* p. 12.

16/ 4   **grave:** G.B.S. to O'Bolger, February 1916, *CL*3 p. 366.

16/ 6   **for it:** *Bernard Shaw: A Chronicle* p. 13.

16/ 8   **over her:** *SSS* p. 13; *CL*3 p. 364.

16/15   **about her:** Preface to *Misalliance*; see *CP*4 p. 109.

16/19   **at all**: G.B.S. to Frank Harris, 5 June 1930; see *The Playwright and the Pirate* p. 227.

16/20   **in it**: G.B.S. marginal comment on p. 19 of O'Bolger's 'The Real Shaw' (Houghton bMS Eng.1046.9).

16/22   **exist**: G.B.S. to O'Bolger, February 1916, *CL*3 p. 366.

16/30   **situation**: G.B.S. to O'Bolger, 7 August 1919, *CL*3 p. 627.

16/31   **children**: *SSS* p. 13; cf *CL*3 p. 365.

16/38   **sentimentality!**: MS of Archibald Henderson's *Playboy and Prophet* (North Carolina).

17/ 8   **anybody**: *SSS* p. 13.

17/11   **long-suffering**: The first draft of this was a letter G.B.S. wrote to O'Bolger dated February 1916, *CL*3 p. 364.

17/12   **admirable**: 'Shaw's astonishing and admirable mother'; this description was borrowed by G.B.S. from Sydney Olivier. See *Sydney Olivier: Letters and Selected Writings* (ed. Margaret Olivier 1948).

17/17   **realities**: G.B.S. to Ellen Terry, 11 June 1897, *CL*1 p. 773, *Ellen Terry and Bernard Shaw: A Correspondence* (ed. Christopher St John 1931) pp. 214–16.

17/37   **beginning**: G.B.S. to O'Bolger, February 1916, *CL*3 p. 365. Shaw rewrote this passage in the published version; cf *SSS* p. 13.

18/10   **vocation**: G.B.S. to Marie Stopes, 27 November 1943, BL Add. MS 58493.

18/22   **life**: G.B.S. to O'Bolger, February 1916, *CL*3 p. 365.

18/32   **love**: G.B.S. to Frank Harris, 5 June 1930, *The Playwright and the Pirate* p. 227.

18/37   **close**: G.B.S. to Henry Salt, 7 December 1934, *CL*4 p. 392.

19/ 4   **world**: G.B.S. marginal comment on O'Bolger's 'The Real Shaw' (Houghton bMS Eng.1046.9).

19/ 8   **one another**: G.B.S. to Henry T. Bellow, 18 December 1925. See *Dear Mr Shaw; Selections from Bernard Shaw's Postbag* (compiled and ed. Vivian Elliot 1988) p. 363.

19/36   **dead**: Preface to *Immaturity* p. xliii.

19/39   **I do?**: See G.B.S. to Janet Achurch, 9 December 1897, *CL*1 p. 828.

20/15   **my mother**: G.B.S. to Gilbert Murray, 14 March 1911, *CL*2 pp. 17–18.

20/19   **God!**: G.B.S. to O'Bolger, February 1916, *CL*3 p. 365. Cf *SSS* p. 13 and G.B.S. to Frank Harris, 5 June 1930, *The Playwright and the Pirate* p. 227.

20/33   **excursion**: Written in 1935 as a preface to *London Music in 1888–89* (1937), *SM*1 pp. 38–9.

21/ 6   **forget:** G.B.S. to Ada Tyrrell, 14 July 1949, *CL*4 p. 352.

21/13   **humor:** G.B.S. to O'Bolger, 7 August 1919, *CL*3 p. 628.

21/34   **brimstone:** 'Disposal of the Dead', *The World* 14 February 1894. See *SM*3 pp. 133–4; see also *Shaw: An Autobiography 1856–1898* (selected from his writings by Stanley Weintraub 1970) pp. 16–17.

21/last   **about:** G.B.S. to Daniel G. Day, 9 May 1949, *CL*4 p. 849.

22/19   **faces:** G.B.S. to Edith [The Hon. Mrs Alfred] Lyttelton, 5 July 1913, *CL*3 pp. 187–8.

22/Ep.   **certificate:** G.B.S. to Denis Johnston, 1 April 1938 (Trinity College, Dublin).

23/17   **defect:** G.B.S. to O'Bolger, February 1916, *CL*3 p. 360.

23/19   **institution:** Ibid., p. 372.

23/38   **Caroline Row:** Now renamed and renumbered 4 Portland Row.

24/ 4   **Harrington Street:** In 1858–9 Harrington Street was renumbered and no. 16 became no. 48.

24/32   **public:** *The Diary of Beatrice Webb* vol. 3 (ed. Norman and Jeanne MacKenzie 1984), entry 12 May 1911, p. 158.

25/13   **dislike it:** G.B.S. to Thomas Armstrong, Editor of *The English Digest*, 30 October 1940 (Texas).

25 / 14   **George:** G.B.S. to Mary P. Ussher of the BBC, 2 April 1937 (BBC, Caversham).

25/33   **live for:** *SSS* p. 14.

26/11   **Synge-street:** Written in 1935 as a preface to *London Music in 1888–89*, *SM*1 p. 35.

26/16   **us:** Ibid., p. 41.

26/18   **sort:** G.B.S. to O'Bolger, February 1916, *CL*3 p. 358.

26/36   **character:** Ibid., p. 356.

26/37   **sexless:** G.B.S. to Frank Harris, 5 June 1930, *The Playwright and the Pirate* p. 224.

26/last   **to them:** 'Rungs of the Ladder IX', *The Listener* VIII, 20 July 1932, pp. 74–5.

27/ 2   **misunderstood:** Written in 1935 as a preface to *London Music in 1888–89*, *SM*1 p. 37.

27/ 4   **inspired:** G.B.S. to O'Bolger, 7 August 1919, *CL*3 p. 628.

27/ 9   **ghost:** G.B.S. to O'Bolger, February 1916, *CL*3 p. 357.

27/11   **work:** O'Donovan, *Shaw and the Charlatan Genius* (1965) p. 27.

27/Ep.   **environment:** G.B.S. to H. G. Wells, 17 May 1917, *CL*3 p. 473.

27/19   **loathed it:** G.B.S. to Hesketh Pearson, 27 December 1942 (Texas).

27/23   **suggested:** Stephen Winsten, *Jesting Apostle: The Life of Bernard Shaw* (1956) p. 11.

27/29   **Hill:** G.B.S. interview, 9 November 1931 (Bucknell).

28/ 4   **world:** G.B.S. to John G. Fitzgerald, 12 April 1947, *CL4* p. 794.

28/ 6   **over:** G.B.S. to Patricia Devine, c. May 1944, BL Add. MS 50524 rev.f.47, shorthand version. A different version appears 3 May 1944, *CL4* pp. 706–7.

28/ 8   **imagination:** G.B.S. to Edith Livia Beatty, 20 September 1907, *CL2* p. 714; also partly quoted in St John Ervine, *Bernard Shaw: His Life, Work and Friends* (1956) p. 28.

28/11   **nobody:** G.B.S. to John G. Fitzgerald, 22 November 1947 (Ireland).

28/14   **outlook:** *Bernard Shaw: A Chronicle* p. 17.

28/19   **work:** G.B.S. to Archibald Henderson, 30 June 1904, *CL2* p. 427.

28/24   **inhabitants:** *Bernard Shaw: His Life, Work and Friends* p. 18.

28/32   **one:** Written in 1935 as a preface to *London Music in 1888–89*, *SM1* p. 37.

28/37   **thing:** G.B.S. answer to O'Bolger, 23 June 1915 (Houghton).

28/last   **Synge St.:** *The Playwright and the Pirate* p. 232.

29/ 5   **bed:** The forty-nine-page text of Edward McNulty's 'Memoirs of G.B.S.', which is at North Carolina, has been edited and annotated by Dan H. Laurence in *The Annual of Bernard Shaw Studies* vol. 12 (ed. Fred D. Crawford 1992) pp. 1–46, together with additional McNulty material. A shorter reminiscence, 'George Bernard Shaw as a Boy', printed in *Candid Friend* 6 July 1901, appears with Shaw's marginal comments in *Shaw: Interviews and Recollections* (ed. A. M. Gibbs 1990).

29/28   **church:** 'Working Men and Sacred Music', *The Star* 8 November 1889; see *SM1* p. 830 for partial quote.

30/ 1   **repartee:** G.B.S. to O'Bolger, February 1916, *CL3* pp. 366–7; cf *SSS* p. 15.

30/ 4   **parables:** Preface to *Immaturity* p. xxii.

30/15   **gentlemen:** *SSS* p. 45.

30/21   **year:** G.B.S. to Frank Harris, 5 June 1930, *The Playwright and the Pirate* p. 228.

30/23   **way:** G.B.S. to O'Bolger, February 1916, *CL3* p. 373.

30/26   **snobbery:** G.B.S. to St John Ervine, 31 October 1942, *CL4* p. 645.

30/40   **laughter:** G.B.S. to O'Bolger, 7 August 1919, *CL3* p. 628.

31/20   **to him:** G.B.S. note for Kingston Barton, 25 October 1879, BL Add. MS 50710 B.

31/33   **tragedies:** In Hesketh Pearson, *Bernard Shaw* (1975 revised edn) p. 16.

32/ 7   **to be:** George Carr Shaw to Lucinda Elizabeth Shaw, 28 July and 8 August 1857, BL Add. MS 50508.

32/13   **time:** George Carr Shaw to Lucinda Elizabeth Shaw, 2 August 1857, ibid.

32/27   **alter it:** G.B.S. to O'Bolger, February 1916, *CL*3 p. 357.

32/36   **Shaw:** G.B.S. to Charles MacMahon Shaw, 17 November 1937, *CL*4 p. 479. Another version is published in *SSS*.

33/ 3   **Street:** Bessie's father was similarly bigoted and would spit whenever he uttered the word 'Papist'.

33/Ep.   **schooling:** *CP*4 p. 36.

33/19   **fly:** Written in 1935 as a preface to *London Music in 1888–89*, *SM*1 p. 40.

33/28   **conjecture:** G.B.S. to H. B. Higgins, 22 August 1928 (copy privately owned. The Higgins papers are in the National Library of Australia, Canberra).

33/32   **day:** Written in 1935 as a preface to *London Music in 1888–89*, *SM*1 p. 40.

33/33   **nothing:** *Nine Answers by G. Bernard Shaw*, with an Introduction by Christopher Morley (unauthorized publication with unnumbered pages privately printed for Jerome Kern, 1923). See also Laurence, *Bernard Shaw. A Bibliography*, vol. I, pp. 151–2; and *Shaw: Interviews and Recollections* pp. 22–9.

34/14   **headmaster:** G.B.S. to John Araben, 1 November 1944, *CL*4 p. 727. A slightly different version of this letter is in the British Library, BL Add. MS 50709.

34/27   **such:** BL Add. MS 50709.

34/34   **incorrigible:** These words were supplied by G.B.S. See the notes on Henderson's biography (North Carolina).

35/ 9   **drop:** G.B.S. to Hesketh Pearson, 15 March 1939, *CL*4 p. 527.

35/13   **for me:** Note by G.B.S. for Archibald Henderson (North Carolina).

35/22   **day:** G.B.S. to Sidney Webb, 26 March 1946 (LSE).

35/25   **fact:** *Nine Answers by G. Bernard Shaw*.

35/27   **Forget it:** G.B.S. to Wesley College, 16 May 1945, *Wesley College Magazine* p. 26.

36/21   **ignored:** G.B.S. to Frank Harris, 5 June 1930, *The Playwright and the Pirate* p. 224.

36/last   **mad:** *Senior Teachers' World and Schoolmistress* 19 October 1938, p. 1.

37/ 3   **genius:** G.B.S. to Lucinda Frances Shaw, 4 March 1874, *CL*1 p. 8.

37/ 8   **glance:** Edward McNulty, 'Memoirs of G.B.S.'

37/16   **answered:** G.B.S. to Archibald Henderson, 3–17 January 1905, *CL*2 p. 504.

37/30   **drawing:** Shaw attended the 'evening freehand class' during the sessions 1 October 1870–28 February 1871, and 6 March 1872–31 July 1872. He had also gone there before the autumn of 1870, but for unspecified reasons.

38/23   **good:** 'Utopias', a paper read to the Hampstead Historical Club, 25 May 1887 (Houghton).

38/36   **Church:** 'If we could only forget for a moment that we are Irish, and become really Catholic Europeans, there would be some hope for us': G.B.S. to Lady Gregory, 3 December 1917. A volume of Shaw's correspondence with Lady Gregory (ed. Nicholas Grene and Dan H. Laurence) is shortly to be published.

39/ 3   **practices:** Preface to *Immaturity* pp. xix–xx.

39/19   **cry:** 'Rungs of the Ladder IX', *The Listener* VIII, 20 July 1932, pp. 73–5.

40/20   **attitude:** 'The Best Books for Children', BL Add. MS 50673.

40/31   **strongly:** Ibid.

40/39   **Dickens:** *SSS* p. 20.

40/40   **end:** Shaw's Introduction to *Great Expectations* (1936).

41/ 1   **one:** G.B.S. reply to O'Bolger questionnaire, 14 December 1916 (Houghton).

41/ 4   **nonage:** Preface to *Misalliance*, *CP*4 p. 132.

41/ 8   **humor:** 'A Barrie and Conan Doyle Comic Opera', *The World* 24 May 1893, *SM*2 p. 891.

41/10   **world:** Preface to *Farfetched Fables*, *CP*7 p. 385.

41/12   **life:** Preface to *The Doctor's Dilemma*, *CP*3 p. 441.

41/15   **relative:** Preface to *Farfetched Fables*, *CP*7 p. 385.

42/Ep.   **senses:** 'The Religion of the Pianoforte' (*Fortnightly Review* February 1894): 'How to Become a Musical Critic', *SM*3 p. 116.

42/ 4   **colleges:** *Nine Answers by G. Bernard Shaw.*

42/10   **rehearsals:** G.B.S. reply to O'Bolger questionnaire, 14 February 1916.

42/18   **character:** Edward McNulty, 'Memoirs of G.B.S.'

42/27   **love:** *Bernard Shaw: A Chronicle* p. 15.

42/33   **characters:** Written in 1935 as a preface to *London Music in 1888–89, SM*1 pp. 44–5.

43/19   **existence:** 'Some Instruments and How to Play Them', *The Star* 8 March 1889, *SM*1 p. 574.

43/23   **voice:** Ibid.

43/28   **music:** Written in 1935 as a preface to *London Music in 1888–89, SM*1 p. 51.

43/33   **abeyance:** 'The 789th Performance of *Dorothy*', *The Star* 13 September 1889, a review of B. C. Stephenson and Alfred Cellier's pastoral comedy opera in which Dorothy was sung by Lucy Shaw; collected in *London Music, SM*1 p. 781.

44/ 3   **time:** Deena Hanson, 'The Sister of G.B.S.', Radio Éireann, Dublin.

44/ 6   **faded:** Edward McNulty, 'Memoirs of G.B.S.'

44/ 9   **own:** G.B.S. to Charles MacMahon Shaw, 17 November 1937, *CL*4 p. 480.

44/15   **melancholy!:** G.B.S. to Harriet Cohen, 2 April 1931 (photocopy from Society of Authors' files). Shaw's correspondence to Harriet Cohen is in the British Library. Some letters appear in her memoirs, *A Bundle of Time.* 'Many ordinary men cannot bear contradiction, especially if they have no sisters; but geniuses cannot bear agreement, perhaps because it is an assertion of equality' (Commonplace Book, Berg).

44/24   **than I:** *The Irrational Knot* (1931) p. 323.

45/10   **guineas:** G.B.S. to Viola Tree, 17 December 1911, *CL*3 pp. 65–6.

45/25   **husband:** Editor's note, *CL*1 p. 133.

45/33   **tinted:** *Saunders' News-Letter* 27 December 1869.

45/37   **purpose:** Written in 1935 as a preface to *London Music in 1888–89, SM*1 p. 43.

45/last   **Street:** See *Shaw and the Charlatan Genius*, Appendix G, pp. 142–8.

46/10   **sympathy:** Preface to *Immaturity* p. xxxi.

47/ 6   **re-election:** *The Irish Times* 13 November 1871.

47/15   **THEATRE:** Ibid., 9 December 1871.

47/25   **expression:** Ibid., 17 January 1866.

47/26   **bouquets:** *Shaw and the Charlatan Genius* p. 76.

47/27   **eroticism:** G.B.S. to Frank Harris, 5 June 1930, *The Playwright and the Pirate* p. 225.

47/30   **artiste:** *The Irish Times* 16 March 1869.

47/last   **charity:** See, for example, public announcement in *The Irish Times* 9 December 1871.

48/ 3   **concert:** *Shaw and the Charlatan Genius*, Appendix E, p. 131.

48/10   **galleries:** *The Irish Times* 7 January 1873.

48/12   **deserve:** Ibid., 13 January 1873.

48/14   **Opera:** Ibid.

48/29   **chance:** Written in 1935 as a preface to *London Music in 1888–89, SM*1 p. 49.

48/32   **harmoniously:** *The Irish Times* 15 May 1873.

48/37   **of it:** *Daily Express* 15 May 1873.

48/38   **Dublin:** In the City of Dublin Library.

49/ 3   **away:** O. J. Vignoles, *Memoir of Sir Robert Prescott Stewart* (n.d. [1898]) pp. 118–19.

49/ 7   **Times:** *The Irish Times* 27 May 1873.

49/11   **Stewart:** An appointment enthusiastically welcomed by the anonymous critic of the *Daily Express*. As critic, Sir Robert Prescott Stewart found himself more than once anonymously obliged to praise the beautiful compositions and fine conducting of Sir Robert Prescott Stewart. Having removed Lee, he later ousted the founder of the old Philharmonic, ending up as Dublin's 'only Great Panjandrum of orchestral music' until his death in 1894. See O'Donovan, *Shaw and the Charlatan Genius* pp. 81–4 and 123–4.

49/14   **her:** *The Irish Times* 18 June 1873, p. 3 lists Mrs Shaw and Miss Shaw among passengers departing from Ireland the previous day. See B. C. Rosset, *Shaw of Dublin: The Formative Years* (Pennsylvania State University Press, 1964) pp. 238–48.

49/14   **ceased:** G.B.S. to Archibald Henderson, 3–17 January 1905, *CL*2 p. 501.

49/Ep.   **inhumanity:** *CP*2 pp. 87–8.

49/18   **back:** Written in 1935 as a preface to *London Music in 1888–89*, *SM*1 p. 54.

49/26   **heartily:** Ibid., p. 36.

49/30   **success:** Ibid., p. 49.

49/32   **about it:** G.B.S. reply to O'Bolger questionnaire, 14 June 1922, *CL*3 p. 774.

50/ 4   **house:** G.B.S. to Frank Harris, 20 June 1930, *CL*4 p. 188, *The Playwright and the Pirate* p. 232.

50/25   **Lane:** G.B.S. reply to O'Bolger questionnaire, 14 June 1922, *CL*3 pp. 774–6.

50/28   **life:** G.B.S. to O'Bolger, 7 August 1919, *CL*1 p. 627. See also G.B.S. to C. M. Shaw (Ireland), and *SSS* pp. 87–8.

50/38   **Petitioner:** Edward McNulty, 'Memoirs of G.B.S.'

51/13   **Marshall:** Julian Marshall, musicologist and tennis player, was a director of Simpkin, Marshall & Co. which had managed the London distribution of *The Voice*. He paid £300 for Torca Cottage (the same as Lee had paid for it two years before).

51/17   **nothing:** G.B.S. reply to O'Bolger questionnaire, 14 February 1916 (Houghton).

51/22   **music:** 'The Religion of the Pianoforte', *Fortnightly Review* February 1894, 'How to Become a Musical Critic', *Scottish Musical Monthly* December 1894, *SM*3 p. 111.

51/27   **life:** G.B.S. reply to O'Bolger questionnaire, 14 February 1916 (Houghton).

51 / 31   **mad:** 'The Religion of the Pianoforte', 'How to Become a Musical Critic', *SM*3 p. 111.

51 / 36   **cost:** Ibid., p. 112.

51 / last   **told:** G.B.S. to Archibald Henderson, 3–17 January 1905, *CL*2 p. 505. In the Shaw Collection at the British Library there is a note by Shaw that c. 1875–6 he took a few piano lessons from T. Moore 'without result', BL Add. MS 50710 f. 4.

52 / 3   **colleagues:** Written in 1935 as a preface to *London Music in 1888–89*, *SM*1 p. 55.

52 / 10   **work:** *SSS* p. 33.

52 / 19   **others:** Preface to *Immaturity* pp. xxxi–xxxii.

52 / 24   **myself:** Ibid., p. xxxii.

52 / 34   **thing:** G.B.S. to Archibald Henderson, 3–17 January 1905, *CL*2 p. 502.

53 / 9   **worst:** *Misalliance*, *CP*4 pp. 214–15.

53 / 12   **loathed:** G.B.S. to Archibald Henderson, 3–17 January 1905, *CL*2 p. 502.

53 / 17   **tomfoolery:** G.B.S. to Mazzini Beatty, 15 December 1899, *CL*2 p. 120.

53 / 19   **to me:** *SSS* p. 33.

53 / 22   **position:** See 'Bernard Shaw as a Clerk: By Himself', *The Clerk* January 1908, pp. 7–8. Cf *SSS* p. 37.

53 / 25   **shopkeepers:** *Bernard Shaw: A Chronicle* p. 24.

53 / 36   **situation:** *SSS* pp. 31–2.

53 / 39   **snobbery:** Edward McNulty, 'Memoirs of G.B.S.'

53 / last   **Dublin:** *SSS* p. 32.

54 / 3   **permanently:** Ibid.

54 / 25   **side:** G.B.S. to Frank Harris, 20 June 1930, *CL*4 p. 189.

54 / 33   **August:** BL Add. MS 50710 f. 2. G.B.S. dates the Catastrophe as August 1877, but is probably repeating 1877 for the date on which he burnt his letter (25 October 1877) and the year in which he wrote this note. He almost certainly meant August 1875.

55 / 25   **tell:** BL Add. MS 50720.

55 / 35   **hate:** G.B.S.'s inscription on his copy of The Ashendene Press edn of Dante's *Tutte le Opere* (Texas); his flyleaf inscriptions were published as *Flyleaves* (ed. with an introduction by Dan H. Laurence and Daniel J. Leary, W. Thomas Taylor, Austin, Texas, 1977).

55 / 38   **them:** G.B.S. to Beatrice Webb, 7 February 1942 (LSE); see also *The Mentor* March 1930, pp. 16–20 and 68–9.

56 / 4   **alone:** Edward McNulty, 'Memoirs of G.B.S.'

56 / 12   **impatience:** Ibid.

56/16   **London W.C:** *Young Men of Great Britain*, no. 34, vol. II, 15 September 1868, p. 515 (Trinity College, Dublin).

56/17   **theatre:** Deena Hanson, 'The Sister of G.B.S.'; see also her 'About G.B.S.' broadcast for the centenary of Shaw's birth on Radio Éireann, 26 July 1956.

56/20   **Theatre:** This shop was 'Kept in tremendous order by a maitresse femme whom I still remember well enough to put into a play if occasion shall arise': G.B.S. to Conal O'Riordan, 13 July 1910 (Texas).

56/23   **demon:** See Edward McNulty, 'George Bernard Shaw as a Boy', *The Candid Friend* 6 July 1901, p. 384. See *Shaw: Interviews and Recollections* pp. 17–21.

56/35   **them:** G.B.S. to Gabrielle Enthoven, 13 February 1948 (Theatre Museum, Victoria and Albert Museum).

57/13   **splendid:** Preface to *Ellen Terry and Bernard Shaw: A Correspondence* (ed. Christopher St John 1931) pp. xxv–xxvi.

57/25   **ecstasy:** 'Lorenzaccio', *Saturday Review* 26 June 1897, *OTN*3 p. 171.

57/33   **tones:** BL Add. MS 50699 f. 375.

57/last   **writing:** *Bernard Shaw: A Chronicle* p. 20; see also Martin Meisel, *Shaw and the Nineteenth-Century Theater* (Princeton University Press 1963) pp. 11–61.

58/ 8   **stars:** Edward McNulty, 'Memoirs of G.B.S.'

58/15   **alone:** McNulty to G.B.S., 17–18 February 1883, *The Annual of Bernard Shaw Studies* vol. 12, 1992, p. 31.

58/20   **Entertainment:** Edward McNulty, 'Memoirs of G.B.S.'

58/29   **man:** Ibid.

59/ 3   **cured:** 'Bernard Shaw as a Clerk: By Himself', pp. 7–8.

59/15   **right:** G.B.S. to C. Uniacke Townshend, 29 February 1876, *CL*1 p. 14.

59/37   **ambition:** Preface to *Immaturity* p. xxxiii.

59/40   **gifts:** G.B.S. to St John Ervine, 27 October 1948 (Texas).

60/ 7   **compulsory:** G.B.S. to St John Ervine, 19 November 1937 (copy supplied by Janet Dunbar).

60/10   **England:** Lady Keeble, 'Bernard Shaw as I Remember Him' (Columbia).

60/15   **office:** *Bernard Shaw: A Chronicle* p. 27.

60/22   **BETTER:** See B. C. Rosset, *Shaw of Dublin* (1964) p. 278.

60/29   **heaven?:** G.B.S. to Margaret Mackail, 11 November 1933, *CL*4 p. 355.

CHAPTER II

61/Ep.   **discouraging:** G.B.S. to Miss Rhoda Halkett, 14 August 1894 (W. E. Hill Collection, Dallas Public Library).

61 / 4   **Unoccupied:** *Diaries* 1, notes for 1876, p. 30.

61 / 6   **result:** Ibid.

61 / 8   **again:** G.B.S. to Edward [E. M.] McNulty. This letter, first published in Stephen Winsten's *Jesting Apostle: The Life of Bernard Shaw* (1956, p. 33) and included in *CL*1 (p. 19), was in fact penned from memory by Shaw at the request of Winsten in the late 1940s.

61 / 13   **grinder:** G.B.S. to Arnold White, 5 October 1879, *CL*1 p. 23.

61 / 19   **hatstand:** G.B.S. to Demetrius O'Bolger, February 1916, *CL*3 p. 357.

61 / 21   **marry her:** G.B.S. to William Archer, 7 November 1905, *CL*2 p. 574. This story, apropos *Mrs Warren's Profession*, is quoted along with a story of incest and an episode involving a prostitute who slept with a father and his son.

61 / 29   **outrageous:** G.B.S. to Lucy Shaw, 24 February 1875, *CL*1 pp. 9–10.

62 / 2   **often:** G.B.S. to Bessie Shaw, 24 February 1875, *CL*1 p. 12.

62 / 6   **in it:** G.B.S. to Lucy Shaw, 24 February 1875, *CL*1 p. 9.

62 / 9   **backs:** H. G. Farmer, *Bernard Shaw's Sister and Her Friends* (1959) p. 31.

62 / 17   **authorship:** G.B.S., *'The Voice': An Autobiographical Explanation* (1952); unnumbered pages.

62 / 29   **faculty:** 'Musical Notes' [unsigned review of Frederic Cowen's opera *Pauline*], *The Hornet* XXI, 29 November 1876, *SM*1 p. 62.

62 / 30   **end:** Ibid., p. 64.

62 / 31   **triplets:** 'Messiah in the Albert Hall', *The Hornet* 27 December 1876, *SM*1 p. 77.

62 / 35   **another:** 'Opera in Italian', *The Saturday Musical Review* 22 February 1879, *SM*1 p. 192.

62 / 37   **England:** 'Vocalists of the Season: M. Capoul', *The Hornet* XXIII, 11 July 1877, *SM*1 p. 156.

63 / 1   **5.15:** 'Madame Schumann's Art', *The Hornet* 7 March 1877, *SM*1 p. 99.

63 / 2   **shouting:** 'Opera and Empty Bravado', *The Hornet* 13 June 1877, *SM*1 p. 133.

63 / 3   **bagpipes:** 'A Semi-Passion', *The Hornet* 21 March 1877, *SM*1 p. 105.

63 / 6   **signal:** 'Her Majesty's Opera' [unsigned review of Etelka Gerster and the production of Donizetti's *Lucia di Lammermoor*], *The Hornet* 11 July 1877, *SM*1 p. 154.

63 / 9   **third:** Ibid.

63 / 17   **articles:** 'How to Become a Musical Critic', *Scottish Musical Monthly* December 1894, *SM*3 p. 343.

63/19 **possess:** G.B.S. to Karl Pearson, 20 June 1893 (Pearson Papers, UCL).

63/20 **criticisms:** Ibid.

63/23 **incompetence:** 'How to Become a Musical Critic', *SM*3 p. 343.

63/25 **hands:** G.B.S. note for F. E. Loewenstein, February 1949, for a reply to Gerald H. Ogle (Texas); see also Preface to *Immaturity* (1930) p. xxxv.

63/29 **world:** See John Stewart Collis, *Bound Upon a Course* (1971) p. 85.

63/38 **Lady:** Donald Shaw to Vandeleur Lee, 11 May 1877, BL Add. MS 50508 ff. 53–53v.

64/ 3 **copy:** Donald Shaw to Lee, early summer 1877, BL Add. MS 50508 ff. 85v–86v.

64/11 **ruined:** G.B.S. to Arnold White, 5 October 1879, *CL*1 p. 23.

64/15 **starve:** G.B.S. to O'Bolger, 7 August 1919, *CL*3 p. 628.

64/26 **time:** G.B.S. reply to O'Bolger questionnaire, 14 June 1922, *CL*3 p. 775.

64/29 **up:** G.B.S. to O'Bolger, 7 August 1919, *CL*3 p. 628.

64/36 **again:** G.B.S. to O'Bolger, February 1916, *CL*3 p. 358.

65/ 5 **attitude:** Written in 1935 as a preface to *London Music in 1888–89* (1937), *SM*1 p. 50.

65/ 7 **tragedy:** G.B.S. reply to O'Bolger questionnaire, 14 June 1922, *CL*3 p. 775.

65/13 **despised:** G.B.S. to O'Bolger, February 1916, *CL*3 p. 358.

65/23 **forgave it:** G.B.S. reply to O'Bolger questionnaire, 14 June 1922, *CL*3 p. 776. Also, 1935 preface to *London Music in 1888–89*, *SM*1 p. 52.

65/25 **pressure:** G.B.S. to O'Bolger, February 1916, *CL*3 p. 358.

65/34 **room:** G.B.S. to Frank Harris, 20 June 1930, *CL*4 p. 189.

65/38 **imagined:** O'Donovan, *Shaw and the Charlatan Genius* pp. 85–6 and 149.

65/40 **opera:** Lee to G.B.S., 4 May 1882, BL Add. MS 50509 f. 171.

66/ 6 **Svengali:** 1935 preface to *London Music in 1888–89*, *SM*1 p. 50.

66/ 6 *Trilby*: Information from Mr Somerset Sullivan.

66/18 **life:** 'Trilby and l'Ami des Femmes', *Saturday Review* 9 November 1895, *OTN*1 pp. 240–1.

66/24 **terms:** G.B.S. to O'Bolger, February 1916, *CL*3 p. 358.

67/ 2 **resumed:** Ibid., pp. 359–60.

67/ 4 **loneliness:** Ibid., p. 360.

67/ 6 **influence:** Lee to G.B.S., 4 May 1882, BL Add. MS 50509 f. 171.

67/ 8   **songs:** Lee to G.B.S., 20 March 1883, *Shaw and the Charlatan Genius* p. 90.

67/10   **Ireland:** Lee to G.B.S., 4 May 1882, BL Add. MS 50509 f. 171.

67/25   **time:** Written in 1935 as a preface to *London Music in 1888–89*, *SM*1 p. 50.

67/26   **statement:** John O'Donovan has pointed out that Shaw's confusion of memory may be attributable to the fact that Lee's presumed father, Colonel Vandeleur, who died on 8 November 1881, did have long-term brain disease ('Softening of the Brain, 3 years certified').

67/31   **after all:** Written in 1935 as a preface to *London Music in 1888–89*, SM1 p. 50; see also G.B.S. reply to O'Bolger questionnaire, 14 June 1922, *CL*3 p. 776.

67/34   **at all:** G.B.S. to O'Bolger, February 1916, *CL*3 p. 360.

67/35   **ever:** G.B.S., '*The Voice*'.

69/Ep.   **would be!:** 'Ideal London', *Pall Mall Gazette* 5 October 1886, p. 5, *Bernard Shaw's Book Reviews Originally Published in the Pall Mall Gazette from 1885 to 1888* (ed. Brian Tyson 1991) pp. 204–8.

69/12   **obscenity?:** G.B.S. to Sylvia Beach, 11 June 1921, *CL*3 p. 719.

69/34   **stomach:** Leonard Woolf, *Sowing: An Autobiography of the Years 1880–1904* (1960) pp. 56–7.

70/10   **Newman-street:** 'Mr Payn's Robinsoniad', *Pall Mall Gazette* 12 January 1888, p. 3, *Bernard Shaw's Book Reviews* pp. 386–90.

70/26   **use it:** 'Ideal London', *Pall Mall Gazette* 5 October 1886, p. 5, *Bernard Shaw's Book Reviews* pp. 204–8.

70/33   **write:** G.B.S. to Donald Suddaby, 3 May 1922 (Texas).

70/34   **planes:** Ibid.

70/36   **mile:** G.B.S. to H. G. Wells, 6 September 1913 (Illinois); see also G.B.S. to Pharall Smith, 17 February 1902 (Colby).

71/ 5   **self delusion:** *CP*7 p. 508. The manuscript of this play is in the Shaw Collection at the British Library (BL Add. MS 50593). First published by the Windhover Press of the University of Iowa in an edition of 350 copies (1971), it subsequently appeared in *CP*7 pp. 487–527.

71/16   **universe:** *CP*7 p. 504.

71/25   **waking:** Ibid., p. 519.

71/28   **black:** Ibid., p. 504.

71/33   **man:** Ibid., p. 502.

71/39   **luxuries:** G.B.S. to Karl Pearson, 20 June 1893 (Pearson Papers, UCL).

72/ 1   **in it:** 'In Five Acts and in Blank Verse', *Pall Mall Gazette* 14 July 1887, p. 3, *Bernard Shaw's Book Reviews* pp. 295–9.

72/15   **dumb:** *CP*6 p. 614.

72/23   **impossible:** G.B.S. to J. A. Hughes, 5 January 1938, *CL*4 p. 488.

72/40   **anybody:** Bernard Shaw, *My Dear Dorothea: A Practical System of Moral Education for Females Embodied in a Letter to a Young Person of That Sex* (1956) p. 15.

73/20   **of her:** Ibid., pp. 13–19.

73/23   **Smith:** Stevie Smith, 'Proud and Fearful', *The Observer* 2 December 1956.

73/33   **Shanachie:** 'The Miraculous Revenge', first published in *Time*, March 1885, was reprinted in *Short Stories, Scraps and Shavings* in 1932. Its appearance in *The Shanachie* was in (Spring) 1906.

73/37   **hand:** '67 Years Later', March–April 1946, Preface to *Immaturity* manuscript (Ireland).

74/ 7   **failure:** *Immaturity* p. 285.

74/ 8   **book:** '67 Years Later'.

74/15   **literature:** *Immaturity* manuscript (Ireland).

74/22   **solitude:** *Immaturity* p. 83.

74/30   **Huddart:** Elinor Huddart to G.B.S., 10 March 1881, BL Add. MS 50535.

75/ 2   **end:** *Immaturity* p. 267.

75/ 6   **good:** Ibid., p. 220.

75/14   **elsewhere:** Ibid., pp. 201–2.

75/21   **truth:** Ibid., p. 126.

75/25   **directed:** G.B.S. to Macmillan & Co., 1 February 1880, *CL*1 p. 27.

75/28   **everything:** *Immaturity* p. 359.

75/31   **minority:** Ibid. See also p. 385.

76/ 4   **immaturity:** Ibid., p. 423.

76/27   **mob:** George Carr Shaw to G.B.S., 28 September 1879, BL Add. MS 50508 f. 161v.

76/32   **conception:** Shaw quotation for *The Standard* 10 May 1930.

77/ 1   **calling:** R. H. Horne to Lucinda Shaw, 7 October 1878, BL Add. MS 50508 ff. 126–126v.

77/21   **acquainted:** G.B.S. to Arnold White, 5 October 1879, *CL*1 p. 23.

77/35   **to me:** Preface to *Immaturity* p. xxxvi.

78/14   **capacities:** 'Meredith on Comedy', *Saturday Review* 27 March 1897, *OTN*3 pp. 85–6.

78/18   **forthwith:** G.B.S. to Mr Dauglish, 31 December 1879, *CL*1 p. 26.

78/22   **myself:** Preface to *Immaturity* p. xxxvi.
78/37   **wrong:** Preface to *The Irrational Knot* (1931) p. vii.
79/ 6   **encouraging:** G.B.S. to Joseph Fels, 8 July 1910, *CL*2 p. 930.
79/14   **fiction:** BL Add. MS 50508 f. 195.
79/28   **failure:** '67 Years Later'.
80/ 1   **wanted:** Preface to *The Irrational Knot* pp. vi–vii.
80/ 6   **forgotten:** '67 Years Later'.
80/15   **shillings:** Editor's note; see *CL*1 p. 21.
80/19   **journalism:** G.B.S. to John Morley, 15 June 1880, ibid., p. 32.
80/21   **pen:** Preface to *The Irrational Knot* p. xi.
80/24   **faithfully:** G.B.S. to John Morley, 15 June 1880, *CL*1 p. 32.
80/30   **gravitation:** Preface to *The Irrational Knot* p. xiii. Cf Preface to
         Immaturity pp. xxxiii–xxxiv: 'I am so poor a hand at pushing
         and struggling, and so little interested in their rewards, that I
         have risen by sheer gravitation . . .'
80/39   **blush:** Preface to *The Irrational Knot* pp. xv–xvi.
81/ 2   **unsaleable:** See 'Sixty Years in Business as an Author': proof
         copy in Berg Collection; *The Author* LV, Summer 1945,
         pp. 56–8.
81/ 5   **in me:** *Nine Answers by G. Bernard Shaw*, with an Introduction
         by Christopher Morley (unauthorized publication with
         unnumbered pages privately printed for Jerome Kern, 1923).
         See also *Shaw: Interviews and Recollections* (ed. A. M. Gibbs
         1990) pp. 22–9.
81/11   **sing:** G.B.S. to Viola Tree, 29 November to 5 December 1911,
         *CL*3 p. 60.
81/20   **use:** G.B.S. to D. Lewin Mannering, 7 December 1927
         (Boston).
81/23   **of us:** See, for example, letters from George Carr Shaw to his
         son dated 4 December 1882 and 29 August 1884: BL Add.
         MS 50509 ff. 248v–249v and 50510 ff. 258–9.
81/31   **fail:** Mary McNulty to G.B.S., 30 March 1881, BL Add. MS
         50509 ff. 19, 18v.
82/ 1   **reversed:** *The Irrational Knot* p. 175.
82/ 2   **down:** Ibid., pp. 243–4.
82/11   **existence:** Ibid., p. 162.
82/17   **ready-made:** Preface to *The Irrational Knot* p. xvii.
82/21   **English:** Ibid., p. xix.
82/24   **nails:** G.B.S. to Charlotte Payne-Townshend, 4 April 1898,
         *CL*2 p. 26.
82/37   **them:** *The Irrational Knot* p. 331.
82/37   **life:** Ibid., p. 335.
82/39   **wife:** 'Mr Bernard Shaw's Works of Fiction: Reviewed by
         Himself', *The Novel Review* no. 33, February 1892, p. 239.

82 / 40   **prodigiously long:** G.B.S. to Swan Sonnenschein & Co., 16 March 1885, *CL*1 p. 125.

83 / 3   **apostrophe:** *The Irrational Knot* manuscript (Ireland).

83 / 8   **matters:** Charles Morgan, *The House of Macmillan (1843–1943)* (1944) p. 120.

83 / 9   **had:** G.B.S. to Scott Ellis, 24 September 1917 (Texas).

83 / 18   **phrase:** '66 Years Later', March–April 1946, Preface to *The Irrational Knot* manuscript (Ireland).

83 / 23   **damns:** G.B.S. to J. R. Osgood, 7 February 1887, *CL*1 p. 162.

83 / 25   **conversational:** Smith Elder to G.B.S., 30 July 1881, BL Add. MS 50509 f. 43.

83 / 27   **unripe:** William Heinemann to G.B.S., 19 January 1893, BL Add. MS 50513 f. 3.

83 / 29   **too:** William Heinemann files.

83 / last   **kind:** 'Mr Bernard Shaw's Works of Fiction: Reviewed by Himself', *The Novel Review* no. 33, February 1892, pp. 236–42.

84 / Ep. 1   **condition:** G.B.S. to Charlotte Payne-Townshend, 4 April 1898, *CL*1 p. 27.

84 / Ep. 2   **vegetarian:** G.B.S. to D. Radford, 27 February 1884, Sotheby's Catalogue, 10 June 1961, item 543.

84 / 15   **nothing:** G.B.S. to R. Golding Bright, 30 January 1895, *CL*1 p. 480.

84 / 25   **inestimable:** G.B.S. to E. Craig, 1929, BL Add. MS 43800 f. ii.

84 / 27   **diet:** *SSS* p. 88.

85 / 12   **restaurant:** 'Failures of Inept Vegetarians', signed 'By an Expert', *Pall Mall Gazette* 26 January 1886, pp. 4–5.

85 / 36   **meat:** Ibid.

86 / 8   **undressing:** G.B.S. to Lady Moya Campbell, n.d. (Texas). There is a shorthand note of this letter in the British Library.

86 / 13   *Fables:* *CP*7 pp. 445–8.

86 / 17   **dead:** G.B.S. to Trebitsch, 23 August 1950, Shaw/Trebitsch letters p. 468.

86 / 30   **cannibalism:** *CP*7 p. 445.

86 / 31   **omitted:** 'Failures of Inept Vegetarians'. See also Archibald Henderson, *George Bernard Shaw: His Life and Works* (1911) p. 50.

86 / 39   **undesirable:** This note (Texas), dated 29 October 1946, was written for F. E. Loewenstein for a reply to a correspondent named L. D. Kelsey.

87 / 11   **poor:** G.B.S. to Symon Gould, 31 August 1948; published in *The American Vegetarian* 1 February 1953, p. 1.

87/14   **people:** Shaw reply to O'Bolger questionnaire, 3 January 1913 (Houghton).

87/17   **exempt:** G.B.S. to Symon Gould, 31 August 1948, published in *The American Vegetarian* 1 February 1953, p. 1.

87/22   **bull:** Preface to *Androcles and the Lion, CP*4 p. 474.

87/24   **life:** Archibald Henderson, *George Bernard Shaw: Man of the Century* (1956) p. 780.

87/29   **indignation:** *Strand Magazine* July 1945, pp. 15–17; cf *The Daily Chronicle* 1 March 1918.

87/31   **believe it:** Ibid.

87/40   **remorse:** G.B.S. to Fenner Brockway, 6 January 1922, *Outside the Right* (1963) Appendix, p. 196.

88/31   **anything:** G.B.S. to André Blaireau, 5 December 1945 (Texas).

88/33   **eat it:** G.B.S. to R. B. Haldane, 20 January 1896 (Scotland, MS 5904).

89/16   **can get:** G.B.S. to E. D. Girdlestone, 18 September 1890, *CL*1 p. 263.

89/17   **get it:** G.B.S. reply to O'Bolger questionnaire, 3 January 1913 (Houghton).

89/17   **mediocre:** G.B.S. to Ralph Ishem, 13 May 1946 (Texas).

89/20   **too much:** G.B.S. note for *The Evening Moscow* 24 July 1931. See Michael Holroyd, *Bernard Shaw* vol. 3 (1991) p. 239.

89/25   **nails:** G.B.S. to Janet Achurch, 8 January 1895 (Texas).

89/27   **diminished:** Ibid.

89/30   **utmost:** G.B.S. to Robertson Scott, 8 January 1947, *CL*4 p. 791.

89/35   **beer:** G.B.S. letter for electorate in South St Pancras where he was standing as one of the Progressive candidates in the London County Council elections, 20 February 1904 (LSE).

89/36   **house:** The Fox and Pelican at Hindhead.

89/37   **control:** See *Manchester Guardian* 23 October 1931.

89/last   **anaesthetic:** G.B.S.'s copy of *The Life and Death of Mr Badman* is at Cornell. See *Flyleaves* (ed. with an introduction by Dan H. Laurence and Daniel J. Leary, W. Thomas Taylor, Austin, Texas 1977) p. 51.

90/28   **in it:** G.B.S. to Robertson Scott, 8 January 1947, *CL*4 p. 791.

90/last   **different:** G.B.S. to Ellen Terry, 3 March 1897, *CL*1 p. 729.

91/Ep.   **myself:** G.B.S. to Charlotte Payne-Townshend, 1 April 1898, *CL*2 p. 26.

91/33   **virulent:** G.B.S., 'Jenner', *The Nation* XXXII, 3 February 1923, pp. 678–9; reprinted in *Doctors' Delusions* (1932) pp. 69–70.

92/ 9   **murder:** G.B.S. to Charles Gane, 22 February 1906, *CL*2 pp. 606–7.

92/11   **practice:** G.B.S. to Trebitsch, 4 June 1929, Shaw/Trebitsch letters pp. 299–300.

92/15   **hat:** Written in 1935 as a preface to *London Music in 1888–89*, *SM*1 p. 42.

92/27   **distribution:** 'Heartbreak Hospital', *The Observer* 14 October 1945.

92/32   **fear:** Pakenham Beatty to G.B.S., 3 June 1881, BL Add. MS 50530 ff. 29–29v.

93/24   **less:** Aileen Bell to G.B.S., 28 January 1883, BL Add. MS 50510 f. 13v.

93/27   **shave:** G.B.S. note for Loewenstein for a reply to Mary Furlong Moore, July 1946 (Texas).

93/last   **boyhood:** Preface to *Immaturity* p. xx.

94/10   **face:** Elinor Huddart to G.B.S., 19 November 1891, BL Add. MS 50537 ff. 139–139v.

94/19   **forget:** *Brave Spirits* (privately printed, London 1952, by Georgina Sims and Frank Nicholson) p. 13; quoted in J. Percy Smith, *The Unrepentant Pilgrim: A Study of the Development of Bernard Shaw* (1966) p. 100.

94/32   **at it:** 'The Old Revolutionist and the New Revolution', *Nation* 19 February 1921. See *Pen Portraits and Reviews* (1931) p. 131.

96/18   **thinker:** '66 Years Later'.

96/20   **Materialism:** 'Mr Bernard Shaw's Works of Fiction: Reviewed by Himself' p. 240.

96/22   **anti-Rationalist:** G.B.S. to Manson Gibson, 12 August 1904 (Edward Laurence Doheny Memorial Library, St John's Seminary, Camarillo, California).

96/28   **nature:** *An Unsocial Socialist* (1930) p. 96.

97/ 6   **against us:** G.B.S. to Joseph H. Levy, 4 June 1902 (Texas).

97/ 9   **entertained:** 'Mr Bernard Shaw's Works of Fiction: Reviewed by Himself' p. 240.

97/13   **gentleman:** '66 Years Later'.

97/20   **praise it:** Edward Garnett's reader's report to T. Fisher Unwin (Berg).

97/27   **please:** G.B.S. to Richard Bentley & Son, 18 February 1882, *CL*1 p. 48.

97/32   **attention:** Edward Garnett's reader's report.

97/34   **invented:** G.B.S. to Archibald Henderson, 3 January 1905, *CL*2 p. 484.

97/36   **himself:** G.B.S. note for Loewenstein for a reply to Lorain Scott, July 1949 (Texas).

97/40   **him:** Gilbert Murray to G.B.S., 1 October 1941, BL Add. MS 50542 f. 64v.

98/20   **radical:** G.B.S. to C. Payne, 20 August 1882.

98/23   **shorthand:** G.B.S. to Messrs G. Street & Co., 23 August 1882 (Texas).

98/30   **young:** *Shaw: An Exhibit*, a Catalog by Dan H. Laurence (University of Texas at Austin 1977), item no. 563.

98/37   **ended:** *Nine Answers by G. Bernard Shaw.*

99/ 9   **outsider:** Henderson, *George Bernard Shaw: Man of the Century* p. 118.

99/18   **society:** Shaw to Hermon Ould, Gen. Sec. of P.E.N., 8 October 1943; see *P.E.N. Broadsheet* no. 4, Winter 1977, p. 9.

99/27   **abortions:** G.B.S. to John Galsworthy, 9 June 1924 (University of Birmingham Library).

100/ 3   **for it:** G.B.S. to Lady Gregory, 12 June 1909, *CL*2 p. 846.

100/ 5   **myself:** *George Bernard Shaw: Man of the Century* p. 119.

100/19   **at last:** 'A Typical Concert', *The Star* 17 May 1889, *SM*1 p. 629.

100/25   **friend:** G.B.S. to Charles McEvoy, 26 March 1916, *CL*3 p. 391.

101/15   **insufferable:** Preface to *Immaturity* p. xlii.

101/29   **virgins:** *Cashel Byron's Profession* (1932) p. 26.

101/33   **pieces:** 'Letter to the Author from Mr Sidney Trefusis', *An Unsocial Socialist* (1932) pp. 254–9.

101/37   **funeral:** G.B.S. to Mrs Crowe, 23 June 1903 (Texas).

101/40   **with:** G.B.S. to Charles Charrington, 13 October 1916 (Texas).

103/12   **mouse:** G.B.S. to Jane ('Jenny') Patterson, 10 March 1886, *CL*1 p. 152.

103/22   **reformed:** G.B.S. to William Archer, 27 April 1890, *CL*1 p. 250.

103/27   **jokes:** G.B.S. to Pakenham Beatty, February 1912 (Alwin J. Scheuer catalog, Serial no. A 2155).

104/ 6   **unto you:** Pakenham Beatty to G.B.S., 16 September 1881, BL Add. MS 50530 ff. 48–48v.

104/12   **published:** Ibid., f. 50.

104/13   **exhibitions:** '64 Years Later', March–April 1946, Preface to manuscript of *Cashel Byron's Profession* (Ireland).

104/30   **subject:** 'Note on Modern Prizefighting' (1901), *Cashel Byron's Profession* (1932) pp. 237–50.

104/35   **of it:** Benny Green, *Shaw's Champions* (1978) p. 131.

105/17   **sake:** G.B.S. to Henry Arthur Jones, 23 August 1899 (Texas).

105/34   **himself:** G.B.S. to 'Ida' Beatty, 8 February 1887, *CL*1 p. 163.

105/last   **resilience:** Ibid., p. 164.

106/ 5   **you:** G.B.S. to Diana Watts, 17 July 1921 (copy privately owned).

106/ 9   **to do?:** Aileen Bell to G.B.S., 29 May 1885, BL Add. MS 50511 ff. 81–81v.

106/14   **Shaw:** Aileen Bell to G.B.S., n.d. [postmark 29 March 1883], BL Add. MS 50510 f. 39v.

106/31   **Carbonaja:** *Diaries* 1, notes for 1877, p. 30.

106/32   **repose:** Ibid.

106/36   **11th:** Ibid.

107/18   **cleverly:** BL Add. MS 50721B f. 9v.

107/28   **book:** For a description of Elinor Huddart's letters to G.B.S. in the British Library see Margot Peters, *Bernard Shaw and the Actresses* (1980) p. 417 n. 11.

107/31   **conceive:** BL Add. MS 50537 f. 7.

108/ 1   **good:** Elinor Huddart to G.B.S., 15 May 1885, ibid., f. 110.

108/ 4   **revive it:** Elinor Huddart to G.B.S., 28 July 1886, ibid., ff. 129–129v.

108/ 9   **All right:** Ibid., f. 153v.

108/14   **much:** Aileen Bell to G.B.S., 11 June 1883, BL Add. MS 50510 f. 75v.

108/17   **coarseness:** BL Add. MS 50537 f. 104.

108/26   **bloodthirsty:** Elinor Huddart to G.B.S., 18 September 1882, BL Add. MS 50535.

109/36   **hesitate:** Alice Lockett to G.B.S., 15 October 1884, *CL*1 p. 98.

110/ 7   **egotistical:** BL Add. MS 50721A f. 121.

110/31   **from her:** G.B.S. to Alice Lockett, 11 September 1883, *CL*1 p. 65.

110/37   **contact:** Ibid.

110/39   **Alice:** Ibid.

111/ 1   **power:** G.B.S. to Alice Lockett, 19 November 1883, *CL*1 p. 73.

111/ 4   **lies:** Ibid.

111/ 6   **character:** G.B.S. to Alice Lockett, 26 September 1884, *CL*1 p. 96.

111/ 8   **heart:** G.B.S. to Alice Lockett, 9 September 1883, *CL*1 p. 64.

111/14   **economy:** G.B.S. to Alice Lockett, 20 October 1883, *CL*1 p. 69.

111/22   **to me:** G.B.S. to Alice Lockett, 9 September 1883, *CL*1 p. 62.

111/37   **exercising it:** Alice Lockett to G.B.S., 11 September 1883, *CL*1 p. 65.

111/39   **something:** G.B.S. to Alice Lockett, 29 November 1883, *CL*1 p. 76.

112/ 9   **work?:** Alice Lockett to G.B.S., 15 January 1884; *Shaw: An Exhibit*, item no. 13.

112/16   **mood:** Alice Lockett to G.B.S., 7 October 1883, *CL*1 p. 67.

112/25   **flatter?:** G.B.S. to Alice Lockett, 5 November 1883, *CL*1 p. 70.

112/32   **question:** G.B.S. to Alice Lockett, 9 July 1884, *CL*1 p. 91.

112/33   **happens:** *The Irrational Knot* (1931) p. 272.

112/last **moment:** G.B.S. to Alice Lockett, 19 August 1884, *CL*1 p. 95.

113/ 4   **lightning:** G.B.S. to Alice Lockett, 8 October 1885, *CL*1
          p. 143.

113/ 5   **Samson:** G.B.S. to Alice Lockett, 29 November 1883, *CL*1
          p. 75.

113/21   **house:** G.B.S. to Archibald Henderson, 7 July 1911, *George
          Bernard Shaw: Man of the Century* pp. 82–3.

114/17   **odds:** '64 Years Later'.

114/34   **please:** G.B.S. to Richard Bentley & Son, 31 May 1883, *CL*1
          p. 60.

115/ 8   **shocker:** G.B.S. to Alma Murray, 20 October 1886, *CL*1
          p. 161.

115/11   **after all:** G.B.S. to Tighe Hopkins, 31 August 1889, *CL*1
          p. 221.

115/19   **know:** G.B.S. to Alma Murray, 20 October 1886, *CL*1 p. 161.

115/20   **fool:** G.B.S. to Archibald Henderson, 3 January 1905, *CL*2
          p. 481.

115/27   **myself:** 'Mr Bernard Shaw's Works of Fiction: Reviewed by
          Himself' p. 240.

115/28   **soul:** G.B.S. to T. Fisher Unwin, 19 November 1888, *CL*1
          p. 202.

116/38   **civilization!:** *An Unsocial Socialist* (1932 edn) pp. 76, 180.

117/ 2   **desks:** Preface to *Immaturity* p. xl.

117/14   **scenery:** G.B.S. to Alice Lockett, 12 August 1884, *CL*1 p. 93.

117/35   **remains:** G.B.S. to unidentified correspondent, 11 August
          1888 (Princeton).

118/29   ***laughter*:** *Man and Superman*, *CP*2 p. 733.

118/32   **catastrophe:** Foreword to *An Unsocial Socialist* p. v.

118/33   **job:** Blanche Patch/G.B.S. note (Cornell).

118/37   **Lenin:** Cf G.B.S.'s Foreword to Standard Edition of *An
          Unsocial Socialist* (1932) p. v.

118/last **interesting:** Kegan Paul, Trench & Co. to G.B.S., 2 January
          1884, BL Add. MS 50510 f. 166.

119/ 3   **Socialism:** Smith Elder & Co. to G.B.S., 14 January 1884, BL
          Add. MS 50510 f. 171.

119/10   **eloquent:** Charles Morgan, *The House of Macmillan (1843–1943)*
          p. 127.

119/15   **away:** G.B.S. to Macmillan & Co., 14 January 1885, *CL*1
          p. 111.

119/24   **at them:** G.B.S. to Macmillan & Co., 22 January 1885, *CL*1 p. 114.

119/last   **bad:** '63 Years Later', March–April 1946, Preface to manuscript of *An Unsocial Socialist* (Ireland).

120/11   **Shaw:** J. L. Joynes to G.B.S., 27 January 1884, BL Add. MS 50510 f. 181v.

120/15   **started me:** G.B.S. inscription in copy of *To-Day* (Bucknell).

121/ 9   **now:** G.B.S. to Mrs T. P. O'Connor, 17 May 1888, *CL*1 p. 189.

121/28   **opinion:** Swan Sonnenschein to G.B.S., n.d. [January 1888], F. E. Loewenstein, *The History of a Famous Novel* (1946) pp. 14–15.

122/ 3   **recovered:** G.B.S. to Cyril Clemens, 12 August 1938 (Pattee Library, Pennsylvania State University).

122/10   **begun:** George Orwell to Brenda Salkeld, March 1933, *The Collected Essays, Journalism and Letters* vol. 1 (ed. Sonia Orwell and Ian Angus 1970 edn) p. 143. See also *Shaw: The Critical Heritage* (ed. T. F. Evans 1976) p. 332.

122/23   **Jail:** George Carr Shaw to G.B.S., 29 August 1884, BL Add. MS 50510 f. 259.

122/25   **in you:** George Carr Shaw to G.B.S., 28 March 1881, BL Add. MS 50509 f. 17.

122/28   **remorse:** *SSS* p. 92.

122/35   **suffering:** Edward McNulty, 'Memoirs of G.B.S.' See *The Annual of Bernard Shaw Studies* vol. 12, 1992, pp. 1–46.

123/ 3   **Orphan:** G.B.S. to J. Kingston Barton, 19 April 1885, *CL*1 p. 132.

123/ 7   **man:** Foreword to *An Unsocial Socialist* p. vi.

CHAPTER III

124/Ep.   **Socialism:** G.B.S. to Archibald Henderson, 3 January 1905, *CL*2 pp. 486–7.

125/22   **comrade:** G.B.S. to J. L. Mahon, 13 April 1885, *CL*1 p. 131.

125/25   **decay:** G.B.S. to Henry A. Barker, 9 February 1887, *CL*1 p. 164.

125/28   **Individualism:** *Major Critical Essays* (1986 edn) p. 126.

125/33   **Individualist:** G.B.S. to J. H. Levy, 31 March 1898 (privately owned).

126/10   **business:** G.B.S. to Archibald Henderson, 3–17 January 1905, *CL*2 p. 486.

126/26   **the Z.S:** G.B.S. to J. M. Fells, 6 August 1881 (Cornell).

126/38 **Browning:** G.B.S. to F. E. Loewenstein, 14 November 1941, *CL*4 p. 621.

127/ 4 **skins:** *Our Corner* June 1886, pp. 371–2.

127/ 5 **type:** 'Shaming the Devil about Shelley', *The Albemarle* II, no. 3, September 1892, p. 91. See *Pen Portraits and Reviews* (1931) pp. 236–46.

127/10 **verse:** G.B.S. note to F. E. Loewenstein for Stephen Winsten, June 1950 (Texas).

127/11 **Vegetarian:** G.B.S. to G. K. Chesterton, 1 March 1908, *CL*2 p. 760.

127/35 **police:** 'Songs of a Revolutionary Epoch', unsigned review by G.B.S. of J. L. Joynes' translations of *Songs of A Revolutionary Epoch, Pall Mall Gazette* XLVII, 16 April 1888, p. 3. See *Bernard Shaw's Book Reviews Originally Published in the Pall Mall Gazette from 1885 to 1886* (ed. Brian Tyson 1991) pp. 405–7.

128/23 **on me:** Archibald Henderson, *George Bernard Shaw: His Life and Works* (1911) p. 96.

129/26 **reconstruction:** G.B.S. to Gerrit Johnson, 7 March 1918, *Everyman* April 1918, p. 8.

130/30 **life:** Hesketh Pearson, *Bernard Shaw* (1975 revised edn) p. 68.

130/32 **read it:** BL Add. MS 50699 f. 271.

130/33 **down:** G.B.S. to Mary Somerville, 24 February 1941 (BBC, Caversham).

130/37 **genius:** G.B.S. to *Labour Forum* vol. 1, no. 2, September– December 1946, pp. 10–11.

131/17 **training:** Doris Langley Moore, *E. Nesbit: A Biography* (1933) p. 72 n. 1.

132/24 **fruitless:** Edward R. Pease, *The History of the Fabian Society* (1916) p. 39.

134/ 2 **English!:** G.B.S. to H. H. Champion, 1 November 1884, *CL*1 p. 101.

134/ 5 **press:** G.B.S. to Alexander Smith, 19 January 1885, *CL*1 p. 112.

134/17 **deplorably:** *Diaries* 1, notes for 1884, p. 33.

134/20 **mind:** G.B.S. to Alexander Smith, 1 July 1884, *CL*1 p. 90.

134/23 **Index:** *Diaries* 1, entry 5 May 1885, p. 86.

134/24 **born:** G.B.S. to Alexander Smith, 19 January 1885, *CL*1 p. 112.

134/27 **sold:** Preface to *The Dark Lady of the Sonnets, CP*4 pp. 271–2.

134/30 **forgetfulness:** *CP*4 p. 273.

134/33 **leisure:** G.B.S. to James B. Murdoch, 28 July 1885, *CL*1 p. 136.

134/37   **journalism:** *Diaries* 1, notes for 1885, p. 54.

135/ 9   **friends:** *Drama* Autumn 1956, p. 34.

135/37   **doing:** William Archer to G.B.S., October 1891, *CL*1 p. 319.

136/ 1   **jampot:** See Hesketh Pearson, *Bernard Shaw* p. 108.

136/ 2   **publicly:** G.B.S. to William Archer, 21 August 1893, *CL*1 p. 402.

136/ 6   **season:** *Drama* Autumn 1956, p. 36.

136/12   **appeal:** William Archer to G.B.S., 22 June 1921, BL Add. MS 50528 ff. 63–4.

136/17   **cause:** G.B.S. to Archer, 29 April 1895 (Fales).

136/19   **about it?:** G.B.S. to Archer, 11 May 1893, *CL*1 p. 395.

136/24   **CENTURY:** Archer to G.B.S., 6 September 1919, BL Add. MS 50528 f. 61.

134/28   **sacrifices:** 'How William Archer Impressed Bernard Shaw', Foreword to William Archer, *Three Plays* (1927) p. xxxii; see also *Pen Portraits and Reviews* (1931) pp. 1–30.

136/29   **impossible:** Ibid., p. xxxi.

136/39   **accomplish:** Max Beerbohm, *More Theatres* (1969) p. 27; see also *Shaw: The Critical Heritage* (ed. T. F. Evans 1976) p. 80.

137/ 1   **of him:** William Archer notice, *The World* 30 May 1905. See *Shaw: The Critical Heritage* p. 117.

137/ 8   **form:** Ibid., pp. 116–17.

137/14   **literature:** G.B.S. to Trebitsch, 19 January 1903, Shaw/Trebitsch letters p. 37.

137/16   **brain:** *Drama* Autumn 1956, pp. 32–6.

137/last   **thought:** Ibid., p. 36.

138/ 4   **hand:** *SSS* p. 39.

138/ 6   **brilliant:** *Drama* Autumn 1956, pp. 32–6.

138/18   **them:** *Diaries* 1, notes for 1885, p. 53.

138/25   ***nil*:** William Archer to G.B.S., 12 November 1885, BL Add. MS 50528 f. 33v.

138/30   **career:** G.B.S. to R. Golding Bright, 2 December 1894, *CL*1 p. 465.

139/ 1   **inexpugnable:** G.B.S. to William Archer, 12 December 1885, *CL*1 p. 145.

139/17   **logic:** Archer to G.B.S., 13 December 1885, BL Add. MS 50528 ff. 35–8.

139/20   **re-re-re-return it:** G.B.S. to Archer, 14 December 1885, *CL*1 pp. 146–7.

139/25   **articles:** Ibid.

139/28   **educated:** Preface to *Misalliance*, *CP*4 p. 124.

140/10   **longer:** *Drama* Autumn 1956, p. 35.

140/22   **main point:** Ibid.

140/23   **analysis:** G.B.S. to D. S. McColl, 26 May 1916 (Glasgow).

140/32   **points:** G.B.S., 'Acting, By One Who Does not Believe in it', *Platform and Pulpit* (ed. with an Introduction by Dan H. Laurence 1962) p. 19.

140/37   **volume:** G.B.S. to Holbrook Jackson, 13 October 1909 (Texas).

141/ 3   **pleeceman:** G.B.S. to D. S. McColl, 9 June 1926 (Glasgow).

141/14   **red tape:** 'In the Picture-Galleries: The Holman Hunt Exhibition', *The World* no. 612, 24 March 1886, p. 10. See *Bernard Shaw on the London Art Scene 1885–1950* (ed. Stanley Weintraub 1989).

141/26   **right!:** 'In the Picture-Galleries: The Academy and the Grosvenor (First Notice)', *The World* no. 618, 5 May 1886, pp. 18–19. See *Bernard Shaw on the London Art Scene 1885–1950* pp. 102–6.

141/30   **lawn-mower:** 'In the Picture-Galleries', *The World* no. 668, 20 April 1887, p. 9. See *Bernard Shaw on the London Art Scene 1885–1950* pp. 153–6.

141/36   **upon?:** 'In the Picture-Galleries', *The World* no. 669, 27 April 1887, pp. 9–10. See *Bernard Shaw on the London Art Scene 1885–1950* pp. 156–60.

142/ 4   **mammoth:** 'In the Picture-Galleries: The Grosvenor-Meissonier Press Day at the Academy', *The World* no. 722, 2 May 1888, pp. 19–20. See *Bernard Shaw on the London Art Scene 1885–1950* pp. 219–22.

142/ 9   **canvasses:** 'In the Picture-Galleries: The Royal Institute—French Gallery—Tooth's—M'Lean's—Gainsborough Gallery', *The World* no. 768, 20 March 1889, pp. 22–3. See *Bernard Shaw on the London Art Scene 1885–1950* pp. 265–9.

142/12   **metaphor:** 'In the Picture-Galleries: The Arts and Crafts—The Old Water-Colour Society', *The World* no. 798, 9 October 1889, p. 26. See *Bernard Shaw on the London Art Scene 1885–1950* pp. 292–4.

142/15   **artist-philosopher:** G.B.S. to Hesketh Pearson, 27 December 1942 (Texas).

142/18   **condition:** 'Ruskin's Politics', *Platform and Pulpit* p. 131.

142/21   **moralizing:** G.B.S. insert on proof of Archibald Henderson's *Playboy and Prophet* (North Carolina).

142/33   **labour:** Shaw's lecture on 'Art' at Bedford Debating Society, December 1885; *Diaries* 1, entry 10 December 1885, p. 130.

142/37   **quality?:** G.B.S. to Austin Spare, 7 January 1917 (Colby).

142/38   **foot:** See, for example, *Daily Mail* 26 September 1929.

143/ 2   **in them:** 'In the Picture-Galleries: The New English Art

Club—Monet at the Goupil Gallery', *The World* no. 773, 24 April 1889, p. 18. See *Bernard Shaw on the London Art Scene 1885–1950* pp. 272–5.

143 / 5   **impertinence**: G.B.S. to Phelan Gibb, 16 March 1917 (Colby).

143 / 10   **in them**: *Diaries* 2, entry 20 September 1893, p. 968.

143 / 12   **excessive**: 'Art Corner' [Sir John Millais exhibit at Grosvenor Gallery; old masters at the Royal Academy], *Our Corner* VII, February 1886, p. 125. See *Bernard Shaw on the London Art Scene 1885–1950* pp. 69–73.

143 / 14   **electioneering**: 'The Effects of Electioneering', *The World* 6 July 1892, *SM2* p. 665.

143 / 22   **classicism**: Ibid.

143 / 23   **mundane**: 'In the Picture-Galleries: The Academy and the Grosvenor (First Notice)', *The World* no. 618, 5 May 1886, pp. 18–19. See *Bernard Shaw on the London Art Scene 1885–1950* pp. 102–6.

143 / 31   **situation**: 'In the Picture-Galleries. The Academy—The British Artists', *The World* no. 723, 9 May 1888, p. 16. See *Bernard Shaw on the London Art Scene 1885–1950* pp. 223–7.

144 / 3   **countenance**: 'In the Picture-Galleries: The Royal Institute and the British Artists', *The World* no. 700, 30 November 1887, p. 20. See *Bernard Shaw on the London Art Scene 1885–1950* pp. 191–5.

144 / 10   **Suffolk Street**: *Diaries* 1, entry 1 April 1887, p. 256.

144 / 12   **ladies**: Ibid., entry 3 September 1886, p. 195.

144 / 16   **last two**: Ibid., entry 4 May 1888, p. 373.

144 / 32   **painter**: 'In the Picture-Galleries: The Holman Hunt Exhibition', *The World* no. 612, 24 March 1886, p. 10. See *Bernard Shaw on the London Art Scene 1885–1950* pp. 81–3.

144 / 36   **work**: 'In the Picture-Galleries: The New Gallery—The Kakemonos in Bond Street', *The World* no. 724, 16 May 1888, p. 22. See *Bernard Shaw on the London Art Scene 1885–1950* pp. 227–30.

144 / 40   **sheep**: 'In the Picture-Galleries: The Holman Hunt Exhibition', *The World* no. 612, 24 March 1886, p. 10. See *Bernard Shaw on the London Art Scene 1885–1950* pp. 81–3.

144 / 40   **depth**: 'Art Corner', *Our Corner* VII, May 1886, p. 311. See *Bernard Shaw on the London Art Scene 1885–1950* pp. 99–101.

145 / 2   **brother**: 'Art Corner' [Sir John Millais exhibit at Grosvenor Gallery; old masters at the Royal Academy], *Our Corner* VII, February 1886, p. 123. See *Bernard Shaw on the London Art Scene 1885–1950* pp. 69–73.

145/ 7　　**flawless:** 'Art Corner', *Our Corner* VII, May 1886, p. 310. See
　　　　　Bernard Shaw on the London Art Scene 1885–1950 pp. 99–101.

145/11　　**streets:** G.B.S., 'William Morris', *Pen Portraits and Reviews*
　　　　　p. 207.

145/13　　**at that:** G.B.S. to D. S. McColl, 26 May 1916 (Glasgow).

145/16　　**public:** Archibald Henderson, *Bernard Shaw: Playboy and
　　　　　Prophet* (1932) p. 266.

145/21　　**world:** Ibid.

145/last　**can be:** 'In the Picture-Galleries: Arts and Crafts', *The World*
　　　　　no. 744, 3 October 1888, p. 23. See *Bernard Shaw on the
　　　　　London Art Scene 1885–1950* pp. 237–40.

146/ 9　　**and art:** 'Literature and Art', *Platform and Pulpit* p. 41.

146/12　　**didactic:** Ibid., p. 44.

146/23　　**music:** Ibid., p. 45.

146/33　　**person:** G.B.S. to Austin Sparc, 7 January 1917 (Colby).

147/12　　**handiwork:** 'In the Picture-Galleries: The Holman Hunt
　　　　　Exhibition', *The World* no. 612, 24 March 1886, p. 10. See
　　　　　Bernard Shaw on the London Art Scene 1885–1950 pp. 81–3.

147/23　　**houses:** BL Add. MS 50699 f. 243.

147/32　　**Laureate:** Ibid., f. 246.

147/36　　**beauty:** Ibid., f. 247.

147/38　　**carpets:** Ibid., f. 246.

148/16　　**discordant:** G.B.S., note on Hesketh Pearson's manuscript
　　　　　(Texas).

148/21　　**Burne-Jones:** 'More About Morris', *The Observer* 6 November
　　　　　1949.

148/25　　**sensible:** BL Add. MS 50699 f. 245.

148/28　　**commonsense:** Ibid., f. 241.

148/36　　**policy:** G.B.S. to unidentified correspondent, 20 June 1887
　　　　　(Boston); see also G.B.S. to H. G. Wells, 8 May 1941
　　　　　(Illinois).

150/13　　**the race:** 'The Sanity of Art', *Major Critical Essays* p. 343.

150/Ep.　**alone:** 'Don Giovanni Explains', *Short Stories, Scraps and
　　　　　Shavings* (1932) p. 100. The story was written between 25 July
　　　　　and 2 August 1887.

151/ 8　　**soul:** Ibid., pp. 104–5.

151/18　　**associations:** *Diaries* 1, entry 29 September 1888, p. 416.

151/24　　**feet:** *Drama* Autumn 1956, p. 34.

151/25　　**man:** William Rothenstein, *Men and Memories* vol. 1: *1872–1900*
　　　　　(1931) p. 208.

152/ 3　　**fail:** Grace Black to G.B.S., 24 May 1887, BL Add. MS 50511
　　　　　ff. 321–2.

153/ 6　　**serious:** Grace Black to G.B.S., 25 May 1887, ibid., ff. 323–4.

153/14 **loved:** G.B.S. to Erica Cotterill, 27 November 1907, *CL*2 p. 733.

153/24 **Black:** Grace Black to G.B.S., 31 March 1889, BL Add. MS 50512 ff. 117–117v.

153/31 **car:** G.B.S. to Erica Cotterill, 27 November 1907, *CL*2 p. 733.

153/37 **idol:** Ibid.

154/ 4 **lent him?:** G.B.S. to Ellen Terry, 5 January 1898, *CL*2 p. 8. See *Ellen Terry and Bernard Shaw: A Correspondence* (ed. Christopher St John 1931) p. 286.

154/ 6 **recognize:** See St John Ervine, *Bernard Shaw: His Life, Work and Friends* (1956) pp. 408–9.

154/ 8 **fibre:** BL Add. MS 50699 f. 238.

154/ 9 **existed:** G.B.S. to Lloyd Eric Grey, n.d. (Texas; transcript by Sir James Pitman, University of Bath Library).

154/11 **man:** G.B.S. to Preger, 22 February 1946 (Berg).

154/23 **euphonium:** Ibid.

154/33 **cynics:** Eleanor Marx Aveling to G.B.S., 2 June 1885, BL Add. MS 50511 ff. 88–89v.

154/35 **myself:** Ibid.

155/27 **money:** G.B.S.'s 'almanack' of activities addressed to Charlotte Payne-Townshend, 4 April 1898, *CL*2 p. 26.

155/37 **person:** G.B.S. to Edward Rose, 14 March 1900, *CL*2 p. 156.

155/last **everybody:** G.B.S. to Archibald Henderson, 3 January 1905, *CL*2 p. 496.

156/ 4 **society:** G.B.S. to Edward Rose, 14 March 1900, *CL*2 p. 156.

156/ 8 **husband:** G.B.S. to T. T. Tucker, 6 January 1925. Sotheby's Catalogue, 6 July 1971, item 655.

156/22 **irresistible:** Doris Langley Moore, *E. Nesbit: A Biography* p. 72.

156/24 **circle:** Ibid., p. 62.

156/32 **women:** G.B.S. to Edith Nesbit Bland, 18 October 1886 (Columbia).

156/36 **Bland:** *Diaries* 1, entry 4 September 1885, p. 109.

157/14 **shrewishness:** Written in 1886. The original is in Southern Historical Collection (North Carolina).

157/23 **ever met:** *E. Nesbit: A Biography* p. 73.

158/27 **compromise her:** *Diaries* 1, entry 11 May 1887, p. 268.

158/37 **understand:** G.B.S. to Frank Harris, 20 June 1930, *CL*4 p. 189. See *The Playwright and the Pirate: Bernard Shaw and Frank Harris: A Correspondence* (ed. Stanley Weintraub 1982) p. 233.

159/26 **successfully:** G.B.S. to Ellen Terry, 12 October 1896, *CL*1 p. 677 (*A Correspondence* pp. 98–9).

159/36 **breath:** Gustav Jaeger, 'Preface', *Health-Culture* (1911) p. 111.

160/17   **concerned:** G.B.S. to Ellen Terry, 31 December 1897, *CL*1
           p. 840 (*A Correspondence* p. 282).

160/24   **animal:** G. K. Chesterton, *Shaw* (1910) p. 96.

160/38   **cerements:** Edward Carpenter, *England's Ideal* (1887), quoted
           by Robert Skidelsky in 'The Fabian Ethic', *The Genius of
           Shaw* (ed. Michael Holroyd 1979) p. 115.

160/40   **parts:** Robert Skidelsky, 'The Fabian Ethic', *The Genius of
           Shaw* p. 115.

160/last   **Juan:** Frank Harris, *Bernard Shaw: An Unauthorised Biography
           …* (1931) p. 119.

161/39   **dreamland:** *SSS* p. 113.

162/38   **to you:** Jenny Patterson to G.B.S., 12 May 1886, BL Add. MS
           50544 f. 78.

163/16   **humanity:** *OTN*2 p. 93.

164/ 1   **Mrs Patterson:** May Morris to G.B.S., 12 and 14 February
           1886, BL Add. MS 50541 ff. 56–60.

164/11   **see you?:** Jenny Patterson to G.B.S., 20 March 1886, BL Add.
           MS 50544 f. 38.

164/14   **savage:** Jenny Patterson to G.B.S., 17 December 1886, ibid.,
           ff. 174–5.

164/17   **please:** Jenny Patterson to G.B.S., 5 February 1886, ibid.,
           ff. 17–18.

164/19   **without Me:** Jenny Patterson to G.B.S., 13 April 1886, ibid.,
           f. 54.

164/20   **but me:** Jenny Patterson to G.B.S., 14 April 1886, ibid., f. 56.

164/25   **harmed you:** Jenny Patterson to G.B.S., 31 March 1886, ibid.,
           f. 48.

164/31   **share:** Written on 1 August 1885; quoted in Jenny Patterson's
           letter to G.B.S., 28 May 1886, ibid., ff. 87–8.

164/32   **love you:** Jenny Patterson to G.B.S., 6 January 1886, ibid.,
           ff. 3–4.

165/ 1   **intimacy:** Jenny Patterson to G.B.S., 8 May 1886, ibid., f. 65.

165/ 1   **scene:** *Diaries* 1, entry 9 May 1886, p. 168.

165/ 4   **platonic:** Ibid.

165/ 9   **of it:** Quoted in Jenny Patterson's letter to G.B.S., 28 May
           1886, BL Add. MS 50544 ff. 87–8.

165/19   **knew me:** Jenny Patterson to G.B.S., 10 and 11 May 1886,
           ibid., ff. 67–81.

165/25   **but that:** Quoted in Jenny Patterson's letter to G.B.S., 28 May
           1886, ibid., ff. 87–8.

165/27   **soul:** Jenny Patterson to G.B.S., 11 May 1886, ibid., f. 70.

165/34   **relations:** *Diaries* 1, entry 15 May 1886, p. 168.

165/38   **nature:** Jenny Patterson to G.B.S., 17 May 1886, BL Add. MS
           50544 ff. 80–1.

166/ 4   **wish it:** Jenny Patterson to G.B.S., 24 June 1886, ibid., f. 103.

166/ 10   **with *me*:** Jenny Patterson to G.B.S., 29 July 1886, ibid., f. 105.

166/ 13   **society:** *Diaries* 1, entry 23 September 1886, p. 200.

166/ 14   **general:** Ibid., entry 10 October 1886, p. 204.

166/ 16   **awful:** Jenny Patterson to G.B.S., 17 December 1886, BL Add. MS 50544 ff. 174–9.

166/ 24   **to be:** Jenny Patterson to G.B.S., 24 November 1886, ibid., f. 160.

166/ 27   **for me:** Jenny Patterson to G.B.S., 22 January 1887, BL Add. MS 50545 f. 12.

166/ 29   **arms:** Jenny Patterson to G.B.S., 8 July 1887 and 12 September 1887, ibid., ff. 48 and 77v.

166/ 30   **faithful??:** Jenny Patterson to G.B.S., 30 September 1887, ibid., f. 83v.

166/ 32   **about you:** Jenny Patterson to G.B.S., 21 September 1887, ibid., f. 81.

166/ 36   **to me:** Jenny Patterson to G.B.S., 30 September 1887, ibid., f. 84.

167/ 9   **action:** G.B.S. to Elizabeth Robins, 28 November 1936, *CL*4 p. 449.

167/ 11   **appeal:** Hesketh Pearson, *Bernard Shaw* p. 459.

167/ 20   **England:** 'Woman Suffrage', letter to *The Times* 31 October 1906. See *Bernard Shaw: Agitations: Letters to the Press 1875–1950* (ed. Dan H. Laurence and James Rambeau 1985) p. 84.

167/ 22   **conscience:** G.B.S., 'Annie Besant's Passage Through Fabian Socialism', from *Dr Annie Besant: Fifty Years in Public Work* (1924), p. 4. An earlier version of this essay was first published in *The Theosophist* (October 1917) as 'Mrs Besant as a Fabian Socialist'.

167/ 31   **detestation:** Annie Besant, *An Autobiography* (1939) p. 402.

167/ 37   **lost:** 'Annie Besant's Passage Through Fabian Socialism', *Dr Annie Besant* (1924) p. 7.

167/ last   **violet:** See G.B.S. to Lady Rhondda, 9 February 1927, *CL*4 p. 48.

168/ 5   **him:** 'Annie Besant's Passage Through Fabian Socialism' p. 7.

168/ 7   **decisions:** Ibid., p. 3.

168/ 12   **candidate:** G.B.S. to F. Keddell, 4 June 1885. Sotheby's Catalogue, 6 July 1971, item 653.

168/ 18   **hod:** Annie Besant, *An Autobiography* p. 402.

168/ 20   **benefactress:** Preface to *Cashel Byron's Profession* (1930) p. 9.

168/ 23   **habit:** Ibid.

168/ 25   **alms-giving:** Ibid.

168/ 30   **scoundrel:** Annie Besant, *An Autobiography* p. 402.

168/last largesse: 'Annie Besant's Passage Through Fabian Socialism' p. 7.
169/12 times: Ibid., pp. 5–6.
169/18 last: G.B.S. to Elizabeth Robins, 17 November 1936 (Fales).
169/25 survived: Arthur H. Nethercot, *The First Five Lives of Annie Besant* (1961) p. 240.
169/32 time: Ibid., p. 239.
170/ 3 century: *The Diary of Beatrice Webb* vol. 4 (ed. Norman and Jeanne MacKenzie 1985), entry 8 June 1933, p. 307.
170/ 5 time: G.B.S. to *The Freethinker* 28 November 1947 (Berg).
170/ 9 did: 'Annie Besant's Passage Through Fabian Socialism' p. 7.
170/15 Besant: Ibid., p. 8.
170/26 earth: Hesketh Pearson, *Bernard Shaw* p. 117.
170/27 over: Ibid., p. 8.
170/31 table: *Diaries* 1, entry 24 December 1887, p. 326.
171/ 9 them: Ibid., entry 25 December 1887, p. 326.
171/17 history: 'A Life of Madame Blavatsky', *Pall Mall Gazette* XLV, 6 January 1887, p. 4. See *Bernard Shaw's Book Reviews* pp. 231–5.
171/21 women: *Diaries* 1, notes for 1887, p. 230.
171/Ep. salt: G.B.S. to Pakenham Beatty, 27 May 1887.
171/29 committee: *SSS* p. 103.
171/34 mistaken: H. M. Hyndman to G.B.S., 15 November 1888, BL Add. MS 50538 ff. 110–110v.
171/last agree: Hyndman to G.B.S., [1920] ibid., f. 149.
172/ 5 religion: See H. M. Hyndman, *Further Reminiscences* (1912) p. 204.
172/11 pseudo-Marxists: *SSS* p. 97.
172/19 anybody: G.B.S. note on Henderson manuscript (North Carolina).
172/32 Shaw: *SSS* pp. 107–8.
172/38 miraculous: Ibid., p. 107.
173/ 5 life: Sidney Webb to G.B.S., 29 January 1934 (LSE).
173/12 do it: G.B.S. to Sidney Webb, 26 March 1946 (LSE).
173/29 for him: There are thirty-two letters from G.B.S. to Kingsley Martin at the University of Sussex Library, Brighton.
173/32 himself: G.B.S. to Lady Londonderry, 29 June 1944 (Public Record Office of Northern Ireland, Belfast).
173/34 lie: 'This History of a Happy Marriage', *The Times Literary Supplement* 20 October 1945, pp. 493–4.
174/ 9 socialism: See Norman and Jeanne MacKenzie, *The First Fabians* (1977) p. 60.
174/14 became: G.B.S. to Kingsley Martin, 14 October 1946 (University of Sussex).

174/17   **work:** Sidney Webb to Archibald Henderson, 6 July 1905 (North Carolina).

174/18   **Socialism:** BL Add. MS 50698 f. 245; see also *Daily Herald* 9 March 1943.

174/21   **another:** Manuscript at University of North Carolina.

174/24   **action:** Sidney Webb to Edward Pease, 24 October 1886. See *The First Fabians* p. 83.

175/27   **human race:** *Diaries* 1, entry 21 January 1885, p. 56.

176/13   **England:** G.B.S. to Havelock Ellis, 24 August 1888, BL Add. MS 61891L.

176/21   **later:** G.B.S. to Sidney Webb, 29 October 1945 (LSE).

176/24   **contain:** *The Diary of Beatrice Webb* vol. 4, entry 9 August 1932, p. 288.

176/30   **grip:** BL Add. MS 50699 f. 53. Reminiscence of Lord Olivier written for Lady Olivier and dated 22 September 1944, and subsequently published as a preface to *Sydney Olivier: Letters and Selected Writings* (1948) p. 9.

176/34   **shoestrings:** BL Add. MS 50699 f. 69, *Sydney Olivier*, p. 20.

176/39   **mercy:** G.B.S. to Havelock Ellis, 24 August 1888, BL Add. MS 61891L.

177/7   **older:** G.B.S. to Janet Achurch, 27 November 1894 (Texas).

177/12   **concerned:** 'Annie Besant's Passage Through Fabian Socialism' p. 6.

177/21   **herself:** Ibid.

177/29   **Musketeers:** G.B.S. to Margaret Cole questionnaire, BL Add. MS 50699 f. 182 (ii) and (iii).

177/32   **bloodshed:** *Practical Socialist* I, January 1886, p. 15.

178/34   **education:** Robert F. Whitman, *Shaw and the Play of Ideas* (1977) p. 84.

178/40   **Socialism:** *Christian Life* 25 March 1927; see also BL Add. MS 50699.

179/3   **them:** G.B.S. note in response to Hesketh Pearson's biography (Texas).

179/6   **gentleman:** 'Some Socialist Fallacies', *The Times* 6 August 1929.

179/29   **idleness:** Preface to the 1908 reprint of *Fabian Essays in Socialism*. This Preface was extracted and itself reprinted in *Essays in Fabian Socialism* (p. 292) in the Standard Edition of the Works of Bernard Shaw (1932).

180/16   ***Barbara:*** *CP*3 pp. 19–22; see also Archibald Henderson, *George Bernard Shaw: Man of the Century* (1956) p. 841, and *CL*2 p. 554.

180/24   **effect:** *E. Nesbit: A Biography* p. 74.

180 / last   **subject:** 'Bluffing the Value Theory', *To-Day* XI, May 1889.
              See also *Bernard Shaw and Karl Marx: a Symposium, 1884–
              1889* (ed. R. W. Ellis, New York 1930).

181 / 27   **gentleman:** G.B.S. to Mrs Pakenham Beatty, 4 September
              1885, *CLi* p. 138.

181 / 31   **Achilles-like:** G.B.S. to Pakenham Beatty, 23 January 1896,
              CLi p. 588.

181 / 34   **convictions:** G.B.S. to Henry Seymour, 5 January 1885, *CLi*
              p. 109.

181 / 36   **past:** See, for example, Geoffrey Ostergaard, 'G.B.S.—
              Anarchist', *New Statesman and Nation* 21 November 1953.

182 / 39   **No. 45:** Reprinted in Shaw's *Essays in Fabian Socialism* (1932)
              pp. 63–99.

183 / 3   **politics:** G.B.S., *The Fabian Society: Its Early History*, Fabian
              Tract no. 41 (1892; reprinted 1899) p. 7; in *Essays in Fabian
              Socialism* p. 131.

183 / 24   **tomb:** Ibid., p. 131.
183 / 29   **demonstrators:** N. and J. MacKenzie, *The First Fabians* p. 79.
183 / 35   **shop:** *Practical Socialist* October 1886.
184 / 6   **agreeable:** G.B.S. to Mrs Pakenham Beatty, 22 September
              1885, *CLi* pp. 140–1.

184 / 12   **capital:** *The First Fabians* p. 80.
184 / 20   **ridiculous:** See *The First Fabians* p. 85.
184 / 33   **attacked:** 'Sir Charles Warren's Courage', *Pall Mall Gazette*
              XLVI, 16 November 1887 p. 11.

185 / 4   **herself:** Hesketh Pearson, *Bernard Shaw* p. 82.
185 / 6   **farce:** Preface to 1908 reprint of *Fabian Essays in Socialism*; in
              Essays in Fabian Socialism p. 291.

185 / 13   **one:** G.B.S. to William Morris, 22 November 1887, *CLi*
              p. 177.

185 / 21   **can:** Hesketh Pearson, *Bernard Shaw* p. 82.
185 / 24   **appearance:** G.B.S. to William Morris, 22 November 1887,
              CLi p. 177.

186 / 18   **come on:** G.B.S. to E. T. Cook, 14 November 1887, Sotheby's
              Catalogue, 16 July 1923, item 758.

186 / 32   **suppression:** Fabian Tract no. 233 (1930) p. 11. This part of
              the Tract, entitled 'Fabianism', was reprinted from *Chambers
              Encyclopaedia* (1930).

187 / 9   **of that:** G.B.S. to William Morris, 22 November 1887, *CLi*
              p. 177.

187 / 16   **model:** Arthur H. Nethercot, *The First Five Lives of Annie
              Besant* p. 273.

187 / 18   **Unionism:** G. M. Trevelyan, *British History in the Nineteenth
              Century and After: 1782–1919* (1965) p. 386.

187/30 **money:** G.B.S. to Jim Connell, 11 December 1888, *CL1*
p. 202.

187/last **work go:** G.B.S. to William Sanders, 23 March 1889, *CL1*
pp. 206–7.

188/ 2 **present:** Ibid.

188/27 **inextinguishable:** Preface to 1931 reprint of *Fabian Essays in Socialism*; see *Essays in Fabian Socialism* p. 301.

188/35 **Britain:** Margaret Cole, *The Story of Fabian Socialism* (1961)
p. 39.

189/ 5 **evolution:** Fabian Tract no. 233 (1930) p. 12.

189/ 9 **party:** 'The Outlook', *Fabian Essays in Socialism* (1889) p. 217.

189/12 **country:** Fabian Tract no. 41 p. 23; reprinted in *Essays in Fabian Socialism* p. 152.

189/19 **individuality:** Preface to *Fabian Essays in Socialism* (1889) p. iv.

CHAPTER IV

191/Ep. **happiness:** G.B.S. to Jules Magny, 16 December 1890, *CL1*
p. 277.

191/23 **Saturday:** G.B.S. to Edith Nesbit Bland, 15 February 1887
(Boston).

191/32 **hall:** *Diaries* 1, entry 7 March 1887, p. 248.

192/11 **house:** G.B.S. to Ellen Terry, 28 August 1896, *CL1* p. 646.
See *Ellen Terry and Bernard Shaw: A Correspondence* (ed.
Christopher St John 1931) p. 44.

192/14 **at all:** Foreword by G.B.S. to *Mars: New Architecture: An Exhibition of the Elements of Modern Architecture* by the Modern Architectural Research Group, New Burlington Galleries, 11–29 January 1938, p. 3. See *Bernard Shaw on the London Art Scene 1885–1950* (ed. Stanley Weintraub 1989) pp. 447–9.

192/23 **State:** 13 March 1887. See BL Add. MS 50702 ff. 162–251.

192/28 **expression:** See *Bernard Shaw: Agitations: Letters to the Press 1875–1950* (ed. Dan H. Laurence and James Rambeau 1985)
p. xiii.

192/30 **face:** 'Blood Money to Whitechapel', *The Star* 24 September 1888, *Agitations* pp. 10–11.

192/38 **world:** Ernest Rhys, *Wales England Wed* (1940) p. 85.

193/ 9 **man:** This description, which originally appeared in the *Workman's Times* in 1894, is quoted in *Platform and Pulpit* (ed. Dan H. Laurence 1961) p. ix, and *CL1* p. 107.

193/17 **to it:** See *Platform and Pulpit* p. x.

193/19 **consonant:** G.B.S. to Lady Rhondda, 9 February 1927, *CL4*
p. 48.

193/21 **theorist:** *The Star* 8 September 1888.

193/23 **Socialists:** G. C. Moore Smith. See *Diaries* 1, entry 9 February 1889, p. 467.

193/28 **perfection:** G.B.S. to Lady Rhondda, 9 February 1927, *CL*4 p. 46.

193/35 **hair:** G.B.S. to Siegfried Trebitsch, 14 January 1926, Shaw/Trebitsch letters p. 268.

193/38 **them:** G.B.S. note on manuscript of Hesketh Pearson's biography (Texas).

193/40 **ornament:** G.B.S. to Muriel J. Robson, 1 March 1917 (Pattee Library, Pennsylvania State University).

194/ 5 **expense:** G.B.S. to Irene Vanbrugh, 22 November 1932 (Princeton).

194/29 **degeneracy:** 'A Refutation of Anarchism', *Our Corner* XI, May 1888, pp. 289–96; June 1888, pp. 374–81; XII, July 1888, pp. 8–20. Revised as a paper, 'The Difficulties of Anarchism', read to the Fabian Society on 16 October 1891; published with further revisions as Fabian Tract no. 45, *The Impossibilities of Anarchism* (1893).

195/13 **increase!:** 'The Economic Basis of Socialism', *Fabian Essays in Socialism* (1889) pp. 3–29 and *Essays in Fabian Socialism* (1932) pp. 3–29.

195/30 *Bernard Shaw*: Arthur and E. M. Sidgwick, *Henry Sidgwick: A Memoir* (1906) pp. 497–8.

195/last **selfishness:** 'The Transition to Social Democracy', an address delivered on 7 September 1888 to the Economic Section of the British Association at Bath, later published in *Fabian Essays in Socialism* (1889) pp. 173–201 and *Essays in Fabian Socialism* (1932) pp. 31–61.

196/16 **broken up:** *SSS* p. 60.

196/19 **stage:** G.B.S. to Irene Vanbrugh, 23 November 1932 (Princeton).

196/20 **tongue work:** *Diaries* 1, entry 26 January 1890, p. 583.

196/24 **vice:** G.B.S. to Lena Ashwell, 2 March 1924 (Texas).

196/29 **politically:** 'The Telltale Microphone', *Political Quarterly* VI, October 1935. See BL Add. MS 50698 for corrected galley proofs.

196/36 **in it:** Ibid.

197/ 4 **Socialism:** G.B.S. to Charles Charrington, 28 January 1890, *CL*1 p. 238.

197/14 **my ability:** G.B.S. to Havelock Ellis, 21 August 1888, BL Add. MS 61891L.

197/23 **this rate:** G.B.S. to Havelock Ellis, 6 February 1889, ibid.

197/32 **series:** G.B.S.'s Preface to the first edition of *The Quintessence of Ibsenism*, in *Bernard Shaw: Major Critical Essays* (1986) p. 34.

197/36 **overwhelming:** See Edward R. Pease, *The History of the Fabian Society* (1916) p. 94; Norman and Jeanne MacKenzie, *The First Fabians* (1977) p. 170.

197/36 **terms:** Ibid.

198/ 2 **distresses me:** Sidney Webb to Beatrice Webb, 18 September 1891, *The Letters of Sidney and Beatrice Webb* (ed. Norman MacKenzie 1978) vol. 1, p. 305.

198/ 6 **creep:** 'Mainly about People', *The Star* 19 July 1890.

198/ 9 **selfishness:** 'Socialism of the Sty', *Justice* 26 July 1890.

198/19 **Ibsenism:** See *CL*1 pp. 275–7. Also *Shaw and Ibsen* (ed. J. L. Wisenthal, University of Toronto Press 1979) pp. 15–16.

198/26 **Rationalism:** G.B.S. to G. K. Chesterton, 1 March 1908, *CL*2 p. 759.

198/27 **document:** G.B.S. to Dr Octavia Wilberforce, 13 January 1943 (Boston).

198/29 **directions:** G.B.S. to Lena Ashwell, 10 May 1913 (Texas).

198/36 **fact:** William Archer to Charles Archer, 25–28 July 1887. See Charles Archer, *William Archer: Life, Work and Friendships* (1931) p. 156.

198/38 **awe:** ' "The Quintessence of Ibsenism": An Open Letter to George Bernard Shaw', *New Review* 5, November 1891, p. 464.

199/ 4 **theatre:** G.B.S. to Elizabeth Robins, 20 April 1891, *CL*1 p. 292.

199/12 **Globe:** 'Ibsen Triumphant', *Saturday Review* 22 May 1897, *OTN*3 p. 138.

199/18 **holiday:** Huntly Carter, *The New Spirit in Drama and Art* (1912) p. 36.

199/23 **Ibsenism:** Preface to the first edition of *The Quintessence of Ibsenism*, June 1891. See 1913 edition completed to death of Ibsen, p. xix.

199/last **name:** William Archer, 'Ibsen As I Knew Him', *Monthly Review* 23 June 1906, p. 14.

200/21 **conscience:** Preface to *Fanny's First Play*, *CP*4 p. 345.

201/ 7 **lies:** 4 July entry, *The G.B.S. Calendar* (1907).

201/ 8 **ideals:** G.B.S. to William Archer, 19 April 1919, *CL*3 p. 602.

201/15 **advantage:** Preface to the first edition of *The Quintessence of Ibsenism*.

201/22 **sacrifices:** *The Quintessence of Ibsenism* (1913 edn) p. 94.

201/29 **devilish:** Ibid., p. 41.

201/37 **madhouse:** Ibid., p. 168.

202/13   **race:** Ibid., pp. 135–7.

202/18   **spirit:** Ibid., p. 12n. This footnote was added for the 1913 edition.

202/23   **prescription:** G.B.S. reply to Mrs V. O. Plenazár, 15 July 1929, *CL*4 p. 154.

202/30   **eighties:** BL Add. MS 50522, shorthand draft rev. of f. 55, typescript 63, dated 1 April 1938. Appeared in *Nordisk-Tidende* 23 May 1938.

203/14   **baffled:** *The Quintessence of Ibsenism* (1913 edn) p. 63.

204/Ep.   **in it:** 'Van Amburgh Revived', *Saturday Review* 7 May 1898, *OTN*3 pp. 377–8.

204/ 7   **criticism:** *The Quintessence of Ibsenism* (1913 edn) p. 45.

204/10   **life's work:** *Diaries* 1, notes for 1885, 'Family circumstances', p. 54.

204/21   **credit:** G.B.S. to Frederic Whyte, 2 July 1922 (Detroit).

204/39   **ground:** Ibid.

205/ 3   **prophesy:** 'The Progress of Despotism in London: Prophetic Calendar for the Next Month', *Pall Mall Gazette* XLVI, 22 November 1887.

205/ 4   **ignoramus:** G.B.S. to J. Robertson Scott, 5 February 1944 (Cornell).

205/ 5   **murder:** G.B.S. to C. Kinloch-Cooke, 14 September 1888, *CL*1 pp. 194–5.

205/ 7   **to do:** 'A New Novel By Bertha Thomas', *Pall Mall Gazette* XLV, 30 March 1887, p. 5. See *Bernard Shaw's Book Reviews Originally Published in the Pall Mall Gazette from 1885 to 1888* (ed. Brian Tyson 1991) pp. 254–7.

205/12   **empty:** 'Painter and Partners', *The Observer* 23 December 1945.

205/14   **staff:** 'A Socialist on the Unemployed', *Pall Mall Gazette* XLIII, 11 February 1886, pp. 4–5.

205/18   **fog:** Ibid.

205/24   **basket:** 'Proletarian Literature', *Pall Mall Gazette* XLVIII, 5 September 1888, p. 5. See *Bernard Shaw's Book Reviews* pp. 436–40.

205/31   **history:** 'Memoirs of an Old-Fashioned Physician', *Pall Mall Gazette* XLII, 25 November 1885, pp. 4–5. See *Bernard Shaw's Book Reviews* pp. 62–9.

205/39   **police:** 'The Truth About Shakespeare', *Pall Mall Gazette* XLIII, 7 January 1886, pp. 4–5. See *Bernard Shaw's Book Reviews* pp. 79–83.

205/last   **rubbish:** G.B.S. to C. Kinloch-Cooke, 14 September 1888, *CL*1 pp. 194–5.

206/20   **as such:** 'The Truth About Shakespeare', *Pall Mall Gazette* XLIII, 7 January 1886, pp. 4–5. See *Bernard Shaw's Book Reviews* pp. 79–83.

207/18   **papers:** 'The Year of Jubilee', *Pall Mall Gazette* XLIV, 16 November 1886, p. 6. See *Bernard Shaw's Book Reviews* pp. 213–18.

207/27   **Mudie:** 'Fiction and Truth', lecture prepared by Shaw for delivery in April 1887. Published in *Bernard Shaw's Nondramatic Literary Criticism* (ed. Stanley Weintraub, University of Nebraska Press, Lincoln 1972) pp. 3–20.

207/28   **at Mudie's:** 'Three New Novels', *Pall Mall Gazette* XLVII, 26 March 1888, p. 3. See *Bernard Shaw's Book Reviews* pp. 399–404.

207/35   **themselves:** 'Folk Lore, English and Scotch', *Pall Mall Gazette* XLII, 25 August 1885, p. 5. See *Bernard Shaw's Book Reviews* pp. 37–40.

208/15   **initiated:** 'Fiction and Truth'. See *Bernard Shaw's Nondramatic Literary Criticism* p. 316.

210/ 9   **prolonged:** 'A Son of Hagar', *Pall Mall Gazette* XLV, 3 February 1887, pp. 4–5. See *Bernard Shaw's Book Reviews* pp. 245–8.

210/23   **purposes:** 'Realism, Real and Unreal', *Pall Mall Gazette* XLVI, 29 September 1887, p. 3. See *Bernard Shaw's Book Reviews* pp. 340–3. See also *Bernard Shaw's Nondramatic Literary Criticism* pp. 110–13.

210/31   *Macbeth:* See *Pen Portraits and Reviews* (1931) pp. 43–52.

210/last   **machine made:** 'A New Novel by Wilkie Collins', *Pall Mall Gazette* XLIV, 18 September 1886, p. 5. *Bernard Shaw's Book Reviews* pp. 199–202.

211/20   **gutter:** 'Realism, Real and Unreal', *Pall Mall Gazette* XLVI, 29 September 1887, p. 3. *Bernard Shaw's Book Reviews* pp. 340–3. See also *Bernard Shaw's Nondramatic Literary Criticism* pp. 110–13.

211/24   **sake:** Preface to *Man and Superman*, *CP*2 p. 527.

211/36   **better:** G.B.S. reply to questionnaire from Floryan Sobieniowski about *The Apple Cart*, 2–10 April 1929 (Berg).

211/last   **effort:** G.B.S. to Ernest Newman, 5 October 1917, *CL*3 p. 509.

212/ 4   **live:** Preface to 'The Sanity of Art', *Major Critical Essays* (1932) p. 283; Penguin (1986) p. 312.

212/ 9   **first:** 'Edgar Allan Poe', *Pen Portraits and Reviews* pp. 220–6.

212/11   **typewriter:** G.B.S. to Esmé Percy. See 'Bernard Shaw: A Personal Memory', *The Listener* 26 May 1955, pp. 929–31.

212/21   **at him:** *Diaries* 1, entry 12 June 1886, p. 176.

212/27   **tact:** 'G.B.S. on Literature—and Other Things' by Norman Clark, 31 December 1931 (North Carolina).

212/40   **Swift:** 'Cobbett's Rural Rides', *Pall Mall Gazette* XLII, 27 July 1885, pp. 4–5. See *Bernard Shaw's Book Reviews* pp. 30–7.

212/last   **Belfort Bax:** See 'Professor Sidgwick and Mr Belfort Bax', *Pall Mall Gazette* XLVI, 26 September 1887, pp. 2–3; and 'Darwin Denounced', *Pall Mall Gazette* XLV, 31 May 1887, p. 5. See *Bernard Shaw's Book Reviews* pp. 331–8, 277–81.

214/31   **Acts:** 'Occasional Notes', *Pall Mall Gazette* XLVIII, 17 September 1888, p. 5. See also *CL*1 pp. 194–5.

215/ 4   **vehicle:** G.B.S. to T. P. O'Connor, 9 February 1888, *CL*1 pp. 183–5.

215/ 7   **my own:** G.B.S. to H. W. Massingham, 9 February 1888, *CL*1 pp. 185–6.

215/ 9   **sulky:** *Diaries* 1, entry 6 February 1888, p. 346.

215/ 9   **immensely:** G.B.S. to H. W. Massingham, 9 February 1888, *CL*1 pp. 185–6.

215/12   **T. P. O'Connor:** St John Ervine, *Bernard Shaw: His Life, Work and Friends* (1956) p. 274.

215/13   **last time:** *Diaries* 1, entry 10 February 1888, pp. 347–8.

215/23   **flight:** Sotheby's Catalogue, 14 March 1979, item 436.

215/28   **some time:** *Diaries* 1, entry 18 October 1889, p. 550.

216/ 3   **hear:** 'In the Picture-Galleries: Pastels at the Grosvenor', *The World* no. 800, 23 October 1889, pp. 25–6. See *Bernard Shaw on the London Art Scene* pp. 294–7.

216/Ep.   **devil:** 11 October entry, *The G.B.S. Calendar* (1907).

216/20   **dictionary:** 'La Princesse Lointaine', *Saturday Review* 22 June 1895, *OTN*1 p. 156.

216/24   **freely:** *Diaries* 1, notes for 1887, p. 230.

217/22   **pleased:** Ibid., entry 15 March 1890, p. 599.

217/27   **annoyance:** Ibid., entry 28 March 1890, p. 603.

217/29   **over it:** Ibid.

217/31   **oiling:** Ibid., entry 3 June 1890, p. 623.

217/35   **procrastination:** Ibid., notes for 1886, p. 135.

217/36   **laziness:** Ibid., entry 1 February 1887, p. 238.

217/38   **fate:** Ibid., entry 13 July 1887, p. 284.

217/last   **until 11:** Ibid., entry 28 November 1888, p. 438.

218/13   **hard:** Ibid., entry 9 November 1890, p. 666.

218/20   **for me:** Ibid., notes for 1892, p. 782.

218/21   **freely:** Ibid., notes for 1887, p. 230.

218/31   **cemetery:** 'A Sunday on the Surrey Hills', *Short Stories, Scraps and Shavings* (1932) p. 217.

218/34   **Nature:** Ibid.

218/37   **manage it:** *Diaries* I, entry 22 January 1889, p. 461.

218/last   *The Star:* See 'Opera in Amsterdam', *The Star* 27 April 1889, *SM*I pp. 609–13.

218/last   **realized:** G.B.S. to William Archer, 18 April 1889, *CL*I p. 208.

219/ 1   **terrible:** *Diaries* I, entry 19 April 1889, p. 491.

219/ 2   **duller:** G.B.S. to William Archer, 18 April 1889, *CL*I p. 208.

219/ 3   **Hague:** *Diaries* I, entry 20 April 1889, p. 491.

219/ 4   **dogholes:** G.B.S. to Archer, 18 April 1889, *CL*I p. 208.

219/ 7   **success:** Ibid.

219/ 9   **successfully:** *Diaries* I, entry 3 August 1889, p. 528.

219/21   **duties:** G.B.S. to Archer, 17 August 1890, *CL*I p. 256.

219/22   **Germany:** Ibid., p. 258.

219/27   **incompetence:** G.B.S. to William Morris, 23 September 1891, *CL*I p. 309.

219/33   **another:** Ibid.

220/ 2   **with you:** Marjorie Davidson to G.B.S., 3 June 1888, BL Add. MS 50547 ff. 26–7. Marjorie Davidson later married Edward Pease, the secretary and historian of the Fabian Society.

220/13   **on me:** *Diaries* I, entry 1 April 1888, p. 362.

220/19   **letters:** Emma Brooke to G.B.S., 5 and 10 April 1888, BL Add. MS 50512.

220/23   **the day:** *Diaries* I, entry 12 April 1888, p. 365.

220/24   **Gilchrist:** Ibid., entry 23 April 1888, p. 369.

221/ 5   **Spooner:** Ibid., entry 14 April 1888, p. 366.

221/ 8   **with Geraldine:** Ibid., entry 21 April 1890, p. 609.

221/18   **love Geraldine:** 'Rain, rain, rain, rain / Damn the rain!' Manuscript verses, 77 lines, 27–29 August 1892, *Shaw: An Exhibit* (University of Texas at Austin 1977) item 564.

221/30   **practised:** Stephen Winsten, *Salt and His Circle* (1951) p. 14. Preface by G.B.S.

221/33   **revolutionist:** G.B.S. to Archibald Henderson, 3–17 January 1905, *CL*2 p. 489.

221/35   **wildflowers:** Henry Salt to G.B.S., 6 July 1924, BL Add. MS 50549 f. 12.

222/11   **never shall:** G.B.S. to Salt, 25 February 1919, *CL*3 pp. 590–1.

222/12   **friends:** G.B.S. to Catherine Mandeville Salt, 8 May 1939, *CL*4 p. 529.

222/15   **creature:** Winsten, *Salt and His Circle* p. 9.

222/16   **profile:** Edward Carpenter, *My Days and Dreams* (1916) p. 237.

222/23   **at home:** 'Salt on Shaw', March 1929. Manuscript at Texas, printed as Appendix to *Salt and His Circle* pp. 205–17 (p. 209).

222/33   **Millthorpe:** G.B.S. to Salt, 19 August 1903, *CL*2 p. 348.

222/34   **impostor:** Ibid.

222/38   **highstrung:** *Diaries* 1, entry 4 January 1889, p. 455.

223/10   **weary:** G.B.S. to Janet Achurch, 24 March 1896, *CL*1 p. 615.

223/16   **lions:** 'More About Morris', *The Observer* 6 November 1949.

223/22   **Philistine:** *William Morris 1834–1934: Some Appreciations* (William Morris Centenary Celebrations, Walthamstow, 1934) pp. 30–1.

223/23   **paradise:** 'Morris as I Knew Him', G.B.S. introduction to May Morris, *William Morris, Artist, Writer, Socialist* vol. 2 (1936).

223/26   **houses:** G.B.S. note on the manuscript of Hesketh Pearson's biography (Texas).

223/27   **May Morris:** *Diaries* 1, entry 27 September 1885, p. 114.

224/ 8   **both of us:** 'Morris as I Knew Him' p. xxviii.

224/15   **understandingly:** May Morris to G.B.S., 5 May 1936 (Texas).

224/20   **women:** G.B.S. to Mrs Pakenham Beatty, 22 September 1885, *CL*1 p. 140.

224/24   **at her:** Eleanor Marx to G.B.S., 2 June 1885, BL Add. MS 50511.

224/37   · **think so:** May Morris to G.B.S., n.d. [c. 1886], BL Add. MS 50541 f. 38.

225/ 7   **teacher:** May Morris to G.B.S., 21 July 1885, ibid., ff. 43–4.

225/ 7   **compliments:** May Morris to G.B.S., 25 October 1885, ibid.

225/ 8   **shallow:** May Morris to G.B.S., 12 June 1885, ibid., f. 34.

225/12   **vanity:** May Morris to G.B.S., 28 April 1886, ibid., ff. 65–6.

225/16   **impossible:** May Morris to G.B.S., n.d. [November 1885], ibid., f. 48.

225/18   **to me:** May Morris to G.B.S., 10 November 1885, ibid., f. 47.

225/20   **relations:** May Morris to G.B.S., 23 April 1936 (copy, Texas).

225/26   **May Morris:** *Diaries* 1, entry 4 April 1886, p. 158.

225/32   **them:** 'Private Note by G.B.S.' (Texas).

225/39   **has me:** May Morris to G.B.S., 5 May 1886, BL Add. MS 50541 ff. 67–8.

226/ 3   **friend Shaw:** Ibid.

226/ 5   **man:** Pakenham Beatty to G.B.S., 28 April 1887, BL Add. MS 50530 ff. 194–5.

226/ 9   **time:** 'Morris as I Knew Him' p. xxviii.

226/22   **situation:** Ibid., p. xxix.

226/26   **elsewhere:** 'Private Note by G.B.S.' (Texas).

226/32   **imagination:** 'Morris as I Knew Him' p. xxix.

226/39   **left Hammersmith:** *Diaries* 2, entry 26 July 1891, p. 742.

227/ 3   **unbearable:** Ibid., entry 1 November 1892, p. 867.

227/ 9   **Sparling:** Ibid., entry 2 November 1892, p. 868.

227/22   **vanish:** 'Morris as I Knew Him' p. xxx.

227/33   **complicated:** Ibid.

227/37 **was not:** 'Private Note by G.B.S.' (Texas).

228/ 5 **May:** *Diaries* 2, entry 7 May 1893, p. 931.

228/ 8 **G[eorge]:** H. G. Farmer, *Bernard Shaw's Sister and Her Friends* (1959) p. 140.

228/12 **blistered:** *Diaries* 2, entry 19 June 1893, p. 947.

229/ 9 **went:** Hesketh Pearson, *Bernard Shaw* p. 101.

229/15 **behind:** G.B.S. to Eva Christy, n.d., BL Add. MS 50527 ff. 47–50.

229/16 **play:** Preface to *Plays Pleasant*, *CP*1 p. 372.

229/16 **'A Mystery':** *Plays Pleasant and Unpleasant* II (1931) p. xix.

229/17 **heart:** *CP*1 p. 594.

229/19 **drawn:** Ibid., p. 572.

229/19 **evening:** Ibid.

229/31 **predicted:** 'Morris as I Knew Him' p. xxxi.

230/ 9 **by his:** 'William Morris as Actor and Playwright', *Pen Portraits and Reviews* (1931) p. 217.

230/14 **fly:** G.B.S. to Charlotte Payne-Townshend, 13 March 1898, BL Add. MS 50550 f. 69.

230/17 **of life:** May Morris to G.B.S., 23 April 1936 (copy, Texas).

230/19 **world:** Jan Marsh, *Jane and May Morris* (1986) p. 295.

230/Ep. **for me:** G.B.S. to Neville Cardus, 6 January 1939 (property of Elizabeth Grice).

230/25 **instrument:** Written in 1935 as a preface to *London Music in 1888–89* (1937), *SM*1 p. 30.

230/30 **family:** 'Musical Mems: by The Star's Own Captious Critic', *The Star* 15 February 1889, *SM*1 p. 557.

230/32 **melancholy:** Written in 1935 as a preface to *London Music in 1888–89*, *SM*1 p. 30.

231/ 5 **damned:** *Man and Superman*, Act 3, *CP*2 p. 646.

231/ 8 **symphony:** G.B.S. to Jules Magny, 18 December 1890, *CP*1 p. 280.

231/15 **Crystal Palace:** *Diaries* 1, entry 29 October 1887, p. 310.

231/18 **feeling:** 'Wagner's Theories', *The World* 17 January 1894, *SM*3 p. 91.

231/19 **arts:** *Man and Superman*, Act 3, *CP*2 p. 646.

231/24 **influence:** 'Music for the People', *The Musical Review* 10 March 1883, *SM*1 p. 196.

231/25 **rectitude:** G.B.S. to W. H. Dircks, 3 September 1890, *CL*1 pp. 259–60.

231/38 **Association:** Written in 1935 as a preface to *London Music in 1888–89*, *SM*1 p. 58.

232/ 8 **attention:** G.B.S. to August Manns, 19 December 1888, *CL*1 pp. 202–3.

232 / 18   **turn:** 'In the Days of Our Youth', *The Star* 19 February 1906, *SSS* pp. 42–7.

232 / 25   **nonsensical:** Written in 1935 as a preface to *London Music in 1888–89*, *SM*1 p. 58.

232 / 36   **at first:** 'Fine Strokes of Comedy', *The World* 15 February 1893, *SM*2 p. 809.

233 / 4   **life:** 'An Embarrassment of Riches', *The Star* 1 March 1889, *SM*1 p. 567.

233 / 8   **himself:** 'Absolute Pitchers', *The Star* 24 May 1889, *SM*1 p. 640.

233 / 12   **bed:** 'The Interval is the Act', *The Star* 7 June 1889, *SM*1 p. 657.

233 / 13   **accurate:** 'Poor Old Philharmonic', *The Star* 5 April 1890, *SM*2 p. 1.

233 / 14   **bigness:** 'Liszt's Variations', *The Star* 14 February 1890, *SM*1 p. 921.

233 / 15   **humor:** 'A Word More About Verdi', *The Anglo-Saxon Review* March 1901, *SM*3 p. 578.

233 / 16   **goodnatured:** 'A Defence of Ballet', *The Star* 4 October 1889, *SM*1 p. 806.

233 / 22   **throne:** 'Beethoven, Brahms, and Banjo', *The Star* 14 March 1890, *SM*1 p. 956.

233 / 27   **lie:** 'Proms at Her Majesty's', *The Star* 19 August 1889, *SM*1 p. 754.

233 / 32   **chests:** 'Too Popular', *The Star* 23 January 1889, *SM*1 p. 550.

233 / 35   **operas:** 'A Typical Concert', *The Star* 17 May 1889, *SM*1 p. 629.

234 / 16   **poor:** 'The Popular Musical Union', *The Star* 13 April 1889, *SM*1 p. 603.

234 / 19   **Congo:** 'Liszt's Variations', *The Star* 14 February 1890, *SM*1 p. 924.

234 / 28   **belong:** 'Paris: A Pedant-Ridden Failure', *The Star* 11 April 1890, *SM*2 pp. 26–7.

234 / 31   **enterprise:** 'Sumptuary Regulations at the Opera'; G.B.S. letter to *The Times*, 3 July 1905, *SM*3 p. 586.

235 / 4   **place:** G.B.S. to the Covent Garden Manager c. July 1888, *CL*1 pp. 190–2.

235 / 9   **satisfaction:** 'Sumptuary Regulations at the Opera'; G.B.S. letter to *The Times*, 3 July 1905, *SM*3 pp. 585–6.

235 / 29   **bird:** Ibid., p. 585.

236 / 14   **dead:** 'Opera in Amsterdam', *The Star* 27 April 1889, *SM*1 pp. 611–12.

236 / 21   **leg:** 'Knighthood and Dancing', *The Star* 21 February 1890, *SM*1 p. 933.

236/29 **themselves:** 'Economics and Music', *The Star* 1 June 1889, *SM*1 p. 651.

236/32 **flat:** 'The Captious Frolic', *The Star* 30 March 1889, *SM*1 p. 593.

236/39 **guineas:** G.B.S. to H. W. Massingham, 28 February 1890, *CL*1 pp. 243–4.

236/last **flood:** T. P. O'Connor, *Memoirs of an Old Parliamentarian* (1929) vol. 2, p. 267.

237/ 8 **week:** 'The Opera Season and Its Lessons', *The Star* 26 July 1889, *SM*1 p. 712.

237/12 **mistake:** G.B.S. to T. P. O'Connor, 5 February 1890, *CL*1 pp. 241–2.

237/13 **hold on:** G.B.S. to O'Connor, 4 March 1890, *CL*1 pp. 244–6.

237/16 **mortals:** 'Bassetto's Valediction', *The Star* 16 May 1890, *SM*2 p. 71.

237/29 **Fabian:** Ibid., p. 70.

238/ 2 **di Bassetto:** Ibid., p. 71.

238/ 8 **absurdity:** 'From Mozart to Mario', *Pall Mall Gazette* 2 February 1887, *SM*1 pp. 481–4.

238/19 **harmony:** 'Paris: A Pedant-Ridden Failure', *The Star* 11 April 1890, *SM*2 p. 26.

238/26 **criticism:** *Nine Answers by G. Bernard Shaw* (1923; unnumbered pages).

238/33 **affairs:** 'Maid Marian and Ivanhoe', *The World* 11 February 1891, *SM*2 p. 264.

238/35 **people:** 'A Barrie and Conan Doyle Comic Opera', *The World* 24 May 1893, *SM*2 p. 893.

239/ 6 **door:** 'Buddha Sings', *The World* 22 June 1892, *SM*2 p. 654.

239/ 7 **horses:** 'Bayreuth's Indifference to Beauty', *The World* 1 August 1894, *SM*3 p. 306.

239/23 **quarters:** 'Irish Patriotism and Italian Opera', *The World* 15 November 1893, *SM*3 pp. 31–2.

239/26 **ears:** 'Mr Henschel in a Bad Light', *The World* 2 March 1892, *SM*2 p. 561.

239/31 **laity:** 'How to Become A Musical Critic', *Scottish Musical Monthly* December 1894, *SM*3 p. 342.

239/last **full stop:** 'Form and Design in Music', *The World* 31 May 1893, *SM*2 p. 898.

240/ 9 **again:** 'Advice for Mr De Lara', *The World* 29 July 1891, *SM*2 p. 408.

240/15 **musicians?:** 'The Birmingham Festival', *The World* 14 October 1891, *SM*2 p. 429.

240/23 **Stanford:** Ibid.

241 / 6   **religious:** 'The Search For Another Messiah', unsigned notes in *The Dramatic Review* 29 August 1885, *SM*1 pp. 346–8.

241 / 8   **funds:** 'Oratorios and Shams', *The World* 25 June 1890, *SM*2 p. 99.

241 / 13   **Handel:** Ibid., p. 98.

241 / 19   **dress:** 'A Dismal Saturday', *The World* 19 November 1890, *SM*2 pp. 202–3.

241 / 27   **destructor:** 'A Sulphurous Sublimity', *The World* 8 November 1893, *SM*3 p. 28.

241 / 39   **whistle:** 'Modern Men: Sir Arthur Sullivan', *The Scots Observer* 6 September 1890, unsigned, *SM*2 p. 174.

242 / 1   **scandalous:** 'Going Fantee', *The World* 10 May 1893, *SM*2 p. 876.

242 / 3   **Professor:** Ibid., p. 879.

243 / 4   **boy:** Ibid., pp. 876–8.

243 / 14   **Mendelssohn:** G.B.S. to Hilda McCleary, 18 September 1948 (Texas).

243 / 21   **tenderness:** 'Liszt the Charlatan', *The Hornet* XXI, 20 December 1876, unsigned, *SM*1 p. 74.

243 / 25   **Maiden:** 'The Hindhead Hall Concerts', *The Farnham, Haslemere and Hindhead Herald* 3 December 1898, *SM*3 p. 403.

243 / 28   **words:** 'Brahms's Verbosity', *The World* 11 May 1892, *SM*2 p. 614.

243 / 31   **lively:** *SM*1 p. 19.

243 / 32   **corpse:** 'A Legion of Pianists', *The World* 18 June 1890, *SM*2 p. 93.

243 / 39   **mine:** G.B.S. to F. J. Kelly, 5 February 1947 (Cornell).

244 / 4   **nails:** 'The Pistol of the Law', *The World* 9 November 1892, *SM*2 p. 729.

244 / 14   **pianoforte:** 'What Impression Do I Produce?', *The World* 4 May 1892, *SM*2 pp. 607–8.

245 / 4   **ruin him:** 'The Stock Exchange Concert', *The World* 24 February 1892, *SM*2 p. 555.

245 / 10   **hospital:** 'Culture for the Provinces', *The World* 9 August 1893, *SM*2 p. 959.

245 / 17   **soles:** 'How Handel is Sung', *The Star* 3 January 1889, unsigned, *SM*1 p. 541.

245 / last   **incomes:** 'The Superiority of Musical to Dramatic Critics', *The Players* 6 January 1892, *SM*2 p. 504.

246 / 3   **well:** G.B.S. to T. T. Watson, 21 November 1893 (Pennsylvania State University). See *Dear Mr Shaw: Selections from Bernard Shaw's postbag* (compiled and ed. Vivian Elliot 1987) p. 337.

246/12   **sympathetic:** 'Maid Marian and Ivanhoe', *The World* 11 February 1891, *SM*2 p. 261.

246/Ep.   **affair:** 'Beethoven's *Unsterbliche Geliebte*', *The World* 1 November 1893, *SM*3 p. 15.

246/17   **eyebrows:** G.B.S. to Ellen Terry, 25 September 1896, *CL*1 p. 668 (*A Correspondence* p. 83).

246/21   **self-respect:** *CP*1 pp. 137–8.

247/ 3   **laughed:** Josephine Johnson, *Florence Farr* (1975) p. 64.

247/11   **herself:** *Diaries* 2, entry 12 June 1892, p. 825.

247/31   **ease:** 'How William Archer Impressed Bernard Shaw', G.B.S.'s Foreword to *Three Plays* by William Archer (1927) p. xxviii. Reprinted in *Pen Portraits and Reviews* (1931) p. 20.

247/37   **very self:** G.B.S. to Florence Farr, 1 May 1891, *CL*1 pp. 295–7.

247/38   **loves:** G.B.S. to Florence Farr, 4 May 1891, *CL*1 p. 298.

248/ 8   **diary:** G.B.S. to Florence Farr, 7 October 1891, *CL*1 p. 313.

248/11   **lost:** *Diaries* 1, entry 11 March 1891, p. 705.

248/15   **back:** Ibid., entry 9 May 1891, p. 720.

248/15   **darkness:** Ibid., entry 4 May 1891, p. 718.

248/16   **time:** Ibid.

248/21   **lot:** G.B.S. to Florence Farr, 4 May 1891, *CL*1 p. 298.

248/24   **biographers:** G.B.S. to Stephen Winsten, quoted in Margot Peters, *Bernard Shaw and the Actresses* (1980) p. 46.

248/27   **voice:** W. B. Yeats, *Autobiographies* (1955) p. 121.

248/29   **lovers:** G.B.S. to Clifford Bax, 9 August 1940 (Texas).

248/30   **love:** Josephine Johnson, *Florence Farr* p. 36.

248/31   **performance:** George Yeats, 'A Foreword to the Letters of W. B. Yeats', *Florence Farr, Bernard Shaw and W. B. Yeats* (1946) p. 34.

248/36   **yes:** Florence Farr, *The Solemnization of Jacklin* (1912), p. 78.

248/40   **usual:** *Diaries* 1, entry 22 October 1890, p. 661.

249/11   **peace:** G.B.S. to Florence Farr, 1 May 1891, *CL*1 p. 297.

249/14   **I did:** Jane Patterson to G.B.S., 7 April 1886, BL Add. MS 50544.

249/17   **games:** Jane Patterson to G.B.S., 29 January 1888, BL Add. MS 50545.

249/21   **enough?:** Jane Patterson to G.B.S., 22 February 1888, ibid.

249/24   **jours:** Jane Patterson to G.B.S., 30 September 1888, ibid.

249/31   **letters:** Jane Patterson to G.B.S., 20 October 1888, ibid.

249/37   **know it:** Jane Patterson to G.B.S., 10 November 1888, ibid.

249/39   **to me:** Jane Patterson to G.B.S., 25 September 1888, ibid.

250/ 7   **for you:** Jane Patterson to G.B.S., 27 May 1886, BL Add. MS 50544.

250/ 8   **price:** Jane Patterson to G.B.S., 23 August 1887, BL Add. MS 50545.

250/17   **to me:** Jane Patterson to G.B.S., 25 September 1888, ibid.

250/26   **with him:** *The Quintessence of Ibsenism* (1913 edn) p. 130.

250/35   **without:** Ibid., pp. 32–3.

250/38   **them:** G.B.S. to George Yeats, 29 August 1940 (copy privately owned).

251/ 6   **promiscuously:** 'To Frank Harris on Sex in Biography', *CL*4 p. 190. Cf. *SSS* p. 113.

251/31   **Miss Farr:** G.B.S. to Janet Achurch, 6 January 1891 (Texas).

251/32   **imagined:** *Diaries* 2, entry 3 June 1891, p. 727.

251/33   **revulsion:** *Diaries* 1, entry 9 January 1886, p. 136.

251/34   **Disillusion:** *Diaries* 2, entry 2 June 1891, p. 727.

252/ 9   **is you:** 'Portrait d'une Femme' by Ezra Pound. See Josephine Johnson, *Florence Farr* pp. 169–70.

252/17   **know:** G.B.S. to Janet Achurch, 23 March 1895, *CL*1 p. 504.

252/26   **die:** G.B.S. to Janet Achurch, 6 January 1891 (Texas).

252/31   **smitten:** *Diaries* 1, entry 21 April 1885, p. 78.

252/38   **soul:** G.B.S. to Mary Grace Walker, 23 January 1885, *CL*1 p. 115.

253/ 9   **perfection:** G.B.S. to Florence Farr, 1 May 1891, *CL*1 p. 296.

253/22   **enterprise:** G.B.S. to Charles Charrington, 30 March 1891, *CL*1 p. 287.

253/22   **certainty:** Ibid.

253/24   **originality:** Ibid.

253/28   **repertory:** G.B.S. to Janet Achurch, 6 January 1891 (Texas).

253/29   **elocution:** *Diaries* 2, entry 10 August 1891, p. 745.

253/36   **vacuity:** G.B.S. to Janet Achurch, 23 March 1895, *CL*1 p. 504.

253/last   **play-acting:** Josephine Johnson, *Florence Farr* p. 57.

254/11   **talked:** G.B.S. to Florence Farr, 27 April 1893, *CL*1 p. 392.

254/14   **Beatrice:** 'The Shelley Celebration', *Daily Chronicle* 16 July 1892, p. 3.

254/20   **sentence!:** Autograph note from G.B.S. to Clifford Bax (Texas).

254/22   **woman:** *Diaries* 1, entry 16 June 1889, p. 512.

254/26   **manner:** 'An Angry Critic and a Very Quiet Lady', *The Star* 21 June 1889, *SM*1 p. 677.

254/31   **bewitched:** G.B.S. to Janet Achurch, 17 June 1889, *CL*1 p. 216.

254/32   **woman:** Ibid.

254/35   **to be had:** Ibid.

255/16   **is you:** G.B.S. to Janet Achurch, 6 January 1891 (Texas).

255/19   **tresses:** Sir Frank Benson, *My Memoirs* (1930) p. 226.

255 / 20   **brow:** Margot Peters, *Bernard Shaw and the Actresses* p. 145.

255 / 22   **career:** 'Charles Charrington's account of his wife, Janet (after her death)', BL Add. MS 50532 ff. 299–306.

255 / 28   **refused:** Ibid.

256 / 3   **my life:** G.B.S. to Janet Achurch, 21 June 1889 (Texas).

256 / 11   **faster:** G.B.S. to Elizabeth Robins, 9 November 1891 (Fales).

256 / 12   **will:** G.B.S. to Janet Achurch, 21 June 1889 (Texas).

256 / 15   **Ibsen:** G.B.S. to Janet Achurch, 6 January 1891 (Texas).

256 / 23   **conceited:** Ibid.

256 / last   **help you?:** Ibid.

257 / 8   **notes:** G.B.S. to Janet Achurch, 21 April 1892, *CL*1 p. 337.

257 / 9   **band:** Ibid., p. 338.

257 / 12   **abated:** Ibid., p. 339.

257 / 16   **man:** G.B.S. to Janet Achurch, 3 March 1893, *CL*1 p. 384.

257 / 20   **invalided:** G.B.S. to Ellen Terry, 5 July 1892, *CL*1 p. 349.

257 / 21   **indomitable:** Ibid.

257 / 26   **appear:** G.B.S. to Janet Achurch, 22 May 1893 (Texas).

257 / 28   **folly:** G.B.S. to Janet Achurch, 24 April 1894 (Texas).

257 / 35   **money:** G.B.S. to Charles Charrington, 11 March 1900, BL Add. MS 50532 f. 204.

257 / 40   **yourself:** G.B.S. to Charles Charrington, 24 November 1910 (Texas).

258 / 1   **England:** G.B.S. to Charles Charrington, 23 July 1905 (Texas).

258 / 3   **world:** Gilbert Murray to G.B.S., 16 March 1901, BL Add. MS 50542 ff. 9–11.

258 / 25   **wanted her:** G.B.S. to Charles Charrington, 20 July 1918 (Texas).

258 / 37   **useful:** G.B.S. to Janet Achurch, 24 April 1894 (Texas).

258 / last   **tell you:** G.B.S. to Charles Charrington, fragment, n.d. (Texas).

259 / 3   **married?:** G.B.S. to Charles Charrington, 3 May 1905 (Texas).

259 / 5   **you are!:** G.B.S. to Charles Charrington, 24 November 1910 (Texas).

259 / 16   **lasts:** G.B.S. to Florence Farr, 27 April 1893, *CL*1 pp. 391–2.

259 / 23   **sentimentalize:** *Diaries* 2, entry 27 July 1891, p. 742.

259 / 29   **description:** 'Christmas in Broadstairs', *The Star* 27 December 1889, *SM*1 p. 881.

259 / 40   **upset me:** *Diaries* 2, entry 4 December 1891, p. 773. See also ibid., entry 5 November 1892, p. 869.

260 / 21   **with it:** Ibid., entry 8 February 1893, p. 904.

261 / 3   **or worse:** 'Bernard Shaw's Reply Shows That, Spite of all his

Critics Have Said, He is no Hater of Women', *The Star* 25
July 1893, *Bernard Shaw: Agitations: Letters to the Press 1875–
1950* pp. 25–30 and *Diaries* 2, entry 24 July 1893 p. 960.

CHAPTER V

262 / Ep. **mind:** 'Why a Labor Year Book?', *The Labour Year Book 1916*
pp. 10–12.

262 / 9 **desert me:** Sidney Webb to Beatrice Potter, 29 July 1890, *The
Letters of Sidney and Beatrice Webb* (ed. Norman MacKenzie
1978) vol. 1, p. 161.

262 / 10 **for you:** Sidney Webb to Beatrice Potter, 2 August 1890, ibid.,
p. 160.

262 / 12 **love:** G.B.S. to Margaret Cole questionnaire, BL Add. MS
50699 f. 184(i).

262 / 24 **family:** Beatrice Potter to Mary Playne, April 1888. Jeanne
MacKenzie, *A Victorian Courtship* (1979) p. 1.

262 / 26 **nautical:** Kitty Muggeridge and Ruth Adam, *Beatrice Webb: A
Life* (1967) p. 13.

262 / 29 **woman:** *A Victorian Courtship* p. 44.

262 / 30 **nature:** *Beatrice Webb: A Life* p. 80.

262 / 32 **one:** *A Victorian Courtship* p. 6.

263 / 2 **intelligence:** *Beatrice Webb: A Life* p. 28.

263 / 15 **to me:** *A Victorian Courtship* p. 27.

263 / 16 **dominate:** Ibid., p. 31.

263 / 19 **happiness:** Ibid., p. 26.

263 / 21 **welcome:** Norman and Jeanne MacKenzie, *The First Fabians*
(1977) p. 129.

263 / 22 **ended:** *A Victorian Courtship* p. 28.

263 / 31 **Napoleon:** *The Diary of Beatrice Webb* vol. 1 (ed. Norman and
Jeanne MacKenzie 1982) entry 26 April 1890, p. 330.

263 / 35 **repulsive:** Sidney Webb to Marjorie Davidson, 12 December
1888, *The Letters of Sidney and Beatrice Webb* vol. 1, p. 118.

263 / 37 **against him:** *The Diary of Beatrice Webb* vol. 1, entry 26 April
1890, pp. 329–30.

263 / last **ludicrous:** Ibid.

264 / 5 **great:** Sidney Webb to Beatrice Potter, 16 June 1890, *The
Letters of Sidney and Beatrice Webb* vol. 1, p. 152.

264 / 8 **Economics:** *A Victorian Courtship* p. 77.

264 / 13 **despatches:** Sidney Webb to Beatrice Potter, 19 September
1890, *The Letters of Sidney and Beatrice Webb* vol. 1, p. 191.

264 / 14 **feeling:** Beatrice Potter to Sidney Webb, 2 May 1890, ibid.,
p. 133.

264/15   **unendurable:** Sidney Webb to Beatrice Potter, 24 May 1890, ibid., p. 139.

264/18   **influence:** Beatrice Potter to Sidney Webb, 11 August 1890, ibid., p. 166.

264/22   **man:** *A Victorian Courtship* p. 107.

264/24   **position?:** Beatrice Potter to Sidney Webb, December 1890, *The Letters of Sidney and Beatrice Webb* vol. 1, p. 238.

264/25   **suicide:** *A Victorian Courtship* p. 107.

264/28   **dream:** Sidney Webb to Beatrice Potter, 21 May 1891, *The Letters of Sidney and Beatrice Webb* vol. 1, p. 271.

264/37   **marrying:** Beatrice Potter to Sidney Webb, 20 August 1891, ibid., p. 281.

264/38   **beginning:** Sidney Webb to Beatrice Potter, 14 September 1891, ibid., p. 299.

264/40   **ceremony:** Kate Courtney diary note, 23 July 1892, *The Letters of Sidney and Beatrice Webb* vol. 1, p. 436.

265/ 2   **race:** Ibid., p. 437.

265/ 6   **paradise:** Bernard Shaw, 'The Webbs and Social Evolution', *New York Times* 18 November 1945, VII, p. 1.

265/16   **disliked me:** BL Add. MS 50699 f. 183 D. See also G.B.S. to Beatrice Potter, 6 October 1890, *CL*1 p. 267.

265/20   **ugly:** *A Victorian Courtship* p. 131.

265/29   **discuss:** G.B.S. to Janet Achurch, 31 August 1895, *CL*1 p. 555.

265/36   **from him:** *The Diary of Beatrice Webb* vol. 2 (ed. Norman and Jeanne MacKenzie 1983), entry 8 May 1897, p. 114.

265/37   **to me:** BL Add. MS 50699 f. 183.

266/ 3   **true:** G.B.S. to Ellen Terry, 8 September 1897, *CL*1 p. 801. See *Ellen Terry and Bernard Shaw: A Correspondence* (ed. Christopher St John 1931) pp. 253–4.

266/ 7   **self-possessed:** *CP*1 p. 273.

266/ 8   **petticoats:** Ibid., p. 271.

266/ 9   **play:** *Beatrice Webb: A Life* p. 142.

266/13   **Socialism:** G.B.S. to Beatrice Webb, 30 July 1901, *CL*2 p. 233.

266/18   **circumstances:** *The Diary of Beatrice Webb* vol. 1, entry 30 September 1889, p. 298.

266/19   **Society:** Sidney Webb to Beatrice Potter, 14 December 1890, *The Letters of Sidney and Beatrice Webb* vol. 1, p. 242.

266/21   **contempt:** BL Add. MS 50699 f. 183.

266/25   **moderation:** Beatrice Webb diaries, 15 February 1890 (LSE).

266/32   **1906:** Edward R. Pease, *The History of the Fabian Society* (1916) p. 213.

267/ 2   **asceticism:** *New York Times* 18 November 1945, VII, p. 1.

267/ 4 **breakfast:** *The Listener* 31 July 1952, p. 18.

267/11 **bicycle:** G.B.S. to F. H. Evans, 27 August 1895, *CL*1 p. 551.

267/21 **machine:** G.B.S. to Janet Achurch, 13 April 1895, *CL*1 p. 519.

267/24 **work:** *The Diary of Beatrice Webb* vol. 2, entry 9 September 1895, p. 80.

267/28 **man:** G.B.S. to R. Golding Bright, 26 September 1896, *CL*1 p. 670.

267/35 **time:** G.B.S. to Mrs Mallet, 5 October 1895 (Texas).

267/38 **harmless:** G.B.S. note to F. E. Loewenstein for a reply to Robert Williamson, 3 October 1948 (Texas).

268/ 5 **boots:** *CP*1 p. 677.

268/18 **miraculous:** G.B.S. note to F. E. Loewenstein for a reply to Robert Williamson, 3 October 1948 (Texas).

268/19 **your leg:** G.B.S. to Elliott O'Donnell, 6 May 1899 (Boston).

268/34 **months:** G.B.S. to Janet Achurch, 16 September 1895, *CL*1 p. 559.

268/38 **Ivanhoe:** G.B.S. to R. Golding Bright, 22 September 1896, *CL*1 p. 663.

268/last **physically:** G.B.S. to anon., 19 April 1899. Christie's Catalogue, Wednesday 23 June 1976.

269/ 6 **books:** *Beatrice Webb: A Life* p. 134.

269/12 **qualifications:** *The Diary of Beatrice Webb* vol. 2, entry 1 February 1895, p. 67.

269/17 **undertake it:** G.B.S. to Sidney Webb, 12 August 1892, *CL*1 p. 360.

269/24 **eater:** Beatrice Webb to Georgina Meinertzhagen, 7 December 1903, *The Letters of Sidney and Beatrice Webb* vol. 2, p. 195.

269/32 **thinking:** *The Diaries of Beatrice Webb* vol. 2, entry 24 July 1903, p. 290.

269/35 **served:** N. and J. MacKenzie, *The First Fabians* p. 347.

270/33 **London:** G.B.S. to Cunninghame Graham, 1 October 1890 (Scotland).

270/35 **S.D.F.O:** G.B.S. to Graham Wallas, 20 September 1892, *CL*1 p. 367.

270/40 **Progressivism:** G.B.S. to Edward Pease, 11 January 1893, *CL*1 p. 377.

271/ 6 **self-defence:** *Sir James Sexton: Agitator* (1936), see *CL*1 p. 376.

271/23 **wages:** Edward Pease, *The History of the Fabian Society* (1916) pp. 114–15.

271/32 **field:** G.B.S. to Graham Wallas, 8 September 1893, *CL*1 p. 405.

272/ 1 **way:** *A Plan of Campaign for Labor* (Fabian Tract no. 49), January 1894, p. 9.

272/11   **election:** Ibid., p. 19.

272/25   **laps:** *The Diary of Beatrice Webb* vol. 2, entry 8 July 1895, p. 76.

273/ 6   **or not:** *Report on Fabian Policy* (Fabian Tract no. 70), July 1896,
            pp. 3–4.

273/11   **with us:** Charlotte Shaw to Edward Pease, 20 July 1911
            (Nuffield).

273/16   **ourselves:** 15 July 1894. See *Labour Leader* 28 July 1894.

273/29   **advisable:** G.B.S. to T. H. S. Escott, January 1902, *CL*2
            p. 253.

274/Ep.   **one:** G.B.S. to Karl Pearson, 20 June 1893 (Pearson Papers,
            UCL).

274/18   **literature:** 'Mr Besant's Literary Paradise: From a Socialist's
            Point of View', *Pall Mall Gazette* XLVI, 12 November 1887,
            p. 3. See *Bernard Shaw's Book Reviews* ... (ed. Brian Tyson
            1991) pp. 355–9.

274/19   **Ida:** See *CP*7 pp. 528–32.

274/27   **comedy:** William Archer's description. *The World* 14
            December 1892, *CP*1 p. 38.

275/ 5   **boyish:** *CP*1 p. 47.

275/16   **Socialism:** G.B.S. to Janet Achurch, 17 June 1889, *CL*1
            p. 216.

275/21   **classes:** *The Fabian Society: What It Has Done* (Fabian Tract no.
            41), August 1892, p. 7.

275/32   **Hooray!:** *Diaries* 1, entry 14 May 1887, p. 269.

276/ 9   **life:** G.B.S. to William Archer, 4 October 1887, *CL*1
            pp. 175–6.

276/19   **out:** 'How William Archer Impressed Bernard Shaw', G.B.S.'s
            Foreword to *Three Plays* by William Archer (1927) p. xiv.
            Reprinted in *Pen Portraits and Reviews* (1931) p. 7.

276/23   **name:** William Archer, 'Ibsen as I Knew Him', *Monthly Review*
            June 1906, p. 14.

276/27   **inventor:** 'The Author's Preface' to 1893 edition of *Widowers'
            Houses*, *CP*1 p. 41.

276/39   **legs:** *CP*1 p. 38.

277/ 6   **socialism:** *Diaries* 1, notes for 1887, 'Habits', p. 228.

277/20   **soon:** G.B.S. gave the manuscript of the novel together with
            this explanatory note to the National Library of Ireland in
            1946. An edition of one thousand copies of *An Unfinished
            Novel*, with an introduction and notes on the text by Stanley
            Weintraub, was published in 1958.

277/23   **with it:** *Diaries* 1, entry 24 December 1890, p. 679.

277/24   **heavy:** G.B.S. to William Sonnenschein, 28 December 1887,
            *CL*1 p. 179.

277/27   **fiction:** G.B.S. to T. Fisher Unwin, 19 November 1888, *CL*1 p. 201.

277/30   **unreal:** G.B.S. to Tighe Hopkins, 31 August 1889, *CL*1 p. 222.

277/34   **of it:** *Diaries* 1, entry 10 September 1888, p. 411.

277/37   **at all:** G.B.S. to Havelock Ellis, 27 September 1888, BL Add. MS 61891L.

278/ 1   **work:** *Diaries* 1, entry 18 December 1888, p. 446.

278/ 5   **postponed:** G.B.S. to Havelock Ellis, 6 February 1889, BL Add. MS 61891L.

278/21   *The Cassone*: See *CP*7 pp. 533–58.

278/31   **considerations:** G.B.S. to Tighe Hopkins, 31 August 1889, *CL*1 p. 222.

278/33   **play:** G.B.S. to Charles Charrington, 28 January 1890, *CL*1 p. 241.

279/ 4   **possible:** G.B.S. to Alma Murray, 24 February 1888, *CL*1 p. 188.

279/10   **dialogue:** From Sydney Olivier to Archibald Henderson, 6 August 1931 (North Carolina).

279/27   **them:** 'Is Mr Buchanan a Critic with a Wooden Head?' *Pall Mall Gazette* XLIX, 13 June 1889, p. 2. See also *Shaw and Ibsen: Bernard Shaw's 'The Quintessence of Ibsenism' and Related Writings* (ed. with an introductory essay by J. L. Wisenthal 1979) pp. 78–80.

279/34   **success:** *CP*7 p. 485.

279/36   **time:** 'Ibsen', *The Clarion* 1 June 1906, p. 5.

279/37   **Road:** 'Build Another Opera House', *The World* 18 March 1891, *SM*2 p. 295.

280/ 2   **gloriously:** Ibid.

280/17   **manager:** Archibald Henderson, *Playboy and Prophet* (1932) pp. 455–6.

280/36   **realism:** G.B.S. to William Archer, 4 October 1887, *CL*1 p. 176.

280/38   **title:** 'Preface: Mainly About Myself', *CP*1 p. 18. See the first edition of *Widowers' Houses* (1893) p. [xxl].

281/ 6   **round it:** G.B.S. to William Archer, 30 December 1916, *CL*3 p. 445.

281/19   **brainpower:** *The World* 4 May 1893.

281/29   *News*: Elinor Huddart to G.B.S., 31 December 1892, BL Add. MS 50537 ff. 152–153v.

281/31   **sensation:** *CP*1 p. 18.

281/31   **playwright:** Ibid.

282/18   **child:** See William Archer notice, *The World* December 1892. *Shaw: The Critical Heritage* (ed. T. F. Evans 1976) p. 51.

282/21   pity: Ibid., p. 54.

282/25   friendliness: G.B.S. to Ben Iden Payne, 8 June 1909,
          Unpublished Letters of George Bernard Shaw, University of
          Buffalo Studies, vol. XVI no. 3 (September 1939) pp. 120–1.

282/32   hands: G.B.S. to Archer, 14 December 1892, *CL*1 p. 373.

282/37   damnation: Matthew 23:14.

282/39   artistically: G.B.S. to R. Golding Bright, 10 June 1896, *CL*1
          p. 632.

283/ 1   lecture: See unsigned notice, *Daily Telegraph* 10 December
          1892. *Shaw: The Critical Heritage* p. 42.

283/ 8   work: Ibid., pp. 55–6.

283/ 9   pamphlet: Charles Morgan, 'Mr Shaw in London, too', *New
          York Times* 12 April 1931.

283/12   art: *CP*1 p. 46.

283/14   London: Ibid.

283/18   rhythm: Margery Morgan, *The Shavian Playground* (1972)
          p. 23.

283/30   Blanche: *CP*1 p. 110.

283/37   creatures: *The Letters of Oscar Wilde* (ed. Rupert Hart-Davis
          1979) p. 112.

284/ 7   footlights: *Shaw: The Critical Heritage* pp. 51–3.

286/13   critics: 'Good Old Don Giovanni', *The Star* 14 June 1889,
          *SM*1 p. 666.

286/29   Philanderer: G.B.S. to Janet Achurch, 10 December 1894,
          BL Add. MS 50561 ff. 51–2.

286/33   foregoing: BL Add. MS 50596.

287/30   crying: See Brian Tyson, 'Shaw's First Discussion Play: An
          Abandoned Act of *The Philanderer*', *Shaw Review* XII,
          September 1969, pp. 90–103.

288/19   stage: G.B.S. to William Archer, 24 January 1900, *CL*2 p. 138.

288/30   away: G.B.S. to Hugo Vallentin, 8 November 1907, *CL*2
          p. 721.

288/33   mad: G.B.S. to Granville Barker, 28 December 1906, *Bernard
          Shaw's Letters to Granville Barker* (1957 edn, New York) p. 73.

288/35   me: G.B.S. to Ellen Terry, 28 August 1896, *CL*1 p. 644 (*A
          Correspondence* p. 42).

289/ 7   eagerly: G.B.S. to Charles Charrington, 6 April 1893 (Texas).

289/18   nowadays: Note by G.B.S. on Henderson manuscript of
          Playboy and Prophet (North Carolina).

289/20   tract: G.B.S. insert on Henderson manuscript of *Playboy and
          Prophet* (North Carolina).

289/22   something: G.B.S. to Archer, 11 May 1893, *CL*1 p. 395.

289/35   account: G.B.S., 'The Root of the White Slave Traffic', *The*

Awakener vol. 1, no. 1, 16 November 1912, pp. 7–8.
Reprinted in *Fabian Feminist: Bernard Shaw and Woman* (ed.
Rodelle Weintraub 1977) p. 256.

290/ 3   **livelihood:** *Cashel Byron's Profession* (Penguin 1979) p. 278.

290/ 6   **conducted:** Morgan, *The Shavian Playground* p. 19.

290/28   **London:** Frederic Whyte, *Life of W. T. Stead* vol. 1 (1925)
p. 175.

290/30   **game:** G.B.S. to Frederic Whyte, 2 July 1922 (Detroit).

291/15   **money:** 'Are Morals Deteriorating?': *Six Questions by Dorothy
Royal Answered by Bernard Shaw*, 10 January 1944. *World
Review* (May 1944) pp. 3–5.

291/17   **prostitution:** Ibid.

291/19   **unemployed:** *Fabian Feminist: Bernard Shaw and Woman*
pp. 7–8.

291/25   **came:** *Diaries* 2, entry 18 August 1893, p. 962.

291/30   **new play:** Ibid., entry 20 August 1893, p. 963.

291/31   **a play:** Ibid., entry 21 August 1893, p. 963.

291/36   **write:** Ibid., entry 22 August 1893, p. 963.

291/38   **mother:** 'Mr Shaw's Method and Secret', *Daily Chronicle* 30
April 1898, p. 3.

291/last   **Unions:** *Diaries* 2, entry 26 August 1893, p. 964.

292/ 6   **T[heatre]:** G.B.S. to William Archer, 30 August 1893, *CL*1
p. 403.

292/ 9   **could:** *Diaries* 2, entry 30 August 1893, p. 965.

292/14   **to be:** 'Mr Shaw's Method and Secret', *Daily Chronicle* 30 April
1898, p. 3.

292/15   **Warren:** Ibid.

292/28   **planned:** G.B.S. to Janet Achurch, *CL*1 p. 404.

293/26   **Rowe:** 'Art Corner', *Our Corner* VII, June 1886, p. 371. See *The
Theatre of Bernard Shaw* (ed. Alan S. Downer, 2 vols 1961).

293/28   **figures:** 'An Old New Play and a New Old One', *Saturday
Review* 23 February 1895, *OTN*1 p. 46.

293/37   **person:** Ibid.

293/last   **morals:** Ibid., pp. 46–7.

294/ 2   **skin:** 'Art Corner', *Our Corner* VII, June 1886, p. 371. See *The
Theatre of Bernard Shaw*.

294/ 2   **rules:** 'The Season's Moral', *Saturday Review* 27 July 1895,
*OTN*1 p. 192.

294/10   **stage:** Martin Meisel, *Shaw and the Nineteenth-Century Theater*
(1963) p. 146.

294/23   **without it:** G.B.S.'s addition to Archibald Henderson's *Playboy
and Prophet* manuscript p. 146 (North Carolina).

294/32   **leaves:** *CP*1 p. 324.

295/ 4 **part of:** *Mrs Warren's Profession* (Garland Facsimile edn 1981) pp. 205–6.

295/23 **creep:** *CP*1 p. 321.

295/25 **disgust:** Ibid., p. 334.

295/28 **difference:** Ibid., p. 339.

295/40 **Ugh!:** G.B.S. to Gertrude Kingston, 16 February 1925 (King's College Library, Cambridge)

296/ 2 **contamination:** J. I. M. Stewart, *Eight Modern Writers* (Oxford History of Modern Literature 1963) p. 132.

296/19 *figures:* *CP*1 p. 356.

296/25 **play:** G.B.S. to Elizabeth Robins, 14 November 1893 (Fales).

296/26 **licensed:** G.B.S. to J. T. Grein, 12 December 1893, *CL*1 p. 413.

296/29 **by me:** G.B.S. to Elizabeth Robins, 14 November 1893 (Fales).

296/30 **ears:** See Archibald Henderson, *George Bernard Shaw: Man of the Century* (1956) pp. 460–1.

296/31 **suicide:** Ibid.

296/32 **mine:** G.B.S. to Elizabeth Robins, 14 November 1893.

296/37 **afternoon:** *Man of the Century* p. 460.

296/38 **late:** *CP*1 p. 366.

297/ 3 **disgrace:** *The New York Dramatic Mirror* 11 November 1905.

297/ 3 **amoral:** See *The Times* 23 February 1955.

297/15 **destiny:** 'A Dramatic Realist to His Critics', *New Review* XI, July 1894, pp. 56–73. See *CP*1 pp. 485–511.

297/Ep.1 **trouble:** *The World Wide News Service Inc.*, Boston, Mass., 16 November 1924.

297/Ep.2 **grown-up:** G.B.S. to Alma Murray, 27 December 1904, *CL*2 p. 473.

298/ 8 **to-day:** *The Star* 14 April 1894, *CP*1 p. 476.

299/ 4 **failure:** G.B.S. to Henry Arthur Jones, 24 December 1894 (Texas), *CL*1 pp. 461–2 (where it is dated 2 December 1894).

299/34 **myself:** Florence Farr to G.B.S., 5 December 1905, BL Add. MS 50533 ff. 103–4.

299/35 **harm:** Annie Horniman to G.B.S., 22 June 1907, BL Add. MS 505387 ff. 7–8.

300/ 1 **ever made:** G.B.S. to Janet Achurch, 2 December 1893, *CL*1 p. 409.

300/ 5 **unwell:** *Diaries* 2, entry 9 January 1894, p. 1005.

300/16 **in it:** G.B.S. to Trebitsch, 16 January 1905, Shaw/Trebitsch letters p. 77.

300/21 **wanted:** *To-Day* 28 April 1894, p. 373.

300/28 **Russian:** G.B.S. to Charles Charrington, n.d. [March 1894] (Texas).

300/29   **name:** *Diaries* 2, entry 17 March 1894, p. 1019.
300/34   **end:** G.B.S. to Charles Charrington, n.d. [March 1894]
          (Texas).
300/38   **time:** Ibid.
300/39   **Bulgaria:** 'G. B. Shaw on Heroes', *Irish Times* 17 February
          1925.
301/ 7   **circumstances:** *Diaries* 2, entry 29 March 1894, p. 1022.
301/15   **part:** W. B. Yeats, *Autobiographies* (1979 edn) p. 281.
301/22   **impossible:** William Archer, *The Theatrical World of 1894*
          (1895) pp. 91–3.
301/32   **steel:** G.B.S. to Elizabeth Robins, 29 March 1894 (Cornell).
301/38   **typewritten:** *Diaries* 2, entry 30 March 1894, p. 1023.
302/ 9   **character:** G.B.S. to A. B. Walkley, 23 April 1894 (Bancroft).
302/10   **itself:** G.B.S. to Alma Murray, 19 February 1901 (Princeton).
302/13   **sight:** G.B.S. to C. M. S. McLellan, 24 October 1894
          (Bucknell).
302/19   **box:** G.B.S. to C. T. H. Helmsley, 17 April 1894, *CL*1 p. 424.
302/21   **lost:** Ibid.
302/22   **Blackheath:** Ibid., p. 425.
302/38   **perpetually:** W. B. Yeats, *Autobiographies* pp. 282–3.
303/ 1   **plausible:** G. K. Chesterton, *George Bernard Shaw* (1949 edn)
          p. 51.
303/ 3   **school:** W. B. Yeats, *Autobiographies* pp. 282–3.
303/ 6   **vintage:** Ibid., p. 283.
303/15   **hand:** 'A Dramatic Realist to His Critics', see *CP*1 p. 508.
303/23   **family:** Ibid.
303/25   **life:** Ibid.
303/39   **detect:** Margery Morgan, *The Shavian Playground* pp. 48–50.
304/18   **affections:** G.B.S. to William Archer, 23 April 1894, *CL*1
          p. 427.
304/22   **voice:** *CP*1 p. 447.
304/23   **believes in it:** Ibid.
304/31   **life:** G.B.S. to C. M. S. McLellan, 24 October 1894
          (Bucknell).
305/ 1   **play:** *Diaries* 2, entry 30 March 1894, p. 1023.
305/ 3   **water:** 'Folkweave Treatment' by Irving Wardle, *The Times* 22
          July 1976.
305/25   **withdraw:** G.B.S. to A. B. Walkley, 23 April 1894 (Bancroft).
305/27   **serious:** *CP*1 p. 460.
305/29   **world:** Ibid., p. 446.
305/30   **machine:** Ibid., p. 460.
305/36   **idiot:** Ibid., p. 469.

305 / last   **laughing:** G.B.S. to Ellen Terry, 21 September 1896, *CL*1
p. 660 (*A Correspondence* p. 72).

306 / 9   **farce:** G.B.S. to Doré Lewin Mannering, 28 June 1912
(Texas).

306 / 12   *cocottes*: G.B.S. to Dr Julio Broutá, 7 February 1911
(Houghton).

306 / 12   **plagiarism:** G.B.S. to John Maxwell, 24 May 1932 (private
collection).

306 / 15   **comedies:** Programme, Lyric Theatre, London 1910.

306 / 23   **successes:** G.B.S. to Edward McNulty, 2 July 1894, *CL*1
p. 447.

306 / 26   **like:** Note on Henderson manuscript (North Carolina).

306 / 38   **criticism:** *Diaries* 2, note for 1894, p. 1003.

307 / 2   **open with:** G.B.S. to C. T. H. Helmsley, 12 July 1894, *CL*1
p. 451.

307 / 8   **at last:** G.B.S. to Edward McNulty, 2 July 1894, *CL*1 p. 448.

307 / Ep.   **conversation:** G.B.S. to Florence Farr, 14 October 1896, *CL*1
p. 679.

307 / 22   **eye:** G.B.S. to Charles Charrington, 20 February 1896, *CL*1
p. 603.

308 / 16   **statute:** G.B.S. to Janet Achurch, 3 May 1895, *CL*1 p. 532.

308 / 33   **idiot-banshee:** G.B.S. to Florence Farr, 6 June 1902, *CL*2
p. 275.

308 / 35   **Emery:** W. B. Yeats to Lady Gregory, n.d., 1902. Josephine
Johnson, *Florence Farr: Bernard Shaw's 'New Woman'* (1975)
p. 107.

308 / 38   **another:** G.B.S. to Florence Farr, 6 June 1902, *CL*2 p. 275.

308 / last   **thing:** *The Letters of W. B. Yeats* (ed. Allan Wade 1954) p. 394.

309 / 6   **wise:** Florence Farr to John Quinn, June 1912 (Berg).

309 / 19   **desperation:** G.B.S. to Florence Farr, 12 October 1896, *CL*1
pp. 674–5.

309 / 34   **religion:** G.B.S. to Janet Achurch, 23 March 1895, *CL*1
p. 504.

309 / last   **opportunities:** G.B.S. to Florence Farr, 14 October 1896,
*CL*1 p. 679.

310 / 3   **emptiness:** G.B.S. to Elizabeth Robins, 29 March 1894
(Cornell).

310 / 11   **at all:** G.B.S. to Jayanta Padmanabha, 4 June 1947, *CL*4 p. 795.

310 / 20   **life:** Ibid.

310 / Ep.   **chastity is:** G.B.S. to Barbara Low, 17 September 1917, BL
RP2299(ii).

311 / 5   **Janet:** G.B.S. to Janet Achurch, 29 January 1896, *CL*1 p. 591.

311 / 29   **pessimism:** See Michael Meyer, *Ibsen* (Pelican edn 1974)
p. 692.

311/32   **theatre:** G.B.S. to Elizabeth Robins, 20 April 1891, *CL*1
          p. 292.
312/10   **time:** Elizabeth Robins to G.B.S., 5 February 1893 (Texas).
312/35   **&c. &c. &c.:** G.B.S. to Elizabeth Robins, 5 February 1893,
          *CL*1 pp. 379–81.
313/ 9   **name:** Elizabeth Robins to G.B.S., 7 January 1895 (Texas).
313/15   **flatter me:** G.B.S. to Elizabeth Robins, 9 November 1891
          (Fales).
313/17   **perambulator:** G.B.S. to Elizabeth Robins, 30 October 1893
          (Fales).
313/18   **into:** G.B.S. to Elizabeth Robins, 4 December 1894 (Fales).
313/24   **content:** G.B.S. to Elizabeth Robins, 29 March 1894
          (Cornell).
313/30   **accessible:** Elizabeth Robins to G.B.S., 20 November 1893
          (Fales).
314/ 2   **of you:** G.B.S. to Elizabeth Robins, 30 October 1893 (Fales).
314/ 5   **frightened you?:** G.B.S. to Elizabeth Robins, 13 February
          1899, *CL*2 p. 78.
314/17   **as yet:** G.B.S. to Janet Achurch, 24 April 1894 (Texas).
314/23   **ruin him:** Ibid.
314/38   **it out:** *CP*1 p. 372.
315/ 9   **hysterical:** G.B.S. to Janet Achurch, 23 March 1895, *CL*1
          p. 506.
315/10   **feeling:** Ibid.
315/11   **unknown:** *CP*1 p. 575.
315/22   **model:** Ibid., p. 603.
316/10   **unspoken:** Margot Peters, *Bernard Shaw and the Actresses*
          (1980) p. 140.
316/12   **instinct:** *CP*1 p. 374.
316/18   **mistakes:** G.B.S. to Osman Edwards, 17 December 1901.
316/25   **intellectually:** G.B.S. to W. T. Stead, 23 January 1905.
316/27   **imagined:** G.B.S. to *Evening Standard*, 28 November 1944,
          *CP*1 p. 603.
316/31   **Mother:** Manuscript of *Candida*, BL Add. MS 50603A f. 3.
          See also facsimile of the holograph manuscript published by
          Garland in 1981.
316/33   **prostitute:** See Ellen Terry to G.B.S., 24 October 1896, *Ellen
          Terry and Bernard Shaw: A Correspondence* (ed. Christopher St
          John 1931) p. 108.
316/35   **more?:** *CP*1 p. 575.
317/ 5   **is not:** G.B.S. to W. T. Stead, 23 January 1905.
317/13   **about 30:** *CP*1 p. 518.
317/19   **can:** Ibid., p. 523.

317/24   **ones:** G.B.S. to James Huneker, 6 April 1904, *CL*2 p. 415.

317/29   **life:** G.B.S. to Eva Christy, n.d., BL Add. MS 50527 f. 50.

317/32   **impatient:** *CP*1 pp. 593–4.

317/36   **world:** G.B.S. to Eva Christy, n.d., BL Add. MS 50527 f. 48.

318/ 2   **religion:** G.B.S. to Janet Achurch, 23 March 1895, *CL*1 p. 506.

318/ 7   **nobler:** *CP*1 p. 594.

318/ 8   **starlight:** G.B.S. to William Archer, 22 May 1904, BL Add. MS 45296 ff. 151–5.

318/ 9   **done:** *CP*1 p. 593.

318/Ep.   **on it:** 'Not Worth Reading', *Saturday Review* 24 April 1897, *OTN*3 p. 114.

319/10   **no Candida:** G.B.S. to Janet Achurch, 13 April 1895, *CL*1 p. 519.

319/31   **uncle:** G.B.S. to Archibald Henderson, 15 March 1909 (North Carolina).

319/36   **advertisement:** G.B.S. to Richard Mansfield, n.d. [October 1894], *CL*1 p. 458.

319/37   **account:** G.B.S. to Elizabeth Marbury, n.d., *CL*1 p. 484. Shaw's diaries record that he received £341-15-2 in 1894 from *Arms and the Man*, £246-5-0 in 1895, £139-10-6 in 1896 and £123-11-9 in 1897.

319/39   **failure:** G.B.S. to Archibald Henderson, 15 March 1909 (North Carolina).

320/12   **piece:** G.B.S. to Richard Mansfield, 22 February 1895, *CL*1 p. 486.

320/16   **fire:** Ibid.

320/22   **yourself:** G.B.S. to Janet Achurch, 3 January 1895 (Texas).

320/30   **drink:** Ibid.

321/11   **sermon:** G.B.S. to Janet Achurch, 8 January 1895 (Texas).

321/21   MANSFIELD: See G.B.S. to Charringtons, 6 March 1895 (Texas).

321/24   **made:** Ibid.

321/32   **parts:** G.B.S. to Richard Mansfield, 16 March 1895, *CL*1 p. 498.

321/last   **trumpet:** Ibid.

322/ 3   **artist:** G.B.S. to Janet Achurch, 23 March 1895, *CL*1 p. 507.

322/11   **to do:** G.B.S. to Janet Achurch, 20 March 1895, *CL*1 p. 503.

322/16   **wig:** Ibid., p. 502.

322/19   **wife:** G.B.S. to Janet Achurch, 23 March 1895, *CL*1 p. 505.

322/24   **please her:** G.B.S. to Richard Mansfield, 27 March 1895, *CL*1 p. 508.

322/32   **qualities:** Richard Mansfield to G.B.S., n.d. [April 1895], *CL*1 p. 523.

322/34   **talk-talk-talk:** Ibid.
323/ 3   **fruit?:** Ibid.
323/ 7   **from you:** Ibid., p. 524.
323/18   **chins:** Ibid.
323/27   **indiscreet:** Ibid., p. 522.
323/last   **conquers:** G.B.S. to Janet Achurch, 3 April 1895, *CL*1 p. 514.
324/ 9   **comes?:** G.B.S. to Janet Achurch, 5 April 1895, *CL*1 p. 515.
324/11   *me:* Ibid.
324/18   **wave:** Ibid., p. 517.
324/24   **unchanged:** G.B.S. to Richard Mansfield, 19 April 1895, BL
                Add. MS 50543 f. 70.
324/26   **senses:** G.B.S. to Beatrice Mansfield, 1 January 1898
                (Philadelphia).
324/28   **pleasanter:** G.B.S. to Beatrice Mansfield, 19 March 1898
                (Philadelphia).
324/31   *me:* G.B.S. to Richard Mansfield, 16 July 1898 (Philadelphia).
324/35   **consequences:** G.B.S. to Beatrice Mansfield, 1 January 1898
                (Philadelphia).
325/ 1   **New York:** G.B.S. to Charles Charrington, 16 April 1895, *CL*1
                p. 519.

CHAPTER VI

326/Ep.   **gallery:** Dan Rider, *Adventures with Bernard Shaw* (1929) p. 22.
326/10   **imagination:** *Evening News* 8 July 1885.
326/12   **hideous:** Ibid.
326/27   **scholar:** Frank Harris, *My Life and Loves* (Grove Press edn
                1964) p. 573.
327/10   **lamentable:** Frank Harris, *Contemporary Portraits* (1915) p. 73.
327/19   **Fortnightly:** Frank Harris to G.B.S., 11 November 1891, BL
                Add. MS 45296 f. 39.
327/25   **anathema:** *My Life and Loves* p. 639.
327/28   **men:** Philippa Pullar, *Frank Harris* (1975) p. 154.
327/29   **life:** *My Life and Loves* p. 639.
327/31   **Desborough:** Ibid., p. 640.
328/ 7   **column:** 'Sardoodledom', *Saturday Review* 1 June 1895, *OTN*1
                p. 139.
328/12   **Shaw:** *My Life and Loves* p. 703.
328/21   **decisive:** Frank Harris, *Bernard Shaw* (1931) p. 126.
328/25   **him:** *SSS* p. 69.
328/35   **income:** G.B.S. to Edward McNulty, 2 July 1894, *CL*1 p. 448.
328/36   **inducement:** G.B.S. to W. T. Stead, 8 July 1894, *CL*1 p. 451.

329/ 6   **days:** *SSS* p. 69.

329/ 7   **theatre:** G.B.S. to McNulty, 2 July 1894, *CL*1 p. 448.

329/14   **[k]ill them:** G.B.S. to Janet Achurch, 6 January 1891 (Texas).

329/18   **people:** 'The Case for the Critic-Dramatist', *Saturday Review* 16 November 1895, *OTN*1 p. 246.

329/35   **incorruptible:** Ibid., pp. 247–8.

329/37   **criticship:** G.B.S. to Janet Achurch, 27 December 1894 (Texas).

329/last   **Harris:** *Diaries* 2, notes for 1895, p. 1059.

330/21   **activity:** 'Slaves of the Ring', *Saturday Review* 5 January 1895, *OTN*1 pp. 1–4.

330/Ep. 1   **none:** 'Mr William Archer's Criticisms', *Saturday Review* 13 April 1895, *OTN*1 p. 91.

330/Ep. 2   **door:** 'Toujours Shakespear', *Saturday Review* 5 December 1896, *OTN*2 pp. 267–8.

330/Ep. 3   **unfortunately:** 'Mrs Tanqueray Plays the Piano', *The World* 20 December 1893, *SM*3 pp. 67–74.

331/ 9   **seats:** 'The Independent Theatre Repents', *Saturday Review* 23 March 1895, *OTN*1 p. 68.

331/25   **house:** 'Vegetarian and Arboreal', *Saturday Review* 30 October 1897, *OTN*3 p. 229.

331/35   **propriety:** 'Mr Arthur Roberts as a Gentleman', *Saturday Review* 9 March 1895, *OTN*1 p. 58.

331/39   **tried to:** 'Plays That Are No Plays', *Saturday Review* 5 October 1895 *OTN*1 p. 205.

332/ 2   **theatre:** 'Alexander the Great', *Saturday Review* 12 June 1897, *OTN*3 p. 162.

332/ 6   **public:** 'Two Bad Plays', *Saturday Review* 20 April 1895, *OTN*1 p. 94.

332/13   **from:** 'Two Plays', *Saturday Review* 8 June 1895, *OTN*1 p. 142.

332/20   **crimes:** 'Told You So', *Saturday Review* 7 December 1895, *OTN*1 pp. 266–7.

332/26   **covered up:** 'The Living Pictures', *Saturday Review* 6 April 1895, *OTN*1 p. 86.

332/33   **over:** 'The Two Latest Comedies', *Saturday Review* 18 May 1895, *OTN*1 p. 123.

332/last   **fellow-creatures:** 'Gallery Rowdyism', *Saturday Review* 6 March 1897, *OTN*3 p. 68.

333/ 8   **himself:** 'Two Bad Plays', *Saturday Review* 20 April 1895, *OTN*1 p. 94.

333/10   **please it:** Ibid.

333/12   **to him:** 'Told You So', *Saturday Review* 7 December 1895, *OTN*1 p. 267.

333/20   **popularity:** 'Mr Bancroft's Pilgrimage', *Saturday Review* 19 December 1896, *OTN*2 p. 284.

333/27   **public:** 'The Natural and the Stage Villain', *Saturday Review* 12 March 1898, *OTN*3 p. 335.

333/30   **existence:** Ibid.

333/36   **dare do:** 'The Late Censor', *Saturday Review* 2 March 1895, *OTN*1 p. 48.

334/13   **was:** Ibid., pp. 49–54.

334/15   **man:** G.B.S. to Charles Charrington, 1 March 1895, *CL*1 p. 489.

334/20   **balderdash:** 'The Late Censor', *Saturday Review* 2 March 1895, *OTN*1 p. 53.

334/23   **Charles I:** Ibid., p. 50.

334/29   **abortion:** 'A Purified Play', *Saturday Review* 16 February 1895, *OTN*1 p. 37.

335/ 7   **Palace:** 'The Censorship of the Stage in England', *North American Review* CLXIX, August 1889, pp. 251–62. See *Shaw on Theatre* (ed. E. J. West 1958) p. 66.

335/10   **parentage:** 'Nietzsche in English', *Saturday Review* 11 April 1896, *OTN*2 p. 96.

335/14   **authors:** 'The Censorship of the Stage in England', *North American Review* CLXIX, August 1899, pp. 251–62. See *Shaw on Theatre* pp. 66–80.

335/17   **wield:** 'Mr Heinemann and the Censor', *Saturday Review* 2 April 1898, *OTN*3 p. 348.

335/24   **Ages:** 'The Author's Apology' (1906) *OTN*1 p. vi.

335/30   **years:** 'Michael and His Lost Angel', *Saturday Review* 18 January 1896, p. 18, *OTN*2 pp. 14–21.

335/last   **art:** 'The Drama Purified', *Saturday Review* 23 April 1898, *OTN*3 p. 367.

336/ 5   **co-operation:** 'Hamlet Revisited', *Saturday Review* 18 December 1897, *OTN*3 pp. 273–4.

336/26   **play:** 'More Masterpieces', *Saturday Review* 26 October 1895, *OTN*1 p. 228.

336/31   **vile:** 'A Purified Play', *Saturday Review* 16 February 1895, *OTN*1 pp. 36–7.

337/ 9   **Impossibilists:** 'The Independent Theatre', *Saturday Review* 26 January 1895, *OTN*1 p. 19.

337/16   **Club:** 'Mr Daly Fossilizes', *Saturday Review* 29 June 1895, *OTN*1 p. 168.

337/26   **public:** 'The Old Acting and the New', *Saturday Review* 14 December 1895, *OTN*1 p. 274.

337/34   *nos jours*: G.B.S. to Ellen Terry, 8 September 1897, *CL*1

p. 801. See *Ellen Terry and Bernard Shaw: A Correspondence* (ed. Christopher St John 1931) p. 253.

338/ 4   **literature:** 'Mr Heinemann and the Censor', *Saturday Review* 2 April 1898, *OTN*3 p. 347.

338/ 9   **characters:** 'An Old New Play and a New Old One', *Saturday Review* 23 February 1895, *OTN*1 p. 46.

338/13   **them:** Ibid., p. 47.

338/16   **consequences:** 'Mr Pinero's New Play', *Saturday Review* 16 March 1895, *OTN*1 p. 63.

338/18   **really is:** 'Pinero As He Is Acted', *Saturday Review* 19 October 1895, *OTN*1 p. 218.

338/22   **generation:** 'Michael and His Lost Angel', *Saturday Review* 18 January 1896, *OTN*2 p. 15.

338/31   **theatre:** 'Quickwit on Blockhead', *Saturday Review* 5 June 1897, *OTN*3 p. 156.

339/ 5   **misrepresented:** 'At Several Theatres', *Saturday Review* 9 October 1897, *OTN*3 p. 212.

339/13   **cry:** 'Michael and His Lost Angel', *Saturday Review* 18 January 1896, *OTN*2 p. 17.

339/16   **pygmies:** 'At Several Theatres', *Saturday Review* 9 October 1897, *OTN*3 p. 211.

339/26   **style:** 'The Season's Moral', *Saturday Review* 27 July 1895, *OTN*1 pp. 192–3.

339/last   **nobody:** 'The Theatres', *Saturday Review* 16 October 1897, *OTN*3 p. 218.

340/ 5   **ease:** 'The Independent Theatre Repents', *Saturday Review* 23 March 1895, *OTN*1 p. 66.

340/15   **integrity:** 'Ibsen Ahead!', *Saturday Review* 7 November 1896, *OTN*2 p. 237.

340/21   **circumstances:** *Shaw on Theatre* pp. 60–5.

340/29   **ventilated:** Ibid., p. 60.

340/38   **streets:** 'Chin Chon Chino', *Saturday Review* 6 November 1897, *OTN*3 pp. 236–7.

341/ 7   **nature:** 'Told You So', *Saturday Review* 7 December 1895, *OTN*1 p. 265.

341/16   **graves:** 'Romance in its Last Ditch', *Saturday Review* 23 October 1897, *OTN*3 p. 225.

341/24   **me:** 'Some Other Critics', *Saturday Review* 20 June 1896, *OTN*2 p. 161.

341/33   **work:** Ibid.

341/35   **manner:** Ibid., p. 162.

341/last   **disliked:** Ibid.

342/Ep.1   **else:** G.B.S. to Janet Achurch, 30 March 1895, *CL*1 p. 511.

342/Ep.2   **mankind:** 'The Season's Moral', *Saturday Review* 27 July 1895, *OTN*1 p. 196.

342/10   **educated:** 'The New Century Theatre', *Saturday Review* 10 April 1897, *OTN*3 p. 102.

342/12   **tramways:** 'Mr Bancroft's Pilgrimage', *Saturday Review* 19 December 1896, *OTN*2 p. 282.

342/28   **world:** 'Satan Saved at Last', *Saturday Review* 16 January 1897, *OTN*3 pp. 16–17.

343/12   **thought:** *CP*1 p. 249.

343/20   **dynamics:** Martin Meisel, *Shaw and the Nineteenth-Century Theater* (1963) p. 46.

343/26   **stage:** 'The Independent Theatre Repents', *Saturday Review* 23 March 1895, *OTN*1 p. 71.

343/27   **conciseness:** 'The Red Robe', *Saturday Review* 24 October 1896, *OTN*2 p. 226.

343/34   **'Bonco':** ' "Macbeth" at the Olympic', *Pall Mall Gazette* XLIV, 9 September 1886, p. 4.

344/ 2   **Juliet:** 'Henry IV', *Saturday Review* 16 May 1896, *OTN*2 p. 131.

344/ 4   **teetotaller:** 'Plays of the Week', *Saturday Review* 11 January 1896, *OTN*2 p. 11.

344/10   **behaved:** 'Romeo and Juliet', *Saturday Review* 28 September 1895, *OTN*1 p. 201.

344/22   **memory:** 'Mr John Hare', *Saturday Review* 21 December 1895, *OTN*1 p. 281.

344/27   **depths:** 'Romeo and Juliet', *Saturday Review* 28 September 1895, *OTN*1 p. 202.

344/36   **here:** 'The New Magdalen and the Old', *Saturday Review* 2 November 1895, *OTN*1 p. 233.

344/39   **herself:** 'The Immortal William', *Saturday Review* 2 May 1896, *OTN*2 p. 111.

344/last   **intelligence:** 'Mr Bancroft's Pilgrimage', *Saturday Review* 19 December 1896, *OTN*2 p. 283.

345/ 1   **us:** 'Sardoodledom', *Saturday Review* 1 June 1895, *OTN*1 p. 138.

345/ 6   **action:** 'La Princesse Lointaine', *Saturday Review* 22 June 1895, *OTN*1 p. 161.

345/10   **stage:** Ibid.

345/16   **them:** 'At Several Theatres', *Saturday Review* 9 October 1897, *OTN*3 p. 210.

345/17   **humanity:** 'Duse and Bernhardt', *Saturday Review* 15 June 1895, *OTN*1 p. 150.

345/19   **themselves:** 'Toujours Daly', *Saturday Review* 13 July 1895, *OTN*1 p. 183.

345/22   **gifts:** 'The New Magda and the New Cyprienne', *Saturday Review* 6 June 1896, *OTN*2 p. 146.

345/38   **ladies:** 'Two Plays', *Saturday Review* 8 June 1895, *OTN*1 p. 146.

346/ 6   **envied:** See *Shaw on Theatre* p. 52.

346/14   **partial:** 'Mr John Hare', *Saturday Review* 21 December 1895, *OTN*1 p. 282.

346/23   **delightfully:** 'Kate Terry', *Saturday Review* 30 April 1898, *OTN*3 p. 372.

346/39   **piffling:** 'Mr John Hare', *Saturday Review* 21 December 1895, *OTN*1 p. 282.

346/last   **conquered:** G.B.S.'s Preface to *A Correspondence* p. xxxii.

347/ 8   **to go:** Ellen Terry to G.B.S., 7 December 1896, *A Correspondence* p. 137.

347/19   **needed me:** Marguerite Steen, *A Pride of Terrys* (1962) p. 185.

347/24   **for gentlemen:** 'King Arthur', *Saturday Review* 19 January 1895, *OTN*1 p. 17.

347/27   **respecting her:** 'Blaming the Bard', *Saturday Review* 26 September 1896, *OTN*2 p. 201.

347/29   **humanity:** *CP*2 p. 331.

347/35   **Act:** 'Two Plays', *Saturday Review* 8 June 1895, *OTN*1 p. 145.

347/37   **woman:** Shaw's Preface to *A Correspondence* p. xiv.

347/38   **New Woman:** 'Mr Grundy's Improvements on Dumas', *Saturday Review* 17 July 1897, *OTN*3 p. 193.

347/last   **than I:** G.B.S.'s Preface to *A Correspondence* p. xiii.

348/ 1   **goddesslike:** Ibid., p. xiv.

348/ 4   **Strindberg:** Ibid., pp. xiii–xiv.

348/ 5   **insufferable:** Ibid., p. xiv.

348/10   **talent:** 'Mr Grundy's Improvements on Dumas', *Saturday Review* 17 July 1897, *OTN*3 p. 193.

348/18   **lady:** G.B.S. to Ellen Terry, 1 November 1895, *CL*1 p. 565 (*A Correspondence* p. 19).

348/20   **sounds:** Ellen Terry to G.B.S., 18 November 1895, *A Correspondence* p. 19.

348/22   **sample:** G.B.S. to Ellen Terry, 28 November 1895, *CL*1 p. 572 (*A Correspondence* p. 20).

348/23   **Ellen:** G.B.S. to Bertha Newcombe, 31 March 1896, *CL*1 p. 620.

348/29   **adorations:** Ibid.

348/29   **audacities:** Ibid.

348/30   **safe:** G.B.S. to Edith Evans, 8 August 1935 (copy Society of Authors).

348/31   **fear:** *CP*1 p. 630.

348/38 **love:** Preface to *A Correspondence* pp. xlv–xlvi.

349/ 4 **play:** G.B.S. to Janet Achurch, 8 July 1895, *CL*1 p. 539.

349/10 **nights:** G.B.S. to Ellen Terry, 28 August 1896, *CL*1 p. 645.

349/14 **lance:** Richard Mansfield to G.B.S., April 1895, *CL*1 p. 524.

349/19 **pantaloon:** G.B.S. to Janet Achurch, 24 August 1895, *CL*1 p. 546.

349/21 **descended:** G.B.S. to Janet Achurch, 31 August 1895, *CL*1 p. 553.

349/23 **ignorance:** G.B.S. to T. Fisher Unwin, 27 August 1895, *CL*1 p. 552.

349/35 **exhibition:** G.B.S. to Richard Mansfield, 8 September 1897, BL Add. MS 50543 ff. 84v–87v. See *CL*1 p. 803.

350/ 3 **Sans-Gêne:** G.B.S. to Janet Achurch, 8 July 1895, *CL*1 p. 539.

350/ 3 **thing:** G.B.S. to John Martin-Harvey, 1 May 1911 (Houghton).

350/ 4 **length:** G.B.S. to Madge McIntosh, 22 October 1902 (Princeton).

350/ 7 **bill:** G.B.S. to John Martin-Harvey, 1 May 1911 (Houghton).

350/10 **business:** G.B.S. to Ellen Terry, 9 March 1896, *CL*1 p. 610 (*A Correspondence* p. 22).

350/13 **Delicious:** Ellen Terry to G.B.S., n.d. [c. November 1895], *A Correspondence* p. 19.

350/22 **beauty:** *CP*1 pp. 622–3.

350/32 **finely:** G.B.S. to Ellen Terry, 9 March 1896, *CL*1 p. 609 (*A Correspondence* p. 21).

350/35 **to it:** G.B.S. to Ellen Terry, 9 March 1896, *CL*1 pp. 609–10 (*A Correspondence* p. 22).

350/39 **left:** Ibid.

350/40 **simple?:** G.B.S. to Ellen Terry, 6 April 1896, *CL*1 p. 622 (*A Correspondence* p. 27).

351/ 1 **incorruptible:** Vide supra, reference p. 329/35.

351/ 3 **brutality:** G.B.S. to Ellen Terry, 6 April 1896, *CL*1 p. 623 (*A Correspondence* p. 29).

351/14 **patrons:** 'Build Another Opera House', *The World* 18 March 1891, *SM*2 p. 294.

351/17 **for him:** G.B.S. to Laurence Irving, 28 November 1946, *CL*4 p. 787.

351/19 **for me:** Laurence Irving, *Henry Irving: The Actor and his World* (1951) p. 174.

351/22 **astonish us:** 'Mainly About Shakespear', *Saturday Review* 29 May 1897, *OTN*3 p. 145.

351/26 **in me:** G.B.S. to Laurence Irving, n.d. (Theatre Museum, Victoria and Albert Museum).

351 / 27   **couple:** Ibid.

351 / 29   **day:** G.B.S. to Laurence Irving, 28 November 1946, *CL*4 p. 787.

351 / 33   **rant:** Ibid.

352 / 9   **behind:** 'The Old Acting and the New', *Saturday Review* 14 December 1895, *OTN*1 p. 273.

352 / 20   **accomplished:** 'Mainly About Shakespear', *Saturday Review* 29 May 1897, *OTN*3 p. 145.

352 / 27   **accomplishment:** Ibid., p. 146.

352 / 35   **for him!:** Ibid.

352 / last   **dramas:** 'Madame Sans-Gêne', *Saturday Review* 17 April 1897, *OTN*3 p. 110.

353 / 7   **to him:** G.B.S. to Laurence Irving, n.d. (Theatre Museum, Victoria and Albert Museum).

353 / 8   **in them:** G.B.S. to Laurence Irving, 12 March 1948 (private collection).

353 / 22   **people:** G.B.S. to Laurence Irving, 18 January 1949, *CL*4 p. 838.

353 / 24   **shelf:** G.B.S. to Ellen Terry, 6 April 1896, *CL*1 p. 622 (*A Correspondence* p. 27).

353 / 33   **buy it:** Ellen Terry to G.B.S., 9 July 1896, *A Correspondence* p. 33.

353 / 36   **fortunate:** G.B.S. to Henry Irving, 12 July 1896 (Texas).

353 / 37   **Miss T's:** Ibid.

353 / last   **occasion:** Ibid.

354 / 2   **terms:** Ibid.

354 / 5   **reasonable:** G.B.S. to Henry Irving, 17 July 1896 (Texas).

354 / 8   **position:** Ibid.

354 / 15   **superfluous:** Ibid.

354 / 29   **time:** G.B.S. to Henry Irving, 23 September 1896, *CL*1 p. 667.

355 / 2   **himself:** 'Blaming the Bard', *Saturday Review* 26 September 1896, *OTN*2 p. 198.

355 / 17   **flesh:** Ellen Terry to G.B.S., 23 September 1896, *A Correspondence* p. 76.

355 / 19   **in that:** G.B.S. to Ellen Terry, 25 September 1896, *A Correspondence* p. 82.

355 / 22   **I am:** Ellen Terry to G.B.S., 23 September 1896, *A Correspondence* p. 77.

355 / 25   **bodyless:** Ellen Terry to G.B.S., 24 September 1896, *A Correspondence* p. 80.

355 / 26   **one!:** Ellen Terry to G.B.S., 7 September 1896, *A Correspondence* p. 52.

355 / 27   **way:** G.B.S. to Ellen Terry, 8 September 1896, *CL*1 p. 651 (*A Correspondence* p. 53).

355/29   **beard:** G.B.S. to Ellen Terry, 6 April 1896, *CL*1 p.623 (*A Correspondence* p.29).

355/32   **laughing:** Ellen Terry to G.B.S., 1 December 1896, *A Correspondence* p.132.

355/33   **with me:** Ellen Terry to G.B.S., 18 September 1896, *A Correspondence* p.67.

355/34   **unfulfilment:** G.B.S. to Ellen Terry, 5 November 1896, *CL*1 p.695 (*A Correspondence* p.118).

356/ 1   **rapture:** G.B.S. to Ellen Terry, 21 September 1896, *CL*1 p.659 (*A Correspondence* p.71).

356/ 5   **meeting:** G.B.S. to Ellen Terry, 2 October 1896, *CL*1 p.672 (*A Correspondence* p.88).

356/ 7   **meet:** Ellen Terry to G.B.S., 19 October 1896, *A Correspondence* p.107.

356/ 8   **tenderness:** G.B.S. to Ellen Terry, 14 June 1897, *CL*1 p.775 (*A Correspondence* p.216).

356/ 9   **you:** G.B.S. to Ellen Terry, 8 December 1896, *CL*1 p.712 (*A Correspondence* p.141).

356/11   **arm:** Ellen Terry to G.B.S., 26 March 1897, *A Correspondence* p.172.

356/14   **don't:** G.B.S. to Ellen Terry, 16 April 1897, *CL*1 p.746 (*A Correspondence* pp.186–7).

356/16   **of business:** G.B.S. to Ellen Terry, 9 March 1896, *CL*1 p.610 (*A Correspondence* pp.22–3).

356/17   **on business:** Ellen Terry to G.B.S., 3 October 1896, *A Correspondence* p.89.

356/24   **copy:** Ellen Terry to G.B.S., 10 October 1896, *A Correspondence* p.94.

356/29   **come:** Ellen Terry to G.B.S., 28 October 1896, *A Correspondence* p.112.

356/31   **G.B.S:** G.B.S. to Ellen Terry, 10 April 1897, *CL*1 p.742 (*A Correspondence* p.178).

356/35   **asleep:** G.B.S. to Ellen Terry, 13 March 1897, *CL*1 p.735 (*A Correspondence* p.170).

356/37   **deaf?:** G.B.S. to Ellen Terry, 26 March 1896, *CL*1 p.617 (*A Correspondence* pp.25–6).

356/39   **moment?:** G.B.S. to Ellen Terry, 6 April 1896, *CL*1 p.622 (*A Correspondence* p.28).

356/last **met?:** G.B.S. to Ellen Terry, 2 October 1896, *CL*1 p.672 (*A Correspondence* p.88).

357/ 5   **much:** *Memoirs* by Ellen Terry (ed. Edith Craig and Christopher St John 1933) pp.268–70.

357/ 9   **for him:** Margot Peters, *Bernard Shaw and the Actresses* (1980) p.167.

357/17   **work**: G.B.S. to Robert Buchanan, n.d., 1895, *CL*1 p. 585.

357/27   **soul**: G.B.S. to H. B. Irving, 10 November 1905 (Theatre Museum, Victoria and Albert Museum).

357/35   **favorites**: 'Why Not Sir Henry Irving?', *Saturday Review* 9 February 1895, *OTN*1 p. 31.

358/ 3   **ridiculous**: 'Shakespear in Manchester', *Saturday Review* 20 March 1897, *OTN*3 p. 75.

358/ 8   **fustian**: 'Why Not Sir Henry Irving?', *Saturday Review* 9 February 1895, *OTN*1 p. 34.

358/10   **aberration**: 'The Shooting Star Season', *Saturday Review* 10 July 1897, *OTN*3 p. 185.

358/20   **mistaken**: 'Olivia', *Saturday Review* 6 February 1897, *OTN*3 pp. 39–40.

358/24   **literature**: G.B.S. to Ellen Terry, 6 September 1896, *CL*1 p. 650 (*A Correspondence* p. 51).

358/31   **genius**: 'On Pleasure Bent', *Saturday Review* 20 November 1897, *OTN*3 p. 253.

358/32   **lip-honor**: Ibid.

358/36   **volcano**: 'Olivia', *Saturday Review* 6 February 1897, *OTN*3 p. 38.

358/last   **consequence**: 'Quickwit on Blockhead', *Saturday Review* 5 June 1897, *OTN*3 p. 154.

359/16   **eminence**: *CP*7 p. 469.

359/32   **ends**: Ibid., pp. 476–7.

359/36   **Swan**: 'Hamlet', *Saturday Review* 2 October 1897, *OTN*3 p. 207.

360/ 4   **against his**: 'Blaming the Bard', *Saturday Review* 26 September 1896, *OTN*2 p. 195.

360/ 7   **Board**: 'Tappertit on Caesar', *Saturday Review* 29 January 1898, *OTN*3 p. 298.

360/10   **susceptibility**: Hilary Spurling, 'The Critic's Critic', in *The Genius of Shaw* (ed. Michael Holroyd 1979) p. 138.

360/15   **feeling**: Ibid.

360/36   **in me**: 'Mr Irving Takes Paregoric', *Saturday Review* 11 May 1895, *OTN*1 pp. 113–15.

361/ 6   **heartlessness**: G.B.S. to Ellen Terry, 7 March 1897, *CL*1 p. 732 (*A Correspondence* p. 165).

361/13   **honor**: G.B.S. to Ellen Terry, 16 April 1897, *CL*1 p. 745 (*A Correspondence* p. 185).

361/16   **failure**: G.B.S. to Ellen Terry, 28 August 1896, *CL*1 p. 645 (*A Correspondence* p. 43).

361/34   **speed**: G.B.S. to Ellen Terry, 17 April 1897, *CL*1 p. 747 (*A Correspondence* p. 190).

361/35 **chuckle:** Ibid.

361/38 **win:** Ellen Terry to G.B.S., April 1897, *A Correspondence* p. 190.

362/ 9 **then:** Ibid., pp. 190–1.

362/20 **standing by:** G.B.S. to Ellen Terry, 21 April 1897, *CL1* p. 748 (*A Correspondence* pp. 191–2).

362/28 **us:** Ibid.

362/37 **artificially:** Ellen Terry to G.B.S., 22 April 1897, *A Correspondence* p. 193.

363/15 **scenes:** 'Richard Himself Again', *Saturday Review* 26 December 1896, *OTN2* pp. 290–1.

363/20 **absence:** Laurence Irving, *Henry Irving: The Actor and his World* (1951) p. 601.

363/38 **present:** *Glasgow Herald* 4 May 1897.

363/last **swear:** G.B.S. to R. Golding Bright, 7 May 1897, *CL1* p. 753.

364/ 7 **unhappiness:** Ellen Terry to G.B.S., April 1897, *A Correspondence* p. 191.

364/10 **happen:** G.B.S. to Ellen Terry, 21 April 1897, *CL1* pp. 748–9 (*A Correspondence* pp. 191–3).

364/15 **thing:** G.B.S. to Henry Irving, 29 April 1897, *CL1* p. 751.

364/21 **pen:** Laurence Irving, *The Actor and his World* p. 604.

364/26 **been:** G.B.S. to R. Golding Bright, 7 May 1897, *CL1* pp. 754–5.

364/32 **happen?:** G.B.S. to Ellen Terry, 4 May 1897, *CL1* p. 752 (*A Correspondence* p. 196).

365/ 3 **know:** G.B.S. to Sir Henry Irving, 10 May 1897, *CL1* p. 756.

365/11 **tussle:** G.B.S. to Ellen Terry, 11 May 1897, *CL1* p. 759 (*A Correspondence* p. 198).

365/16 **patiently:** G.B.S. to Ellen Terry, 11 May 1897, *CL1* pp. 759–60 (*A Correspondence* pp. 197–8).

365/21 **hopeless:** Ellen Terry to G.B.S., 22 April 1897, *A Correspondence* p. 194.

365/27 **self-assertion:** G.B.S. narrative, *A Correspondence* p. 189.

365/33 **bit:** Ellen Terry to G.B.S., 9 May 1897, *A Correspondence* p. 196.

365/last **know it:** Ellen Terry to G.B.S., 11 May 1897, *A Correspondence* pp. 199–200.

366/12 **beaten:** G.B.S. to Ellen Terry, 12 May 1897, *CL1* p. 760 (*A Correspondence* p. 201).

366/15 ***that*:** G.B.S. to Ellen Terry, 16 May 1897, *CL1* p. 763 (*A Correspondence* p. 205).

366/16 **people:** Ibid.

366/21 **might do:** G.B.S. to Ellen Terry, 12 May 1897, *CL1* pp. 760–1 (*A Correspondence* p. 201).

366/23   **teacup:** G.B.S. to Sir Henry Irving, 10 May 1897, *CL*1 p. 756.

366/34   **Ellen:** G.B.S. to Ellen Terry, 12 May 1897, *CL*1 p. 761 (*A Correspondence* p. 203).

366/last   **himself:** G.B.S. to Ellen Terry, 13 May 1897, *CL*1 p. 762 (*A Correspondence* p. 204).

367/ 7   **Destiny:** G.B.S. to Ellen Terry, 12 May 1897, *CL*1 p. 761 (*A Correspondence* p. 203).

367/11   **genius:** *CP*1 p. 663.

367/17   **won't:** G.B.S. to Ellen Terry, 13 May 1897, *CL*1 p. 762 (*A Correspondence* pp. 203–4).

367/25   **Henry!:** Ellen Terry to G.B.S., 25 May 1897, *A Correspondence* p. 209.

367/33   **with you:** Ellen Terry to G.B.S., n.d. [between 13 and 16 May 1897], *A Correspondence* p. 205.

367/37   **proceed:** G.B.S. to Ellen Terry, 28 August 1896, *CL*1 p. 646 (*A Correspondence* p. 44).

368/ 2   **ways:** Ellen Terry to G.B.S., n.d. [between 13 and 16 May 1897], *A Correspondence* p. 205.

368/ 6   **by you:** Ellen Terry to G.B.S., 31 May 1899, *A Correspondence* p. 324.

368/11   **lightning:** G.B.S. to Ellen Terry, 16 May 1897, *CL*1 pp. 763–4 (*A Correspondence* p. 206).

368/15   **absurd:** Ellen Terry to G.B.S., 3 July 1897, *A Correspondence* p. 224.

368/16   **alerts me:** Ellen Terry to G.B.S., 27 September 1897, *A Correspondence* p. 258.

368/18   **this:** Ellen Terry to G.B.S., 20 October 1897, *A Correspondence* p. 263.

368/20   **passed:** Ellen Terry to G.B.S., 29 May 1897, *A Correspondence* p. 212.

368/23   **them:** Ellen Terry to G.B.S., 25 May 1897, *A Correspondence* p. 209.

368/27   **to me:** Ellen Terry to G.B.S., 3 July 1897, *A Correspondence* p. 224.

369/12   **say:** G.B.S. to Ellen Terry, 14 June 1897, *CL*1 p. 775 (*A Correspondence* p. 217).

369/21   **else:** Ellen Terry to G.B.S., 29 May 1897, *A Correspondence* p. 212.

369/24   **oh no:** Ellen Terry to G.B.S., 17 October 1897, *A Correspondence* p. 261.

369/26   **him:** G.B.S. to Ellen Terry, 13 May 1897, *CL*1 p. 763 (*A Correspondence* p. 204).

369/Ep.   **anti-climax:** G.B.S. to Janet Achurch, 29 January 1896, *CL*1 p. 591.

370/ 7 **tigress:** 'The New Magdalen and the Old', *Saturday Review* 2 November 1895, *OTN*1 p. 234.

370/ 7 **victim:** Ibid.

370/ 8 **possess:** Ibid., p. 232.

370/ 19 **appalled us:** Ibid., pp. 233–5.

370/ 32 **Play:** G.B.S. to Ellen Terry, n.d. [c. 20–26 August 1896], *CL*1 p. 641 (*A Correspondence* p. 37).

370/ 37 **result:** G.B.S. to Janet Achurch, 30 October 1895 (Texas).

370/ last *overdo* it: Ellen Terry to G.B.S., 7 December 1896, *A Correspondence* p. 137.

371/ 9 **Charringtons:** *Diaries* 2, notes for 1895, pp. 1059–60.

371/ 15 **languages:** G.B.S. to Sydney Cockerell, 24 June 1895, *CL*1 p. 539.

371/ 34 **himself:** Bertha Newcombe, 'Memories of Janet Achurch', April 1928, BL Add. MS 50532 ff. 307–9. The evening was on 30 December 1895.

372/ 5 **hovis:** G.B.S. to Janet Achurch, 23 December 1895, *CL*1 pp. 581–4.

372/ 12 **same:** G.B.S. to Janet Achurch, 24 May 1895, *CL*1 pp. 534–8.

372/ 14 **yourself:** Ibid.

372/ 33 **Heinemann:** G.B.S. to Charles Charrington, 27 February 1896 (Texas).

372/ 37 **voice:** G.B.S. to William Heinemann, 18 February 1896, *CL*1 p. 600.

373/ 1 **position:** G.B.S. to Heinemann, 24 February 1896 (Texas).

373/ 7 **on it:** G.B.S. to Janet Achurch, 14 April 1896, *CL*1 p. 625.

373/ 25 **suddenness:** Ibid.

373/ 32 **incontinence:** Ibid.

373/ last: **mother:** G.B.S. to Ellen Terry, 12 October 1896, *CL*1 p. 677 (*A Correspondence* p. 98).

374/ 9 **Limited:** G.B.S. to Janet Achurch, 30 October 1896, *CL*1 p. 687.

374/ 24 **extraordinary:** 'Little Eyolf', *Saturday Review* 28 November 1896, *OTN*2 p. 260.

374/ 27 **disappointingly:** Ibid., p. 262.

374/ 29 **domestic:** Ibid.

375/ 2 **audience:** Ibid., p. 260.

375/ 31 **genius:** Ibid., pp. 261–3.

375/ 33 **Goodbye:** Ellen Terry to G.B.S., 28 October 1896, *A Correspondence* p. 112.

375/ 37 **fleet?:** G.B.S. to Janet Achurch, 30 October 1896, *CL*1 p. 687.

376/ 2 **baby-play:** 'The New Magda and the New Cyprienne', *Saturday Review* 6 June 1896, *OTN*2 p. 148.

376/ 8   **speculation:** 'Ibsen Without Tears', *Saturday Review* 12 December 1896, *OTN*2 p. 271.

376/17   **circumstances:** G.B.S. to Ellen Terry, 5 December 1896, *CL*1 p. 708.

376/21   **enemy:** G.B.S. to Charlotte Payne-Townshend, 5 December 1896, *CL*1 p. 709.

376/23   **effect:** 'Ibsen Without Tears', *Saturday Review* 12 December 1896, *OTN*2 p. 276.

377/ 3   **souls:** Ibid., pp. 272–4.

377/ 9   **organization:** Ibid., p. 278.

377/18   **clever:** Ellen Terry to G.B.S., 7 December 1896, *A Correspondence* p. 137.

377/21   **rampage:** G.B.S. to Charles Charrington, 18 March 1897 (Texas).

377/22   **fat:** 'Shakespear in Manchester', *Saturday Review* 20 March 1897, *OTN*3 p. 81.

377/30   **with:** G.B.S. to Ellen Terry, 28 May 1897, *CL*1 p. 770 (*A Correspondence* p. 211).

377/last   **end:** 'Shakespear in Manchester', *Saturday Review* 20 March 1897, *OTN*3 pp. 77–83.

378/25   **us:** 'A Doll's House Again', *Saturday Review* 15 May 1897, *OTN*3 p. 133.

379/ 2   **dramatically:** Ibid., pp. 129–32.

379/24   **in it?:** 'Ibsen Triumphant', *Saturday Review* 22 May 1897, *OTN*3 pp. 139–40.

379/31   **pioneer:** 'The New Ibsen Play', *Saturday Review* 30 January 1897, *OTN*3 p. 34.

379/33   **anything:** 'The New Century Theatre', *Saturday Review* 10 April 1897, *OTN*3 p. 101.

380/13   **Charrington:** Ibid., pp. 101–2.

380/16   **woman:** G.B.S. to Janet Achurch, 24 May 1895, *CL*1 p. 536.

380/23   **you!:** G.B.S. to Janet Achurch, 20 May 1897, *CL*1 pp. 765–6.

380/26   **dislike me:** G.B.S. to Ellen Terry, 14 July 1897, *CL*1 p. 783 (*A Correspondence* p. 232).

380/28   **hands:** 'Ghosts at the Jubilee', *Saturday Review* 3 July 1897, *OTN*3 p. 179.

380/30   **dog:** G.B.S. to Ellen Terry, 14 July 1897, *CL*1 p. 782 (*A Correspondence* p. 231).

380/37   **come:** G.B.S. to Ellen Terry, 14 July 1897, *CL*1 pp. 782–3 (*A Correspondence* p. 231).

381/10   **mother:** Margot Peters, *Bernard Shaw and the Actresses* (1980) p. 186.

381/16   **string:** Ibid., p. 187.

381 / 21   **sweetheart-Mother:** Holograph, British Library, n.d. [11 November 1896]. *Shaw and the Actresses* p. 192; see also p. 430 n. 22.

381 / 31   **in it:** Ellen Terry to G.B.S., 19 October 1896, *A Correspondence* p. 107.

381 / 32   **heart:** G.B.S. to Janet Achurch, 23 July 1897, *CL*1 p. 787.

382 / 4   **efficiently:** *Northern Figaro* 7 August 1897.

382 / 18   **Ellen:** G.B.S. to Ellen Terry, 4 July 1897, *CL*1 pp. 778–9 (*A Correspondence* pp. 225–6).

382 / 22   **it all:** Ellen Terry to G.B.S., 30 August 1897, *A Correspondence* p. 248.

382 / 24   **over:** Ibid., p. 249.

382 / 26   **face it:** G.B.S. to Janet Achurch, 1 November 1897, *CL*1 p. 820.

382 / 32   **would:** G.B.S. to Janet Achurch, 4 August 1897 (Texas).

382 / 34   **vacuum:** G.B.S. to Janet Achurch, 29 May 1897, *CL*1 p. 771.

382 / 35   **London:** Ellen Terry to G.B.S., 4 September 1897, *A Correspondence* p. 250.

382 / last   **play:** G.B.S. to Charrington, undated fragment (Texas).

383 / 2   **successfully:** G.B.S. to Ellen Terry, 10 July 1900, *CL*2 p. 178 (*A Correspondence* p. 381).

383 / 4   **parson:** G.B.S. to Ellen Terry, 8 November 1900, *CL*2 p. 198 (*A Correspondence* p. 389).

383 / 18   **farewell:** G.B.S. to Janet Achurch, 9 December 1897, *CL*1 p. 828.

383 / Ep.   **performed:** *CP*1 p. 666.

383 / last   **tom-cat:** R. F. Rattray, *Bernard Shaw: A Chronicle* (1951) p. 116n.

384 / 11   **drama:** *CP*1 p. 376.

384 / 18   **in one:** Charles Archer, *William Archer: Life, Work and Friendships* (1931) p. 295.

384 / 21   **sorrow:** *CP*1 p. 694.

384 / 29   **I can:** Allan Chappelow, *Shaw the Villager and Human Being* (1961) p. 218.

384 / 30   **plays:** G.B.S. to Eric Walter White, 2 July 1944 (privately owned).

385 / 5   **outburst:** 'An Old New Play and a New Old One', *Saturday Review* 23 February 1895, *OTN*1 pp. 42–3.

385 / 16   **alone:** George Shaw to Lucinda Shaw, 17 July 1857, BL Add. MS 50508 ff. 1–2v.

385 / 38   **George-Eliotism:** G.B.S. to Harley Granville Barker, 6 December 1904, *CL*2 p. 471 (Shaw / Barker letters p. 45).

386 / 11   **voice:** *CP*1 p. 691.

386/13   **mother:** G.B.S. to William Archer, 22 May 1904, BL Add. MS 45296 ff. 151–5.

386/17   **affections:** *CP*1 pp. 679–80.

386/20   **her youth:** Ibid., p. 680.

386/20   **creature:** Ibid., p. 669.

386/22   **prepossessing youth:** Ibid., pp. 672–3.

386/34   **die:** Ibid., p. 793.

386/35   **wisdom!:** Ibid.

387/18   **described:** *You Never Can Tell* (Garland facsimile edn 1981) pp. 180–8.

387/26   **since:** G.B.S. to Janet Achurch, 9 December 1897, *CL*1 p. 828.

387/29   **pieces:** *CP*1 pp. 761–2.

388/ 2   **Limited:** G.B.S. to Janet Achurch, 30 October 1896, *CL*1 p. 687.

388/12   **tell:** *CP*1 p. 794.

388/15   **coming:** G.B.S. to Janet Achurch, 8 July 1895, *CL*1 p. 539.

388/17   **life:** G.B.S. to Janet Achurch, 23 December 1895, *CL*1 p. 583.

388/21   **happy:** G.B.S. to Janet Achurch, 14 April 1896, *CL*1 p. 624.

388/23   **stage:** G.B.S. to Edward Carpenter, 19 August 1896, *CL*1 p. 640.

388/24   **brilliant:** 'The Red Robe', *Saturday Review* 24 October 1896, *OTN*2 p. 222.

388/26   **with it:** G.B.S. to Ellen Terry, 8 September 1896, *CL*1 p. 653 (*A Correspondence* p. 57).

388/31   **fatuity:** 'The Red Robe', *Saturday Review* 24 October 1896, *OTN*2 p. 222.

388/39   **again:** G.B.S. to Ellen Terry, 5 November 1896, *CL*1 p. 695 (*A Correspondence* p. 119).

389/ 2   **comedian:** G.B.S. to Beatrice Mansfield, 8 January 1897, *CL*1 p. 718.

389/ 7   **performance:** G.B.S. to Ellen Terry, n.d. [assigned to 1 March 1897], *CL*1 p. 728 (*A Correspondence* p. 158).

389/ 9   **hour:** G.B.S. to Ellen Terry, 9 April 1897, *CL*1 p. 740 (*A Correspondence*, p. 175).

389/12   **sufferings:** G.B.S. to Ellen Terry, 12 and 21 April 1897, *CL*1 pp. 743, 749 (*A Correspondence* pp. 181, 193).

389/16   **exits:** G.B.S. to William Archer, 14 December 1924, *CL*3 p. 893.

389/18   **before:** *CP*1 p. 802.

389/23   **try:** G.B.S. to Archer, 14 December 1924, *CL*3 p. 892.

389/25   **whole:** Ibid.

390/ 8   **humanity:** Ibid., p. 893.

390/17   **play:** Frederick Harrison to G.B.S., 18 May 1897. See *Shaw:*

An Exhibit (University of Texas at Austin 1977), item no. 234.

390/31 **available:** G.B.S. to Beatrice Mansfield, 21 October 1899 (Philadelphia).

390/32 **sepulchre:** G.B.S. to Henry Arthur Jones, 23 August 1899. See *Shaw: An Exhibit*, item no. 237 (Texas).

390/34 **death:** G.B.S. to Florence Farr, 8 September 1897, *CL*1 pp. 799–800.

390/36 ***nos jours:*** G.B.S. to Ellen Terry, 8 September 1897, *CL*1 p. 801 (*A Correspondence* p. 253).

390/last **pantomime:** George Moore to Frank Harris, n.d. See *Moore versus Harris* (privately printed, Chicago 1925) p. 18.

391/3 **soul:** G.B.S. to Beatrice Mansfield, 12 June 1900, *CL*2 p. 173.

391/6 **with them:** G.B.S. to Yorke Stephens, 21 May 1900, *CL*2 p. 166.

391/11 **money-maker:** G.B.S. to Lady Gregory, 4 May 1917 (Cornell).

391/29 **efforts:** *CP*1 pp. 98–9.

391/37 **deserted him:** Ibid., p. 801.

392/11 **blame him:** Ibid., pp. 802–3.

392/21 **issue:** Harrison to G.B.S., 18 May 1897. See *Shaw: An Exhibit*, item no. 234 (Texas).

392/32 **seriously:** *Shaw: The Critical Heritage* (ed. T. F. Evans 1976) p. 84.

392/35 **comedy:** G.B.S. to R. G. Walford, n.d. (BBC, Caversham).

393/10 **situation:** 'The Devil's Disciple'. Holograph dated Malvern, 18 August 1930 (Boston). Written for the 1930 production starring John Martin-Harvey, Edmund Gwenn and Margaret Webster.

393/26 **lines:** Ibid.

393/35 **force:** G.B.S. to Janet Achurch, 14 April 1896, *CL*1 p. 625.

393/37 **14/4/96:** See BL Add. MS 50606 A–D.

393/last **Irvingism:** G.B.S. to John Martin-Harvey, 4 November 1933 (Houghton).

394/9 **to A:** *The Devil's Disciple* (Garland facsimile edn 1981) p. 2.

394/17 **at work:** G.B.S. to Ellen Terry, 16 October 1896, *CL*1 p. 680 (*A Correspondence* p. 103).

394/28 **centuries:** 'Two Bad Plays', *Saturday Review* 20 April 1895, *OTN*1 p. 93.

394/31 **Macbeth:** G.B.S. to Ellen Terry, 26 March 1896, *CL*1 p. 617 (*A Correspondence* p. 25).

394/last **restaurant:** Preface to *Three Plays for Puritans*, *CP*2 p. 31.

395/8 **effect:** G.B.S. to Ellen Terry, 30 November 1896, *CL*1 pp. 705–6 (*A Correspondence* pp. 129–31).

395/13   **play:** G.B.S. to Hesketh Pearson, 25 October 1918 (Texas).

395/23   **black:** G.B.S. to Theatre Guild, n.d. (Yale).

395/23   **interest:** *CP*2 p. 113.

395/31   **gallows:** Ibid.

395/last   **moments:** G.B.S. to Mrs O'Byrne, 14 October 1909 (Harvard Theater Collection).

396/ 2   **melodrama:** *CP*2 p. 32.

396/ 3   **day:** Ibid.

396/10   **part:** G.B.S. to Beatrice Mansfield, 8 January 1897, *CL*1 p. 717.

396/14   **copied:** See Gerald Howson, *Burgoyne of Saratoga* (1979) pp. xvii, 299–300. 'The germ of the play was probably suggested to Shaw by the Jane McCrae affair. She, a Tory going to meet her fiancé in Burgoyne's army, was shot in error by an Indian who thought he had been sent to get her scalp. Her father was a clergyman; her aunt was a Tory, but her brother was a colonel in the rebel militia...'

396/18   **usual:** *CP*2 p. 131.

396/26   **Puritanism:** Ibid., p. 53.

396/27   **in it:** Ibid., p. 32.

397/10   **Disciple:** 'The Devil's Disciple'. Holograph dated Malvern 18 August 1930 (Boston). See also G.B.S. to Hesketh Pearson, 25 October 1918 (Texas).

397/16   **concerned:** G.B.S. to Ellen Terry, 13 March 1897, *CL*1 p. 735 (*A Correspondence* p. 170).

397/21   **newspapers:** G.B.S. to Ellen Terry, 24 December 1897, *CL*1 p. 831 (*A Correspondence* p. 274).

397/23   **sympathy:** G.B.S. to Charles Charrington, 7 March 1898, *CL*2 p. 12.

397/27   **here:** G.B.S. to Beatrice Mansfield, 1 January 1898 (Philadelphia).

397/31   **of it?:** *CP*2 p. 12.

397/36   **success:** G.B.S. to Charles Charrington, 19 February 1896, *CL*1 p. 604.

398/ 8   **disappointed:** *CP*2 p. 36.

398/22   **now:** G.B.S. to Janet Achurch, 14 April 1896, *CL*1 p. 627.

398/last   **artist:** G.B.S. to Siegfried Trebitsch, 16 October 1902, Shaw/Trebitsch letters p. 23.

399/ 3   **theatre:** G.B.S. to R. Golding Bright, 7 May 1897, *CL*1 p. 754.

399/ 9   **them:** G.B.S. to Frederick Evans, 14 August 1895, *CL*1 p. 543.

399/12   **copies!:** G.B.S. to John Lane, 16 April 1894, *CL*1 p. 424.

399/17   **Farr?:** Ibid., p. 423.

399/39   **copy:** G.B.S. to Frederic Whyte, 11 April 1928 (Detroit).

400/15   **work:** G.B.S. to T. Fisher Unwin, 22 April 1891, *CL*1 p. 293.

400/25   **speculation:** G.B.S. to T. Fisher Unwin, 9 September 1895, *CL*1 pp. 556–7.

400/29   **reads plays?:** Ibid., p. 557.

400/33   **Cameo:** G.B.S. to T. Fisher Unwin, 11 February 1896, *CL*1 p. 595.

400/37   **new plays:** G.B.S. to T. Fisher Unwin, 16 February 1896, *CL*1 p. 598.

401/ 1   **extraordinary:** Grant Richards, *Author Hunting* (1960 edn) p. 29.

401/ 2   **read plays:** G.B.S. to Grant Richards, 8 November 1896, *CL*1 p. 698.

401/ 3   **G.B.S:** *Author Hunting* p. 28.

401/21   **presence:** G.B.S. to Ellen Terry, 13 March 1897, *CL*1 p. 736 (*A Correspondence* p. 171).

401/28   **profanation:** G.B.S. to Janet Achurch, 23 December 1895, *CL*1 p. 583.

401/30   **heard of:** G.B.S. to Grant Richards, 12 March 1899 (Texas). See also BL Add. MS 50561 f. 130.

401/32   **life:** Richards to G.B.S., 22 May 1897 (Berg).

401/33   **villain:** G.B.S. to Samuel Butler, 24 March 1901, *CL*2 p. 224.

401/36   **Literature:** G.B.S. to Grant Richards, 23 May 1934 (Texas).

401/38   **somehow:** G.B.S. to Frederick Whelen, 24 December 1899 (Texas).

402/ 2   **affairs:** *Author Hunting* p. 105.

402/ 6   **circumstances:** G.B.S. to Richards, 17 January 1905 (Texas).

402/ 7   **judgment:** G.B.S. to Richards, 25 September 1897, *CL*1 p. 808.

402/14   **seasons:** G.B.S. to Richards, 24 September 1897.

402/26   **terms:** G.B.S. to Robert Buchanan, n.d. [late 1895], *CL*1 pp. 584–5.

402/28   **production:** G.B.S. to Grant Richards, 28 August 1897, *CL*1 p. 799.

402/31   **mind:** G.B.S. to Grant Richards, 8 October 1897, *CL*1 p. 811.

402/33   **suicidal:** Ibid.

402/last   **teetotaller:** Archibald Henderson, *Playboy and Prophet* (1932) p. 277.

403/ 2   **used:** G.B.S. to Holbrook Jackson, 29 July 1907 (Texas).

403/10   **novel:** G.B.S. to Grant Richards, 26 August 1897, *CL*1 p. 798.

403/30   **sense:** G.B.S. to Nugent Monck, 16 April 1924 (privately owned).

403/32   **plays:** G.B.S. to George Sylvester Viereck, 2 June 1926 (Cornell).

403/37   **embroidered:** 'Shaw Looks at Life at 70'. Interview by G. S. Viereck, 1927 (Holograph, Cornell) extensively revised by G.B.S. In *Liberty* IV, 13 August 1927, pp. 7–10. Also in *London Magazine* LIX, December 1927, pp. 615–23.

403/last   **lunch:** G.B.S. to Ellen Terry, 9 April 1897, *CL1* p. 740 (*A Correspondence* p. 175).

404/4   **falling:** G.B.S. to Ellen Terry, 5 August 1897, *CL1* p. 791 (*A Correspondence* p. 244).

404/5   **calls:** G.B.S. to Henry Lowenfeld, 1 December 1897, *CL1* p. 825.

404/8   **stop:** G.B.S. to Ellen Terry, 5 January 1898, *CL2* p. 8 (*A Correspondence* p. 287).

404/16   **myself?:** *CP2* p. 29.

404/24   **rich:** *Author Hunting* p. 115.

404/34   **contumely:** See St John Ervine, *Bernard Shaw: His Life, Work and Friends* (1956) pp. 329–30.

404/37   **audience:** Doris Arthur Jones, *The Life and Letters of Henry Arthur Jones* (1930) p. 348.

405/15   **theatre:** Max Beerbohm, *More Theatres* (1969) pp. 25–6.

405/19   **Max:** 'Valedictory', *Saturday Review* 21 May 1898, *OTN3* p. 386.

405/22   **bags:** Philippa Pullar, *Frank Harris* (1975) p. 161.

405/30   **rigging:** Max Beerbohm to G.B.S., 12 February 1914, BL Add. MS 50529 ff. 38–40.

405/32   **Shelley:** G.B.S. to Archibald Henderson, 29 August 1925 (North Carolina).

405/37   **directions:** G.B.S. to Hesketh Pearson, 7 September 1916 (Cornell).

406/8   **liar:** G.B.S. to Hesketh Pearson, 22 December 1916 (Cornell).

406/11   **understand it:** G.B.S. to Lord Alfred Douglas, 21 January 1942, *Bernard Shaw and Alfred Douglas: A Correspondence* (ed. Mary Hyde 1982) p. 151.

406/15   **impossible:** G.B.S. to Lord Alfred Douglas, 18 April 1938, ibid., p. 30.

406/last   **him:** G.B.S. to Hugh Kingsmill, 16 June 1932 (copy privately owned).

407/1   **furious:** G.B.S. to Hesketh Pearson, 22 December 1916 (Cornell).

407/5   **left:** G.B.S. to Douglas, 19 July 1938, *Bernard Shaw and Alfred Douglas: A Correspondence* p. 70.

407/16   **self:** Hesketh Pearson, *The Life of Oscar Wilde* (1975 edn) p. 385.

407/24   **talk:** *Diaries* 2, notes for 1895, p. 1060.

407/31   **again:** Ibid.
407/34   **articles:** Philippa Pullar, *Frank Harris* p. 187.
408/24   **am I:** 'Valedictory', *Saturday Review* 21 May 1898, *OTN*3 pp. 384–6.

CHAPTER VII

409/Ep. 1   **in it:** Ellen Terry to G.B.S., 29 May 1897, *Ellen Terry and Bernard Shaw: A Correspondence* (ed. Christopher St John 1931) p. 212.
409/Ep. 2   **councillor:** *New York Times* 24 March 1933, p. 20.
409/16   **accordingly:** G.B.S. to Frank R. Lewis, n.d. (shorthand version, University of Bath. Transcript at Texas).
410/ 4   **advisable:** Henry Hunt Hutchinson's last will and testament.
410/ 9   ***thinking:*** Beatrice Webb, *Our Partnership* (1948) pp. 85–6.
410/14   **vans:** G.B.S. note to F. E. Loewenstein for letter to A. W. Morledge-Hadfield, November 1949 (Texas).
410/20   **blow:** G.B.S. to Sidney Webb, 28 September 1894. See Sidney Caine, *The History of the Foundation of the London School of Economics & Political Science* (1963).
411/ 6   **bequests:** Ibid.
411/ 9   **Socialism:** Ibid.
411/18   **scientific:** *Our Partnership* p. 92.
411/22   **done:** G.B.S. to Frank R. Lewis, op.cit.
412/31   **claim me:** G.B.S. to John Burns, 28 May 1897, *CL*1 p. 768.
412/35   **folly:** G.B.S. to Ellen Terry, 28 May 1897, *CL*1 p. 770 (*A Correspondence* p. 211).
412/40   **will be!:** G.B.S. to John Burns, 28 May 1897, *CL*1 p. 769.
413/11   **ill-fame:** Preface, 'Memories of Early Years', to E. W. Walters, *Ensor Walters and the London He Loves* (1937) p. 9.
413/17   **slums:** See *St Pancras Journal* vol. 1, no. 1, May 1947, p. 4.
413/31   **minimum:** *Ensor Walters and the London He Loves* p. 9.
413/39   **changed:** *IWG* (Penguin 1965) p. 365.
414/ 5   **socialized:** G.B.S. to Hannen Swaffer, 7 August 1936 (see Sotheby's Catalogue, 24 July 1979, item 274).
414/20   **better:** *Ensor Walters and the London He Loves* pp. 10–12.
414/28   **vote:** *IWG* p. 365.
414/37   **jury:** G.B.S. to Pakenham Beatty, 3 December 1894, *CL*1 p. 467.
415/16   **views:** *EPWW* pp. 270–1.
415/27   **respected:** H. M. Geduld, 'Bernard Shaw, Vestryman and Borough Councillor', *The California Shavian* vol. 3, no. 3, May–June 1962.

415/36   **idleness:** G.B.S. to J. E. Brydone, 23 February 1904 (Cornell).

416/25   **enormous:** G.B.S. to R. Golding Bright, 2 November 1900, *CL*2 p. 191.

416/26   **labor:** G.B.S. to Ellen Terry, 3 November 1900, *CL*2 p. 192 (*A Correspondence* p. 386).

417/13   **present:** 'The Unmentionable Case for Women's Suffrage', *Englishwoman* March 1909 (reprinted in *Bernard Shaw Practical Politics* ed. Lloyd J. Hubenka 1976, pp. 101–8).

417/36   **deputation:** *St Pancras Gazette* 8 September 1900, p. 5.

417/last   **tactics:** G.B.S. to J. H. Cripps-Day, 3 February 1903 (privately owned).

418/24   **Vestry:** *St Pancras Gazette* 10 November 1900, p. 5.

418/32   **Mayor:** Ibid., 1 December 1900, p. 5.

419/ 2   **afford it:** Ibid., 1 August 1903, p. 5.

419/12   **boxes:** Ibid., 9 February 1901, p. 5.

419/29   **anyone (laughter):** Ibid., 13 October 1902, p. 5.

419/34   **to have:** Ibid.

420/ 3   **attention:** *CP*1 p. 267.

420/23   **calculations:** G.B.S. to Dr Collins, 3 November 1901 (Sotheby's Catalogue, 21 February 1978, item 438).

420/31   **subject:** *EPWW* p. 239.

421/ 3   **for him:** 'Socialism and Medicine', *Platform and Pulpit* (ed. with an Introduction by Dan H. Laurence 1962) p. 59.

421/ 8   **excluded:** *Vaccination Inquirer* 2 December 1901, p. 167.

421/16   **parallel:** *St Pancras Gazette* 28 September 1901, p. 5.

421/20   **Council:** *Doctors' Delusions* (1931) p. 1.

421/24   **Press:** 'Smallpox in St Pancras', *The Times* 21 September 1901, p. 12.

421/29   **evidence:** *EPWW* p. 240.

421/33   **electioneers:** 'Mr Bernard Shaw on Small-Pox Prevention', *British Medical Journal* 26 October 1901, p. 1289.

421/34   **vaccination:** *St Pancras Gazette* 28 September 1901, p. 5.

421/35   **murder:** *Shaw: An Exhibit*, A Catalog by Dan H. Laurence for an Exhibit Selected and Prepared by Lois B. Garcia (University of Texas at Austin 1977), item no. 160. ·

422/ 2   **at all:** *British Medical Journal* 25 October 1901, p. 1290.

422/17   **meeting:** *Shaw: An Exhibit*, item no. 159 (Texas).

422/31   **present:** G.B.S. to J. H. Cripps-Day, 7 July 1903 (privately owned).

422/35   **theatres:** G.B.S. to Ellen Terry, 28 May 1897, *CL*1 p. 770 (*A Correspondence* p. 210).

422/38   **exasperation:** G.B.S. to Charlotte Payne-Townshend, 16 March 1898, *CL*2 p. 16.

423/ 1   **respectability:** Ibid.

423/ 8   **contrary:** BL Add. MS 50550.

423/26   **manners:** *CP*1 p. 269.

423/20   **inhabitants:** G.B.S. to Frederick Sinclair, 22 September 1938 (Camden Public Library).

423/35   **&c, &c, &c:** G.B.S. to Archibald Henderson, 30 June 1904, *CL*2 p. 426.

424/10   **Trading:** G.B.S. to W. B. Yeats, 23 June 1903 (copy privately owned).

424/22   **foxhounds:** *St Pancras Municipal Journal* (undated item, Camden Public Library).

424/30   **work:** Preface to *Ensor Walters and the London He Loves* p. 12.

425/34   **applause:** 'Mr Bernard Shaw's Last Words', *St Pancras Gazette* 15 November 1902, p. 5.

426/Ep.   **know:** *The Diary of Beatrice Webb* vol. 2 (ed. Norman and Jeanne MacKenzie 1983), entry 8 May 1897, p. 114.

426/24   **thought:** Ibid., entry 25 September 1895, p. 82.

426/last   **plays:** 'The History of a Happy Marriage', *The Times Literary Supplement* 20 October 1945, p. 493. See also BL Add. MS 50699.

427/ 2   **unhappiness:** G.B.S. to Janet Achurch, 31 August 1895, *CL*1 p. 554.

427/26   **inartistic:** See Janet Dunbar, *Mrs G.B.S.: A Biographical Portrait of Charlotte Shaw* (1963) p. 135.

428/12   **mind:** BL Add. MS 50532 f. 307.

428/21   **half-conscious:** Ibid., f. 311.

428/last   **endearments:** Ibid., f. 310.

429/21   **brokenheartedness:** G.B.S. to Janet Achurch, 24 August 1895, *CL*1 p. 547.

429/22   **hers:** G.B.S. to Charles Charrington, 20 July 1918, *CL*3 p. 559.

429/28   **forgotten you:** G.B.S. to Bertha Newcombe, 31 March 1896, *CL*1 p. 618.

430/15   **death:** *The Diary of Beatrice Webb* vol. 2, entry 9 March 1897, p. 111.

430/28   **ashamed?:** G.B.S. to Bertha Newcombe, 9 June 1909, *CL*2 p. 846.

430/38   **grievance:** Margot Peters, *Bernard Shaw and the Actresses* (1980) p. 316.

431/ 6   **patience:** G.B.S. to Charles Charrington, 17 July 1918, *CL*3 p. 555.

431/14   **of me:** G.B.S. to Bertha Newcombe, 16 April 1922 (Texas).

431/19   **letters:** Ibid.

431/24   **grievance:** G.B.S. to Beatrice Webb, 29 December 1918 (LSE).

432 / 10   **pain:** Beatrice Webb, *Our Partnership* p. 90.

432 / 25   **part:** G.B.S.'s answer to Demetrius O'Bolger questionnaire, 12 April 1916 (Houghton).

432 / 29   **furniture:** Ibid.

432 / 39   **possible:** Ibid.

433 / 2   **uneasy:** *The Diary of Beatrice Webb* vol. 2, entry 16 September 1896, p. 101.

433 / 3   **youth:** Charlotte Shaw to T. E. Lawrence, 17 May 1927, BL Add. MS 45922 f. 68.

433 / 6   **patience:** Ibid.

433 / 12   **action:** Janet Dunbar, *Mrs G.B.S.* p. 57.

433 / 18   **home:** Charlotte Shaw to T. E. Lawrence, 17 May 1927, BL Add. MS 45922 f. 68.

433 / 24   **enough:** Ibid.

433 / last   **marry:** Ibid.

434 / 9   **call her:** G.B.S. to Ellen Terry, 28 August 1896, *CL*1 p. 645 (*A Correspondence* p. 44).

434 / 27   **killing her:** Charlotte Shaw to T. E. Lawrence, 17 May 1927, BL Add. MS 45922 f. 70.

434 / 39   **tendencies:** *The Diary of Beatrice Webb* vol. 2, entry 16 September 1896, p. 101.

435 / 17   **St Andrew:** G.B.S. to Janet Achurch, 7 September 1896 (Texas).

435 / 22   **money:** G.B.S. to Ellen Terry, 12 October 1896, *CL*1 p. 676 (*A Correspondence* p. 98).

435 / 25   **after me:** G.B.S. to Ellen Terry, 28 August 1896, *CL*1 pp. 645–6 (*A Correspondence* p. 44).

435 / 29   *love* **me:** G.B.S. to Ellen Terry, 5 November 1896, *CL*1 p. 695 (*A Correspondence* p. 119).

435 / 38   **do it:** Ibid., *CL*1 pp. 695–6 (*A Correspondence* p. 119).

436 / 2   **grateful:** G.B.S. to Charlotte Payne-Townshend, 17 November 1896, *CL*1 p. 703.

436 / 7   **consequences:** *The Diary of Beatrice Webb* vol. 2, p. 101.

436 / 16   **bed!:** G.B.S. to Charlotte Payne-Townshend, 21 September 1896, *CL*1 p. 660.

436 / 22   **train:** G.B.S. to Charlotte Payne-Townshend, n.d. [possibly 21 September 1896 or April or May 1897], *CL*1 p. 657.

436 / 31   **dearest!:** G.B.S. to Charlotte Payne-Townshend, 7 November 1896, *CL*1 p. 697.

436 / 37   **arms:** G.B.S. to Charlotte Payne-Townshend, 27 October 1896, *CL*1 p. 686.

437 / 2   **hills:** G.B.S. to Charlotte Payne-Townshend, 2 and 4 November 1896, *CL*1 689, 691.

437/ 5   **writing:** G.B.S. to Charlotte Payne-Townshend, 21 and 27 October 1896, 2 November 1896, *CL*1 pp. 682, 686, 689.

437/29   **villainy:** G.B.S. to Charlotte Payne-Townshend, 9 November 1896, *CL*1 p. 699.

437/35   **heart:** G.B.S. to Charlotte Payne-Townshend, 10 November 1896, *CL*1 p. 700.

437/39   **greediness:** Ibid.

438/ 1   **maid:** G.B.S. to Ellen Terry, 5 November 1896, *CL*1 p. 695. This passage was omitted from *A Correspondence.*

438/ 8   **off:** G.B.S. to Ellen Terry, 16 November 1896, *CL*1 p. 702 (*A Correspondence* p. 126).

438/11   **use me:** G.B.S. to Ellen Terry, 12 October 1896, *CL*1 p. 676 (*A Correspondence* p. 97).

438/13   **depths:** G.B.S. to Charlotte Payne-Townshend, 17 November 1896, *CL*1 p. 703.

138/17   **made:** Ibid.

438/24   **nervously:** Ibid.

438/27   **maternity:** G.B.S.'s answer to O'Bolger questionnaire, 12 April 1916 (Houghton).

438/28   **breeding:** Ibid.

438/34   **TIMES:** G.B.S. to Charlotte Payne-Townshend, 17 October 1896, *CL*1 p. 681.

438/39   **mad:** G.B.S. to Janet Achurch, 30 October 1896, *CL*1 p. 687.

438/last   **freedom?:** G.B.S. to Charlotte Payne-Townshend, 16 and 18 November 1896, *CL*1 pp. 700–1, 704.

439/ 3   **dictation:** G.B.S.'s answer to O'Bolger questionnaire, 12 April 1916 (Houghton).

439/ 5   **for me:** Ibid.

439/12   **friends:** Ibid.

439/17   **baby:** G.B.S. to Charlotte Payne-Townshend, 11 January 1897, *CL*1 p. 719.

439/31   **can be:** *The Diary of Beatrice Webb* vol. 2, entry 1 May 1897, p. 112.

440/20   **friendship:** Ibid., pp. 112–13.

440/22   **shop:** G.B.S. to Ellen Terry, 28 May 1897, *CL* p. 771 (*A Correspondence* p. 211).

440/27   **look:** *The Diary of Beatrice Webb* vol. 2, entry 8 May 1897, p. 115.

440/33   **for her:** Beatrice Webb diaries p. 1491 (LSE).

441/ 3   **situation?:** G.B.S. to Ellen Terry, 8 March 1897, *CL*1 p. 733. This passage was omitted from *A Correspondence.*

441/ 8   **endowment:** G.B.S.'s answer to O'Bolger questionnaire, 12 April 1916, p. 2 (Houghton).

441/12 **marriage:** G.B.S. to Ellen Terry, 2 June 1897, *CL*1 p. 777 (*A Correspondence* p. 208).

441/25 **conventionality:** G.B.S.'s answer to O'Bolger questionnaire, 12 April 1916 (Houghton).

441/35 **met:** G.B.S. to Ellen Terry, 24 May 1897, *CL*1 pp. 767, 768 (*A Correspondence* p. 208).

442/ 4 **for me:** G.B.S. to Ellen Terry, 5 August 1897, *CL*1 p. 792. This passage was omitted from *A Correspondence*.

442/ 6 **Australia:** Ibid.

442/22 **wrong:** G.B.S. to Charlotte Payne-Townshend, 13 July 1897, *CL*1 pp. 783–4.

443/13 **rooms:** G.B.S. to Ellen Terry, 11 July 1897, *CL*1 p. 783 (*A Correspondence* p. 231).

443/19 **marry:** Ellen Terry to G.B.S., 19 June 1897, *A Correspondence* p. 220.

443/21 **blessing:** G.B.S. to Charlotte Payne-Townshend, 21 July 1897, *CL*1 p. 787.

443/29 **Friday:** G.B.S. to Ellen Terry, 27 July 1897, *CL*1 p. 790 (*A Correspondence* p. 240).

443/34 **round:** G.B.S. to Ellen Terry, 8 September 1897, *CL*1 p. 802 (*A Correspondence* p. 255).

443/36 **journey:** Ibid., *CL*1 p. 801 (*A Correspondence* p. 253).

444/21 **person:** G.B.S. to Ellen Terry, 8 September 1897, *CL*1 pp. 801–2 (*A Correspondence* p. 254).

444/30 **money:** Ibid., p. 801 (*A Correspondence* p. 253).

445/ 7 **dishonourable:** *The Diary of Beatrice Webb* vol. 2, entry 27 September 1897, p. 123.

445/15 **evenings?:** G.B.S. to Charlotte Payne-Townshend, 7 October 1897, *CL*1 p. 810.

445/18 **talk to:** G.B.S. to Charlotte Payne-Townshend, 15 October 1897, *CL*1 p. 814.

445/25 **Terrace:** G.B.S. to Charlotte Payne-Townshend, 29 October 1897, *CL*1 p. 817.

445/31 **spare them:** G.B.S. to Charlotte Payne-Townshend, 4 November 1897, *CL*1 p. 821.

445/34 **reach:** G.B.S. to Charlotte Payne-Townshend, 7 November 1897, *CL*1 p. 822.

446/ 3 **time:** Ellen Terry to G.B.S., 15 December 1897, *A Correspondence* p. 270.

446/ 8 **to me:** G.B.S. to Charlotte Payne-Townshend, 29 November 1897, *CL*1 p. 824.

446/ 9 **eleven:** G.B.S. to Charlotte Payne-Townshend, 6 December 1897, *CL*1 p. 826.

446/21   **as I am:** Ibid.
446/25   **aberrations:** G.B.S. to Pinero, 6 October 1912 (Texas).
446/37   **foundered?:** G.B.S. to Charlotte Payne-Townshend, 8
          December 1897, *CL*1 p. 827.
447/14   **GBS:** Ibid.
448/ 5   **tomorrow:** G.B.S. to Charlotte Payne-Townshend, 4 January
          1898, *CL*2 p. 7.
448/ 8   **victim:** G.B.S. to Charlotte Payne-Townshend, 4 March 1898,
          *CL*2 p. 12.
448/10   **intentions:** G.B.S. to Ellen Terry, 18 January 1898, *CL*2 p. 9
          (*A Correspondence* p. 292).
448/12   **democracy:** *The Diary of Beatrice Webb* vol. 2, entry 15 June
          1897, p. 118.
448/15   **affair:** G.B.S. to Ellen Terry, 18 January 1898, *CL*2 p. 9 (*A
          Correspondence* p. 291).
448/24   **left:** G.B.S. to Sidney Webb, 11 April 1898, *CL*2 p. 29.
448/Ep.1 **married?:** G.B.S. to Henry Arthur Jones, 20 May 1898, *CL*2
          p. 44.
448/Ep.2 **to do:** G.B.S.'s answer to O'Bolger questionnaire, 12 April
          1916 (Houghton).
448/31   **women:** G.B.S. to Eileen O'Casey, 4 October 1939, Eileen
          O'Casey, *Cheerio, Titan* (1989) p. 105.
449/13   **theatre:** *SSS* p. 150.
449/17   **was over:** *Diaries* 1, entry 17 December 1887, p. 324.
449/31   **encored him:** 'The 789th Performance of *Dorothy*', *The Star*
          13 September 1889, *SM*1 p. 780.
450/20   **souls?:** Ibid., pp. 781–2.
450/22   **act:** H. G. Farmer, *Bernard Shaw's Sister and Her Friends*
          (1959) p. 72.
450/27   **uncritical:** Judy Musters to Archibald Henderson, 23 August
          1952 (North Carolina).
450/38   **lard:** *SSS* p. 150.
451/ 1   **invalid:** St John Ervine, *Bernard Shaw: His Life, Work and
          Friends* (1956) p. 198.
451/ 9   **world:** Ibid., p. 320.
451/11   **mad:** G.B.S. to Charles Charrington, 8 November 1895, *CL*1
          p. 569.
451/14   **inclination:** G.B.S. to Charlotte Payne-Townshend, 4
          February 1897, *CL*1 p. 725.
451/18   **hell:** G.B.S. to Charles Charrington, 8 November 1895, *CL*1
          p. 569.
451/28   **mother:** G.B.S.'s answer to Hayden Church, 27 October 1928
          (Houghton).

451/29   **mute:** 'A Handbook of Physiognomy', *Pall Mall Gazette* 23 September 1885, p. 5. See *Bernard Shaw's Book Reviews Originally Published in the Pall Mall Gazette from 1885 to 1950* (ed. Brian Tyson 1991) pp. 48–52.

451/35   **years:** *Diaries* 1, entries 13 January 1888 and 16 February 1889, pp. 338 and 469.

451/last   **solid:** 'A Science of Ghosts', *Pall Mall Gazette* 24 November 1886, p. 6. See *Bernard Shaw's Book Reviews* pp. 218–22.

452/ 2   **witchcraft:** 'Mr Laurence Oliphant's New Novel', *Pall Mall Gazette* 16 June 1886, p. 5. See *Bernard Shaw's Book Reviews* pp. 147–50.

452/ 7   **health:** G.B.S.'s answer to Hayden Church, 27 October 1928 (Houghton).

452/13   **London:** 'A Scotland Yard For Spectres', *Pall Mall Gazette* 23 January 1886, p. 4. See *Bernard Shaw's Book Reviews* pp. 100–5.

452/16   **stories:** 'A Runaway From Civilization', *Pall Mall Gazette* 15 July 1887, p. 3. See *Bernard Shaw's Book Reviews* pp. 299–302.

452/25   **veracity:** 'A Science of Ghosts', *Pall Mall Gazette* 24 November 1886, p. 6. See *Bernard Shaw's Book Reviews* pp. 218–22.

452/30   **place:** 'Mr Laurence Oliphant's New Novel', *Pall Mall Gazette* 16 June 1886, p. 5. See *Bernard Shaw's Book Reviews* pp. 147–50.

452/last   **finance:** 'Physical Expression', *Pall Mall Gazette* 17 September 1885. See *Bernard Shaw's Book Reviews* pp. 44–8.

453/ 8   **done it:** *CP*7 p. 309.

453/14   **America:** 'The Devil's Disciple'. Untitled manuscript on the play's history dated 'Malvern 18 August 30' (Boston).

453/16   **matter:** G.B.S. to Richard Mansfield, n.d., BL Add. MS 50543 f. 85.

453/23   **inch:** G.B.S. to Beatrice Mansfield, 19 March 1898 (Philadelphia).

453/28   **Shaw?:** 'The Devil's Disciple'. Untitled manuscript (Boston).

453/31   **gamble:** Ibid.

453/38   **improve:** G.B.S.'s answer to O'Bolger questionnaire, 12 April 1916 (Houghton).

454/ 2   **season:** G.B.S. to Sidney Webb, 11 April 1898, *CL*2 p. 30.

454/ 3   **say:** G.B.S. to Lena Ashwell, 1 June 1898 (Texas).

454/11   **life:** G.B.S. to Charlotte Payne-Townshend, 23 April 1898, *CL*2 pp. 35–6.

454/13   **wreck:** G.B.S. to Charlotte Payne-Townshend, 21 April 1898, *CL*2 p. 33.

454/17   **brilliancy:** G.B.S. to Karl Pearson, 4 July 1898 (UCL).

454/18   **form:** G.B.S. to Charlotte Payne-Townshend, 14 April 1898, *CL*2 p. 32.

454/22   **damnable:** G.B.S. to Charlotte Payne-Townshend, 30 March 1898, *CL*2 p. 24.

454/23   **inconvenient:** G.B.S. to Charlotte Payne-Townshend, 15 March 1898, *CL*2 p. 15.

454/32   **famously:** G.B.S. to Charlotte Payne-Townshend, 16 March 1898, *CL*2 p. 16.

454/34   **myself:** G.B.S. to Charlotte Payne-Townshend, 30 March 1898, *CL*2 pp. 24–5.

455/ 1   **a secretary:** BL Add. MS 50550 ff. 73–4.

455/ 3   **your secretary:** G.B.S. to Charlotte Payne-Townshend, 22 March 1898, *CL*2 p. 21.

455/ 6   **off:** G.B.S. to Charlotte Payne-Townshend, 30 March 1898, *CL*2 p. 23.

455/ 9   **Rome!:** G.B.S. to Charlotte Payne-Townshend, 4, 5 and 7 April 1898, *CL*2, pp. 27–8.

455/29   **with her:** G.B.S. to Charlotte Payne-Townshend, 30 March 1898, *CL*2 p. 24.

456/ 1   **bachelordom:** G.B.S. to Karl Pearson, 4 July 1898 (UCL).

456/11   **self-defence:** G.B.S. to Sidney Webb, 7 May 1898 (LSE).

456/26   **mutton:** G.B.S. to Charlotte Payne-Townshend, 19 April 1898, *CL*2 p. 32.

456/29   **soon:** G.B.S. to Philip Wicksteed, 2 November 1898.

456/30   **church bell:** G.B.S. to Emery Walker, 22 April 1898 (Texas).

456/34   **any use:** G.B.S. to Charlotte Payne-Townshend, 22 April 1898, *CL*2 p. 35.

456/38   **thing:** G.B.S. to Charlotte Payne-Townshend, 23 April 1898, *CL*2 p. 36.

457/ 3   **tamer:** G.B.S. to Charlotte Payne-Townshend, 26 April 1898, *CL*2 p. 37.

457/ 6   **nurse me:** G.B.S. to Karl Pearson, 4 July 1898 (UCL).

457/ 9   **enjoy *you*:** Janet Dunbar, *Mrs G.B.S.* (1963) p. 163.

457/11   **leg:** G.B.S. to Charlotte Payne-Townshend, 22 April 1898, *CL*2 p. 35.

457/13   **need:** G.B.S. to Charlotte Payne-Townshend, 25 April 1898, *CL*2 p. 37.

457/18   **bell:** G.B.S. to Charlotte Payne-Townshend, 1 May 1898, *CL*2 p. 38.

457/24   **telegraphed:** Ibid.

457/32   **Charlotte:** Charlotte to G.B.S., May 1898, Janet Dunbar, *Mrs G.B.S.* p. 167.

457/34 **least:** G.B.S. to Charlotte Payne-Townshend, 2 May 1898, BL
Add. MS 46505 f. 143.

458/ 7 **chair:** G.B.S. to Clarence Rook, 24 April 1898 (Princeton).

458/30 **Rome:** G.B.S. to Sidney Webb, 7 May 1898, *CL*2 p. 40.

459/ 6 **coquetting:** G.B.S. to Blanchamp, 18 May 1898.

459/12 **curiosity:** Charlotte Shaw to O'Bolger, 10 April 1921 and 1
May 1921 (Houghton).

459/22 **critical condition:** G.B.S. to Janet Achurch, 11 May 1898,
*CL*2 p. 42.

459/24 **superhuman condition:** G.B.S. to Philip Wicksteed, 2
November 1898.

459/25 **vegetarianism!:** Janet Dunbar, *Mrs G.B.S.* p. 181.

459/39 **exhausted condition:** 'G.B.S. Vivisected', *Saturday Review* 14
May 1898, *OTN*3 pp. 381–4.

460/32 **loss?:** Ibid., pp. 381–2.

460/35 **lately:** *The Star* 2 June 1898.

461/ 3 **marriage:** G.B.S. to Karl Pearson, 4 July 1898 (UCL).

461/ 9 **myself:** G.B.S. to Philip Wicksteed, 2 November 1898.

461/12 **widow:** G.B.S. to Beatrice Mansfield, 2 January 1899 (New
York Public Library).

461/22 **existence:** G.B.S. to Karl Pearson, 4 July 1898 (UCL).

461/24 **vulgarities:** G.B.S. to Beatrice Webb, 21 June 1898, *CL*2
p. 51.

461/27 **Destiny:** Ibid.

461/30 **man:** G.B.S.'s answer to O'Bolger questionnaire, 12 April
1916, p. 8 (Houghton).

461/34 **goose:** 'Valedictory', *Saturday Review* 21 May 1898, *OTN*3
p. 384.

462/ 1 **to me:** G.B.S. to Beatrice Webb, 21 June 1898, *CL*2 p. 50.

462/ 6 **country:** Grant Richards, *Author Hunting* (1960) p. 116.

462/12 **spelling:** G.B.S. to Beatrice Webb, 21 June 1898, *CL*2 p. 51.

462/13 **to me:** Ibid.

462/21 **family:** G.B.S. to Ada Tyrrell, 21 November 1943, *CL*4 p. 685.

462/35 **arrangement:** G.B.S.'s answer to O'Bolger questionnaire, 12
April 1916, p. 8 (Houghton).

462/40 **parasite:** G.B.S. to O'Bolger, 28 June 1922, *CL*3 p. 777.

463/ 5 **marry me:** G.B.S. to Karl Pearson, 4 July 1898 (UCL).

463/ 8 **else:** G.B.S. to O'Bolger, 28 June 1922, *CL*3 p. 777.

463/30 **yours:** G.B.S. to N. F. W. Fisher, 5 May 1910, *CL*2 pp. 924–5.

463/34 **fortune:** G.B.S. to Philip Wicksteed, 2 November 1898.

464/11 **married her:** G.B.S. to O'Bolger, 28 June 1922, *CL*3 p. 778.

464/16 **affair:** G.B.S. to Beatrice Webb, 21 June 1898, *CL*2 p. 51.

464/32 **use:** G.B.S. to Graham Wallas, 26 May 1898, *CL*2 p. 46.

464/35   **proceeding:** Ibid.

464/38   CONTRACT: G.B.S. to Henry S. Salt, 31 May 1898, *CL*2 p. 46.

465/ 6   **to me:** Archibald Henderson, *George Bernard Shaw: Man of the Century* (1957) p. 418.

465/ 9   **secretly:** G.B.S. to Max Hecht, 23 May 1898, *CL*2 pp. 44–5.

465/10   **Gladstone:** G.B.S. to Beatrice Webb, 21 June 1898, *CL*2 p. 51.

465/23   **to them:** *The Star* 2 June 1898.

465/25   **adventure:** G.B.S. to Elizabeth Scott-Ellis, 24 July 1935 (privately printed rehearsal copy of *The Millionairess*, Cornell). The play was not published in England until 1936. See Laurence, *Bernard Shaw: A Bibliography* (1983) vol. I, AA21a, p. 404.

465/25   **man:** G.B.S. to Henry Arthur Jones, 22 March 1902 (Texas).

VOLUME TWO
The Pursuit of Power

CHAPTER I

3/Ep. 1   **forty:** G.B.S. to Hesketh Pearson, 25 October 1918 (Texas).

3/Ep. 2   **never was:** G.B.S. to Mrs Walker, 21 June 1898 (Texas).

3/ 5   **house:** Janet Dunbar, *Mrs G.B.S.: A Biographical Portrait of Charlotte Shaw* (1963) p. 181.

3/ 7   **begun:** G.B.S. to Beatrice Webb, 21 June 1898, *CL*2 p. 52.

3/18   **book:** G.B.S. to Grant Richards, 19 June 1898, *CL*2 p. 48.

3/26   **well:** G.B.S. to Beatrice Webb, 21 June 1898, *CL*2 p. 52.

4/ 3   **foot:** G.B.S. to Karl Pearson, 4 July 1898 (Pearson Papers, UCL).

4/11   **quiet:** Charlotte Shaw to Henry Salt, 28 July 1898, *CL*2 p. 56.

4/19   **calamities:** G.B.S. to Charles Charrington, 13 October 1898, *CL*2 p. 65.

4/24   **nurse:** G.B.S. to Mrs Walker, 21 June 1898 (Texas).

4/25   **baby:** G.B.S. to Philip Wicksteed, 2 November 1898.

4/38   **Janet:** G.B.S. to Charles Charrington, 20 June 1898, *CL*2 p. 49.

5/ 5   **marriage:** Janet Dunbar, *Mrs G.B.S.* p. 189.

5/10   **work:** Charlotte Shaw to Nancy Astor, 3 October 1929 (Reading).

5/11   **pieces:** Charlotte Shaw to Nancy Astor, 7 January 1929 (Reading).

5/18   **work:** G.B.S. to Beatrice Mansfield, 2 January 1899 (Philadelphia).

5/24   **right:** G.B.S. to Sidney Webb, 18 October 1898, *CL*2 p. 67.

5/36   **convictions:** Ibid., p. 66.

6/ 2   **luxury:** G.B.S. to George Samuel, undated [c. 23–24 December 1899], *CL*2 p. 123.

6/ 4   **dream:** G.B.S. to Charles Charrington, 23 October 1898, *CL*2 p. 70.

6/ 9   **with:** G.B.S. to Elizabeth Robins, 13 February 1899, *CL*2 p. 77.

6/22   **activity:** *The Diary of Beatrice Webb* vol. 2 (ed. Norman and Jeanne MacKenzie 1983), entry 5 February 1899, p. 156.

6/33   **off them:** G.B.S. to Henry Salt, 16 October 1898 (Berg).

7/ 2   **were here:** Charlotte Shaw to Beatrice Webb, 6 November 1898 (LSE).

7/14   **waiting:** G.B.S. to Henry Arthur Jones, 2 December 1898, BL Add. MS 50561 f. 123.

7/20   **we say?:** Ibid.

7/26   **bone:** G.B.S. to Mrs Pat. Campbell, 12 April 1899, *CL*2 p. 85.

7/31   **spirits:** G.B.S. to Charles Charrington, 27 April 1899 (Texas).

7/35   **ankle:** G.B.S. to Ellen Terry, 14 July 1899, *Ellen Terry and Bernard Shaw: A Correspondence* (ed. Christopher St John 1931) p. 332.

8/ 2   **community:** G.B.S. to Grant Allen, 14 August 1899 (Bucknell).

8/ 5   **sake:** G.B.S. to Charrington, 22 August 1899 (Texas).

8/ 7   **neck:** G.B.S. to Graham Wallas, 24 August 1899, *CL*2 p. 100.

8/12   **avalanche:** G.B.S. to Graham Wallas, 9 September 1899 (LSE).

8/13   **myself up:** G.B.S. to Graham Wallas, 24 August 1899, *CL*2 p. 100.

8/17   **success:** Charlotte Shaw to Grant Richards, 5 October 1899 (Texas).

8/25   **pleasures:** G.B.S. to Beatrice Mansfield, 21 October 1899 (Philadelphia).

8/30   **machine:** G.B.S. to Edward Rose, 25 September 1899, *CL*2 p. 103.

8/32   **air:** G.B.S. to Sydney Cockerell, 17 October 1899, *CL*2 p. 111.

8/35   **life:** Ibid.

8/last   **pang:** *CL*2 p. 112.

9/ 4   **existence:** G.B.S. to Karl Pearson, 4 July 1898 (UCL).

9/ 8   **mine:** G.B.S. to Rayner Storr, 14 August 1899 (Sotheby's Catalogue, 16 July 1973, item 737).

9/14   **bath:** Janet Dunbar, *Mrs G.B.S.* p. 180.

9/29   **questionable:** 'Shaw Looks at Life at 70', interview by G. S. Viereck, 1927 (Holograph, Cornell). Extensively revised by G.B.S. In *Liberty* IV, 13 August 1927, pp. 7–10. Also in *London Magazine* LIX, December 1927, pp. 615–23.

9/37   **afternoons:** G.B.S. to William Rothenstein, 13 June 1900 (Houghton).

10/ 1   **busy:** Ibid.

10/ 6   **policy:** G.B.S. to Edward Rose, 14 December 1899, *CL*2 p. 119.

10/ 8   **honeymoon:** G.B.S. to William Archer, 24 June 1898, BL Add. MS 45296 f. 75.

10/13   **times:** G.B.S. to Robert Loraine, 4 August 1918; in Winifred Loraine, *Robert Loraine, Soldier. Actor. Airman* (1938) p. 243.

10/Ep.   **plenty:** *The Diary of Beatrice Webb* vol. 2, entry 30 October 1899, p. 166.

10/30   **passion:** 'Night Falls on the Gods', *The Perfect Wagnerite: A Commentary on the Niblung's Ring, SM*3 p. 498 (*Major Critical Essays*, 1986 edn p. 236).

10/33   **lives:** 'Siegfried as Protestant', *The Perfect Wagnerite: A Commentary on the Niblung's Ring, SM*3 p. 481 (*Major Critical Essays* p. 221).

10/35   **passion:** Ibid., *SM*3 p. 479 (*Major Critical Essays* p. 220).

11/18   **mind:** Preface to the Third Edition: *The Perfect Wagnerite: A Commentary on the Niblung's Ring, SM*3 p. 414 (*Major Critical Essays* p. 160).

11/21   **personal:** Thomas Mann, 'He was Mankind's Friend', *The Listener* 18 January 1951, p. 99.

11/33   **Churches:** 'Wagner as Revolutionist', *The Perfect Wagnerite: A Commentary on the Niblung's Ring, SM*3 p. 445 (*Major Critical Essays* p. 189).

12/13   **Heros:** Ibid.

12/37   **grasp:** 'The Rhine Gold', *The Perfect Wagnerite: A Commentary on the Niblung's Ring, SM*3 pp. 424–7 (*Major Critical Essays* pp. 171, 173).

13/26   **death:** 'Siegfried as Protestant', *The Perfect Wagnerite: A Commentary on the Niblung's Ring, SM*3 p. 479 (*Major Critical Essays* p. 219).

13/38   **men:** Ibid., pp. 481–2 (*Major Critical Essays* pp. 221–2).

14/ 5   **generation:** 'Why He Changed His Mind', *The Perfect Wagnerite: A Commentary on the Niblung's Ring, SM*3 p. 506 (*Major Critical Essays* p. 271).

14/10   **complete:** Ibid., *SM*3 p. 508 (*Major Critical Essays* p. 273).

14/11   **better:** Gilbert Murray to G.B.S., 30 July 1900, BL Add. MS 50542 ff. 1–2.

14/19   **word:** G.B.S. to Beatrice Mansfield, 3 May 1899, *CL*2 p. 90.

14/19   **in it:** G.B.S. to Charles Charrington, 23 October 1898, *CL*2 p. 70.

14/26   **action:** *CP*2 p. 261.

14/36   **work:** Ibid., p. 215.

15/ 8   **to him:** Ibid., p. 187.

15/10   **children:** Ibid., p. 257.

15/12   **gifts:** 'Why Do the Ungodly Prosper', *Eagle and the Serpent*, Special Issue, no. 18, c. December 1902, pp. 69–70.

15/19   **present him:** Hesketh Pearson, *Bernard Shaw* (1975 rev. edn) p. 223.

15/26   **Holinshed:** Ibid.
15/30   **girl Cleopatra:** G.B.S. to Charles Charrington, 1 April 1897
        (Cornell).
15/32   **hero:** 'Caesar and Cleopatra', G.B.S. letter to *The Times*, 31
        December 1945, p. 5.
15/34   **braggart:** 'Tappertit on Caesar', *Saturday Review* 29 January
        1898, *OTN*3 p. 298.
15/last **by it:** *CP*2 p. 277.
16/ 7   **executions:** 'Hamlet', *Saturday Review* 20 October 1897,
        *OTN*3 p. 201.
16/11   **comedian:** 'Caesar and Cleopatra', Theatre Guild Press
        Release. Two typescript pages by G.B.S. (Yale).
16/35   **occasions:** 'Bernard Shaw and the Heroic Actor', *The Play
        Pictorial* no. 62, October 1907, pp. 110–11. Reprinted in *CP*2
        pp. 306–10.
17/ 6   **Antony:** *CP*2 p. 292.
17/26   **child:** G.B.S. to Gabriel Pascal, 15 March 1944 (Texas).
17/30   **absurdity:** 'Caesar and Cleopatra', G.B.S. letter to *The Times*,
        31 December 1945, p. 5.
17/31   **witchery:** Ibid.
18/10   **wane:** 'The Perfect Wagnerite', *SM*3 p. 495n. See also *Major
        Critical Essays* p. 369.
18/15   **other men:** BL Add. MS 50609B f. 33. See *The Man of
        Destiny & Caesar and Cleopatra* (Garland facsimile edition
        1981) p. 251.
18/18   **understand:** *CP*2 p. 278.
18/28   **despair:** Ibid., p. 280.
19/ 2   **Pessimism:** 'Wagner's Own Explanation', 'The Perfect
        Wagnerite', *SM*3 p. 511 (*Major Critical Essays* p. 276).
19/ 7   **place:** *CP*2 pp. 301, 298.
19/16   **moralists:** Ibid., p. 304.
19/22   **ever:** Ibid., p. 291.
19/25   **speech!:** Ibid., p. 254.
19/28   **question:** Ibid., p. 191.
19/31   **attraction:** G.B.S. to Gabriel Pascal, 15 March 1944 (Texas).
19/32   **horror:** *CP*2 p. 290.
19/39   **another:** Ibid., pp. 181–2.
20/ 2   **of it:** 1921 Preface to *Immaturity* (1931) p. xliii.
20/ 7   **months:** *CP*2 p. 396.
20/11   **of it:** Ibid., pp. 357–8.
20/14   **fuming:** Ibid., p. 369.
20/18   **marry me:** Ibid., p. 339.
20/19   **nursery:** Ibid., p. 347.

20/22   **gentle:** Ibid., p. 356.

20/36   **at all:** Ibid., p. 331.

20/38   **manners:** G.B.S. to S. J. C. Russell, 23 October 1907 (Texas).

21/ 6   **explorer?:** G.B.S.'s answer to questionnaire dated 3 October 1929 (Colby).

21/18   **drifters:** G.B.S. to Ellen Terry, 8 August 1899, *CL*2 p. 98 (*A Correspondence* p. 340).

21/21   **woman:** *CP*2 p. 428.

21/23   **men:** Ibid.

22/ 2   **world:** G.B.S. to Ellen Terry, 8 August 1899, *CL*2 pp. 98–9 (*A Correspondence* pp. 339–41).

22/11   **steamer:** 'Notes to *Captain Brassbound's Conversion*', *CP*2 p. 418.

22/15   **tomorrow:** *CP*2 p. 338.

22/23   **by it:** G.B.S. to Ellen Terry, 8 August 1899, *CL*2 p. 99 (*A Correspondence* p. 341).

22/30   **she said:** *CP*2 p. 430.

22/34   **written:** G.B.S.'s answer to questionnaire dated 3 October 1929 (Colby).

23/11   **actors:** G.B.S. to Max Hecht, 27 February 1899, *CL*2 p. 78.

23/20   **pantomime:** *CL*2 pp. 78–9.

23/23   **part:** 'Caesar and Cleopatra', Theatre Guild Press Release. Two typescript pages by G.B.S. (Yale).

23/24   **play:** 'Caesar and Cleopatra', G.B.S. letter to *The Times* 31 December 1945.

23/25   **lunch:** G.B.S. to Mrs Patrick Campbell, 12 April 1899, *CL*2 p. 85 (*Their Correspondence* p. 11).

23/36   **prize:** G.B.S. to Ellen Terry, 7 July 1899, *CL*2 p. 92 (*A Correspondence* p. 329).

23/39   **thing:** Ellen Terry to G.B.S., 10 July 1899, *A Correspondence* p. 330.

24/ 9   **Mrs A?:** Ellen Terry to G.B.S., 18 February 1898, *A Correspondence* p. 301.

24/33   **present:** Ellen Terry's *Memoirs* (1933) pp. 271–2.

24/last   **do it!:** Ellen Terry to G.B.S., 15 January 1899, *A Correspondence* p. 318.

25/ 7   **personality:** G.B.S. to Ellen Terry, 1 June 1899, *A Correspondence* p. 327.

25/15   **Mrs Pat:** Ellen Terry to G.B.S., 3 August 1899, *A Correspondence* p. 336.

25/29   **projects:** G.B.S. to Ellen Terry, 4 August 1899, *CL*2 pp. 96–7 (*A Correspondence* pp. 337–8).

25/33   **for me:** Ellen Terry to G.B.S., 6 August 1899, *A Correspondence* p. 338.

26/15   **everything**: G.B.S. to Ellen Terry, 8 August 1899, *CL*2 pp. 97–9 (*A Correspondence* pp. 339–41).

26/20   **convictions**: Ellen Terry, *The Story of My Life* (1908) p. 322.

26/26   **you do!**: Ellen Terry to G.B.S., 9 August 1899, *A Correspondence* p. 342.

26/29   **to me?**: Ibid.

26/39   **like you!**: Ellen Terry to G.B.S., 20 August 1899, *A Correspondence* p. 344.

27/ 1   **speak of**: Ellen Terry to G.B.S., 27 August 1899, *A Correspondence* p. 349.

27/ 5   **before me**: Ellen Terry to G.B.S., 27 August 1899, 17 September 1899, *A Correspondence* pp. 350, 351.

27/ 9   **right**: G.B.S. answer to questionnaire, 3 October 1929 (Colby).

27/17   **do it**: Ellen Terry to G.B.S., 2 October 1899, *A Correspondence* p. 359.

27/20   **of him**: Ellen Terry to G.B.S., 11 October 1899, *A Correspondence* p. 365.

27/21   **wrong**: Ibid., p. 364.

27/36   **manner**: G.B.S. to Graham Wallas, 24 August 1899, *CL*2 p. 100.

27/last   **his life**: G.B.S. to Beatrice Mansfield, 21 October 1899 (Philadelphia).

28/ 6   **beholders**: Desmond MacCarthy, *Shaw* (1951) p. 63.

28/11   **do it?**: *CP*2 p. 415.

28/15   **dangerous!**: Ibid., p. 416.

28/21   **secret**: Ibid.

28/22   **freedom!**: Ibid., p. 417.

28/29   *mise-en-scène*: G.B.S. to R. B. Cunninghame Graham, 19 July 1899 (Scotland).

29/ 1   **satisfactory**: Ellen Terry to G.B.S., 28 January 1900, *A Correspondence* p. 371.

29/21   **bidder**: G.B.S. to Ellen Terry, 9 February 1900, *CL*2 pp. 147–8 (*A Correspondence* pp. 373–4).

29/27   **stay**: Ibid.

29/30   **Fabian**: Ibid.

29/34   **contemptuous**: Ellen Terry's *Memoirs* p. 274.

30/ 5   *Opera!*: Ellen Terry to G.B.S., 7 November 1900, *A Correspondence* pp. 387–8. See also BL Add. MS 43802 ff. 115–115v, 117.

30/13   **alarm**: G.B.S. to Ellen Terry, 8 November 1900, *CL*2 p. 198 (*A Correspondence* p. 389).

30/16   **see it**: Ellen Terry to G.B.S. [some time in December 1900], *A Correspondence* p. 391.

30/25 **stage:** Ellen Terry to G.B.S., 10 December 1902, *A Correspondence* p. 402.

30/30 **myself:** Ibid.

30/35 **salt:** Ellen Terry to G.B.S., 18 December 1902, BL Add. MS 43802 f. 139.

31/ 7 **herself:** *A Correspondence* pp. xxxviii–xxxix.

31/10 **Lady C.:** Ellen Terry to G.B.S. [some time in December 1900], *A Correspondence* p. 392.

31/13 **wrote:** G.B.S. to Ada Rehan, 29 June 1901 (Texas).

31/16 **Cicely:** G.B.S. to Ellen Terry, 3 April 1902, *CL*2 p. 272 (*A Correspondence* p. 399).

31/18 **play:** Ellen Terry to G.B.S., 5 April 1902, *A Correspondence* p. 400.

31/22 **delighted:** G.B.S. to Ellen Terry, 12 June 1904, *CL*2 p. 421 (*A Correspondence* p. 407).

31/29 **love you:** G.B.S. to Ellen Terry, 27 February 1906; G.B.S. to Ellen Terry 16 March 1906, *A Correspondence* pp. 427, 429.

31/31 **memory:** *The Times* 23 March 1906.

31/33 **effect:** Desmond MacCarthy, *Shaw* p. 62.

31/36 **while:** Ellen Terry to G.B.S., 18 April 1906, *A Correspondence* p. 430.

31/37 **humility:** Ibid., p. 429.

32/ 3 **successful:** G.B.S. to Siegfried Trebitsch, 28 March 1906 and 21 November 1907, Shaw/Trebitsch letters pp. 96, 129.

32/ 7 **world:** Ellen Terry to G.B.S., 7 April 1907, *A Correspondence* p. 434.

32/ 9 **sight:** G.B.S. to Ellen Terry, 16 March 1906, *A Correspondence* p. 429.

32/12 **history:** G.B.S. to Ellen Terry, 14 October 1907, *A Correspondence* p. 438.

32/15 **adoration?:** Ibid., pp. 438–9.

32/20 **disappointment!:** Archibald Henderson, *George Bernard Shaw: Man of the Century* (1957) p. 562n.

32/25 **ever did:** G.B.S. to Gertrude Kingston, 15 October 1929 (King's College, Cambridge).

32/35 **something:** G.B.S. to Richard Mansfield, 28 April 1899, *CL*2 p. 86.

33/ 6 **succeed:** G.B.S. to Edy (Edith) Craig, 17 July 1940, *CL*4 p. 570.

33/26 **fascinates me:** G.B.S. to Ellen Terry, 8 November 1900, *CL*2 p. 198 (*A Correspondence* p. 389).

33/29 **composition:** G.B.S. to Grant Richards, 8 May 1900, *CL*2 p. 163.

33/32   **my life:** G.B.S. to Ellen Terry, 10 July 1900, *CL*2 p. 179 (*A Correspondence* p. 382).

34/ 4   **narrative:** 'How to Make Plays Readable', *The Author*, December 1901, pp. 59–62.

34/13   **costs:** G.B.S. to R. Golding Bright, 2 November 1900, *CL*2 p. 191.

34/18   **publishing it:** G.B.S. to Ellen Terry, 1 August 1899, *CL*2 p. 95 (*A Correspondence* p. 334).

34/27   **spectator:** *Morning Leader* 16 February 1901.

34/31   **stage:** *CP*2, p. 18.

34/32   **allowed:** Ibid.

34/39   **today:** Ibid., p. 21.

34/40   **vices:** Ibid., p. 19.

35/ 3   **in it:** Ibid., p. 25.

35/ 6   **sensuousness:** Ibid., p. 27.

35/ 8   **upon:** Ibid., p. 26.

35/ 9   **honesty:** Ibid., p. 28.

35/11   **edification:** Ibid., p. 14.

35/16   **plays?:** Ibid., pp. 15–16.

35/21   **killed me:** Ibid., pp. 20–1.

36/14   **cremated:** G.B.S. to Ellen Terry, 4 August 1899, *CL*2 p. 97 (*A Correspondence* pp. 337–8).

36/19   **dramatist:** G.B.S. to Ellen Terry, 1 August 1899, *CL*2 p. 96 (*A Correspondence* p. 335).

36/29   **silly:** G.B.S. to Edward R. Pease, 30 October 1899, *CL*2 p. 115.

37/ 4   **Jingoism:** Hesketh Pearson, *Conan Doyle* (1943) p. 126.

37/ 8   **put down:** G.B.S. to Arthur Conan Doyle, 24 January 1899, *CL*2 p. 73.

37/38   **destiny:** Margaret Cole, *The Story of Fabian Socialism* (1963) p. 97.

38/22   **Society:** Norman and Jeanne MacKenzie, *The First Fabians* (1977) p. 271.

39/ 7   **blue-books:** Beatrice Webb, *Our Partnership* (1948) pp. 218–19.

40/34   **view:** G.B.S. to Edward Rose, 13 March 1900, *CL*2 p. 154.

41/ 8   **damned:** G.B.S. to Ramsay MacDonald, 30 November 1899, Ramsay MacDonald Papers, Public Record Office 5/9. See also David Marquand, *Ramsay MacDonald* (1977) pp. 65–6.

41/19   **off us:** G.B.S. to Walter Crane, 22 March 1900 (Cornell).

41/32   **pals:** G.B.S. to Gilbert Murray, 28 July 1900, *CL*2 p. 180.

42/ 7   **another:** G.B.S. to Walter Crane, 22 March 1900 (Cornell).

42/32   **wins:** G.B.S. to George Samuel, undated [c. 23–24 December 1899], *CL*2 pp. 121–2.

43/ 1   **Destiny:** G.B.S. to Hubert Bland, 30 December 1899, *CL*2 p. 126.

43/ 4   **Socialism:** G.B.S. to George Samuel, undated [c. 23–24 December 1899], *CL*2 p. 123.

43/14   **for it:** *Fabianism and the Empire: A Manifesto by the Fabian Society* (ed. G.B.S. 1900) pp. 23–4.

43/24   **bad man:** G.B.S. to G. F. McCleary, 24 May 1900, *CL*2 p. 169.

43/last   **reversed:** G.B.S. to Henry S. Salt, 12 March 1900, *CL*2 p. 153.

44/10   **immense one:** Edward Pease, *The History of the Fabian Society* (1916) p. 134.

44/11   **masterpiece:** G.B.S. to H. T. Muggeridge, 31 August 1900, *CL*2 p. 182.

44/19   **Empire:** *The History of the Fabian Society* p. 135.

44/31   **author:** G.B.S. to Grant Richards, 26 September 1900, *CL*2 p. 185.

44/33   **date:** Beatrice Webb, *Our Partnership* p. 194.

45/ 5   **Government:** Ibid., p. 202.

45/ 9   **worth:** G.B.S. to Sidney Webb, 26 July 1901, *CL*2 p. 230.

45/10   **flattery:** *Our Partnership* p. 220.

CHAPTER II

46/Ep.   **ever:** G.B.S. to William Archer, 26 March 1902, BL Add. MS 45296 ff. 119 and v.

46/11   **abolished:** G.B.S. to John Burns, 11 September 1903, *CL*2 p. 369.

46/21   **supporters:** Beatrice Webb, *Our Partnership* (1948) p. 282.

46/23   **defeat:** Ibid.

46/25   **get in:** Ibid., p. 283.

46/30   **known:** *St Pancras Guardian* 19 March 1904.

47/ 3   **disgruntled:** *Our Partnership* p. 284.

47/ 8   **furious:** G.B.S. to Siegfried Trebitsch, 14 March 1904, *CL*2 p. 411 (Shaw/Trebitsch letters p. 68).

47/16   **war:** *Our Partnership* p. 284.

47/23   **way:** Ibid., p. 283.

47/25   **won:** Ibid., p. 284.

47/29   **whatever:** G.B.S. to William Platts, 24 June 1904 (Berg).

48/16   **mind:** Siegfried Trebitsch, *Chronicle of a Life* (1953) pp. 122–3.

48/22   **vanished:** Ibid.

48/28   **poetic:** Ibid.

48/29   **days:** Trebitsch to Archibald Henderson, 19 January 1905 (North Carolina).

48/30   **with me?:** *Chronicle of a Life* p. 123.

48/32   **Europe:** *CP5* p. 719.

48/33   **for him:** *Chronicle of a Life* p. 123.

48/35   **mind:** Trebitsch to Archibald Henderson, 13 May 1924 (North Carolina).

49/3   **to me:** *Chronicle of a Life* p. 123.

49/27   **to him:** Ibid., pp. 124–5.

49/29   **see him:** *CP5* p. 719.

49/34   **grammar:** G.B.S. to Trebitsch, 22 October 1902, Shaw/Trebitsch letters p. 24.

49/35   **dictionary:** G.B.S. to Julius Bab, 21 December 1925 (Berg).

49/38   **carefully:** G.B.S. to Trebitsch, 2 July 1903 (Berg).

49/39   **errors:** G.B.S. to Siegfried Trebitsch, 26 December 1902, *CL2* p. 297 (Shaw/Trebitsch letters p. 30).

50/2   **sea:** G.B.S. to Trebitsch, 7 January 1903 and 10 January 1907, Shaw/Trebitsch letters pp. 33, 117.

50/9   **purpose:** G.B.S. to Trebitsch, 26 July 1903, Shaw/Trebitsch letters p. 55.

50/10   **laugh:** G.B.S. to Siegfried Trebitsch, 26 December 1902, *CL2* p. 298 (Shaw/Trebitsch letters p. 31).

50/14   **cleverer:** G.B.S. to Trebitsch, 21 February 1903 and 26 December 1902, Shaw/Trebitsch letters pp. 42, 31; *CL2* p. 298.

50/16   **questions:** G.B.S. to Trebitsch, 1 July 1902, Shaw/Trebitsch letters p. 19.

50/27   **better:** G.B.S. to Trebitsch, 7 January, 18 September 1903, Shaw/Trebitsch letters pp. 32–3, 62.

50/31   **women:** G.B.S. to Trebitsch, 28 March 1904, Shaw/Trebitsch letters p. 69.

50/34   **slay:** G.B.S. to Trebitsch, 26 December 1902, *CL2* p. 297 (Shaw/Trebitsch letters p. 30).

51/3   **well:** G.B.S. to Trebitsch, 18 November 1902, *CL2* p. 288 (Shaw/Trebitsch letters p. 24).

51/11   **artist:** G.B.S. to Trebitsch, 16 October 1902, Shaw/Trebitsch letters p. 23.

51/14   **producers:** Siegfried Trebitsch, *Chronicle of a Life* p. 126.

51/15   **trouble:** Ibid., p. 127.

51/21   **time:** Ibid., p. 98.

51/22   **heart:** Ibid., p. 127.

51/28   **yourself:** Ibid., p. 126.

52/7   **counterpart:** Thomas Mann, 'He was Mankind's Friend', *The Listener* 18 January 1951.

52/ 9   **to do:** *Chronicle of a Life* p. 130.

52/20   **incalculable:** *CP*5 pp. 719, 720.

52/25   **sake:** Trebitsch to Archibald Henderson, 18 August 1905 (North Carolina).

52/28   **invention:** G.B.S. to Trebitsch, 16 October 1902, Shaw/Trebitsch letters p. 22.

52/last   **sensation:** *Chronicle of a Life* pp. 128–9, 130, 147.

52/19   **translating:** G.B.S. to Trebitsch, 16 October 1902; 23 February 1903; 6 March 1903; 24 March 1903; 10 August 1903; 18 September 1903; 22 October 1903; 11 April 1905, Shaw/Trebitsch letters pp. 22, 44, 46–7, 50, 57–8, 62, 65, 79.

53/25   **bluff him:** Note on Archibald Henderson manuscript p. 127A (North Carolina).

54/ 5   **suffered:** G.B.S. to Archibald Henderson, 1 August 1932. Note for his manuscript of *Playboy and Prophet* (North Carolina).

54/ 6   **plays:** G.B.S. to Trebitsch, 14 June 1905, Shaw/Trebitsch letters p. 82.

54/11   **to you:** G.B.S. to Trebitsch, 22 October 1903, ibid., p. 65.

54/17   **younger:** G.B.S. to Trebitsch, 9 September 1904, ibid., p. 73.

54/38   **bother:** G.B.S. to Henry Arthur Jones, 25 July 1908 (copy, BL Add. MS 50562 ff. 56–7).

55/ 5   **Spain:** G.B.S. to Julio Broutá, 30 June 1907, *CL*2 p. 696.

55/ 9   **money:** G.B.S. to Gerald Gould, 25 January 1919 (copy privately owned).

55/21   **live on:** G.B.S. to Arnold Bennett, 16 July 1910, *CL*2 p. 933.

55/22   **théâtre:** G.B.S. to Augustin Hamon, 15 May 1908, *CL*2 p. 783.

55/23   **devils:** G.B.S. to Hamon, 1 May 1908, *CL*2 p. 777.

55/32   **into it:** G.B.S. to Arnold Bennett, 16 July 1910, *CL*2 p. 933.

55/35   **about:** Archibald Henderson, *George Bernard Shaw: Man of the Century* (1956) p. 495.

56/ 6   **dramatist:** G.B.S. to Hamon, 9 January 1907, *CL*2 pp. 668–9.

56/13   **painful:** G.B.S. to Hamon, 24 January 1910, *CL*2 p. 893.

56/18   **combating:** G.B.S. to Hamon, n.d. (Hofstra).

57/20   **Germans:** G.B.S. to Henry D. Davray, 8 November 1922 (Ella Strong Denison Library, Scripps College, Claremont, California).

57/32   **abstractions?:** G.B.S. to Augustin Hamon, 29 October 1910, *CL*2 p. 950.

57/36   **comfort:** G.B.S. to Trebitsch, c. 1940. See *Shaw: An Exhibit*, a Catalog by Dan H. Laurence for an Exhibit Selected and

Prepared with Lois B. Garcia (University of Texas at Austin 1977), item 639.

58/11   **hands:** G.B.S. to Augustin Hamon, 9 January 1907, *CL*2 p. 670.

58/Ep.1   **at all:** G.B.S. to Trebitsch, 16 February 1904, Shaw/Trebitsch letters p. 67.

58/Ep.2   **everything:** G.B.S. to Trebitsch, 16 August 1903, *CL*2 p. 345 (Shaw/Trebitsch letters p. 59).

59/10   **residences:** G.B.S. to Henry Salt, 2 August 1903, *CL*2 p. 341.

59/37   **explained:** Lord David Cecil, *Max* (1964) p. 166.

60/ 3   **anything:** 'A Letter from Sir Max Beerbohm', *G.B.S. 90: Aspects of Shaw's Life and Work* (ed. Stephen Winsten 1946) p. 56.

60/ 5   **curses:** Ibid.

60/17   **matter:** Max Beerbohm, *Letters to Reggie Turner* (ed. Rupert Hart-Davis 1964) p. 230.

60/30   **disgusted:** G.B.S. to Siegfried Trebitsch, 7 October 1903, *CL*2 p. 375 (Shaw/Trebitsch letters p. 63).

60/38   **individual:** G.B.S. to J. N. Pasara, 24 April 1929 (Cornell).

61/ 6   **bathing:** G.B.S. to Beatrice Webb, 24 July 1901 (LSE).

61/ 9   **sea:** G.B.S. to May Morris, 14 January 1934, BL Add. MS 45348 f. 45.

61/13   **critic:** G.B.S. to Rev. Ensor Walters, 19 September 1902, *CL*2 p. 283.

61/21   **day:** Janet Dunbar, *Mrs G.B.S.: A Biographical Portrait of Charlotte Shaw* (1963) p. 204.

61/25   **three weeks:** G.B.S. to Janet Achurch, 8 May 1903, *CL*2 p. 323.

61/31   **loch:** G.B.S. to Trebitsch, 16 August 1903, *CL*2 p. 348 (Shaw/Trebitsch letters p. 61).

61/34   **chance:** G.B.S. to R. C. Phillimore, 2 April 1912 (Texas).

61/39   **Charing +:** G.B.S. to Henry Salt, 9 August 1901, *CL*2 p. 236.

62/ 3   **hill:** G.B.S. to Ellen Terry, 26 July 1904, *Ellen Terry and Bernard Shaw: A Correspondence* (ed. Christopher St John 1931) p. 411.

62/18   **holidays!:** G.B.S. to Harley Granville Barker, 12 August 1904, *CL*2 p. 443 (Shaw/Barker letters p. 23).

62/22   **wrong:** G.B.S. to Siegfried Trebitsch, 4 August 1911, *CL*2 p. 47 (Shaw/Trebitsch letters p. 154).

62/30   **surface:** G.B.S. to Charles Charrington, 4 March 1900, *CL*2 p. 150.

62/Ep.1   **just now:** G.B.S. to Alma Murray, 19 February 1901 (Princeton).

62/Ep.2   **now:** G.B.S. to Max Beerbohm, 30 December 1900, *CL*2 p.216.

63/ 4   **of it:** G.B.S. to Trebitsch, 21 June 1903, Shaw/Trebitsch letters p.53.

63/ 7   **style:** *CP*2 p.433.

63/ 9   **foolishnesses:** G.B.S. to William Wyes, 5 June 1903 (Sotheby's Catalogue, 25 July 1978, item 453).

63/14   **masterpiece:** *CP*2 p.485.

63/18   **fond:** Ibid.

63/22   **for me:** Ibid., p.484.

63/23   **play:** G.B.S. to Trebitsch, 12 June 1903, *CL*2 p.331 (Shaw/Trebitsch letters p.52).

63/24   **letters:** G.B.S. to Hilaire Belloc, 8 January 1904, *CL*2 p.506.

63/31   **intentions:** G.B.S. to William Archer, 6 June 1901, BL Add. MS 45296 ff. 101 and v.

64/ 5   **dwell:** *CP*2 p.475.

64/12   **MPs:** Ibid., p.455.

64/33   **poisonous:** Ibid., pp.456–7.

64/37   **season:** G.B.S. to Trebitsch, 21 June 1903, Shaw/Trebitsch letters p.53.

65/12   **Shakespeare:** G.B.S. to Granville Barker, 23 April 1903, Shaw/Barker letters p.12.

65/18   **end:** G.B.S. to Siegfried Trebitsch, 12 June 1903, *CL*2 p.331 (Shaw/Trebitsch letters p.52).

65/24   **Drury Lane:** G.B.S. to Trebitsch, 21 June 1903, Shaw/Trebitsch letters p.53.

65/29   **performed:** *Saturday Review* 13 June 1903. Max Beerbohm, *More Theatres: 1898–1903* (1969) pp.580–2.

66/10   **Shaw:** *Saturday Review* 2 November 1901. Max Beerbohm, 'A Cursory Conspectus of G.B.S.', *Around Theatres* (1953) p.172.

66/31   **again:** Ibid., pp.174–5.

66/36   **at all:** Ibid., p.175.

67/ 2   **saying:** G.B.S. to William Archer, 8 September 1903, *CL*2 p.366.

67/Ep.   **alone:** G.B.S. to Siegfried Trebitsch, 7 July 1902, *CL*2 p.280 (Shaw/Trebitsch letters p.20).

67/12   **generation:** G.B.S. to Beatrice Mansfield, 12 July 1900, *CL*2 p.174.

67/22   **omitted:** G.B.S. to Gilbert Murray, 12 January 1903, *CL*2 p.299.

67/28   **idea:** Beatrice Webb, *Our Partnership* p.256.

67/32   **stand it:** G.B.S. to Augustin Hamon, n.d. (LSE).

67/last   **anything?:** G.B.S. to Frederick H. Evans, 6 May 1903, *CL*2
pp. 321–2.

68/10   **author-duffer:** G.B.S. to Grant Richards, 30 March 1904,
*CL*2 p. 412.

68/13   **right:** G.B.S. to Constable & Company, 26 March 1907, *CL*2
pp. 678–9.

68/17   **do it:** G.B.S. to Constable & Co., 15 July 1903, *CL*2
pp. 337–8.

68/33   **accent?:** William Archer to G.B.S., between 27 August and 2
September 1903. See *CL*2 pp. 356–7; also 'Mr Pinero and
Mr Bernard Shaw', *Morning Leader* 22 August 1903, p. 4.

69/ 5   **worship:** G. K. Chesterton, review, *Daily News* 22 August
1903. See *Shaw: The Critical Heritage* (ed. T. F. Evans 1976)
pp. 99–100.

69/13   **salaries:** G.B.S. to Archibald Henderson, 30 June 1904, *CL*2
p. 426.

69/15   **unreality:** *CP*2 p. 506.

69/23   **remains:** Ibid., p. 527.

69/32   **aforetime:** Ibid.

69/37   **patches!:** J. G. Riewald, *Beerbohm's Literary Caricatures* (1977)
p. 81. Also *A Catalogue of the Caricatures of Max Beerbohm*,
compiled Rupert Hart-Davis (1972) item no. 1500.

70/ 2   **write:** Max Beerbohm, *Around Theatres* (1953) pp. 268–72.

70/ 7   **art:** Ibid.

70/13   **success:** Ibid.

70/27   **immediately:** G.B.S. to Max Beerbohm, 15 September 1903,
*CL*2 pp. 372–4.

70/last   **won't do:** Max Beerbohm to G.B.S., 21 September 1903, BL
Add. MS 50529 f. 29.

71/15   **theatre:** Beerbohm, *Around Theatres* p. 354.

71/33   **technique:** Ibid., pp. 413–14.

72/ 2   **brave:** G.B.S. to Mrs Patrick Campbell, 27 November 1912,
*CL*3 p. 129. See also *Bernard Shaw and Mrs Patrick Campbell:
Their Correspondence* (ed. Alan Dent 1952) p. 59.

72/15   **of it:** *Immaturity* (1931) p. xliii.

72/17   **time:** G.B.S. to Archibald Henderson, 3 January 1905, *CL*2
p. 506.

72/33   **individualism:** *Pall Mall Gazette* 19 March 1888, p. 3.

72/36   **fellow-heretic:** Archibald Henderson, *Bernard Shaw: Playboy
and Prophet* (1932) p. 753.

72/37   **morality:** *CP*3 p. 20.

73/28   **epoch:** G.B.S. to Charles Trevelyan, 14 March 1918, *CL*3
pp. 542–3.

73/31   **Evolutionists:** Hesketh Pearson, *Bernard Shaw* (rev. edn 1975) p. 237.

73/32   **Time:** *CP*2 p. 492.

74/ 7   **institutions:** Ibid., p. 670.

74/19   **purpose:** Ibid., p. 509.

74/21   **tragic:** Ibid.

74/27   **penalties:** Ibid., p. 672.

75/ 3   **develop her:** Ibid., p. 509.

75/12   **human:** Ibid., p. 687.

75/19   **romance:** Ibid., pp. 650–1.

75/28   **questions:** Ibid.

76/ 8   **lately?:** Ibid., p. 653.

76/25   **complete:** E. Belfort Bax, *The Ethics of Socialism* (1893) p. 216. Quoted in Robert F. Whitman, *Shaw and the Play of Ideas* (1977) p. 159.

76/27   **plane:** *CP*2 p. 661.

76/31   **talk:** Ibid., p. 682.

76/33   **Superman!:** Ibid., p. 689.

77/11   **pianissimos:** Winifred Loraine, *Robert Loraine, Soldier. Actor. Airman* (1938) p. 90.

77/25   **Figaro:** G.B.S. to Arnold Bennett, 27 February 1925 (Sotheby's Catalogue, 25 May 1936).

77/39   **self-understanding:** *CP*2 pp. 679–80.

78/ 6   **happy:** Ibid., p. 523.

78/22   **Superman:** Ibid., p. 743.

78/37   **from them:** Ibid., pp. 744–5.

79/30   **comedy:** G.B.S. interview, 20 January 1926 (Harvard Theater Collection).

79/31   **played:** G.B.S. to Charles Pabst, 25 February 1949 (North Carolina).

79/32   **to it:** G.B.S. note on Henderson proofs of *Playboy and Prophet* (North Carolina).

79/33   **of it:** See *Daily Sketch* 7 February 1930.

79/37   **founded:** G.B.S. to William Archer, 19 April 1919, *CL*3 p. 79.

80/last **plays:** Undated typescript statement (Texas).

81/Ep.   **absurdities:** '*John Bull's Other Island*: The Author's Instructions to the Producer', 25 December 1904, BL Add. MS 50615 f. 3.

81/15   **stage:** G.B.S. to Johnston Forbes-Robertson, 21 and 22 December 1903, *CL*2 p. 382.

81/18   **Candidamania:** G.B.S. to Ada Rehan, 29 June 1904, *CL*2 p. 424.

81/19   **me now:** G.B.S. to Harley Granville Barker, 2 September 1903, *CL*2 p. 361 (Shaw/Barker letters p. 18).

81 / 27   **leprechauns:** G.B.S. to W. B. Yeats, 23 June 1903 (Cornell).

81 / 33   **England:** Lady Gregory, *Our Irish Theatre* (1914 edn) p. 9.

81 / 35   **commerce:** *Beltaine* May 1899, pp. 7, 20–1.

82 / 1   **Irishwoman:** 'The Irish Players', *Evening Sun* (New York) 9 December 1911. See *The Matter with Ireland* (ed. with an introduction by David H. Greene and Dan H. Laurence 1962) p. 68.

82 / 7   **world:** George Moore, *Ave* (1937) p. 31.

82 / 28   **Dublin:** W. G. Fay and C. Carswell, *The Fays of the Abbey Theatre* (1935) p. 152.

82 / 33   **Morgue:** Hugh Hunt, *The Abbey: Ireland's National Theatre* (1979) p. 57.

82 / 39   **ideal:** Lennox Robinson, *Ireland's Abbey Theatre: A History, 1899–1951* (1951) p. 45.

83 / 1   **Theatre:** *CP2* p. 808.

83 / 4   **backer:** G.B.S. to W. B. Yeats, 31 August 1904, *CL2* p. 452.

83 / 5   **paper:** G.B.S. to Lady Gregory, 20 June 1904, *CL2* p. 423.

83 / 10   **rate:** G.B.S. to Arnold Daly, 13 July 1904 (Houghton).

83 / 13   **Germany:** G.B.S. to Siegfried Trebitsch, 7 October 1903, *CL2* p. 376 (Shaw/Trebitsch letters p. 64).

83 / 15   **cranks:** G.B.S. to Ada Rehan, 5 July 1904, *CL2* p. 430.

83 / 18   **time:** G.B.S. to Harley Granville Barker, 24 August 1904, *CL2* p. 444 (Shaw/Barker letters p. 26).

83 / 22   **bridges:** G.B.S. to W. B. Yeats, 31 August 1904, *CL2* p. 452.

83 / 23   **contretemps:** G.B.S. to Barker, 7 September 1904, Shaw/Barker letters p. 31.

83 / 25   **curtain-raiser:** G.B.S. to Barker, 18 August 1904, Shaw / Barker letters p. 23.

83 / 36   **collapse:** G.B.S. to W. B. Yeats, 7 September 1904 (Sotheby's Catalogue, 25 July 1978, p. 330).

83 / last   **time:** G.B.S. to Barker, 7 September 1904, Shaw/Barker letters p. 31.

84 / 20   **unreal:** *CP2* p. 919.

84 / 29   **life:** Ibid., p. 894.

84 / 31   **penance:** Ibid., pp. 990–1.

84 / 39   **Oxford Street:** Ibid., p. 992.

84 / last   **grab it:** Ibid., p. 716.

85 / 10   **absurdities:** 'Instructions to the Producer' [of *John Bull's Other Island*], typed manuscript dated 'Christmas 1904', BL Add. 50615.

85 / 11   **irresistible:** *CP2* p. 894.

85 / 15   **incorporeal:** G.B.S. to Barker, 29 July 1906, Shaw/Barker letters p. 67.

85/16   **priest:** '*John Bull's Other Island*: The Author's Instructions to the Producer'.

85/22   **Catholic:** G.B.S. to Alfred Douglas, 28 August 1940, *Bernard Shaw and Alfred Douglas: A Correspondence* (ed. Mary Hyde 1982) p. 131. See also *CL4* p. 575.

85/35   **pleasure:** *CP2* p. 991.

85/38   **future:** Ibid., p. 1012.

85/39   **at all:** Ibid.

85/40   **damnation:** Ibid., p. 1020.

86/ 1   **efficient:** Ibid., pp. 1013, 1017.

86/ 4   **minerals:** Ibid., p. 1016.

86/ 9   *inspiration*: Ibid., p. 1017.

86/12   **everything:** Ibid., p. 1011.

86/13   **often:** Ibid., p. 1020.

86/18   **be done:** Ibid., p. 1018.

86/20   **doing it:** Ibid., p. 918.

86/21   **live:** Ibid., p. 1018.

86/21   **vote:** Ibid., p. 1015.

86/22   **yours:** Ibid., p. 1013.

86/23   **cowed:** Ibid.

86/25   **traitors:** Ibid., p. 1016.

86/30   **dreaming!:** Ibid., p. 909.

86/34   *confidence*: Ibid., pp. 909–10.

86/last   **anybody:** Ibid., p. 1005.

86/4   **world:** Ibid., pp. 963, 1009.

87/ 9   **devil:** Ibid., p. 1015.

87/19   **sexless:** Ibid., p. 927.

87/20   **chest:** Ibid., p. 999.

87/21   **figure:** Ibid., p. 1005.

87/22   **fanciful:** Ibid., p. 1010.

87/23   **home:** Ibid., p. 1004.

87/29   **separate them:** Ibid., p. 914.

87/32   **understand:** Ibid., p. 913.

87/38   **Irishman:** Ibid.

88/ 4   **Time:** Ibid., p. 1021.

88/ 5   **truth:** Ibid., p. 930.

88/ 8   **come:** Ibid., p. 1018.

88/13   **one:** Bernard Shaw, *The Quintessence of Ibsenism* (1913) pp. 65, 67. *Major Critical Essays* (1986) pp. 78, 79.

88/20   **madman:** *CP2* p. 1021.

88/23   **against me:** Ibid.

89/14   **else:** W. B. Yeats to G.B.S., 5 October 1904, BL Add. MS 50553, vol. XLVI, ff. 144–5.

89/25   **Ireland:** *CP*2 p. 808.

89/27   **amused:** W. B. Yeats to Lady Gregory, 7 November 1904, *The Letters of W. B. Yeats* (ed. Allan Wade 1954) p. 442.

89/30   **shapeless:** Ibid.

89/last   **classed:** William Archer, notice, *The World* 8 November 1904. See *Shaw: The Critical Heritage* (ed. T. F. Evans 1976) p. 129.

90/ 2   **extravaganza:** Ibid.

90/15   **barricades:** W. B. Yeats to Florence Farr, 7 October 1907, *The Letters of W. B. Yeats* p. 500.

90/20   **of it:** *CP*2 p. 927.

90/24   **elephant:** W. B. Yeats to G.B.S., 1 May 1905 (Parke-Bernet Catalogue, 10 April 1962. Reprinted in *CL*2 p. 453).

90/25   **admire it:** Ibid.

90/31   **man:** W. B. Yeats to Florence Farr, 7 October 1907, *The Letters of W. B. Yeats* p. 500.

90/32   **interests:** W. B. Yeats to Edmund Gosse, 12 April 1910, *The Letters of W. B. Yeats* p. 549.

91/ 6   **neck:** G.B.S. to Lady Gregory, 26 June 1928. The Rendells Inc. Catalogue item 26, p. 48.

91/Ep.   **theatre:** G.B.S. to Harley Granville Barker, 24 August 1904, *CL*2 p. 444 (also Shaw/Barker letters p. 26).

91/15   **unpublished:** G.B.S. to Charles Charrington, 23 October 1905 (Texas).

91/26   **done:** G.B.S. to Charles Charrington, 6 June 1900, *CL*2 p. 170.

91/31   **yrs GBS:** G.B.S. to Charrington, 9 June 1900, *CL*2 p. 171.

91/last   **substitute:** G.B.S. to Charrington, 11 June 1900, *CL*2 p. 172.

92/ 7   **on him:** G.B.S. to William Archer, 8 July 1900, *CL*2 p. 175.

92/33   **ambition:** G.B.S. to Gilbert Murray, 15 March 1901, *CL*2 p. 221.

92/37   **Powers:** G.B.S. to Barker, 22 August 1900, Shaw/Barker letters p. 6.

93/ 2   **part:** G.B.S. to Barker, 7 December 1900, Shaw/Barker letters p. 7.

93/ 8   **of it:** G.B.S. to Barker, 2 January 1901, Shaw/Barker letters p. 8.

93/14   **literature:** G.B.S. to William Archer, 27 August 1903, *CL*2 p. 352.

93/20   **forty:** Doris Arthur Jones, *The Life and Letters of Henry Arthur Jones* (1930) p. 211.

93/25   **time:** 'Granville-Barker: Some Particulars by Shaw', *Drama* no. 3, Winter 1946 p. 8.

93/28   **indeed:** G.B.S. to Mrs Patrick Campbell, 18 September 1901, *Their Correspondence* p. 13.

93/32   **actor:** G.B.S.'s answer to Alan S. Downer questionnaire, 14 April 1947 (Cornell).

94/ 3   **naturally:** G.B.S. to Siegfried Trebitsch, 22 October 1903, Shaw/Trebitsch letters p. 65.

94/ 6   **melodramatic:** Miscellaneous manuscript for Hesketh Pearson (Texas).

94/14   **father:** G.B.S.'s answer to Alan S. Downer questionnaire, 14 April 1947 (Cornell).

94/24   **talent:** G.B.S. note for Henderson (North Carolina).

94/34   **soul:** Beatrice Webb diaries p. 2434 (LSE).

95/ 9   **nature:** G.B.S.'s answer to Alan S. Downer questionnaire, 14 April 1947 (Cornell).

95/23   **son?:** G.B.S. to William Archer, 14 December 1924, *CL*3 pp. 893–4.

95/36   **ability:** G.B.S.'s answer to Alan S. Downer questionnaire, 14 April 1947 (Cornell).

96/11   **soldiers:** G.B.S. to Gertrude Elliott, 8 June 1903, *CL*2 p. 328.

96/32   **architecture:** Quoted in C. B. Purdom, *Harley Granville Barker* (1955) p. 20.

96/39   **feature:** Desmond MacCarthy, *The Court Theatre 1904–1907* (University of Miami Press 1966 edn) p. 18.

96/last   **feeling:** *Dictionary of Literary Biography* vol. 10: *Modern British Dramatists* (1982) p. 67.

97/ 1   **heart:** Ben Iden Payne, *A Life in a Wooden O* (1966) p. 110.

97/ 5   **knew:** Wilfred Scawen Blunt, *My Diaries*, Part II (1922) p. 104.

97/ 9   **anon:** C. B. Purdom, *Harley Granville Barker* p. 21.

97/11   **career:** Ibid.

97/20   **arts:** Margery M. Morgan, *A Drama of Political Man* (1961) p. 2.

97/40   **Folly:** G.B.S. to Harley Granville Barker, 28 August 1904, *CL*2 p. 447 (Shaw/Barker letters p. 29).

97/last   **howling:** G.B.S. to Barker, 24 August 1904, *CL*2 p. 444 (Shaw/Barker letters p. 26).

98/ 3   **play:** G.B.S. to Barker, 3 October 1904, *CL*2 p. 457 (Shaw/Barker letters p. 39).

98/12   **happening:** G.B.S. to Ada Rehan, 27 October 1904, *CL*2 p. 458.

98/16   **opens:** G.B.S. to J. E. Vedrenne, 25 August 1904, *CL*2 p. 445.

98/30   **tricks:** G.B.S. to J. L. Shine, 29 October 1904, *CL*2 p. 461.

98/38   **saying so:** G.B.S. to Ellen O'Malley, 1 November 1904, *CL*2 p. 463.

99/ 8   **to me:** J. L. Shine to G.B.S., 30 October 1904, *CL*2 p. 462.

99/11   **Best:** Max Beerbohm, *Around Theatres* p. 353.

99/12 **success:** Desmond MacCarthy, *The Court Theatre* p. 67.

99/15 **recognised:** William Archer, notice, *The World* 8 November 1904. See *Shaw: The Critical Heritage* pp. 127–9.

99/26 **remedy:** G.B.S. to Vedrenne and Barker, 14 March 1905, *CL*2 p. 522.

99/35 **April:** G.B.S. to Florence Farr, 5 March 1905, *CL*2 p. 519.

99/40 **revolutionist:** G.B.S. to Pearl Craigie, 6 March 1905 (Lincoln Center, New York).

100/13 **noise:** *CP*2 pp. 1023–5.

100/18 **three:** G.B.S. to Trebitsch, 22 August 1919, Shaw/Trebitsch letters p. 207.

100/21 **debates:** G.B.S. to Charrington, 23 October 1905 (Texas).

100/22 **would be!:** G.B.S. to Eleanor Robson, 13 April 1905, *CL*2 p. 524.

100/Ep. **morality:** G.B.S. to Gilbert Murray, 5 September 1941, *CL*4 p. 613.

100/29 **saint too:** Eleanor Robson, *The Fabric of Memory* (1957) p. 39.

100/33 **artist:** G.B.S. to Eleanor Robson, 1 December 1904. Archibald Henderson, *George Bernard Shaw: Man of the Century* p. 586 (*The Fabric of Memory* p. 33).

101/16 **except you:** Henderson, *Shaw: Man of the Century* pp. 586–7 (*The Fabric of Memory* p. 36).

101/27 **purpose:** *The Diary of Beatrice Webb* vol. 3 (ed. Norman and Jeanne MacKenzie 1984), entries 29 November and 2 December 1905, pp. 13–14.

102/7 **producing:** G.B.S. to James Huneker, 9 May 1905, *CL*2 p. 526.

102/16 **overwhelmed:** G.B.S. to Eleanor Robson, 21 June 1905, *CL*2 p. 532.

102/18 **trains:** Henderson, *Shaw: Man of the Century* p. 566.

102/31 **cat:** G.B.S. to William Archer, 17 June 1905, BL Add. MS 45296 f. 157.

102/31 **nonsense:** G.B.S. to Harry Furniss, 12 August 1905 (Illinois).

102/36 **territory:** Irving Wardle, 'The Plays', in Michael Holroyd, *The Genius of Shaw* (1979) p. 145.

102/38 **Booths:** Raymond Mander and Joe Mitchenson, *Theatrical Companion to Shaw* (1954) p. 112.

102/39 **tent:** Henderson, *Shaw: Man of the Century* p. 514.

102/last **success:** *CP*3 p. 203.

103/2 **remorseless:** G.B.S. to Paul Reynolds, 8 February 1923 (Columbia).

103/10 **Pole:** *CP*2 p. 907.

103/14   **sea:** Preface to *Immaturity* p. xxxiii.
103/22   **land:** Janet Dunbar, *Mrs G.B.S.* p. 20
103/28   **by scrap:** G.B.S. to Louis Calvert, 23 July 1905, *CL2* p. 542.
103/29   **or so:** G.B.S. to J. E. Vedrenne, 21 July 1905 (Texas).
103/31   **dreaded:** G.B.S. to Eleanor Robson, 21 July 1905, *The Fabric of Memory* p. 41.
103/34   **chances:** G.B.S. to Granville Barker, 3 August 1905, Shaw/Barker letters p. 50.
103/35   **emotions:** *The Diary of Beatrice Webb* vol. 3, entry 29 November 1905, p. 13.
103/39   **heaven:** G.B.S. to Eleanor Robson, 21 August 1905, *CL2* p. 550.
103/last   **concerning it:** G.B.S. to Vedrenne, 17 September 1905, Shaw/Barker letters p. 54.
104/6   **non-economist:** G.B.S. to Demetrius O'Bolger, 7 August 1919, *CL3* p. 629.
104/28   **matter:** G.B.S. to Pharall Smith, 30 December 1902 (Princeton).
104/last   **created:** Louis Crompton, *Shaw the Dramatist* (1969) p. 116.
105/14   **play:** Maurice Valency, *The Cart and the Trumpet: The Plays of George Bernard Shaw* (1973) p. 250.
106/4   **itself:** *CP3* p. 157.
106/20   **poet:** Robson, *The Fabric of Memory* p. 39.
106/27   **stupendous:** G.B.S. to Louis Calvert, 23 July 1905, *CL2* pp. 542–3.
106/28   **Play:** *Major Barbara* (Garland facsimile edition 1981) p. 239.
106/32   **morals:** G.B.S. to Gilbert Murray, n.d. (Texas).
107/23   **buried:** Janet Dunbar, *Mrs G.B.S.* pp. 209–10.
108/13   **offensive:** Gilbert Murray to G.B.S., 3 December 1905. Sidney Albert, 'In More Ways Than One: *Major Barbara*'s Debt to Gilbert Murray', *Educational Theatre Journal* vol. XX no. 2, May 1968, p. 139.
108/24   **thing:** Gilbert Murray: 'The Early G.B.S.', *New Statesman and Nation* 16 August 1947. *Drama* Spring 1951.
108/28   **no use:** G.B.S. to Murray, 1 October 1905, *CL2* p. 564.
108/37   **tomorrow:** Ibid.
109/8   **uncertain:** 'In More Ways Than One: *Major Barbara*'s Debt to Gilbert Murray', *Educational Theatre Journal* vol. XX no. 2, May 1968, p. 126.
109/14   **country:** G.B.S. to Murray, 7 October 1905, *CL2* pp. 565–6.
109/21   **room:** *Major Barbara* (Garland facsimile edition) p. 195.
109/25   **for me:** Ibid., p. 199.
109/29   **for it:** *CP3* p. 180.

109/32   decide: *Major Barbara* (Garland facsimile edition) p. 215.
109/37   forsaken me?: *CP*3 p. 136.
110/ 6   sometimes: Ibid., p. 156.
110/ 9   all one: Ibid., p. 183.
110/13   lives?: Gilbert Murray, *Euripides and his Age* (1913) p. 189.
110/30   in it: *CP*3 p. 174.
110/32   conviction: Ibid., p. 169.
110/33   Hell: Ibid., p. 154.
110/35   hellish one: Ibid., p. 158.
110/last hunters: Ibid., p. 169.
111/ 6   evil, too: Ibid., p. 181.
111/11   again: Ibid., p. 169.
111/16   Greek: Ibid., p. 178.
111/21   fools: *Major Barbara* (Garland facsimile edition) p. 206.
111/30   perish: Ibid., pp. 316–17.
111/33   good: *CP*3 p. 181.
112/ 1   character: Duncan Wilson, *Gilbert Murray OM* (1988) p. 95.
112/ 6   coarseness: *CP*3 pp. 79–80.
112/17   in it: *Gilbert Murray OM* p. 110.
112/24   melodrama: G.B.S. to Gilbert Murray, 7 October 1905, *CL*2 p. 566.
112/34   *man*: Beatrice Webb, *Our Partnership* p. 315.
112/last places: G.B.S. to Gordon Wormald, 11 August 1941 (copy, privately owned).
113/ 9   for you: *Major Barbara* (Garland facsimile edition) p. 225.
113/23   convince me: *Our Partnership* p. 315.
113/26   convictions: Beatrice Webb to G.B.S., 4 December 1905, *The Letters of Sidney and Beatrice Webb* (ed. Norman MacKenzie 1978) vol. 2, p. 216.
113/30   part: G.B.S. to Eleanor Robson, 21 August 1905, *CL*2 p. 549.
113/32   war: *CP*3 p. 178.
113/34   battleships: Ibid., p. 165.
113/last movement: Introduction by Bernard F. Dukore to Garland facsimile edition of *Major Barbara*, p. xx.
114/ 2   with it: Robert Morley to Michael Holroyd, 7 October 1977.
114/ 5   world: G.B.S. to Gilbert Murray, 7 October 1905, *CL*2 p. 566.
114/ 9   means: *CP*3 pp. 169–70.
114/11   end: Robson, *The Fabric of Memory* p. 39.
114/13   skies: *CP*3 p. 185.
114/18   heaven!: Ibid., p. 182.
114/21   something: Ibid., p. 156.
114/25   understands: G.B.S. to Eleanor Robson, 24 December 1905, *CL*2 p. 589.

114/40   **let it go:** *CP*3 p. 183.
115/ 3   **gas:** *CP*2 p. 656.
115/ 6   *explosion*: *CP*5 p. 180.
115/10   **dreams:** *CP*3 p. 172.
115/11   **conviction:** Ibid., p. 174.
115/13   **aim:** R. F. Rattray, *Bernard Shaw: A Chronicle* (1951) p. 165.
115/18   **point:** G.B.S. to Eleanor Robson, 24 December 1905, *CL*2 p. 589.
115/22   **playing it:** *CP*3 p. 190.
115/23   **company:** G.B.S. to R. Golding Bright, 7 May 1910, *Advice to a Young Critic: Letters 1894–1928* (1956) p. 124.
115/26   **kill you:** G.B.S. to Eleanor Robson, 24 December 1905, *CL*2 p. 589.
115/36   *you* **like:** G.B.S. to Annie Russell, 20 November, 27 November 1905, *CL*2 pp. 581, 583.
115/last **away:** *CP*3 p. 186.
116/ 3   **adultery:** Ibid., p. 187.

CHAPTER III

117/Ep. **preserve us!:** *The Diary of Beatrice Webb* vol. 2 (ed. Norman and Jeanne MacKenzie 1983), entry 14 October 1905, pp. 355–6.
117/ 9   **bedfellow!:** Beatrice Webb to Georgina Meinertzhagen, 7 December 1903, *The Letters of Sidney and Beatrice Webb* (ed. Norman MacKenzie 1978) vol. 2, p. 196.
117/13   **people:** Norman and Jeanne MacKenzie, *The First Fabians* (1977) p. 296.
118/ 3   **extinction:** G.B.S. to Edward Pease, 14 November 1911 (Texas).
118/10   **not alone:** *The Times* 20 July 1901.
119/ 3   **change:** Sidney Webb to Beatrice Webb, 14 July 1902, *The Letters of Sidney and Beatrice Webb* vol. 2, p. 162.
119/10   **politics:** Beatrice Webb, *Our Partnership* (1948) p. 382.
119/20   **Empire!:** Ibid., p. 271.
119/33   **conversation:** Ibid., p. 309.
119/39   **things:** Ibid., p. 271.
119/last **interest him:** Ibid., p. 248.
120/ 2   **questions:** Ibid., p. 249.
120/32   **surprise:** Edward Pease, *The History of the Fabian Society* (1916) pp. 145–6.
122/ 1   **franchise:** Fabian Society pamphlet, drafted by G.B.S.,

Fabianism and the Fiscal Question: An Alternative Policy (Fabian Tract no. 116, 1904) p. 9.

122 / 24   **crisis:** G.B.S. to Edward Pease, 30 September 1903. See C. M. Joad, *Shaw and Society* (1953) pp. 171–2.

122 / 29   **boots:** G.B.S. to John Burns, 11 September 1903, *CL2* p. 369.

122 / 31   **nonsense:** 'The Solidarity of Social-Democracy', *Practical Politics: Twentieth-Century Views on Politics and Economics* (ed. Lloyd J. Hubenka 1976) p. 14.

122 / 36   **do:** G.B.S. to Beatrice Webb, 8 October 1903, *CL2* p. 377.

123 / 1   **saying:** *Shaw and Society* p. 172.

123 / 10   **incomes:** Ibid., p. 173.

123 / 16   **administration:** Ibid., p. 174.

123 / 23   **abroad:** *Fabianism and the Fiscal Question* p. 9.

123 / 39   **know:** Graham Wallas to G.B.S., 13 December 1908, BL Add. MS 50553 ff. 3–4.

123 / last   **collective:** *Fabianism and the Fiscal Question*, deluxe issue, p. 5. This Preface is not included in the ordinary issue.

124 / 4   **suddenness:** G.B.S. to Beatrice Webb, 8 October 1903, *CL2* p. 377.

124 / 10   **masterpiece:** A. M. McBriar, *Fabian Socialism and English Politics 1884–1918* (1962) p. 133.

124 / 12   **Society:** Edward Pease, *The History of the Fabian Society* p. 160.

124 / 23   **futurist:** Ibid.

124 / 29   **politics:** *Fabianism and the Fiscal Question* p. 13.

124 / 36   **weal:** Ibid., p. 38.

124 / 39   **Pitt:** Ibid., p. 37.

125 / 4   **reaction:** Ibid., pp. 37–8.

125 / 17   **pitied:** Ibid., p. 88.

126 / 12   **cobbler:** Margaret Cole, *The Story of Fabian Socialism* (1963) p. 114.

126 / 21   **party:** 'Fabian Notes, The Election', *Clarion* 2 February 1906, p. 5.

126 / Ep.   **circumstances:** Discarded section of G.B.S.'s leaflet, *Election of Executive Committee 1907–8* (8 February 1907), BL Add. MS 50681 ff. 9–10.

127 / 12   **help us:** S. G. Hobson to G.B.S., 30 October 1906, BL Add. MS 50514 f. 366.

127 / 17   **ossified:** Norman and Jeanne MacKenzie, *The First Fabians* p. 326.

127 / 36   **desirable:** Hobson to G.B.S., 30 October 1906, BL Add. MS 50514 f. 366.

128 / 3   **permeated:** The Fabian Society, *Election of Executive Committee* (8 February 1907), BL Add. MS 50681, f. 6v.

128/ 8   **of it:** Ibid., f. 6.

128/26   **science:** G.B.S.'s note for Augustin Hamon, December 1911
(Texas). See Hamon, *Le Molière du XXᵉ Siècle* (Paris, 1913).

129/ 5   **fighting:** BL Add. MS 50661 ff. 87–8: 'Fabian Darwin
Discard'.

129/14   **else:** G.B.S. to Sidney Webb, 25 November 1906, *CL2* p. 661.

129/19   **moment:** Ibid., p. 662.

129/28   **face:** H. G. Wells, *Experiment in Autobiography* (1934) vol. 1,
p. 244.

130/ 7   **drama:** Ibid., vol. 2, p. 535.

130/11   **defiance:** Leon Edel, *The Life of Henry James* (1977 edn) vol. 2,
p. 151.

130/15   **whiskers:** *Experiment in Autobiography* vol. 2, p. 539.

130/23   **verities:** Ibid.

130/29   **serenity:** 'Two New Plays', *Saturday Review* 12 January 1895,
OTN1 p. 6.

130/32   **line:** Ibid., pp. 7–8.

130/36   **hand:** 'Bernard Shaw by H. G. Wells', *Daily Express* 3
November 1950.

130/40   **mind:** *Experiment in Autobiography* vol. 2, p. 541.

131/15   **feet:** *Saturday Review* January 1898.

131/17   **pigmies:** G.B.S. to Beatrice Webb, 15–16 November 1939
(LSE).

131/25   **fulfilled:** G.B.S.'s Preface to *Great Expectations* (1937, revised
1947).

131/40   **heating:** Norman and Jeanne MacKenzie, *The Time Traveller:
The Life of H. G. Wells* (1973) p. 162.

132/ 4   **forward:** Beatrice Webb, *Our Partnership* p. 226.

132/21   **chapters:** Sidney Webb to H. G. Wells, 8 December 1901, *The
Letters of Sidney and Beatrice Webb* vol. 2, pp. 144–5.

132/27   **co-operation:** H. G. Wells, *The New Machiavelli* (1911) p. 212.

132/34   **world:** *Our Partnership* pp. 230–1.

133/16   **stuffed one:** G.B.S. to H. G. Wells, 26 January 1902 (Illinois).

133/22   **assimilated it:** Charlotte Shaw to Wells, 15 March 1903
(Illinois).

133/28   **treatment:** *The Time Traveller* p. 185.

133/35   **friendship:** G.B.S. to Wells, 10 November 1903 (Illinois).

133/last   **other:** *Experiment in Autobiography* vol. 2, pp. 539–40.

134/ 3   **esteem:** Wells to G.B.S., n.d. [1901], BL Add. MS 50552
f. 4v.

134/ 6   **like you:** Wells to G.B.S., n.d. [1906], BL Add. MS 50552,
ff. 30 and 30v.

134/11   **play:** Wells to G.B.S., 5 November 1905 (copy, Illinois).

134/14   **forward:** 'I Score over Mr Wells' [contribution to 'Rights of Man' national debate, 'chaired' by H. G. Wells], *Daily Herald* 19 February 1940, p. 4.

134/16   **boat:** G.B.S. to Wells, 19 March 1932, *CL*4 p. 280.

134/21   **plays:** G.B.S. to Wells, 6 September 1913 (Illinois).

134/25   **unsurpassable:** 'Bernard Shaw by H. G. Wells', *Daily Express* 3 November 1950.

134/32   **matters:** Ibid.

134/35   **dinner:** Wells to G.B.S., 30 July 1929, BL Add. MS 50552 f. 53.

134/36   **science?:** Wells to G.B.S., 8 December 1916, BL Add. MS 50552 f. 42.

134/40   **reject that:** G.B.S. to Wells, 19 March 1932, *CL*4 p. 279.

135/ 3   **mind:** Wells to G.B.S., n.d. [c. 1909], BL Add. MS 50552 f. 26.

135/ 6   **ignorance:** Wells to G.B.S., 17 November 1915, BL Add. MS 50552 f. 41.

135/16   **debate:** Norman and Jeanne MacKenzie, *The First Fabians* p. 325.

135/25   **individuals:** G.B.S. to Wells, 26 March 1904 (Illinois).

135/27   **Society:** *The First Fabians* p. 325.

135/35   **useful:** *The Diary of Beatrice Webb* vol. 2, entry 19 April 1904, p. 320.

136/ 6   **instincts:** Ibid., entry 17 April 1905, p. 342.

136/13   **drudgers:** *The Diary of Beatrice Webb* vol. 3, entry 15 July 1906, p. 43.

136/15   **way:** *The Time Traveller* p. 196.

136/17   **focus:** Ibid., p. 195.

136/19   **compatriots:** *The First Fabians* p. 326.

136/20   **again:** G.B.S. to Edward Pease, 4 July 1905, *CL*2 p. 536.

136/25   **dustbin:** *The Time Traveller* p. 195.

137/ 4   **within me:** H. G. Wells, *Faults of the Fabian* (privately printed 1906) p. 6.

137/25   **found:** Ibid., pp. 9–10.

137/32   **plant:** Ibid., p. 9.

137/36   **organization:** Ibid., p. 4.

138/ 5   **hear me:** Ibid., p. 6.

138/11   **giggle:** Ibid., p. 9.

138/34   **joke:** Ibid., p. 8.

139/ 6   **appear:** See *The Time Traveller* p. 198.

139/17   **report:** G.B.S. to Wells, 14 February 1906 (Illinois).

140/ 1   **Charlotte:** G.B.S. to Wells, 24 March 1906, *CL*2 p. 612.

140/25   **else:** 'H. G. Wells on the Rest of us', *The Christian*

Commonwealth, 19 May 1909. See *Pen Portraits and Reviews* (1931) pp. 279–80.

140/30 **unemployed:** *New Statesman* 17 August 1946.

140/33 **soul:** 'H. G. Wells on the Rest of us'. See *Pen Portraits and Reviews* p. 279.

140/34 **friends:** *The New Statesman* 17 August 1946.

140/last **fight:** *The Time Traveller* p. 204.

141/13 **condemned:** Charlotte Shaw to Wells, 4 September 1906 (Illinois).

141/16 **done:** *The First Fabians* p. 332.

141/20 **glad!:** Charlotte Shaw to Wells, 7 October 1906 (Illinois).

141/25 **scheme:** Edward Pease, *The History of the Fabian Society* p. 168.

142/12 **achievements:** 'Reconstruction of the Fabian Society'.

142/19 **agenda:** *The Time Traveller* p. 209.

142/11 **affairs:** 'Reconstruction of the Fabian Society'.

142/23 **for ever:** G.B.S. to H. G. Wells, undated [assigned to 14 September 1906], *CL2* pp. 651–2.

143/36 **ILP?:** *The Time Traveller* p. 204.

144/ 6 **sinners:** Keir Hardie to G.B.S., 5 December 1906, BL Add. MS 50538 ff. 20–1.

144/12 **things?:** *The Time Traveller* p. 212.

144/15 **vindictive:** G.B.S. to Hubert Bland, 10 December 1906, *CL2* p. 666.

144/23 **of them:** Ibid.

144/26 **overworked:** Ibid.

145/ 5 **consequences:** 'Members' Meetings', *Fabian News* XVII, January 1907, pp. 11–13.

145/ 9 **Wells:** Ibid.

145/21 **laughing:** S. G. Hobson, *Pilgrim to the Left: Memoirs of a Modern Revolutionary* (1938) pp. 106–7.

145/28 **joke:** Ibid.

145/32 **gallery:** *The First Fabians* p. 338.

145/34 **business:** *The Diary of Beatrice Webb* vol. 3, entry 15 December 1906, p. 62.

145/37 **succeeded:** Ibid.

146/ 1 **right:** *The Time Traveller* p. 206.

146/ 4 **G.B.S.:** *The Diary of Beatrice Webb* vol. 3, entry 15 December 1906, p. 62.

146/13 **man:** G.B.S. to St John Ervine, 21 October 1920 (copy provided by Janet Dunbar).

146/15 **without him:** *The First Fabians* p. 338.

146/21 **undisliked:** 'H. G. Wells on the Rest of us'. See *Pen Portraits and Reviews* p. 280.

146/22   **exchange:** 'The Man I Knew', *New Statesman* 17 August 1946, p. 115.

146/27   **forgotten:** G.B.S. to Edward Pease, 18 March 1916 (Texas).

146/33   **tell you:** G.B.S. to Wells, 17 December 1906, *CL*2 p. 667.

146/36   **time:** *The First Fabians* p. 338.

147/ 8   **H. G.:** Wells to G.B.S., 9 June 1928, BL Add. MS 50552 f. 50.

147/10   **fun:** G.B.S. to St John Ervine, 21 October 1920 (copy provided by Janet Dunbar).

147/13   **made so:** Wells to G.B.S., n.d., BL Add. MS 50552 f. 22.

147/15   **blue:** 'H. G. Wells on the Rest of us'. See *Pen Portraits and Reviews* p. 283.

147/26   **watch:** *The Diary of Beatrice Webb* vol. 3, entry 15 July 1906, p. 44.

147/32   **lessen:** Desmond MacCarthy, *Shaw* (1951) p. 55.

147/35   **emotion:** From an unsigned notice, *Pall Mall Gazette* 29 November 1905. See *Shaw: The Critical Heritage* (ed. T. F. Evans 1976) pp. 142–3.

148/ 1   **forgiven:** Unsigned notice, *Morning Post* 29 November 1905. See *Shaw: The Critical Heritage* p. 146.

148/ 3   **about:** Sir Oliver Lodge, '*Major Barbara*, G.B.S., and Robert Blatchford', *Clarion* 29 December 1905. See *Shaw: The Critical Heritage* p. 160.

148/ 9   **revolting:** J. T. Grein, from a notice, *Sunday Times* 3 December 1905. See *Shaw: The Critical Heritage* p. 149.

148/17   **attack:** Max Beerbohm, notice, *Saturday Review* 9 December 1905. See *Shaw: The Critical Heritage* p. 157.

148/40   **Republican:** *CP*2 p. 811.

149/15   **brutal:** *The Letters of Rupert Brooke* (ed. Geoffrey Keynes 1968) pp. 62, 74, 38.

149/16   **youth:** Leonard Woolf, *Sowing: An Autobiography of the Years 1880 to 1904* (1960) p. 164.

149/27   **Dreyfus:** Ibid., p. 152.

149/36   **London:** Rupert Brooke to St John Lucas, October 1906, *The Letters of Rupert Brooke* p. 62.

149/39   **names:** Desmond MacCarthy, *The Court Theatre 1904–1907* (ed. Stanley Weintraub, University of Miami Press 1966) p. xx.

150/28   **Court:** Ibid., Appendix II, p. 164.

151/ 5   **Tennyson:** Hesketh Pearson, *The Pilgrim Daughters* (1961) pp. 305–7.

151/10   **you do?:** Margaret Webster, *The Same Only Different* (1969) p. 239.

151/20   **place:** 'Rules for Play Producers', *Strand Magazine* CXVII, July 1949, pp. 17–25.

151/27   **voice:** Hesketh Pearson, *Bernard Shaw* (rev. edn 1975) p. 243.

152/12   **amusement:** 'Rules for Play Producers', *Strand Magazine*
          CXVII, July 1949, pp. 17–25.

152/35   **recklessly:** G.B.S. to Granville Barker, 19 September 1907,
          Bernard Shaw's Letters to Granville Barker (ed. C. B. Purdom
          1957) pp. 105–6.

152/39   **play?:** G.B.S. to Barker, 19 July 1906, Shaw/Barker letters
          p. 65.

153/ 3   **written for:** G.B.S. to Barker, 19 January 1908, Shaw/Barker
          letters p. 115.

153/13   **without:** G.B.S. to Barker and Vedrenne, 21 April 1907,
          Shaw/Barker letters p. 81.

153/28   **freshness:** 'Granville Barker: Some Particulars by Shaw',
          Drama, Winter 1946, p. 14.

153/last **Suggestion:** Hesketh Pearson, *Modern Men and Mummers*
          (1921) pp. 177–8.

154/ 6   **form:** C. B. Purdom, *Harley Granville Barker* (1955) p. 164.

154/18   **actresses:** 'An Aside by Bernard Shaw', Lillah McCarthy,
          Myself and My Friends (1933) p. 5.

154/26   **the stage:** 'A New Lady Macbeth and a New Mrs Ebbsmith',
          Saturday Review 25 May 1895, *OTN1* pp. 132–3.

154/36   **Diana:** *Myself and My Friends* p. 5.
154/37   **Whitefield:** Ibid., p. 55.
155/ 7   **surpassed:** Ibid., pp. 5–6.
155/15   **income.** Margot Peters, *Bernard Shaw and the Actresses* (1980)
          p. 280.

155/17   **women:** *Myself and My Friends* p. 57.
155/28   **time:** Ibid., pp. 59–61.
155/35   **of me:** Ibid., pp. 63–4.
156/ 4   **happiness:** Ibid., p. 65.
156/ 9   **well:** E. A. Baughan, initialled notice, *Daily News* 24 May 1905.
          See *Shaw: The Critical Heritage* p. 109.

156/12   **existed:** *Myself and My Friends* p. 6.
156/23   **for him:** 'Granville Barker: Some Particulars by Shaw', *Drama*,
          Winter 1946, p. 10.

156/28   **welcome:** Ibid., pp. 10–11.
156/34   **another:** Ibid., p. 10.
157/ 6   **marriage:** *The Diary of Beatrice Webb* vol. 3, entry 4 September
          1906, p. 48.

157/10   **hate:** *Myself and My Friends* pp. 78–9.
157/12   **universe:** G.B.S. to Lillah McCarthy, 1 September 1906, *CL2*
          p. 644.

157/Ep.   **reasons:** *CP3* p. 59.

158/ 6   **sauce:** Preface to *The Doctor's Dilemma, CP3* p. 313.

158/21   **theory:** G.B.S. to Almroth Wright, 15 September 1905 (Sotheby's Catalogue, 28 July 1977, item 518).

158/27   **discovery:** G.B.S. to A. B. Walkley, 18 November 1906, *CL2* p. 660.

158/36   **Cox:** G.B.S. to William Archer, 19 November 1906, BL Add. MS 45296 f. 177v.

159/24   **saving:** *Sunday Times* 7 June 1981.

159/37   **women:** Almroth Wright, *Alethetropic Logic* (1953) p. 217.

160/ 2   **world:** Almroth Wright, *The Unexpurgated Case Against Woman Suffrage* (1913) pp. 35–6.

160/29   **enemy:** Lord Moran, Annual Address delivered to the Royal College of Physicians by the President, 1948. Quoted in Leonard Colebrook, *Almroth Wright: Provocative Doctor and Thinker* (1954) p. 196.

160/last   **horror:** G.B.S. to Wright, 15 May 1941 (copy privately owned).

161/11   **all this:** Ibid.

161/21   **too:** G.B.S. to Gilbert Murray, 11 October 1912, BL Add. MS 50542 f. 34.

161/27   **biologist:** G.B.S. to Wright, 15 May 1941 (copy privately owned).

161/33   **laboratory:** G.B.S. to Dr Arthur Gregson, 29 October 1930 (Texas).

161/34   **instruction:** Ibid.

161/35   **play:** Almroth Wright to G.B.S., BL Add. MS 50553 f. 119. See Margery Morgan's Introduction to Garland facsimile edition of *The Doctor's Dilemma* (1981) p. xiv.

161/last   **wares:** Wright to G.B.S., 12 November 1906, BL Add. MS 50553 ff. 118–19.

162/13   **sense:** *CP3* p. 328.

162/17   **proud of:** Ibid., p. 329.

162/27   **aesthetic:** 'Aesthetic Science', *Design '46: Survey of British Industrial Design as Displayed at the 'Britain Can Make It' Exhibition* (1946) pp. 143–4.

162/34   **again:** 'The Socialist Criticism of the Medical Profession', *The Medico-Legal Society: Transactions 1908–09* (1909) pp. 202–28.

162/last   **scientific:** G.B.S. to Almroth Wright, 15 May 1941 (copy privately owned).

163/11   **everywhere:** 'Aesthetic Science', loc. cit.

163/25   **alternative:** Louis Crompton, *Shaw the Dramatist: A Study of the Intellectual Background of His Plays* (1971) p. 126.

163/32   **himself:** Almroth Wright to G.B.S., 12 November 1906, BL Add. MS 50553 f. 118.

163/37   **murder!:** *CP3* p. 436.

163/38   **responsible:** Ibid., p. 443.

163/last   **science:** G.B.S. to Almroth Wright, 11 November 1910 (privately owned).

164/ 6   **theories:** *Shaw the Dramatist* p. 124.

164/17   **gold:** Leonard Colebrook, *Almroth Wright: Provocative Doctor and Thinker* (1954) p. 189.

164/20   **immunology:** *British Medicine* 21 November 1978.

164/35   **realise:** G.B.S. to Hentschl, 17 January 1907 (North Carolina).

165/ 3   **them:** 'Memoirs of an Old-fashioned Physician', *Pall Mall Gazette* 25 November 1885, pp. 4–5.

165/13   **Ralph:** *CP3* p. 407.

165/16   **honor:** Ibid., p. 421.

165/34   **tradesman's:** G.B.S. to Countess Feodora Gleichen, 22 March 1906, *CL2* p. 610.

165/37   **himself:** Introduction to the Garland facsimile edition of *The Doctor's Dilemma* (1981) p. xvi.

165/38   **Shaw:** *CP3* p. 393.

166/16   **defence:** G.B.S. to Hentschl, 17 January 1907 (North Carolina). See also G.B.S. to R. D. Blumenfeld, 8 November 1906 (Texas).

166/22   **without them:** G.B.S. to Hugo Vallentin, 13 February 1921 (Texas).

166/34   **distribution:** 'Heartbreak Hospital', *The Observer* 14 October 1945, p. 3.

167/ 3   **importance:** Archibald Henderson, *Bernard Shaw: Playboy and Prophet* (1932) p. 616.

167/12   **Jennifer:** G.B.S. to Lillah McCarthy, 1 September 1906, *CL2* p. 644.

167/15   **in me:** *CP3* p. 377.

167/18   **Guinevere:** Ibid., p. 357.

167/28   **immortals:** *The Tribune* 14 July 1906.

167/29   **taste:** G.B.S. to Mrs Patrick Campbell, 12 December 1906 (Boston). Quoted in Sotheby's Catalogue, 18 July 1972, item 344.

167/last   **Finn:** *Bernard Shaw: Playboy and Prophet* pp. 616–17.

168/ 3   ***macabre*:** See Margery Morgan's Introduction to the Garland facsimile edition of *The Doctor's Dilemma* (1981) p. xix.

168/ 9   **pathos:** Ibid.

168/18   **spectacle:** G.B.S. to Siegfried Trebitsch, 17 May 1910, *CL2* p. 926 (Shaw/Trebitsch letters p. 150).

168/21   ***inspired*:** G.B.S. to Mrs Patrick Campbell, 12 December 1906 (Boston). Quoted in Sotheby's Catalogue, 18 July 1972, item 344.

168/25   **Paris:** G.B.S. to Cecil Lewis, 15 December 1926 (Texas).

168/31   **hears:** *CP*3 p. 411.

168/34   **thrill:** *The Times* 21 November 1906.

169/14   **G. Bernard Shaw:** 'Mr G. B. Shaw on the Original of his "Artist's Creed", letter to the Editor, *The Standard* 22 November 1906, *CP*3 pp. 438–9.

169/Ep.   **damned:** *As You Like It*, Act III, Scene 2 (quoted as epigraph to Desmond MacCarthy's *The Court Theatre*).

169/25   **quickly:** G.B.S. to Archibald Henderson, 11 August 1906, *CL*2 pp. 639–41.

169/31   **inked:** Shaw to Siegfried Trebitsch, 28 August 1906, Shaw/Trebitsch letters p. 111.

169/32   **play:** G.B.S. to Lillah McCarthy, 1 September 1906, *CL*2 p. 644.

170/last **genius:** Louis A. Sargent to G.B.S., 18 August 1906, BL Add. MS 50514 ff. 337–40. See also Sargent to G.B.S., 28 August 1906, BL Add. MS 50514 ff. 340–1.

171/10   **Student:** Royal Academy to G.B.S., 23 August 1906, BL Add. MS 50514 f. 339.

171/15   **was:** G.B.S. to Granville Barker, 24 September 1906, Shaw/Barker letters p. 72.

171/31   **thoroughly?:** Granville Barker to Neville Lytton, 12 October 1906 (Berg).

171/38   **others:** Desmond MacCarthy, notice, *Speaker* 24 November 1906. See *Shaw: The Critical Heritage* p. 169.

172/18   **shore:** A transcript of Shaw's speech at the Complimentary Dinner to J. E. Vedrenne and Granville Barker on 7 July 1907. Reprinted as Appendix II to the 1966 edition (ed. Stanley Weintraub, University of Miami Press) of Desmond MacCarthy's *The Court Theatre*.

172/19   **edge:** Unsigned notice, *Morning Post* 22 November 1906. See *Shaw: The Critical Heritage* p. 165.

172/32   **nation:** *The Times* 10 May 1909, p. 12.

172/36   **movement:** John Elsom and Nicholas Tomalin, *The History of the National Theatre* (1978) p. 28.

173/16   **Bankside:** Hesketh Pearson, *Modern Men and Mummers* (1921) p. 179.

173/38   **arrived:** G.B.S. to J. E. Vedrenne, 26 February 1907, Shaw/Barker letters p. 78.

174/ 2   **nuisance:** Josephine Johnson, *Florence Farr* (1975) p. 126.

174/ 6   **egotistic:** *The Journals of Arnold Bennett: 1896–1910* (ed. Newman Flower 1932), entries 19 January and 24 January 1908, pp. 275–6.

174/13 **verdict:** G.B.S. to J. E. Vedrenne, undated [c. May 1907], Shaw/Barker letters, p. 78.

174/16 **pessimism:** *Drama*, Spring 1959 pp. 28–31.

174/21 **simultaneously:** 'Granville Barker: Some Particulars By Shaw', *Drama*, Winter 1946 pp. 9–10.

174/26 **loathe it:** G.B.S. to Vedrenne and Barker, 19 August 1908 *CL*2 p. 809.

174/38 **situation:** G.B.S. to Vedrenne, 16 September 1907 (Enthoven Collection, Theatre Museum, Victoria and Albert Museum).

175/ 1 **destruction:** G.B.S. to Vedrenne, 9 April 1908 (Texas).

175/ 5 **Vedrenne?:** G.B.S. to Lillah McCarthy, 4 May 1907 (Texas).

175/ 6 **Barker:** G.B.S. to Vedrenne, 26 May 1908 (Texas).

175/ 8 **of it:** G.B.S. to Gertrude Kingston, 4 December 1912 (King's College Library, Cambridge).

175/13 **world:** G.B.S. to Lee Matthews, 29 February 1908 (Texas).

175/18 **recommends:** G.B.S. to Vedrenne, undated [May 1907], Shaw/Barker letters pp. 77–8.

175/21 **actor:** G.B.S. to Cedric Hardwicke, 9 May 1949 (Texas).

175/26 **loved them:** Eric Salmon, *Granville Barker: A Secret Life* (1983) p. 123.

175/32 **volume:** G.B.S. to Granville Barker, 5 August 1906, Shaw/Barker letters p. 68.

176/ 2 **feet:** G.B.S. to Lillah McCarthy, 17 April 1907 (Texas).

176/18 **failures:** G.B.S. to Ellen O'Malley, 30 March 1907 (Texas).

176/23 **through:** G.B.S. to Granville Barker, 5 August 1906, Shaw/Barker letters p. 68.

176/25 **Savoy:** G.B.S. to Barker and Vedrenne, 21 April 1907, ibid., p. 82.

176/38 **partnership:** G.B.S. to Vedrenne, 3 May 1907 (Enthoven Collection, Theatre Museum, Victoria and Albert Museum).

176/39 **usurer:** G.B.S. to J. E. Vedrenne, 1 August 1907, *CL*2 p. 706.

177/ 3 **superiority:** G.B.S. to J. E. Vedrenne, 27 July 1907, *CL*2 p. 703.

177/11 **propagandist:** Hesketh Pearson, *Bernard Shaw* (rev. edn 1975) p. 256.

177/22 **week:** G.B.S. to Vedrenne and Barker, 19 August 1908, *CL*2 p. 807.

177/30 **block it:** G.B.S. to Granville Barker, 18 September 1907, Shaw/Barker letters p. 105.

177/40 **spectacle:** Eric Salmon, *Granville Barker: A Secret Life* p. 127.

178/13 **immortal:** *CP*3 pp. 663–4.

178/16 **here:** G.B.S. to Edward McNulty, 29 June 1908, *CL*2 p. 792.

178/17 **Repertory:** G.B.S. to J. E. Vedrenne, 3 October 1909, *CL*2 p. 871.

178/19   **later on:** G.B.S. to Vedrenne, 5 March 1909 (Bucknell).
178/27   **hanging-up:** G.B.S. to J. E. Vedrenne, 3 October 1909, *CL*2
          p. 871.
179/11   **stop:** *A Draft Letter to Millionaires*, c. 1911, BL Add. MS
          45296 f. 220.

CHAPTER IV

180/Ep.   **master:** Rainer Maria Rilke to Elizabeth von der Heydt, 26
          April 1906, BL Add. MS 50548 f. 136.
180/ 9   **handy:** G.B.S. to H. G. Wells, 5 April 1904, *CL*2 p. 414.
180/27   **Molière:** *Three Plays by Brieux* (1911) with a Preface by G.B.S.,
          p. ix.
181/ 3   **poses:** 'Rodin', *The Nation* 9 November 1912 and 24
          November 1917. See Bernard Shaw, *Pen Portraits and Reviews*
          (1931) p. 228.
181/25   *porte*: Charlotte Shaw to Auguste Rodin, 27 February 1907
          (Musée Rodin).
181/28   **me!!!!!:** G.B.S. to Siegfried Trebitsch, 1 March 1906,
          Shaw/Trebitsch letters p. 95.
181/31   **for us:** G.B.S.'s note on Archibald Henderson's *Playboy and
          Prophet* manuscript (North Carolina).
181/36   *poser*: Charlotte Shaw to Rodin, 8 April 1906 (Musée Rodin).
182/ 2   **give you:** 'How Frank ought to have done it', *SSS* pp. 124–5.
182/11   **for it:** Rainer Maria Rilke to Clara Rilke, 26 April 1906, BL
          Add. MS 50548 f. 136.
182/16   **zest:** Rilke to Elizabeth von der Heydt, 26 April 1906, BL Add.
          MS 50548 f. 136.
182/19   *extraordinaire*: Rilke to William Rothenstein, 26 April 1906,
          William Rothenstein, *Men and Memories* vol. 2 (1932) p. 108.
182/20   **movements:** Siegfried Trebitsch, *Chronicle of a Life* (1953)
          p. 188.
182/22   **goat:** Rilke to S. Fischer, 19 April 1906, BL Add. MS 50548
          f. 135.
182/23   *caractère*: William Rothenstein, *Men and Memories* vol. 2
          (1932) p. 108.
182/25   **a day:** 'Rodin'. See *Pen Portraits and Reviews* p. 228.
182/last **delight:** Rilke to Clara Rilke, 19 April 1906, BL Add. MS
          50548 ff. 135–6.
183/ 3   **life:** G.B.S. to Sydney Cockerell, 20 April 1906, *CL*2 p. 618.
183/ 6   **read:** Ibid.
183/ 8   **simple:** 'Rodin'. See *Pen Portraits and Reviews* p. 231.

183/11   **s'impose:** Robert Boothby, *I Fight to Live* (1947) p. 102.
183/12   **languages:** G.B.S. to Jacob Epstein, undated, Hesketh
          Pearson, *Bernard Shaw* (rev. edn 1975), p. 320.
183/17   **Rodin:** Rothenstein, *Men and Memories* vol. 2, p. 108.
183/19   **great man:** *Men and Memories* vol. 1 (1931) p. 208.
183/22   **universe:** Trebitsch, *Chronicle of a Life* p. 188.
183/26   **world:** G.B.S. to Archibald Henderson, 29 July 1907, *CL*2
          p. 704.
183/34   **Le Penseur:** *Alvin Langdon Coburn, Photographer: An
          Autobiography* (1967) p. 40.
183/37   **parliament:** 'Rodin'. See *Pen Portraits and Reviews* p. 227.
183/40   **reputation:** Ibid.
184/ 4   **plea:** Archibald Henderson, *Bernard Shaw: Playboy and Prophet*
          (1932) p. 736.
184/10   **unknown:** *Table-Talk of G.B.S.* (ed. Archibald Henderson
          1925) pp. 90–1.
184/17   **himself:** G.B.S. to Jacob Epstein, undated, Hesketh Pearson,
          Bernard Shaw p. 320.
184/30   **seeing:** *Chronicle of a Life* p. 190.
184/31   **Sunday:** G.B.S. to Granville Barker, 7 May 1906, *CL*2 p. 621
          (Shaw/Barker letters p. 62).
185/ 2   **revolutionists:** 'Bernard Shaw's Message: "The People *Won't*
          Revolt"', *Labour Leader* 11 May 1906, p. 750.
185/ 9   **stones:** G.B.S. to Granville Barker, 7 May 1906, *CL*2 p. 621
          (Shaw/Barker letters p. 62).
185/13   **away:** Ibid.
185/14   **the way:** Janet Dunbar, *Mrs G.B.S.: A Biographical Portrait of
          Charlotte Shaw* (1963) p. 216.
185/19   **full one:** G.B.S. to Trebitsch, 1 May 1906, Shaw/Trebitsch
          letters p. 100.
185/26   **immortel:** Charlotte Shaw to Auguste Rodin, 15 November
          1906 (Musée Rodin).
185/35   **better:** G.B.S. to Lady Hilton Young (formerly Scott, also
          Kennet), 24 April 1931 (Cambridge University Library).
186/ 3   **nobleman:** G.B.S. to Jacob Epstein, undated, Hesketh
          Pearson, *Bernard Shaw* p. 321.
186/ 6   **trebled:** Ibid., p. 322.
186/22   **Superman:** 'Rodin'. See *Pen Portraits and Reviews* p. 228.
186/27   **face:** G.B.S. to Margaret Epstein, 29 December 1937, *CL*4
          p. 487.
186/28   **of it:** G.B.S. to Jacob Epstein, undated, Hesketh Pearson,
          Bernard Shaw p. 322.
186/34   **flesh:** G.B.S.'s Preface to *Portraits and Figures by Sigismund de
          Strobl* (exhibition catalogue, 1935).

186/37   **sitter:** G.B.S. to Sean O'Casey, 15 March 1942 (copy, Society of Authors).

186/39   **materially:** *Epstein: An Autobiography* (second edn 1963) p. 81.

187/ 5   **of it:** G.B.S. to Margaret Epstein, 29 December 1937, *CL*4 p. 487.

187/ 9   **condition:** G.B.S. to Jacob Epstein, undated, Hesketh Pearson, *Bernard Shaw* (revised edn 1975), p. 322.

187/11   **portrait:** Ibid.

187/13   **Shaw:** Ibid.

187/19   **life:** 'Rodin'. See *Pen Portraits and Reviews* p. 226.

187/21   **model:** G.B.S. to Jacob Epstein, undated, Hesketh Pearson, *Bernard Shaw* p. 322.

187/39   **fire:** Winifred Loraine, *Robert Loraine, Soldier. Actor. Airman* (1938) p. 82.

188/ 6   **detestable:** Ibid., pp. 90–1.

188/10   **property:** Ibid.

188/Ep.   **jobs:** G.B.S. to Beatrice Webb, 9 December 1910 (LSE).

188/29   **them:** *Shaw the Villager and Human Being: A Biographical Symposium* (ed. Allan Chappelow 1961) p. 30.

188/33   **Flood:** Ibid., p. 98.

189/ 2   **thing:** Ibid.

189/13   **to us:** Ibid., p. 56.

190/ 6   **good:** G.B.S. to Sydney Cockerell, undated [assigned to 3 April 1907], *CL*2 p. 682.

190/ 9   **burst:** G.B.S. to Mrs Grainger, 8 November 1907 (Texas).

190/35   **rule:** G.B.S. to Anthony Tuke, 12 June 1939 (privately owned).

191/37   **America:** 'Orage: Memories', *New English Weekly* 15 November 1934, pp. 99–100.

191/last   **insolvent:** G.B.S. to Graham Wallas, 28 November 1908 (LSE).

192/ 8   **astonishing:** *New English Weekly* 15 November 1934, pp. 99–100.

193/ 6   **promised:** G.B.S. to Granville Barker, 10 August 1907, *Bernard Shaw's Letters to Granville Barker* (ed. C. B. Purdom 1957) p. 98.

193/10   **house:** G.B.S. to Granville Barker, 3 August 1907, Shaw/Barker letters p. 98.

193/27   **last:** G.B.S. to H. G. Wells, 14 August 1907, *CL*2 pp. 709–10.

193/last   **of me:** Winifred Loraine, *Robert Loraine* p. 95.

194/ 4   **family:** *The Journals of Arnold Bennett: 1896–1910* (ed. Newman Flower 1932), entry 24 January 1908, p. 276.

194/10   **address:** G.B.S. to William Archer, 3 July 1908, *CL*2 p. 801.

194/12   **mediocrity:** Ibid., p. 802.

194/15   **oil:** *Dagens Nyheter* 12 July 1908.

194/17   **before:** 1 August 1908. See Sotheby's Catalogue, 4 November 1929, item 607.

194/28   **affable:** Maurice Collis, *Somerville and Ross* (1968) pp. 127–8.

194/38   **independent:** Lady Gregory, *Seventy Years* (1974) p. 474.

195/10   **restaurant:** See Sotheby's Catalogue, 4 November 1929, item 608.

195/12   **murder me:** G.B.S. to Granville Barker, 11 August 1908, Shaw/Barker letters p. 133.

195/17   **it is:** G.B.S. to Granville Barker, 12 August 1908, *CL*2 p. 807 (Shaw/Barker letters pp. 134–5).

195/23   **divorce:** G.B.S. to Granville Barker, 19 August 1908, Shaw/Barker letters p. 136.

195/32   **time:** 'When "G.B.S." Met Strindberg', *Manchester Guardian* 2 March 1928, p. 11 and *Baltimore Sun* 4 March 1928.

195/33   **impossible:** G.B.S. to William Archer, undated [assigned to 16 July 1908], *CL*2 p. 802.

195/38   **man?:** *Baltimore Sun* 4 March 1928.

196/ 2   **shy:** Ibid.

196/ 4   **German:** *New York Times* 25 March 1928.

196/16   **theatre:** *Sweden Now* no. 5, 1981, pp. 29–31.

196/22   **broke up:** G.B.S. to Granville Barker, c. 16 July 1908, Shaw/Barker letters p. 130.

196/34   **great:** *Adam* XVII no. 190–1, January–February 1949, p. 1.

196/36   **dramatist:** *CP*2 p. 38.

196/38   **living:** Ibid.

197/ 1   **spirit:** Ibid.

197/14   **beyond him?:** 'He was Mankind's Friend', *The Listener* 18 January 1951. In *Shaw: The Critical Heritage* (ed. T. F. Evans 1976) pp. 395–402.

197/29   **murdering him:** 'Europa om August Strindberg', written on 30 April 1912, just before Strindberg's death on 14 May. *Dagens Nyheter* 15 May 1912.

198/Ep.   **discoveries:** Strindberg, *Miss Julie* (translated by Michael Meyer 1964) p. 22.

198/ 7   **intervals:** Ibid.

198/11   **drama:** *CP*3 p. 449.

198/21   **play:** 'Sardoodledom', *Saturday Review* 1 June 1895, *OTN*1 p. 133.

198/23   **rules:** 'The Season's Moral', *Saturday Review* 27 July 1895, *OTN*1 p. 192.

198/24   **situation:** 'Michael and His Lost Angel', *Saturday Review* 18 January 1896, *OTN*2 p. 14.

198/26   **for it**: 'Madame Sans-Gêne', *Saturday Review* 17 April 1897, *OTN*3 p. 110.

198/27   **ever saw**: 'Two Bad Plays', *Saturday Review* 20 April 1895, *OTN*1 p. 97.

198/33   **play**: 'The New Magda and the New Cyprienne', *Saturday Review* 6 June 1896, *OTN*2 p. 151.

198/last   **details**: Martin Meisel, *Shaw and the Nineteenth-Century Theater* (1963) p. 266.

199/ 5   **telegrams**: 'Two Bad Plays', *Saturday Review* 20 April 1895.

199/12   **drama**: 'Toujours Daly', *Saturday Review* 13 July 1895, *OTN*1 p. 177.

199/32   **of it**: G.B.S.'s own account written to Archibald Henderson (172 F and 172 G) for inclusion in *Playboy and Prophet*, where it appears (pp. 559–60) as Henderson's narrative (North Carolina).

199/35   **form**: Eric Bentley, *Bernard Shaw* (1967 edn) p. 87.

199/37   **Laughter**: *CP*2 p. 733.

200/ 6   **else**: Henderson, *Playboy and Prophet* pp. 559–60.

200/11   **play**: *Diaries* 2, entry 17 June 1893, p. 946.

200/35   **parts**: G.B.S. to Mrs Patrick Campbell, 19 December 1915, *CL*3 p. 335. See *Bernard Shaw and Mrs Patrick Campbell: Their Correspondence* (ed. Alan Dent 1952) p. 182.

200/38   **drama**: G.B.S. to William Faversham, 20 December 1915, *CL*3 p. 338.

201/ 6   **irresistible**: *CP*3 p. 622.

201/20   **life**: G.B.S. to Erica Cotterill, 28 September 1905, *CL*2 p. 563.

201/31   **mother**: G.B.S. to Gilbert Murray, 13 March 1911, *CL*3 p. 17.

201/35   **strain**: Ibid., pp. 17–18.

201/38   **lips**: G.B.S. to Maud Churton Braby, 18 May 1908, *CL*2 p. 786.

202/ 7   **Sonny**: *CP*3 p. 655.

202/11   **amusing**: Ibid., p. 582.

202/13   **fool**: Ibid., p. 625.

202/15   **need**: Ibid., p. 626.

202/18   **pressed it**: Ibid.

202/25   **mother**: Ibid., p. 627.

202/26   **for you**: Ibid., p. 655.

202/27   **obey you**: Ibid., p. 631.

202/38   **at all**: Ibid., p. 661.

203/18   **George**: Ibid., p. 553.

203/20   **decent**: Ibid., p. 619.

203/22   **some day**: Ibid., p. 581.

203/25   **divine**: Ibid., p. 597.

203 / 27   **another:** Ibid., p. 657.

203 / 30   **people:** Ibid., pp. 611–12.

204 / 8   **keeping:** G.B.S. to Granville Barker, 23 September 1907, Shaw/Barker letters p. 108.

204 / 12   **Equality:** G.B.S. to Lillah McCarthy, 13 May 1908, *CL2* p. 781.

204 / 28   **Press:** *CP3* pp. 665–6.

204 / 30   **denunciation:** G.B.S. to Siegfried Trebitsch, 29 June 1908, *CL2* p. 794 (Shaw/Trebitsch letters p. 138).

205 / 2   **fidget:** Max Beerbohm, *Around Theatres* (1953) pp. 509–10.

205 / 8   **funny:** Desmond MacCarthy, *Shaw* (1951) p. 159.

205 / 10   **home:** *Bernard Shaw and Alfred Douglas: A Correspondence* (ed. Mary Hyde 1982), Appendix I p. 207.

205 / 15   **really are:** G.B.S. to C. H. Norman, 15 May 1908 (Cornell).

205 / 23   **institution:** G.B.S. to J. E. Vedrenne, 22 [early a.m. 23] May 1908, *CL2* p. 786.

205 / 29   **isnt it?:** *CP3* p. 616.

205 / 33   **over-straining:** J. T. Grein cited, Shaw/Barker letters p. 122.

205 / 36   **all day:** *CP3* p. 616.

205 / last   **press:** G.B.S. to Edward McNulty, 29 June 1908, *CL2* p. 792.

206 / Ep.   **night:** *Man and Superman, CP2* p. 586.

206 / 4   **presently:** G.B.S. to Mrs Cornwallis-West, 24 June 1908 (Churchill College, Cambridge).

206 / 13   **graceful:** *The Autocar* 5 December 1908. See *CL2* p. 822.

206 / 32   **Drive:** 'George Bernard Shaw says—"They Shouldn't Allow Me to Drive"', *The Motor* LXVIII, 22 October 1935, pp. 563–5.

206 / 34   **I'm dead:** 'Mr Shaw's Telegram', *Daily Mail* 23 January 1909.

207 / 8   **Widening It:** *The Car* no. 440, 26 October 1910, p. 374.

207 / 13   **unbounded:** G.B.S. to Beatrice Webb, 24 October 1910, *CL2* pp. 949–50.

207 / 23   **still:** 'George Bernard Shaw says—"They Shouldn't Allow Me to Drive"', *The Motor* LXVIII, 22 October 1935, pp. 563–5.

207 / 28   **driving:** G.B.S. to Granville Barker, 26 April 1909 (Texas).

207 / 30   **superb:** G.B.S. to Granville Barker, undated [assigned to 1 April 1909], *CL2* p. 840 (Shaw/Barker letters pp. 152–3).

207 / 36   **force:** G.B.S. to Granville Barker, 3 April 1909, Shaw/Barker letters p. 151.

208 / 6   **Mediterranean:** G.B.S. to Granville Barker, 14 April 1909, Shaw/Barker letters p. 152; G.B.S. to Edward McNulty, undated [assigned to 20 April 1909], *CL2* p. 841.

208 / 11   **sulphur:** G.B.S. to Granville Barker, 18 April 1909, Shaw/Barker letters p. 153.

208/25   **about them:** G.B.S. to Granville Barker, 26 July 1910, *CL*2
         p. 940 (Shaw/Barker letters p. 167).

208/35   **place:** G.B.S. to Frederick Jackson, 18 September 1910, *CL*2
         pp. 941–2.

209/ 8   **world:** Ibid.

209/20   **I left:** G.B.S. to Granville Barker, 1 April 1910, *CL*2 p. 919.

209/23   **to place!:** Charlotte Shaw to Barker, 24 April 1910 (Texas).

209/27   **grave:** G.B.S. to Granville Barker, undated [assigned to 14
         April 1910], *CL*2 p. 921.

210/ 4   **activity:** G.B.S. to Granville Barker, 30 April 1910,
         Shaw/Barker letters p. 164.

210/10   **after all:** G.B.S. to Granville Barker, 5 April 1910, *CL*2 p. 919.

210/Ep. **suggestive:** G.B.S. to Ensor Walters, 1 November 1903; to
         Siegfried Trebitsch, 20 July 1903 (Shaw/Trebitsch letters
         p. 54); to Lady Gregory, 16 April 1920.

210/15   **rum one:** *Shaw the Villager and Human Being* p. 165.

210/26   **with him:** Ibid., p. 166.

210/last **ago:** Ibid., p. 167.

211/ 9   **country:** Note on Archibald Henderson's *Playboy and Prophet*
         manuscript (North Carolina).

211/35   **for the job:** *Playboy and Prophet* p. 4.

211/last **do the job:** Ibid., p. 5.

212/ 8   **significance:** Ibid., p. xvii.

212/23   **century:** G.B.S. to Archibald Henderson, 10 February 1905,
         *CL*2 p. 511.

212/27   **own times:** G.B.S. to Henderson, 3 January 1905, *CL*2 p. 506.

212/29   **is Shaw:** G.B.S. to Henderson, 30 June 1904, *CL*2 p. 427.

212/34   **Who's Who:** *The Playwright and the Pirate* (ed. Stanley
         Weintraub 1982) p. 219.

213/17   **interesting:** G.B.S. to Henderson, 22 May 1907 (North
         Carolina).

213/25   **indeed:** 'Chesterton on Shaw', *Nation* 25 August 1909. See *Pen
         Portraits and Reviews* p. 84.

213/26   **with me:** G.B.S. to Hesketh Pearson, 14 June 1916 (Cornell).

213/27   **after him:** 'Chesterton on Shaw', See *Pen Portraits and Reviews*
         p. 88.

213/34   **the two:** G.B.S. to St John Ervine, 23 May 1936 (Texas).

214/ 1   **put in:** *Letters to T. E. Lawrence* (ed. A. W. Lawrence 1962)
         p. 177.

214/ 5   **biographers:** *The Playwright and the Pirate* p. 219.

214/27   **optimism:** G. K. Chesterton, *George Bernard Shaw* (1909).
         From 'The Problem of a Preface', 'The Irishman', 'The
         Puritan', 'The Progressive', 'The Critic'.

215/ 1   **mind:** G. K. Chesterton to Ronald Knox. See Evelyn Waugh, *Monsignor Ronald Knox* (Boston 1959) p. 208.

215/14   **next:** Bernard Shaw, *Short Stories, Scraps and Shavings* (1934) p. 147 (*CP5* p. 637).

215/20   **earnest:** Ibid., p. 183 (*CP5* pp. 678–9).

215/27   **possess:** G.B.S., 'The Rectorial Contest', *The Student Leader* no. 2, October 1925, p. 12.

216/15   **ideal:** 'The Religion of the Future', *The Religious Speeches of Bernard Shaw* (ed. Warren Sylvester Smith, Pennsylvania 1963) pp. 29–37.

216/24   **time:** *The Religious Speeches of Bernard Shaw* p. xxiii.

216/last   **horror:** Ibid., p. xx.

217/13   **our time:** *Fortnightly Review* July 1911.

217/17   **Cam:** *The Academy* 3 June 1911.

217/33   **fine man:** 'G. K. Chesterton's Reply to Bernard Shaw', November 1911. See also William B. Furlong, *Shaw and Chesterton: The Metaphysical Jesters* (1970) p. 87.

217/38   **of me:** G.B.S. to Cyril Clemens, 1 April 1937, *CL4* p. 463.

218/ 7   **Man:** G. K. Chesterton, *Autobiography* (1936) pp. 227–8.

218/32   **owners:** 'Shaw vs. Chesterton', *Christian Commonwealth* 6, 13 December 1911. See *Platform and Pulpit* (ed. with an introduction by Dan H. Laurence 1962) pp. 86–93.

219/ 4   **Socialist:** Ibid.

219/25   **gesture:** G.B.S., 'The Rectorial Contest', *The Student Leader* no. 2, October 1925, p. 12.

219/29   **falsehood:** G. K. Chesterton, *Autobiography* pp. 338–9.

219/32   **impossible:** G.B.S. to H. G. Wells, 19 March 1932, *CL4* p. 278.

220/ 1   **question:** 'Shaw vs. Chesterton'. See *Platform and Pulpit* p. 91.

220/ 2   **of ours:** Maisie Ward, *Gilbert Keith Chesterton* (1944) p. 312.

220/ 7   **with him:** G. K. Chesterton, *George Bernard Shaw* (1909 edn) p. 1.

220/20   **match:** Maisie Ward, *Gilbert Keith Chesterton* p. 312.

220/33   **debate:** G. K. Chesterton and Bernard Shaw, *Do We Agree?* (1928) p. 18.

220/36   **manners:** Ibid., p. 8.

220/37   **are mad:** Ibid., p. 10.

220/last   **express:** Ibid., pp. 11–12.

221/ 1   **position:** Ibid., p. 16.

221/11   **revelation:** Ibid., p. 11.

221/13   **negative:** Ibid., p. 17.

221/19   **antiquated:** Ibid., p. 45.

221/Ep. 1   **books:** 'Meeting the Immortals: Which Classic Author Would

You Most Like to Meet', *John O' London's Weekly* XVIII, 17 March 1928, p. 812.

221/Ep. 2   **public:** G.B.S. to Maud Churton Braby, 18 May 1908 (The Rendells Inc. Catalogue no. 121, item 42).

222/ 4   **to Authors:** *The Bookseller* 5 June 1884.

222/14   **book:** *The Author* XIII, July 1903, p. 263.

222/22   **methods:** 'Confessions of a Benevolent and High-Minded Shark', *The Author* XV, July 1905, p. 306.

222/32   **for you:** Maisie Ward, *Gilbert Keith Chesterton* pp. 206–7.

222/39   **Association:** 'Theatre Managers and Film Rights', *The Author* XLI, Spring 1931, p. 88.

223/16   **pressure:** G.B.S. to Arthur W. Pinero, 7 January 1909 (Texas).

223/33   **profession:** 'The Annual Dinner', *The Author* XVI, June 1906, p. 269.

223/last   **backs:** 'Theatre Managers and Film Rights', *The Author* XLI, Spring 1931, p. 88.

224/ 9   **profiteers:** *The Author* XXIX, July 1919, p. 149.

224/27   **I know:** 'Sixty Years in Business as an Author', *The Author* LV, Summer 1945, p. 58.

224/37   **abuse it:** G.B.S. to Evacustus Phipson Jr., 8 March 1892 (Malcolm A. Love Library, San Diego State University).

225/ 8   **Presidents:** G.B.S. statement dated 17 May 1948 (Texas).

225/15   **treason:** *Chief Constables' Association ... Reports of the General Conference 7th June, 1928, and Special General Conference 8th June, 1928.*

226/13   **continued:** 'The Solution of the Censorship Problem', *The Academy* LXXII, 29 June 1907, pp. 628–31.

226/23   **of us:** Ibid.

226/39   **surgery:** '"Waste" and the Censor', *The Nation* II, 8 February 1908, pp. 675–6.

226/last   **back:** G.B.S. to Gilbert Murray, 10 October 1907, *CL*2 p. 715.

227/ 2   **better:** G.B.S. to Edward Garnett, 15 July 1907, *CL*2 p. 702.

227/ 5   **concession:** G.B.S. to Lena Ashwell, 4 November 1907, *CL*2 pp. 718–19.

227/ 7   **load:** G.B.S. to Archibald Henderson, 2 July 1908 (North Carolina).

227/14   **round him:** Hesketh Pearson, *Beerbohm Tree* (1956) p. 173.

227/21   **horrified:** Ibid., pp. 173–4.

227/23   **mean one:** *CP*3 p. 774.

227/25   **town:** Ibid., p. 784.

227/27   **prostitute:** Hesketh Pearson, *Beerbohm Tree* p. 175.

227/36   **intended:** G.B.S. to Archibald Henderson, 15 March 1909, *CL*2 p. 835.

227/38 **America:** *CP3* p. 671.

228/ 3 **people:** G.B.S. to John Martin-Harvey, 1 April 1925 (Cornell).

228/11 **form:** *CP3* p. 674.

228/18 **Censorship:** G.B.S. to Siegfried Trebitsch, 28 June 1909, Shaw/Trebitsch letters p. 144.

228/29 **Posnet:** *CP3* pp. 800–2.

228/37 **sensitive:** Lady Gregory to G.B.S., 6 July 1909, BL Add. MS 50534 f. 171.

229/24 **accepted:** *The Observer* 22 August 1909.

229/29 **Ireland:** G.B.S. to Lady Gregory, 17 August 1909, BL Add. MS 50534 f. 182.

229/39 **nation:** *The Arrow* no. 5, vol. 1, 25 August 1909.

230/13 **reality:** *The Times* 25 August 1909.

230/22 **with joy:** See *Shaw: The Critical Heritage* pp. 197–8.

230/34 **order:** Ibid.

231/ 6 **feelings:** *The Times* 27 August 1909.

231/11 *Posnet*: *Irish Times* 26 August 1909.

231/15 **to it:** G.B.S. to Lady Gregory, 29 August 1909.

231/25 **decision:** G. A. Redford to Iden Payne, 8 September 1909, *CL2* p. 866.

231/33 **destruction:** *CP3* p. 804.

232/ 1 **imagine:** Desmond MacCarthy, *Shaw* p. 133.

232/ 5 **we can:** Max Beerbohm, *Last Theatres* (1970) p. 466.

232/ 7 **can be:** *CP3* p. 803.

232/10 **blackguard:** G.B.S. to Iden Payne, 12 September 1909, *CL2* p. 867.

232/22 **stage:** *Shaw: An Exhibit*, a Catalog by Dan H. Laurence for an Exhibit Selected and Prepared with Lois B. Garcia (Texas, 1977), item 350.

232/29 *Punch*: 'The Censor's Revenge', *The Times* 26 June 1909, p. 10.

232/33 **Lord Roberts:** Ibid.

232/37 **both:** *CP3* p. 839.

233/13 **Bones:** Ben Iden Payne, *A Life in a Wooden O* (1977) p. 101.

233/32 **at law:** G.B.S. multigraphed letter, 'The Select Committee on the Censorship', 6 August 1909 (Houghton). See *The Times* 2 August 1909.

233/36 **censorship:** G.B.S. to Edith Lyttelton, 28 July 1909 (Churchill College, Cambridge).

234/19 **The Times:** G.B.S. to Herbert Samuel, 31 July 1909, *CL2* p. 854.

234/32 **to speak:** G.B.S. to Herbert Samuel, 5 August 1909 (House of Lords Record Office).

235/ 1   **word:** Joseph Conrad to John Galsworthy, 6 August 1909 (University of Birmingham Library).

235/11   **of it:** G.B.S. to Herbert Samuel, 31 July 1909, *CL*2 p. 854.

235/14   **myself:** G.B.S. to Samuel, 5 August 1909 (House of Lords Record Office).

235/16   **through:** G.B.S. to Samuel, 13 August 1909 (House of Lords Record Office).

235/18   **part:** Ibid.

235/23   **case:** Ibid.

235/26   **tell them!:** G.B.S. to Samuel, 31 July 1909, *CL*2 p. 855.

235/32   **liked:** G.B.S. to Lord Lytton, n.d.; written on his copy of the printed edition (July 1909) of his Evidence in Chief before the Joint-Committee on Stage Plays (privately owned). See Dan H. Laurence, *Bernard Shaw: A Bibliography* (1983) vol. 1, A98, pp. 91–2.

235/last   **from him:** G.B.S. to Samuel, 5 August 1909 (House of Lords Record Office).

236/28   **fashion:** G.B.S. to Douglas Goldring, 8 January 1918 (Maggs Booksellers, London).

236/last   **innovation:** G.B.S. to Samuel, 11 November 1909 (House of Lords Record Office).

237/13   **problems:** Interview with M. K. Wisehart, *The Mentor* March 1930, p. 68.

237/30   **seriously:** *CP*3 p. 696.

237/35   **as possible:** G.B.S. to C. H. Norman, 28 January 1916 (Texas).

CHAPTER V

239/Ep.   **abhorrence:** Preface to *The Shewing-up of Blanco Posnet*, *CP*3 p. 698.

239/23   **ourselves:** G.B.S. to Leo Tolstoy, 14 February 1910, *CL*2 pp. 901–2.

240/ 3   **letter:** Ibid., pp. 900–2.

240/ 9   **its own:** Leon Edel, *The Life of Henry James* (1977 edn) vol. 2, p. 667.

240/12   **in it:** G.B.S. to Leo Tolstoy, 14 February 1910, *CL*2 pp. 901–2.

240/26   **changing it:** G.B.S. to Henry James, 17 January 1909, *CL*2 pp. 827–8.

240/33   **wrote:** Leon Edel, *The Life of Henry James* vol. 2, p. 174.

240/35   **since:** G.B.S. to Henry James, 17 January 1909, *CL*2 p. 827.

241 / 11   **environment:** Ibid.
241 / 16   **other:** G.B.S. to Henry James, 21 January 1909, *CL2* p. 830.
241 / 23   **myself:** G.B.S. to H. G. Wells, 13 March 1914, *CL3* p. 223.
241 / 28   **death:** G.B.S. to Henry James, 21 January 1909, *CL2* p. 830.
242 / 8   **jokes:** G.B.S. to Leo Tolstoy, 14 February 1910, *CL2* p. 902.
242 / 19   **of man:** Janet Dunbar, *J. M. Barrie: The Man Behind the Image* (1970) p. 128.
242 / 22   **word:** Andrew Birkin, *J. M. Barrie and the Lost Boys* (1980 edn) p. 47.
242 / 31   **Theatricalities:** G.B.S. to Granville Barker, 4 April 1909, *Bernard Shaw's Letters to Granville Barker* (ed. C. B. Purdom 1957) p. 151.
242 / 35   **practicable:** C. B. Purdom, *Harley Granville Barker* (1955) p. 100.
242 / last **that is:** Ibid.
243 / 14   **for him:** 'The National Shakespeare Theatre and the New Repertory Theatres', *The Times* 10 May 1909, p. 12.
243 / 25   **broken men:** G.B.S. to Waters, 5 January 1910 (see *Daily Mail* 8 February 1910).
243 / 29   **babies:** G.B.S. to Granville Barker, 30 June 1912, *CL3* p. 96 (Shaw/Barker letters p. 183).
243 / 34   **into it:** *CP4* p. 209.
243 / 36   **father:** Ibid., p. 246.
243 / 40   **to bits!:** Ibid., p. 182.
244 / 5   **impossible:** G.B.S. page 172J on Henderson proof of *Playboy and Prophet* (North Carolina).
244 / 29   **keep to:** *The Times* 24 February 1910.
244 / 31   **inconclusive:** Desmond MacCarthy, *Shaw* (1951) p. 160.
244 / 36   **everything:** Max Beerbohm, *Around Theatres* (1953) pp. 561–5.
244 / last **merit:** *The Times* 24 June 1939.
245 / 7   **sky:** Introduction to Luigi Pirandello, *Naked Masks* (1952).
245 / 14   **as well:** *CP4* p. 199.
245 / 15   **Titmus:** Ibid., p. 209.
245 / 18   **absurd:** *G. B. Shaw: A Collection of Critical Essays* (ed. Ralph J. Kaufmann 1965), p. 11.
245 / 28   **Butler Saw:** *The Guardian* 30 June 1980, p. 9.
245 / 32   **itself:** *Around Theatres* p. 564.
245 / 36   **both:** G.B.S. page 172J on Henderson proof of *Playboy and Prophet* (North Carolina).
246 / 12   **directions:** Edward McNulty to G.B.S., 17 June 1914, BL Add. MS 50517.
246 / 20   **impulses:** *CP4* p. 206.
246 / 21   **England:** Ibid., p. 168.

246/24   **delicacy?:** Ibid., p. 180.

246/27   **books?:** Ibid., p. 203.

246/30   **talk!:** Ibid., p. 237.

246/35   **sky:** Ibid., p. 185.

246/37   **universe:** *CP2* p. 689.

246/38   **wonderful:** *CP4* p. 200.

247/ 6   **love:** G.B.S. to Irene Vanbrugh, 26 March 1930, *CL4* p. 181.

247/ 8   **cloak:** G.B.S. to Nugent Monck, 26 April 1944 (privately owned).

247/15   **tennis?:** *CP4* p. 169.

247/23   **some tea?:** Ibid., p. 191.

247/25   **magic:** Ibid., p. 240.

247/29   **young:** Ibid., p. 197.

247/31   **nonsense:** Ibid., p. 195.

247/32   **myself:** Ibid., p. 196.

247/37   **humour:** Bertolt Brecht, 'Ovation for Shaw'. See *G. B. Shaw: A Collection of Critical Essays* p. 15 and n.

247/last   **comedy:** *CP4* p. 262.

248/11   **Underwear!:** Ibid., pp. 172–3.

248/17   **plays:** Ibid., p. 169.

248/29   **mind:** Ibid., p. 214.

248/32   **for you:** Ibid., p. 210.

248/34   **bound!:** Ibid., p. 219.

248/38   **will come:** Ibid.

249/ 3   **for me:** Ibid., p. 241.

249/10   **her part:** G.B.S. to Irene Vanbrugh, 26 March 1930, *CL4* p. 181.

249/17   **torrent:** Ibid.

249/21   **ought to be:** *CP4* p. 249.

249/25   **her sins:** Margot Peters, *Bernard Shaw and the Actresses* (1980) p. 317.

249/28   *gaiety:* G.B.S. to Lena Ashwell, 11 March 1910, *CL2* p. 905.

249/36   **life:** Lena Ashwell, *Myself a Player* (1927) pp. 254–6.

249/40   **presence:** G.B.S. to Mona Limerick, n.d. [c. March 1910] (Sotheby's Catalogue, 15 February 1932, item 568).

251/ 8   **frontier:** G.B.S. to Granville Barker, 9 May 1910, Shaw/Barker letters p. 166.

251/18   **to-morrow?:** *The English Review* April–July 1910, pp. 631–48. See C. B. Purdom, *Harley Granville Barker* pp. 109–10.

251/24   **enterprise:** *CP4* p. 260.

251/Ep.   **generations:** 'Art and Public Money', *Sussex Daily News* 7 March 1907, pp. 2–4.

252/ 2   **abstain:** G.B.S. to H. G. Wells, 14 August 1907, *CL2* p. 711.

252/11   **too much:** H. G. Wells to G.B.S., 23 August 1907, BL Add. MS 50552 ff. 17–18.

252/13   **opponent:** G.B.S. to Wells, 16 January 1907 (Illinois).

252/26   **of the lot:** *Bernard Shaw's Nondramatic Literary Criticism* (ed. Stanley Weintraub 1972) p. 100.

252/34   **days:** Edward Pease, *The History of the Fabian Society* (1916) p. 182.

253/ 3   **character:** *The Diary of Beatrice Webb*, vol. 3 (ed. Norman and Jeanne MacKenzie 1984), entry 9 February 1906, p. 25.

253/ 5   **things:** Ibid., entry 23 November 1905, p. 12.

253/22   **really is:** Ibid., entry 14 September 1908, p. 98.

254/ 1   **society:** Ibid., entry 13 March 1910, p. 137.

254/20   **phantasies:** Leonard Woolf, *Beginning Again: An Autobiography of the Years 1911 to 1918* (1964) p. 120.

254/25   **other men:** Norman and Jeanne MacKenzie, *The Time Traveller: The Life of H. G. Wells* (1973) p. 229.

254/32   **melancholy man:** Ibid., p. 225.

254/35   **for Rosamund:** Ibid.

254/39   **give them:** Norman and Jeanne MacKenzie, *The First Fabians* (1977) p. 351.

255/ 1   **ease:** *The Time Traveller* p. 228.

255/ 4   **I can:** Ibid.

255/34   **vote:** *Fabian Feminist: Bernard Shaw and Woman* (ed. Rodelle Weintraub 1977) pp. 248, 237.

256/ 1   **women:** Ibid., p. 239.

256/ 6   **a man:** *Shaw: An Exhibit*, a Catalog by Dan H. Laurence for an Exhibit Selected and Prepared with Lois B. Garcia (Texas, 1977) item 538.

256/10   **timetable:** Frank Harris, *Bernard Shaw* (1931) p. 189.

256/16   **behaviour:** St John Ervine, *Bernard Shaw: His Life, Work and Friends* (1956) p. 383.

256/21   **occasions:** *Village Wooing*, CP6 p. 541.

257/ 5   **question:** *Fabian News* 7 February 1907, p. 22.

257/24   **amusing:** MacKenzie, *The Time Traveller* pp. 247–8.

257/last   **ever met:** *The First Fabians* p. 351.

258/11   **nose:** G.B.S. to H. G. Wells, 22 March 1908, CL2 p. 764.

258/23   **aptitude:** Wells to G.B.S., n.d. (Illinois).

258/35   **movement:** *The Time Traveller* p. 232.

259/34   *Ann Veronica*: Beatrice Webb to Sidney Webb, late November 1909, *The Letters of Sidney and Beatrice Webb* (ed. Norman MacKenzie 1978) vol. 2, p. 338.

259/last   **known them:** *The Diary of Beatrice Webb* vol. 3, entry 20 March 1910, p. 138.

260/ 6   **person:** H. G. Wells, *Experiment in Autobiography: Discoveries and Conclusions of a Very Ordinary Brain (Since 1866)* (1934) vol. 2, p. 470.

260/10   **society:** *The Diary of Beatrice Webb* vol. 3, entry 22 August 1909, p. 124.

260/15   **talent:** Ibid.

260/17   **mire:** Ibid., entry 27 September 1909, p. 126.

260/21   **common cause:** Beatrice Webb to H. G. Wells, 28 February 1909, *The Letters of Sidney and Beatrice Webb* vol. 2, p. 325.

260/35   **mischief:** G.B.S. to Beatrice Webb, 30 September 1909, *CL2* pp. 869–71.

260/37   **approval!:** *The Diary of Beatrice Webb* vol. 3, entry 4 October 1909, p. 128.

260/last   **or so:** *The Time Traveller* p. 254.

261/10   **gallantry:** 'Modern Novels and Sex', *Evening Standard* 26 May 1922, p. 5. See *Bernard Shaw's Nondramatic Literary Criticism* p. 210.

261/18   **about:** *The Diary of Beatrice Webb* vol. 3, entry early August 1909, p. 121.

261/28   **start:** *Fabian News* June 1909.

261/32   **life!:** Beatrice Webb to Sidney Webb, 11 June 1890, *The Letters of Sidney and Beatrice Webb* vol. 1, p. 150.

262/ 8   **directions:** Beatrice Webb to Millicent Fawcett, 2 November 1906, ibid., vol. 2, p. 242.

262/17   **superior:** *The Diary of Beatrice Webb* vol. 3, entry 15 December 1908, p. 104.

262/24   **Poor Law:** Ibid., entry 2 December 1905, p. 16.

262/36   **will stand:** Ibid., entry 26 November 1907, p. 73.

263/14   **generation:** 'What I Think of the Minority Report', *Christian Commonwealth* XXIX, 30 June 1909, p. 685.

263/36   **ideas:** *The First Fabians* p. 354.

264/ 4   **Society:** 'What I Think of the Minority Report', *Christian Commonwealth* XXIX, 30 June 1909, p. 683.

264/11   **after 50!:** Beatrice Webb to Georgina Meinertzhagen, 8 August 1909, *The Letters of Sidney and Beatrice Webb* vol. 2, p. 332.

264/17   **personality:** *The Diary of Beatrice Webb* vol. 3, entry 22 July 1909, p. 120.

264/29   *limelight*: Ibid., entry 30 November 1910, p. 149.

264/33   **rest:** 'What I Think of the Minority Report', *Christian Commonwealth* XXIX, 30 June 1909, p. 683.

264/34   **malicious way:** *The Diary of Beatrice Webb* vol. 3, entry 5 November 1910, p. 147.

264/39	**S[ociety]:** G.B.S. to Sidney and Beatrice Webb, 22 March 1911 (LSE).
265/12	**health:** 'What I Think of the Minority Report', *Christian Commonwealth* XXIX, 30 June 1909, p. 685.
265/26	**Socialism:** *Bernard Shaw: The Road to Equality: Ten Unpublished Lectures and Essays, 1884–1918* (ed. Louis Crompton 1971) p. 155.
265/last	**standard:** Ibid., p. 191.
266/ 7	**our time:** 'What I Think of the Minority Report', *Christian Commonwealth* XXIX, 30 June 1909, p. 685.
266/22	**Shaw:** *The Diary of Beatrice Webb* vol. 3, entry 21 April 1911, pp. 157–8.
266/33	**indifference:** Ibid., entry 7 March 1911, p. 154.
267/ 1	**filter:** G.B.S. to Sidney and Beatrice Webb, 22 March 1911 (LSE).
267/ 5	**Society:** Ibid.
267/10	**not there!:** *The Diary of Beatrice Webb* vol. 3, entry 7 March 1911, p. 154.
267/16	**resign:** G.B.S. to Edward Pease, 3 March 1911, *CL*3 p. 13.
267/28	**accompaniment:** G.B.S. to Sidney Webb, 5 March 1911 (LSE).
267/32	**lictors:** Ibid.
268/ 4	**done it:** See F. E. Loewenstein, 'The Shaw–Wells Controversy of 1904–1908', *Fabian Quarterly* no. 41, April 1944, p. 20.
268/Ep.	**amused:** G.B.S. to Greenhaugh Smith, 29 December 1904 (Princeton).
268/10	**thinking:** Virginia Woolf, *The Flight of the Mind* (1975) p. 423.
268/24	**Chancery:** *CP*3 p. 900.
268/28	**notions:** Ibid., p. 902.
268/32	**Park Lane:** Ibid., p. 909.
269/ 6	**Mine!:** Ibid., p. 914.
269/12	**death:** G.B.S. note for F. E. Loewenstein, May 1950 (Texas).
269/26	**anything:** *CP*3 p. 828.
269/32	**really are:** Ibid., pp. 832–3.
270/ 3	**in it:** G.B.S. to Leo Tolstoy, 14 February 1910, *CL*2 pp. 900–1.
270/ 9	**defend us!:** *CP*4 p. 309.
270/16	**woman:** Ibid., p. 310.
270/19	**trifles:** Ibid., p. 311.
270/23	**hand:** Ibid., p. 312.
270/40	**takes him:** Ibid., p. 320.
271/ 3	**for you:** Ibid., p. 322.
271/11	**wish:** Ibid., p. 325.
271/21	**genius:** Ibid., p. 285.

271 / 26   **myself:** Ibid., p. 275.
272 / 1   **life:** Ibid., p. 892.
272 / 14   **world:** G. K. Chesterton, *Autobiography* (1936) p. 202.
272 / 18   **afford:** *CP*4 p. 880.
272 / 23   **this time:** Ibid., p. 885.
272 / 35   **woman:** Ibid., pp. 892–3.
272 / 39   **to me:** Ibid.
273 / 6   **at all:** Ibid., p. 878.
273 / 13   **and w----s:** Byron, *Don Juan*, Stanza XCII, Canto vi.
273 / 16   **everybody's Catherine:** *CP*4 p. 898.
273 / 21   **clown:** Ibid.
273 / 24   **ingenues:** Ibid., p. 903.
273 / 26   **famous:** Gertrude Kingston to G.B.S., 18 November 1913
            and 7 May 1915, BL Add. MS 50539
            ff. 51–2 and 50539 ff. 91–4.
273 / 27   **at that:** G.B.S. to Gertrude Kingston, 15 December 1913
            (King's College, Cambridge).
273 / 36   **too far:** *CP*4 p. 923.
273 / last **ridiculous:** Ibid., p. 944.
274 / 14   **subjects:** Ibid., p. 900.
274 / 31   **probable:** G.B.S. to Edith Lyttelton [The Hon. Mrs Alfred], 1
            February 1910 (Churchill College, Cambridge).
274 / 33   **Foundling:** G.B.S. to Lillah McCarthy, 10 January 1916
            (Texas).
274 / 34   **trash:** G.B.S. to Rosalind Ivan, 18 December 1914 (Colby).
274 / 35   **unbearable:** G.B.S. to William Armstrong, 27 March 1914
            (copy, Society of Authors).
274 / 36   **bad play:** G.B.S. to Gertrude Kingston, 21 November 1913,
            *CL*3 p. 208.
275 / 19   **street:** G.B.S. to Arthur W. Pinero, 15 October 1912 (Texas).
275 / 22   **ever had:** G.B.S. to R. C. Carton, 26 December 1915 (Texas).
275 / 24   **dog:** Ibid.
275 / 32   **cert:** Ibid.
275 / 34   **merit:** G.B.S. to Austin Harrison, 27 December 1912, BL
            Add. MS 50538 f. 62.
275 / 38   **involved:** St John Ervine, *Bernard Shaw: His Life, Work and
            Friends* (1956) p. 443.
276 / 14   **part us:** *CP*4 p. 855.
276 / 22   **people:** Ibid., p. 827.
276 / 36   **lounge:** Desmond MacCarthy, *Shaw* pp. 177–8.
277 / 6   **omit:** *The Times* 7 May 1975.
277 / 11   **pair:** 'Slaves of the Ring', *Saturday Review* 5 January 1895,
            *OTN*1 pp. 3–4.

277 / 12	**comedy:** *CP*4 p. 844.
277 / 18	**tells the truth:** Ibid., p. 833.
277 / 22	**for the truth:** Ibid., p. 834.
277 / 28	**gaiety:** Desmond MacCarthy, *Shaw* p. 176.
277 / 33	**in love:** *CP*4 p. 848.
277 / 36	**romance:** Ibid., p. 857.
277 / 39	**to you:** Ibid., p. 868.
277 / last	**love me:** Ibid., p. 872.
278 / 8	**kind:** Ibid., p. 827.
278 / Ep.	**true:** G.B.S. to Cliff Keene, 12 June 1914 (Detroit).
278 / 18	**England!:** G.B.S. to Ernest Parke, 23 December 1910, *CL*2 p. 958.
278 / last	**move, this:** G.B.S. to Granville Barker, 11 January 1911, *CL*3 p. 7.
279 / 2	**January:** *Kingston Gleaner* 12 January 1911.
279 / 37	**argument:** Maurice Valency, *The Cart and the Trumpet: The Plays of George Bernard Shaw* (1973) p. 299.
280 / 22	**Theatre:** *CP*4 p. 341.
280 / 33	**gentleman:** G.B.S. to Charles Ricketts, 10 April 1911 (BL Ricketts Collection, misc. correspondence, Add. MSS 58090–1).
281 / 6	**critic:** G.B.S. to Demetrius O'Bolger, 9 February 1916 (Houghton).
281 / 15	**originals:** *The Times* 20 April 1911.
281 / 19	**at all:** E. A. Baughan notices, *Daily News* 24 May 1905, 2 November 1904, 26 November 1907. See *Shaw: The Critical Heritage* (ed. T. F. Evans 1976) pp. 108, 126, 182.
281 / 33	**about him:** *CP*4 pp. 437–8.
282 / 11	**Vedrenne:** G.B.S. to J. E. Vedrenne, 21 April 1911 (Theatre Museum, Victoria and Albert Museum).
282 / 14	**wrote it:** G.B.S. to F. C. Whitney, 9 May 1911, *CL*3 p. 35.
282 / 20	**note:** Beerbohm Tree to G.B.S., 5 May 1911. See *Shaw: An Exhibit*, item 364.
282 / 26	**or die:** G.B.S. to Julio Broutá, 26 June 1911 (Houghton).
282 / 34	**revive:** G.B.S. to Siegfried Trebitsch, 4 August 1911, *CL*3 p. 47 (Shaw/Trebitsch letters p. 154).
282 / last	**like it!:** Charlotte Shaw to Edward Pease, 12 July 1911 (Nuffield College).
283 / 6	**breaking up:** G.B.S. to Granville Barker, 21 June 1911, Shaw/Barker letters p. 173.
283 / 10	**idiotic:** G.B.S. to Henry Hyde Champion, 3 September 1911 (Boston).
283 / 13	**genius:** G.B.S. to Rutland Boughton, 12 July 1911, BL Add. MS 52365 f. 5.

283 / 18   **martyrs:** G.B.S. to Frances Chesterton, 5 April 1912. See
        Hesketh Pearson, 'The Origin of "Androcles and the Lion"',
        The Listener 13 November 1952, pp. 803–4.

283 / 22   **arena?:** G.B.S. to Arthur W. Pinero, 5 January 1912. Hesketh
        Pearson copy (privately owned).

283 / 30   **howlers:** G.B.S. to Gilbert Murray, 3 February 1912, *CL*3
        p. 74.

283 / 36   **conversions:** Desmond MacCarthy, *Shaw* p. 205.

283 / 38   ***Play!:*** *The Diary of Beatrice Webb* vol. 3, entry 13 July 1913,
        p. 190.

283 / 39   **work:** Lillah McCarthy, *Myself and My Friends* (1933) p. 136.

283 / last   **performance:** *The Diary of Beatrice Webb* vol. 3, entry 21 April
        1911, p. 157.

284 / 2   **farces:** Desmond MacCarthy, *Shaw* p. 203.

284 / 5   **religious pantomime:** Ibid., p. 102.

284 / 7   **Christmas pantomime!:** *CP*4 p. 356.

284 / 9   **death:** 'Children in Theatres', *The Star* 24 January 1890, *SM*1
        p. 903.

284 / 13   **together:** Desmond MacCarthy, *Shaw* p. 102.

284 / 19   **lion:** *CP*4, pp. 611, 619, 629.

284 / 27   **like:** Hesketh Pearson, 'The Origin of "Androcles and the
        Lion"', *The Listener* 13 November 1952, p. 803.

284 / 33   **failure:** G.B.S. to the Children's Theater, New York, 30
        August 1947, *Christian Science Monitor* 30 September 1947.

284 / 35   **occasionally:** G.B.S. note for Loewenstein, August 1948
        (Texas).

285 / 11   **stage:** 'Plays of the Week', *Saturday Review* 11 January 1896,
        *OTN*2 p. 13.

285 / 16   **crucified yet:** 'Mrs Wilson Barrett as the Messiah', *Saturday
        Review* 13 February 1897, *OTN*3 p. 45.

285 / 23   **be done:** Ibid., p. 43.

285 / 29   **Christianity:** Martin Meisel, *Shaw and the Nineteenth-Century
        Theater* (1963) p. 341.

285 / 36   **passion:** *CP*4 p. 597.

285 / 39   **nothing:** Ibid., p. 625.

286 / 3   **dreams:** Ibid., p. 624.

286 / 4   **for nothing?:** Ibid., p. 625.

286 / 19   **joke:** Ibid., p. 591.

286 / 37   **upon me:** Ibid., p. 599.

286 / 40   **moves us:** Ibid., p. 597.

287 / 4   **religion:** *The Religious Speeches of Bernard Shaw* (ed. Warren
        Sylvester Smith 1963) pp. 54–5.

287 / 11   **crucifixion:** Ibid., p. 55.

287/16   **they do:** Ibid.
287/20   **personage:** *CP*4 p. 594.
287/23   **with him:** Ibid., p. 583.
287/25   **madness:** Ibid., p. 601.
287/30   **will be:** Ibid., pp. 633–4.
287/36   **little:** Ibid., p. 585.
287/40   **imitation:** Wells to G.B.S., 4 September 1913, BL Add. MS 50552 f. 37.
288/ 4   **even yet:** *The Religious Speeches of Bernard Shaw* p. 56.
288/10   **suffering:** Stevie Smith, 'Proud and Fearful', *The Observer* 2 December 1956.
288/21   **real:** G.B.S. to Rosina Filippi, 16 September 1913, *CL*3 p. 203.
288/25   **religion:** 'Androcles: How Divines Differ about Shaw', *Daily News* 29 September 1913, p. 6.
288/29   **Androcles:** *CP*4 p. 589.
288/35   **Christianity:** Ibid., p. 587.
288/40   **jungle:** Ibid., p. 590.
289/ 5   **minutes:** Ibid.
289/ 9   **Strauss:** G.B.S. to Trebitsch, 7 March 1912, Shaw/Trebitsch letters p. 159.
289/31   **inculcation:** 'Industrial Malingering', *Saturday Review* CXIII, 16 March 1912, pp. 336–7.
290/ 9   **conditions:** *Liverpool Daily Courier* 11 March 1912.
290/28   **Pole:** G.B.S. to Beatrice Webb, 10 July 1912, *CL*3 p. 99.
290/32   **nowhere:** Ibid.
290/38   **country:** G.B.S. to Trebitsch, 10 April 1912, Shaw/Trebitsch letters p. 160.
290/40   **for me:** G.B.S. to Beatrice Webb, 10 July 1912, *CL*3 p. 99.
291/ 4   **bachelor too:** G.B.S. to Charlotte Shaw, 19 April 1912, *CL*3 p. 84.
291/27   **sane:** G.B.S. to Charlotte Shaw, 24 April 1912, BL Add. MS 50550 f. 124 (TS), 46506 ff. 7–8 (orig.).
291/34   **manner:** G.B.S. to Charlotte Shaw, 26 April 1912, BL Add. MS 50550 f. 127 (TS), 46506 f. 9 (orig.).
291/38   **daughter:** Ibid.
292/ 3   **stones:** G.B.S. to Charlotte Shaw, 28 April 1912, *CL*3 p. 86.
292/12   **ah-ooh-ow!!!!!:** G.B.S. to Trebitsch, 30 April 1912, Shaw/Trebitsch letters p. 161.
292/15   **ah-oo-ow!:** G.B.S. to Charlotte Shaw, 30 April 1912, *CL*3 p. 87.
292/21   **business:** Charlotte Shaw to Trebitsch, undated [c. April/May 1912]. See Janet Dunbar, *Mrs G.B.S.: A Biographical Portrait of Charlotte Shaw* (1963) p. 240.

292/26   **anyone else:** G.B.S. to Charlotte Shaw, 8 May 1912, *CL*3
p. 90.

292/32   **Kilsby:** G.B.S. to Charlotte Shaw, 2 May 1912, *CL*3 p. 89.

293/ 2   **motoring:** G.B.S. to Charlotte Shaw, 3 May 1912, BL Add.
MS 50550 ff. 136, 137 (TS), 46506 ff. 23, 23v (orig.).

293/ 5   **infant:** G.B.S. to Charlotte Shaw, 5 May 1912, BL Add. MS
50550 f. 141 (TS), 46506 f. 25v (orig.).

293/14   **holiday:** Ibid.

293/27   **laborers:** G.B.S. to Charlotte Shaw, 8 May 1912, *CL*3 p. 91.

293/36   **open:** G.B.S. to Charlotte Shaw, 3 May 1912, BL Add. MS
50550 f. 137 (TS), 46506 f. 23v (orig.).

294/11   **truth:** 'The Titanic. Some Unmentioned Morals', *Daily News
and Leader* 14 May 1912, p. 6.

294/20   **Shaw:** Hesketh Pearson, *Conan Doyle* (1977 edn) p. 148.

294/24   **bullfinch:** Blanche Patch, *Thirty Years with G.B.S.*
[ghostwritten by Robert Williamson] (1951) p. 23.

294/32   **rather die:** Hesketh Pearson, *Bernard Shaw* (rev. 1975 edn)
p. 305.

294/37   **may be:** G.B.S. to Ellen Terry, 20 August 1912, *CL*3 p. 110.
See *Ellen Terry and Bernard Shaw: A Correspondence* (ed.
Christopher St John 1931) p. 448.

294/last   **thrilling:** Ellen Terry to G.B.S., 16 September 1912, *A
Correspondence* p. 451.

295/Ep. 1   **humanizing:** G.B.S. to Mrs Patrick Campbell, 20 March
1913, *CL*3 p. 158. See *Bernard Shaw and Mrs Patrick
Campbell: Their Correspondence* (ed. Alan Dent 1952) pp. 97–8.

295/Ep. 2   **survived it:** G.B.S. to Mrs Patrick Campbell, 8 February 1914
(privately owned).

295/Ep. 3   **over it:** G.B.S. to Mrs Patrick Campbell, 23 October 1912,
Their Correspondence p. 48.

295/18   **woman:** 'Mr Pinero's New Play', *Saturday Review* 16 March
1895, *OTN*1 p. 61.

295/19   **wonderful:** 'Romeo and Juliet', *Saturday Review* 28 September
1895, *OTN*1 p. 202.

295/28   **deeds:** 'The Return of Mrs Pat', *Saturday Review* 7 March
1896, *OTN*2 p. 65.

295/33   **with it:** 'Mr Pinero's New Play', *Saturday Review* 16 March
1895, *OTN*1 p. 61.

296/ 8   **Ulysses:** 'Sardoodledom', *Saturday Review* 1 June 1895, *OTN*1
p. 135.

296/26   **feathers:** G.B.S. to Ellen Terry, 8 September 1897, *CL*1
p. 803 (*A Correspondence* p. 256).

296/28   **flower girl:** Ibid.

297/10   **surely:** Mrs Patrick Campbell to G.B.S., 27 June 1912, *Their Correspondence* p. 19.

297/17   **business:** G.B.S. to Granville Barker, 30 June 1912, *CL3* p. 95 (Shaw/Barker letters pp. 182–3).

297/20   **twentieth:** G.B.S. to Ellen Terry, 13 August 1912, *A Correspondence* p. 449.

297/22   **grown up:** G.B.S. to Mrs Patrick Campbell, 3 July 1912, *Their Correspondence* p. 25.

297/23   **limit?:** G.B.S. to Lady Gregory, 18 November 1912, *CL3* p. 127.

297/24   **world:** G.B.S. to Granville Barker, 30 June 1912, *CL3* p. 95.

297/32   **hours:** G.B.S. to Mrs Patrick Campbell, 30 June 1912, *CL3* pp. 96–7 (*Their Correspondence* p. 20).

297/35   **hides:** G.B.S. to Mrs Patrick Campbell, 30 June 1912, *CL3* p. 96 (*Their Correspondence* p. 20).

297/last **herself:** G.B.S. to Mrs Patrick Campbell, 3 July 1912, *Their Correspondence* pp. 24–5.

298/ 6   **Society:** G.B.S. to Erica Cotterill, 5 April 1906, *CL2* p. 615.

298/11   **soul:** The character Ursula Windridge in Erica Cotterill's play, *A Professional Socialist* (1908); *CL2* p. 562.

298/17   **love?:** Erica Cotterill, *An Account* II (Erica Cotterill, c. 1916), 93 Sydney Street, Chelsea, n.d.

298/29   **people:** G.B.S. to Erica Cotterill, 27 June 1912 (Texas).

298/32   **you are 40:** G.B.S. to Erica Cotterill, 30 October 1910, *CL2* p. 951.

299/ 5   **pull them:** Erica Cotterill, *An Account Through Letters*. Printed by J. B. Shears, 64 Sydney Street, Chelsea, c. 1916, p. 108.

299/ 6   **cried:** Ibid., p. 137.

299/12   **feeling it?:** Erica Cotterill, *Letter to Bernard Shaw* (1908) pp. 23–4. Printed by J. B. Shears, 64 Sydney Street, Chelsea.

299/19   **time:** G.B.S. to Erica Cotterill, 14–16 December 1907, *CL2* p. 741.

299/38   **mother:** G.B.S. to Erica Cotterill, 27 April 1908, *CL2* p. 774.

300/ 1   **impossible:** Ibid.

300/ 5   **ever met:** G.B.S. to Erica Cotterill, 22 April 1908, *CL2* p. 772.

300/ 7   **you are:** G.B.S. to Erica Cotterill, 11 July 1907, *CL2* p. 700.

300/30   **for it:** *An Account Through Letters* pp. 134–6.

300/36   **herself:** G.B.S. to Erica Cotterill, 22 June 1909, *CL2* p. 847.

301/ 7   **possible:** G.B.S. to Mrs Patrick Campbell, 5 July 1912, *CL3* p. 97 (*Their Correspondence* p. 26).

301/18   **empty:** G.B.S. to Mrs Patrick Campbell, 9 August 1912, *CL3* p. 102 (*Their Correspondence* pp. 32–3).

301/23   **life:** G.B.S. to Mrs Patrick Campbell, 9 August 1912, *CL3* p. 103 (*Their Correspondence* p. 33).

301/37   **treatments:** Ibid.

302/12   **station:** G.B.S. to Charlotte Shaw, 12–14 August 1912, BL Add. MS 50550 ff. 147, 150–3 (TS), 46506 ff. 28, 36, 38–9, 42–3 (orig.). See also *CL3* pp. 105–6.

302/22   **work:** G.B.S. to Charlotte Shaw, 22 August 1912, *CL3* p. 114.

302/31   **help:** G.B.S. to Mrs Patrick Campbell, 19 August 1912, *Their Correspondence* pp. 37, 41.

302/39   **boyhood:** G.B.S. to Mrs Patrick Campbell, 9 June 1913, *CL3* p. 185 (*Their Correspondence* p. 119).

303/21   **nerves:** G.B.S. to Mrs Patrick Campbell, 20 March 1913 (*CL3* p. 158), 26 March 1913, 9 April 1913 (*CL3* p. 165). *Their Correspondence* pp. 98, 104, 108.

303/22   **writer:** Mrs Patrick Campbell to G.B.S., 25 March 1913, *Their Correspondence* p. 101.

303/27   **sunlight:** Rebecca West, 'A Very Strange Story', *The Times* 2 November 1952.

304/29   **ending:** G.B.S. to Edith Lyttelton [The Hon. Mrs Alfred], 27 December 1912, *CL3* p. 141.

305/ 4   **burying her:** G.B.S. to Archibald Henderson, 22 February 1911, *CL3* p. 9.

305/12   **contingencies:** G.B.S. to Beatrice Webb, 10 June 1912, *CL3* p. 100.

305/18   **procrastinator:** Archibald Henderson, *Bernard Shaw: Playboy and Prophet* (1932) p. 182.

305/18   **idler:** Lucy Shaw to Janey Crichton, 31 December [1900] (Texas).

305/25   **blows:** Lucy Shaw to Janey Crichton, 21 June [1909] (Texas).

305/31   **married:** Lucy Shaw to Janey Crichton, n.d. (Texas).

305/last **disappointment:** Lucy Shaw to Janey Crichton, 31 December [1900] (Texas).

306/ 9   **infidelity:** Lucy Shaw to Janey Crichton, 21 June [1909] (Texas).

306/15   **alone knows:** Ibid.

306/17   **want it:** G.B.S. to Lucy Carr Shaw, 9 March 1910, *CL2* p. 904.

306/32   **up here:** Archibald Henderson, *Bernard Shaw: His Life and Works* (1911) p. 38.

307/ 3   **doubt:** Lucinda Shaw to G.B.S., 16 October 1908 (Texas).

307/ 5   **experiment:** Hayden Church questionnaire, 27 October 1928 (Houghton).

307/ 8   **letter:** Henderson, *Playboy and Prophet* pp. 181–2.

307/11   **slept:** G.B.S. to Mrs H. R. Beeton, 23 October 1912 (Texas).

307/16   **terrible:** Lucy Shaw to Janey Crichton, 6 December [1912] (Texas).

307/18   **fits:** G.B.S. to Lady Gregory, 18 November 1912, *CL*3 p. 127.
307/27   **gone:** Lucy Shaw to Janey Crichton, 14 April 1913 (Texas).
307/34   **sand:** Ibid.
307/39   **certainly did:** Ibid.
308/ 7   **affect me:** *Shaw: An Exhibit*, item 584.
308/10   **as yet:** G.B.S. to Mrs Patrick Campbell, 22 February 1913,
          *CL*3 p. 152 (*Their Correspondence* p. 86).
308/28   **fire:** Ibid., *CL*3 pp. 151–3 (*Their Correspondence* pp. 85–9).
309/ 2   **wonder!:** Ibid.
309/13   **anything:** Ibid.
309/16   **sea:** G.B.S. to Mrs Patrick Campbell, 7 February 1913, *CL*3
          p. 149 (*Their Correspondence* p. 84).
309/21   **lifetime:** G.B.S. to Archibald Henderson, 22 February 1911,
          *CL*3 p. 9.
309/24   **dead:** G.B.S. to Demetrius O'Bolger, February 1916, *CL*3
          p. 361.
309/26   **childhood:** G.B.S. to Mrs Patrick Campbell, 3 January 1913,
          *CL*3 p. 143.
309/27   **mortality:** G.B.S. to Mrs Patrick Campbell, 26 February 1913,
          Their Correspondence p. 89.
310/ 2   **anything:** G.B.S. to Mrs Patrick Campbell, 13 March 1913,
          *CL*3 pp. 155–6 (*Their Correspondence* pp. 96–7).
310/ 7   **came:** Helen Spinola, *Nothing But the Truth* (1961) p. 123.
310/ 8   **want me:** G.B.S. to Mrs Patrick Campbell, 12 March 1913,
          Their Correspondence p. 95.
310/ 9   **darling:** G.B.S. to Mrs Patrick Campbell, 4 January 1913, *CL*3
          p. 145 (*Their Correspondence* p. 72).
310/10   **with you:** G.B.S. to Mrs Patrick Campbell, 8 December 1912,
          Their Correspondence p. 61.
310/15   **very ill:** Mrs Patrick Campbell to G.B.S., 26 November 1912,
          Their Correspondence p. 57.
310/16   **with me:** Mrs Patrick Campbell to G.B.S., 4 November 1912,
          Their Correspondence p. 53.
310/18   **to see:** Mrs Patrick Campbell to G.B.S., 2 December 1912,
          Their Correspondence p. 60.
310/19   **Stella:** G.B.S. to Mrs Patrick Campbell, 10 December 1912,
          *CL*3 p. 136 (*Their Correspondence* p. 69).
310/23   **scandalously:** G.B.S. to Mrs Patrick Campbell, 29 November
          1912, *CL*3 p. 130 (*Their Correspondence* p. 59).
310/26   **kill:** Margot Peters, *Mrs Pat* (1984) p. 320.
310/31   **for me:** Mrs Patrick Campbell, *My Life and Some Letters* (1922)
          p. 249.
310/32   **heart:** Mrs Patrick Campbell to G.B.S., 31 January 1913, *Their
          Correspondence* p. 76.

310/33 **again:** G.B.S. to Mrs Patrick Campbell, 6 February 1913, *CL3* p. 148 (*Their Correspondence* p. 83).

310/35 *love* you: Mrs Patrick Campbell to G.B.S., 1 November 1912, *Their Correspondence* p. 52.

310/36 **world:** G.B.S. to Mrs Patrick Campbell, 31 January 1913, *Their Correspondence* p. 77.

310/38 **shining:** Mrs Patrick Campbell to G.B.S., 5 February 1913 (Sotheby's Catalogue, 23 February 1983, item 94, p. 43).

310/last **like me:** Mrs Patrick Campbell to G.B.S., 9 December 1912, *Their Correspondence* p. 64.

311/ 4 **without us:** G.B.S. to Mrs Patrick Campbell, 24 May 1913, *CL3* p. 182 (*Their Correspondence* pp. 117–18).

311/30 **Mrs Mouse:** Sotheby's Catalogue, 23 February 1983, item 94, p. 43.

311/31 *blind* man: Mrs Patrick Campbell to G.B.S., 26 October 1912, *Their Correspondence* p. 49.

311/32 **dare!:** Mrs Patrick Campbell to G.B.S., 18 November 1912, *Their Correspondence* p. 56.

311/34 **mean that:** Mrs Patrick Campbell to G.B.S., 31 January 1913, *Their Correspondence* p. 77.

311/38 **colour:** Mrs Patrick Campbell to G.B.S., n.d. [24 February 1913]. See Sotheby's Catalogue, 23 February 1938, item 94, where it is dated 24 March 1918.

311/last **will:** Mrs Patrick Campbell to G.B.S., 18 January 1913, *Their Correspondence* p. 73.

312/ 3 **victims:** G.B.S. to Mrs Patrick Campbell, 8 November 1912, *CL3* p. 126 (*Their Correspondence* p. 54).

312/ 5 **nature:** G.B.S. to Mrs Patrick Campbell, 4 February 1913, *Their Correspondence* p. 80.

312/ 5 **help it:** G.B.S. to Mrs Patrick Campbell, 3 April 1913, *Their Correspondence* p. 106.

312/ 7 **success:** G.B.S. to Mrs Patrick Campbell, 22 March 1913, *Their Correspondence* p. 101.

312/11 **accident:** G.B.S. to Mrs Patrick Campbell, 26 March 1913, *Their Correspondence* p. 103.

312/15 **things:** G.B.S. to Mrs Patrick Campbell, 3 April 1913, *Their Correspondence* p. 106.

312/24 **liked her:** G.B.S. to M. Digby, 16 June 1948 (Plunkett).

312/27 **letters:** G.B.S. to Mrs Patrick Campbell, 2 April 1913, *CL3* p. 163 (*Their Correspondence* p. 104).

312/32 **grudge her:** Ibid., *CL3* pp. 163–4 (*Their Correspondence* p. 105).

312/39 **Eliza:** G.B.S. to Mrs Patrick Campbell, 18 November 1912 (Sotheby's Catalogue, 23 February 1983).

313/12   **triumph:** G.B.S. to Sylvia Brooke, 12 November 1911, *CL3* pp. 57–8.

313/17   **children:** Mrs Patrick Campbell to G.B.S., 24 January 1913, *Their Correspondence* p. 74.

313/21   **with you?:** G.B.S. to Mrs Patrick Campbell, 27 October 1912, *Their Correspondence* pp. 50–1.

313/24   **love?:** Mrs Patrick Campbell to G.B.S., 21 April 1913, *Their Correspondence* p. 110.

313/27   **property:** G.B.S. to Mrs Patrick Campbell, 28 September 1912, *CL3* p. 118 (*Their Correspondence* p. 45).

313/30   **I am:** Mrs Patrick Campbell to G.B.S., 24 February 1913 (Sotheby's Catalogue, 23 February 1983, item 94, where it is dated 24 March 1918).

313/38   **help me:** Margot Peters, *Mrs Pat* p. 320.

314/ 7   **dream out:** G.B.S. to Mrs Patrick Campbell, 9 June 1913, *CL3* pp. 184–5 (*Their Correspondence* pp. 119–20).

314/23   **murder her:** G.B.S. to Mrs Patrick Campbell, 24 May 1913, *CL3* p. 181 (*Their Correspondence* p. 117).

314/36   **easygoing man:** G.B.S. to Mrs Patrick Campbell, 21 September 1913, *CL3* p. 204 (*Their Correspondence* p. 149).

315/ 2   **alternatively:** *Mrs Pat* p. 329.

315/ 6   **lucrative:** G.B.S. to Mrs Patrick Campbell, 28 April 1913, *Their Correspondence* p. 113.

315/18   **iron:** G.B.S. to the Hon. Mrs Alfred Lyttelton, 25 July 1913, *CL3* pp. 192–3.

315/24   **somewhere:** Mrs Patrick Campbell to G.B.S., 31 July 1913, *Their Correspondence* p. 134.

315/26   **I be?:** G.B.S. to Mrs Patrick Campbell, 6 August 1913, *Their Correspondence* p. 137.

315/29   **you know:** Mrs Patrick Campbell to G.B.S., 7 August 1913, *Their Correspondence* p. 137.

315/30   **forgotten:** G.B.S. to Mrs Patrick Campbell, 2 July [August] 1913, *CL3* p. 194 (*Their Correspondence* p. 135).

316/10   **despise you:** Mrs Patrick Campbell to G.B.S., 10 August 1913, *Their Correspondence* p. 137.

316/25   **than I:** Mrs Patrick Campbell to G.B.S., 11 August 1913, *Their Correspondence* p. 138.

317/15   **hurt me:** G.B.S. to Mrs Patrick Campbell, 11–13 August 1913, *Their Correspondence* pp. 138–43. See also *CL3* pp. 195–7.

317/17   **claws:** Mrs Patrick Campbell to G.B.S., 30 August 1913, *Their Correspondence* p. 145.

317/23   **self:** Mrs Patrick Campbell to G.B.S., 13 August 1913, *Their Correspondence* pp. 141–2.

317/26   **a man:** Ibid., *Their Correspondence* p. 142.

317/last   **years:** G.B.S. to Mrs Lily Nightingale-Duddington (J. Wilson Catalogue, 8 July 1969).

CHAPTER VI

318/Ep.   **Spenlow:** G.B.S. to St John Ervine, n.d. [1912] (Texas).

318/6   **way:** *The Diary of Beatrice Webb* vol. 3, entry 13 July 1913, p. 189.

318/29   **adorned:** G.B.S. to Beatrice Webb, 10 July 1912, *CL*3 pp. 98–9.

318/32   **success:** Beatrice Webb to G.B.S., 19 February 1913, *The Letters of Sidney and Beatrice Webb* (ed. Norman MacKenzie 1978) vol. 3, p. 10.

319/22   **slow:** Sidney Webb to Beatrice Webb, 7 December 1912, *The Letters of Sidney and Beatrice Webb* vol. 3, p. 11.

319/23   **safe:** *The Diary of Beatrice Webb* vol. 3, entry 25 May 1913, p. 187.

319/32   **dog:** Leonard Woolf, *Beginning Again* (1964) p. 129.

319/37   **success:** G.B.S. to Kenyon n.d. [1913] (Fales).

320/8   **gentlemen:** Edward Hyams, *The New Statesman: The History of the First Fifty Years: 1913–1963* (1963) p. 25.

320/16   **Tax:** Ibid., p. 27.

320/19   **paper:** G.B.S. to Beatrice Webb, 22 May 1913, *CL*3 p. 176.

320/22   **of me:** *CL*3 p. 178.

320/25   **equality:** *The Diary of Beatrice Webb* vol. 3, entry 5 July 1913, p. 188.

320/37   **interesting:** Edward Hyams, *The New Statesman* p. 27.

321/5   **across:** Ibid., p. 65.

321/9   **for that:** *The Diary of Beatrice Webb* vol. 3, entry 2 January 1914, p. 194.

321/14   **fancy:** Ibid., entry 5 July 1913, p. 188.

321/16   **to me:** G.B.S. to Beatrice Webb, 22 May 1913, *CL*3 p. 178.

321/31   **savage:** Ibid., *CL*3 p. 179.

322/3   **opinion:** G.B.S. to Robert Ross, 13 September 1916, *CL*3 p. 414.

322/6   **years:** Beatrice Webb to G.B.S., 17 June 1913, *The Letters of Sidney and Beatrice Webb* vol. 3, p. 24.

322/7   **brain:** Beatrice Webb to G.B.S., 13 June 1914, ibid., p. 31.

322/9   **egotism:** *The Diary of Beatrice Webb* vol. 3, entry 5 July 1913, p. 188.

322/11   **affair:** Mrs Patrick Campbell to G.B.S., 3 June 1913, *Bernard*

Shaw and Mrs Patrick Campbell: Their Correspondence (ed. Alan Dent 1952) p. 118.

322 / 14 **spider:** *The Diary of Beatrice Webb* vol. 3, entry 13 July 1913, p. 190.

322 / 19 **God:** G.B.S. to Mrs Patrick Campbell, 31 December 1913, *CL3* p. 212 (*Their Correspondence* pp. 148, 155).

322 / 27 **terms:** *The Diary of Beatrice Webb* vol. 3, entry 4 December 1913, pp. 191–2.

322 / 30 **failure:** G.B.S. to Gertrude Kingston, 21 November 1913, *CL3* p. 208.

322 / 32 **more:** *The Times* 19 November 1913.

322 / 36 **thing?:** Desmond MacCarthy, *Shaw* (1951) p. 107.

322 / last **not a few:** *The Morning Post* 2 September 1913.

323 / 3 **ideas:** E. A. Baughan on *Androcles and the Lion*, *Daily News* 2 September 1913. See *Shaw: The Critical Heritage* (ed. T. F. Evans 1976) p. 210.

323 / 7 **succession:** Desmond MacCarthy, *Shaw* p. 102.

323 / 10 **talks:** *The Times* 2 September 1913.

323 / 16 **fun of it:** *Manchester Guardian* 2 September 1913.

323 / 18 **hair:** G.B.S. to Mrs Patrick Campbell, 21 September 1913, *CL3* p. 205 (*Their Correspondence* p. 150).

323 / 26 **ashamed?:** Letter from R. F. Birmingham-Clements, *The Sketch* 4 September 1913.

323 / 30 **shocked:** *London Budget* 7 September 1913.

323 / 34 **charm:** G.B.S. to Charlotte Shaw, 29 December 1913, *CL3* p. 211.

324 / 3 **we are:** *The Diary of Beatrice Webb* vol. 3, entry 2 January 1914, p. 194.

324 / 8 **happy:** G.B.S. to Charlotte Shaw, 29 December 1913, *CL3* p. 211.

324 / 10 **since:** G.B.S. to Mrs Patrick Campbell, 31 December 1913, *CL3* p. 212 (*Their Correspondence* p. 155).

324 / 13 **company:** *The Diary of Beatrice Webb* vol. 3, entry 2 January 1914, p. 194.

324 / 16 **thats all:** Mrs Patrick Campbell to G.B.S., 19 October 1913, *Their Correspondence* p. 151.

324 / 18 **upon one:** Mrs Patrick Campbell to G.B.S., 1 December 1913, *Their Correspondence* p. 153.

324 / 21 **prettiness:** Mrs Patrick Campbell to G.B.S., 4 November 1913, *Their Correspondence* p. 152.

324 / 22 **fool of me:** Mrs Patrick Campbell to G.B.S., 20 December 1913, *Their Correspondence* p. 154.

324 / last **out of me:** Mrs Patrick Campbell to G.B.S., 10 February 1914, *The Correspondence* p. 156.

325/Ep.   **Pygmalion:** G.B.S. to William Archer, 19 April 1919, *CL*3 p. 604.

325/18   **what it is:** Richard Huggett, *The Truth about 'Pygmalion'* (1969) p. 111.

325/23   **enthusiast:** *CP*4 p. 659.

325/28   **present:** Ibid., p. 663.

325/35   **myself:** G.B.S. to Archibald Henderson, 3 January 1905, *CL*2 p. 484.

325/last   **hopes of:** G.B.S. to Robert Bridges, 4 February 1910, *CL*2 p. 897.

326/17   **House:** G.B.S. to Henry Sweet, 2 February 1911, BL Add. MS 50549 ff. 243–5.

326/21   **anything:** Ibid.

326/29   **Eliza?:** *CP*4 pp. 694–5.

326/35   **rest of us:** Ibid., p. 763.

327/ 3   **Governor:** Ibid., p. 710.

327/ 4   **like it:** Ibid., p. 711.

327/13   **about him:** Ibid., p. 710.

327/15   **gentleman:** Ibid., p. 759.

327/21   **basis:** Eric Bentley, *Bernard Shaw* (1967) p. 25.

327/30   **morality:** *CP*4 pp. 761–2.

327/35   **tone:** Ibid., p. 727.

327/36   **dressmaker's:** Ibid., p. 733.

327/39   **work:** Ibid., p. 779.

328/2–3   **parthenogenetically:** Arnold Silver, *Bernard Shaw: The Darker Side* (1982) p. 197.

328/15   **slippers:** *CP*4 pp. 747–8.

328/20   **position:** Ibid., pp. 701–2.

328/30   **care of you:** Ibid., p. 694.

329/3–4   **of him:** *Florence Farr, Bernard Shaw and W. B. Yeats* (ed. Clifford Bax 1946) pp. 23–4.

329/16   **sacred:** *CP*4 p. 702.

329/23   **bird's nes':** Ibid., p. 689.

329/35   **changed:** Ibid., p. 722.

330/ 4   **you like:** Ibid., p. 749.

330/ 8   **battleship:** Ibid., p. 781.

330/24   **character:** G.B.S. to Demetrius O'Bolger, n.d. [February 1916], *CL*3 p. 356.

330/39   **gutter:** *CP*4 pp. 774–9.

331/10   **rather:** Ibid., p. 775.

331/23   ***manner:*** *Androcles and the Lion, Overruled, Pygmalion* (Constable 1916) p. 191.

331/35   **agreed:** *The Truth about 'Pygmalion'* p. 111.

331/37   **unbearable:** *CP*4 p. 782.

332/ 3   **disgusting:** G.B.S. to Trebitsch, 15 June 1934,
　　　　　Shaw/Trebitsch letters p. 342.

332/22   **Pygmalion!:** G.B.S. to Julio Broutá, 3 February 1920
　　　　　(Houghton).

332/30   ***play ends*:** G.B.S. to William Maxwell, 19 August 1939
　　　　　(Scotland). See *CP*4 p. 782.

332/34   **tragedy:** G.B.S. to R. and R. Clark, 25 October 1932, *CL*4
　　　　　p. 311.

332/37   **Liza:** *The Collected Screenplays of Bernard Shaw* (ed. with an
　　　　　introduction by Bernard F. Dukore 1980) p. 71.

333/ 1   **ending:** *Brooklyn Daily Eagle* 8 December 1938.

333/ 3   **scenario:** *CP*4 p. 822.

333/11   **repeated:** G.B.S. to Trebitsch, 23 July 1921, Shaw/Trebitsch
　　　　　letters p. 224.

333/14   **music:** G.B.S. to anon., 3 February 1948. See *Dear Mr Shaw:
　　　　　Selections from Bernard Shaw's postbag* (compiled and ed.
　　　　　Vivian Elliot 1987) p. 124.

333/34   **intolerable:** G.B.S. to Waters, 5 January 1910.

334/ 4   **failure:** G.B.S. to Trebitsch, 29 January 1913, *CL*3 p. 146
　　　　　(Shaw/Trebitsch letters p. 163).

334/16   **hammer:** 'Mr Shaw's New Play', *The Observer* 2 November
　　　　　1913, p. 11.

334/31–2 **welcome to it:** *CP*4 p. 799.

334/34   **needed it:** Hesketh Pearson, *Beerbohm Tree* (1956) p. 176.

334/37   **Handel:** *CP*4 p. 799.

334/39   **detectives:** G.B.S. note for Loewenstein, August 1946
　　　　　(Texas).

335/ 4   **originality:** G.B.S. to Cecil Lewis, 15 December 1926
　　　　　(Texas).

335/11   **feeling:** Beerbohm Tree to G.B.S., 21 November 1913, BL
　　　　　Add. MS 50551 f. 63.

335/33   **Christmas:** G.B.S. to Edmund Gurney, 6 March 1914, *CL*3
　　　　　p. 222.

335/last **rebuff:** Margot Peters, *Mrs Pat* (1984) p. 502.

336/ 4   **next time:** *CP*4 p. 807.

336/ 7   **kill him:** G.B.S. to Mrs Patrick Campbell, 11 April 1914, *CL*3
　　　　　p. 225 (*Their Correspondence* p. 161).

336/10   **pages:** Hesketh Pearson, *Beerbohm Tree* p. 180.

336/12   **call you out:** Mrs Patrick Campbell to G.B.S., 2 March 1914,
　　　　　Their Correspondence p. 158.

336/13   **paper:** *The Truth about 'Pygmalion'* p. 88.

336/19   **Joey:** *Mrs Pat* p. 337.

336/23 **bruise:** *The Truth about 'Pygmalion'* p. 70.

336/28 **for you:** Mrs Patrick Campbell to G.B.S., 21 February 1914, *Their Correspondence* p. 157.

336/40 **seriously!:** Mrs Patrick Campbell to G.B.S., 2 March 1914, *Their Correspondence* p. 158.

337/10 **over it:** Sir Herbert Tree to G.B.S., 6 March 1914, *CL3* p. 221.

337/19 **time:** Michael Holroyd interview with Margaret Halford, 11 July 1976.

337/22 **fight:** G.B.S. to Ellen Pollock, 10 November 1942, *CL4* pp. 648–9.

337/27 **anxiety:** Mrs Patrick Campbell to G.B.S., undated [30 March 1914], *Their Correspondence* pp. 159–60.

337/38 **harmony:** *The Truth about 'Pygmalion'* p. 107.

338/13 **emotion:** C. F. Shaw, *Knowledge is the Door: A Forerunner* p. 12.

338/17 **chance:** G.B.S. to Mrs Patrick Campbell, 11 April 1914, *CL3* p. 225 (*Their Correspondence* pp. 161–2).

338/19 **finish:** Mrs Patrick Campbell to G.B.S., 11 April 1914, *Their Correspondence* p. 162.

338/28 **funny here:** G.B.S. to Charlotte Shaw, 12 April 1914, *CL3* p. 227.

338/35 **go on:** Ibid.

338/40 **his life:** Ibid.

339/9 **down:** Ibid., *CL3* pp. 227–8.

339/14 **hang fire:** Ibid., *CL3* p. 227.

339/24 **uncle:** Ibid., *CL3* p. 228.

339/29 **Higgins:** Mrs Patrick Campbell to G.B.S., 11 May 1914, *Their Correspondence* p. 164.

339/30 **again:** G.B.S. to Charlotte Shaw, 12 April 1914, *CL3* p. 228.

339/35 **play:** Mrs Patrick Campbell to G.B.S., 17 April 1914, *Their Correspondence* p. 162.

339/36 **no more:** G.B.S. to Charlotte Shaw, 27 April 1914, *CL3* p. 228.

340/3 **fold:** Mrs Patrick Campbell to G.B.S., 29 April 1914, *Their Correspondence* p. 163.

340/4 **longer:** G.B.S. to Viola Tree, 27 February 1920, *CL3* p. 666.

340/14 **Higgins:** Nicholas Grene, *Bernard Shaw: A Critical View* (1984) p. 111.

340/21 **to me:** G.B.S. to Viola Tree, 25 February 1920 (Texas).

340/30 **expletive:** G.B.S. to Charlotte Shaw, 19 April 1914, *CL3* p. 229.

341/9 **flower-girl:** *The Truth about 'Pygmalion'* pp. 158–9.

341/17 **week!:** Mrs Patrick Campbell to G.B.S., 28 June 1914, *Their Correspondence* pp. 164–5.

341 / 22	**situation:** Richard Huggett, *The Truth about 'Pygmalion'* p. 158.
341 / 23	**further:** G.B.S. to Charlotte Shaw, 19 April 1914, *CL*3 p. 229.
341 / Ep. 1	**about it?:** G.B.S. to Rowley, 7 January 1916 (Berg).
341 / Ep. 2	**lives:** 'Common Sense About the War', Supplement to *New Statesman* 14 November 1914. See Bernard Shaw, *What I Really Wrote about the War* (1931) p. 69.
342 / 9	**figures:** 'The German Case against Germany', *New Age* 25 May 1916, ibid., p. 155.
342 / 12	**necessary:** Ibid., p. 156.
342 / 15	**conductors:** 'On British Squealing, and the Situation after the War', *New Republic* 6 January 1917, ibid., p. 194.
342 / 19	**dangerous:** 'Chestertonism and the War', *New Statesman* 23 January 1915, ibid., p. 180.
343 / 18	**of man:** *The Times* 9 October 1911.
343 / 33	**persons:** G.B.S. to Carl Heath, n.d. [c. 13 October 1911] (Texas).
344 / 7	**future:** *What I Really Wrote about the War* pp. 216–17.
344 / 11	**effectively:** G.B.S. to R. C. Phillimore, 12 January 1912, *CL*3 p. 72.
344 / 17	**Germany:** 'Armaments and Conscription. A Triple Alliance against War', *Daily Chronicle* 18 March 1913, *What I Really Wrote about the War* p. 11.
344 / 30	**personally:** 'The Peace of Europe and How to Attain it', *Daily News* 1 January 1914, ibid., pp. 15–16.
344 / 33	**of me:** 'Common Sense About the War', ibid., p. 78.
344 / last	**campaign:** Ibid., p. v.
345 / 11	**way out:** 'The Madness of this War', *Daily Citizen* 1 August 1914. See *Bernard Shaw: Agitations: Letters to the Press 1875–1950* (ed. Dan H. Laurence and James Rambeau 1985) pp. 159–60.
345 / 20	**went mad:** Preface to *Heartbreak House*, *CP*5 p. 23.
345 / 26	**fist:** See Hugh Kingsmill, *What They Said at the Time* (1935) p. 167.
346 / 2	**good one:** Ibid.
346 / 4	**morphia:** *What I Really Wrote about the War* p. 111.
346 / 22	**circumstances:** G.B.S. to George Cornwallis-West, 2 October 1914, *CL*3 p. 252.
346 / 25	**taxpayer:** G.B.S. to Siegfried Trebitsch, 28 July 1915, *CL*3 p. 305.
346 / 33	**annihilated:** G.B.S. to Trebitsch, 14 October 1915, Shaw/Trebitsch letters p. 193.
346 / 38	**CIRCUMSTANCES:** G.B.S. to Siegfried Trebitsch, 4 August 1914, *CL*3 p. 243.

347/ 2 **hand:** G.B.S. to Beatrice Webb, 14 August 1914 (LSE).

347/ 7 **easily:** 'Common Sense About the War', *What I Really Wrote about the War* p. 22.

347/23 **destruction:** Manuscript statement dated 6 August 1914 (Cornell). See *New Statesman* III, 8 August 1914, p. 546.

347/29 **later on:** G.B.S. to Beatrice Webb, 14 August 1914 (LSE).

348/ 3 **licked:** 'Mr Shaw's Contribution to the "Daily News"', *Saturday Review* CXVIII, 22 August 1914, p. 222.

348/17 **nations:** 'Open Letter to the President of the United States of America', *Nation* 7 November 1914. *What I Really Wrote about the War* pp. 122–7.

348/23 **HOME:** *New York Call* 1 November 1914.

348/29 **divide:** C. P. Scott to G.B.S., 16 September 1914, BL Add. MS 50517. Cited in *CL*3 p. 250.

348/40 **delirium:** G.B.S. to S. K. Ratcliffe, 2 September 1918, *CL*3 p. 564.

349/ 5 **rid of it:** G.B.S. to Perriton Maxwell, 9 November 1917, *CL*3 p. 516.

349/ 7 **over:** G.B.S. to W. F. Rean, undated [c. August 1915], *CL*3 p. 308.

349/16 **case for it:** G.B.S. to Alexander M. Thompson, 22 December 1917, *CL*3 p. 519.

349/23 **board:** G.B.S. to Lucy Carr Shaw, 13 October 1914, *CL*3 p. 256.

349/25 **circumstances:** G.B.S. to Beatrice Webb, 14 August 1914 (LSE).

349/36 **it all:** Alfred Sutro, *Celebrities and Simple Souls* (1933) p. 266.

350/ 4 **in fact:** G.B.S. to Beatrice Webb, 12 August 1914, *CL*3 pp. 244–5.

350/16 **war:** G.B.S. to Hall Caine, 13 November 1914, *CL*3 p. 267.

350/26 **nation:** 'Common Sense About the War', *What I Really Wrote about the War* p. 45.

350/27 **ideas:** G.B.S. to Charles Trevelyan, 28 February 1918, *CL*3 p. 529.

350/32 **Churchill:** 'Common Sense About the War', *What I Really Wrote about the War* p. 41.

350/34 **Yankee:** Ibid., p. 25.

351/ 4 **temper:** *The Autobiography of Bertrand Russell: 1914–1944* (vol. 2 1968) p. 49.

351/11 **Prussia:** Stanley Weintraub, *Bernard Shaw 1914–1918: Journey to Heartbreak* (1973) p. 38.

351/13 **intellectuals:** G.B.S. to Beatrice Webb, 26 August 1914, *CL*3 p. 247.

351 / 22   **case:** G.B.S. to Alexander M. Thompson, 14 January 1916, *CL3* p. 350.

351 / 24   **joke:** G.B.S. to Hesketh Pearson, 24 June 1919 (Cornell).

351 / 27   **treaties:** 'Common Sense About the War', *What I Really Wrote about the War* p. 42.

352 / 2   **powers:** G.B.S. to Siegfried Trebitsch, 9 June 1915, *CL3* p. 299.

352 / 3   **if you can:** G.B.S. to Hugo Vallentin, 6 August 1914, *CL3* p. 243.

352 / 4   **little:** Archibald Henderson, *Table-Talk of G.B.S.* p. 144.

352 / 15   **Capitalism:** 'Common Sense About the War', *What I Really Wrote about the War* p. 86.

352 / 26   **peace:** Ibid., p. 101.

352 / 28   **before us:** *The Diary of Beatrice Webb* vol. 3, entry 3 January 1915, p. 221.

352 / 39   **feeling:** 'Common Sense About the War', *What I Really Wrote about the War* pp. 89–90.

353 / 7   **advocated them:** Ibid., p. 67.

353 / 27   **get five:** G.B.S. to Mrs Patrick Campbell, 6 October 1914, *Their Correspondence* p. 167.

354 / 4   **cause:** G.B.S., 'Call You This Discipline', letter to the *Daily Citizen* 26 November 1914, p. 2. See *Agitations* pp. 161–3.

354 / 5   **against you:** Doris Arthur Jones, *The Life and Letters of Henry Arthur Jones* (1930) pp. 312–13.

354 / 15   **eye:** 'Blatchford's Reply to Pro-German Outburst', *Weekly Dispatch* 22 November 1914. See *Agitations* p. 166.

354 / 19   **country?:** *The Times* 26 November 1914.

354 / 25   **creatures:** Theodore Roosevelt, *Letters* vol. 8 (ed. E. Elting Morison 1954), 14 September 1914.

354 / 28   **sour:** Granville Barker to G.B.S., 19 February 1915, BL Add. MS 50534 ff. 123–4.

354 / 36   **battlefield:** 'Shaw Empty of Good Sense', *New York Times Current European History of the War* I, 12 December 1914, pp. 68–72.

354 / last   **sick-bed?:** *The Life and Letters of Henry Arthur Jones* pp. 312–13.

355 / 5   **procreation:** R. F. Rattray, *Bernard Shaw: A Chronicle* (1951) p. 197. See also Henry Arthur Jones, *My Dear Wells* (1921) pp. 274–7.

355 / 12   **thieves:** G.B.S. to William Archer, 11 November 1914, *CL3* p. 265.

355 / 15   **believed:** Stanley Weintraub, *Bernard Shaw 1914–1918: Journey to Heartbreak* p. 49.

355/17   **job:** G.B.S. to Frances Chesterton, 5 May 1915, *CL*3 p. 294.
355/20   **will:** Maisie Ward, *Gilbert Keith Chesterton* (1944) p. 332.
355/23   **life:** Ibid., p. 333.
356/ 3   **nuisance:** *Journey to Heartbreak* p. 78.
356/ 5   **attended to it:** G.B.S. to Beatrice Webb, 6 July 1915 (LSE).
356/14   **anti-German:** G.B.S. to Siegfried Trebitsch, 28 July 1915,
          19 January 1915, *CL*3 pp. 304, 286 (Shaw/Trebitsch letters
          pp. 189, 183).
356/32   **symmetry:** *Journey to Heartbreak* p. 125.
356/36   **key:** *The Autobiography of Bertrand Russell* vol. 2, p. 49.
356/last **harlequinading:** 'The Nonsense about Belgium', *Daily News
          & Leader* 18 November 1914.
357/16   **go mad:** G.B.S. to Robert Loraine, undated [c. 10 August
          1918]; G.B.S. to Lucy Carr Shaw, 13 May 1916, *CL*3
          pp. 560, 401.
357/27   **can bear:** G.B.S. to Clifford Sharp, 24 October 1914, *CL*3
          p. 260.
357/34   **madmen:** G.B.S. to Bertrand Russell, 9 November 1914, *CL*3
          p. 261.
358/ 3   *office*: Hall Caine to G.B.S., 20 October 1914 and 28
          November 1914, BL Add. MS 50531 ff. 15, 18–19.
358/ 5   **stand it:** Hall Caine to G.B.S., 4 December 1914, BL Add.
          MS 50531 f. 20.
358/11   **cap:** Hall Caine to G.B.S., 19 December 1914, BL Add. MS
          50531 f. 21.
358/15   **of you:** James F. Muirhead to G.B.S., 15 January 1915, BL
          Add. MS 50517 ff. 236–7.
358/26   **meet:** James F. Muirhead to G.B.S., 23 January 1915, BL
          Add. MS 50517 ff. 248–9.
358/30   **thing:** G.B.S. to R. C. Carton, 2 November 1915, *CL*3 p. 326.
358/37   **good-naturedly:** Desmond MacCarthy, *Shaw* p. 216.
358/38   **unpopularity:** G.B.S. to Beatrice Webb, 6 July 1915 (LSE).
358/last **savage:** G.B.S. to Beatrice Webb, 22 May 1913, *CL*3 p. 179.
359/ 2   **completely:** G.B.S. to Kathleen Hilton Young [formerly
          Scott], 12 October 1922 (on deposit, University of
          Cambridge).
359/ 4   **angry:** Stanley Weintraub, *Journey to Heartbreak* p. 45.
359/ 9   **subjects:** *New Statesman* 14 November 1914, p. 124.
359/14   **wrecker:** G.B.S. to Beatrice and Sidney Webb, 5 October
          1916, *CL*3 p. 423.
359/21   **as I do:** Ibid., p. 424.
359/24   **anything:** G.B.S. to H. G. Wells, 7 December 1916, *CL*3
          p. 439.
359/28   **sun:** G.B.S. to Chesterton, 22 June 1915, BL Add. MS 50522
          ff. 472–472v.

359/32 **so much:** G.B.S. to James F. Muirhead, 16 January 1915, BL Add. MS 50517 f. 243.

359/33 **popular:** G.B.S. to C. D. Medley, 29 December 1916 (Cornell).

359/38 **do it:** G.B.S. to H. M. Paull, 28 October 1915, *CL*3 p. 316.

359/last **footstool:** G.B.S. to Mrs Patrick Campbell, 20 December 1914, *Their Correspondence* p. 171.

360/ 9 **lost:** G.B.S. to Augustin Hamon, 14 April 1921, *CL*3 p. 716.

360/11 **effective:** 'Mr Bernard Shaw on the War!', *New Statesman* 19 December 1914. Reprinted under general title 'Nonsense About Neutrality' in *What I Really Wrote about the War* p. 147.

360/13 **Labor party:** G.B.S. to Augustin Hamon, 9 March 1918, *CL*3 p. 536.

360/15 **backing:** G.B.S. to Lady Gregory, 14 November 1918, *CL*3 p. 573.

360/18 **their own:** 'Common Sense About the War', *What I Really Wrote about the War* p. 68.

360/23 **help him:** G.B.S. to Sidney Webb, 11 December 1916, *CL*3 p. 443.

360/24 **passed:** Blanche Patch note of a reply G.B.S. sent during the Second World War to a man who thought his talents were wasted in the army (Cornell).

361/ 3 **on you:** G.B.S. to Beatrice Webb, 3 July 1915 (LSE).

361/ 5 **desk:** G.B.S. to Gilbert Murray, 14 July 1915, *CL*3 p. 301.

361/10 **withdraw:** 'I have Nothing to Withdraw', *The Star* 25 October 1916. See *Agitations* p. 207.

361/20 **with it:** G.B.S. to Henry Arthur Jones, 2 November 1915, *CL*3 p. 322.

361/33 **combatants:** Preface to *Heartbreak House*, *CP*5 p. 34.

362/ 1 **reasons:** 'More Common Sense about the War', BL Add. MS 50669.

362/13 **wars:** Bernard Shaw, *Fabianism and the War* (pamphlet 1917; copy, BL).

362/25 **recruit on:** 'The Pro-Germanism of Bernard Shaw', *Daily Dispatch*, Manchester, 7 December 1914. See *Agitations* p. 175.

362/27 **recruits:** G.B.S. to James F. Muirhead, 16 January 1915, BL Add. MS 50517 f. 242.

363/ 3 **patriot:** Michael Holroyd, *Lytton Strachey* (1971 edn) p. 612.

363/22 **of one:** *Punch* 25 November 1914, p. 430.

363/25 **matter:** G.B.S. to W. F. Rean, undated [c. August 1915], *CL*3 p. 308.

363/29 **still:** *What I Really Wrote about the War* p. 176.

363/32   **join them:** Ibid., p. 177.

363/35   **management:** *Journey to Heartbreak* p. 118.

364/ 2   **organization:** 'Conscription: Mr Bernard Shaw on Safeguards', *Daily News* 5 January 1916, p. 4. *What I Really Wrote about the War* pp. 219–22.

364/13   **coward:** *What I Really Wrote about the War* p. 215.

364/17   **serve:** Ibid., p. 214.

364/25   **war:** 'Conscientious Objectors', *Nation* 27 May 1916, ibid., pp. 223–4.

364/31   **thinking:** 'Glastonbury Festival and the Military Authority', *Western Daily Press* 29 August 1916, ibid., p. 231.

364/last   **discredited:** 'The Case of Stephen Hobhouse', *Nation* 25 November 1916, ibid., p. 234.

365/13   **inside:** G.B.S. to Clive Bell, 7 July 1916 (King's College, Cambridge).

365/22   **indulgence:** G.B.S. to P. Beaumont Wadsworth, 3 June 1919 (privately owned).

365/25   **service:** 'Glastonbury Festival and the Military Authority', *What I Really Wrote about the War* p. 230.

365/33   **evasion:** 'Conscientious Objectors', ibid., p. 229.

366/ 7   **politics:** 'Mrs Shaw's Diverted Genius', *The New Republic* 5 December 1914, pp. 13–14.

366/10   **habit:** H. G. Wells to G.B.S., early March 1914, *CL3* p. 223.

366/12   **thing:** G.B.S. to Ernest Newman, 25 October 1917, *CL3* p. 512.

366/14   **fortissimos:** G.B.S. to Edward Elgar, 8 March 1919, *CL3* p. 593.

366/18   **soul:** G.B.S. to Mrs Patrick Campbell, 9 December 1915, *CL3* p. 337 (*Their Correspondence* p. 184).

366/25   **said to it:** G.B.S. to H. G. Wells, 17 May 1917, *CL3* p. 471.

366/27   **friction:** G.B.S. to Rutland Boughton, 26 April 1916, *CL3* p. 396.

366/30   **world:** *The New Republic* 5 December 1914, pp. 13–14.

366/35   **on this:** Leonard Woolf, *Beginning Again* (1964) p. 187.

367/Ep.   **play:** 'Joy Riding at the Front', II: 'The Technique of War', *Daily Chronicle* 7 March 1917, *What I Really Wrote about the War* p. 258.

367/32   **the war:** *Ellen Terry and Bernard Shaw: A Correspondence* (ed. Christopher St John 1931) p. 453.

368/ 3   **to come:** Keir Hardie to G.B.S., 26 November 1914, BL Add. MS 50538 ff. 24–5.

368/ 8   **uttered:** 'The Nonsense about Belgium', *Daily News & Leader* 18 November 1914.

368/12   **gardens:** G.B.S. to Arnold Bennett, 9 November 1916
          (Sotheby's Catalogue, 25 May 1936).

368/28   **For ages:** H. G. Wells, *Experiment in Autobiography: Discoveries
          and Conclusions of a Very Ordinary Brain (Since 1866)* (1934)
          vol. 2, pp. 677–8.

368/34   **way:** *Shaw the Villager and Human Being: A Biographical
          Symposium* (ed. Allan Chappelow 1961) p. 166.

369/ 4   **'top ten':** Ibid., pp. 166–9.

369/12   **paying:** G.B.S. to Beatrice and Sidney Webb, 5 October 1916,
          *CL*3 p. 426.

369/15   **German:** M. MacDonagh, *In London during the Great War*
          (1935) p. 138.

369/28   **we are!:** G.B.S. to Beatrice and Sidney Webb, 5 October 1916,
          *CL*3 p. 426.

369/35   **hiss:** Michael Holroyd, *Augustus John* (1976) p. 525.

369/40   **Mrs Webb:** Virginia Woolf to Vanessa Bell, 28 June 1916, *The
          Question of Things Happening: The Letters of Virginia Woolf*, vol.
          2: *1912–1922* (1976) p. 104.

370/ 4   **within you:** *The Diary of Beatrice Webb* vol. 4, entry 24 May
          1927, p. 124.

370/ 6   **religion:** Virginia Woolf to Vanessa Bell, 28 June 1916, *The
          Question of Things Happening* p. 104.

370/10   **Mrs Shaw:** Ibid.

370/14   **environment:** *The Diary of Beatrice Webb* vol. 4, entry 24 May
          1927, p. 124.

371/22   **refuse:** *What I Really Wrote about the War* p. 240.

371/30   **experience:** G.B.S. to Lady Gregory, 4 May 1917 (Cornell).

371/32   **continuously:** 'Joy Riding at the Front', I: 'Bombardment',
          Daily Chronicle 5 March 1917, *What I Really Wrote about the
          War* p. 253.

372/ 1   **trams:** Ibid., p. 241.

372/30   **than I:** 'Joy Riding at the Front', III: 'Consolations and
          Responsibilities', *Daily Chronicle* 8 March 1917, ibid., p. 266.

372/last **horror:** Ibid., p. 267.

373/ 6   **pig:** 'Joy Riding at the Front', II: 'The Technique of War',
          ibid., p. 259.

373/ 8   **war:** 'Joy Riding at the Front', III: 'Consolations and
          Responsibilities', ibid., p. 261.

373/16   **ambition:** Ibid., p. 267.

373/24   **proud of it:** 'Mr Bernard Shaw's Visit to the Front', *The Times*
          9 May 1917, ibid., p. 269.

373/31   **views:** *Private Papers of Douglas Haig* (ed. Robert Blake 1952)
          pp. 194–5.

373/34   **months:** 'The New Book That Interested Me Most', *The Sun* (New York) 14 April 1918, p. 10.

374/ 2   **superannuated:** *What I Really Wrote about the War* p. 244.

374/20   **enough:** G.B.S. to Trebitsch, 21 April 1922, Shaw/Trebitsch letters p. 232.

374/27   **successful:** G.B.S. to Lord Kennet (Hilton Young), 21 February 1948 (on deposit, University of Cambridge).

374/32   **perfection:** Ibid., 28 February 1948.

374/39   **abominable war:** G.B.S. to Charles Charrington, 3 December 1914, *CL*3 p. 273.

374/40   **about the war:** G.B.S. to Charles Delme-Radcliffe, 23 April 1917, *CL*3 p. 464.

375/ 8   **fiasco:** G.B.S. to Charlotte Shaw, 30 August 1917, BL Add. MS 50550 f. 215 (TS), 46506 f. 124 (orig.).

375/15   **expected:** G.B.S. to Henry Salt, 30 October 1919 (Berg).

375/17   **gramophone:** G.B.S. to Charlotte Shaw, 31 August 1917, BL Add. MS 50550 f. 216 (TS), 46505 f. 125 (orig.).

375/20   **politics:** G.B.S. to Charles Delme-Radcliffe, 23 April 1917, *CL*3 p. 465.

375/26   **victory:** G.B.S. to Beatrice Webb, 27 November 1917 (LSE).

375/27   **Labor:** G.B.S. to Augustin Hamon, 9 March 1918, *CL*3 p. 536.

375/28   **P.M.:** G.B.S. to Kathleen Young [formerly Scott, also Kennet], 12 October 1922 (on deposit, University of Cambridge).

375/30   **mad:** G.B.S. to Ernest Newman, 10 August 1917, *CL*3 p. 500.

375/33   **have met:** G.B.S. to Charlotte Shaw, 31 August 1917, BL Add. MS 50550 f. 216 (TS), 46505 f. 125 (orig.).

375/last   **priest:** G.B.S. to Beatrice Webb, 2 October 1917 (LSE).

376/Ep.   **patriotism:** *CP*5 p. 58.

376/ 9   **judgments:** Stanley Weintraub, *Journey to Heartbreak* pp. 90–1.

376/20   **hear:** Cyril Scott, *My Years of Indiscretion* (1924) p. 231.

376/33   **bewildered him:** *CP*5 p. 46.

377/22   **intellect:** G.B.S. to Austin Harrison, 14 May 1917, BL Add. MS 50538 f. 69.

377/27   **continent:** *CP*4 p. 971.

377/39   **doing!:** *CP*4 pp. 980–1.

378/ 1   **recommend it:** G.B.S. to J. E. Vedrenne, 19 December 1916 (Theatre Museum, Victoria and Albert Museum).

378/ 8   **Emperor!:** Stanley Weintraub, *Journey to Heartbreak* p. 130.

378/11   **fair?:** *CP*4 p. 981.

378/16   **at first:** G.B.S. to Vedrenne, 19 December 1916 (Theatre Museum, Victoria and Albert Museum).

378/18   **enough:** G.B.S. to Lord Dunsany, 11 October 1916 (Berg).

378/27   **Farce:** Raymond Mander and Joe Mitchenson, *Theatrical*

Companion to Shaw: A Pictorial Record of the First Performances
of the Plays of George Bernard Shaw (1954) p. 176.

378/27   **appeal:** *CP5* p. 227.

378/31   **to date:** G.B.S. to Vedrenne, 19 December 1916 (Theatre
Museum, Victoria and Albert Museum).

378/37   **imagination:** *The Times* 23 January 1917.

379/ 5   **duchess:** *Theatrical Companion to Shaw* p. 177. The title was
subsequently changed to *Annajanska, the Bolshevik Empress.*

379/16   **silly:** *What I Really Wrote about the War* p. 271.

379/21   **anonymity:** Lillah McCarthy, *Myself and My Friends* (1933)
p. 190.

379/26   **tired:** Ibid., p. 193.

379/30–1 **misunderstandings:** G.B.S. to Lady Gregory, 14 September
1915, *CL3* p. 309.

379/39   **adventure:** *CP4* p. 1016.

380/ 2   **gloriously on:** G.B.S. to Lady Gregory, 14 September 1915,
CL3 p. 309.

380/ 3   **see him:** Lady Gregory to G.B.S., 19 September 1925 (Texas).

380/ 8   **harm:** G.B.S. to W. B. Yeats, 12 October 1915 (Sotheby's
Catalogue, 7 December 1966, item 649).

380/18   **king:** *CP4* p. 986.

380/24   **run?:** G.B.S. to Lance-Corporal W. J. Wells, 28 May 1917,
CL3 p. 477.

380/34   **life:** *CP4* p. 1008.

380/38   **hen:** Ibid., p. 1009.

380/40   **patch:** Ibid., p. 987.

381/ 3   **disposition:** Ibid., p. 1013.

381/ 9   **is right:** Ibid., p. 996.

381/10   **race:** Ibid., p. 1000.

381/18   **surroundings:** Matthew Nathan to G.B.S., 16 November
1915, BL Add. MS 50517 ff. 320–1.

381/24   **theatre:** Horace Plunkett to G.B.S., 15 November 1915, BL
Add. MS 50547 ff. 126–7.

381/33   **nothing:** G.B.S. to Lady Gregory, 27 November 1917, *CL3*
p. 517.

382/20   **about:** G.B.S. to Mrs Patrick Campbell, 14 May 1916, *Their
Correspondence* p. 186.

382/26   **before:** G.B.S. to William Archer, 30 December 1916, *CL3*
p. 445.

382/30   **them:** G.B.S. to Hugo Vallentin, 27 October 1917, *CL3* p. 513.

382/last **bit:** G.B.S. to Lillah McCarthy, 24 June 1918, *CL3* p. 553.

383/Ep.   **governing me:** G.B.S. to Sá, 4 November 1917 (Sotheby's
Catalogue, 21 February 1978, item 441).

383 / 12   **nationality:** 'A Note on Aggressive Nationalism', *New Statesman* 12 July 1913. See Bernard Shaw, *The Matter with Ireland* (ed. with an introduction by Dan H. Laurence and David H. Greene 1962) p. 81.

383 / 17   **metropolis:** G.B.S. to Ignatius MacHugh, 19 August 1921, *CL*3 p. 729.

383 / 22   **week:** Andrew Wilson to Michael Holroyd, 14 March 1975.

383 / 28   **dust heap:** Lady Gregory, *Seventy Years: Being an Autobiography of Lady Gregory* (ed. Colin Smythe 1974) p. 447.

383 / last **England:** G.B.S. to Sylvia Beach, 11 June 1921, *CL*3 p. 719.

384 / 2   **passed:** G.B.S. to Mrs Patrick Campbell, 3 April 1913, *Their Correspondence* p. 106.

384 / 9   **hopeless:** G.B.S. to Lady Gregory, n.d. [1916] (Cornell).

384 / 11   **forgotten:** 'War Issues for Irishmen', written 1918 and published 1962, *The Matter with Ireland* p. 180.

384 / 19   **for him?:** G.B.S. to R. D. Blumenfeld, 24 August 1921 (Texas).

384 / 37   **lands:** Nicholas Grene, 'Shaw in Ireland: Visitor or Returning Exile?' See *Shaw: The Annual of Bernard Shaw Studies*, vol. 5: *Shaw Abroad* (ed. Rodelle Weintraub 1985) p. 59.

385 / 6   **camps:** *CP*2 p. 829.

385 / 8   **political:** G.B.S. note on Hesketh Pearson typescript of biography (Texas).

385 / 10   **English:** 'The Gaelic League', *The Freeman's Journal* 17 October 1910. See *The Matter with Ireland* p. 61.

385 / 15   **city!:** 'Neglected Morals of the Irish Rising', *New Statesman* 6 May 1916. See *The Matter with Ireland* p. 109.

385 / 19   **Ireland:** 'The Irish Censorship', *Time and Tide* 16 November 1928. See *The Matter with Ireland* pp. 273–9.

385 / 22   **O'Dogherty:** G.B.S. to Bearnard O'Dubhthaigh, 1 October 1948 (privately owned).

385 / 27   **period:** 'The Gaelic League'. See *The Matter with Ireland* p. 60.

385 / 31   **settled:** 'Why Devolution Will Not Do', *The Irish Statesman* 22 November 1919. See *The Matter with Ireland* p. 207.

385 / 38   **Englishmen:** 'The Protestants of Ireland', lecture 6 December 1912. See *The Matter with Ireland* p. 72.

386 / 5   **rancor:** *CP*2 p. 846.

386 / 7   **command:** 'Neglected Morals of the Irish Rising'. See *The Matter with Ireland* p. 111.

386 / 19   **party:** 'Shall Parnell Go?' *The Star* 20 November 1890. See *The Matter with Ireland* p. 25.

386 / 26   **criminals:** 'Shall Parnell Go?' *The Star* 27 November 1890. See *The Matter with Ireland* pp. 28, 27.

386/last **them:** 'A Crib for Home Rulers', *Pall Mall Gazette* 25
         September 1888. See *The Matter with Ireland* p. 23.
387/ 9 **sends them:** *CP2* pp. 819–20.
387/15 **angels:** 'A Note on Aggressive Nationalism'. See *The Matter
         with Ireland* p. 82.
387/18 **love:** *King Richard III* Act II, Scene 1.
387/24 **done:** *CP2* pp. 831–2.
387/31 **war:** 'The Easter Weekend Executions'. See *The Matter with
         Ireland* pp. 113, 112.
387/35 **Commonwealth:** E. R. Dodds, *Missing Persons* (1972) p. 66.
388/ 6 **defiance:** *The Diary of Beatrice Webb* vol. 3, entry 21 May 1916,
         p. 256.
388/15 **Crown:** 'Roger Casement'. See *The Matter with Ireland* p. 118.
388/20 **mourning:** *The Diary of Beatrice Webb* vol. 3, entry 21 May
         1916, p. 256.
388/32 **turn:** 'Roger Casement'. See *The Matter with Ireland* pp. 121–3.
389/ 3 **to you:** Brian Inglis, *Roger Casement* (1973) pp. 329–30.
389/10 **G.B.S.:** Ibid., p. 331.
389/18 **better:** G.B.S. to Henry W. Nevinson, 6 July 1916, *CL3* p. 405.
389/24 **consecration:** 'Roger Casement'. See *The Matter with Ireland*
         p. 124.
389/38 **the way:** 'Irish Novelist Replies to Mr Shaw', *Irish Press* 13
         February 1937.
390/ 4 **that way:** 'Brogue-Shock', *The Nation* 24 March 1917. See *The
         Matter with Ireland* p. 139.
390/15 **kingdoms:** G.B.S. to R. B. Haldane, 12 July 1917, *CL3* p. 482.
390/18 **at once:** G.B.S. to Henry Salt, 3 October 1917 (Texas).
390/25 **of him:** Plunkett Diaries (Plunkett).
390/28 **settlement:** G.B.S. to Plunkett, 9 November 1917 (Plunkett).
390/39 **pickaxe:** Ibid.
391/ 2 **England:** G.B.S. to R. E. Muirhead and Robert Smillie,
         undated [assigned to 16 November 1920], *CL3* p. 699.
391/ 8 **alike:** Bernard Shaw, *Irish Nationalism and Labour
         Internationalism* (1920) p. 14. For publication details, see
         Laurence, *Bernard Shaw: A Bibliography* (1983) A156.
391/13 **nervousness:** G.B.S. to Horace Plunkett, 15 March and 31
         March 1918, *CL3* pp. 543, 548.
391/29 **right:** *CP2* p. 844.
391/33 **discussion:** 'A Crib for Home Rulers'. See *The Matter with
         Ireland* p. 22.
391/37 **accept:** Ibid., p. 21.
391/last **people:** *CP2* p. 843.
392/ 5 **Powers:** 'How to Settle the Irish Question', *The Matter with*

Ireland p. 144. See Laurence, *Bernard Shaw: A Bibliography* A145.

392/13   **Home Rule:** *CP2* pp. 841–2.

392/21   **malady:** 'How to Settle the Irish Question'. See *The Matter with Ireland* p. 145.

392/29   **chance:** G.B.S. to Lady Gregory, 14 November 1918, *CL*3 p. 573.

392/33   **services:** G.B.S. to Mabel Fitzgerald, 1 December 1914, *CL*3 p. 272.

392/last   **Socialism:** G.B.S. to Patrick O'Reilly, 30 March 1949, *CL*4 p. 844.

393/Ep.   **at war:** G.B.S. to Henry Newbolt, 25 July 1920, *CL*3 p. 685.

393/9   **all:** G.B.S. to Lady Gregory, 14 November 1918, *CL*3 pp. 573–4.

393/16   **mother:** G.B.S. to Lady Mary Murray, 8 February 1918, *CL*3 p. 528.

393/19   **killed:** Mrs Patrick Campbell to G.B.S., 7 January 1918, *Their Correspondence* p. 198.

393/23   **dearest!:** G.B.S. to Mrs Patrick Campbell, 7 January 1918, *CL*3 p. 525 (*Their Correspondence* p. 199).

393/35   **to him:** G.B.S. to Lady Gregory, 5 February 1918, *CL*3 p. 527.

394/19   **Archer:** 'William Archer', *Pen Portraits and Reviews* (1931) p. 16.

394/27   **occasions:** *What I Really Wrote about the War* p. 176.

394/32   **elbow:** G.B.S. to Mrs Patrick Campbell, 13 January 1915, *CL*3 p. 282 (*Their Correspondence* p. 172).

394/36   **years:** G.B.S. to Robert Loraine, 13 December 1914, *CL*3 pp. 278–9.

395/3   **leg:** Winifred Loraine, *Robert Loraine, Soldier. Actor. Airman* (1938) p. 243.

395/9   **better:** G.B.S. to Robert Loraine, undated [c. 10 August 1918], *CL*3 pp. 559–60.

395/19   **service:** G.B.S. to St John Ervine, 22 May 1918, *CL*3 p. 551.

395/21   **war:** *Robert Loraine* p. 243.

395/28   **like me:** G.B.S. to Charles Charrington, 14 September 1916, *CL*3 p. 415.

395/35   **manner:** *Drama*, Winter 1946 p. 12.

396/6   **went back:** Mrs Patrick Campbell to G.B.S., 3 February and 20 September 1915, *Their Correspondence* pp. 173, 180.

396/11   **salaries:** C. B. Purdom, *Harley Granville Barker* (1955) p. 172.

396/15   **theatre:** G.B.S. to Gilbert Murray, 14 July 1915, *CL*3 p. 301.

396/26   **loose end:** G.B.S. to Arthur W. Pinero, 22 October 1915 (Texas).

396/29   **count:** C. B. Purdom, *Harley Granville Barker* p. 173.
396/last   **much more:** Ibid., pp. 174–5.
397/19   **insult:** *Drama*, Winter 1946 p. 12.
397/25   **refuse it:** G.B.S. to Lillah McCarthy, 19 January 1916, *CL*3
                p. 352.
397/36   **sorry:** Granville Barker to G.B.S., 4 April 1916, *Granville
                Barker and His Correspondents* (ed. Eric Salmon, Detroit 1986)
                pp. 148–9.
397/38   **time of it:** *Drama*, Winter 1946 p. 12.
397/last   **effort:** Granville Barker to G.B.S., 4 April 1916, *Granville
                Barker and His Correspondents* pp. 148–9.
398/ 5   **devil:** G.B.S. to Mrs Patrick Campbell, 14 May 1916, *Their
                Correspondence* p. 186.
398/11   **would?:** Granville Barker to G.B.S., 26 May 1916, *Granville
                Barker and His Correspondents* p. 151.
398/22   **letter:** Hesketh Pearson, *Bernard Shaw* (1975 edn) p. 495.
398/32   **myself:** G.B.S. to Lillah McCarthy, 19 June 1918, *CL*3 p. 552.
398/37   **your age:** G.B.S. to Granville Barker, 26 August 1918, *CL*3
                p. 561 (Shaw/Barker letters p. 197).
399/11   **playreading:** G.B.S. to Granville Barker, 18 December 1918,
                *CL*3 pp. 575–6 (Shaw/Barker letters pp. 198–9).
399/13   **again:** *Drama*, Winter 1946 p. 13.
399/16   **happy:** Ibid.
399/19   **woman:** G.B.S. to Lillah McCarthy, 21 August 1932 (Texas).
399/21   **re-born:** Lillah McCarthy to G.B.S., 10 October 1936, BL
                Add. MS 50534 f. 169.
399/27   **unalterable:** *Drama*, Winter 1946 p. 13.
399/29   **six years:** G.B.S. to Lillah McCarthy, 18 June 1918, *CL*3
                p. 552.
399/30   **into me:** Hesketh Pearson, *Bernard Shaw* (1975 edn) p. 496.
399/37   **Henryjamesism:** G.B.S. to William Archer, 8 June 1923, BL
                Add. MS 45296 f. 264.
399/39   **stage:** G.B.S. to St John Ervine, 10 July 1923 (copy privately
                owned).
400/ 1   **earth:** G.B.S. to William Archer, 14 December 1924, *CL*3
                p. 895.
400/ 4   **herself:** Florence Hardy to G.B.S., 1 June 1924, BL Add. MS
                50519 ff. 141–2.
400/12   **of me:** Hesketh Pearson, *Bernard Shaw* (1975 edn) p. 496.
400/15   **poker:** *Time and Tide* 11 August 1956, p. 953.
400/20   **done for:** Hesketh Pearson, *Bernard Shaw* p. 496.
400/27   **before:** *Time and Tide* 11 August 1956.
400/30   **known:** Hesketh Pearson, *Bernard Shaw* p. 495.

400 / 34   **soul:** G.B.S. to William Archer, 14 December 1924, *CL*3
          p. 894.

401 / 11   **alone:** Granville Barker to G.B.S., 19 September 1917,
          Granville Barker and His Correspondents p. 151.

401 / 20   **tolerate me:** G.B.S. to Lillah McCarthy, 19 June 1918, *CL*3
          p. 552.

401 / 26   **to her:** Hesketh Pearson, *Bernard Shaw* p. 495.

401 / 32   **Harley's:** Raymond Mortimer, 'Shaw and Barker', *Sunday
          Times* 31 March 1957.

401 / 35   **revive:** *The Times Literary Supplement* 12 September 1946. See
          also *Granville Barker and His Correspondents* p. 163.

402 / 3   **knowing it:** G.B.S. to Henry Salt, 25 February 1919, *CL*3
          p. 591.

402 / 15   **everything else:** G.B.S. to H. A. Des Voeux, 9 May 1913,
          *CL*3 p. 171.

402 / 24   **looked:** H. G. Farmer, *Bernard Shaw's Sister and Her Friends*
          (1959) p. 201.

402 / 30   **Thought:** Copy of letter dated 14 February 1918 found with
          Lucy's will.

402 / 35   **possess:** G.B.S. to Mrs Patrick Campbell, 19 December 1915,
          *CL*3 p. 336 (*Their Correspondence* p. 183).

402 / last **Golders Green:** G.B.S. to Mrs Patrick Campbell, 14 May
          1916, *Their Correspondence* p. 186.

403 / 22   ***wish for:*** *Bernard Shaw's Sister and Her Friends* pp. 237–8.

403 / 32   **minute:** Mrs Patrick Campbell to G.B.S., 23 February 1920,
          Their Correspondence p. 208.

403 / 39   **dead:** *SSS* p. 95.

VOLUME THREE
The Lure of Fantasy

CHAPTER I

3 / Ep. **armistice:** Memorandum issued by Admiral Beatty, reported in *The Times* 21 November 1918.

3 / 18 **morality:** *The Diary of Beatrice Webb* vol. 3 (ed. Norman and Jeanne MacKenzie 1984), entry 12 December 1918, p. 326.

4 / 9 **other leg:** 'The Croaking Raven Doth Bellow for Revenge', *Manchester Guardian* 21 November 1918, collected in *Bernard Shaw: Agitations: Letters to the Press 1875–1950* (ed. Dan H. Laurence and James Rambeau 1985) p. 227.

4 / 11 **reparations?:** *Manchester Guardian* 3 December 1923.

4 / 18 **in vain:** 'What To Do With the Kaiser', *Sunday Evening Telegram* 6 July 1919, p. 5.

4 / 23 **enemies:** 'Bury the Hatchet', *Manchester Guardian* 3 February 1919, *Agitations* p. 232.

4 / 28 **pacific:** 'Peace Conference Hints', *New York American* 19 January–23 March 1919, *What I Really Wrote about the War* (1931) p. 295.

4 / 30 **success:** G.B.S. to Archibald Henderson, n.d., BL Add. MS 50564 f. 119.

4 / 39 **Ha ha!:** G.B.S. to Henry Salt, 25 February 1919, *CL*3 p. 591.

4 / last **politics:** William Irvine, *The Universe of G.B.S.* (1968) p. 306.

5 / 10 **nor man's?:** Hugh Kingsmill, *What They Said at the Time* (1935) p. 206.

5 / 24 **restorations:** 'Peace Conference Hints', *What I Really Wrote about the War* p. 347.

5 / 29 **to evil:** Ibid., p. 308.

5 / 36 **the way:** Ibid., p. 315.

6 / 4 **absurdity:** Ibid., p. 308.

6 / 11 **crime:** Ibid., p. 338.

6 / 17 **own way:** 'The League of Nations', *Daily News* 15 April 1919, *Agitations* p. 236.

7 / 3 **now:** G.B.S. to Kathleen Scott, 30 July 1919 (copy privately owned).

7 / 10 **world:** William Gerhardie, *God's Fifth Column* (1981) p. 265.

7 / 25 **Nations:** *What I Really Wrote about the War* p. 356.

7/32   **Europe:** Robert Skidelsky, *John Maynard Keynes: Hopes Betrayed* (1983) pp. 374–5.

7/38   **dispute this:** G.B.S. to Siegfried Trebitsch, 15 January 1920, *CL*3 p. 655 (Shaw/Trebitsch letters p. 210).

8/ 2   **circles:** Roy Harrod, *John Maynard Keynes* (1951) p. 254.

8/ 6   **the peace:** *The Universe of G.B.S.* p. 308.

8/17   **dried up:** John Maynard Keynes, *The Economic Consequences of the Peace* (1919) pp. 44–5.

8/20   **people:** 'Peace Conference Hints', *What I Really Wrote about the War* p. 312.

8/24   **Europe:** G.B.S. to Kathleen Scott, 30 July 1919 (copy privately owned).

8/Ep.   **madhouse:** *CP*5 p. 164.

8/32   **nightmare:** T. E. Lawrence to Charlotte Shaw, 8 May 1928, BL Add. MS 45904 f. 3.

8/33   **atmosphere:** Archibald Henderson, *George Bernard Shaw: Man of the Century* (1956) p. 625.

9/ 4   **playgoer:** G.B.S. to George Moore, n.d. [assigned to October 1911], *CL*3 p. 53.

9/ 8   **poets:** BL Add. MS 50699 f. 370.

9/11   **futility:** *CP*5 p. 13.

9/14   **war:** Ibid., p. 12.

9/20   **people:** Ibid., p. 173.

9/33   **in comedy:** *Bernard Shaw and Alfred Douglas: A Correspondence* (ed. Mary Hyde 1982) p. 192.

10/ 1   **farce:** Richard Denham, *Stars in my Hair: Being Certain Indiscreet Memoirs* (1958) p. 112.

10/ 3   **my Lear:** *CP*7 p. 475.

10/ 5   **tragic:** 'Tolstoy: Tragedian or Comedian?' Extemporized speech at Tolstoy Commemoration, 30 November 1921. See *Pen Portraits and Reviews* (1931) p. 261.

10/ 8   **of 88:** G.B.S. to Lillah McCarthy, 10 August 1917, *CL*3 p. 498.

10/12   **rode them:** *CP*5 p. 14.

10/21   **household:** Ibid., p. 160.

10/27   **senses:** Ibid., p. 165.

10/32   **wounds?:** Ibid., p. 172.

11/ 6   **bang?:** Ibid., p. 103.

11/10   **of 18:** G.B.S. to Lillah McCarthy, 10 August 1917, *CL* 3 p. 498.

11/14   **handsome:** *CP*5 p. 79.

11/18   **broken:** Ibid., p. 85.

11/20   **lady-killer:** Ibid., p. 97.

11/34   **at all:** Ibid., p. 110.

11/35	**income:** Ibid., p. 162.
11/38	**take you:** Ibid., p. 167.
12/ 1	**father:** Ibid., p. 168.
12/ 7	**nothing:** Ibid., p. 148.
12/15	**years ago:** Ibid., p. 176.
12/17	**concentration:** Ibid., p. 63.
12/22	**contemplation:** *Heartbreak House* (Garland facsimile edition 1981) p. 9.
12/34	**misery:** Desmond MacCarthy, *Shaw* (1951) p. 144.
12/last	**feeling:** *CP*5 p. 140.
13/18	**break:** Ibid., pp. 140–1.
13/22	**progeny:** Ibid., p. 156.
13/26	**shock:** See Louis Crompton, *Shaw the Dramatist: A Study of the Intellectual Background of His Plays* (1971) pp. 156–7.
13/31	**peace:** *CP*5 p. 140.
13/39	**together:** Ibid., p. 148.
14/ 2	**devil:** Ibid., p. 175.
14/ 5	**Parsifal:** G.B.S. to J. C. Squire, 14 October 1919, *CL*3 p. 638.
14/ 6	**work:** G.B.S. to Edward Elgar, 12 August 1929 (copy privately owned).
14/10	**atmosphere:** G.B.S. to Nugent Monck, 4 September 1927 (copies received from Frank Hildy).
14/14	**Tchekov's plays:** G.B.S. to Siegfried Trebitsch, 16 September 1920, Shaw/Trebitsch letters p. 216.
14/25	**naturally:** *CP*5 p. 134.
15/ 7	**dreams:** Ibid., p. 127.
15/11	**naked:** Ibid., p. 166.
15/18	**anyone else:** Ibid., p. 129.
15/20	**young:** Ibid., p. 143.
15/21	**outside them:** Ibid., p. 88.
15/32	**with us?:** Ibid., pp. 104–5.
15/35	**pose:** Ibid., p. 151.
15/37	**what we are:** Ibid., p. 94.
15/40	**about her:** Ibid., p. 119.
16/ 1	**on purpose:** Ibid., p. 113.
16/ 3	**him myself:** Ibid., pp. 138–9.
16/ 5	**harshly:** Ibid., p. 180.
16/25	**survive:** Ibid.
16/26	**mixed:** Ibid., p. 85.
16/35	**his work:** G.B.S. to A. C. Howard, *Shaw the Villager and Human Being: A Biographical Symposium* (ed. Allan Chappelow 1961) p. 186.
17/ 8	**department:** *CP*5 p. 163.

17/18   **everything:** G.B.S. to Mrs Patrick Campbell, 28 July 1929, *CL*4 p. 157. See *Bernard Shaw and Mrs Patrick Campbell: Their Correspondence* (ed. Alan Dent 1952) p. 291.

17/21   **freedom:** *CP*5 p. 172.

17/26   **world:** Ibid., p. 123.

17/30   **what for?:** Margot Peters, *Mrs Pat* (1984) pp. 26, 408, 447.

17/33   **Shotover:** Mrs Patrick Campbell to G.B.S., 25 June 1917, *Their Correspondence* p. 196.

17/36   **would:** G.B.S. to Mrs Patrick Campbell, 13 January 1920 [1921], *CL*3 p. 707 (*Their Correspondence* p. 219).

18/ 2   **person:** G.B.S. to Clare Winsten, 3 May 1950 (Texas).

18/11   **hell:** *CP*5 p. 142.

18/14   **heaven:** Ibid., p. 99.

18/31   **out of it:** Virginia Woolf to Katherine Cox, 25 June 1916; Virginia Woolf to Vanessa Bell, 28 June 1916, *The Question of Things Happening: The Letters of Virginia Woolf*, vol. 2: *1912– 1922* (1976) pp. 102, 104.

18/33   **knee:** Stanley Weintraub, *Bernard Shaw: 1914–1918: Journey to Heartbreak* (1973) p. 165.

18/39   **creatures:** *CP*5 p. 159.

19/ 5   **with you:** Leonard Woolf, *Beginning Again* (1964) p. 126.

19/13   **pococurantism:** Crompton, *Shaw the Dramatist* p. 154.

19/25   **something:** *CP*5 p. 175.

19/27   **boots:** C. T. Watts and Laurence Davies, *Cunninghame Graham* (1979) p. 134.

20/ 2   **world:** *CP*5 p. 145.

20/18   **bauble yet:** *The Collected Poems of W. B. Yeats* (1933) pp. 239–40.

21/ 5   **inspired:** Mrs Patrick Campbell to G.B.S., 25 June 1917, *Their Correspondence* pp. 195–6.

21/36   **broken:** *CP*5 p. 184.

22/ 8   **cretins?:** G.B.S. to Mrs Patrick Campbell, 13 November 1914, *Their Correspondence* p. 169.

22/23   **footlights:** A. B. Walkley, 'The English Marivaux', *TLS* 2 October 1919. See *Shaw: The Critical Heritage* (ed. T. F. Evans 1976) p. 239.

22/29   **lunatics:** John Middleton Murry, review, *Athenaeum* 17 October 1919. See *Shaw: The Critical Heritage* pp. 244–5.

22/34   **Captain:** G.B.S. to Esmé Percy, 29 March 1920 (Fitzwilliam Museum, Cambridge).

22/last   **blunder:** Lawrence Langner, *G.B.S. and the Lunatic* (1964) p. 25.

23/11   **success:** G.B.S. to Augustin Hamon, 14 April 1921, *CL*3 pp. 715–16.

23 / 22   **end:** *Christian Science Monitor* 14 December 1920.

23 / last   **same time:** Naomi Royde-Smith, from an initialled notice, *Westminster Gazette* 19 October 1921. See *Shaw: The Critical Heritage* p. 248.

24 / 5   **years ago:** *CP5* p. 190.

24 / 9   **ever was:** See Bryan Forbes, *Ned's Girl: The Life of Edith Evans* (1977) pp. 59–60.

24 / 11   **smell:** Sydney W. Caroll, *Sunday Times* notice, 23 October 1921. See *Shaw: The Critical Heritage* p. 255.

24 / 21   **dud:** G.B.S. to James B. Fagan, 20 October 1921, *CL3* p. 738.

24 / 29   **testaments:** James Agate, *Saturday Review* 21 October 1921. See *Shaw: The Critical Heritage* pp. 252–3.

24 / 34   **entertainment:** *Sunday Express* 13 November 1921.

25 / 2   **prosperity:** G.B.S. to Martineau and Reid, n.d. [c. 22 June 1922], *CL3* p. 776.

25 / 17   **dislike it:** *CP5* pp. 194–6.

25 / Ep.   **too famous:** Blanche Patch, *Thirty Years with G.B.S.* [ghostwritten by Robert Williamson 1951] p. 61.

26 / 6   **then:** Ibid., p. 19.

26 / 11   **vacant?:** G.B.S. to Blanche Patch, 8 June 1920, *CL3* p. 677.

26 / 18   **by me:** *Thirty Years with G.B.S.* p. 22.

26 / 24   **on her:** G.B.S. to Mrs Patrick Campbell, 6 December 1921, *Their Correspondence* p. 230.

26 / 31   **developed:** *Shaw the Villager and Human Being* p. 263.

26 / 33   **Pierrot:** G.B.S. to Beatrice Webb, 6 September 1922 (LSE).

26 / 39   **from him:** *Thirty Years with G.B.S.* p. 236.

27 / 4   **I do:** Ibid.

27 / 5   **much:** Blanche Patch to G.B.S., 17 June 1920, BL Add. MS 50518 f. 203.

27 / 16   **rate:** G.B.S. to Ann M. Elder, 1 January 1914, *CL3* p. 213.

27 / 24   **thousands:** *Thirty Years with G.B.S.* pp. 199–200, 203.

27 / 32   **I had:** Ibid., p. 201.

28 / 6   **paper:** Ibid., pp. 46, 48.

28 / 13   **too much:** Ibid., p. 243.

28 / 22   **novels:** Ibid.

29 / 9   **he did:** Ibid., p. 164.

29 / 17   **time:** Ibid., p. 178.

29 / 30   **your work:** Ibid., p. 235.

30 / 3   **table also:** G.B.S. to Blanche Patch, 16 September 1925 (Texas).

30 / 7   **more rest:** G.B.S. to Blanche Patch, 9 June 1926 (Texas).

30 / 11   **without you:** G.B.S. to Blanche Patch, 1 June 1926 (Cornell).

30 / 22   **Patch:** G.B.S. to Lady Astor, 2 February 1935 (Reading).

31 / 10   **blame:** *Shaw the Villager and Human Being* p. 39.

31 / 23   **terrified:** Ibid., p. 40.

32 / Ep. 1   **as I do:** G.B.S. to Beatrice and Sidney Webb, 5 October 1916, *CL*3 p. 424.

32 / Ep. 2   **at my age:** *Back to Methuselah* (Constable 1921) p. lxxxvii.

32 / 20   **world:** 1921 *Back to Methuselah*, press release (Texas).

33 / 3   *magnum opus*: Charlotte Shaw to Apsley Cherry-Garrard, 1 September 1920 (Texas).

33 / 5   **fancy:** G.B.S. to Karel Mušek, 13 August 1920 (Princeton).

33 / 7   **produce:** Ibid.

33 / 23   **civilization:** G.B.S. to Julius Bab, 21 December 1925, *CL*3 p. 925.

33 / 34   **Poland:** Ibid.

34 / 2   **we die:** G.B.S. to William Poel, 4 June 1919 (Folger).

34 / 4   **money in it:** G.B.S. to Siegfried Trebitsch, 20 July 1919, *CL*3 p. 625.

34 / 7   **considerations:** *CP*5 p. 691.

34 / 10   **anything:** G.B.S. to Julius Bab, 21 December 1925, *CL*3 p. 925.

34 / 15   **widow:** G.B.S. to Sister Ethna, 10 October 1920, *CL*3 p. 692.

34 / 23   **civilization!:** G.B.S. to Perriton Maxwell, n.d. [c. March 1921], *CL*3 pp. 712–13.

34 / 27   **myself:** G.B.S. to West Edinburgh Labour Party, n.d. [c. 20 February 1922], *CL*3 p. 763.

34 / 33   **dreadful:** Untitled lecture, April 1887, BL Add. MS 50702 ff. 238–9. Quoted in Louis Crompton, *Shaw the Dramatist* p. 182.

35 / 2   **slaughter:** G.B.S. to Maurice Ernest, 30 June 1945, BL Add. MS 50524 ff. 320–4.

35 / 7   **job too:** G.B.S. to Oliver Lodge, 14 June 1924, *CL*3 p. 879.

35 / 10   **follies:** G.B.S. to Bertha Newcombe, 16 April 1922 (Texas).

35 / 16   **flappers:** G.B.S. to Cecil Lewis, 27 November 1928 (Texas).

35 / 20   **drink:** G.B.S. to Cecil Lewis, 18–20 November 1928 (Texas).

35 / last   **extravagant one:** G.B.S. to Norman Clark, n.d. [c. 1929]. See *Detroit News* 5 May 1929, pp. 8, 12.

36 / 8   **time:** 'A Final Statement of Faith', *Liberty* (New York) XIII, 1 August 1936, pp. 18–19.

36 / 14   **gratified:** G.B.S. to Beatrice and Sidney Webb, 5 October 1916, *CL*3 p. 424.

36 / 25   **writings:** *CP*5 p. 714.

36 / 31   **discouragement:** Ibid., p. 696.

36 / 32   **death:** Ibid., p. 337.

37 / 14   **beaten:** G.B.S. to W. J. Bassett-Lowke, 1 November 1916, *CL*3 p. 435.

37/28 **stultifying one:** G.B.S. to H. Reinheimer, 20 July 1929 (Texas).

37/last **tomorrow:** *Commonplace Book* (Berg).

38/ 2 **looking:** *CP*5 p. 269.

38/12 **Selection:** 'Mr Gilbert Cannan on Samuel Butler', *New Statesman* 8 May 1915. See *Pen Portraits and Reviews* p. 66.

38/18 **own way:** G.B.S. to Kurt Eitzen, 5 September 1919 (Texas).

38/33 **everything:** 'Darwin Denounced', *Pall Mall Gazette* 31 May 1887, p. 5.

39/ 4 **modification:** Ibid.

39/13 **to me:** 2 January 1897, *Samuel Butler's Notebooks* (ed. Geoffrey Keynes and Brian Hill 1951) pp. 45–6.

39/21 **pertinacity:** *Manchester Guardian* 4 December 1935.

39/25 **cared:** Ibid.

39/31 **Barbara:** G.B.S. to Kurt Eitzen, 5 September 1919 (Texas).

39/33 **century:** *CP*3 p. 32.

39/39 **charitably:** 'Samuel Butler: The New Life Reviewed', *Manchester Guardian* 1 November 1919. See *Pen Portraits and Reviews* p. 53.

40/ 3 **revelation:** 'Mr Gilbert Cannan on Samuel Butler', *New Statesman* 8 May 1915. See *Pen Portraits and Reviews* p. 65.

40/ 5 **as well:** G.B.S. to Festing Jones, 2 January 1923 (Chapin Library, Williams College, Williamstown, Mass.).

40/11 **the line:** *Clarion* 17 July 1914, p. 4.

40/21 **biography:** 'Samuel Butler: The New Life Reviewed', *Manchester Guardian* 1 November 1919. See *Pen Portraits and Reviews* p. 64.

40/32 **anybody:** *CP*5 pp. 298–300.

40/36 **Shavian:** *The Observer* 26 March 1950, p. 8.

40/last **chief method:** *CP*5 p. 299.

41/ 3 **unintentionally:** Ibid., p. 306.

41/15 **down:** 'Mr Gilbert Cannan on Samuel Butler', *New Statesman* 8 May 1915. See *Pen Portraits and Reviews* p. 70.

41/19 **prototype:** Ibid.

41/20 **laboratories:** *CP*5 p. 306.

41/29 **Butler:** 'A Lesson in the "Obvious"', *The Observer* 1 May 1932, *Agitations* p. 285.

41/32 **head:** Ibid., pp. 281–2.

42/ 2 **creation:** *CP*5 p. 348.

42/ 6 **work:** 'A Lesson in the "Obvious"', *The Observer* 1 May 1932, *Agitations* p. 282.

42/12 **verdict:** G.B.S. to Hesketh Pearson, 13 September 1939 (Texas).

42 / 20   **had not read**: Cover copy written by G.B.S. for 1939 Penguin
            edn of *Back to Methuselah*.

42 / 23   **Magus**: 'A Final Statement of Faith', *Liberty* (New York) XIII,
            1 August 1936, pp. 18–19.

42 / 35   **for ever**: *CP*5 p. 339.

43 / 3   **Ring**: G.B.S. to Siegfried Trebitsch, 15 September 1920, *CL*3
            p. 688 (Shaw/Trebitsch letters p. 213).

43 / 14   **writing**: Maurice Valency, *The Cart and the Trumpet: The Plays
            of George Bernard Shaw* (1973) p. 352.

43 / 15   **playwright**: Eric Bentley, *Bernard Shaw* (1967 edn) p. 104.

43 / 22   **yours**: *CP*5 p. 347.

43 / 29   **possible**: Ibid., p. 346.

44 / 3   **myself**: Ibid., p. 343.

44 / 5   **certainty**: Ibid., p. 356.

44 / 17   **immortality**: Ibid., p. 422.

44 / 21   *in her hands*: Ibid., p. 359.

44 / 33   **them**: St John Ervine, *Bernard Shaw: His Life, Work and Friends*
            (1956) p. 383.

45 / 17   **agriculture**: *CP*5 pp. 424–5.

45 / 22   **adventures!**: Ibid., p. 361.

45 / 26   **vein**: H. M. Geduld, 'Edition of Bernard Shaw's *Back to
            Methuselah*' (unpublished thesis, University of London, 1961)
            vol. II, appendix K, p. 87.

45 / 32   **drudge**: *CP*5 pp. 363–4.

45 / 36   **killing**: Ibid., p. 369.

45 / 39   **digger**: Ibid., p. 372.

46 / 2   **least**: Ibid.

46 / 19   **destroyer**: Ibid., p. 370.

46 / 31   **science**: Ibid., p. 422.

46 / 38   **future**: Ibid., p. 680.

47 / 2   **my own**: Ibid., p. 682.

47 / 8   **wedlock**: Ibid., p. 675.

47 / 11   **together**: Ibid., p. 674.

47 / 17   **despised**: Ibid., p. 676.

47 / 40   **lemons**: Ibid., p. 432.

48 / 6   **politics**: Ibid., p. 437.

48 / 14   **two men**: Ibid., p. 439.

48 / 26   **joke**: Ibid., p. 460.

48 / 30   **sure**: Ibid., p. 433.

48 / 34   **chumps**: 'A Final Statement of Faith', *Liberty* (New York) XIII,
            1 August 1936, pp. 18–19.

49 / 6   **manias**: G.B.S. to Christina Walshe [Richardson], 15
            September 1934 (Texas).

49/11   **to us:** *CP5* pp. 474, 475.
49/19   **of life:** Ibid., p. 527.
49/37   **world:** Ibid., p. 525.
50/ 4   **common one:** Ibid., p. 538.
50/12   **Mahatma:** Ibid., p. 95.
50/21   **intelligible:** Ibid., p. 624.
50/34   **chin:** Ibid., p. 497.
51/ 3   ***falls dead*:** Ibid., pp. 562–3.
51/23   **refuse:** Ibid., p. 609.
51/25   **Shavianism:** Archibald Henderson, *Bernard Shaw: Playboy and Prophet* (1932) p. 539. The sentence was written by G.B.S. himself. See p. 167 of the proofs (North Carolina).
52/ 1   **years:** *CP5* p. 574.
52/ 4   **dead:** Ibid., p. 567.
52/14   **adult:** G.B.S. to St John Ervine, 21 September 1921, *CL3* p. 732.
52/20   **necessary:** *CP5* p. 623.
52/23   **thought:** Ibid., p. 620.
52/32   **earth:** Ibid., pp. 628, 629.
53/ 4   **beyond:** Ibid., pp. 629–31.
53/ 7   **of life:** Ibid., p. 617.
53/21   **matter:** G.B.S. to H. Reinheimer, 20 July 1929 (Texas).
53/27   **mocked it:** *CP5* p. 630.
53/29   **in one:** *The Quintessence of Ibsenism* (1913 edn) p. 67. *Major Critical Essays* (Penguin edn 1986) p. 79.
53/35   **works:** G.B.S. to Karel Mušek, 26 September 1922 (Houghton).
54/ 7   **decrepit:** William Archer to G.B.S., 22 June 1921, BL Add. MS 50528 ff. 63–4.
54/16   **on earth:** Max Beerbohm to G.B.S., 27 June 1921, *Letters of Max Beerbohm 1892–1956* (ed. Rupert Hart-Davis 1988) pp. 130–1.
54/20   **position:** *The Shavian* vol. 2, no. 7, October 1963, p. 111.
54/26   **disapproval:** *Inostrannia Literatura* no. 4, 1957, pp. 27–32. See also Peter Stepanovich Balashov, *Khudozhestrennyi mir Bernarda Shou* (Moscow 1982) p. 222.
54/30   **soul of man:** Marie Stopes to L. H. S. Jermyn, 20 September 1946.
54/34   **success:** Desmond MacCarthy, *Shaw* (1951) pp. 134–9.
54/35   **discursive:** G.B.S. to William Maxwell, 21 December 1944 (Scotland).
54/37   **superstition:** *Criterion* IV, April 1926, p. 389.
54/last   ***Methuselah*:** *Cambridge Review* 6 June 1928.

55/ 4   **way:** J. C. Squire, *Observer* review 26 June 1921, *Shaw: The Critical Heritage* p. 264.

55/ 9   **done:** Ibid., p. 262.

55/34   **undertaking:** Lawrence Langner, *G.B.S. and the Lunatic* (1964) pp. 32–55.

55/38   **were run:** Walter Prichard Eaton, 'Producing *Back to Methuselah*' (Theatre Guild, New York).

56/ 9   **recognize you:** *G.B.S. and the Lunatic* p. 38.

56/30   **loss:** Ibid., p. 51.

56/33   *Methuselah*!: Ibid., pp. xi, 31.

57/ 5   **centuries:** J. C. Trewin, 'Sir Barry Jackson', *Malvern Festival Programme* (1979) p. 4.

57/13   **patron:** *Birmingham Repertory Theatre 1913–1938* (Souvenir of the 25th Anniversary) p. 6.

57/19   **companions:** J. C. Trewin, loc. cit.

57/37   **terrified!:** Gwen Ffrangçon-Davies to M. Gooden, 12 August 1923 (University of Birmingham Library).

58/ 2   **evils:** G.B.S. to Edith Evans, 17 September 1923, *CL*3 p. 848.

58/21   **fashionable:** G.B.S. to Bache Matthews, 25 June 1923, *CL*3 pp. 840–1.

58/26   **life:** *CP*5 p. 704.

58/29   **mistake:** James Agate, *Sunday Times* review 24 February 1924, *Shaw: The Critical Heritage* p. 272.

58/30   **stage:** 19 February 1924, *Arnold Bennett: The Journals* (ed. Frank Swinnerton, Penguin reprint 1984) p. 474.

58/37   **thoughts most:** Desmond MacCarthy, *Shaw* p. 137.

59/ 2   **living:** Ibid., p. 142.

59/Ep.   **nations:** G.B.S. to Jerome N. Frank, 13 April 1918 (University of Chicago Library).

59/10   **Kilteragh guests:** Horace Plunkett to Charlotte Shaw, 14 March 1928 (Plunkett).

59/12   **situation:** Plunkett to G.B.S., 17 April 1918 (Plunkett).

59/15   **provoked:** Ibid.

59/16   **of Ireland!:** Ibid.

59/23   **to Ireland:** Plunkett to Charlotte Shaw, 28 September 1917 (Plunkett).

59/30   **Politics:** 'The Dominion League', *Irish Statesman* 30 August 1919. See Bernard Shaw, *The Matter with Ireland* (ed. with an introduction by Dan H. Laurence and David H. Greene 1962) p. 189.

59/last   **English-speaking world:** 'Why Devolution Will Not Do', *Irish Statesman* 25 October 1919, *The Matter with Ireland* p. 201.

60/ 4   **country:** Ibid., p. 195.

60/14   **policeman:** 'Wanted: A Strong Government', *Irish Statesman*
11 October 1919, and 'Socialism and Ireland' (Fabian
lecture, 28 November 1919). See *The Matter with Ireland*
pp. 191, 226.

60/24   **self-government:** See *The Matter with Ireland* p. 226.

60/30   **duly sown:** 'The Reign of Terror', *Irish Statesman* 3 January
1920. See *The Matter with Ireland* p. 233.

61/ 3   **beat him:** 'The Irish Crisis', *New York American* 25 December
1921. See *The Matter with Ireland* p. 253.

61/11   **world:** Ibid., pp. 254, 250.

61/19   **stand:** 'The Eve of Civil War', *The Irish Times* 21 August 1922,
The Matter with Ireland p. 257.

61/23   **for him:** G.B.S. to R. D. Blumenfeld, 24 August 1921 (Texas).

61/28   **hatred:** 'The Reign of Terror', *The Matter with Ireland* p. 235.

61/31   **their cause:** 'Socialism and Ireland', *The Matter with Ireland*
p. 216.

61/32   **matters:** 'How Ireland Impressed Mr Chesterton', *Irish
Statesman* 22 November 1919, *The Matter with Ireland*,
p. 209.

62/12   **reflexes:** 'On Throwing Out Dirty Water', *Irish Statesman* 15
September 1923, *The Matter with Ireland* pp. 267–8.

62/17   **ending:** 'The Irish Crisis', *The Matter with Ireland* p. 250.

63/ 2   **lived:** G.B.S. to Johanna Collins, 24 August 1922, *CL*3 p. 783
(*The Matter with Ireland* p. 258).

63/ 8   **to die:** G.B.S. to Beatrice Webb, 6 September 1922 (LSE).

63/29   **luxury:** 'Safe Holidays in Ireland', *The Times* 31 July 1923, *The
Matter with Ireland* pp. 265–6.

64/ 8   **harmless:** 'The Eve of Civil War', *The Matter with Ireland*
p. 257.

64/Ep.   **it is:** *CP*5 p. 796.

64/13   **Europe:** G.B.S. to Henry Newbolt, 25 July 1920, *CL*3 p. 685.

64/18   **it can:** G.B.S. to the Director of the German Society for
Education in State Citizenship, 9 July 1920, *CL*3 p. 680.

64/26   **civilization:** G.B.S. to Carl Otto, 4 October 1919 (Cornell).

64/30   **for you:** G.B.S. to Siegfried Trebitsch, 20 July 1919, *CL*3
pp. 624–5 (Shaw/Trebitsch letters p. 203).

64/last **countries:** G.B.S. to Trebitsch, 24 December 1918,
Shaw/Trebitsch letters p. 201.

65/ 3   **dawn:** G.B.S. to Trebitsch, 20 July 1919, *CL*3 p. 624
(Shaw/Trebitsch letters p. 202).

65/13   **leave-taking:** Siegfried Trebitsch, *Chronicle of a Life* (1953)
p. 257.

65/20   **more:** G.B.S. to Trebitsch, 4 August 1919, Shaw/Trebitsch
letters p. 204.

65/22   **his jaws:** Ibid.

65/28   **faded away:** *Chronicle of a Life* pp. 272–3.

65/29   **of yours:** G.B.S. to Trebitsch, 19 August 1913, Shaw/Trebitsch letters p. 166.

65/39   **the author:** *Chronicle of a Life* p. 263.

66/ 5   **dictionary:** G.B.S. to Trebitsch, 26 May 1920, Shaw/Trebitsch letters p. 212.

66/ 7   **instinct:** G.B.S. to Trebitsch, 15 September 1920, *CL*3 p. 688 (Shaw/Trebitsch letters p. 212).

66/14   **Gitta:** *CP*5 p. 721.

66/19   **furious:** G.B.S. to Trebitsch, 15 September 1920, *CL*3 p. 688 (Shaw/Trebitsch letters p. 213).

66/27   **Harrow:** G.B.S. to Trebitsch, 28 September 1920, *CL*3 pp. 690–1 (Shaw/Trebitsch letters p. 217).

66/36   **your own:** Ibid.

67/ 1   **sequel:** G.B.S. to Trebitsch, 15 September 1920, *CL*3 p. 688 (Shaw/Trebitsch letters p. 213).

67/ 9   **person:** *CP*5 p. 798.

67/14   **naturally:** Ibid., p. 797.

67/25   **comedy!:** *Shaw: An Exhibit* (Texas 1977) item 638.

67/33   **news:** G.B.S. to Trebitsch, 28 August 1921, *CL*3 p. 730 (Shaw/Trebitsch letters p. 224).

68/ 3   **continuation:** G.B.S. to Trebitsch, 2 October 1921, Shaw/Trebitsch letters p. 225.

68/15   **agree?:** *Chronicle of a Life* p. 264.

68/18   **spoil it:** G.B.S. to Trebitsch, 15 May 1922, Shaw/Trebitsch letters p. 232.

68/25   **best:** G.B.S. to Trebitsch, 17 June 1922, Shaw/Trebitsch letters p. 233.

68/28   **genious:** *Shaw: An Exhibit*, item 638.

68/36   **season:** Lawrence Langner, *G.B.S. and the Lunatic* p. 95.

68/38   **comedy:** Ibid., p. 96.

69/ 3   **Theatre:** G.B.S. to Trebitsch, 9 December 1924, Shaw/Trebitsch letters p. 251.

69/ 9   **too well:** G.B.S. to Trebitsch, 16 April 1925, Shaw/Trebitsch letters p. 255.

69/13   **mine:** G.B.S. to Trebitsch, 13 March 1925, Shaw/Trebitsch letters p. 253.

69/15   **most men:** *Daily Telegraph* 1 May 1930.

69/19   **entertainment:** *Nation & Athenaeum* 10 May 1930.

69/23   **wrote:** *Letters of Arnold Bennett*, vol. IV: *Family Letters* (ed. James Hepburn 1986) p. 463.

69/33   **acting:** 31 January 1925, *Arnold Bennett: The Journals* p. 58.

70/ 2   **we need:** G.B.S. to Trebitsch, 17 October 1927,
         Shaw/Trebitsch letters p. 283.

70/ 3   **horribly:** G.B.S. to Trebitsch, 18 June 1926, Shaw/Trebitsch
         letters p. 271.

70/ 6   **Residenztheater:** Trebitsch, *Chronicle of a Life* p. 264.

70/ 7   **'kyboshed':** G.B.S. to J. E. Vedrenne, 18 March 1923 (Texas).

70/ 8   **play:** G.B.S. to Trebitsch, 16 April 1925, Shaw/Trebitsch
         letters p. 255.

70/14   **Joan of Arc?:** G.B.S. to Trebitsch, n.d. [May 1923],
         Shaw/Trebitsch letters p. 242.

70/15   **over here:** G.B.S. to Trebitsch, 2–4 October 1921,
         Shaw/Trebitsch letters p. 228.

70/20   **receive her:** *Chronicle of a Life* p. 264.

70/27   **Joan:** G.B.S. to Trebitsch, 23 September 1923,
         Shaw/Trebitsch letters p. 243.

70/30   **for you:** *Chronicle of a Life* opposite p. 201.

71/ 3   **goodwill:** Ibid., pp. 264–9.

71/ 6   **example:** G.B.S. to Trebitsch, 3 July 1924, Shaw/Trebitsch
         letters p. 248.

71/last   **new play:** G.B.S. to Trebitsch, 23 September 1923,
         Shaw/Trebitsch letters p. 243.

CHAPTER II

72/Ep.1   **us!:** *CP*6 p. 90.

72/Ep.2   **dance:** T. E. Lawrence to Charlotte Shaw, 16 March 1924,
         The Letters of T. E. Lawrence (selected and ed. Malcolm Brown
         1988) p. 259.

72/13   **flapdoodle:** Archibald Henderson, *Table-Talk of G.B.S.:
         Conversations on Things in General between George Bernard Shaw
         and his Biographer* (1925) pp. 44–5.

72/14   **stale:** 'Art Corner', *Our Corner* July 1885, *SM* 1 p. 288.

72/last   **impossible:** Preface to *Ellen Terry and Bernard Shaw: A
         Correspondence* (ed. Christopher St John 1931) p. xxiii.

73/ 5   **day:** *CP*6 p. 40.

73/ 7   **women:** G.B.S. to John Middleton Murry, 1 May 1924, *CL*3
         p. 876.

73/13   **Victorian:** *CP*6 pp. 42–3.

73/14   **sick:** *Comoedia* (Paris) 16 March 1924. Original in Boston
         Public Library. Reprinted in *'Saint Joan': Fifty Years After* (ed.
         Stanley Weintraub 1973) pp. 15–22.

73/17   **insanity:** *CP*2 p. 302.

73 / 19   **sanity:** *CP*3 p. 473.

73 / 23   **your heart:** G.B.S. to Harley Granville Barker, 24 May 1907, *CL*2 p. 690 (Shaw/Barker letters p. 84).

73 / 26   **spirit:** 'La Princesse Lointaine', *Saturday Review* 22 June 1895, *OTN*1 p. 155.

73 / 28   **him!:** G.B.S. to Eleanor Robson, 24 December 1905, *CL*2, p. 587.

73 / 32   **Joan of Arc:** 'Joy Riding at the Front', I: 'Bombardment', *Daily Chronicle* 5 March 1917, *What I Really Wrote about the War* (1930) p. 247.

74 / 2   **leader:** *CP*6 pp. 21–2 and Walter Tittle, 'Mr Bernard Shaw Talks about St Joan', *Outlook* 25 June 1924, pp. 311–13. Reprinted in *'Saint Joan': Fifty Years After* pp. 8–14.

74 / 6   **fighting chin:** *CP*6 p. 85.

74 / 19   **Joan...:** G.B.S. to Mrs Patrick Campbell, 8 September 1913, *CL*3 pp. 201–2 (*Their Correspondence* pp. 146–7).

74 / 21   **epilogue:** Stanley Weintraub, *The Unexpected Shaw* (1982) p. 86.

74 / 23   **the play:** G.B.S. to Dr Arthur Bárdos, n.d., BL Add. MS 50521 f. 121.

74 / 25   **the play:** See *CL*3 p. 201.

74 / 29   **soldier:** G.B.S. to Thea Holme, 2 February 1939, *CL*4 p. 526.

75 / 2   **of principle:** 'Peace Conference Hints', *What I Really Wrote about the War* p. 315.

75 / 18   **masterpiece:** 'Siegfried as Protestant', *The Perfect Wagnerite*. See *Major Critical Essays* (ed. Michael Holroyd, Penguin edn 1986) pp. 241–3.

75 / 24   **calling:** *CP*6 p. 210.

75 / 27   **Inquisition:** Ibid., pp. 228–9.

75 / last   **civilizations:** Ibid., p. 210.

76 / 6   **imagination?:** Ibid., p. 202.

76 / 8   **among you:** Ibid., p. 184.

76 / 16   **madman:** G.B.S. to Siegfried Trebitsch, 7 June 1925, Shaw/Trebitsch letters p. 257.

76 / 20   **my own?:** *CP*6 p. 175.

76 / 27   **miracle:** Ibid., p. 90.

76 / 33   **Court:** Ibid., p. 105.

77 / 1   **I hope not:** Ibid., p. 103.

77 / 3   **shoulder:** Ibid., p. 116.

77 / 15   **play?:** *The Letters of Sean O'Casey: 1910–41* (ed. David Krause 1975) vol. 1, p. 137 n. 3.

77 / 18   **epoch:** *CP*6 p. 107.

77 / 23   **away:** Ibid., p. 95.

77/33 **genius:** Ibid., p. 24.

77/36 **reasons after:** Ibid., p. 143.

78/ 2 **set down:** 'On the Principles that Govern the Dramatist', letter to *The New York Times* 2 June 1912. See *Shaw on Theatre* (ed. E. J. West 1958) p. 116.

78/ 7 **mine:** Corrected proofs of Henderson's *Playboy and Prophet* p. 168 (North Carolina); cf Archibald Henderson, *Bernard Shaw: Playboy and Prophet* (1932) p. 543.

78/15 **Heaven:** Brian Tyson, *The Story of Shaw's 'Saint Joan'* (1982) p. 22.

78/25 **dresser:** Marina Warner, 'Posthumous honours', *The Times Literary Supplement* 2 March 1984, p. 221.

78/31 **oddities:** Desmond MacCarthy, *Shaw* (1951) p. 163.

79/ 2 **moment:** Sybil Thorndike to G.B.S., 1945, BL Add. MS 50531 f. 57.

79/ 7 **housekeeping:** Sheridan Morley, *Sybil Thorndike: A Life in the Theatre* (1977) p. 33.

79/16 **my Joan:** Ibid., p. 68.

79/22 **railway:** 'The Ten Birthplaces of Saint Joan', *Irish Independent* 13 November 1943.

79/28 **Methuselah!:** G.B.S. to Molly Tompkins, 27 August 1923, *To a Young Actress: The Letters of Bernard Shaw to Molly Tompkins* (ed. Peter Tompkins 1960) p. 49.

79/35 **Binyon's:** *Sybil Thorndike: A Life in the Theatre* p. 73.

80/ 2 ***Saint Joan:*** Hesketh Pearson, *Bernard Shaw* (1975 edn) p. 396.

80/10 **people:** *The Story of Shaw's 'Saint Joan'* pp. 3–4.

80/13 **quickly:** Lawrence Langner, *G.B.S. and the Lunatic* (1964) p. 57.

80/31 **with it:** *The Story of Shaw's 'Saint Joan'* p. 5.

80/last **equipped:** G.B.S. to the Rev. Joseph Leonard, 11 December 1922, *CL*3 pp. 795–6.

81/11 **later on:** *CP*6 p. 186.

81/21 **heretic:** G.B.S. to Mr Keble, 28 September 1923, *CL*3 p. 849.

81/30 **queer fish:** *The Story of Shaw's 'Saint Joan'* p. 4.

81/35 **today:** *CP*6 p. 46.

82/ 5 **finished:** G.B.S. to John Middleton Murry, 1 May 1924, *CL*3 p. 875.

82/10 **one third:** Proofs of *Playboy and Prophet* (North Carolina); cf *Playboy and Prophet* p. 543.

82/20 **marvellous play:** John Casson, *Lewis & Sybil: A Memoir* (1972) p. 113.

82/22 **in tears:** Sheridan Morley, *Sybil Thorndike: A Life in the Theatre* p. 74.

83/12   **composed:** St John Ervine, *Bernard Shaw: His Life, Work and Friends* (1956) pp. 496–7.

83/16   **smash:** Brian Tyson, *The Story of Shaw's 'Saint Joan'* p. 8.

83/19   **was:** Mary Hankinson to Mrs Brett Young, 22 January 1951 (University of Birmingham Library).

83/24   **handed:** *The Story of Shaw's 'Saint Joan'* p. 18.

83/34   **whistle:** Matthew Barry Sullivan to Michael Holroyd (20 January 1980).

83/37   **parties:** *The Story of Shaw's 'Saint Joan'* p. 18.

83/38   **George Fox:** G.B.S. to J. E. Whiting, 18 May 1927, *CL*4 p. 53.

83/40   **Saint Joan:** Maurice Valency, *The Cart and the Trumpet: The Plays of George Bernard Shaw* (1973) p. 370.

84/2   **garden city:** Desmond MacCarthy, *Shaw* p. 173.

84/8   **Mrs Pankhurst's:** T. S. Eliot, unsigned article from *Criterion* October 1924; *Shaw: The Critical Heritage* (ed. T. F. Evans 1976) p. 294.

84/15   **Joan:** *CP*6 p. 228.

85/6   **burn it:** T. E. Lawrence to G.B.S., 17 August 1922, *Selected Letters of T. E. Lawrence* (ed. David Garnett 1941) pp. 144–5.

85/8   **old friends:** G.B.S. to T. E. Lawrence, 25 August 1922, *CL*3 p. 784.

85/15   **with it:** T. E. Lawrence to G.B.S., 27 August 1922, *Selected Letters of T. E. Lawrence* p. 151.

85/17   **the Bible:** G.B.S. to Sydney Cockerell, 13 April 1923, *The Best of Friends: Further Letters to Sydney Carlyle Cockerell* (ed. Viola Meynell 1956) p. 29.

85/23   **read it:** T. E. Lawrence to G.B.S., 30 September 1922, BL Add. MS 50540 f. 4.

85/29   **with you:** G.B.S. to T. E. Lawrence, 1 December 1922, *CL*3 pp. 787–9.

85/34   **improvement:** T. E. Lawrence to Sydney Cockerell, 15 October 1924. See Dan H. Laurence, *Bernard Shaw: A Bibliography* vol. 1 (1983), BB30, p. 504.

85/38   **world:** *Lady Gregory's Journals*, vol. 1: Books One to Twenty-Nine, 10 October 1916–24 February 1925 (ed. Daniel Murphy 1978) p. 454.

86/8   **circumstances:** G.B.S. to Stanley Baldwin, 31 May 1923, *CL*3 pp. 829–31.

86/9   **help:** T. E. Lawrence to G.B.S., 2 January 1923, *The Letters of T. E. Lawrence* (ed. Malcolm Brown 1988) p. 217.

86/23   **thoughts:** *Selected Letters of T. E. Lawrence* pp. 80–1.

86/29   **nation-state:** Stanley Weintraub, *Private Shaw and Public Shaw* (1963) p. 48.

86 / 37   **Domremy:** *CP*6 p. 66.

86 / 38   **monastery:** *T. E. Lawrence by his Friends* (ed. A. W. Lawrence 1937) p. 244.

86 / last **present day:** *CP*6 p. 226.

87 / 5   **maturity:** *T. E. Lawrence by his Friends* pp. 246–7.

87 / 25   **really?:** G.B.S. to T. E. Lawrence, 23 June 1928 (Texas).

87 / 29   **opportunity:** G.B.S. to T. E. Lawrence, 4 January 1923, *CL*3 pp. 804–5.

87 / 35   **her own:** 'Vision of Everest', *The Times* 17 February 1984.

87 / 38   **the Maid:** *New York Times* 1 January 1928.

88 / 3   **put them down:** Lawrence Langner, *G.B.S. and the Lunatic* p. 60.

88 / 10   **eyes:** Beatrice Webb diary, entry 21 May 1936 (LSE).

88 / 18   **tricks:** *T. E. Lawrence by his Friends* p. 247.

88 / 20   **understand:** G.B.S. to Charles Sarolea, 2 January 1925, *New York Times* 19 September 1926. See also Weintraub, *'Saint Joan': Fifty Years After* p. 100.

88 / 33   **scoundrel:** Archibald Henderson, *George Bernard Shaw: Man of the Century* (1956) p. 741.

89 / 1   **1920:** *CP*6 p. 203.

89 / 14   **audience:** Louis L. Martz, 'The Saint as Tragic Hero', *G. B. Shaw: A Collection of Critical Essays* (ed. Ralph J. Kaufmann 1965) p. 160.

89 / 17   **illusion:** *George Bernard Shaw: Man of the Century* p. 600.

89 / 35   **TO THEM:** *G.B.S. and the Lunatic* p. 68.

90 / 9   **in Shaw:** Luigi Pirandello, notice, *New York Times* 13 January 1924, *Shaw: The Critical Heritage* pp. 279–84.

90 / 11   **Six Characters:** *The Shavian* vol. 2, no. 8, February 1964, p. 7.

90 / 15   **success:** *G.B.S. and the Lunatic* p. 72.

90 / 24   **injustice:** A. B. Walkley, unsigned notice, *The Times* 27 March 1924, *Shaw: The Critical Heritage* p. 285.

90 / 37   **the thing:** J. G. Paul Delaney, 'Charles Ricketts and his Unlikely Friendship with George Bernard Shaw', *The Pen* no. 15, Autumn 1983, pp. 3–5.

91 / 11   **the second:** Ibid.

91 / 35   **ever known:** Siegfried Trebitsch, *Chronicle of a Life* (1953) p. 271.

92 / 1   **materialism:** See Introduction to *Shaw: The Critical Heritage* p. 22.

92 / 12   **author:** Lawrence Langner, *G.B.S. and the Lunatic* p. 79.

92 / 25   **typical of Shaw:** Daniel C. Gerould, *'Saint Joan* in Paris', *Shaw Review* VII, January 1964, pp. 11–23. Reprinted in *'Saint Joan': Fifty Years After* pp. 213–14.

92/26   **enemy:** *Revue hebdomadaire* 13 June 1925, p. 226.

92/35   **of the play:** Daniel C. Gerould, '*Saint Joan* in Paris', '*Saint Joan': Fifty Years After* p. 211.

92/36   **praise me!:** *CP6* p. 206.

93/3   **great one:** See Stanley Weintraub, *The Unexpected Shaw* (1982) p. 191.

93/5   **70th birthday:** G.B.S. to Hamon, n.d. (copy, Cornell).

93/8   **works of art:** G.B.S. to A. Eaglefield Hall, 29 September 1918 (Hofstra).

93/16   **the better:** G.B.S. to Ebba Low, 14 November 1926, *CL4* p. 33.

93/18   **emphatically:** G.B.S. to H. G. Wells, 12 November 1926 (Illinois).

93/29   *hors concours*: G.B.S. to the Permanent Secretary of the Royal Swedish Academy, 18 November 1926, *CL4* p. 34.

94/3   **mistresses:** G.B.S. to Hamon, n.d. (copy, Hofstra).

94/11   **Mephistophelean:** *Evening Standard* 12 November 1926.

94/17   **after St Joan:** G.B.S. to Edith Evans, n.d. [assigned to 29 August 1924], *CL3* p. 883.

94/Ep.   **really G.B.S.:** G.B.S. to Beatrice Mansfield, 3 August 1927 (Philadelphia).

94/23   **come back:** G.B.S. to Otto Kyllmann, 16 December 1924 (North Carolina).

94/28   **at all:** Ibid.

94/29   **theatres:** G.B.S. to Lawrence Langner, n.d. [c. January 1925] (Yale).

94/33   **you are:** G.B.S. to William Archer, 14 December 1924, *CL3* p. 895.

95/2   **Decay:** G.B.S. to George Sampson, 2 February 1924, *CL3* p. 864.

95/6   **anxiety:** Max Beerbohm, *More Theatres* (1969) p. 27.

95/13   **knowledge box:** G.B.S. to William Archer, 19 June 1923, *CL3* p. 832.

95/27   **jelly-fish:** William Archer to G.B.S., 20 June 1923, *CL3* p. 836.

95/31   **got it yet:** G.B.S. to William Archer, 22 June 1923, *CL3* pp. 836–7.

96/14   **intimacy:** 'The Psychology of G.B.S.', *Bookman* LXVIII, December 1924, pp. 399, 139. Reprinted in *Shaw: The Critical Heritage* pp. 300–4.

96/16   **about me:** 'How William Archer Impressed Bernard Shaw', *Three Plays* by William Archer (1927). See *Pen Portraits and Reviews* (1931) p. 11.

96/23 **talk to:** Ibid., p. 29.

96/25 **business:** William Archer to Granville Barker, 17 December 1924, *CL3* p. 895.

96/36 **comradeship:** C. Archer, *William Archer: Life, Work and Friendship* (1931) pp. 402–3.

96/39 **Madeira:** 'How William Archer Impressed Bernard Shaw', *Pen Portraits and Reviews* p. 30.

97/10 **midwinter:** G.B.S. to William Rothenstein, n.d. (Houghton).

97/15 **bereavement:** 'How William Archer Impressed Bernard Shaw', *Pen Portraits and Reviews* p. 30.

97/24 **reasoning:** G.B.S. to Molly Tompkins, 24 February 1925, *CL3* p. 905 (*To A Young Actress* p. 83).

97/30 **superfluous:** 'How William Archer Impressed Bernard Shaw', *Pen Portraits and Reviews* p. 30.

98/ 8 **be off:** Alistair Cooke to Michael Holroyd, 18 May 1976.

98/23 **forty:** G.B.S. to Noël Coward, 27 June 1921 (Texas).

98/35 **hump:** Forster to G. H. Ludolf, 11 July 1926. Quoted in P. N. Furbank, *E. M. Forster: A Life* (1978) vol. 2, p. 331.

99/ 4 **there!:** G.B.S. to Floryan Sobieniowski, 29 February 1924 (Berg) and 26 September 1926 (*CL3* p. 884).

99/10 **with him:** 'How William Archer Impressed Bernard Shaw', *Pen Portraits and Reviews* p. 30.

99/21 **something else:** Charlotte Shaw to T. E. Lawrence, BL Add. MS 45922 ff. 60–1. See Philip Knightley and Colin Simpson, *The Secret Lives of Lawrence of Arabia* (1969) p. 249.

99/23 **understanding:** Janet Dunbar, *Mrs G.B.S.: A Biographical Portrait of Charlotte Shaw* (1963) p. 265.

99/29 **of my life:** Charlotte Shaw to Dorothy Walker, 6 March 1939. See *Mrs G.B.S.* p. 265.

100/ 7 **intoxicate me:** T. E. Lawrence to Charlotte Shaw, 17 June 1926, *The Letters of T. E. Lawrence* (ed. Malcolm Brown 1988) p. 302.

100/ 8 **its head:** Dunbar, *Mrs G.B.S.* p. 277.

100/11 **about myself:** Knightley and Simpson, *The Secret Lives of Lawrence of Arabia* p. 256.

100/15 **such a help:** Charlotte Shaw to T. E. Lawrence, 31 May 1927, BL Add. MS 45922 ff. 74–9.

100/22 **of my being:** Charlotte Shaw to T. E. Lawrence, 9 April 1928, BL Add. MS 45922 ff. 104–7.

100/26 **heap on me:** *The Secret Lives of Lawrence of Arabia* p. 254.

100/32 **a soul:** Ibid., p. 258.

100/34 **your mother:** Ibid., p. 249.

100/36 **at all:** Ibid., p. 254.

100/38   **brains out:** T. E. Lawrence to Charlotte Shaw, 21 April 1927, BL Add. MS 45903 f. 135v.

100/last   **somehow:** *The Secret Lives of Lawrence of Arabia* p. 254.

101/ 2   **difficult:** T. E. Lawrence to Charlotte Shaw, 15 April 1932, BL Add. MS 45904 f. 168.

101/ 3   **best:** T. E. Lawrence to Charlotte Shaw, 29 March 1927, *The Letters of T. E. Lawrence* (ed. Malcolm Brown) p. 322.

101/ 5   **not G.B.S.:** T. E. Lawrence to Charlotte Shaw, 8 December 1927, BL Add. MS 45903 f. 188.

101/11   **grudge:** T. E. Lawrence to Charlotte Shaw, 27 November 1928, BL Add. MS 45904 f. 50.

101/16   **both ways:** T. E. Lawrence to Charlotte Shaw, 17 May 1928, 25 December 1928, 2 February 1934, BL Add. MS 45904 ff. 4, 56, 208.

101/19   **over one:** T. E. Lawrence to Charlotte Shaw, 26 March and 31 August 1924, *The Letters of T. E. Lawrence* (ed. Malcolm Brown) pp. 262, 272.

101/20   **circumstances:** T. E. Lawrence to Charlotte Shaw, 6 October 1928, BL Add. MS 45904 f. 45.

101/23   **with it:** T. E. Lawrence to his mother, 10 July 1928, *The Letters of T. E. Lawrence* (ed. Malcolm Brown) p. 379.

101/25   **will pass:** T. E. Lawrence to Charlotte Shaw, 24 April 1933, BL Add. MS 45904 f. 188.

101/30   **pores:** *The Letters of T. E. Lawrence* (ed. David Garnett 1938), letter 240, p. 452.

101/32   **work:** Charlotte Shaw to Nancy Astor, 2 January 1931 (Reading).

102/ 1   **degree:** Charlotte Shaw to T. E. Lawrence, 17 May 1927, BL Add. MS 45922 ff. 5–12.

102/ 7   **Lawrence:** Hesketh Pearson, *Bernard Shaw* (1975 edn) p. 456.

102/12   **earth:** Ibid., p. 415 n. 1.

102/15   **enchanting:** Osbert Sitwell, *Laughter in the Next Room* (1975) p. 187.

102/22   **character-actors:** G.B.S. to T. E. Lawrence, 7 March 1927.

102/23   **sink my ship:** *The Letters of T. E. Lawrence* (ed. David Garnett), letters 363 and 357.

102/29   **atom:** T. E. Lawrence to Charlotte Shaw, 10 July 1929, *The Letters of T. E. Lawrence* (ed. Malcolm Brown) p. 424.

102/35   **limelight:** *Mrs G.B.S.* p. 300.

102/last   **dead:** T. E. Lawrence to Charlotte Shaw, 3 August 1927, BL Add. MS 45903 f. 165.

103/ 8   **genetic theory:** G.B.S. to *The Freethinker*, 30 June 1945. See *Bernard Shaw: Agitations: Letters to the Press 1875–1950* (ed. Dan H. Laurence and James Rambeau 1985) p. 338.

103/20   **experience:** *T. E. Lawrence By His Friends* (ed. A. W. Lawrence 1937) p. 192.

103/21   **Cherry-Garrard:** T. E. Lawrence to Charlotte Shaw, 17 June 1926, *The Letters of T. E. Lawrence* (ed. Malcolm Brown) p. 303.

103/28   **we are away:** G.B.S. to Lillah McCarthy, 2 September 1917, *CL*3 p. 504.

104/ 2   **heroic Scott:** G.B.S. to Lord Kennet (Hilton Young), 21 February 1948 (Cambridge).

104/ 6   **his bolt:** *T. E. Lawrence By His Friends* p. 191.

104/14   **persons:** G.B.S. to Lord Kennet, 2 March 1948 (Cambridge).

104/30   **world:** 'The Latest from Colonel Lawrence', *The Spectator* 12 March 1927. See *Bernard Shaw's Nondramatic Literary Criticism* (ed. Stanley Weintraub 1972) p. 164.

104/33   **himself:** G.B.S.'s jacket blurb to the 1929 Chatto & Windus edn of Apsley Cherry-Garrard's *The Worst Journey in the World*.

104/38   **moment:** 'The Latest from Colonel Lawrence', *Bernard Shaw's Nondramatic Literary Criticism* pp. 164–5.

105/ 6   **ridiculous:** G.B.S. to Apsley Cherry-Garrard, 26 April 1922, *CL*3 p. 768.

105/12   **exploration:** G.B.S. to Lord Kennet, 21 February 1948 (Cambridge).

105/17   **more or less:** Lord Kennet to Peter Scott, Whitmonday 1957 (Cambridge). See Editor's Note, *CL*3 p. 818.

105/32   **you:** *T. E. Lawrence By His Friends* p. 191.

106/ 4   **problem:** Beatrice Webb diaries, entry 4 May 1932 (LSE).

106/ 9   **me:** G.B.S. to Kathleen Hilton Young [formerly Scott, also Kennet], 20 May 1926, *CL*4 p. 22.

106/11   **me behind:** Ibid.

106/15   **a poet:** See 'Morality: A Document', *New Statesman and Nation* 1 August 1936, *Bernard Shaw's Nondramatic Literary Criticism* p. 170.

106/17   **of my life:** Cecil Lewis, *Never Look Back* (1974) p. 87.

106/last   **hundreds:** 'The Telltale Microphone', *Political Quarterly* VI, October 1935, pp. 463–7.

107/ 8   **Democracy:** *CP*6 p. 256.

107/21   **among us:** *Never Look Back* pp. 82–7.

107/32   **occasion:** G.B.S. to Friedrich Sthamer, 28 July 1926, *CL*4 pp. 25–6.

108/ 4   **event:** G.B.S. to William Maxwell, 15 August 1926 (Scotland).

108/34   **Party:** G.B.S. to Ramsay MacDonald, 16 July 1929 (privately owned).

108/38   **England:** 'MacDonald Ablest Leader in England, Says Bernard Shaw', *New York American* 13 January 1924, pp. 4–5.

109/ 8   **to me:** G.B.S. to Stanley Baldwin, 28 April 1925, *CL*3 p: 910.

109/13   **his age:** G.B.S. to Fenner Brockway, 13 September 1933 (copy, Society of Authors).

110/18   **political world:** *The Diary of Beatrice Webb* vol. 4 (ed. Norman and Jeanne MacKenzie 1985) entry 25 February 1931, p. 239.

110/25   **suicide!:** Robert Skidelsky, *Oswald Mosley* (1975) p. 278.

110/38   **strength:** G.B.S. to St John Ervine, 28 January 1932 (Texas).

111/ 5   **settled:** G.B.S. to Nancy Astor, 10 October 1931 (Reading).

111/14   **for ever:** G.B.S. to St John Ervine, 28 January 1932 (Texas).

111/17   **party system:** 'Mr Shaw on the Election Landslide', *Manchester Guardian* 29 October 1931, p. 4.

111/25   **different ways:** G.B.S. to Emery Walker, 25 January 1932, *CL*4 p. 274.

111/29   **Ramsay:** Charlotte Shaw to Nancy Astor, 26 October 1931 (Reading).

111/36   **sincerely:** 'Mr Shaw on the Election Landslide', *Manchester Guardian* 29 October 1931, p. 4.

112/12   **tirade:** *The Diary of Beatrice Webb* vol. 4, entry 28 November 1932, p. 292.

112/19   **offence:** 'In Praise of Guy Fawkes', *The New Clarion* 3 and 10 December 1932. See *Platform and Pulpit* (ed. with an introduction by Dan H. Laurence and Rupert Hart-Davis 1962) p. 235.

112/34   **with him:** Ibid., pp. 241–3.

113/ 8   **for words:** 'Mosley, by Shaw', *Daily Express* 26 November 1943, p. 2.

113/13   **business:** 'George Bernard Shaw ... Answers Eight Questions on the Future', *Sunday Express* 25 July 1943, p. 2.

113/16   **in Italy:** G.B.S. to Public Affairs News Service, 5 August 1933 (Cornell).

113/17   **enterprise:** G.B.S. to Lady Rhondda, 1 January 1945, *CL*4 p. 734.

113/18   **exploiters:** G.B.S. to Rutland Boughton, 16 October 1944, BL Add. MS 52365 f. 71.

113/21   **industrialists:** 'Mosley, by Shaw', *Daily Express* 26 November 1943, p. 2.

113/35   **it all?:** *The Diary of Beatrice Webb* vol. 4, entry 2 July 1934, p. 334.

113/37   **politics:** Ibid., p. 335.

114/11   **happiness:** *The Diary of Beatrice Webb* vol. 4, entry 1 July 1935, p. 354.

114/Ep. **woman:** G.B.S. to Mary Hamilton, 23 November 1918, *Carnegie Magazine* July/August 1988, p. 29.

114/15 **see you:** *Shaw and Molly Tompkins* (ed. Peter Tompkins 1962) p. 13.

114/18 **shape:** G.B.S. to Molly Tompkins, 27 December 1921, *CL*3 pp. 753–5, *To a Young Actress: The Letters of Bernard Shaw to Molly Tompkins* (ed. Peter Tompkins 1960) p. 12.

114/30 **idea!:** *Shaw and Molly Tompkins* pp. 13–14.

115/ 1 **occasionally:** G.B.S. to Forbes-Robertson, 1 October 1923; G.B.S. to Molly Tompkins, 27 December 1921, *CL*3 p. 753. See *To a Young Actress* pp. 55, 11, 12.

115/ 5 **skate:** G.B.S. to Molly Tompkins, 20 April 1922, *To a Young Actress* p. 21.

115/16 **instant dislike:** *Shaw and Molly Tompkins* pp. 16, 22.

115/22 **properly:** G.B.S. to Molly Tompkins, 16 July 1922, *To a Young Actress* p. 23.

115/28 **as yet:** G.B.S. to Molly Tompkins, 27 January, 16 July, 12 September, 27 September 1922, *To a Young Actress* pp. 16, 24, 25.

115/33 **ago:** G.B.S. to Molly Tompkins, 16 July 1922, *To a Young Actress* p. 23.

116/ 1 **or both?:** G.B.S. to Mrs Patrick Campbell, 20 January 1921, *CL*3 p. 708. See *Bernard Shaw and Mrs Patrick Campbell: Their Correspondence* (ed. Alan Dent 1952) p. 221.

116/ 4 **be silly:** Mrs Patrick Campbell to G.B.S., February 1921, *Their Correspondence* p. 223.

116/ 6 **pound note:** G.B.S. to Otto Kyllmann, 27 February 1921, *CL*3 p 711.

116/17 **bonnet:** Mrs Patrick Campbell to G.B.S., 24 December 1921, *Their Correspondence* p. 234.

116/21 **street:** G.B.S. to Mrs Patrick Campbell, 30 December 1921, *CL*3 pp. 755–6 (*Their Correspondence* p. 235).

116/25 **worry:** Mrs Patrick Campbell to G.B.S., 12 and 13 January 1922, *Their Correspondence* pp. 241–2.

116/35 **heroine:** G.B.S. to Mrs Patrick Campbell, 16 January 1922, *Their Correspondence* p. 243.

116/39 **delicious letters:** Mrs Patrick Campbell to G.B.S. [attributed to January 1922], *Their Correspondence* pp. 243–4.

117/ 2 **countenance?:** G.B.S. to Mrs Patrick Campbell, 16 January 1922, *Their Correspondence* p. 243.

117/11 **dreadful thing:** G.B.S. to Mrs Patrick Campbell, 25 February 1922, *Their Correspondence* pp. 248–9.

117/17 **like:** Mrs Patrick Campbell to G.B.S., 24 February 1922, *Their Correspondence* p. 247.

117/22   **mind:** Mrs Patrick Campbell to G.B.S., 5 May 1922, *Their Correspondence* p. 253.

117/31   **to do:** G.B.S. to G. K. Chesterton, 21 May 1922, *CL*3 pp. 770–1.

117/34   **been born:** G.B.S. to Mrs Patrick Campbell, 3 January 1923, *Their Correspondence* p. 259.

118/ 1   **age:** G.B.S. to Molly Tompkins, 27 August 1924, 27 January 1926, *CL*4 pp. 7–9 (*To a Young Actress* pp. 75, 91).

118/ 4   **imprevu:** G.B.S. to Molly Tompkins, 15 December 1925, *To a Young Actress* p. 88.

118/ 7   **evenings:** G.B.S. to Molly Tompkins, 10 June 1924, *To a Young Actress* p. 71.

118/11   **of things:** G.B.S. to Mrs Patrick Campbell, 12 December 1927, *Their Correspondence* p. 262.

118/13   **bore:** G.B.S. to Molly Tompkins, 10 June 1924, *To a Young Actress* p. 71.

118/16   **stories:** G.B.S. to Mrs Patrick Campbell, 3 January 1923, *Their Correspondence* p. 259.

118/20   **shop:** G.B.S. to Molly Tompkins, 22 December 1922, *To a Young Actress* p. 32.

118/37   **right:** G.B.S. to Molly Tompkins, 20 March 1923, 1 May 1932, 26 November 1922, 22 December 1922, 11 January 1922; *To a Young Actress* pp. 37, 158, 27, 33, 15.

119/ 3   **helped:** G.B.S. to Molly Tompkins, 4 August 1923, *To a Young Actress* p. 47.

119/ 4   **themselves:** G.B.S. to Molly Tompkins, 6 May 1924, *To a Young Actress* p. 69.

119/12   **invited:** *Shaw and Molly Tompkins* p. 36.

119/22   **to you:** G.B.S. to Molly Tompkins, 20 April 1922, *To a Young Actress* p. 21.

119/27   **Godalming:** G.B.S. to Molly Tompkins, 27 August 1924, *To a Young Actress* p. 76.

119/29   **skill:** G.B.S. to Molly Tompkins, 24 November 1931, *To a Young Actress* p. 155.

119/30   **shivers:** G.B.S. to Molly Tompkins, 10 February 1924, *To a Young Actress* p. 59.

120/11   **to London:** *Shaw and Molly Tompkins* Chapter 5.

120/28   **done better:** G.B.S. to Molly Tompkins, 1 December 1922, *To a Young Actress* p. 28.

120/33   **roar:** G.B.S. to Molly Tompkins, 27 August 1923, *To a Young Actress* p. 48.

120/last   **wrong:** *Shaw and Molly Tompkins* p. 76.

121/10   **theatre:** G.B.S. to Forbes-Robertson, 1 October 1923, *To a Young Actress* p. 55.

121 / 16   **so there:** *Shaw and Molly Tompkins* p. 97.

121 / 18   ***him*!:** G.B.S. to Molly Tompkins, 27 August 1924, *To a Young Actress* p. 76.

121 / 21   **a day:** *Shaw and Molly Tompkins* p. 99.

121 / 30   **know:** G.B.S. to Molly Tompkins, 25 June 1925, *To a Young Actress* p. 85.

121 / 35   **actress:** *Shaw and Molly Tompkins* p. 107.

121 / last **to Italy:** G.B.S. to Molly Tompkins, 14 July 1924, *To a Young Actress* pp. 74, 73.

122 / 7   **undesirables:** G.B.S. to Molly Tompkins, 24 February 1925, *CL*3 p. 906 (*To a Young Actress* p. 83).

122 / 8   **you again:** Ibid.

122 / 13   **scenery:** G.B.S. to H. G. Wells, 11 September 1925 (Illinois).

122 / 16   **of work:** G.B.S. to Harriet Cohen, 23 December 1926 (copy, Society of Authors).

122 / 22   ***never was warm*:** Charlotte Shaw to Beatrice Webb, August/September 1926 (LSE).

122 / 26   **as well:** G.B.S. to Blanche Patch, 4 September 1926 (Cornell).

122 / 28   **finish me:** G.B.S. to Siegfried Trebitsch, 2 August 1926, Shaw/Trebitsch letters p. 273.

122 / 28   **cold water:** G.B.S. to Kathleen Hilton Young [formerly Kathleen Scott], 20 May 1926, *CL*4 p. 23.

122 / 31   **happy:** Charlotte Shaw to Apsley Cherry-Garrard, 20 August 1926, 12 August 1926 (Texas).

123 / 5   **sitting:** Charlotte Shaw to Beatrice Webb, August / September 1926 (LSE).

123 / 7   **time:** Charlotte Shaw to Apsley Cherry-Garrard, 12 August 1926 (Texas).

123 / 14   **live it:** G.B.S. to Molly Tompkins, 12 July 1926, *To a Young Actress* p. 92.

123 / 17   **again today:** G.B.S. to Molly Tompkins, 10 August 1926, *To a Young Actress* p. 95.

123 / 26   **arrangement:** *Shaw and Molly Tompkins* p. 132.

124 / 5   **immediately:** Ibid., p. 140.

124 / 8   **you live:** G.B.S. to Molly Tompkins, 18 September 1926, *To a Young Actress* pp. 105–6.

124 / 15   **I'd be good:** *Shaw and Molly Tompkins* p. 141.

124 / 17   **everything:** G.B.S. to Molly Tompkins, 19 September 1926, *To a Young Actress* p. 107.

124 / 24   **lake:** *Shaw and Molly Tompkins* p. 142.

124 / 26   **to Paris:** Ibid., p. 143.

124 / 28   **illness:** G.B.S. to Harriet Cohen, 23 December 1926 (copy, Society of Authors).

124/28   **I think:** G.B.S. to Molly Tompkins, 10 January 1927, *To a Young Actress* p. 109.

124/31   **of life:** G.B.S. to Molly Tompkins, 8 January 1928, *CL*4 pp. 82–4 (*To a Young Actress* p. 123).

124/33   **of them:** G.B.S. to Molly Tompkins, 27 August 1924, *To a Young Actress* p. 76.

124/35   **mind me:** G.B.S. to Molly Tompkins, 12 January 1927, *To a Young Actress* p. 111.

124/37   **imposed on:** G.B.S. to Molly Tompkins, 25 June 1925, *To a Young Actress* p. 85.

125/ 1   **gone by:** G.B.S. to Molly Tompkins, 8 August 1926, *To a Young Actress* p. 96.

125/ 3   **tired of her:** G.B.S. to Molly Tompkins, 12 January 1927, *To a Young Actress* p. 110.

125/10   **incurable:** G.B.S. to Molly Tompkins, 22 February 1925, *CL*3 pp. 904–6 (*To a Young Actress* p. 82).

125/12   **Shotover:** G.B.S. to Molly Tompkins, 9 August 1925, *To a Young Actress* p. 87.

125/14   **young friends:** G.B.S. to Molly Tompkins, 7 February 1931, *To a Young Actress* p. 142.

125/19   **consequences:** G.B.S. to Molly Tompkins, 2 February 1927, *To a Young Actress* p. 113.

125/21   **other lady:** G.B.S. to Molly Tompkins, 10 June 1924, *To a Young Actress* p. 71.

125/24   **live here!:** Charlotte Shaw to Molly Tompkins, 22 August 1926, *To a Young Actress* p. 97.

126/ 2   **affection:** *The Diary of Beatrice Webb* vol. 4, entry 24 May 1927, p. 124.

126/10   **at once:** G.B.S. to Molly Tompkins, 27 January 1926, *CL*4 pp. 7–9; 2 February 1927 (*To a Young Actress* pp. 91, 113).

126/14   **understand:** Charlotte Shaw to T. E. Lawrence, 9 September [1926 or 1927], BL Add. MS 45922 f. 56.

127/ 4   **sweetness:** *Shaw and Molly Tompkins* p. 156.

127/12   **river:** Margot Peters, *Bernard Shaw and the Actresses* (1980) pp. 408–9.

127/18   **beggar:** G.B.S. to Molly Tompkins, 2 February 1929, *To a Young Actress* p. 131.

127/22   **grab at it:** G.B.S. to Molly Tompkins, 10 June 1924, *To a Young Actress* p. 71.

127/26   **succeed:** G.B.S. to Molly Tompkins, 31 May 1928, *CL*4 pp. 99–100 (*To a Young Actress* p. 128).

127/29   **voice:** G.B.S. to Molly Tompkins, 8 January 1928, *CL*4 pp. 82–4 (*To a Young Actress* p. 123).

127/35   **nothingness:** G.B.S. to Molly Tompkins, 31 May 1928, *CL*4 pp. 99–100 (*To a Young Actress* p. 127).

128/ 8   **last day came:** *Shaw and Molly Tompkins* pp. 161–2.

128/18   **go their way:** G.B.S. to Molly Tompkins, 31 May 1928, *CL*4 pp. 99–100 (*To a Young Actress* pp. 127–8).

128/29   **including G.B.S.:** G.B.S. to Molly Tompkins, 2 March 1928; 21 September 1930 (*To a Young Actress* pp. 124, 140).

128/Ep.   **of income:** *IWG* p. 500.

129/ 3   *quite plainly*: Mary [Mrs Hugh] Cholmondeley to G.B.S., n.d. [1924], BL Add. MS 50519 ff. 363–4.

129/11   **point:** *IWG* p. 37.

129/14   **dozen plays:** G.B.S. to Augustin Hamon, 3 December 1925, *CL*3 p. 921.

129/16   **writing plays:** G.B.S. to Molly Tompkins, 27 January 1926, *CL*4 pp. 7–9 (*To a Young Actress* p. 90).

129/17   **killed myself:** G.B.S. to R. & R. Clark, 29 July 1926 (Scotland).

129/18   **socialism!:** G.B.S. to Kathleen Hilton Young [formerly Scott], 20 May 1926, *CL*4 p. 23.

129/21   **question:** G.B.S. to Archibald Henderson, 30 January 1926 (North Carolina).

129/22   **its end:** *Letters to T. E. Lawrence* (ed. A. W. Lawrence 1962) p. 174.

129/24   **morning:** Charlotte Shaw to T. E. Lawrence, 16 March 1927, BL Add. MS 45922 f. 4.

129/33   **longer:** G.B.S. to Beatrice Webb, 12 December 1927 (LSE).

129/35   **letters:** G.B.S. to William Maxwell, 8 February 1928 (National Library of Scotland).

129/37   **future ages:** G.B.S. to Otto Kyllmann, January 1931 and 6 November 1930 (North Carolina).

130/ 1   **forearm:** Stanley Weintraub, *Private Shaw and Public Shaw* (1963) p. 135.

130/ 8   **to be:** G.B.S. to Hayden Church, 27 October 1928 (Houghton).

130/12   **nothing:** *IWG* p. 506.

130/16   **Socialism:** G.B.S. to Calman-Lévy, c. November 1928 and n.d. (Berg and Texas).

130/21   **income:** 'The Simple Truth about Socialism', *The Road to Equality: The Unpublished Lectures and Essays, 1884–1918* (ed. Louis Crompton 1971) p. 184.

130/25   **Socialism:** G.B.S. to Edith Lyttelton, 27 December 1912, *CL*3 p. 142.

130/29   **range:** G.B.S. to Beatrice Webb, 13 October 1916, *CL*3 pp. 428–9.

130/33   **write:** G.B.S. to Otto Kyllmann, 12 September 1924 (North Carolina).

130/36   **use:** 'The Future of Western Civilization', *Practical Politics: Twentieth-Century Views on Politics and Economics* (ed. Lloyd J. Hubenka 1976) p. 201.

131/ 3   **flapper vote:** G.B.S. to Fenner Brockway, 28 June 1928 (copy, Society of Authors).

131/18   **Victorian era:** 'Bernard Shaw's *Intelligent Woman's Guide*: Some Opinions', *The Criterion* September 1928, pp. 195–6.

131/22   **freedom:** Ibid., p. 194.

131/38   **literature:** *IWG* p. 506.

132/12   **spare money:** Ibid., p. 501.

132/16   **dialogue:** 'Bernard Shaw's *Intelligent Woman's Guide*: Some Opinions', *The Criterion* September 1928, p. 196.

132/19   **masculine:** *IWG* p. 54.

132/22   **existed:** Ibid., p. 501.

132/26   **really are:** Ibid., p. 83.

132/32   **for it:** Ibid., p. 59.

133/ 3   **her bow:** Ibid., p. 200.

133/ 6   **document:** Introduction to *IWG* p. xxxix.

133/10   **possesses:** Siegfried Trebitsch, *Chronicle of a Life* (1953) p. 277.

133/12   **activity:** *Albert Einstein–Michele Besso: Correspondence 1903–1955*, letter 93. See also letter to Mrs Hedwig Fischer, 1928. See P. de Mendelsohn, *The S. Fischer Verlag* (1970) p. 1164.

133/14   **poetry:** T. E. Lawrence to Charlotte Shaw, 18 December and 23 July 1928, BL Add. MS 45904 ff. 55, 18.

133/35   **to him:** Quoted in E. P. Thompson, *William Morris: Romantic to Revolutionary* (1977) p. 548 and Margaret Walters' Introduction to *IWG* p. xi.

133/38   **periods:** G.B.S. to Molly Tompkins, 4 April 1927, *To a Young Actress* p. 116.

134/11   **themselves:** *IWG* pp. 493–4.

134/13   **sensibility:** Ibid., p. 496.

134/18   **ways:** Ibid., pp. 494–5.

134/21   **horses:** Ibid., p. 496.

134/32   **dirt:** Ibid., p. 500.

135/6   **wealth:** Ibid., p. 83.

136/10   **reluctant one:** Ibid., p. 461.

136/23   **for years:** Ibid., pp. 84, 451.

136/25   **gas-bag:** *The Collected Letters of D. H. Lawrence* (ed. Harry T. Moore 1962) vol. 2, p. 1069.

136/30   **you down:** Hayden Church questionnaire, 27 October 1928 (Houghton).

136/35   **else:** Ibid.

137/ 7   **prosperous:** G.B.S. to J. Armour Macmillan, 12 October 1928, BL Add. MS 50519 ff. 353–6.

137/10   **irritating:** Harold Laski to Holmes, 28 May 1928, *Holmes–Laski Letters: The Correspondence of Mr Justice Holmes and Harold J. Laski 1916–1935* (ed. Mark DeWolfe Howe 1953) vol. 2, p. 1059.

137/14   **equality:** *IWG* p. 25.

137/31   **bad book:** *The Letters of Sidney and Beatrice Webb* (ed. Norman MacKenzie 1978) vol. 3, p. 238.

137/last   **unreality:** *The Diary of Beatrice Webb* vol. 4, entry 9 June 1928, p. 146.

CHAPTER III

138/Ep. 1   **attitude:** G.B.S. to Charles Sarolea, 20 February 1926, *CL*4 p. 13.

138/Ep. 2   **comic:** G.B.S. to Stanley W. Bull, 6 July 1926, *CL*4 p. 24.

138/27   **loved it:** St John Ervine, *Bernard Shaw: His Life, Work and Friends* (1956) p. 515.

139/29   **undernourished:** Unpublished typescript from Mrs Stella Williamson.

139/36   **half an hour:** G.B.S. to Ada Tyrrell, 28 January 1928, *CL*4 p. 87.

139/last   **sometimes does:** G.B.S. to Edith Lyttelton, 8 July 1926 (Churchill College, Cambridge).

140/ 5   **crocks:** Charlotte Shaw to Nancy Astor, 11 December 1927 (Reading). See also Christopher Sykes, *Nancy: The Life of Lady Astor* (1979 edn) p. 341.

140/10   **life:** Charlotte Shaw to Nancy Astor, 10 January 1928 and 19 February 1928 (Reading).

140/34   **don't know why:** Christopher Sykes, *Nancy: The Life of Lady Astor* p. 343.

141/ 3   **life!:** William Douglas Home, *Mr Home Pronounced Hume* (1979) p. 69.

141/11   **Order:** G.B.S. to Nancy Astor, 18 May 1929, *CL*4 p. 142.

141/15   **mind?:** G.B.S. to Nancy Astor, 9 August 1930 (Reading).

141/19   **Labor Party:** G.B.S. to Nancy Astor, 20 November 1929 (Reading).

141/35   **visitors:** G.B.S. to Molly Tompkins, 8 January 1928, *CL*4 p. 83.

141/39   **maidens:** Beatrice Webb diaries, 13 April 1928 (LSE).

142/ 7   **Fabian lot:** G.B.S. to Nancy Astor, 11 February 1929. See
Nancy: The Life of Lady Astor pp. 345–6.

142/24   **aristocracy:** 'G.B.S. Hits Out in Defence of Lady Astor',
Sunday Graphic 5 March 1939, pp. 2–3.

142/30   **America:** 'Bernard Shaw Answers Frederick L. Collins about
Lady Astor', *Liberty* 11 March 1939, pp. 7–8.

142/33   **Charlotte:** *The Diary of Beatrice Webb* vol. 4 (ed. N. and J.
MacKenzie 1985), entry 5 December 1927, p. 136.

142/35   **much tact:** *Arnold Bennett: The Journals* (ed. Frank Swinnerton,
Penguin 1984) entry 28 September 1928, p. 558.

143/ 3   **admirers:** Beatrice Webb diaries, 18 April 1928 (LSE).

143/ 8   **organization:** G.B.S. to Nancy Astor, 1 June 1943 (Reading).

143/35   **tyrant:** 'Bernard Shaw on Mussolini: a Defence', *Daily News*
24 January 1927.

144/ 3   **did:** G.B.S. to Byfield, n.d., BL Add. MS 50560 f. 219.

144/21   **command:** G.B.S. to Ramsay MacDonald, 21 October 1927,
*CL*4 p. 75.

144/24   **police:** 'Bernard Shaw on Mussolini: A Defence', *Daily News*
24 January 1927.

144/28   **Mussolini:** G.B.S. to Molly Tompkins, 2 February 1927, *To a
Young Actress: The Letters of Bernard Shaw to Molly Tompkins*
(ed. Peter Tompkins 1960) p. 112.

144/31   **establish it:** G.B.S. to W. S. Kennedy, 7 February 1927, *CL*4
p. 43.

144/36   **disgust you:** G.B.S. to Friedrich Adler, 2 October 1927, *CL*4
p. 70.

144/40   **enthusiasm:** G.B.S. to W. S. Kennedy, 7 February 1927, *CL*4
p. 44.

145/ 2   **wrong:** G.B.S. to Byfield, n.d., BL Add. MS 50560 f. 219.

145/13   **manners:** 'Bernard Shaw on Mussolini: a Defence', *Daily News*
24 January 1927, cited *CL*4 p. 42.

145/18   **people:** G.B.S. to Ramsay MacDonald, 21 October 1927, *CL*4
p. 75.

145/21   **scoundrel:** G.B.S. to Graham Wallas, 24 December 1927,
*CL*4 p. 81.

145/32   **experience:** Friedrich Adler to G.B.S., c. 7 February 1927,
*CL*4 p. 67.

145/38   **resents it:** Beatrice Webb diaries, 23 October 1935 (LSE).

146/ 8   **queer forms:** *The Diary of Beatrice Webb* vol. 4, entry 5
December 1927, p. 135.

146/Ep.   **pay you:** *CP*6 p. 842.

146/13   **lass:** G.B.S. to Molly Tompkins, 27 January 1926, *CL*4 pp. 7–9
(*To a Young Actress* p. 90).

146/19   *a new play*: G.B.S. to William Maxwell, 5 November 1928
           (Scotland).
146/26   **let it rip:** G.B.S. to William Maxwell, 3 December 1928
           (Scotland).
146/28   **pace with it:** G.B.S. to Cecil Lewis, 27 December 1928
           (Texas).
146/32   **imagine:** Ibid.
146/last   **possibly can be:** G.B.S. to Theresa Helburn, 8 February
           1929, *CL*4 p. 129.
147/18   **financiers:** William Poel, *What is Wrong with the Stage* (1920)
           pp. 9–10.
147/23   **meddle:** G.B.S. to C. B. Purdom, 12 January 1930, *CL*4
           p. 172.
147/32   **ventures?:** Vivian Elliot, '"Genius Loci": The Malvern
           Festival Tradition', *Shaw: The Annual of Bernard Shaw Studies*
           vol. 3: *Shaw's Plays In Performance* (ed. Daniel Leary 1983)
           p. 194.
148/34   **of ideas:** Ibid., p. 197.
148/40   **wisdom:** Malvern Festival 1929 Souvenir Book, p. 3.
149/ 3   **to you:** *Shaw's Plays in Performance* p. 194.
149/ 9   **headlines:** 'Malvern Festival's Future', *Malvern Gazette* 15
           April 1939.
149/16   **witticisms:** *The Times* 17 June 1929.
149/29   **motifs:** Edmund Wilson, *The Triple Thinkers* (1962 Pelican
           edn) p. 206.
150/ 9   **secretaries:** Ibid., pp. 205–6.
150/15   **for it:** Hesketh Pearson, *Bernard Shaw* (1975 edn) p. 411.
150/25   **relations:** G.B.S. to Siegfried Trebitsch, 23 February 1930,
           Shaw/Trebitsch letters p. 311.
150/31   **and on...:** Mrs Patrick Campbell to G.B.S., n.d. [February
           1928], 25 November 1928, *Bernard Shaw and Mrs Patrick
           Campbell: Their Correspondence* (ed. Alan Dent 1952) pp. 267,
           271.
151/38   **courtesy:** *Their Correspondence* pp. 271–87.
152/ 7   **heels:** Margot Peters, *Bernard Shaw and the Actresses* (1980)
           p. 392.
152/26   **struck:** G.B.S. to Mrs Patrick Campbell, 12 July 1929, *CL*4
           p. 153.
152/28   **to it:** Mrs Patrick Campbell to G.B.S., 26 July 1929, *Their
           Correspondence* p. 290.
153/ 2   **game:** G.B.S. to Mrs Patrick Campbell, 28 July 1929 (see *CL*4
           pp. 156–7); Mrs Patrick Campbell to G.B.S., 22 July 1929;
           G.B.S. to Mrs Patrick Campbell, 12 July 1929 (*CL*4
           pp. 152–3), *Their Correspondence* pp. 288–91.

153/15   **ridiculous:** *CP*6 pp. 338, 342.

153/30   **finds me:** G.B.S. to Mrs Patrick Campbell, n.d. [c. 23 July 1929], *CL*4 p. 156 (*Their Correspondence* p. 290).

153/36   **untruthfulness:** Mrs Patrick Campbell to G.B.S., 22 July 1929, *Their Correspondence* p. 289.

154/ 2   **from royalty:** *CP*6 pp. 340, 347, 345.

154/ 6   **Sandwich and all:** *Their Correspondence* pp. 275–6. See *CL*4 p. 133 for G.B.S. to Mrs Patrick Campbell, 6 April 1929.

154/10   **hurting you:** *CP*6 p. 349.

154/14   **the place out:** Ibid., p. 342.

154/34   **fairyland:** Ibid., pp. 342, 338, 345, 347.

155/ 9   **old lady:** G.B.S.'s answer to Sobieniowski questionnaire, 2–10 April 1929 (Berg).

155/18   **England:** *CP*6 p. 330.

155/27   **yours truly:** Ibid., p. 331.

155/35   **personal tie:** Ibid., p. 329.

156/ 2   **every pie:** Ibid.

156/ 6   **station:** Ibid., p. 374.

156/22   **country:** Ibid., pp. 324–5.

156/34   **cucumber:** Ibid., p. 306.

157/14   **to play it:** Ibid., p. 251.

157/18   **type:** Ibid., p. 381.

157/29   **professionalism:** Ibid., p. 326.

157/34   **as I do:** *The Listener* 4 June 1953, p. 936.

157/39   **Magnus:** *CP*6 p. 385.

158/ 2   **Henri Quatre:** G.B.S. to C. H. Norman, 9 January 1930, *CL*4 p. 169.

158/ 5   **myself:** Hesketh Pearson, *Bernard Shaw* pp. 411–12.

158/11   **generalization:** Notes to *Caesar and Cleopatra*, *CP*2 p. 303.

158/13   **ideals:** *CP*1 p. 608.

158/18   **speeches:** G.B.S. to Siegfried Trebitsch, 29 November 1929, Shaw/Trebitsch letters p. 306.

158/39   **as monarch:** G.B.S. to G. W. Bishop, 4 September 1929, *CL*4 p. 157.

159/ 5   **finish:** *CP*6 p. 374.

159/ 9   **his life:** W. B. Yeats on the reception of *The Apple Cart*, letters to Lady Gregory, 21 August and 16 November 1929. See *Shaw: The Critical Heritage* (ed. T. F. Evans 1976) p. 321.

159/12   **Sandringham:** *The Diary of Beatrice Webb* vol. 4, entry 2 October 1929, p. 196.

159/24   **philosophy:** Ivor Brown, an initialled notice, *Manchester Guardian* 20 August 1929, *Shaw: The Critical Heritage* pp. 314–15.

159/34   **money:** *CP6* p. 254.
159/38   **poetry:** G.B.S. to Edward Elgar, 12 August 1929 (Worcester
          Record Office).
160/ 2   **creates:** W. B. Yeats on the reception of *The Apple Cart*, letters
          to Lady Gregory, 21 August and 16 November 1929. See
          Shaw: The Critical Heritage p. 321.
160/15   **King:** Desmond MacCarthy, *Shaw* (1951) pp. 184–5.
160/21   **appreciated:** Edmund Wilson, *Triple Thinkers* p. 205.
160/24   **Sophocles:** Hesketh Pearson, *Bernard Shaw* (1975 edn) p. 411.
160/27   **fresh:** Ivor Brown, an initialled notice, *Manchester Guardian* 20
          August 1929, *Shaw: The Critical Heritage* p. 316.
160/29   **detail:** See Margery Morgan, *The Shavian Playground: An
          Exploration of the Art of George Bernard Shaw* (1972)
          pp. 303–15, and *Bernard Shaw* II: *1907–1950* (Writers and
          Their Work; Profile Books 1982) p. 29.
160/35   **satire:** 'He was Mankind's Friend', *The Listener* 18 January
          1951, *Shaw: The Critical Heritage* p. 400.
161/ 4   **Europe:** R. H. Bruce Lockhart, *Retreat from Glory* (1934)
          p. 348.
161/20   **performed:** G.B.S. to Floryan Sobieniowski, n.d. [assigned to
          8 June 1929], *CL4* p. 147.
162/ 2   **separated:** Charlotte Shaw to Nancy Astor, 26 August 1929
          (Reading).
162/10   **economics:** Beverley Nichols, *All I Could Never Be: Some
          Recollections* (1949) pp. 145–7.
162/17   **gardens:** '"Genius Loci": The Malvern Festival Tradition',
          Shaw's Plays in Performance p. 198.
162/18   **festival:** Ibid., p. 216.
162/37   **plays:** Ibid., p. 203.
162/last **Woolworth's:** Ibid., p. 202.
163/ 1   **world:** Mavis Walker to Michael Holroyd, n.d.
163/23   **Ghosts:** '"Genius Loci": The Malvern Festival Tradition',
          Shaw's Plays in Performance p. 214.
163/29   **good thing...:** G.B.S. to Edward Elgar, 12 August 1929
          (Worcester Record Office).
163/34   **come of it:** *St James's Gazette* 13 December 1907.
163/38   **Shakespeare's:** G.B.S. to Rutland Boughton, 9 August 1932,
          BL Add. MS 52365 f. 41.
164/10   **earth:** Vivian Elliot, 'Shaw and Elgar: Two Famous Friends of
          Malvern', Malvern Festival Programme, 22 May–11 June
          1978 p. 3.
164/15   **much more:** Quoted in Malvern Festival Programme, 1977
          p. 5.

164/18 **many ways:** Jerrold Northrop Moore, *Edward Elgar: A Creative Life* (1984) p. 519.

164/22 **orchestration:** G.B.S. to Conal O'Riordan, 29 July 1944 (Texas).

164/34 **Elgar:** G.B.S. to the Editor of the *Morning Post* [1911]. See Dan H. Laurence, introduction to *SM*1 pp. 19–20.

164/38 **English:** 'The Reminiscences of a Quinquagenarian', *Musical Association Proceedings 1910–11, SM*3 p. 630.

165/ 4 **yourself:** *Edward Elgar: A Creative Life* p. 737.

165/22 **found it:** 'Sir Edward Elgar', *Music and Letters* January 1920, *SM*3 pp. 722–4.

166/ 3 **culture:** G.B.S. to the *Daily News* 9 June 1922, *SM*3 pp. 729–30.

166/16 **experience:** Harriet Cohen, *A Bundle of Time* (1969) p. 150.

166/25 **everything:** G.B.S. to Conal O'Riordan, 29 July 1944 (Texas).

166/32 ***The Apple Cart:*** Edward Elgar to G.B.S., quoted in Malvern Festival Programme, 1977 p. 25.

166/38 **experience:** G.B.S. to Conal O'Riordan, 29 July 1944 (Texas).

167/ 1 **as his own:** 'Severn Suite' score (Texas).

167/ 5 **music:** G.B.S. to Elgar, 28 September 1930, *CL*4 p. 201.

167/16 **King (Queen):** G.B.S. to Elgar, 2 January 1931, *CL*4 p. 225.

167/29 **months:** 'Sir Edward Elgar', *Music and Letters* January 1920, *SM*3 p. 725.

167/36 **Clearing:** G.B.S. to Elgar, 29 June 1932 (Worcester Record Office).

168/ 4 **livelihood:** John Reith, *Into the Wind* (1949) p. 163.

168/ 8 **ninth:** G.B.S. to *The Times*, 20 December 1932, *SM*3 p. 732.

168/24 **myself:** Charlotte Shaw to Elgar, 20 September 1932 (Worcester Record Office).

168/26 **away:** Elgar to the Shaws, 18 April 1933 (Worcester Record Office).

168/last **bear:** Charlotte Shaw to Nancy Astor, 9 September 1934 (Reading).

169/Ep. **used to be:** G.B.S. to Frank Harris, 7 April 1927, *The Playwright and the Pirate: Bernard Shaw and Frank Harris: A Correspondence* (ed. Stanley Weintraub 1982) p. 212.

169/ 9 **royalties:** G.B.S. to T. E. Lawrence, 23 June 1928 (Texas).

169/20 **stay:** Charlotte Shaw to Nancy Astor, 10 August 1928 (Reading).

169/23 **purgatory:** G.B.S. to Blanche Patch, 31 July 1928 (Cornell).

169/27 **arms:** Charlotte Shaw to Nancy Astor, 22 August 1928 (Reading).

169/32 **mostly:** G.B.S. to Siegfried Trebitsch, 24 August 1928, Shaw/Trebitsch letters p. 292.

170/ 6   **town:** Charlotte Shaw to Nancy Astor, 22 August 1928 (Reading).

170/19   **autobiography:** G.B.S. to Frank Harris, 11 November 1915, *The Playwright and the Pirate* p. 22.

170/25   **world:** Harris to G.B.S., 23 November 1917, 14 September 1920, *The Playwright and the Pirate* pp. 71, 154.

170/28   **Casanova:** G.B.S. to Harris, 31 July 1928, *CL4* p. 106 (*The Playwright and the Pirate* p. 213).

170/31   **one into:** G.B.S. to Harris, 5 March 1918, *The Playwright and the Pirate* p. 87.

171/ 3   **words:** Harris to G.B.S., 24 April 1919, *The Playwright and the Pirate* p. 120.

171/12   **generosity:** Harris to G.B.S., 13 November 1919, 29 September 1916, *The Playwright and the Pirate* pp. 149, 46.

171/16   **done:** Harris to G.B.S., 25 August 1915, *The Playwright and the Pirate* p. 19.

171/16   **extant:** Philippa Pullar, *Frank Harris* (1975) p. 326.

171/18   **together:** Harris to G.B.S., 14 July 1918, *The Playwright and the Pirate* p. 100.

171/25   **England:** Harris to G.B.S., 14 July 1918, 24 April 1919, *The Playwright and the Pirate* pp. 99, 120.

171/30   **except you:** Harris to G.B.S., 23 November 1917, 14 July 1918 [March 1923], *The Playwright and the Pirate* pp. 71, 99, 188–9.

171/34   **interesting:** Harris to G.B.S., 14 September 1920, 12 October 1920, *The Playwright and the Pirate* pp. 154, 162.

171/36   **unsatisfactory:** Harris to G.B.S., 2 March 1923, *The Playwright and the Pirate* p. 186.

171/40   **bootlaces:** Harris to G.B.S., 26 March 1923; G.B.S. to Harris, 5 April 1923, *The Playwright and the Pirate*, pp. 187–8, 192. See also *CL3* pp. 819–20.

172/ 5   **incredible:** G.B.S. to Archibald Henderson, 29 August 1925 (North Carolina).

172/ 8   **were:** G.B.S. to Harris, 27 September 1918, *The Playwright and the Pirate* p. 105.

172/11   **on you:** Harris to G.B.S., 22 October 1918, *The Playwright and the Pirate* p. 111.

172/35   **sides:** Harris to G.B.S., 30 January 1929, *The Playwright and the Pirate* pp. 215–16.

172/19   **better:** G.B.S. to Harris, 11 January 1930, *The Playwright and the Pirate* pp. 217, 218.

172/28   **poor:** Harris to G.B.S., 3 April 1927, *The Playwright and the Pirate* p. 211.

172/33 **rich:** G.B.S. to Harris, 15 January 1917, 8 February 1931, *The Playwright and the Pirate* pp. 64, 251. See also *CL*3 pp. 451–4.

173/ 6 **forgive me:** G.B.S. to Harris, 27 January 1930, *The Playwright and the Pirate* p. 219.

173/ 9 **tome:** Harris to G.B.S., 23 September 1930, *The Playwright and the Pirate* p. 242.

173/13 **in you:** Harris to G.B.S., 3 April 1927, 23 September 1930, *The Playwright and the Pirate* pp. 211, 242.

173/18 **flames:** G.B.S. to Harris, 31 July 1928, *CL*4 p. 106 (*The Playwright and the Pirate* p. 213).

173/30 **university:** G.B.S. to Harris, 5 March 1918, *The Playwright and the Pirate* p. 88.

173/36 **questionnaires:** Ibid.

174/ 3 **information:** Demetrius O'Bolger's Introduction to 'The Real Shaw' (Houghton).

174/ 8 **cross-examination:** G.B.S. to Harris, 5 March 1918, *The Playwright and the Pirate* p. 88.

174/17 **lifetime:** G.B.S. to Harris, 4 January 1918, *CL*3 p. 523 (*The Playwright and the Pirate* p. 75).

174/20 **tell me:** Harris to G.B.S., 6 February 1918, *The Playwright and the Pirate* p. 81.

174/23 **questions:** G.B.S. to Harris, 16 October 1916, *The Playwright and the Pirate* pp. 52–3.

174/28 **your MS:** G.B.S. to O'Bolger, 24 February 1916, *CL*3 p. 355.

174/35 **ears:** G.B.S. to Harris, 16 October 1916, *The Playwright and the Pirate* p. 53.

174/40 **strain:** Introduction to 'The Real Shaw' (Houghton).

175/ 2 **Frank Harris:** G.B.S. to O'Bolger, 24 April 1919 (Houghton).

175/ 4 **published:** Introduction to 'The Real Shaw' (Houghton).

175/ 8 **rescuer:** G.B.S. to O'Bolger, 17 July 1919 (Houghton).

175/18 **at it:** G.B.S. to O'Bolger, 23 January 1922, *CL*3 p. 760.

175/23 **have done:** G.B.S. to Harris, 3 March 1930, *The Playwright and the Pirate* p. 221.

175/28 **&c &c:** G.B.S. to O'Bolger, 23 January 1922, *CL*3 p. 760.

175/28 **medically:** G.B.S. to O'Bolger, 3 November 1921, *CL*3 p. 746.

175/last **suffered:** Ibid., pp. 746–7.

176/ 4 **hunter:** G.B.S. to Harris, 3 March 1930, *The Playwright and the Pirate* p. 221.

176/ 8 **construction:** Ibid.

176/16 **time:** G.B.S. to Ignatius MacHugh, 24 August 1923, *CL*3 p. 845.

176/18 **death of me:** G.B.S. to O'Bolger, 7 August 1919, *CL*3 p. 626.

176/23 **rescue him:** G.B.S. to Ignatius MacHugh, 24 August 1923, *CL*3 pp. 844–5.

176/28 **ruining him:** G.B.S. to Harris, 3 March 1930, *The Playwright and the Pirate* p. 221.

176/32 **misunderstood:** G.B.S. to Harris, 16 October 1916, *The Playwright and the Pirate* p. 53.

176/35 **accident:** Ibid.

176/37 **misunderstandings:** G.B.S. to Archibald Henderson, 8 March 1918 (North Carolina).

176/last **vomit:** G.B.S. to Harris, 5 March 1918, *The Playwright and the Pirate* p. 88.

177/16 **matter:** G.B.S. to Archibald Henderson, 30 January 1926, *CL*4 pp. 10–11.

177/21 **flop:** G.B.S. to Henderson, 25 December 1931 (North Carolina).

177/26 **sounds:** G.B.S. to Henderson, 29 August 1925 (North Carolina).

177/40 **on you:** G.B.S. to Harris, 18 September 1930, *The Playwright and the Pirate* p. 240.

178/4 **circumstances:** G.B.S. to Henderson, 25 December 1931 (North Carolina).

178/10 **Esquire:** G.B.S. to Frank Harris, 21 April 1931, *CL*4 pp. 235–6 (*The Playwright and the Pirate* p. 254).

178/14 **parish will:** Ibid.

178/18 **oddest:** Frank Harris, *Bernard Shaw* (1931) p. 387.

178/26 **doctoring:** G.B.S. to Helen (Nellie) Harris, 17 October 1931, *CL*4 p. 262.

178/38 **particular:** Ibid.

178/39 **Harris:** Frank Harris, *Bernard Shaw* p. 395.

179/3 **of them:** G.B.S. to Archibald Henderson, 8 March 1918 (Houghton).

179/16 **foundling:** Frank Harris, *Bernard Shaw* p. 87.

179/17 **Done It?:** *Daily Express* 27 November 1931.

179/33 **sayings!:** G.B.S. to Archibald Henderson, 28 August 1932 (North Carolina).

179/37 **tactfully:** G.B.S. to Molly Tompkins, 3 September 1928, *To a Young Actress* p. 129.

180/3 **journalists:** G.B.S. to Gene Tunney, 31 August 1928 (North Carolina).

180/7 **devours us:** G.B.S. to Blanche Patch, 21 April 1929 (Cornell).

180/9 **us!:** Charlotte Shaw to Blanche Patch, 3 May 1929 (Texas).

180/13 **exhausting:** G.B.S. to Mrs Patrick Campbell, 20 May 1929, *Bernard Shaw and Mrs Patrick Campbell: Their Correspondence* p. 283.

180/17   **statements:** Damir Kalogjera, 'A Political Game: Shaw in Yugoslavia', *Shaw Abroad: The Annual of Bernard Shaw Studies* vol. 5 (ed. Rodelle Weintraub 1985) p. 117.

180/36   **ladies:** *Shaw Bulletin* 4 January 1958, p. 1.

180/39   **worse:** G.B.S. to Sydney Cockerell, 6 June 1929, *CL*4 p. 144.

181/12   **would be:** Kalogjera, 'A Political Game: Shaw in Yugoslavia', *Shaw Abroad* p. 117.

181/22   **Dictatorship:** 'Shaw Upholds Dictatorship', *New York American* 24 May 1929, p. 5.

181/28   **anyhow:** Benny Green, *Shaw's Champions: G.B.S. and Prizefighting from Cashel Byron to Gene Tunney* (1978) p. 178.

181/37   **me?:** Ellen Terry to G.B.S., 16 September 1912, *Ellen Terry and Bernard Shaw: A Correspondence* (ed. Christopher St John 1931) pp. 444–5, 451.

182/ 8   **terror?:** G.B.S. to Ellen Terry, 9 November 1913, *CL*3 p. 206.

182/15   **work:** Ellen Terry to G.B.S., 18 March 1911, *A Correspondence* p. 447.

182/26   **concerned:** See Michael Meyer, *Ibsen* (1974 edn) p. 632.

183/ 8   **withdrawn:** G.B.S. to Ellen Terry, 7 January 1918, *CL*3 pp. 524–5 (*A Correspondence* pp. 455–6).

183/12   **published?:** 'A Plea for G.B.S.' p. 5. Annex to Edward Gordon Craig, *Ellen Terry and Her Secret Self* (1931).

183/18   **executors:** G.B.S. to Edward Gordon Craig, 12 April 1929, *CL*4 p. 136.

183/31   **to me:** G.B.S. to Edward Gordon Craig, 7 September 1929, *CL*4 p. 159.

184/ 6   **dislike him:** Ibid., pp. 160–1.

184/ 9   **few more:** 'A Plea for G.B.S.' p. 24.

184/17   **published:** G.B.S. to Elbridge L. Adams, 17 September 1929, *CL*4 p. 162.

184/23   **of it:** Ibid., p. 159.

184/25   **Craig:** 'Gordon Craig and the Shaw–Terry Letters', *Shaw on Theatre* (ed. E. J. West 1958) pp. 206–12.

184/31   **H.I.:** G.B.S. to Edward Gordon Craig, 3 October 1930, *CL*4 p. 203.

185/ 7   **interviews:** Gordon Craig to G.B.S., 1 October 1930.

185/11   **through:** G.B.S. to Edward Gordon Craig, 3 October 1930, *CL*4 pp. 202–3.

185/28   **expense:** 'Gordon Craig and the Shaw–Terry Letters', *Shaw on Theatre* pp. 209–10.

186/ 5   **there:** *The Times* 2 November 1931.

186/16   **forgive me:** 'Gordon Craig and the Shaw–Terry Letters', *Shaw on Theatre* p. 207.

186/20   **harm:** G.B.S. to Edith Craig, 31 October 1931, *CL*4 p. 266.

186/29   **street:** 'A Plea for G.B.S.' p. 24.

186/37   **sense:** G.B.S. to Frank Harris, 7 April 1931, *The Playwright and the Pirate* p. 252.

186/39   **anticlimax:** G.B.S. to Archibald Henderson, 25 December 1931 (North Carolina).

187/ 4   **enough:** Margot Peters, *Mrs Pat* (1984) pp. 416–17.

187/14   **grave!:** Mrs Patrick Campbell to G.B.S., 29 March 1932, *Their Correspondence* p. 298.

187/18   **about it:** G.B.S. to Mrs Patrick Campbell, 16 April 1932, *Their Correspondence* p. 301.

187/23   **senility:** Ibid.

187/25   **mine:** Mrs Patrick Campbell to G.B.S., 12 May 1932, *Their Correspondence* p. 304.

187/26   **decree it:** G.B.S. to Mrs Patrick Campbell, 12 June 1932, *Their Correspondence* p. 306.

187/30   **operation:** G.B.S. to Mrs Patrick Campbell, 11 August 1937, *CL*4 p. 471 (*Their Correspondence* p. 312).

187/32   **read them:** Mrs Patrick Campbell to G.B.S., 25 August 1937, *Their Correspondence* p. 313.

187/34   **good:** G.B.S. to Mrs Patrick Campbell, 18 March 1938, *CL*4 p. 497 (*Their Correspondence* p. 320).

187/last   **amoureuse:** Margot Peters, *Mrs Pat* p. 466.

188/12   **Beech:** *Shaw: An Autobiography: 1898–1950* (ed. Stanley Weintraub 1971) p. 226.

188/21   **Ellen's:** G.B.S. to Mrs Patrick Campbell, 16 April 1932, *Their Correspondence* p. 300.

188/last   *Stella!*: G.B.S. to Mrs Patrick Campbell, 10 June 1931 (Lockwood Memorial Library, Buffalo).

189/Ep.   **of all:** Sean O'Casey to James Joyce, 30 May 1939, *The Letters of Sean O'Casey, 1910–41*, vol. 1 (ed. David Krause 1975) p. 800.

189/10   **end:** G.B.S. to Otto Kyllmann, 31 May 1930 (North Carolina).

189/23   **masterpieces!:** Charlotte Shaw to Nancy Astor, 31 December 1931 (Reading).

189/24   **now:** G.B.S. to Nancy Astor, 23 September 1929 (Reading).

189/25   **digging:** G.B.S. to Otto Kyllmann, 6 January 1925 (Reading).

189/30   **blast it!:** G.B.S. to Kyllmann, 9 July 1930, *CL*4 p. 193.

189/34   **grave:** G.B.S. to Kyllmann, 20 November 1931 (North Carolina).

190/ 2   **last:** G.B.S., 'My Memories of Oscar Wilde', in Frank Harris, *Oscar Wilde: His Life and Confessions* (1918) vol. 2, pp. 7–32 (after the final chapter).

190/11 **life:** Ibid.

190/22 **unassailable:** Ibid.

190/31 **kind:** 'A Batch of Books', *Pall Mall Gazette* 26 July 1888, p. 3. *Bernard Shaw's Book Reviews* (ed. Brian Tyson 1991) pp. 426–30.

191/17 **seriousness:** 'Two New Plays', *Saturday Review* 12 January 1895, *OTN*1 pp. 9–10.

191/22 **instinct:** Oscar Wilde to G.B.S., 9 May 1893, *The Letters of Oscar Wilde* (ed. Rupert Hart-Davis 1962) p. 339.

191/23 **refreshing:** Oscar Wilde to G.B.S., 23 February 1893, *The Letters of Oscar Wilde* p. 332.

191/28 **friends:** Ibid.

191/31 **occasion:** 'My Memories of Oscar Wilde', vide supra.

191/38 **told them:** Ibid.

192/ 5 **play:** Ibid.

192/10 **than he:** Ibid.

192/17 **good:** *The Letters of Oscar Wilde* p. 789n.

192/32 **language:** 'Two Plays', *Saturday Review* 17 October 1896, *OTN*2 p. 217.

192/37 **School:** Oscar Wilde to G.B.S., 9 May 1893, *The Letters of Oscar Wilde* p. 339.

193/ 4 **De Profundis:** Bernard Shaw, 'Oscar Wilde', *Neue Freie Presse*, 23 April 1905. See *The Matter with Ireland* (ed. with an introduction by David H. Greene and Dan H. Laurence 1962) p. 29.

193/13 **rejoicing:** G.B.S. to David Manderson, 2 December 1938. See *Dear Mr Shaw: Selections from Bernard Shaw's postbag* (compiled and ed. Vivian Elliot 1987) p. 126.

193/33 **drama:** 'My Memories of Oscar Wilde'.

193/39 **himself?:** G.B.S. to Alfred Douglas, 29 May 1931, *Bernard Shaw and Alfred Douglas: A Correspondence* (ed. Mary Hyde 1982) p. 8.

194/ 8 **fathom:** W. B. Yeats, *Autobiographies* (1979) pp. 133–4.

194/17 **results:** W. B. Yeats to Dorothy Wellesley, 23 December 1936, *The Letters of W. B. Yeats* (ed. Allan Wade 1954) p. 876.

194/19 **movement:** 'Preface for Politicians', *CP*2 p. 808.

194/21 **me:** *Irish Renaissance: A Gathering of Essays, Memoirs and Letters from 'The Massachusetts Review'* (ed. Robin Skelton and David R. Clark, Dolmen Press 1965) p. 25.

194/26 **praise:** W. B. Yeats, *Autobiographies* p. 284.

194/28 **question:** Joseph Hone, *W. B. Yeats: 1865–1939* (1965 edn) p. 236.

194/30 **indispensable:** W. B. Yeats to T. Sturge Moore, 25 April

[1911], *W. B. Yeats and T. Sturge Moore: Their Correspondence 1901–37* (ed. Ursula Bridge 1953) p. 19.

194/32   **hands:** W. B. Yeats, *Memoirs* (ed. Denis Donoghue 1972) p. 195.

194/34   **air:** *Yeats and the Theatre* (ed. Robert O'Driscoll and Lorna Reynolds 1975) p. 42.

195/ 2   **corridor:** W. B. Yeats to George Russell, 1 July 1921, *The Letters of W. B. Yeats* p. 671.

195/ 7   **commonplace:** G.B.S. to Stephen Gwynn, 28 August 1940, *CL*4 pp. 576–7.

195/14   **throat:** 'A Coat', from *The Collected Poems of W. B. Yeats* (1971 edn) p. 142.

195/20   **raiser:** 'An Explanatory Word from Mr. Shaw', *Florence Farr, Bernard Shaw and W. B. Yeats* (ed. Clifford Bax 1946) p. ix.

195/34   **at Coole:** G.B.S. to Stephen Gwynn, 28 August 1940, *CL*4 p. 577.

195/38   **him:** Ibid.

196/ 6   **intrude:** Ibid., pp. 576–7.

196/11   **there:** 'Politics', in *The Collected Poems of W. B. Yeats* pp. 392–3.

196/29   **circumstance:** W. B. Yeats, *A Vision* (1981 edn) p. 157.

197/12   **nonsense:** G.B.S. to W. B. Yeats, 20 September 1932, *CL*4 pp. 308–9.

197/25   **writers:** *The Letters of W. B. Yeats* pp. 801–2.

198/ 5   **met:** James Joyce to W. B. Yeats, 5 October 1932, *Selected Letters of James Joyce* (ed. Richard Ellmann 1975) p. 365.

198/ 8   **poetry:** 'G.B.S. Was Not Disgusted', *Picture Post* 3 June 1939 p. 61.

198/10   **quality:** Archibald Henderson, *Table-Talk of G.B.S.: Conversations on Things in General between George Bernard Shaw and his Biographer* (1925) pp. 130, 129.

198/12   **enthusiasm:** 'G.B.S. Was Not Disgusted', *Picture Post* 3 June 1939, p. 61.

198/20   *daimon:* *Table-Talk of G.B.S.* pp. 132–4.

198/28   **countrymen:** G.B.S. to Sylvia Beach, 11 June 1921, *CL*3 p. 719.

198/31   **themselves:** G.B.S. to Ezra Pound, 8 and 16 March 1922, *CL*3 pp. 764, 766.

198/37   **countrymen:** See *James Joyce Quarterly* Winter 1986.

198/38   **us:** Humphrey Carpenter, *A Serious Character: The Life of Ezra Pound* (1988) p. 114.

198/39   **I have:** William Hall, 'Shaw on the Joyce He Scarcely Read', *Shaw Bulletin* September 1954, p. 19.

199/ 4   **informed:** Richard Ellmann, *James Joyce* (1965) p. 791.

199/11   **obscene:** *Shaw: An Exhibit*, item no. 612 (Texas).

199/17   **G.B.S.:** 'George Bernard Shaw, the Stage Society and *Exiles*', *James Joyce: The Critical Heritage*, vol. 1, *1902–1927* (ed. Robert H. Deming 1970) pp. 130–1.

199/31   **playwrighting:** 'James Joyce on *Blanco Posnet* and Shaw the Preacher', *Shaw: The Critical Heritage* (ed. T. F. Evans 1976) p. 199.

199/36   **world:** G.B.S. to Ezra Pound, 24 March 1922, *CL3* p. 767.

200/ 2   **worth:** G.B.S. to Malachi Leonard, March 1948 (Bucknell).

200/ 3   **arrows:** G.B.S. to anon., 13 November 1949. See William White, 'Irish Antitheses: Shaw and Joyce', *The Shavian* February 1961, p. 34.

200/12   **action:** A. M. Gibbs, 'Yeats, Shaw and Unity of Culture', *Southern Review* September 1973, pp. 189–203.

200/16   **Shaw:** Stanislas Joyce, *My Brother's Keeper: James Joyce's Early Years* (1958) p. 114.

200/20   **townsman:** James Joyce to G.B.S., 26 November 1926, *Selected Letters of James Joyce* p. 318.

200/25   **Candidately:** Stanley Weintraub, 'A Respectful Distance: James Joyce and His Dublin Townsman Bernard Shaw', *Journal of Modern Literature* March 1986, pp. 61–75.

200/27   **else:** Sean O'Casey to the Irish Academy of Letters, 11 October 1932, *The Letters of Sean O'Casey* vol. 1, p. 452.

201/Ep.   **first:** 'Bernard Shaw by H. G. Wells', *Daily Express* 3 November 1950.

201/ 5   **Abbey:** Janet Dunbar, *Mrs G.B.S.: A Biographical Portrait of Charlotte Shaw* (1965) p. 294.

201/ 9   **prose:** 'Tributes', *Daily News* 12 January 1928, p. 7.

201/18   **Evolutionist:** Preface to *Heartbreak House*, *CP5* p. 15.

201/27   **epoch:** G.B.S. to Arthur Hadley, 14 November 1918, *CL3* p. 572.

201/32   **to it:** 'Hardy Knew: Mr Bernard Shaw and Westminster Abbey Burial', *Daily News* 17 January 1928, p. 6.

202/ 3   **ashes:** Ibid.

202/ 7   **clothes:** G.B.S. to Mrs Patrick Campbell, 14 January 1928, *Their Correspondence* p. 263.

202/11   **perfectly:** Janet Dunbar, *Mrs G.B.S.* pp. 294–5.

202/18   **thought:** Ibid.

202/20   **head:** G.B.S. to Henry Salt, 20 January 1928, quoted in *CL4* p. 84.

202/26   **material:** Winifred Gérin to Michael Holroyd, 6 February 1980.

202/38   **broken:** Janet Dunbar, *Mrs G.B.S.* p. 295.

203/ 5   **passed him:** G.B.S. to Florence Emily Hardy, 16 January
          1928, *CL*4 p. 84.
203/ 8   **know of:** 'Tributes', *Daily News* 12 January 1928, p. 7.
203/16   *you*: G.B.S. to Florence Emily Hardy, 16 January 1925, *CL*4
          pp. 84–5.
203/28   **Scott:** 'Rudyard Kipling', *The Times* 20 January 1936, p. 19.
203/30   **shortly:** '"One of Those Curious People" – G.B.S.', *Daily
          Herald* 26 December 1935, p. 2.
203/37   **children:** 'The Unhappy Years of Barrie', *Sunday Graphic and
          Sunday News* 20 June 1937, p. 5.
203/last **soul:** Ibid.
204/ 3   **better:** 'Bernard Shaw Pays Tribute to His Friend Barrie',
          Sunday Pictorial 20 June 1937, p. 6.
204/13   **stone:** 'What About the Abbey? Bernard Shaw on What Nation
          Owes to [T. E.] Lawrence', *Natal Mercury* 20 May 1935, p. 9.
          See also 'What about Westminster Abbey', *New York Times* 20
          May 1935, p. 10.
204/32   **about it:** Charlotte Shaw to Dorothy ('Dolly') Walker, 24 June
          1935 (Texas).
204/354   **known:** Charlotte Shaw to H. G. Wells, 30 May 1927. See
          *CL*4 pp. 53–4.
204/38   **blast it!:** G.B.S. to H. G. Wells, 30 May 1927, *CL*4 pp. 54–5.
205/10   **distressed:** G.B.S. to Beatrice Webb, 13 July 1927 [misdated
          1924] (LSE).
205/28   **brief:** G.B.S. to H. G. Wells, 4 August 1927, *CL*4 p. 60.
205/34   **angry:** Charlotte Shaw to H. G. Wells, 1 September 1927. See
          *CL*4 pp. 60–1.
205/38   **meet:** Charlotte Shaw to H. G. Wells, 16 September 1927
          (Illinois).
206/ 5   **let go:** Janet Dunbar, *Mrs G.B.S.* p. 288.
206/ 8   **done:** *Arnold Bennett: The Journals* (ed. Frank Swinnerton,
          Penguin 1984), entry Monday 10 October 1927, p. 543.
206/10   **ceremonies:** Virginia Woolf to Vita Sackville-West, 9 October
          1927, *A Change of Perspective: The Letters of Virginia Woolf*, vol.
          3: *1923–1928* (ed. Nigel Nicolson 1977) p. 428.
206/14   **precious:** *The Diary of Virginia Woolf* vol. 3: *1925–1930* (ed.
          Anne Olivier Bell 1980), entry 22 October 1927, p. 164.
206/23   **howled:** Janet Dunbar, *Mrs G.B.S.* pp. 288–9.
206/31   **for it:** *H. G. Wells in Love* (ed. G. P. Wells 1984) p. 46.
207/ 3   **his due:** *The Diary of Virginia Woolf* vol. 3, p. 164.
207/ 6   **remote:** Janet Dunbar, *Mrs G.B.S.* p. 289.
207/ 9   **splendid:** *The Diary of Virginia Woolf* vol. 3, p. 164.
207/12   **him:** Janet Dunbar, *Mrs G.B.S.* p. 289.

207/15   **death:** H. G. Wells to R. D. Lawrence, 1 August 1943.

207/21   **help you:** Charlotte Shaw to G.B.S., 1 September 1927, *CL4* pp. 60–1.

207/24   **assassinated:** G.B.S. to H. G. Wells, 4 August 1927, *CL4* p. 60.

207/27   **prayer:** Wells to G.B.S., 1 June 1936 and 30 July 1929, BL Add. MS 50552 ff. 64–64v, 53.

207/35   **excessive:** Wells to G.B.S., 9 June 1928, BL Add. MS 50552 ff. 50–50v.

207/36   **to you:** Wells to Charlotte Shaw, 28 November 1934 (copy privately owned).

207/39   **grave:** St John Ervine, *Bernard Shaw: His Life, Work and Friends* (1956) p. 594.

207/last   **environment:** Wells to G.B.S., 22 April 1941, BL Add. MS 50552 ff. 65–66.

208/ 6   **activities:** *H. G. Wells in Love* p. 122.

208/12   **cancer:** 'Bernard Shaw by H. G. Wells', *Daily Express* 3 November 1950.

208/17   **world:** Ibid.

208/21   **deserted him:** Benny Green, *Shaw's Champions* pp. 187–8.

208/33   **generation:** Ibid., p. 160.

208/36   **greatest:** Ibid., p. 154.

209/10   **win:** G.B.S. to Norman Clark, 21 February 1929, *CL4* pp. 130–1.

209/23   **like:** 'G. B. Shaw Answers Tunney's Criticism', *New York Times* 22 November 1926, p. 6.

209/26   **man:** *Colliers Magazine* 23 June 1951.

209/33   **happiness:** Frederick L. Allen, *Only Yesterday* (1931) p. 149.

210/ 5   **master:** Charlotte Shaw to Lady Astor, 23 April 1929 (Reading).

210/ 8   **you:** G.B.S. to Nancy Astor, 13 April 1929, *CL4* p. 137.

210/22   **splendid:** Blanche Patch, *Thirty Years with G.B.S.* p. 154.

210/26   **dialogue:** Green, *Shaw's Champions* p. 180.

210/28   **ground:** Stephen Winsten, *Shaw's Corner* (1952) p. 195.

210/33   **life:** Gene Tunney to Elmer Gertz, 31 August 1956 (Library of Congress, Washington).

210/last   **aesthetic:** S. N. Behrman, *Conversations with Max* (1960) pp. 179–80.

211/ 3   **thesis:** *Shaw's Champions* p. 186.

211/ 4   **myself:** *Colliers Magazine* 23 June 1951.

211/12   **dead:** *Shaw's Champions* p. 183.

211/15   **rush:** Ibid.

211/20   **him then:** *Colliers Magazine* 23 June 1951.

211 / 26   **line:** *Shaw's Champions* p. 187.

211 / 28   **journey:** *Colliers Magazine* 23 June 1951.

211 / 35   **profession:** *Shaw's Champions* p. 188.

211 / 38   **known:** Gene Tunney to D. Felicitas Corrigan, 24 February
1955 (Cornell).

212 / 7   **ever:** D. Felicitas Corrigan, *The Nun, the Infidel and the
Superman* (1985) p. 83.

212 / 28   **touched:** Sydney Cockerell to Laurentia McLachlan, April
1907, Corrigan, *The Nun, the Infidel and the Superman* p. 45.

212 / 30   **fully:** Laurentia McLachlan to Sydney Cockerell, n.d. [c. April
1907], *The Nun, the Infidel and the Superman* p. 56.

212 / 35   **lies:** Ibid.

212 / 38   **meet:** Sydney Cockerell to Laurentia McLachlan, n.d., *The
Nun, the Infidel and the Superman* p. 85.

213 / 5   **one!:** Laurentia McLachlan to Sydney Cockerell, n.d. [1907],
The Nun, the Infidel and the Superman p. 84.

213 / 10   **them:** Sydney Cockerell to Laurentia McLachlan, n.d. [April
1924], *The Nun, the Infidel and the Superman* p. 87.

213 / 15   **please me:** Laurentia McLachlan to Sydney Cockerell, 15
April 1924, *The Nun, the Infidel and the Superman* p. 88.

213 / 20   **see you:** Charlotte Shaw to Laurentia McLachlan, 23 April
1924, *The Nun, the Infidel and the Superman* p. 88.

213 / 32   **really:** Janet Dunbar, *Mrs G.B.S.* p. 295.

213 / 29   **Abbey:** Charlotte Shaw to Nancy Astor, 22 August 1929
(Reading).

214 / 3   **Morris:** *The Nun, the Infidel and the Superman* pp. 96–7.

214 / 17   **lands:** G.B.S. to Laurentia McLachlan, 23 December 1924,
*CL*3 p. 897.

214 / 16   **heresies:** Laurentia McLachlan to Sydney Cockerell, 2 January
1925, *The Nun, the Infidel and the Superman* p. 92.

214 / 18   **ease:** G.B.S. to Laurentia McLachlan, 23 December 1924,
*CL*3 p. 897.

214 / 21   **him:** Laurentia McLachlan to Sydney Cockerell, 3 November
1924, *The Nun, the Infidel and the Superman* p. 91.

214 / 23   **simplicity:** *The Nun, the Infidel and the Superman* p. 89.

214 / 25   **man:** Laurentia McLachlan to Sydney Cockerell, n.d. [April
1924], *The Nun, the Infidel and the Superman* p. 89.

214 / 29   **can be:** G.B.S. to Laurentia McLachlan, 17 August 1948, *The
Nun, the Infidel and the Superman* p. 143.

214 / 33   **kind:** Laurentia McLachlan to G.B.S., 24 January 1935, BL
Add. MS 50543 f. 43.

214 / 36   **of them:** G.B.S. to Laurentia McLachlan, 23 December 1924,
The Nun, the Infidel and the Superman p. 95 (*CL*3 p. 898).

214/39   **sensuality:** *The Best of Friends* (ed. Viola Meynell 1956) p. 38.
214/last   **practised:** Preface to Stephen Winsten, *Salt and His Circle*
           (1951) p. 14.
215/ 2   **about it:** G.B.S. to Laurentia McLachlan, 4 September 1944,
           *CL*4 p. 723.
215/ 5   **himself:** *The Nun, the Infidel and the Superman* p. 97.
215/14   **earnestly:** Laurentia McLachlan to G.B.S., 12 October 1931,
           BL Add. MS 50543 f. 37.
215/21   **you...:** G.B.S. to Laurentia McLachlan, 23 December 1924,
           The Nun, the Infidel and the Superman p. 95 (*CL*3 p. 898).
215/28   **that:** Laurentia McLachlan to G.B.S., 24 January 1935, BL
           Add. MS 50543 f. 43.
215/32   **would be:** Laurentia McLachlan to G.B.S., 9 September 1935,
           The Nun, the Infidel and the Superman p. 141.
216/ 2   **I can:** *The Nun, the Infidel and the Superman* p. 90.
216/ 4   **salvation:** Ibid.
216/16   **Calvary:** Laurentia McLachlan to G.B.S., 1 March 1931, *The
           Nun, the Infidel and the Superman* p. 99.
216/18   **army:** G.B.S. to Sydney Cockerell, 13 March 1931, *CL*4
           p. 229.
216/29   **self:** G.B.S. to Laurentia McLachlan, 17 March 1931, *CL*4
           p. 234.
216/37   **enough?:** G.B.S. to Laurentia McLachlan, 25 October 1931,
           *CL*4 pp. 264–5.
217/16   **like it:** G.B.S. to Laurentia McLachlan, 17 March 1931, *CL*4
           pp. 231–2.
217/20   **Stanbrook:** Laurentia McLachlan to G.B.S., 18 April 1931,
           The Nun, the Infidel and the Superman p. 109.
217/26   **smallmindedness:** G.B.S. to Alfred Douglas, 25 April 1938,
           *CL*4 p. 500 (*Bernard Shaw and Alfred Douglas: A
           Correspondence* p. 37).
217/34   **manner:** *CP*5 p. 278.
218/ 3   **merriment:** *CP*6 p. 68.
218/20   **humanity:** G.B.S., 'Foundation Oration', delivered before the
           Union Society of University College, London, 18 March
           1920. See *Platform and Pulpit* p. 161.
218/26   **thought:** *The Times* 7 November 1920. Quoted in Ronald W.
           Clark, *Einstein: The Life and Times* (1971) p. 231. See also *The
           Times* 15 November 1920.
218/31   **study:** *CP*5 p. 594.
218/33   **intelligence:** Desmond J. McRory, 'Why Shaw Liked
           Einstein', thesis, Penn State University. See also Desmond J.
           McRory, 'Shaw, Einstein and Physics', *Annual of Shaw
           Studies*, vol. 6, 1986, pp. 33–67.

218/36   **hopeful:** Ibid.
218/last   **Einstein:** *CP*6 pp. 499–500.
219/13   **Tensors:** Archibald Henderson, *Bernard Shaw: Man of the Century* (1956) p. 766.
219/18   **form:** Archibald Henderson, *Table-Talk of G.B.S.* pp. 135–6.
219/23   **physicists:** Ibid., p. 139.
219/26   **of us:** *Die Literarische Welt* 23 July 1926. See *CL*4 p. 29.
219/31   **influence:** Einstein to Wolff, 16 January 1929 (Seeley G. Mudd Library, Princeton University, Einstein Duplicate Archive. Correspondence folder box 45 33–248), translated by Desmond J. McRory.
219/38   **guilty of:** 'Religion and Science', 28 October 1930, *The Religious Speeches of Bernard Shaw* (ed. Warren Sylvester Smith 1963) p. 82.
220/ 3   **born!:** BBC Archives 921-SHA.
220/13   **solitude:** Ibid.
220/22   **them:** Ibid.
220/28   **world:** G.B.S. to Albert Einstein, 2 December 1924. Quoted in Desmond J. McRory, 'Shaw, Einstein and Physics'.
220/last   **life:** BBC Archives 921-SHA.

CHAPTER IV

221/Ep. 1   **Catholicism:** D. Felicitas Corrigan, *The Nun, the Infidel and the Superman* (1985) p. 111.
221/Ep. 2   **race:** G.B.S., 'Common Sense About the War', *New Statesman*, Supplement 14 November 1914, *What I Really Wrote about the War* (1931) p. 103.
221/12   **many ways:** G.B.S. to Frank Harris, 30 March 1917, *CL*3 p. 463 (*The Playwright and the Pirate: Bernard Shaw and Frank Harris*, ed. Stanley Weintraub 1977, p. 69).
221/21   **Tolstoy:** G.B.S. to Gilbert Murray, 5 November 1914, *CL*3 p. 261.
221/24   **life:** 'Common Sense About the War', *What I Really Wrote about the War* p. 82.
221/27   **Europe:** 'Assure New Russia of British Regard', *New York Times* 1 April 1917, p. 3.
221/30   **nineteenth:** G.B.S. to Maxim Gorki, 28 December 1915, *CL*3 p. 342.
222/ 7   **pence:** 'The Dictatorship of the Proletariat', *Labour Monthly* October 1921, *Practical Politics: Twentieth-Century Views on Politics and Economics* (ed. Lloyd J. Hubenka 1976) p. 177.

222/ 9 **boast of:** See James Hulse, *Revolutionists in London* (1970) p. 208.

222/13 **England:** 'Assure New Russia of British Regard', *New York Times* 1 April 1917, p. 3.

222/18 **war:** G.B.S. to Maxim Gorki, 24 May 1917, *CL3* p. 474.

222/29 **alive:** Ronald W. Clark, *The Life of Bertrand Russell* (1978 edn) pp. 395–6.

222/33 **fraternity:** Leonard Woolf, *Beginning Again* (1964 edn) p. 207.

222/37 **years:** 'G.B.S. and "World of Fools",' *Daily Herald* 15 May 1922, p. 5.

223/ 9 **process:** *The Clarion* 21 October 1904.

223/18 **sound:** Woolf, *Beginning Again* p. 214.

223/22 **to him:** William Gerhardie, *Memoirs of a Polyglot* (1931 edn) pp. 127–8.

223/33 **important:** 'Socialism and the Labor Party', *Christian Commonwealth*, Supplement 6 February 1920. See *Practical Politics* p. 157.

223/38 **in Russia:** David Caute, *The Fellow Travellers: Intellectual Friends of Communism* (1988 edn) p. 220.

224/ 6 **writer:** Friedrich Engels, *Briefwechsel mit Karl Kautsky* (1955) p. 362.

224/ 7 **Europe:** See *Labour Monthly*, Pamphlet I, 1951 series, p. 14.

224/16 **conviction:** *Practical Politics* p. 165.

224/19 **again:** Ibid., p. 160.

224/32 **dread:** Ibid., p. 165.

224/last **bedevilling:** Ibid., p. 158.

225/ 9 **not wait:** Ibid.

225/14 **Capitalism:** Ibid., p. 178.

225/21 **Utopias:** Preface to Sidney and Beatrice Webb, *The Truth about Soviet Russia* (1942) p. 9.

225/26 **system:** *Practical Politics* pp. 168, 169.

225/37 **Hohenzollern:** 'Russia's Interest in the Work', *Manchester Guardian* (Russian supplement) 7 July 1917, p. 28.

226/ 7 **art:** G.B.S. to John Farleigh, 6 July 1932, *CL4* p. 300.

226/ 9 **Europe:** 'The Dictatorship of the Proletariat', *Practical Politics* p. 157.

226/12 **quality:** G.B.S. to Siegfried Trebitsch, 2 October 1921, Shaw/Trebitsch letters p. 226.

226/15 **terrors:** 'Vernon Lee's War Trilogy', *The Nation* 18 September 1920. See *Pen Portraits and Reviews* (1931) p. 185.

226/20 **what not:** G.B.S. to Boris Lebedeff, n.d. [assigned to 22 November 1920], *CL3* p. 702.

226/24 **conversation:** Winston Churchill, *Great Contemporaries* (1937) p. 47.

226 / 28   **Socialism:** Ibid.

226 / 34   **world:** Ibid., p. 57.

226 / 36   **scoundrel:** 'Maxims for Revolutionists', *CP2* p. 795.

227 / 3   **dreaded:** G.B.S. to Winston Churchill, n.d. [August 1946], *CL4* p. 778.

227 / 9   **truth:** Manfred Weidhorn, 'Churchill and the British Literary Intelligentsia', *Shaw: The Annual of Bernard Shaw Studies* vol. 8 (ed. Stanley Weintraub 1988) p. 122.

227 / 26   **wounded men:** Churchill, *Great Contemporaries* pp. 56–7.

227 / 30   **clown:** Weidhorn in *Shaw Studies* vol. 8, p. 122.

227 / 34   **seriously:** *Great Contemporaries* p. 52.

227 / 38   **shot:** G.B.S. to John Reith, 2 May 1932, *CL4* p. 290.

227 / 39   **solicitors:** G.B.S. to H. G. Wells, 19 March 1932, *CL4* p. 279.

228 / 28   **Winston:** 'The Socialist Fraud. Bernard Shaw Replies to Winston Churchill', *Sunday Chronicle* 13 April 1924, pp. 1–2.

228 / 30   **ear:** David Caute, *The Fellow Travellers* p. 242.

228 / 34   **afraid of:** David Dunn, 'Shaw's Russia', unpublished LSE thesis, pp. 96, 100.

228 / 37   **gentlemen:** 'Socialism and the Labor Party', *Practical Politics*, p. 161.

229 / 2   **Capitalists:** 'Shaw's Russia', pp. 162, 164.

229 / 6   **abuse:** *New York American* 30 September 1919.

229 / 10   **side:** Hesketh Pearson, *Bernard Shaw* (1975 edn) p. 377.

229 / 14   **name:** 'What Indeed?' Lecture delivered at Kingsway Hall, 26 November 1931, *Practical Politics* pp. 211–13.

229 / 26   **boy:** G.B.S. to Huntly Carter, 13 June 1935, BL Add. MS 50521 f. 77.

229 / 38   **indescribable:** *IWC* pp. 466, 468.

230 / 6   **gradualism:** *Practical Politics* p. 219.

230 / 17   **shooting:** *IWG* p. 472.

230 / 23   **peasant's hands:** 'What Indeed?', *Practical Politics* pp. 213–14.

230 / 29   **stop them:** Ibid., p. 232.

230 / 37   **breath:** Leonard Woolf, *International Government* (Brentano, New York, 1916) p. xv. Shaw's Introduction also appears in the 1923 English edition (Allen & Unwin).

230 / 40   **in it:** G.B.S. to Boris Lebedeff, n.d. [assigned to 22 November 1920], *CL3* p. 703.

231 / 2   **problem:** G.B.S. to Henri Barbusse, 4 May 1932, *CL4* p. 292.

231 / 14   **itself:** 'Western Writers about Lenin: Lenin and George Washington (conversation with Bernard Shaw)', *Izvestia* 29 January 1924.

231 / 16   **misunderstandings:** Ibid.

231 / 18   **Moscow:** 'Shaw's Russia', p. 115.

231 / 25   **Labour:** Ibid., p. 106.

231 / 36   **ordinarily:** G.B.S. to Rutland Boughton, 1 July 1928, *CL*4
p. 103.

232 / 3   **Revolution:** G.B.S. to Ramsay MacDonald, 11 November
1925, *CL*3 pp. 915–16.

232 / 5   **notions:** G.B.S. to Charles Sarolea, 19 August 1922, *CL*3
p. 783.

232 / 9   **lunatics:** 'G.B.S. and "World of Fools"', *Daily Herald* 15 May
1922, p. 5.

232 / 14   **consummated:** *New York Times* 14 September 1924.

232 / 24   **competently:** G.B.S. to H. G. Wells, 19 March 1932, *CL*4
p. 279.

232 / 30   **clay:** 'The Dictatorship of the Proletariat', *Practical Politics*
p. 175.

232 / 39   **success:** 'Rebuilding Babel', *The Times* 30 August 1948, p. 5,
Bernard Shaw: Agitations: Letters to the Press 1875–1950 (ed.
Dan H. Laurence and James Rambeau 1985) p. 348.

232 / 40   **presence:** 'Bernard Shaw on Trotsky', *Daily Herald* 26 July
1929, p. 1.

233 / 7   **bourgeois:** G.B.S. to Charles Sarolea, 19 August 1922, *CL*3
p. 782.

233 / 12   **Communism:** G.B.S. to Rutland Boughton, 5 July 1928, *CL*4
p. 104.

233 / 17   **at all:** G.B.S. to Horace Plunkett, 16 July 1931, *CL*4 p. 242.

233 / 21   **rails:** Hesketh Pearson, *Bernard Shaw* pp. 379–80.

233 / 26   **back:** G.B.S. to Horace Plunkett, 16 July 1931, *CL*4 pp. 242–3.

233 / 27   **kill you?:** T. E. Lawrence to Charlotte Shaw, 20 April 1931,
BL Add. MS 45904 f. 144.

233 / 29   **Paris:** G.B.S. to Horace Plunkett, 16 July 1931, *CL*4 p. 242.

233 / 34   **can!:** Charlotte Shaw to Nancy Astor, 28 June 1931 (Reading).

234 / 11   **Moscow:** A. M. Findersley, travel agent, to G.B.S., 7 July
1931, BL Add. MS 50520 f. 80.

234 / 21   **in Moscow:** G.B.S. to Waldorf Astor, 27 June 1931, *CL*4
p. 239.

234 / 34   **so long:** *Shaw: An Autobiography 1898–1950: The Playwright
Years* (selected from his writings by Stanley Weintraub 1971)
p. 193.

235 / 7   **cultivates:** Ibid.

235 / 14   **civilization:** Ibid., pp. 193–4.

235 / 32   **Russia:** Ibid., p. 194.

235 / 37   **Pickford:** Christopher Sykes, *Nancy: The Life of Lady Astor*
(1979 edn) p. 384.

236 / 1   **clubs:** G.B.S., *The Rationalization of Russia* (ed. with an
Introduction by Harry M. Geduld 1964) p. 81.

236/11   **blood:** Caterina Andrassy, 'G.B.S. in Moscow', *New Statesman* 3 March 1951, p. 241.
236/20   **Scotsman:** Quoted in A. L. Tait, 'George Bernard Shaw and the USSR', *Irish Slavonic Studies* (Belfast) no. 5, 1984, p. 90.
236/22   **altogether:** Ibid.
236/23   **cameras:** G.B.S. to Charlotte Shaw, 21 July 1931, *CL*4 p. 246.
236/29   **man!:** *New York Times* 22 July 1931, p. 23.
236/31   **people:** Quoted in Christopher Sykes, *Nancy* pp. 384, 383.
236/36   **wins:** 'Shaw's Russia', p. 204.
236/40   **speed:** G.B.S. to Charlotte Shaw, 21 July 1931, *CL*4 p. 246.
237/ 5   **gallery:** Ibid.
237/14   **myself:** *Shaw: An Autobiography 1898–1950* pp. 197–8.
237/19   **everyday:** G.B.S. to Charlotte Shaw, 21 and 23 July 1931, *CL*4 pp. 246–7, 250.
237/33   **Wells:** Quoted in *Irish Slavonic Studies* (Belfast) no. 5, 1984, pp. 85–6.
238/13   **west:** 'Bernard Shaw – Our Guest', *Izvestia* 21 July 1931, p. 2, cols 6, 7 and 8. Translated by Olivia Lichtenstein.
238/18   **say:** Caterina Andrassy, 'G.B.S. in Moscow', *New Statesman* 3 March 1951.
238/22   **sentences:** G.B.S. to Frederick Wheeler [1936]. Quoted in *New Statesman* 17 March 1951.
238/26   **unemployed:** Christopher Sykes, *Nancy* p. 387.
238/29   **process:** G.B.S. to Waldorf Astor, 27 June 1931, *CL*4 p. 239.
238/37   **country:** 'Touring in Russia', *Nash's (and Pall Mall) Magazine* February 1932, p. 19. See *Shaw: An Autobiography 1898–1950* pp. 192–204.
238/40   **questions:** G.B.S. to Charlotte Shaw, 23 July 1931, *CL*4 p. 249.
239/ 9   **prigs:** *Shaw: An Autobiography 1898–1950* p. 201.
239/15   **Russians:** 'Shaw in Moscow', *American Mercury* XXV, 1932, p. 348. See Dunn, 'Shaw's Russia' thesis.
239/20   EASY: *The Evening Moscow* 24 July 1931. The USSR Central State Archive of Literature and Art, fund no. 562, Inventory no. 1, storage unit no. 744. Shaw's writing is reproduced in facsimile.
239/23   **odd:** Quoted in A. L. Tait's 'George Bernard Shaw and the USSR', *Irish Slavonic Studies* (Belfast) no. 5, 1984, p. 99.
239/25   **terrible:** 'Shaw in Moscow', *American Mercury* XXV, 1932, p. 345.
239/30   **them:** G.B.S. to Charlotte Shaw, 22 July 1931, *CL*4 p. 248.
239/35   **South Pole:** Ibid.
239/36   **under-trammed:** *Shaw: An Autobiography 1898–1950* pp. 194–5.

240/ 4   **mobs:** 'Touring in Russia', *Nash's (and Pall Mall) Magazine*
           January 1932, p. 9.

240/ 9   **existence:** G.B.S. to Fenner Brockway, 3 April 1929, *CL4*
           p. 132.

240/13   **Philadelphia:** *Shaw: An Autobiography 1898–1950* p. 198.

240/15   **tramping:** G.B.S. to Charlotte Shaw, 24 July 1931, *CL4*
           p. 251.

240/20   **flowers:** *CP6* p. 183.

240/26   **count:** Maxim Gorki, 75th birthday greeting to G.B.S., 26 July
           1931, *CL4* p. 254.

240/30   **things:** *The Rationalization of Russia* p. 71. See also *Shaw: An
           Autobiography 1898–1950* p. 199.

240/38   **Lenin:** Ibid.

240/last   **them:** Ibid.

241/ 4   **applause:** G.B.S. to Charlotte Shaw, 23 July 1931, *CL4* p. 249.

241/ 5   **of me:** G.B.S. to Charlotte Shaw, 27 July 1931, *CL4* p. 254.

241/ 6   **inch:** G.B.S. to Charlotte Shaw, 22 July 1931, *CL4* p. 248.

241/ 8   **Opera:** Ibid., p. 247.

241/13   **Horrid!:** Ibid., p. 248.

241/17   **state:** *New York Times* 27 July 1931, p. 8.

241/23   **here:** *New Statesman* 3 March 1951, p. 338.

241/31   **Litvinov:** Ibid., p. 337.

241/33   **telegrams:** G.B.S. to Charlotte Shaw, 24 July 1931, *CL4*
           p. 251.

241/39   **jurisdiction:** Eugene Lyons, *Assignment in Utopia* (1938)
           pp. 431–2.

242/ 1   **Russia:** G.B.S. to Nancy Astor, 2 September 1931, *CL4*
           p. 260.

242/10   **America:** Christopher Sykes, *Nancy* p. 389.

242/17   **horrors:** G.B.S. to Charlotte Shaw, 24 July 1931, *CL4* p. 251.

242/last   **Shaw:** G.B.S. to William Gerhardie, 11 August 1938, *CL4*
           p. 506.

243/17   **dynamite:** G.B.S. to Robert Fraser, 5 August 1933 (Cornell).

243/19   **revolution:** Lewis A. Coser, *Men of Ideas* (1965) p. 239.

243/38   **values:** Beatrice Webb to Lord Haldane, 11 November 1926,
           The Letters of Sidney and Beatrice Webb (ed. Norman
           MacKenzie 1978) vol. 3, p. 272.

244/ 3   **fail:** 'Soviet Leads in World Race, Says Shaw, Back in
           England', *New York American* 3 August 1931, p. 7.

244/11   **gentleman:** 'Shaw in Moscow', *American Mercury* XXV, 1932,
           p. 350.

244/22   **cardinal:** G.B.S., *The Rationalization of Russia* p. 81.

244/27   **innocence:** G.B.S. to Mary Catharine Inge, 18 January 1938,
           CL4 p. 488.

244/37   **whirlwind:** Hesketh Pearson, *Bernard Shaw* (1975 edn) p. 385.

244/last   **credulity:** 'Shaw in Moscow', *American Mercury* XXV, 1932, p. 350.

245/10   **comradeship:** Winston Churchill, *Great Contemporaries* pp. 54–5.

245/15   **perdition:** G.B.S. to Augustin Hamon, 8 January 1932, *CL4* p. 269.

245/20   **cobbler:** *The Rationalization of Russia* p. 81.

245/37   **Pope:** See Allan Chappelow, *Shaw – 'The Chucker-Out': A Biographical Exposition and Critique* (1969) p. 211.

246/19   **friends:** Quoted in Dunn, 'Shaw's Russia', pp. 228–30. See also, for a slightly different version, *Platform and Pulpit* (ed. Dan H. Laurence 1962) pp. 216–18.

246/25   **met:** *Irish Slavonic Studies* (Belfast) no. 5, 1984, p. 87.

246/31   **press:** Ibid., p. 105.

247/11   **surrounded us:** G.B.S.'s Moscow speech delivered 26 July 1931. See *CL4* p. 256.

247/18   **earth:** Ibid., pp. 256–7.

247/20   **vulgarly:** G.B.S. to Charlotte Shaw, 27 July 1931, *CL4* p. 254.

247/32   **ruin:** See *New Statesman* 3 March 1951, and *CL4* pp. 257–8. Also *Pravda* 29 July 1931, p. 2, cols 1–3.

248/ 3   **younger:** G.B.S. to Charlotte Shaw, 27 July 1931, *CL4* p. 255.

248/ 9   **infection:** Charlotte Shaw to Dorothy Walker, 5 August 1931 (Texas).

248/11   **dream:** Charlotte Shaw to William Maxwell, 2 August 1931. See *CL4* p. 259.

248/16   **Ireland?:** *The Star* 1 August 1931.

248/26   **Capitalism:** '"We Want a Five-Year Plan Here": George Bernard Shaw at the I.L.P. National Summer School', *The New Leader* 7 August 1931, p. 67. Reprinted in *Platform and Pulpit* p. 218. See also *The Times* 6 August 1931.

248/32   **right!:** *The Diary of Beatrice Webb* vol. 4 (ed. Norman and Jeanne MacKenzie 1985), entry 8 August 1931, p. 249.

248/36   **movement:** *The Letters of Sidney and Beatrice Webb* vol. 3, p. 286.

249/ 4   **crowds:** *The Diary of Beatrice Webb* vol. 4, entry 28 July 1931, p. 248.

249/ 6   **organization:** Ibid., entry 8 August 1931, p. 249.

249/11   **multitude:** Ibid., p. 250.

249/32   **animal:** 'Look, You Boob! A Little Talk on America', 11 October 1931 broadcast. See *Platform and Pulpit* p. 232.

250/ 9   **good:** *The Diary of Beatrice Webb* vol. 4, entry 18 August 1931, p. 250.

250/18   **by day:** Ibid., entry 1 May 1933, p. 302.

250/26   **profit by:** G.B.S. to Lady Rhondda, 5 October 1931 (Fales).

250/35   **at all:** 'What Indeed?' *Practical Politics* p. 211.

250/38   **are:** G.B.S. to Augustin Hamon, 8 January 1932, *CL*4 p. 270.

250/40   **population:** *The Diary of Beatrice Webb* vol. 4, entry 8 August 1931, pp. 249–50.

251/ 3   **or two:** 'The Only Hope of the World', *The New Leader* 7 August 1931, 'Look, You Boob! A Little Talk on America', *Platform and Pulpit* pp. 225, 228, 234.

251/ 5   **afterlife:** *The Diary of Beatrice Webb* vol. 4, entry 30 June 1930, p. 221.

251/ 5   **Russia:** 'Look, You Boob! A Little Talk on America', *Platform and Pulpit* p. 234.

251/24   **right:** *Essays in Fabian Socialism* pp. 305–6.

251/27   **right after all:** See Michael Holroyd, *Bernard Shaw*, vol. 1 (1988) p. 190. There is a misprint in this quotation which should read 'Morris was right after all.'

251/34   **Fabianism:** *The Diary of Beatrice Webb* vol. 4, entry 8 August 1931, p. 249.

252/ 2   **birth:** Anna Louise Strong to G.B.S., 24 July 1931, BL Add. MS 50520 f. 110.

252/ 6   **construction:** David Caute, *The Fellow Travellers* p. 4.

252/ 7   **Communism:** Ibid., p. 347.

252/13   **survive:** Edgar Snow, *Journey to the Beginning* (1959) p. 138.

252/31   **going on:** Katherine Mansfield to John Middleton Murry, 8 November 1919 (courtesy of Margaret Scott).

253/10   **villainy:** *The Rationalization of Russia* p. 38.

253/13   **favorable:** 'Shaw in Moscow', *American Mercury* XXV, 1932, p. 351.

253/14   **twenty years:** Shaw's Introductory fanfare to *The Soviet–Finnish Campaign* by Major A. S. Hooper (1941).

253/30   **would:** *The Rationalization of Russia* pp. 86–7.

253/38   **person:** Ibid., pp. 112–13.

254/ 2   **simple:** G.B.S. to the Rev. Ensor Walters, 9 January 1932, *CL*4 p. 271.

254/ 4   **world:** 'Look, You Boob! A Little Talk on America', *Platform and Pulpit* p. 233.

254/11   **mercy:** G.B.S. to Charles Sumner, 20 June 1937 (see Sotheby's Catalogue, 22 July 1980, item 572).

254/14   **sincerity:** See advertisement of *Retour de l'URSS* by André Gide, in *Fact* May 1937, p. 7.

254/17   **criticism:** G.B.S. to Rutland Boughton, 15 April 1937, BL Add. MS 52365 f. 58.

254/23   **good:** G.B.S. to Siegfried Trebitsch, 11 March 1940, *CL*4
          pp. 549–50 (Shaw/Trebitsch letters, p. 395).
255/ 7   **thieves:** *The Rationalization of Russia* pp. 112–13.
255/ 8   **paradise:** 'Look, You Boob! A Little Talk on America'. See
          Platform and Pulpit p. 234.
255/10   **got religion:** G.B.S. to the Very Rev. W. R. Inge, 9 January
          1932, *CL*4 p. 273.
255/17   **indescribable:** G.B.S. to the Rev. Ensor Walters, *CL*4 p. 272.
255/22   **neighbours:** *CP*6 p. 525.
255/Ep.   **fictions:** Ibid.
255/last **done:** Charlotte Shaw to Nancy Astor, 27 May 1931 (Reading).
255/last **bounds:** Charlotte Shaw to Nancy Astor, 5 June 1931
          (Reading).
256/ 3   **Good:** G.B.S. to Otto Kyllmann, 2 June 1931 (North
          Carolina).
256/10   **war:** G.B.S. to Ellen Pollock, 11 October 1944 (copy privately
          owned).
256/17   **theatre:** Charlotte Shaw to Nancy Astor, 10 December 1931
          (Reading).
256/22   **purpose:** *The Diary of Beatrice Webb* vol. 4, entry 18 June 1931,
          p. 245.
256/23   **long:** T. E. Lawrence to Charlotte Shaw, 9 December 1931,
          BL Add. MS 45904 f. 161.
256/25   **turns:** G.B.S. to Otto Kyllmann, 2 June 1931 (North Carolina).
256/26   **Farce:** Charlotte Shaw to Nancy Astor, 5 June 1931 (Reading).
256/37   **bring up:** T. E. Lawrence to Charlotte Shaw, 28 October
          1931, BL Add. MS 45904 f. 158.
256/last **scared:** T. E. Lawrence to Charlotte Shaw 27 January 1932,
          BL Add. MS 45904 f. 165.
257/ 4   **unexpected:** G.B.S. to Otto Kyllmann, 4 June 1931 (North
          Carolina). See also *The Times* 6 June 1931, p. 12.
257/13   **islands:** G.B.S. to Francis Younghusband, 28 December 1934,
          *CL*4 p. 395.
257/25   **rods:** *CP*6 p. 430.
257/30   **else:** Ibid., p. 436.
257/37   **infect them:** Ibid., p. 437.
258/10   **bed:** G.B.S. to Blanche Patch, 2 May 1931 (Cornell).
258/27   **again:** See John Bunyan, *The Pilgrim's Progress.*
258/33   **knew:** *CP*6 p. 448.
258/last **proceeds:** Ibid., pp. 449–50.
259/ 3   **destiny:** Ibid., p. 447.
259/ 7   **yourself:** Ibid., p. 452.
259/11   **gentleman:** Ibid., p. 448.

259/22	Ariel: Ibid., p. 453.
259/30	*sleep*: Ibid., pp. 455–6.
259/33	hand: Ibid. p. 446.
259/35	weaklings: Ibid., p. 447.
259/37	dream: Ibid., pp. 451, 452.
259/40	find: Ibid., p. 452.
259/last	country: Ibid., p. 457.
260/15	meekly: See Stanley Weintraub, *Private Shaw and Public Shaw* (1963) p. 197.
260/24	there: *CP6* p. 466.
260/28	inferior: Ibid.
260/30	Lawrence: G.B.S. to St John Ervine, 29 October 1932, *CL4* p. 314.
260/33	subordinate: *CP6* p. 491.
260/39	Meek: Ibid.
261/3	there: Ibid., p. 523.
261/5	country: Ibid., pp. 523–4.
261/17	wrap: Ibid., p. 464.
261/19	ballet: Ibid.
261/23	touch: Ibid., p. 468.
261/30	centres: Ibid., p. 474.
261/32	necessity: Ibid., p. 473.
261/32	affections: Ibid., p. 474.
261/34	man: Ibid., p. 482.
261/37	ladylike: Ibid., p. 475.
261/last	eloquence: Ibid., p. 471.
262/7	miserable: Ibid., pp. 481, 482.
262/8	week: Ibid., p. 481.
262/19	lying: Ibid., p. 469.
262/20	to do: Ibid., p. 482.
262/24	happiness: *CP2* p. 650.
262/27	found!: *CP6* p. 472.
263/4	dejection: Ibid., p. 493.
263/10	century: A. N. Wilson, *Penfriends from Porlock* (1988) p. 183.
263/16	England: Hesketh Pearson, *Bernard Shaw* (1975 edn) pp. 440–1.
263/27	dogma: *CP6* pp. 500–1.
263/38	disconsolate: *The Diary of Beatrice Webb* vol. 4, entries 10 July 1924, 14 April 1926, pp. 33–4, 74.
264/10	attention: *CP6* p. 492.
264/11	Bunyan: Bernard Shaw, *Flyleaves* (ed. with an introduction by Dan H. Laurence and Daniel J. Leary 1977) p. 46.
264/14	meet: *CP6* p. 494.

264/16   **dream:** See *The Pilgrim's Progress* title page.
264/29   **to come:** *CP6* p. 496.
264/34   **truth:** *Flyleaves* p. 48.
264/40   **place:** *CP6* p. 497.
265/14   **do it:** Ibid., pp. 475, 477.
265/18   **marries you:** Ibid., pp. 495, 499.
265/23   **room for:** Ibid., p. 499.
265/30   **both:** *Flyleaves* p. 46.
265/37   **doing it:** *CP6* p. 499.
266/ 7   **manure:** Ibid., p. 482.
266/12   **talk:** Ibid., p. 482.
266/14   **vocal:** Ibid., p. 478.
266/19   **wall:** T. E. Lawrence to Charlotte Shaw, 4 July 1932, BL Add.
         MS 45904 f. 172v.
266/32   **for me:** *CP6* pp. 509, 511, 512.
266/38   **mad:** Ibid., p. 503.
267/ 4   **all:** Ibid., p. 505.
267/18   **do it:** Ibid., pp. 471–2.
267/24   **mistake it:** Ibid., p. 501.
267/34   **about it:** Ibid., pp. 520, 521.
267/37   **been!:** Ibid., p. 513.
267/38   **mother:** Ibid., p. 455.
268/ 5   **perish:** Ibid., p. 527.
268/11   **stomach:** T. E. Lawrence to Charlotte Shaw, 27 January 1932,
         21 October 1932, BL Add. MS 45904 ff. 165, 182.
268/18   **period:** Lawrence Langner, *G.B.S. and the Lunatic* (1964)
         p. 138.
268/20   **made:** T. E. Lawrence to Charlotte Shaw, 9 January 1932, BL
         Add. MS 45904 f. 163.
268/25   **people:** Charlotte Shaw to Nancy Astor, 6 August 1932
         (Reading).
268/33   **praise:** Garry O'Connor, *Ralph Richardson* (1983) p. 91.
268/34   **aeroplane:** Desmond MacCarthy, *Shaw* (1951) p. 190.
268/37   **by it:** Ibid. See also *CP6* p. 530.
269/ 4   **meant to:** Langner, *G.B.S. and the Lunatic* p. 203.
269/ 5   **plays:** 'Shakespeare's Rival', *The Spectator* 25 November 1932.
         See *Shaw: The Critical Heritage* (ed. T. F. Evans 1976) p. 330.
269/ 8   **avant-garde:** *G.B.S. and the Lunatic* p. 138.
269/11   **spot:** *CP6* p. 400.
269/13   **farce:** Charles Morgan, unsigned notice, *The Times* 8 August
         1932. See *Shaw: The Critical Heritage* p. 328.
269/15   **about:** Desmond MacCarthy, *Shaw* p. 190.
269/20   **drivel!:** Charlotte Shaw to Nancy Astor, 14 August 1932
         (Reading).

269/22   **amusing!:** Charlotte Shaw to Dolly Walker, 7 August 1932. See *CL*4 p. 301.

269/24   **strange:** Ibid.

269/26   *St Joan: The Diary of Beatrice Webb* vol. 4, entry 25 September 1932, p. 289.

269/28   **terrified!:** Charlotte Shaw to Nancy Astor, 14 August 1932 (Reading).

269/30   **success:** G.B.S. to Christopher St John, 21 August 1932 (Cornell).

270/ 4   **century:** *CP*6 p. 533.

270/ 9   **whatever:** Ibid., p. 529.

270/12   **redeemer:** *The Diary of Beatrice Webb* vol. 4, entry 25 September 1932, p. 289.

270/22   **play:** *The Observer* 9 October 1932.

270/28   **wilderness!:** Janet Dunbar, *Mrs G.B.S.: A Biographical Portrait of Charlotte Shaw* (1963) pp. 309–10.

270/34   **feat:** Desmond MacCarthy, *Shaw* p. 192.

271/ 1   **advanced:** *CP*6 p. 846.

271/ 3   **preach:** Ibid., p. 527.

271/11   **Aubrey:** S. Weintraub, 'The Two Sides of "Lawrence of Arabia": Aubrey and Meek', *The Shaw Review* vol. 7, May 1964, pp. 54–7. Collected in *Bernard Shaw's Plays* (ed. Warren S. Smith, Norton Critical edn 1970) pp. 472–6.

271/14   **fluency:** *CP*6 p. 846.

271/15   **said:** Ibid., p. 454.

271/Ep.   **missionary:** G.B.S. to Clara M. Kennedy, 27 September 1947, *CL*4 p. 803.

271/34   **am:** *Cape Argus* 11 January 1932, p. 11.

272/ 1   **perishes:** 'Break Down of Morality ... Exclusive Interview', *Cape Times* 12 January 1932, p. 9.

272/ 8   **sunshine:** G.B.S. to Nancy Astor, 28 November 1931, *CL*4 p. 267.

272/10   **Pole:** Ibid., p. 270.

272/13   **sailed:** Ibid.

272/19   **head:** *Cape Argus* 11 January 1932, p. 11.

272/23   **Africa:** See Leon Hugo, 'Upset in a "Suntrap": Shaw in South Africa', *Shaw: The Annual of Bernard Shaw Studies*, vol. 5: *Shaw Abroad* (ed. Rodelle Weintraub 1985) p. 148.

272/35   **lived now:** 'Break Down of Morality ... Exclusive Interview', *Cape Times* 12 January 1932, pp. 9, 10.

273/ 2   **hardships:** Ibid.

273/12   **science:** *Cape Times* 19 January 1932.

273/28   **Russia:** 'Shavianisms at the City Hall', *Cape Times* 2 February 1932.

273/30   **a hair:** G.B.S. to Nancy Astor, 18 February 1932 (Reading).

273/32   **audience:** 'G.B.S. in Cape Town', *The Lantern* December 1972, p. 86.

274/ 5   **happens:** 'G.B.S. Hits Out Again', *Cape Times* 14 January 1932.

274/11   **unbeatable:** G.B.S. to Nancy Astor, 18 February 1932 (Reading).

274/18   **so far:** 'Upset in a "Sun-trap": Shaw in South Africa'. See *Shaw Abroad* p. 154.

274/20   **day:** G.B.S. to A. Nelson, 30 January 1932, *CL*4 p. 275.

274/23   **of it:** 'G.B.S. Hits Out Again', *Cape Times* 14 January 1932.

274/29   **of course:** *The Spectator* (London) 17 November 1956.

275/ 7   **gravely:** Quoted in *Shaw: An Exhibit*, item no. 742 (Texas).

275/12   **Africa:** *Cape Times* 15 January 1932.

275/15   **leave!:** Blanche Patch, *Thirty Years with G.B.S.* [ghostwritten by Robert Williamson 1951] p. 73.

275/27   **moonshine:** 'The Dangers of a "Sun Trap": Mr Bernard Shaw's Warning to South Africa', *Cape Times* 8 February 1932, p. 9.

275/last   **day:** Ibid.

276/ 9   **Heaven:** Ibid.

276/13   **State:** Ibid., p. 10.

276/18   **insoluble:** G.B.S. to Emery Walker, 25 January 1932, *CL*4 p. 274.

276/28   **young:** 'The Dangers of a "Sun Trap"', *Cape Times* 8 February 1932, p. 10.

277/ 9   **civilisation:** Ibid.

277/18   **luck:** Ibid.

277/31   **relationship:** *The Lantern* December 1972, p. 88.

278/11   **miles:** G.B.S. to Nancy Astor, 18 February 1932 (Reading).

278/22   **obstacles:** 'Did Not Drive into Ditch: Indignant Denial by G.B.S.', *Cape Times* 22 February 1932, p. 9.

278/24   **knee:** Blanche Patch, *Thirty Years with G.B.S.* p. 72.

278/31   **bone:** G.B.S. to Nancy Astor, 18 February 1932 (Reading).

279/ 1   **miserable:** Ibid.

279/ 8   **dream:** 'Reminiscence of the Visit of Mr and Mrs Shaw to Knysna' by D. I. Fraser (unpublished).

279/12   **real thing:** 'The Adventures of the Black Girl in her Search for God', *Short Stories, Scraps and Shavings* (1932) p. 237.

279/16   **religions:** G.B.S. inscription on Mabel Shaw's 1932 first edition copy of *The Adventures of the Black Girl in Her Search for God*. See *CL*4 p. 55.

279/21   **Horrors?:** G.B.S. to J. E. Whiting, 5 July 1927, *CL*4 p. 56.

279/26   **Christ:** G.B.S. to Nancy Astor, 12 May 1930, *CL*4 p. 187.

279/29   **contrast:** *Short Stories, Scraps and Shavings* p. 238.

279/31   **lovers:** Ibid., p. 254.

279/34   **hallucination:** Preface to *Mr Fortune's Maggot* (Virago edn 1978).

280/ 7   **Progress:** G.B.S. to John Farleigh, 8 May 1932, *CL*4 p. 297.

280/10   **miracles:** G.B.S. to Laurentia McLachlan, 12 [14] April 1932, *CL*4 p. 281.

280/15   **artist:** *Short Stories, Scraps and Shavings* p. 272.

280/19   **forefathers:** Ibid., p. 303.

280/28   **God:** Ibid., p. 259.

281/ 6   **Messiah:** Ibid., p. 303.

281/ 9   **crazy:** Ibid., p. 259.

281/21   **pray:** G.B.S. to Mabel Shaw, 30 January 1928, *CL*4 p. 89.

281/36   **born:** *Short Stories, Scraps and Shavings* p. 246.

281/37   **civilization:** Ibid., pp. 268–9.

282/ 5   **it:** *Cape Times* 19 March 1932.

282/23   **whites:** *Cape Argus* 18 March 1932, p. 11.

282/28   **plain-sailing:** *The Outspan* 29 June 1934, p. 11.

282/32   **well-kept:** Ibid.

282/36   **exceedingly:** Ibid.

283/ 2   **saw:** Charlotte Shaw to Dr and Mrs Allen, 21 April 1932 (private collection).

283/ 5   **questions:** *Cape Times* 19 March 1932.

283/11   **town:** *Natal Witness* 24 May 1935, p. 6.

283/19   **inferior:** 'Marriage of Whites and Blacks: Startling Plan by Mr Shaw', *Daily Telegraph* 11 June 1935, p. 11.

283/29   **nonsense:** *Cape Times* 11 June 1935.

283/38   **races:** G.B.S. to Siegfried Trebitsch, 27 June 1935, *CL*4 p. 413 (Shaw/Trebitsch letters p. 350).

283/40   **inhabitants:** *Daily Telegraph* 11 June 1935, p. 11

284/ 2   **Mr Shaw:** Ibid.

284/12   **Nazis:** Interview c. 1946, BL Add. MS 50526 f. 32.

284/18   **said it:** G.B.S. to Siegfried Trebitsch, 27 June 1935, *CL*4 p. 413 (Shaw/Trebitsch letters p. 350).

284/24   **place:** *CP*3 p. 658.

284/33   **fail:** *Maurice Collis: Diaries: 1949–1969* (ed. Louise Collis 1977) p. 112.

284/36   **Capitalism:** *CP*2 p. 22.

285/ 4   **missionaries:** *CP*7 p. 64.

285/ 7   **you?:** Ibid., p. 96.

285/14   **place:** Katharine Sansom, *Sir George Sansom and Japan* (Diplomatic Press, Tallahassee, Florida, 1972) p. 58.

285/16   **her:** G.B.S. to Otto Kyllmann, n.d., 1933. See *CL4* p. 221.
285/30   **poisoned:** G.B.S. to Edward Elgar, 7 January 1932 (Hereford and Worcester County Record Office).
285/33   **quality is:** Blanche Patch, *Thirty Years with G.B.S.* p. 74.
285/35   **go mad:** See *CL4* p. 223.
286/ 3   **fight:** G.B.S. to Nancy Astor, 13 January 1933, *CL4* p. 321.
286/23   **floor:** Vincent Sheean, 'My Last Visit with Shaw', *The Atlantic* January 1951, p. 22.
286/29   **earth:** See Valli Rao, 'Seeking the Unknowable: Shaw in India', *Shaw Abroad* p. 184.
286/34   **G.B.S.:** G.B.S. to Nancy Astor, 6 March 1943 (Reading).
286/40   **ours:** G.B.S. note for F. E. Loewenstein, May 1946 (Texas).
287/ 3   **well:** G.B.S. to Rabindranath Tagore, 10 January 1933, *CL4* p. 321.
287/ 9   **daughter:** 'Mr Shaw May Visit Gandhi in Jail', *Daily Herald* 9 January 1933, p. 6.
287/17   **present:** 'Seeking the Unknowable: Shaw in India', *Shaw Abroad* p. 186.
287/21   **death:** *Daily Herald* 9 January 1933, p. 6.
287/24   **man:** 'Seeking the Unknowable: Shaw in India', *Shaw Abroad* p. 184.
287/29   **visit you:** G.B.S. to Rabindranath Tagore, 10 January 1933, *CL4* p. 321.
287/38   **Socialist:** Arthur H. Nethercot, *The Last Four Years of Annie Besant* (1963) p. 412.
288/ 2   **support:** Stephen Winsten, *Jesting Apostle: The Life of Bernard Shaw* (1956) p. 164.
288/ 9   **could:** Hesketh Pearson, *Bernard Shaw* (1975 edn) p. 119.
288/14   **shrine:** G.B.S. to Nancy Astor, 13 January 1933, *CL4* p. 322.
288/15   **Indians:** Nirad C. Chaudhuri, *Thy Hand, Great Anarch!: India 1921–1952* (1987) p. 258.
288/28   **Friendship:** *CP7* p. 204.
288/33   **with him:** S. J. Woolf, *Here I am* (1941) p. 181.
288/34   **denomination:** G.B.S. to J. E. Whiting, 18 May 1927, *CL4* p. 53.
289/ 3   **ago:** *Church of England Newspaper* LXIX, 13 January 1950, pp. 1, 5.
289/22   **comprehension:** *EPWW* pp. 227–30. See also G.B.S. to the Rev. Ensor Walters, 4 February 1933, *CL4* pp. 322–5.
290/20   **gods:** *CP7* pp. 397–8.
290/25   **can:** G.B.S. to Laurentia McLachlan, 12 April 1935, *CL4* p. 411.
290/29   **country:** *Thirty Years with G.B.S.* p. 107.

290/33   **East:** Hesketh Pearson, *Bernard Shaw* (1975 edn) p. 445.

290/34   **conduct:** *CP6* p. 762.

291/ 3   **idolatry:** 'Seeking the Unknowable: Shaw in India', *Shaw Abroad* p. 207.

291/14   **shell:** *South China Morning Post* 13 February 1933, p. 16. Quoted in *Shaw Abroad* p. 212.

291/26   **top:** *New Statesman* 8 September 1934.

291/31   **Nations:** Duncan Wilson, *Gilbert Murray OM* (1987) p. 369.

292/ 6   **bluff:** *Shaw Abroad* p. 212.

292/12   **hongs:** Piers Gray, 'Hong Kong, Shanghai, The Great Wall: Bernard Shaw in China', *Shaw Abroad* p. 213.

292/23   **esthetic:** *Design '46: Survey of British Industrial Design as Displayed at the 'Britain Can Make It' Exhibition* (1946) pp. 143–4.

292/26   **understand:** G.B.S. to H. Reinheimer, 20 July 1929 (Texas).

292/26   **well:** G.B.S. to Rabindranath Tagore, 10 January 1933, *CL4* p. 321.

293/17   **at 40:** *South China Morning Post* 14 February 1933, p. 10. See also *Shaw Abroad* p. 216, and for a variant version *Platform and Pulpit* p. 260.

293/22   **in it?:** Piers Gray, 'Hong Kong, Shanghai, The Great Wall: Bernard Shaw in China', *Shaw Abroad* pp. 216–17.

293/26   **done so:** Ibid., p. 220.

293/last   **force:** *Xiabona zai Shanghai* (Shanghai 1933) compiled by Qu Qiubai, translated by Anita Chan and quoted in *Shaw Abroad* pp. 234–5.

294/ 8   **with him:** Lin Yutang, *With Love and Irony* (1945) pp. 237–8. Quoted in *Shaw Abroad* p. 228.

294/36   **score:** Harold Isaacs, *Re-encounters in China* (M. E. Sharpe 1985) p. 130.

295/ 4   **complaining:** Preface to 'Bernard Shaw in Shanghai', *Selected Works of Lu Hsun* vol. 3 (Peking 1959), p. 223.

295/11   **revealed:** Ibid., p. 224.

295/20   **arrest:** Harold R. Isaacs, Introduction to *Straw Scandals: Chinese Short Stories, 1918–1933* (Cambridge, Mass., 1974) p. xxxiv.

295/34   **handkerchief:** Qian Junrui, 'Great International Fighter', *China Reconstructs*, Special Supplement 'In Memory of Soong Ching Ling', September 1981, p. 45.

296/ 6   **belonged there!:** Charlotte Shaw to Nancy Astor, 21 March 1933 (Reading).

296/10   **ushers:** S. I. Hsiung, 'Through Eastern Eyes', *G.B.S. 90: Aspects of Bernard Shaw's Life and Work* (ed. Stephen Winsten 1946) p. 198.

296/16   **gaiters:** G.B.S. to Edward Edgar, 30 May 1933, *CL*4 p. 341.
296/21   **stupendous:** Ibid., p. 340.
296/37   **basses:** Ibid., pp. 340–1.
297/ 4   **fire:** *Daily Herald* 20 April 1933.
297/11   **kindness:** *The Times* 9 March 1933.
297/12   **pilot:** Sidney P. Albert, with Junko Matoba, 'Shaking the Earth: Shaw in Japan', *Shaw Abroad* p. 241.
297/24   **at that:** *Manchester Guardian* 28 April 1933.
297/30   **thoughts:** *CP*6 p. 608.
297/38   **machinery:** Quoted in 'Shaking the Earth: Shaw in Japan', *Shaw Abroad* p. 242.
298/17   **people:** *Asian Affairs* XIX (Old Series vol. 75, February 1988) p. 47.
298/21   **ago:** 'Shaking the Earth: Shaw in Japan', *Shaw Abroad* p. 251.
298/23   **people:** *Asian Affairs* XIX (Old Series vol. 75, February 1988) p. 48.
298/32   **temple:** Ibid.
298/34   **well:** Ibid.
298/39   **like it:** Katharine Sansom, *Sir George Sansom: a Memoir* (1972) p. 63.
299/ 9   **Japan:** Ibid., p. 68.
299/16   **lunch:** Ibid., p. 56.
299/27   **San!:** Ibid., p. 59.
299/32   **whirlwind!:** *Manchester Guardian* 28 April 1933.
299/36   **at all:** Ibid.
300/13   **ruffians:** Katharine Sansom, *Sir George Sansom and Japan* (1972) p. 64.
300/21   **moments:** Ibid., pp. 64–5.
300/37   **Japan!:** Ibid., p. 66.
300/40   **goal:** Piers Gray, 'Hong Kong, Shanghai, The Great Wall: Bernard Shaw in China', *Shaw Abroad* p. 229.
301/14   **about it:** Sidney P. Albert, with Junko Matoba, 'Shaking the Earth: Shaw in Japan', *Shaw Abroad* p. 257.
301/21   **bell:** G.B.S. to Edward Elgar, 30 May 1933, *CL*4 p. 341.
301/last   **consequences:** 'Shaking the Earth: Shaw in Japan', *Shaw Abroad* p. 260.
302/ 2   **America:** *Dear Mr Shaw: Selections from Bernard Shaw's postbag* (compiled and ed. Vivian Elliot 1987) p. 261.
302/ 4   **time:** G.B.S. to George C. Tyler, 13 February 1924.
302/ 8   **allow me:** G.B.S. to James B. Pond, 7 April 1921 (privately owned).
302/19   **partiality:** G.B.S. note on Archibald Henderson's galleys of *Playboy and Prophet* (North Carolina).

302 / 25   **poison:** Answer to Hayden Church questionnaire dated 27 October 1928 (Houghton).

302 / 26   **off!:** Interview by M. K. Wisehart, *The Mentor* March 1930, pp. 16–20, 68–9.

302 / 30   **that!:** Archibald Henderson, *Playboy and Prophet* (1932) p. 767.

302 / 35   **strength:** *CP2* p. 65.

302/37   **pride:** Ibid., p. 53.

303 / 3   **affirmation:** Ibid., p. 697.

303 / 5   **welcome:** *CP6* p. 352.

303 / 14   **late:** *Dear Mr Shaw: Selections from Bernard Shaw's postbag* p. 261.

303 / 17   **friends:** 'U.S. Thinks it Will Bend Shaw – He Doesn't', *Daily Herald* 12 December 1932, p. 9.

303 / 31   **affairs:** G.B.S. to George C. Tyler, 21 August 1905.

304 / 4   **indifference:** G.B.S. to Robert W. Welch, n.d. [c. 22–23 September 1905], *CL2* p. 559.

304 / 11   **Fathers:** 'A Nation of Villagers', *Everybody's* December 1907, pp. 861–5.

304 / 19   **Go Back:** Ibid.

304 / 29   **neighbor's:** Ibid.

304 / 35   **Irishman:** 'Look, You Boob! A Little Talk on America', *Platform and Pulpit* p. 227.

304 / 40   **world:** *Practical Politics: Twentieth-Century Views on Politics and Economics* (ed. Lloyd J. Hubenka 1976) p. 115.

305 / 8   **Russia:** 'Look, You Boob! A Little Talk on America', *Platform and Pulpit* p. 226.

305 / 11   **funny:** Charlotte Shaw to Nancy Astor, 13 October 1931 (Reading).

305 / 26   **first word:** 'Look, You Boob! A Little Talk on America', *Platform and Pulpit* pp. 226–34.

305 / 29   **foolish:** G.B.S. to St John Ervine, 14 November 1921 (copy from Janet Dunbar).

306 / 3   **assassins:** Hesketh Pearson, *Bernard Shaw* (1975 edn) p. 426.

306 / 6   **sting:** Maurice Colbourne, *The Real Bernard Shaw* (1949 edn) p. 319.

306 / 8   **government:** 'O'P'Shaw', *Rob Wagner's Script* vol. IX, no. 219, 22 April 1933.

306 / 16   **Lenin:** Answer to questionnaire dated 8 December 1932 (Cornell).

306 / 22   **Capitalism:** G.B.S. to Thomas Mooney, 27 March 1933, *CL4* pp. 330–1.

306 / 25   **years:** *New York Times* 25 March 1933.

306 / 34   **P[ress]:** G.B.S. to Fanny Holtzman, 26 October 1946 (privately owned).

307/18   **G.B.S.:** Dan H. Laurence, '"That Awful Country": Shaw in America', *Shaw Abroad* p. 286.

307/24   **performance:** Bernard F. Dukore, 'GBS, MGM, RKO: Shaw in Hollywood', *Shaw Abroad* p. 272.

307/25   **popped:** Edwin Schallert, 'Mr Shaw Shakes up Hollywood', *Movie Classic* 4, June 1933, p. 62.

307/26   **afterward:** Ibid.

307/28   **longer:** Marion Davies, *The Times We Had Then* (1975) p. 142.

307/31   **to cry:** *Daily Herald* 20 April 1933.

307/33   **wake:** *Movie Classic* 4, June 1933, p. 62.

307/35   **detestable:** *The Times We Had Then* p. 138.

307/38   **my stuff:** G.B.S. to Kenneth MacGowan, 7 April 1933, *CL*4 p. 334.

308/ 2   **money:** S. N. Behrman, *The Suspended Drawing Room* (1965) p. 66.

308/ 8   **visit:** G.B.S. to Theresa Helburn, Meridian day 13–14 March 1933, *CL*4 p. 327.

308/10   **Academy:** G.B.S. to Ethel Warner, 14 March 1933, *CL*4 p. 329.

308/19   **world:** *Daily Herald* 20 April 1933.

308/33   **audible:** *CP*6 p. 607.

309/ 4   **GBS:** G.B.S. to the New York Press, n.d. [assigned to 11 April 1933], *CL*4 p. 334.

309/10   **effort:** G.B.S. to Constance Collier, 14 April 1933 (Fales).

309/14   **Shaw:** Howard Lewis to Otto Kyllmann, 17 April 1933 (North Carolina).

309/18   **slip:** Ibid.

309/23   **justice:** Charlotte Shaw to Nancy Astor, 21 March 1933 (Reading).

309/24   **life:** 'The World Shaw Saw – And the Shaw the World Doesn't Know', *Sunday Chronicle* 23 April 1933, p. 4.

309/38   **Claus:** Edmund Wilson, 'Shaw in the Metropolitan', *New Republic* 26 April 1933.

310/ 4   **sing:** *The Political Madhouse in America and Nearer Home: A Lecture by Bernard Shaw* (1933) p. 11; first pub. in USA (1933) as *The Future of Political Science in America*.

310/ 6   **bouquets:** Ibid., p. 31.

310/13   **world:** Ibid., pp. 21, 20.

310/18   **magnate:** Ibid., p. 18.

310/20   **power:** Ibid., p. 43.

310/23   **club:** Ibid., p. 48.

310/29   **order:** Ibid., p. 18.

310/40   **derangement:** Ibid., p. 25.

311/ 4   **decency:** Ibid., p. 26.

'311/10   **sincerity:** 'Truth by Radio', talk filmed for motion picture, 'B.B.C., the Voice of Britain'. See *Platform and Pulpit* pp. 275, 274.

311/17   **gift:** Blanche Patch, *Thirty Years with G.B.S.* p. 156.

311/21   **privacy:** *The Political Madhouse in America and Nearer Home* p. 30.

311/29   **together:** Ibid., p. 52.

311/33   **Communistic:** Ibid., pp. 54–5.

311/38   **pieces:** Ibid., p. 28.

311/last   **arms:** Ibid., p. 24.

312/ 3   **illusion:** Ibid., pp. 40–1.

312/ 9   **prosperity:** Ibid., p. 46.

312/12   **with!:** Ibid., p. 58.

312/18   **first:** Ibid., p. 34.

312/19   **silence:** Ibid., p. 26.

312/23   **radicals:** 'Shaw in the Metropolitan', *New Republic* 26 April 1933.

312/24   **down:** 'Bernard Shaw: an Appreciation by "His Friend and Publisher"', typescript of *Chapter of Autobiography* by William H. Wise (Library of Congress, Washington).

312/27   **talk:** *The Political Madhouse in America and Nearer Home* p. 20.

312/31   **it:** Dan H. Laurence, '"That Awful Country": Shaw in America', *Shaw Abroad* p. 291.

312/38   **before:** 'Shaw in the Metropolitan', *New Republic* 26 April 1933.

312/last   **ship:** G.B.S. to Constance Collier, 14 April 1933 (Fales).

313/ 1   **wave:** 'Bernard Shaw: An Appreciation by "His Friend and Publisher"'.

313/10   **man:** Lawrence Langner, *G.B.S. and the Lunatic* p. 129.

313/14   **door:** 'Bernard Shaw: An Appreciation by "His Friend and Publisher"'.

313/16   **manners:** *G.B.S. and the Lunatic* p. 129.

313/20   **life:** Charlotte Shaw to Nancy Astor, 21 March 1933 (Reading).

313/25   **there:** 'The World Shaw Saw – And the Shaw the World Doesn't Know', *Sunday Chronicle* 23 April 1933, p. 4.

313/33   **age:** *The Diary of Beatrice Webb* vol. 4, entry 20 December 1935, p. 362.

313/35   **hands!:** Charlotte Shaw to Nancy Astor, 16 December 1935 (Reading).

313/39   **do:** Ibid.

314/ 1   **silence:** See '"That Awful Country": Shaw in America', *Shaw Abroad* p. 293.

314/ 5   **sentence:** G.B.S. to Blanche Patch, 20 March 1936, *CL*4
p. 426.

314/11   **sights:** J. B. Priestley, *Margin Released* (1962) p. 166.

314/14   **things:** Charlotte Shaw to Nancy Astor, 21 March 1933
(Reading).

314/23   **with us?:** *The Political Madhouse in America and Nearer Home*
p. 29.

314/27   **backache!!:** Charlotte Shaw to Nancy Astor, 8 March 1934
(Reading).

314/35   **voyage:** Hesketh Pearson, *Bernard Shaw* (1975 edn) p. 418.

315/ 4   **to me:** G.B.S. to Apsley Cherry-Garrard, 1 May 1934, *CL*4
p. 371.

315/ 7   **journalists:** Blanche Patch, *Thirty Years with G.B.S.* p. 88.

315/10   **do!:** Charlotte Shaw to Nancy Astor, 8 March 1934 (Reading).

315/12   **endurance:** G.B.S. to Ethel Warner, 15 May 1933. See *CL*4
p. 328.

315/20   **much less:** G.B.S. to R. M. Campbell, 11 March 1934
(Alexander Turnbull Library, MS Papers 1900, R. M.
Campbell folder 9).

315/33   **Parliament:** *Address by Mr G. Bernard Shaw to the Wellington
Fabians and Members of the N.Z. Labour Party* (Wellington
1934) p. 4.

315/38   **democracy!:** Ibid., pp. 4–5.

316/ 8   **Government:** Ibid., p. 7.

316/12   **say:** *The Dominion* 11 April 1934. *What I Said in N.Z.*
(Wellington 1934) p. 25.

316/24   **New Zealand:** *Evening Post* 13 April 1934. *What I Said in N.Z.*
p. 27.

316/38   **processions:** J. B. Priestley, *Margin Released* (1962) p. 164.

317/ 4   **movement:** '"I'm More at Home Here": Talkies and
Tourists', *Auckland Star* 2 April 1934, p. 7. *What I Said in
N.Z.* p. 11.

317/19   **follies:** 'Be Independent', *Auckland Star* 15 March 1934, p. 8.
What I Said in N.Z. p. 3.

317/26   **myself:** '"I'm More at Home Here": Talkies and Tourists',
Auckland Star 2 April 1934, p. 7. *What I Said in N.Z.* p. 11.

317/30   **themselves:** 'Mr G. B. Shaw Interviewed', *Dominion* 4 April
1934, p. 10. *What I Said in N.Z.* p. 13.

317/32   **city:** Blanche Patch, *Thirty Years with G.B.S.* p. 100.

317/36   **geysers:** Charlotte Shaw to Nancy Astor, March 1934
(Reading).

317/37   **travelling:** Charlotte Shaw to T. E. Lawrence, 14 January
1934, BL Add. MS 45922 f. 49.

317/39 **money:** See *CL*4 p. 221.
318/ 4 **view:** Charlotte Shaw to Nancy Astor, 28 March 1934 (Reading).
318/ 7 **too:** Ibid.
318/15 **us:** Ibid.
318/17 **live in:** *Evening Post*, 14 April 1934. *What I Said in N.Z.* p. 23.
318/26 **miserable:** 'Mr G. B. Shaw Interviewed', *Dominion* 4 April 1934, p. 10. *What I Said in N.Z.* p. 13.
318/32 **jazz:** G.B.S. to W. I. Forde of the *Evening Post*, 2 April 1934 (Alexander Turnbull Library, Acc. 87–72 G.B. Shaw folder 1).
318/34 **King:** Blanche Patch, *Thirty Years with G.B.S.* p. 100.
318/37 **rate:** G.B.S. to Nancy Astor, 28 April 1934, *CL*4 p. 369.
319/ 1 **pouring in:** *What I Said in N.Z.* p. 25.
319/ 5 **food:** Mary King, *Truby King the Man* (1948) p. 208. Quoted by Katrine Keuneman in *The Independent Shavian* vol. 22, nos 2–3, 1984, p. 41.
319/11 **sufficient:** Ibid.
319/20 **sit up:** *What I Said in N.Z.* p. 29.
319/23 **jersey:** *Dominion* 16 April 1934. *What I Said in N.Z.* p. 28.
319/26 **Shavians:** *Auckland Star* 27 March 1934. *What I Said in N.Z.* p. 8.
319/29 **come:** *Christchurch Press* 10 April 1934. *What I Said in N.Z.* p. 21.
319/31 **better:** 'Be Independent', *Auckland Star* 15 March 1934, p. 8. *What I Said in N.Z.* p. 3.
319/33 **Empire:** '"A Civil Folk": Mr Shaw's Opinion of New Zealanders', *Dominion* 27 March 1934, p. 10. *The Independent Shavian* vol. 22, nos 2–3, 1984, p. 38.
319/37 **cocoa:** R. M. Campbell, 'Bernard Shaw in New Zealand: A Broadcast and Some Other Memories' (Alexander Turnbull Library, MS Papers 1900, R. M. Campbell folder 9).
319/39 **persons:** See *CL*4 p. 223.
320/ 1 **Zealand:** G.B.S. to Scanlan, MS Papers 232. N. Scanlan, folder 4, 23 November 1934 (Alexander Turnbull Library).
320/ 4 **house:** See Anthony Trollope, *Australia and New Zealand* (2 vols 1873).
320/ 7 **to me:** *Christchurch Press* 10 April 1934; *Auckland Star* 2 April 1934. *What I Said in N.Z.* pp. 23, 11.
320/12 **been in:** *What I Said in N.Z.* p. 29.
320/Ep. **myself:** G.B.S. to Mrs Patrick Campbell, 16 April 1932, *Their Correspondence* p. 301.
320/18 **property:** *CP*6 p. 583.

320/25	**poorer:** Ibid., p. 405.
320/34	**cruelties:** Ibid., p. 589.
321/ 1	**way:** Ibid., p. 602.
321/ 4	**vulgarities?:** Ibid., p. 857.
321/ 6	**adders:** Ibid., p. 590.
321/ 8	**science:** Ibid., p. 595.
321/11	**community:** Ibid., p. 627.
321/16	**poverty:** Ibid., p. 403.
321/26	**at all?:** Ibid., p. 867.
321/28	**overdue:** Ibid., p. 878.
321/30	**examples:** Ibid., p. 851.
321/40	**to it:** Ibid., p. 626.
322/ 1	**criticism:** Ibid., p. 625.
322/ 3	**does:** Ibid., p. 762.
322/ 5	**mad:** Ibid., p. 871.
322/ 6	**inequality:** Ibid., p. 880.
322/ 7	**people:** Ibid., p. 418.
322/14	**wisdom:** Ibid., p. 624.
322/17	**missionaries:** Ibid., p. 759.
322/18	**justified:** Ibid., p. 613.
322/21	**Church:** Ibid., p. 417.
322/26	**Governments:** Ibid., p. 589.
322/29	**are:** Ibid., p. 859.
322/34	**story:** G.B.S. to R. & R. Clark, 14 May 1932, *CL*4 p. 288.
322/last	**work:** John Farleigh, *Graven Image* (1940) p. 220.
323/ 1	**satirist:** G.B.S. to Siegfried Trebitsch, 25 May 1932, Shaw/Trebitsch letters p. 322.
323/ 5	**volume:** G.B.S. to John Farleigh, 8 May 1932, *CL*4 p. 296.
323/ 9	**possible:** G.B.S. to John Farleigh, 24 May 1932, *Graven Image* p. 238.
323/10	**of it:** G.B.S. to John Farleigh, 24 May 1932, *CL*4 p. 299.
323/11	**rip:** *Graven Image* p. 230.
323/16	**ruefully:** G.B.S. to Michael Sadleir, 25 July 1932 (North Carolina).
323/23	**nothing:** G.B.S. to Otto Kyllmann, 8 August 1932 (North Carolina).
323/27	**intelligence:** Farleigh, *Graven Image* p. 270.
323/33	**ignorant:** Beatrice Webb's diaries, 28 November 1932 (LSE).
323/36	**God:** *Sunday Chronicle* 4 December 1932.
324/ 2	**respectability:** G.B.S. to Floryan Sobieniowski, 24 July 1933, *CL*4 p. 347.
324/ 6	**genuine:** *The Diary of Beatrice Webb* vol. 4, entry 28 November 1932, p. 293.

324/ 9   **come off:** G.B.S. to G. K. Chesterton, 3 December 1932, *CL*4
               p. 318.

324/ 15   **card:** *The Diary of Beatrice Webb* vol. 4, entry 1 December 1932,
               p. 293.

324/ 16   **W.B.A.:** G.B.S. to Floryan Sobieniowski, 24 July 1933, *CL*4
               p. 347.

324/ 22   **obscenity:** G.B.S. to W. B. Yeats, 18 May 1933, *CL*4 p. 340.

324/ 28   **view:** G.B.S. to W. B. Yeats, 4 September 1933, *CL*4 p. 353.

324/ 38   **irreligious:** G.B.S. to Dame Laurentia McLachlan, 14 April
               1932, D. Felicitas Corrigan, *The Nun, the Infidel and the
               Superman* (1985) pp. 117, 119 (*CL*4 pp. 281, 283).

325/ 2   **Shaw:** *The Nun, the Infidel and the Superman* p. 121 (*CL*4
               p. 289).

325/ 8   **later:** G.B.S. to R. & R. Clark, 14 April 1932. See *CL*4 p. 288.

325/ 10   **way:** G.B.S. to Dame Laurentia, c. 2 May 1932, *The Nun, the
               Infidel and the Superman* pp. 121–2 (*CL*4 pp. 289–90).

325/ 15   **you:** Dame Laurentia to G.B.S., 3 May 1932, *The Nun, the
               Infidel and the Superman* p. 122 (see *CL*4 p. 289).

325/ 19   **me:** G.B.S. to Dame Laurentia, 14 December 1932, *The Nun,
               the Infidel and the Superman* p. 126 (*CL*4 p. 344).

325/ 22   **it:** *The Nun, the Infidel and the Superman* p. 125.

325/ 39   **stories:** G.B.S. to Dame Laurentia, 29 June 1933, *The Nun, the
               Infidel and the Superman* pp. 126–7 (*CL*4 pp. 344–5).

326/ 5   **God:** Dame Laurentia to G.B.S., 13 July 1933, *The Nun, the
               Infidel and the Superman* p. 128 (*CL*4 p. 348).

326/ 19   **may be:** G.B.S. to Dame Laurentia, 24 July 1933, *The Nun, the
               Infidel and the Superman* pp. 129–30 (*CL*4 pp. 349–50).

326/ 24   **old:** G.B.S. to the Ladies of Stanbrook Abbey, 3 October 1934,
               The Nun, the Infidel and the Superman p. 132 (*CL*4 p. 380).

327/ 2   **rough:** Ibid.

327/ 8   **future:** Dame Laurentia to G.B.S., 4 October 1934, *The Nun,
               the Infidel and the Superman* p. 133.

327/ 12   **Girl:** G.B.S. to Dame Laurentia, 7 October 1934, *The Nun, the
               Infidel and the Superman* p. 133 (*CL*4 p. 381).

327/ 16   **sort:** G.B.S. to Sydney Cockerell, 17 October 1934. See *CL*4
               p. 380.

327/ 19   **different:** *The Diary of Virginia Woolf* vol. 4, entry 3 June 1932,
               p. 106.

327/ 25   **also:** G.B.S. to Dame Laurentia, 24 July 1933, *The Nun, the
               Infidel and the Superman* p. 130 (*CL*4 p. 350).

327/ 31   **for him:** G.B.S. to Frances Chesterton, 15 June 1936, *CL*4
               p. 433.

327/ 33   **unnoticed:** G.B.S. to Francis Younghusband, 28 December
               1934, *CL*4 p. 393.

CHAPTER V

328/Ep.   **about?:** *CP*6 p. 715.
328/ 9   **anybody:** *Shaw the Villager and Human Being: A Biographical*
            Symposium (ed. Allan Chappelow 1961) p. 48.
328/15   **story:** Ibid., p. 139.
328/23   **work:** Ibid., p. 51.
328/28   **by one:** Ibid., pp. 51, 56.
329/ 2   **or not:** Ibid., p. 49.
329/15   **children:** Ibid., pp. 39, 41.
329/27   **best:** Ibid., p. 99.
329/35.   **serious:** Ibid., p. 156.
330/ 6   **nuisance:** 'Shaw's Pippin', *Countryman*, Spring 1952, p. 130.
330/10   **liked it:** G.B.S. to N. W. Barritt, 21 October 1936,
            Countryman, Spring 1952, p. 131.
330/23   **god:** *Shaw the Villager and Human Being* p. 118.
330/40   **ease:** Ibid., pp. 109, 222, 145.
331/ 6   ˜**uncle:** Ibid., pp. 93, 109, 202, 110.
331/10   **that:** Ibid., p. 93.
332/ 4   **to me:** Ibid., pp. 80–91.
332/ 8   **Conversations:** The title page of proof copy.
332/15   **Strachey:** G.B.S. to Lillah McCarthy, 25 May 1934 (Texas).
332/19   **in it:** *The Diary of Beatrice Webb* vol. 4, entry 1 May 1933,
            p. 302.
332/21   **puzzles:** *Shaw the Villager and Human Being* p. 83.
332/26   **person:** Ibid., p. 231.
332/31   **book:** *CP*6 p. 537.
333/18   **nature?:** *CP*4 pp. 722, 773.
333/23   **moving:** *Theatre Arts* March 1957.
333/30   **contemporary:** Blanche Patch, *Thirty Years with G.B.S.*
            [ghostwritten by Robert Williamson] (1951) p. 74.
333/31   *House*: Frederick P. W. McDowell, 'Crisis and Unreason:
            Shaw's *On the Rocks*', *Educational Theatre Journal* XIII, no. 3,
            October 1961, p. 200.
334/ 4   **them:** *CP*6 p. 636.
334/ 5   **fairyland:** Ibid., p. 645.
334/ 8   **anyhow:** Ibid., p. 644.
334/12   **politician:** Ibid., p. 669.
334/24   **life:** Ibid., p. 642.
334/27   **unattractive?:** Ibid., p. 640.
334/32   **dotty:** Ibid., pp. 638–9.
334/33   **like this:** Ibid., p. 645.
334/last   **incurable:** Ibid., p. 671.

335/ 8   **him:** Ibid., p. 678.

335/26   **head:** Ibid., p. 677.

336/12   **class:** Ibid., p. 702.

336/18   **earth:** Ibid., p. 697.

336/20   **view:** Ibid., p. 699.

336/24   **moving:** Ibid., p. 707.

336/27   **body:** Ibid., p. 692.

337/ 6   **spirit:** Ibid., p. 708.

337/ 8   **do it:** Ibid., p. 706.

337/16   **drama:** Margery M. Morgan, *The Shavian Playground: An Exploration of the Art of George Bernard Shaw* (1972) p. 284.

337/23   **surprises:** *The Times* 6 May 1982.

337/28   **find?:** *CP6* p. 721.

337/31   **bitten:** Ibid., p. 701.

337/35   **Communist:** Richard Nickson, '*On the Rocks:* Messages Given and Received', *The Independent Shavian* vol. 23, nos 2–3, 1985, p. 29.

337/39   **once:** G.B.S. to Theresa Helburn, 27 April 1934 (Yale).

337/40   **ideas:** *Morning Post* 27 November 1933. See *Shaw: The Critical Heritage* (ed. T. F. Evans 1976) p. 336. See also *The Times* 27 November 1933.

338/ 5   **order:** *New Statesman and Nation* 2 December 1933, pp. 694–5.

338/ 9   **genius:** *The Diary of Beatrice Webb* vol. 4, entry 8 December 1933, p. 319.

338/14   **everywhere:** G.B.S. to Theresa Helburn, 23 December 1933 (Yale).

338/17   **London:** *The Observer* 24 August 1975.

338/18   **1933:** *Sunday Times* 24 August 1975.

338/20   **1970s:** *The Times* 23 August 1975.

338/23   **1975:** *The Lady* 11 September 1975.

338/29   **now:** *The Observer* 9 May 1982.

338/35   **best:** *CP6* p. 649.

338/38   **bit:** Ibid., p. 655.

339/ 6   **cocksureness:** Ibid., p. 661.

339/10   **yours:** Ibid., p. 660.

339/13   **heartbreaking one:** Ibid., p. 657.

339/14   **revolution:** Ibid., p. 721.

339/16   **Hipney:** Ibid., p. 719.

339/18   **insidious:** *Sunday Times* 9 May 1982.

339/24   **left:** *New Statesman* 14 May 1982.

339/29   **words:** *CP6* pp. 187–8.

339/33   **police:** Ibid., p. 735.

339/37   **like:** Ibid., p. 734.

340/ 3   **destinies:** Eric Bentley, *Bernard Shaw* (1967 edn) p. 97.
340/23   **Molière:** Edmund Wilson, 'Bernard Shaw at Eighty', *The Triple Thinkers* (1962 edn) p. 219.
341/Ep.   **me:** St John Ervine, *Bernard Shaw: His Life, Work and Friends* (1956) p. 555.
341/20   **England:** Raymond Mander and Joe Mitchenson, *Theatrical Companion to Shaw: A Pictorial Record of the First Performances of the Plays of George Bernard Shaw* (1954) p. 294.
341/33   **to him:** Charlotte Shaw to Nancy Astor, 1 November 1933 (Reading).
341/37   **pleasure:** G.B.S. to Arthur Wontner, 5 December 1944 (Berg).
342/ 3   **pieces:** Christopher Casson to Michael Holroyd (16 February 1976).
342/16   **show:** 'Beloved Slavedriver', *Sunday Times* 21 September 1975.
342/26   **accent:** Russell Sidgwick to Michael Holroyd, 14 April 1975.
342/36   **life:** *Great Acting* (ed. Hal Burton 1967) p. 68.
342/39   **alarmed:** John Gielgud, *Early Stages* (rev. edn 1974) pp. 110–11.
343/ 1   **mine:** *Dear Mr Shaw: Selections from Bernard Shaw's postbag* (compiled and ed. Vivian Elliot 1987) p. 291.
343/ 6   **fortnight:** G.B.S. to Gertrude Kingston, 22 November 1933 (King's College, Cambridge).
343/18   **feet:** 'Beloved Slavedriver', *Sunday Times* 21 September 1975.
343/25   **there:** Charlotte Shaw to T. E. Lawrence, 27 November 1933, BL Add. MS 45922 f. 115.
343/34   **them:** *CP6* p. 636.
343/last **setting:** Beatrice Webb's diaries, 8 December 1933 (LSE).
344/ 2   **increase:** G.B.S. to Otto Kyllmann, 25 January 1934 (North Carolina).
344/12   **impossibility:** G.B.S. to St John Ervine, 28 January 1932 (Texas).
344/25   **habits:** *CP6* p. 765.
344/27   **them:** Ibid., p. 769.
344/36   ***dead*:** Ibid., p. 771.
345/ 3   **myself in:** Ibid., p. 772.
345/ 9   **loveliness:** Ibid., p. 774.
345/29   **trying:** Ibid., p. 777.
345/last **self-understanding:** *CP2* p. 680.
346/ 5   **again:** *CP6* p. 778.
346/ 6   **years:** *The Letters of T. E. Lawrence* (ed. Malcolm Brown 1988) p. 259.
346/12   **for me:** *CP6* p. 779.

346/16   **indescribable:** G.B.S. to Siegfried Trebitsch, 26 June 1934, Shaw/Trebitsch letters p. 342.

346/28   **respectable:** *CP*6 p. 787.

346/33   **trespassing:** Ibid., p. 784.

346/36   **forever:** Ibid., p. 786.

346/last   **kiss you:** Ibid., p. 789.

347/18   **conscience:** Ibid., pp. 793–5.

347/20   **of conscience:** Ibid., p. 796.

347/25   **easily:** Ibid., p. 798.

347/28   **one life:** Ibid., pp. 791, 803.

347/last   **art:** 'Edgar Allan Poe', *The Nation* 16 January 1909. See *Pen Portraits and Reviews* (1931) pp. 225–6.

348/ 7   **race:** G.B.S. to Elmer Pheils, 2 August 1950 (owned by Murray T. Pheils, Professorial Surgical Unit, University of Sydney, New South Wales).

348/15   **glory:** *CP*6 p. 830.

348/21   **sterile:** Ibid., p. 807.

348/31   **fool:** Ibid., p. 812.

348/last   **deluded:** Ibid., pp. 810, 811, 812.

349/ 4   *pourra:* St John Ervine, *Bernard Shaw: His Life, Work and Friends* p. 555.

349/12   **Apocalypse:** Morgan, *The Shavian Playground* p. 299.

349/17   **maturity:** *CP*6 pp. 824, 825.

349/19   **indispensables:** Ibid., p. 769.

349/22   **disappear:** Ibid., p. 822.

349/27   **people:** Ibid., p. 834.

349/35   **degree:** G.B.S. to Floryan Sobieniowski, 13 March 1935 (Texas).

350/ 3   **arms:** *CP*6 p. 832.

350/ 7   **Paradise:** From Coleridge's *Kubla Khan* quoted in *CP*6 p. 789.

350/12   **world:** *CP*6 p. 839.

350/19   **power:** Ibid., pp. 839, 840.

350/26   **writing:** Lawrence Langner, *The Magic Curtain* (1951) p. 293.

350/31   *Isles:* Lawrence Langner, *G.B.S. and the Lunatic* (1964) p. 151.

350/36   **coconuts:** *New York Herald Tribune* 19 February 1935.

351/ 4   **undress:** G.B.S. to Mrs Patrick Campbell, 17 March 1935, *CL*4 pp. 405–6. See *Bernard Shaw and Mrs Patrick Campbell: Their Correspondence* (ed. Alan Dent 1952) p. 308.

351/14   **economics:** 'Utopias', a lecture delivered by G.B.S. to the Hampstead Historical Club, 25 May 1887 (Houghton).

351/23   **confusion:** *The Bulletin* (Sydney) 16 October 1935.

351/27   **mind:** *The Times* 30 July 1935.

351/29   **improprieties:** Langner, *G.B.S. and the Lunatic* p. 152.

351/36   us: See editorial note, Shaw/Trebitsch letters p. 349.

352/ 2   may do: Dame Laurentia McLachlan to G.B.S., 7 February
         1935, D. Felicitas Corrigan, *The Nun, the Infidel and the
         Superman* (1985) p. 136.

352/ 5   the Father?: G.B.S. to Laurentia McLachlan, 12 April 1935,
         *CL*4 p. 410.

352/ 8   divinity: G.B.S. to Sydney Cockerell, 28 February 1935
         (Cornell).

352/11   temples: Ibid.

352/16   no-gods: G.B.S. to the Theatre Guild, 7 April 1935, *CL*4
         p. 408.

352/20   silly: Edmund Wilson, *The Triple Thinkers* p. 220.

352/24   production: G.B.S. to William Armstrong, 14 September 1937
         (copy, Society of Authors).

352/29   soliloquies: Ray Conlogue, *Toronto Globe and Mail* 1 July 1983.

353/ 8   will: 'Joy Riding at the Front', I: 'Bombardment', *Daily
         Chronicle* 5 March 1917. *What I Really Wrote about the War*
         (1931) p. 249.

353/17   surrender: Stanley Weintraub, 'In the Picture Galleries', *The
         Genius of Shaw* (ed. Michael Holroyd 1979) p. 57.

353/24   whatever: *CP*6 pp. 975, 973.

353/26   words: Ibid., p. [992].

353/31   effect: *Shaw: An Exhibit*, a Catalog by Dan H. Laurence
         (Texas, 1977) item 482.

354/ 1   tale: *CP*6 p. 904.

354/ 7   his: Ibid., p. 890.

354/ 8   criminals: Ibid., p. 891.

354/25   property: Ibid., pp. 929, 963.

354/26   fixation: Ibid., p. 930.

354/37   end: St John Ervine, *Bernard Shaw: His Life, Work and Friends*
         p. 555.

356/ 3   devils: Mander and Mitchenson, *Theatrical Companion to Shaw*
         pp. 248–9.

356/ 6   dream: *CP*6 p. 941.

356/18   care for: Ibid., pp. 945–6.

356/27   it up: Ibid., pp. 960, 967.

356/30   money: Ibid., p. 962.

356/36   republic: Ibid., p. 968.

357/ 5   powers!: Ibid.

357/15   daily: Margot Peters, '*The Millionairess*: Capitalism Bankrupt?'
         Shaw: The Neglected Plays (ed. Alfred Turco Jr); *Shaw: The
         Annual of Bernard Shaw Studies* vol. 7 (1987) p. 243.

357/17   Rhodes: *Cape Times* 30 April 1935.

356/18 **species:** *CP*6 p. 927.

356/21 **woman:** G.B.S. to Nancy Astor, 8 April 1935 (Reading).

356/24 **den:** G.B.S. to Sidney Webb, 20 April 1935 (LSE). For Beatrice Webb's comments on Act III of *The Millionairess*, see Beatrice Webb to G.B.S., 30 July 1935, *The Letters of Sidney and Beatrice Webb* vol. 3, pp. 407–8.

356/28 **pulse:** *CP*6 p. 961.

356/32 **found it:** Ibid., p. 962.

356/36 **Mrs Siddons:** G.B.S. to Herbert M. Prentice, 8 July 1937, *CL*4 p. 470.

356/40 **earnest:** Bryan Forbes, *Ned's Girl* (1977) p. 170.

357/ 3 **live with:** *CP*6 p. 899.

357/ 6 **power:** 'Shaw's hymn to tyranny', *Guardian* 13 October 1988.

357/ 9 **silly:** *The Diary of Beatrice Webb* vol. 4, entry 1 July 1935, p. 354.

357/14 **play:** *The Observer* 7 January 1979.

357/17 **one:** *Sunday Dispatch* 10 December 1933. Quoted by Vivian Elliot in *Dear Mr Shaw* p. 227.

357/20 **always are:** G.B.S. to J. C. Squire, 14 October 1919, *CL*3 p. 638.

357/23 **voice:** G.B.S. to John Barrymore, 22 February 1925, *CL*3 p. 903.

357/33 **acting:** 'Mr Shaw on Mr Shaw', *New York Times* 12 June 1927, p. 1, reprinted by E. J. West in *Shaw on Theatre* (1958) p. 185.

357/last **executants:** 'The Play of Ideas', *New Statesman and Nation* 6 May 1950, reprinted by E. J. West in *Shaw on Theatre* p. 294.

358/ 4 **can:** Bryan Forbes, *Ned's Girl* p. 169.

358/14 **knows:** G.B.S. to Sybil Thorndike, 28 April 1937 (copy privately owned).

358/22 **play?:** Lawrence Langner, *G.B.S. and the Lunatic* p. 156.

358/31 **half-playing:** G.B.S. to Hugh ('Binkie') Beaumont, 30 June 1942 (Frederick R. Koch Foundation, Pierpont Morgan Library, New York).

358/last **heart:** Kenneth Tynan, *A View of the English Stage 1944–1965* (1975) pp. 115–18.

359/Ep. **settled:** G.B.S. to Hannen Swaffer, 26 February 1938, *CL*4 p. 495.

359/ 3 **Nov:** G.B.S. to John Reith, 3 December 1935 (BBC, Caversham).

359/ 8 **death:** G.B.S. to Henry Salt, 7 December 1934, *CL*4 pp. 391–2.

359/13 **finger:** *The Diary of Virginia Woolf* vol. 4, entry 6 January 1935, p. 272.

359/22 **Shakespeare:** Virginia Woolf to Vanessa Bell, 8 May 1927, *The*

Letters of Virginia Woolf vol. 3: *A Change of Perspective* (ed. Nigel Nicolson 1977) p. 371.

359/24   **undergraduates:** *The Diary of Beatrice Webb* vol. 4, entry 19 June 1936, p. 371.

359/27   **with me:** G.B.S. to Nancy Astor, 26 January 1935 (Reading).

359/33   **partner:** *The Diary of Beatrice Webb* vol. 4, entry 12 January 1935, p. 347.

360/ 2   **thing:** G.B.S. to Sydney Cockerell, 12 February 1935 (Cornell).

360/ 3   **age:** G.B.S. to Nancy Astor, 27 July 1939 (Reading).

360/ 9   **intimidating:** G.B.S. to H. A. Gwynne, 22 June 1936, *CL4* p. 434.

360/11   **games:** G.B.S. to Hugh ('Binkie') Beaumont, 7 April 1940 (Frederick R. Koch Foundation, Pierpont Morgan Library, New York).

360/17   **long:** Charlotte Shaw to Nancy Astor, 12 September 1937, 7 December 1937 (Reading).

360/20   **worthwhile:** Beatrice Webb's diaries, 5 June 1937 (LSE).

360/28   **or both:** Ibid., 23 May 1936.

360/32   **hurricane:** See *CL4* p. 451.

360/35   **shape:** *The Diary of Virginia Woolf* vol. 4, entry 16 June 1933, p. 164.

360/36   **ungrand:** John Stewart Collis, *Bound Upon a Course* (1971) p. 92.

360/38   **flower:** Valerie Pascal, *The Disciple and His Devil* (1970) p. 141.

361/11   **to me:** Brendan O'Byrne, *The Ancient Britons* (Outposts Publications 1979) p. 5. Revised by the author 1991.

361/13   *old*: Charlotte Shaw to Nancy Astor, 14 December 1936 (Reading).

361/15   **perfection:** G.B.S. to Sydney Cockerell, 12 February 1935 (Texas).

361/17   **pieces:** Charlotte Shaw to Nancy Astor, 10 November 1936 (Reading).

361/19   **soon:** Charlotte Shaw to Nancy Astor, 28 May 1938 (Reading).

361/21   **something:** G.B.S. to Nancy Astor, 27 July 1939 (Reading).

361/23   **immovable!:** Charlotte Shaw to Waldorf Astor, 7 December 1937 and to Nancy Astor, n.d. (Reading).

361/27   **anything:** G.B.S. to Blanche Patch, 24 August 1938 (Cornell).

361/35   **listen to:** *The Diary of Beatrice Webb* vol. 4, entry 2 July 1934, p. 334.

362/ 1   **friend:** Sidney Webb to Beatrice Webb, 29 January 1934, *The Letters of Sidney and Beatrice Webb* (ed. Norman MacKenzie 1978) vol. 3, p. 386.

362/11   **indeed:** Sidney Webb to Bernard Shaw, 29 January 1934.
362/16   **doubts:** *The Diary of Beatrice Webb* vol. 4, entry 29 September 1936, p. 377.
362/20   **Webbs:** Ibid., entry 5 June 1937, p. 390.
362/29   **give it:** Ibid., entry 25 January 1938, p. 407.
362/33   **failure:** G.B.S. to Beatrice Webb, 6 February 1938, *CL*4 p. 493.
362/last **stifle it:** Ibid.
363/ 3   **obituary:** 'Comment from Shaw' [on the death of Maxim Gorki], *New York Times* 19 June 1936, p. 21.
363/ 4   **up:** G.B.S. to Hannen Swaffer, 26 February 1938, *CL*4 p. 495.
363/ 9   **wifes!:** Sidney Webb to G.B.S., 2 June 1938, *The Letters of Sidney and Beatrice Webb* vol. 3, p. 423.
363/17   **doctor!:** Charlotte Shaw to Dorothy Walker, 21 June 1938 (Texas).
363/22   **own:** Gilbert Murray to G.B.S., 13 August 1938, BL Add. MS 50542 f. 56.
363/24   **regions:** G.B.S. to Lady Kennet [Kathleen Hilton Young], 17 February 1947.
363/25   **not:** 'G.B.S. Wants to Eat Acorn Extracts', *Daily Express* 29 June 1938, p. 5.
363/26   **unchanged:** G.B.S. to Frank Wyatt, 28 June 1938, *CL*4 p. 502.
363/33   **already:** Charlotte Shaw to Apsley Cherry-Garrard, 20 June 1938 (Texas).
363/36   **man:** G.B.S. to Henry Salt, 29 August 1938, *CL*4 p. 506.
364/ 2   **pen:** Janet Dunbar, *Mrs G.B.S.: A Biographical Portrait of Charlotte Shaw* (1963) p. 310.
364/ 8   **party:** G.B.S. to Nancy Astor, 1 January 1939 (Reading).
364/10   **resurrected:** G.B.S. to Lady Kennet [Kathleen Hilton Young, formerly Kathleen Scott], 17 February 1947.
364/17   **Cure:** Ibid.
364/27   **death:** G.B.S. to Symon Gould, 31 August 1948, *American Vegetarian* 1 February 1953, p. 1.
364/33   **butter:** G.B.S. to Symon Gould, 8 July 1941, *American Vegetarian* 1 March 1953, pp. 1, 5.
364/34   **stuff:** Commonplace Book (Berg).
364/38   **particularizing:** G.B.S. to Henry Salt, 29 August 1938, *CL*4 p. 507.
364/39   **story:** Commonplace Book (Berg).
365/ 1   **dead:** G.B.S. to Lady Londonderry, 4 December 1938 (Public Record Office of Northern Ireland, Belfast).
365/ 6   **numbers:** *Dear Mr Shaw: Selections from Bernard Shaw's postbag* p. 153.

365/10   **survive:** G.B.S. to Henry Salt, 29 August 1938, *CL4* p. 507.
365/16   **GBS!:** *The Diary of Beatrice Webb* vol. 4, entry 30 June 1938, p. 415.
365/18   **write:** G.B.S. to Beatrice Webb, 17 September 1939, *CL4* p. 538.
365/21   **other:** Beatrice Webb to G.B.S., 19 September 1939, *The Letters of Sidney and Beatrice Webb* vol. 3, pp. 430–1.
365/26   **again:** *The Diary of Beatrice Webb* vol. 4, entry 24 May 1940, p. 452.
365/32   **least so:** Ibid., entry 11 January 1939, p. 426.
365/39   **affectionate:** Ibid., entry 24 May 1940, p. 452.
365/last   **enough:** G.B.S. to Beatrice Webb, 17 September 1939, *CL4* p. 538.
366/ 6   **release:** G.B.S. to Catherine Salt, 8 May 1939, *CL4* p. 529.
366/28   **them:** G.B.S. to St John Ervine, 28 April and 11 May 1936, *CL4* p. 428.
366/35   **spot:** Ibid., p. 429.
366/37   **first:** G.B.S. to St John Ervine, 23 May 1936 (Texas).
366/38   **write it:** St John Ervine, *Bernard Shaw: His Life, Work and Friends* p. vii.
367/ 4   **Dublin:** G.B.S. to St John Ervine, 31 October 1942, *CL4* pp. 645–6.
367/ 6   **century:** Michael Holroyd, *Bernard Shaw* vol. 2 (1989) p. 212.
367/ 8   **about:** G.B.S. to James Elroy Flecker, 6 March 1911, BL Add. MS 50516 ff. 12–13.
367/13   **begun:** St John Ervine, *Bernard Shaw: His Life, Work and Friends* p. vii.
367/31   **Irish:** Ibid.
368/ 5   **Shaw:** Hesketh Pearson, *Modern Men and Mummers* (1921) p. 11.
368/11   **me:** G.B.S. to Hesketh Pearson, 8 October 1938, *CL4* p. 512.
368/15   **field:** G.B.S. to Hesketh Pearson, 2 December 1938, *CL4* p. 520.
368/16   **man:** Introduction by Richard Ingrams to 1975 edn of Hesketh Pearson's *Bernard Shaw* p. 8.
368/18   **clown:** *Hesketh Pearson by Himself* (1965) p. 291.
368/22   **invigorating:** Introduction by Richard Ingrams to 1975 edn of Hesketh Pearson's *Bernard Shaw* p. 8.
368/27   **post:** *Hesketh Pearson by Himself* p. 292.
368/30   **elopement:** G.B.S. to Nancy Astor, 7 April 1939 (Reading).
368/38   **gossip:** G.B.S. to Beatrice Webb, 5 March 1939 (LSE).
369/ 3   **seen it:** *Hesketh Pearson by Himself* pp. 299–300.
369/ 6   **affairs:** G.B.S. to Pearson, 31 December 1940 (Texas).

369/11   **myself:** G.B.S. to Beatrice Webb, 17 February 1941, *CL*4 p. 595.

369/13   **published:** Beatrice Webb's diaries, entry 28 July 1942 (LSE).

369/31   **reticent:** *Hesketh Pearson by Himself* pp. 301, 303.

369/37   **point:** Ibid., p. 294.

370/14   **progressive:** Pearson typescript pp. 605–8 (Texas).

370/27   **betterment:** Hesketh Pearson, *Bernard Shaw* (1975 edn) p. 376.

370/32   **angle:** Ibid., p. 377.

370/35   **promise:** Ibid., p. 381.

371/17   **Shaw's:** G.B.S. to Hesketh Pearson, 12 January 1941, *CL*4 p. 590, and G.B.S. to Pearson, 19 January 1941 (Texas).

371/26   **mad:** G.B.S. to Hesketh Pearson, 18 January 1943, *CL*4 p. 658.

371/29   **Pearson:** G.B.S. note to F. E. Loewenstein for letter to Ernest H. Rasdall, December 1946 (Texas).

371/31   **life:** G.B.S. to Cyril Clemens, 28 November 1941 (copy, Texas).

371/33   **I?:** G.B.S. to Archibald Henderson, 28 April 1941 (North Carolina).

372/Ep. 1   **prices:** G.B.S. to Allen Lane, 20 August 1949 (Penguin Archive).

372/Ep. 2   **endurance:** G.B.S. to Siegfried Trebitsch, 28 April 1931, *CL*4 p. 236 (Shaw/Trebitsch letters p. 319).

372/ 9   **way:** G.B.S. to Beatrice Webb, 10 July 1912, *CL*3 p. 98.

372/24   **slump:** Linda Lloyd Jones, 'Fifty Years of Penguin Books', *Fifty Penguin Years* (1985) p. 15.

372/32   **did:** Michael S. Howard, *Jonathan Cape: Publisher* (1971) p. 164.

373/ 2   **year:** G.B.S. to Otto Kyllmann, 14 August 1945, *CL*4 p. 751.

373/ 8   **words:** F. A. Mumby and Ian Norrie, *Publishing and Bookselling* (rev. edn 1974) p. 367.

373/15   **canon:** J. E. Morpurgo, *Allen Lane: King Penguin* (1979) p. 59.

373/19   **mankind:** G.B.S. to William Maxwell, 20 October 1936 (National Library of Scotland).

373/21   **ways:** G.B.S. to Allen Lane, 3 January 1944 (Penguin Archive).

374/ 6   **pleasure:** Allen Lane to G.B.S., 23 July 1948. Quoted in T. F. Evans, 'Shaw Among the Penguins', *The Shavian*, Spring 1986, p. 8.

374/22   **firms:** G.B.S. answer to Demetrius O'Bolger questionnaire, 14 February 1916 (Houghton).

374/28   **present:** G.B.S. to E. Y. McPeake, 15 December 1920 (Houghton).

374/33   **film:** 'Shaw Not a Film Snob. But Can't Be a Dumb Dramatist', *Daily News* 26 February 1926, p. 5.

375/ 3   **uncompromising:** *Bernard Shaw on Photography: Essays and Photographs by George Bernard Shaw* (ed. Bill Jay 1989) p. 112.

375/15   **film:** 'The Cinema as a Moral Leveller', *New Statesman* Special Supplement on the Modern Theatre 27 June 1914. See also G.B.S. questionnaire by Hayden Church, 27 October 1928 (Houghton).

375/24   **dialogue:** 'Shaw Finds Talkies Opening New Field', *New York Times* 19 May 1929, p. 26.

375/36   **stage:** G.B.S. to Huntly Carter, 9 September 1930 (Yale).

376/ 1   **eroticism:** O'Bolger Manuscript XIV–16 (Houghton).

376/ 4   **altogether:** *The Times* 10 November 1927.

376/ 6   **37:** *CP2* p. 1033.

376/18   **director:** Cecil Lewis, *Never Look Back* (1974) p. 106.

376/21   **suggest:** Quoted in *The Collected Screenplays of Bernard Shaw* (ed. with an introduction by Bernard F. Dukore 1980) p. 21.

376/23   **word:** Ibid., p. 22.

376/28   **pianola:** Cecil Lewis, *Never Look Back* p. 106.

376/31   **screen:** *The Times* 13 January 1931.

376/32   **photography:** *New York Times* 13 January 1931.

377/ 4   **screen:** 'Mr Shaw and the Cinema', *The Times* 26 January 1937, p. 12.

377/17   **climax:** *Shaw on Theatre* (ed. E. J. West 1958) p. 206.

377/21   **result:** Cecil Lewis, *Never Look Back* p. 106.

377/27   **minutes:** *G.B.S. and the Lunatic* p. 222.

377/32   **Hollywood:** G.B.S. to Cecil Lewis, 18 April 1932, *CL4* p. 287.

377/34   **ship:** Quoted in *The Collected Screenplays of Bernard Shaw* p. 33.

378/10   **mistakes:** G.B.S. to Cecil Lewis, 5 June 1937, *CL4* p. 468.

378/14   **on it:** G.B.S. to Siegfried Trebitsch, 24 April 1930, Shaw/Trebitsch letters p. 313.

378/17   **scene:** G.B.S. to Cecil Lewis, 17 April 1932 (Berg).

378/24   **infancy:** *Shaw on Theatre* pp. 212–13.

378/33   **stage:** Ibid.

378/36   **privilege:** *The Star* 25 January 1933.

379/ 3   **needed:** G.B.S. to Kenneth MacGowan, 7 April 1933, *CL4* p. 334.

379/12   **work:** G.B.S. to Kenneth MacGowan, 15 February 1934, *CL4* p. 366.

379/15   **judgement:** *The Collected Screenplays of Bernard Shaw* p. 38.

379/16   **artistically:** G.B.S. to Kenneth MacGowan, 15 February 1934, *CL4* p. 365.

379/24   **despair:** G.B.S. to Kenneth MacGowan, 7 April 1933 and to Theresa Helburn, 15 February 1935, *CL4* pp. 334, 401.

379/34 **Hollywood:** G.B.S. to John Barrymore, 14 November 1933, *CL*4 p. 355.

380/11 **universe:** G.B.S. to Augustin Hamon, 13 February 1935, *CL*4 p. 399.

380/15 **firm:** G.B.S. to Siegfried Trebitsch, 3 July 1934, Shaw/Trebitsch letters p. 342.

380/17 **bits:** G.B.S. to Trebitsch, 22 September 1934, Shaw/Trebitsch letters p. 344.

380/22 **separately:** G.B.S. to Trebitsch, 15 June 1934, Shaw/Trebitsch letters p. 341.

380/26 **basket:** G.B.S. to Augustin Hamon, 13 February 1935, *CL*4 p. 399.

380/32 **film:** *Daily Sketch* 6 June 1936.

380/37 **hint:** G.B.S. to Siegfried Trebitsch, 16 January 1936, *CL*4 p. 423 (Shaw/Trebitsch letters p. 354).

381/ 2 **myself:** G.B.S. to Theresa Helburn, 15 February 1935, *CL*4 p. 401.

381/21 **Irishman:** Quoted in *The Collected Screenplays of Bernard Shaw* p. 53.

381/23 **Vatican:** *CP*6 p. 237.

383/ 3 **such:** Ibid., pp. 232–41.

382/11 **Joan:** G.B.S. to Gabriel Pascal, 1 September 1938, *CL*4 p. 509.

382/18 **director:** G.B.S. to James Bridie, 8 August 1935, *CL*4 p. 415.

382/24 **answered:** *Dear Mr Shaw: Selections from Bernard Shaw's postbag* (compiled and ed. Vivian Elliot 1987) p. 5.

382/25 **signature:** Blanche Patch, *Thirty Years with G.B.S.* (1951) p. 132.

382/38 **flame:** Ibid., p. 131.

382/38 **reputation:** Ibid., p. 133.

383/13 **entity:** *Dear Mr Shaw* pp. 324, 154.

383/18 **aristocrat:** Ibid., p. 322.

383/27 **selfish:** Ibid., pp. 186–7, 349, 174, 169.

383/33 **sort:** *Thirty Years with G.B.S.* p. 136.

383/35 **affairs?:** *Dear Mr Shaw* p. 12.

384/ 7 **infant:** Ibid., pp. 164, 33.

384/20 **MacDonald:** Ibid., pp. 269, 47, 233, 235.

384/26 **brains?:** Ibid., p. 181.

385/23 **interesting:** 'Recollection of GBS', *Time and Tide* (obituary notice, November 1950).

385/25 **Atatürk:** *People* 15 August 1954.

385/32 **rest:** *Frieda Lawrence: the Memoirs and Correspondence* (ed. E. W. Tedlock 1961) p. 148.

385/37 **earth:** *Dear Mr Shaw* p. 297.

386/ 7   **buttocks:** Valerie Pascal, *The Disciple and His Devil* p. 76.
386/ 9   **foreigner:** *Thirty Years with G.B.S.* p. 118.
386/14   **genius:** Foreword to Marjorie Deans, *Meeting at the Sphinx: Gabriel Pascal's Production of Bernard Shaw's 'Caesar and Cleopatra'* (1946) p. vii.
386/15   **rules:** G.B.S. to Siegfried Trebitsch, 28 March 1940, Shaw/Trebitsch letters p. 395.
386/17   **off:** St John Ervine obituary, quoted in *CL4* p. 885.
386/19   **more:** *Thirty Years with G.B.S.* p. 118.
386/25   **anything:** 'Gabriel and his Trump', *Family Circle* vol. 19, no. 2, 11 July 1941, p. 25.
386/36   **Harris:** G.B.S. to Siegfried Trebitsch, 30 December 1935, *CL4* p. 421 (Shaw/Trebitsch letters p. 353).
387/ 4   **lived:** Hesketh Pearson, *Extraordinary People* (1964) p. 191.
387/ 5   **talker:** G.B.S. to Siegfried Trebitsch, 30 December 1935, *CL4* p. 421 (Shaw/Trebitsch letters p. 353).
387/ 8   **heaven:** *The Disciple and His Devil* p. 32.
387/30   **height:** *Family Circle* vol. 19, no. 2, 11 July 1941, p. 27.
388/ 4   **more:** Ibid.
388/ 8   **work:** Ibid.
388/12   **producer:** Ibid., p. 28.
388/20   **films:** Ibid.
388/37   **Hollywood:** Marjorie Deans, *Meeting at the Sphinx* p. vii.
388/39   **with:** Ibid.
389/10   **Pascal:** G.B.S. to Siegfried Trebitsch, 15 December 1935, *CL4* p. 420 (Shaw/Trebitsch letters p. 352).
389/12   **world:** *The Disciple and His Devil* p. 79.
389/14   **village:** G.B.S. to Siegfried Trebitsch, 23 May 1948, *CL4* p. 818 (Shaw/Trebitsch letters p. 444).
389/15   **Shaw:** *The Disciple and His Devil* p. 183.
389/17   **rich:** Ibid., p. 79.
389/22   **of it:** S. N. Behrman, *The Suspended Drawing Room* (1965) p. 68.
389/26   **them:** Ibid., p. 71.
389/29   **anything:** *The Disciple and His Devil* p. 216.
389/31   **sense:** Michael Holroyd, *Bernard Shaw*, vol. 1 (1988) p. 401.
389/31   **nursing:** G.B.S. to Leonard Elmhirst, 5 April 1940, *CL4* p. 552.
389/last **habits:** G.B.S. to John Maxwell, 24 May 1932 (privately owned).
390/ 9   **rock:** G.B.S. to Gabriel Pascal, 21 August 1939, *CL4* p. 533.
390/17   **less:** G.B.S. to Augustin Hamon, 21 November 1936, *CL4* p. 447.

390 / 28   **myself:** *The Collected Screenplays of Bernard Shaw* p. 69.

390 / 31   **years:** G.B.S. to Gabriel Pascal, 18 November 1937. Quoted in S. N. Behrman, *The Suspended Drawing Room* p. 78.

390 / 37   **want:** *The Collected Screenplays of Bernard Shaw* pp. 84, 67.

391 / 7   **stage:** G.B.S. to Gabriel Pascal, 1 September 1938, *CL*4 pp. 508–9.

391 / 26   **well:** *The Shaw Review* XIV, no. 1, January 1971, p. 34.

391 / 37   **work:** *The Suspended Drawing Room* p. 73.

392 / 5   **about:** *CP*4 pp. 822–3.

392 / 12   **production:** *The Disciple and His Devil* p. 85.

392 / 15   **beginning:** G.B.S. to Gabriel Pascal, 24 February 1938, *CL*4 p. 494.

392 / 18   **world:** Lawrence Langner, *G.B.S. and the Lunatic* p. 228.

392 / 22   **insult:** 'G.B.S. Says Film Honour Is "Insult"', *The Star* 24 February 1939.

392 / 26   **film:** G.B.S. to Gabriel Pascal, 24 February 1938, *CL*4 p. 494.

392 / 29   **writers:** *The Disciple and His Devil* p. 85.

392 / 33   **expert:** G.B.S. to Lawrence Langner, 3 April 1940, *CL*4 p. 551.

392 / 36   **triumph:** *The Disciple and His Devil* p. 85.

392 / last   **late:** Ibid., p. 90.

393 / 2   **younger:** *The Suspended Drawing Room* p. 76.

393 / 4   **more:** Ibid., p. 82.

393 / Ep.   **does:** *What I Really Wrote about the War* (1931) p. 411.

393 / 10   **scenarios:** G.B.S. to Siegfried Trebitsch, 30 December 1935, *CL*4 p. 422 (Shaw/Trebitsch letters p. 353).

393 / 13   **studios:** G.B.S. to Kenneth MacGowan, 15 February 1934, *CL*4 p. 366.

393 / 15   **Manners:** Subtitle to *Buoyant Billions*, *CP*7 p. 303.

393 / 23   **haunt me:** *CP*7 p. 180.

393 / 35   **Beethoven:** Ibid., pp. 184–5.

394 / 6   **Shakespeare/Shakspere:** G.B.S. to Ellen Terry, 6 September 1896, *A Correspondence* p. 51 (*CL*1 p. 650).

394 / 9   **Cymbeline:** Ibid., p. 46 (p. 646).

394 / 26   **old:** Hugh Kingsmill, *The Return of William Shakespeare* (1929) p. 202.

395 / 3   **unravel?:** *CP*7 p. 198.

395 / 25   **murders:** Ibid.

395 / 36   **stalls:** Ronald Adam to Michael Holroyd, 13 March 1975.

396 / 6   **began:** *The Times* 17 November 1937.

396 / 12   **itself:** *CP*7 p. 166.

396 / 19   **military:** *The League of Nations*, Fabian Tract no. 226 (1929). See *What I Really Wrote about the War* p. 400.

396/26 **delegate:** R. H. Bruce Lockhart, *Retreat from Glory* (1934) p. 337.

397/ 6 **last:** *The League of Nations.* See *What I Really Wrote about the War* p. 401.

397/20 **diplomacy:** Ibid., pp. 403–4.

397/27 **order:** Ibid., pp. 404–5.

398/ 7 **Government:** Ibid., p. 403.

398/12 **history:** Title page of first edition of *Geneva* (1939).

398/19 **institution:** G.B.S. to Beatrice Webb, 2 September 1923 (LSE).

398/22 **1919:** *The League of Nations.* See *What I Really Wrote about the War* p. 410.

398/35 **nerve:** *What I Really Wrote about the War,* p. 411.

399/13 **of it:** G.B.S. to Henri Barbusse, 4 May 1932, *CL4* p. 292.

399/20 **notice of:** P. N. Furbank, *E. M. Forster: A Life* vol. 2 (1978) p. 196.

399/25 **stiff:** Duncan Wilson, *Gilbert Murray OM* (1987) p. 352.

399/28 **play:** Gilbert Murray, *Unfinished Autobiography* (1960) p. 191.

399/30 **it!:** *Gilbert Murray OM* pp. 352–3.

399/36 **saved:** Ibid., p. 364.

399/37 **telepathy:** *CP7* p. 167.

400/ 4 **about?:** Ibid.

400/10 **drama:** *EPWW* p. 180.

400/13 **stage:** G.B.S. to H. K. Ayliff, 10 May 1938, *CL4* p. 501.

400/17 **drama:** Maurice Colbourne, *The Real Bernard Shaw* (1949) p. 215.

400/22 **rats:** *CP7* p. 45.

400/26 **here:** Ibid., p. 46.

400/28 **remedy:** Ibid., p. 171.

401/16 **law:** Ibid., p. 137.

401/21 **grind:** Ibid., p. 68.

401/29 **killed:** Ibid., pp. 99, 101.

401/33 **personality:** Ibid., p. 74.

401/36 **manner:** Gilbert Murray to G.B.S., 13 August 1938, BL Add. MS 50542 f. 55.

401/37 **whatever:** *CP7* p. 86.

401/last **penance:** See Michael Holroyd, *Bernard Shaw* vol. 2 (1989) p. 84.

402/ 4 **affairs:** *CP7* p. 75.

402/ 8 **with it:** *The League of Nations.* See *What I Really Wrote about the War* p. 403.

402/10 **globe:** G.B.S. to G. S. Viereck, 8 March 1940, *CL4* p. 547.

402/24 **colour:** Shaw's 'Notes on the Way', *Time and Tide* no. 21, 12

October 1940. See *Shaw: The Neglected Plays* (ed. Alfred Turco Jr 1987) p. 327.

402/29	**war:** *CP7* p. 74.
402/33	**love:** Ibid., p. 85.
402/35	**glory:** Shaw's 'Notes on the Way', *Time and Tide*, no. 21, 12 October 1940. See *Shaw: The Neglected Plays* p. 327.
402/36	**play:** *EPWW* p. 44.
402/last	**comedian:** G.B.S. to H. K. Ayliff, 10 May 1938, *CL4* p. 501.
403/ 3	**opportunely:** *CP7* p. 78.
403/ 4	**inch a judge:** Ibid., p. 76.
403/ 5	**am a judge:** Ibid., p. 79.
403/13	**gathered:** Ibid., p. 112.
403/35	**obedience:** Ibid., p. 127.
403/36	**dramatize:** G.B.S. to G. S. Viereck, 8 March 1940, *CL4* p. 547.
404/ 1	**world:** G.B.S. to Nancy Astor, 22 October 1942, *CL4* p. 643.
404/ 6	**semi-idiot:** G.B.S. to Siegfried Trebitsch, 26 January 1939, Shaw/Trebitsch letters p. 381.
404/12	**moron:** *News Chronicle* 21 September 1936.
404/14	**life:** G.B.S. to G. S. Viereck, 8 March 1940, *CL4* p. 547.
404/28	**pioneer:** *CP7* p. 143.
404/32	**mystic:** Beatrice Webb diaries, TS p. 6586 (LSE).
404/35	**wit:** George Sylvester Viereck to G.B.S., 13 February 1940 (Iowa).
405/ 4	**none:** G.B.S. to Trebitsch, 12–15 May 1933, *CL4* p. 336 (Shaw/Trebitsch letters p. 333).
405/14	**form:** Beatrice Webb diaries, 23 May 1936 (LSE).
405/15	**all:** G.B.S. to Beatrice Webb, 18 May 1936 (LSE).
405/19	**side:** Beatrice Webb diaries, 5 June 1937 (LSE).
405/24	**right:** *The Diary of Beatrice Webb* vol. 4, entry 27 October 1937, p. 396.
405/25	**want to:** G.B.S. to Mrs Patrick Campbell, 19 December 1938, *Bernard Shaw and Mrs Patrick Campbell: Their Correspondence* (ed. Alan Dent 1952) p. 329.
405/27	**nearly:** G.B.S. to Roy Limbert, 29 May 1938 (Texas).
405/33	**Play:** 'Mussolini Makes Shaw Re-write Play', *Daily Herald* 12 October 1938, p. 9.
405/35	**bone:** G.B.S. to H. K. Ayliff, 10 May 1938, *CL4* p. 501.
405/last	**time:** 'Bernard Shaw Tells Us All About—My Plays, My Work, My Novels, My Money', *Sunday Graphic* 17 December 1933, pp. 12, 23.
406/ 5	**burlesques:** G.B.S. to H. K. Ayliff, 6 March 1939 (Hofstra).
406/10	**trick:** G.B.S. to Roy Limbert, 17 September 1939 (Texas).

406/14 **week:** G.B.S. to Maurice Colbourne, 17 September 1939 (Theatre Museum, Victoria and Albert Museum).

406/20 **futile:** Brooks Atkinson, notice, *New York Times* 31 January 1940. See *Shaw: The Critical Heritage* (ed. T. F. Evans 1976) p. 359.

406/23 **confused:** *The Spectator* 28 August 1938.

406/29 **whisper:** *CP7* p. 116.

406/34 **useless:** G.B.S. to Lawrence Langner, 20 September 1938, *CL4* p. 511.

407/ 5 **side:** Lawrence Langner, *G.B.S. and the Lunatic* pp. 162, 165.

407/ 6 **bit:** G.B.S. to Lawrence Langner, 20 September 1938, *CL4* p. 511.

407/23 **enormously:** G.B.S. to Roy Limbert, 5 January 1939, *CL4* p. 523.

407/31 **view:** *CP1* p. 373.

408/ 2 **life:** Desmond MacCarthy, *Shaw* (1951) pp. 194–5.

408/15 **living in:** *CP7* pp. 100, 106.

408/16 **race:** Ibid., p. 101.

408/23 **execution:** Ibid., p. 154.

408/28 **round:** Gilbert Murray to G.B.S., 13 August 1938, BL Add. MS 50542 f. 55.

409/ 1 **of it:** *CP7* p. 166.

409/ 5 **at them:** Ibid., p. 142.

409/11 **to die:** G.B.S. to H. K. Ayliff, 11 December 1938 (Cornell).

409/17 **have not:** *CP7* p. 138.

409/19 **domination:** Ibid., p. 154.

409/34 **now?:** Ibid., p. 158.

410/ 5 **about it:** Charlotte Shaw to Dorothy Walker, 15 November 1938 (Texas).

410/10 **A.1:** *The Diary of Beatrice Webb* vol. 4, entry 11 January 1939, p. 426.

410/16 **finished:** G.B.S. to Roy Limbert, 24 December 1938, *CL4* p. 522.

410/24 **quality:** J. M. Keynes, 'G.B.S. and Isaac Newton', in *G.B.S. 90: Aspects of Bernard Shaw's Life and Work* (ed. Stephen Winsten 1946) pp. 109, 106.

410/29 **thing:** Lytton Strachey, *Biographical Essays* (1948) p. 11.

410/36 **temporal:** *CP7* p. 219.

411/ 3 **sorts:** Ibid., p. 110.

411/ 7 **civilization:** Ibid., p. 295.

411/21 **follow:** Ibid., pp. 261, 263, 266, 262, 276, 284.

412/ 5 **guest:** *The Religious Speeches of Bernard Shaw* (ed. Warren Sylvester Smith 1963) pp. 84, 86.

412/17   **anachronism:** *CP*7 p. 205.
412/18   **profession:** Ibid., p. 270.
412/25   **gravitation:** Ibid., pp. 279–80.
412/32   **myself:** *EPWW* p. 181.
412/35   **annals:** G.B.S. to Upton Sinclair, 12 December 1941 (Lilly Library, Indiana University).
412/last **same:** *CP*2 p. 306.
413/ 6   **thought:** *CP*7 p. 461.
413/ 9   **light:** See Michael Holroyd, *Bernard Shaw* vol. 1 (1988) p. 121.
413/11   **intelligible:** *EPWW* p. 186.
413/15   **exist:** G.B.S. to Upton Sinclair, 12 December 1941 (Lilly Library, Indiana University).
413/25   **of him:** J. L. Wisenthal, *Shaw's Sense of History* (1988) p. 93.
413/28   **pages:** G.B.S. to Upton Sinclair, 12 December 1941 (Lilly Library, Indiana University).
413/36   **known:** G.B.S. to Beatrice Webb, 17 January 1939, *CL*4 p. 524.
414/16   **appeal:** G.B.S. to Edith Evans, 4 May 1939 (copy privately owned).
414/20   **unfaithfulness?:** *CP*7 pp. 289, 291.
414/23   **to me:** Ibid., pp. 291–2.
414/27   **love:** See Michael Holroyd, *Bernard Shaw* vol. 2, p. 312.
414/39   **jealous:** *CP*7 p. 292.
414/40   **now:** Ibid., p. 296.
414/last **husbands:** G.B.S. to William Maxwell, 23 April 1939 (Scotland).
415/ 6   **ever!:** *CP*7 p. 301.
415/12   ***Methuselah*:** James Agate, notice, *Sunday Times* 13 August 1939. See *Shaw: The Critical Heritage* p. 362.
415/13   ***Saint Joan*:** Hesketh Pearson, *Bernard Shaw* (1975 revised edn) p. 416.
415/17   **survive:** Sydney Cockerell to G.B.S., 10 December 1939, BL Add. MS 50531 ff. 71–2.
415/23   **U.S.A.:** Lawrence Langner, *G.B.S. and the Lunatic* p. 213.
415/29   **giant:** James Agate, notice, *Sunday Times* 13 August 1939. See *Shaw: The Critical Heritage* p. 362.
415/last **knowledge:** Maurice Colbourne, *The Real Bernard Shaw* p. 219.
416/ 8   **incomprehensible!:** Siegfried Trebitsch, *Chronicle of a Life* (1953) p. 273.
416/26   **towered:** Ibid., p. 284.
416/34   **language:** Ibid., pp. 284, 285, 287, 288.
417/ 3   **supreme:** *Neue Rundschau*, 1929; *Literary Digest* 7 January 1928. See editorial note, Shaw/Trebitsch letters p. 201.

417/ 8   **effacement:** G.B.S. to Siegfried Trebitsch, 19 March 1926, *CL4* p. 20 (Shaw/Trebitsch letters p. 269).

417/14   **misrepresentation:** G.B.S. to Trebitsch, 6 January 1925, Shaw/Trebitsch letters p. 253.

417/18   **profession:** G.B.S. to Trebitsch, 29 April 1927, Shaw/Trebitsch letters p. 278.

417/24   **mamselle:** G.B.S. to Trebitsch, 23 February 1930, Shaw/Trebitsch letters p. 311.

417/28   **Reinhardt:** G.B.S. to Trebitsch, 19 December 1929, Shaw/Trebitsch letters p. 307.

417/34   **Schiller:** *Hitler's Secret Conversations* (1953), quoted in Shaw/Trebitsch letters p. 331.

418/ 9   **can you:** G.B.S. to Siegfried Trebitsch, 19 December 1929, 23 February 1930, 23 April 1930, 1 August 1930, 30 November 1931. Shaw/Trebitsch letters pp. 307, 311, 312, 315, 321.

418/11   **confusing:** *Chronicle of a Life* p. 327.

418/14   **comedy:** Quoted, editorial note Shaw/Trebitsch letters p. 325.

418/19   **mistake?:** G.B.S. to Siegfried Trebitsch, 29 November 1929, Shaw/Trebitsch letters p. 305.

418/28   **repertory:** Editorial note, Shaw/Trebitsch letters p. 339.

418/32   **trifles:** Quoted Shaw/Trebitsch letters p. 331.

418/35   **imperishable:** *Chronicle of a Life* p. 291.

418/35   **future:** Ibid., p. 277.

419/ 4   **gold:** G.B.S. to Siegfried Trebitsch, 24 April 1930, Shaw/Trebitsch letters p. 314.

419/ 8   **remit:** G.B.S. to Trebitsch, 15 December 1935, *CL4* p. 420 (Shaw/Trebitsch letters p. 352).

419/15   ***nobile*:** G.B.S. to Trebitsch, 30 November 1931, 20 July 1934, Shaw/Trebitsch letters pp. 320, 343.

419/19   **pleased:** G.B.S. to Trebitsch, 10 July 1933, 8 April 1938, Shaw/Trebitsch letters pp. 336, 373.

419/24   **other:** *Chronicle of a Life* p. 324.

419/25   **meant:** Ibid., p. 275.

419/29   **cookery:** Ibid., pp. 275–6.

420/ 2   **criticism!:** Ibid., p. 394.

420/11   **censorship:** Ibid., pp. 328–9.

420/12   **success:** Ibid., p. 348.

420/18   **attend:** Ibid., p. 351.

420/22   **fatal:** *CP6* p. 869.

420/30   **spirit:** Editorial note, Shaw/Trebitsch letters p. 331.

421/ 2   **opinions:** G.B.S. to Siegfried Trebitsch, 12–15 May 1933, *CL4* pp. 336–7 (Shaw/Trebitsch letters p. 333).

421/ 8   **disease:** 'Halt, Hitler', *Sunday Dispatch* 4 June 1933, p. 12.

421 / 11   **publication:** 'Bernard Shaw ... Says We Will Have Peace', *Daily Express* 26 July 1939, p. 8.

421 / 14   **England is:** G.B.S. to H. C. Duffin, 29 November–2 December 1937 (Sotheby's Catalogue, 20–21 July 1981, item 581).

421 / 18   **unpopular:** G.B.S. to Siegfried Trebitsch, 27 June 1935, *CL*4 p. 413 (Shaw/Trebitsch letters p. 350).

421 / 21   **foreigners:** 'The Empire and Self-government', *Shaw: Interviews and Recollections* (ed. A. M. Gibbs, 1990) p. 362.

421 / 28   **Europe:** 'Bernard Shaw Answers Eight Questions', *Daily Express* 26 March 1938, p. 12.

421 / 35   **dream:** 'Bernard Shaw ... Says We Will Have Peace', *Daily Express* 26 July 1939, p. 8.

421 / 39   **Nations:** 'Shaw's Mistake', *New Statesman* 5 July 1941. See *Bernard Shaw: Agitations: Letters to the Press 1875–1950* (ed. Dan H. Laurence and James Rambeau 1985) p. 324.

422 / 4   **respectable:** 'Bernard Shaw Discusses Foreign Policy', *Daily Herald* 3 March 1939, p. 10.

422 / 9   **inevitable:** Stanley Weintraub, *The Last Great Cause: The Intellectuals and the Spanish Civil War* (1968) pp. 145–6.

422 / 10   **Africans!:** 'Bernard Shaw Discusses Foreign Policy', *Daily Express* 26 March 1938, p. 10.

422 / 13   **undesirable:** G.B.S. to Beatrice Webb, 6 February 1938, *CL*4 p. 493.

422 / 16   **party:** 'G.B.S. on the Nazis: "A Mentally Bankrupt Party"', *Jewish Chronicle* no. 3321, 2 December 1932, p. 23.

422 / 25   **jealousies:** Ibid.

422 / 27   **created it:** 'Bernard Shaw Answers Eight Questions', *Daily Express* 26 March 1938, p. 12.

423 / 3   **purpose:** 'Persecution of the Jews: (3) How to Deal with the Jewish Difficulty', *Time and Tide* XIX, 26 November 1938, Supplement.

423 / 10   **begin:** *Chronicle of a Life* p. 365.

423 / 11   **Germany:** G.B.S. to Siegfried Trebitsch, 12–15 May 1933, *CL*4 p. 338 (Shaw/Trebitsch letters p. 334).

423 / 15   **spring?:** G.B.S. to Trebitsch, 15 March 1938, Shaw/Trebitsch letters p. 370.

423 / 18   **persecution:** G.B.S. to Trebitsch, 18 March 1938, *CL*4 p. 496 (Shaw/Trebitsch letters p. 372).

423 / 24   **harm:** G.B.S. to Trebitsch, 7 December 1938, 31 January 1939, *CL*4 p. 525 (Shaw/Trebitsch letters pp. 380, 383).

423 / 27   **electric:** G.B.S. to Trebitsch, 25 March 1939, Shaw/Trebitsch letters p. 386.

423/33   **authenticity:** *CP*7 p. 168.

424/ 7   **war:** G.B.S. to Trebitsch, 25 March 1939, Shaw/Trebitsch
            letters p. 386.

424/18   **mad:** 'Can Anyone Explain?', *The Times* 28 August 1939, p. 11.

424/24   **time:** *Chronicle of a Life* p. 372.

424/25   **again:** Ibid., p. 375.

424/29   **!!!!!:** G.B.S. to Siegfried Trebitsch, 3 November 1939,
            Shaw/Trebitsch letters p. 390.

424/last **business:** G.B.S. to Trebitsch, 28 September 1942,
            Shaw/Trebitsch letters p. 413.

CHAPTER VI

425/Ep. 1   **itself:** G.B.S. to C. H. Norman, 22 April 1940, *CL*4 p. 554.

425/ 8   **time:** G.B.S. to Beatrice Webb, 17 September 1939, *CL*4
            p. 538.

425/14   **lives:** G.B.S. to Blanche Patch, 6 September 1939, *CL*4 p. 536.

425/15   **Says:** '"War is Over," Shaw Says: Sees Stalin Outwitting Both
            Sides', *New York Journal-American* 6 October 1939, p. 1. See
            also 'War is Over, Stalin Victor, Shaw Claims', *Daily Mirror*
            (New York) 7 October 1939, p. 4.

425/18   **Lights:** 'Cease Fire, Turn Up the Lights', *Daily Worker* 14
            October 1939, p. 1: 'The sooner the order is given to Cease
            Fire and Turn Up the Lights the better'.

425/25   **through it:** G.B.S. to Blanche Patch, 5 and 6 September 1939,
            *CL*4 pp. 535–6.

426/ 4   **1914:** Leonard Woolf, *The Journey Not the Arrival Matters: An
            Autobiography of the Years 1939 to 1969* (1969) p. 9.

426/ 7   **happen:** Cecil Beaton, *The Years Between: Diaries 1939–44*
            (1965) p. 13.

426/10   **it is:** *Chips: The Diaries of Sir Henry Channon* (ed. Robert
            Rhodes James 1967) p. 226.

426/14   **together:** Frances Partridge, *A Pacifist's War* (1978) p. 23.

426/18   **do:** G.B.S. to Siegfried Trebitsch, 11 April 1940,
            Shaw/Trebitsch letters p. 397.

426/25   **owls:** G.B.S. to Trebitsch, 7 April 1940, 18 April 1940
            [postmarked], Shaw/Trebitsch letters pp. 396, 398.

426/29   **us:** G.B.S. to Kingsley Martin, n.d. [1939] (University of
            Sussex).

426/33   **species:** 'Break Germany For Ever? Nonsense!' *Sunday
            Pictorial* 13 August 1944, p. 4.

427/ 2   **Baltic:** G.B.S. to Nancy Astor, 28 September 1939, *CL*4
            p. 539.

427/11   **before it:** 'Uncommon Sense about the War', *New Statesman*
          21 October 1939, pp. 549–50.

427/16   **'great war:** *The Diary of Beatrice Webb* vol. 4, entry 5 October
          1939, pp. 442–3.

427/23   **pride:** Harold Nicolson, *Diaries and Letters 1939–45* (ed. Nigel
          Nicolson 1967) p. 30.

427/26   **dry up:** Samuel Courtauld to Christabel Aberconway, 20
          October 1939, BL Add. MS 52434 f. 55.

427/34   **useful:** G.B.S. to J. M. Keynes, 5 October 1939, *CL*4 p. 541.

427/37   **war:** Kingsley Martin, *Editor: a second volume of autobiography
          1931–45* (1968) p. 268.

428/ 7   **Tie:** Ibid., p. 269.

428/10   **Hitlerism:** 'Capitalism in the Future', *Sunday Express* 8
          October 1944, p. 4.

428/12   **grasp:** 'Uncommon Sense about the War', *New Statesman* 21
          October 1939, pp. 549–50. See also *Editor* p. 270.

428/22   **intermission:** 'Authors and the War: Exploited Patriotism', *The
          Author*, Spring 1940, p. 6.

428/27   **skilled:** G.B.S. to the Editor, *Daily Telegraph* 6 February 1940,
          Bernard Shaw: Agitations: Letters to the Press 1875–1950 (ed.
          Dan H. Laurence and James Rambeau 1985) p. 312.

428/32   **ritual:** Kenneth Clark, *The Other Half* (1977) p. 1.

428/last **them?:** G.B.S. to the Editor, *The Times* 5 September 1939,
          Agitations p. 306.

429/21   **warriors:** Ashley Dukes, *Theatre Arts* January 1945.

429/23   **ruin me:** G.B.S. to Roy Limbert, 21 March 1943 (Texas).

429/30   **Street:** 'Conscription of Wealth', *The Times* 24 December
          1941, p. 5.

429/33   **commission:** 'G.B.S. on L.S.D.', *Daily Herald* 22 May 1941,
          p. 2.

430/11   **appearance:** Typescript by Basil Langton (copy privately
          owned).

430/17   **again:** G.B.S. to Beatrice Webb, 17 February 1941, *CL*4
          p. 595.

430/18   **controversy:** G.B.S. to Siegfried Trebitsch, 18 October 1939,
          Shaw/Trebitsch letters p. 389.

430/26   **prevail:** 'G.B.S. – If I were Churchill!: Shaw Discusses War
          Strategy', *Cavalcade* 1 November 1941, p. 1.

430/30   **allusions:** 29 May 1940 entry, 'War-time Diary', *The Collected
          Essays, Journalism and Letters of George Orwell*, vol. 2: *My
          Country Right or Left 1940–1943* (ed. Sonia Orwell and Ian
          Angus 1970 edn) p. 386.

430/34   **events:** Emrys Hughes, 'George Bernard Shaw', *Forward* 11
          November 1950.

431 / 3   **with him:** 'How to Talk Intelligently about the War' (typescript, Cornell). Also BL Add. MS 50698 f. 145.

431 / 7   **line:** *Chips: The Diaries of Sir Henry Channon* p. 235.

431 / 14   **do not:** '"Mouthpiece for the Nation": Bernard Shaw on Our Propaganda', *The Observer* 15 October 1939, p. 12.

431 / 20   **name:** G.B.S. to Beatrice Webb, 17 June 1940, *CL*4 p. 559.

431 / 23   **Munich:** 'G.B.S. – If I were Churchill!: Shaw Discusses War Strategy', *Cavalcade* 1 November 1941, p. 1.

431 / 29   **definition:** *Bernard Shaw and Alfred Douglas: A Correspondence* (ed. Mary Hyde 1982) p. 159.

431 / 36   **Communism:** *Shaw: Interviews and Recollections* (ed. A. M. Gibbs 1990) p. 470. Also 'How to Talk Intelligently about the War', BL Add. MS 50698 f. 146.

432 / 2   **gratify:** 'To Bomb or Not to Bomb?', *Sunday Chronicle* 4 May 1941, p. 1.

432 / 8   **them:** 'Reprisals', *Sunday Dispatch* 3 November 1940, p. 11.

432 / 15   **shelled:** 'But Shaw Isn't Dismayed', *Daily Mail* 2 December 1939, p. 6.

432 / 20   **situation:** G.B.S. to the Editor, *Yorkshire Evening Post* 14 March 1940, *Agitations* p. 317.

432 / 23   **Jingoes:** 'Uncommon Sense about the War', *New Statesman* 21 October 1939, pp. 549–50; 'Peace Aims', *New Statesman* 18 November 1939, pp. 711–12.

432 / 30   **lie:** G.B.S. to Anthony Weymouth, 20 March 1940 (privately owned).

433 / 3   **Russia:** 'The Unavoidable Subject', June 1940. See *Platform and Pulpit* (ed. with an introduction by Dan H. Laurence 1962) pp. 286–92.

433 / 9   **right:** Harold Nicolson to Sir Frederick Ogilvie, 5 July 1940 (BBC, Caversham).

433 / 14   **him:** Sir Stephen Tallents to Ministry of Information, 12 June 1940 (BBC, Caversham).

433 / 15   **across:** Harold Nicolson to Ogilvie, 5 July 1940 (BBC, Caversham).

433 / 21   **cause:** Tallents to Harold Nicolson, n.d. (BBC, Caversham). See also Asa Briggs, *The War of Words* (1970) p. 212.

433 / 22   **air:** Cited *CL*4 p. 563.

433 / 23   **Worker:** G.B.S. to Ivo Geikie-Cobb, 24 June 1940, *CL*4 p. 563.

433 / 33   **importance:** 'What About "Daily Worker"? Stalin and Lindbergh', *Forward* 1 February 1941, p. 3.

433 / 35   **products:** *Daily Film Renter* 1 January 1946. See *Shaw: Interviews and Recollections* p. 392.

434/ 4   **country:** Ibid.

434/ 7   **concerned:** Valerie Pascal, *The Disciple and His Devil* (1970) p. 93.

434/13   **films:** G.B.S. to Kenneth Clark, 11 June 1941 (privately owned).

434/20   **propaganda:** Kenneth Clark, *The Other Half* (1977) p. 38.

434/25   **them:** G.B.S. to Blanche Patch, 5 September 1939, *CL4* p. 535.

434/30   **Guinness:** G.B.S. to Gabriel Pascal, 28 February [June] 1940, *CL4* p. 565.

434/34   **insured?:** S. N. Behrman, *The Suspended Drawing Room* (1965) p. 76.

434/40   **Middlesex:** *The Disciple and His Devil* p. 89.

435/ 3   **plays:** Ibid., p. 91.

435/14   **pantomime:** G.B.S. to Leonard Elmhirst, 5 April 1940, *CL4* p. 553.

435/18   **fire:** *The Collected Screenplays of Bernard Shaw* (ed. with an introduction by Bernard F. Dukore 1980) p. 98.

435/23   **Whitehall:** *The Disciple and His Devil* p. 97.

435/28   **production:** *The Shaw Review* XIV, no. 1, January 1971, p. 35.

435/30   **friends:** *The Collected Screenplays of Bernard Shaw* p. 98.

435/40   **me!:** Ibid., pp. 95, 99.

435/last   **mad?:** G.B.S. to Wendy Hiller, 4 December 1940, *CL4* p. 589.

436/ 2   **me:** *The Shaw Review* XIV, no. 1, January 1971, p. 35.

436/ 4   **virgin:** *The Collected Screenplays of Bernard Shaw* p. 100.

436/12   **director:** *The Shaw Review* XIV, no. 1, January 1971, p. 35.

436/17   **takes:** *The Collected Screenplays of Bernard Shaw* p. 100.

436/20   **pictures:** Cited *CL4* p. 565 (*The Disciple and His Devil* p. 95).

436/25   **Hollywood:** *The Collected Screenplays of Bernard Shaw* p. 92.

436/28   **movies:** Gabriel Pascal to G.B.S., 3 July 1940. Cited *CL4* p. 565.

436/31   **can:** G.B.S. to Gabriel Pascal, 6 July 1940, *CL4* p. 566.

436/36   **that:** *The Collected Screenplays of Bernard Shaw* p. 94.

437/10   **couldn't:** *The Disciple and His Devil* p. 96.

437/15   **extravagance:** *The Suspended Drawing Room* p. 78.

437/22   **dream:** G.B.S. to Gabriel Pascal, 6 July 1940, *CL4* p. 566.

437/25   **Windsor:** *The Disciple and His Devil* p. 99.

437/32   **missing:** *The Collected Screenplays of Bernard Shaw* p. 111.

437/37   **profiteer:** G.B.S. to Gilbert Murray, 5 September 1941, *CL4* p. 613.

437/38   **disappointment:** *The Shaw Review* XIV, no. 1, January 1971, p. 35.

437/39   **thrilled:** Gilbert Murray to G.B.S. 26 July 1941 (Texas).

438/11   **reason:** H. G. Wells to G.B.S., 16 April 1941. *Shaw: An Exhibit*, a catalog by Dan H. Laurence for an Exhibit Selected and Prepared with Lois B. Garcia (Texas, 1977), item 735.

438/20   **his:** Rex Harrison, *Rex: an Autobiography* (1974) p. 70.

438/23   **one:** 'George Bernard Shaw on Will Hitler Invade?', *Daily Express* 24 September 1940, p. 4.

438/28   **hunt:** G.B.S. to F. R. Brown Jr, 7 July 1941 (Cornell).

438/32   **destroyers:** *CP3* p. 64.

438/last   **marching on:** Ibid., p. 65.

439/13   **farewell!:** Ibid.

439/Ep.   **were:** G.B.S. to Lillah McCarthy, 24 October 1942 (Berg).

439/16   **Adolf:** G.B.S. to Ada Tyrrell, 27 June 1940, *CL4* p. 564.

439/18   **invasion:** G.B.S. to Siegfried Trebitsch, 20 August 1940, Shaw/Trebitsch letters p. 399.

439/23   **dressing:** G.B.S. to Alfred Douglas, 28 August 1940, *CL4* p. 575 (*Bernard Shaw and Alfred Douglas: A Correspondence* p. 131).

439/29   **good:** Charlotte Shaw to Nancy Astor, 1 October 1940 (Reading).

439/31   **routine:** G.B.S. to Nancy Astor, 21 September 1940 (Reading).

439/34   **trouble:** G.B.S. to F. N. Hornsby, 4 December 1940 (Texas).

440/ 3   **insults:** G.B.S. to Nancy Astor, 21 September 1940 (Reading).

440/ 6   **matter:** G.B.S. to Maurice Colbourne, 11 October 1940 (Theatre Museum, Victoria and Albert Museum).

440/15   **to go:** Blanche Patch, *Thirty Years with G.B.S.* [ghostwritten by Robert Williamson 1951] p. 39.

440/25   **hurt:** G.B.S. to Nancy Astor, 30 January 1941, *CL4* p. 593.

440/34   **to him:** *Thirty Years with G.B.S.* p. 39.

440/38   **telephone:** G.B.S. to Nancy Astor, 16 April 1942 (Reading).

441/ 8   **of it:** *Thirty Years with G.B.S.* p. 40.

441/11   **them:** G.B.S. to Upton Sinclair, 12 December 1941 (Lilly Library, Indiana University).

441/16   **did:** G.B.S. to Alfred Douglas, 27 December 1941, *CL4* p. 623 (*Bernard Shaw and Alfred Douglas: A Correspondence* p. 147).

441/23   **scoundrels:** G.B.S. to Beatrice Webb, 4 August 1941 (LSE).

441/31   **Providence:** G.B.S. to Siegfried Trebitsch, 8 August 1942, Shaw/Trebitsch letters p. 412.

441/36   **paths:** G.B.S. to Robertson Scott, 2 September 1939 (Princeton). See also 'Strength and Stay', *Countryman* XX, January 1940, p. 419.

442/ 2   **smiling:** Charlotte Shaw to Nancy Astor, 27 October 1940 (Reading).

442/ 5   **him:** *Thirty Years with G.B.S.* p. 37.

442/ 9   **out:** Blanche Patch to G.B.S., 4 August 1942 (Texas).

442/15   **again:** G.B.S. to Beatrice Webb, 7 February 1942 (Texas).

442/19   **place:** Charlotte Shaw to F. N. Hornsby, 26 October 1940 (Texas).

442/33   **here!:** Charlotte Shaw to Nancy Astor, n.d. (Reading).

442/26   **intensely:** *Thirty Years with G.B.S.* p. 38.

442/28   **posture:** G.B.S. to Beatrice Webb, 17 February 1941, *CL*4 p. 594.

442/32   **does:** Charlotte Shaw to Hugh Walpole, 6 April 1941 (Texas).

442/37   **cant:** Charlotte Shaw to Nancy Astor, 1 October 1940 (Reading).

442/39   **cellar:** Charlotte Shaw to Nancy Astor, 10 August 1941 (Reading).

443/ 2   **corner:** G.B.S. to Nancy Astor, 19 July 1941 (Reading).

443/12   *fortissimo*: Joyce Grenfell, *Joyce Grenfell Requests the Pleasure* (1976) pp. 160–1.

443/13   **prison:** Charlotte Shaw to Nancy Astor, 30 August 1941 (Reading).

443/16   **repetitions:** G.B.S. to H. G. Wells, 3 January 1941 (Illinois).

443/18   **not:** G.B.S. to H. G. Wells, 16 March 1942 (Illinois).

443/20   **barren:** G.B.S. note to Loewenstein for Roy Limbert and J. Baxter Somerville, April 1940 (Texas).

443/29   **of it:** *G.B.S. 90: Aspects of Bernard Shaw's Life and Work* (ed. Stephen Winsten 1946) p. 178.

443/36   **dejection:** Manuscript of *An Abiding Curiosity* by Laurence Irving (privately owned).

444/ 2   **ignorance:** G.B.S. to Sidney Webb, 24 May 1943 (LSE).

444/ 9   **hither:** G.B.S. to Kenneth Barnes, 23 July 1941, *CL*4 p. 607.

444/20   **day:** Charlotte Shaw to Nancy Astor, 15 December 1941 (Reading).

444/21   **bear:** Ibid.

444/27   **job:** Charlotte Shaw to Beatrice Webb, 10 October 1940 (LSE).

444/29   **worrying:** G.B.S. to Nancy Astor, 22 October 1942, *CL*4 p. 643.

444/36   **stoop:** G.B.S. to Nancy Astor, 22 April 1942 (Reading).

444/38   **both:** G.B.S. to H. G. Wells, 7 December 1939 (Illinois).

444/40   **wrinkled:** G.B.S. to H. G. Wells, 12 September 1943, *CL*4 p. 677.

445/ 5   **skeleton:** G.B.S. to Beatrice Webb, 17 February 1941, *CL*4 p. 596.

445/ 7   **anything:** G.B.S. to Nancy Astor, 4 March 1942 (Reading).

445/ 9   **through:** Charlotte Shaw to Nancy Astor, 10 February 1942 (Reading).

445/14   **sort:** G.B.S. to Upton Sinclair, 12 December 1941 (Lilly Library, Indiana University).

445/19   **hands:** G.B.S. to Nancy Astor, 11 July 1942 (Reading).

445/23   **limb:** G.B.S. to Beatrice Webb, 26 November 1942 (LSE).

445/27   **age:** Ibid.

445/29   **pneumonia:** G.B.S. to H. G. Wells, 12 September 1943, *CL*4 p. 677.

445/31   **dull:** G.B.S. to Nancy Astor, 17 August 1942 (Reading).

445/32   **Spitfires:** G.B.S. to Nancy Astor, 11 April 1943 (Reading).

445/37   **darling:** G.B.S. to Nancy Astor, 17 August 1942 (Reading).

446/ 6   **end:** G.B.S. to Sidney Webb, 29 April 1943, *CL*4 p. 668.

446/13   **heartbreaking:** G.B.S. to Nancy Astor, 17 June 1943 (Reading).

446/14   **diminish:** G.B.S. to Sidney Webb, 24 May 1943 (LSE).

446/24   **realised:** *Shaw the Villager and Human Being: A Biographical Symposium* (ed. Allan Chappelow 1961) p. 128.

446/28   **them:** Michael Holroyd, *Bernard Shaw* vol. 1 (1988) p. 465.

446/31   **slopes:** *Shaw: Interviews and Recollections* p. 171.

446/35   **seems:** Maurice Collis, *Somerville and Ross: a Biography* (1968) p. 127.

447/ 1   **etiquette:** *Shaw the Villager and Human Being* p. 154.

447/ 3   **Queen:** *Shaw: Interviews and Recollections* p. 187.

447/ 8   **conduct:** *Shaw the Villager and Human Being* p. 259, 259n.

447/10   **day:** *Marlborough Express* (New Zealand) 11 April 1934.

447/14   **point:** Hesketh Pearson, *Bernard Shaw* (1975 rev. edn) p. 454.

447/29   **lives:** Lena Ashwell, *Myself a Player* (1936) pp. 282, 191.

447/35   **other:** Hesketh Pearson, *Bernard Shaw* p. 456.

447/37   **conscience:** Obituary for Charlotte Shaw by Lady Rhondda in *Time and Tide* 18 September 1943.

447/39   **dreams:** Interview with Charlotte Shaw in *Boston Post* 29 April 1914. See *Shaw: Interviews and Recollections* p. 180.

447/last   **indestructible:** Hesketh Pearson, *Bernard Shaw* p. 456.

448/ 2   **life:** Janet Dunbar, *Mrs G.B.S.: A Biographical Portrait of Charlotte Shaw* (1963) p. 313.

448/ 9   **beliefs:** *Boston Post* 29 April 1914. See *Shaw: Interviews and Recollections* p. 180.

448/17   **audience:** Lawrence Langner, *G.B.S. and the Lunatic* (1963) p. 59.

448/27   **to me:** Hesketh Pearson, *Bernard Shaw* p. 452.

448/35   **lights:** *Mrs G.B.S.* p. 312.

448/37   **lasts:** G.B.S. to Nancy Astor, 25 July 1941 (Reading).

448 / last   **together:** G.B.S. to Beatrice Webb, 4 August 1941 (LSE).

449 / 13   **advise me:** *Shaw the Villager and Human Being* p. 75.

449 / 14   **for her:** G.B.S. to Sidney Webb, 29 April 1943, *CL*4 p. 668.

449 / 17   **age:** Beatrice Webb's diaries, 17 August 1942 (LSE).

449 / 19   **interest:** *The Diary of Beatrice Webb* vol. 4, entry 19 April 1943, p. 496.

449 / 26   **else:** G.B.S. to Sidney Webb, 24 May 1943 (LSE).

449 / 32   **properly:** *Shaw the Villager and Human Being* p. 76.

449 / 33   **witch:** Ibid., p. 285.

449 / 38   **done:** G.B.S. to Nancy Astor, 1 June 1943 (Reading).

450 / 2   **about her:** G.B.S. to Ethel Shaw, 25 August 1943 (Cornell).

450 / 4   **here:** G.B.S. to H. G. Wells, 4 August 1943 (Illinois).

450 / 8   **for her:** G.B.S. to Nancy Astor, 21 August 1943 (Reading).

450 / 12   **dying:** 'Tributes to Bernard Shaw', no. 1 by St John Ervine, *The Listener* 9 November 1950.

450 / 22   **worse:** G.B.S. to Almroth Wright, 17 September 1943 (privately owned).

450 / 24   **mornings:** *Shaw the Villager and Human Being* p. 77.

450 / 39   **over:** G.B.S. to Almroth Wright, 17 September 1943 (privately owned).

451 / 6   **young:** Ibid.

451 / 7   **help:** Ronald Mavor, *Dr Mavor and Mr Bridie* (1988) p. 117.

451 / 10   **please her:** *Shaw the Villager and Human Being* p. 78.

451 / 16   **beautiful:** Hesketh Pearson, *Bernard Shaw* p. 454.

451 / 21   **dead:** Ibid.

451 / 25   **heaven:** G.B.S. to H. G. Wells, 12 September 1943, *CL*4 p. 677.

451 / 28   **to you:** *Bernard Shaw's Letters to Granville Barker* (ed. C. B. Purdom 1957) p. 200. See also *Granville Barker and his Correspondents* (ed. Eric Salmon 1986) p. 162.

451 / 32   **moved:** G.B.S. to H. G. Wells, 12 September 1943, *CL*4 p. 678.

452 / 5   **more:** Ibid.

452 / 8   **sight:** Blanche Patch to W. R. Rodgers, 21 September 1954 (Texas).

452 / Ep.   **party:** G.B.S. to Nancy Astor, 11 August 1944 (Reading).

452 / 14   **Green:** G.B.S. to H. G. Wells, 12 September 1943, *CL*4 p. 678.

452 / 18   **serenity:** Notice in 'Personal' column, acknowledging messages of sympathy on the death of Charlotte F. Shaw, *The Times* 20 September 1943 p. 1.

452 / 20   **congratulations:** G.B.S. to Sean O'Casey, 29 September 1943 (copy, Society of Authors).

452/21   **distress:** G.B.S. to Sidney Webb, 12 September 1943 (LSE).
452/25   **desolate:** *Bernard Shaw and Alfred Douglas: A Correspondence* p. 174.
452/28   **P[atch]:** G.B.S. to Nancy Astor, 27 December 1943 (Reading).
452/29   **happened:** G.B.S. to Edith Evans, 15 September 1943 (copy, Society of Authors).
452/33   **forget:** G.B.S. to Lord Melchett, 28 September 1948 (Theatre Museum, Victoria and Albert Museum).
452/last **anybody:** St John Ervine, *Bernard Shaw: His Life, Work and Friends* (1956) p. 576.
453/ 5   **like:** G.B.S. to Sidney Webb, 26 October 1945, *CL4* p. 757.
453/ 7   **either:** *Shaw the Villager and Human Being* p. 28.
453/13   **melancholy:** G.B.S. to William Maxwell, 15 September 1943 (Cornell).
453/17   **life:** G.B.S. to Otto Kyllmann, 15 September 1943 (North Carolina).
453/19   **died:** G.B.S. to Rutland Boughton, 4 September 1946, BL Add. MS 52365 f. 74. G.B.S. to Nancy Astor, 15 October 1943 (Reading).
453/22   **free:** *Bernard Shaw and Alfred Douglas: A Correspondence* pp. 174–5.
453/26   **obviously:** *Shaw the Villager and Human Being* p. 214.
453/32   **marriage:** Keith Bryant, *Marie Stopes, a Biography* (1962) p. 7.
454/ 3   **chairman:** Blanche Patch, *Thirty Years with G.B.S.* p. 114.
454/ 8   **quiet:** Blanche Patch to W. R. Rodgers, 21 September 1954 (Texas).
454/ 9   **with us:** Ibid.
454/11   **to me:** *Thirty Years with G.B.S.* p. 114.
454/16   **conversations:** G.B.S. to Nancy Astor, 17 October 1947 (Reading) and 21 October 1947, *CL4* p. 804.
454/25   **Cliveden:** G.B.S. to Nancy Astor, 27 December 1943 (Reading).
454/31   **mouth:** Lilli Palmer, *Change Lobsters – and Dance: An Autobiography* (1976) p. 191.
454/35   **alone:** G.B.S. to Nancy Astor, 2 January 1944 (Reading).
454/38   **you can!:** Charlotte Shaw to Nancy Astor, 28 June 1931 (Reading).
454/last **teatime:** G.B.S. to Nancy Astor, 2 January 1944 (Reading).
455/33   **for them:** Ibid.
455/ 6   **world now:** G.B.S. to Nancy Astor, 17 April 1945 (Reading).
455/27   **sleepless nights:** Blanche Patch to Hesketh Pearson, 7 July 1944 (copy privately owned).
455/32   **week:** G.B.S. to Nancy Astor, 29 June 1944 (Reading).

455/35   **for us:** *Shaw the Villager and Human Being* p. 56.
455/last   **Hitler:** Ibid., p. 52.
456/ 4   **else:** Ibid., p. 51.
456/ 9   *I* **die:** Ibid., p. 25.
456/12   **him:** Ibid., pp. 29, 36.
456/18   **pieces:** G.B.S. to Nancy Astor, 6 October 1944 (Reading).
456/26   **hand:** Ibid.
456/28   **years:** Ibid.
456/33   **altogether:** G.B.S. to Blanche Patch, 21 February 1945, *CL*4
           p. 740.
456/34   **Mrs Laden:** G.B.S. to Nancy Astor, 8 May 1944 (Reading).
457/ 3   **effect:** G.B.S. to Nancy Astor, 27 August 1944 (Reading).
457/ 9   **mine:** *Shaw the Villager and Human Being* pp. 27–8.
457/13   **well:** Ibid., p. 309.
457/15   **views:** Ibid., p. 27.
457/20   **watchdog:** Ibid., p. 26.
457/37   **doing it:** G.B.S. to Nancy Astor, 6 October 1944 (Reading).
457/38   **ladies:** G.B.S. to Nancy Astor, 11 August 1944 (Reading).
457/40   **pin pricks:** Blanche Patch to Hesketh Pearson, 31 March 1945
           (copy privately owned).
458/ 1   **Zadist:** Ibid.
458/ 4   **demand:** G.B.S. to Nancy Astor, 12 March 1944 (Reading).
458/ 5   **happiest:** Act III, *Buoyant Billions*; *CP*7 p. 357.
458/11   **widowhood:** G.B.S. to Lady Rhondda, 8 December 1948
           (Fales).
458/12   **wife:** Ibid.
458/15   **house:** G.B.S. to Eleanor O'Connell, 15 July 1950 (copy
           privately owned).
458/19   **days:** G.B.S. to Molly Tompkins, 4 December 1944, *To a
           Young Actress: The Letters of Bernard Shaw to Molly Tompkins*
           (ed. Peter Tompkins 1960) p. 180.
458/31   **this:** G.B.S. to Brownrigg, 4 September 1932, 2 August 1932
           (copy privately owned).
458/39   **with you?:** G.B.S. to Molly Tompkins, c. November 1931, *To a
           Young Actress* p. 151.
459/ 1   **than ever:** Peter Tompkins, *Shaw and Molly Tompkins* (1961)
           p. 214.
459/ 5   **triumph!:** Charlotte Shaw to Molly Tompkins, undated, *Shaw
           and Molly Tompkins* p. 224.
459/ 8   **near us:** G.B.S. to Molly Tompkins, 21 December 1937, *To a
           Young Actress* p. 168.
459/18   **letters:** G.B.S. to Molly Tompkins, 4 December 1944, *To a
           Young Actress* p. 181.

459/21   **shocks:** G.B.S. to Molly Tompkins, 18 December 1946, *To a Young Actress* p. 185.

459/29   **gates:** G.B.S. to Molly Tompkins, 30 October 1945, *To a Young Actress* p. 184.

459/33   **heart:** Partially quoted in Margot Peters, *Bernard Shaw and the Actresses* (1980) pp. 408–9, from the originals in the British Library.

459/34   **correspondent:** G.B.S. to Molly Tompkins, 3 February 1949, *To a Young Actress* p. 187.

459/35   **lost:** Molly Tompkins to G.B.S., November 1945, BL 50551 ff. 21–25.

459/last **of them:** G.B.S. to Molly Tompkins, 15 July 1931, *To a Young Actress* p. 149.

460/ 1   **job:** Blanche Patch to Hesketh Pearson, 6 January 1945 (copy privately owned).

460/ 7   **mad:** Blanche Patch to Hesketh Pearson, 19 November 1944 (copy privately owned).

460/ 9   **abolition:** 'How I Like to Spend Christmas', *People's National Theatre Magazine* IV, December 1937, p. 22.

460/17   **move off:** Blanche Patch to Hesketh Pearson, 19 November 1944 (copy privately owned).

460/24   **suffer:** Blanche Patch to Hesketh Pearson, 1 November 1944 (copy privately owned).

460/28   **own:** G.B.S. to Blanche Patch, 23 November 1945, *CL*4 p. 759.

460/33   **heart:** John Wardrop recollection [assigned to 1942] for G.B.S. of their first meeting; undated transcription. See *CL*4 p. 636.

460/35   **complete:** Ibid.

461/ 2   **them all?:** G.B.S. to John Wardrop, 21 December 1939 (National Library of Wales).

461/ 9   **nonpareil:** G.B.S. to John Wardrop, 3 September 1942, *CL*4 p. 638.

461/12   **the other:** G.B.S. to Blanche Patch, n.d. [assigned to 17 February 1945], *CL*4 p. 739.

461/12   **of me?:** John Wardrop to G.B.S., 11 November 1941 (copy Bucknell).

461/19   **polish:** G.B.S. to Blanch Patch, n.d. [assigned to 17 February 1945], *CL*4 p. 739.

461/31   **safety:** Blanche Patch typescript, 'Eleanor O'Connell' (copy Bucknell).

461/32   **died:** Blanche Patch to Hesketh Pearson, 1 November 1944 (copy privately owned).

461/34   **hair:** John Wardrop recollection [assigned to 1942] for G.B.S. of their first meeting; undated transcription. See *CL*4 p. 636.

461/last **you up:** G.B.S. to John Wardrop, n.d. (copy Bucknell).

462/ 2 **on me:** Blanche Patch to Hesketh Pearson, 1 November 1944 (copy privately owned).

462/ 6 **scholarship:** Dan H. Laurence, *Bernard Shaw: A Bibliography* (1983) vol. 1, p. ix.

462/ 7 **digging:** Ibid., p. x.

462/ 9 **to it:** G.B.S. to F. E. Loewenstein, 10 December 1936, *CL*4 p. 450.

462/16 **mechanic-trainee:** Loewenstein to G.B.S., 19 September 1942 (Boston).

462/18 **goods:** Ibid.

462/23 **principles:** Shaw Society prospectus (1941).

462/27 **proceedings:** G.B.S. to F. E. Loewenstein, 11 September 1942, *CL*4 p. 640.

462/33 **Shaw:** G.B.S. to Loewenstein, 1 February 1943 (Boston).

462/36 **Society:** Loewenstein to G.B.S., 19 September 1942 (Boston).

463/ 1 **fool:** G.B.S. to Loewenstein, 13 June 1942, 2 November 1943, 17 January 1944 (Boston).

463/ 3 **creature:** G.B.S. to the Sheffield Shaw Society, 31 December 1943, *CL*4 p. 687.

463/12 **struggles:** Blanche Patch to Hesketh Pearson, 7 July 1944 (copy privately owned).

463/15 **retired:** Ibid.

463/17 **works:** Ibid.

463/20 **in for:** Ibid.

463/25 **heir:** G.B.S. to Blanche Patch, n.d. [assigned to 17 February 1945], *CL*4 p. 739.

463/26 **world:** G.B.S. to Blanche Patch, n.d. (Texas).

463/33 **time:** G.B.S. to Blanche Patch, 17 January 1945 (Bucknell).

463/38 **Jew:** Blanche Patch to Hesketh Pearson, 19 November 1944 (copy privately owned).

464/ 2 **attendance:** G.B.S. to Blanche Patch, 17 January 1945 (Bucknell).

464/ 4 **W[ardrop]:** G.B.S. to Blanche Patch, 10 February 1945 (Texas).

464/ 9 **sanity:** G.B.S. to Blanche Patch, 17 February 1945, *CL*4 p. 738.

464/13 **for it:** G.B.S. to Blanche Patch, n.d. [assigned to 17 February 1945], *CL*4 p. 739.

464/17 **Swift:** Denis Johnston 1954 B.B.C. interview. See *CL*4 p. 692.

464/29 **Splendid:** G.B.S. to Nancy Astor, 13 April 1945, CL4 p. 742.

464/ 3 **traced:** Blanche Patch to Hesketh Pearson, 7 July 1944 (copy privately owned).

464/34 **Wardrop:** G.B.S. to Nancy Astor, 6 April 1945 (Reading).

464/36 **bedroom:** G.B.S. to Eleanor O'Connell, 8 April 1945 (copy Bucknell).

465/ 4 **Loewenstein:** F. E. Loewenstein to Nancy Astor, 5 April 1945 (Reading).

465/10 **life:** Christopher Sykes, *Nancy: The Life of Lady Astor* (1979 edn) p. 555.

465/14 **does:** Ibid., pp. 557–8.

465/22 **steps:** Nancy Astor to G.B.S., 25 June 1945 and n.d. (Cornell).

465/25 **Germans:** Blanche Patch to Hesketh Pearson, 31 March 1945 (copy privately owned).

465/37 **able:** Alice Laden to Blanche Patch, March 1945 (copy privately owned).

466/ 2 **pass out:** Blanche Patch to Stanley Clench, 13 August 1945 (Cornell).

466/ 9 **see it:** 'Six Sorts of Genius', *The Spectator* 27 July 1956.

466/10 **conventional:** G.B.S. to R. & R. Clark, 4 May 1944 (Texas).

466/12 **visitors:** G.B.S. to Lord Brocket, n.d. [c. 1948] (copy privately owned).

466/22 **to me:** G.B.S. to Ivo Currall, 5 January 1949, *CL*4 p. 837.

466/23 **Loew:** Blanche Patch to William Maxwell, 22 November 1945 (Scotland).

466/27 **friends:** Eleanor O'Connell memorandum, 29 September 1950 (privately owned).

466/28 **hates them:** Ibid.

466/30 **Jew:** See *CL*4 p. 694.

466/31 **lamb:** Blanche Patch quotation in a letter to Hesketh Pearson, 18 November 1945 (copy privately owned).

466/34 **things:** G.B.S. to R. & R. Clark, 4 May 1944 (Texas).

466/36 **with him:** *The Quintessence of G.B.S.: The Wit and Wisdom of Bernard Shaw* (ed. Stephen Winsten 1949) p. 7.

466/38 **about me:** Stephen Winsten, *Days with Bernard Shaw* (1951 edn) p. 7.

466/last **friendship:** Ibid.

467/ 2 **art:** Jacket flap copy, Stephen Winsten, *Jesting Apostle: The Life of Bernard Shaw* (1956).

467/ 5 **beside him:** *Days with Bernard Shaw* p. 7.

467/11 **nature:** 'Conversation Pieces', *The Times Literary Supplement* 15 January 1949, p. 41.

467/15 **apologetic:** *Days with Bernard Shaw* pp. 7–8.

467/18 **inventions:** G.B.S. to S. K. Ratcliffe, 9 January 1949 (Texas).

467/19 **Shawland:** G.B.S. to Robert E. Sherwood, *New York Times Book Review* 1 May 1949. See *CL*4 p. 836.

467 / 23   **himself:** Stephen Winsten, *Shaw's Corner* (1952) p. ix.

467 / 26   **fiction:** *Jesting Apostle* p. 7.

467 / 28   **contact:** *Shaw's Corner* p. viii.

467 / 33   **artist:** Quoted in a letter from G.B.S. to Nancy Astor, 31 August 1946 (Reading).

468 / 2   **pounds:** G.B.S. to Clare Winsten, 11 September 1944 (Cornell).

468 / 17   **entirely:** Blanche Patch to William Maxwell, 18 October 1945 (Texas).

468 / 31   **offstage:** G.B.S. to Blanche Patch, 13 October 1945, *CL*4 p. 754.

469 / 5   **shorthand-typist:** Blanche Patch to G.B.S., November 1945 (Cornell).

469 / 18   **what will?:** G.B.S. to Blanche Patch, 23 November 1945, *CL*4 pp. 758–9.

469 / 23   **duties:** Blanche Patch to G.B.S., 26 November 1945 (Cornell).

469 / 31   **books?:** G.B.S. to Blanche Patch, n.d. (Texas).

469 / 38   **for it:** *Shaw the Villager and Human Being* p. 31.

469 / last   **terms:** G.B.S. to Nancy Astor, 31 August 1946 (Reading).

470 / 4   **fact:** G.B.S. to Blanche Patch, 24 August 1946 (copy privately owned).

470 / 7   **freedom:** *CP*6 p. 919.

470 / 14   **money?:** *CP*1 p. 84.

470 / 22   **the other:** Blanche Patch to G.B.S., 26 November 1945 (Cornell).

470 / 29   **of me:** G.B.S. to Blanche Patch, 11 December 1948, *CL*4 p. 833.

470 / last   **for ever:** G.B.S. to Clare Winsten, 6 November 1949 (Cornell).

471 / 4   **established:** *Life Digest* November 1948, p. 17.

471 / 11   **without him:** G.B.S. to Blanche Patch, 30 November 1945, *CL*4 p. 760.

471 / 16   **assistance:** Dan H. Laurence, *Bernard Shaw: A Bibliography* (1983) vol. 2, D16 (a) and (b), p. 835.

471 / 31   **mortgage:** G.B.S. to Ivo Currall, 18 October 1949 (copy privately owned).

471 / last   **you:** Nancy Astor to G.B.S., n.d. (Cornell).

472 / 2   **Keep off:** G.B.S. to Nancy Astor, 5 May 1949 (Reading).

472 / 6   **old man:** Eleanor O'Connell memorandum, 29 September 1950 (privately owned).

472 / 21   **G.B.S.:** G.B.S. to Nancy Astor, 8 May 1949, *CL*4 p. 848.

472 / 24   **work:** Blanche Patch to Hesketh Pearson, 27 April 1945 (copy privately owned).

472/31   **welcome:** G.B.S. to Blanche Patch, 15 January 1949 (Texas).

472/39   **gone:** Blanche Patch, *Thirty Years with G.B.S.* p. 248.

473/Ep.   **get out:** S. N. Behrman, *The Suspended Drawing Room* (1965) p. 92.

473/13   **come back:** Valerie Pascal, *The Disciple and His Devil* (1970) p. 100.

473/17   **himself:** Ibid., p. 103.

473/19   **West:** G.B.S. to Gabriel Pascal, 1 September 1938, *CL*4 p. 508.

473/21   **gentleman:** *Dear Mr Shaw: Selections from Bernard Shaw's postbag* (compiled and ed. Vivian Elliot 1987) p. 190.

473/24   **reassuring:** *The Collected Screenplays of Bernard Shaw* (ed. with an introduction by Bernard F. Dukore 1980) p. 120.

473/30   **Cleopatra:** *The Suspended Drawing Room* p. 85.

473/last   **million:** G.B.S. to Gabriel Pascal, 1 July 1944, *CL*4 p. 713.

474/ 2   **Wonderful, no?:** *The Suspended Drawing Room* p. 85.

474/ 9   **confidence:** *The Collected Screenplays of Bernard Shaw* p. 127. See also Ronald Hayman, *John Gielgud* (1971) p. 143.

474/11   **Caesar:** E. W. & M. M. Robson, *Bernard Shaw Among the Innocents* (1945) p. 23.

474/31   **teeth:** Hugo Vickers, *Vivien Leigh* (1990 edn) p. 169.

474/last   **love it:** *The Collected Screenplays of Bernard Shaw* p. 414.

475/ 5   **seduce him:** Lucy Hughes-Hallett, *Cleopatra: Histories, Dreams and Distortions* (1990) p. 254.

475/19   **wonder:** G.B.S. to Gabriel Pascal, 1 July 1944, *CL*4 p. 714.

475/23   **with!:** Marjorie Deans, *Meeting at the Sphinx: Gabriel Pascal's Production of Bernard Shaw's 'Caesar and Cleopatra'* (1948) p. 28.

475/25   **creation:** G.B.S. to Gabriel Pascal, 1 July 1944, *CL*4 p. 713.

475/38   **film:** Hugo Vickers, *Vivien Leigh* p. 170.

476/ 4   **saboteurs:** *The Disciple and His Devil* p. 106.

476/ 8   **blitz:** *Meeting at the Sphinx* p. 41.

476/20   **clouds:** Stanley Holloway, *Wiv' a Little Bit of Luck* (1967) p. 267.

476/22   **quality:** *Meeting at the Sphinx* p. 96.

476/36   **music:** G.B.S. to Arthur Bliss, 7 May 1944, *CL*4 p. 708.

476/last   **England:** 'Radio Music', *Musical Times* January 1947, *SM*3 p. 758.

477/ 2   **elegance:** G.B.S. to Gabriel Pascal, 16 December 1944, *CL*4 p. 730.

477/ 7   **mark:** *The Disciple and His Devil* p. 96.

477/ 8   **Blissfullest:** G.B.S. to Arthur Bliss, 7 May 1944, *CL*4 p. 709.

477/15   **Handelian:** *Meeting at the Sphinx* p. 107.

477 / 25   **Like this:** *The Suspended Drawing Room* p. 91.

477 / 32   **opinion:** *Thirty Years with G.B.S.* p. 128.

477 / 35   **cinema:** *The Collected Screenplays of Bernard Shaw* p. 146.

478 / 2   **control:** Ibid., p. 147.

478 / 9   **nothing:** G.B.S. to Dorothy Walker, 8 February 1947 (Texas).

478 / 14   **film:** *CP*7 p. 202.

478 / 16   **Mille:** Kenneth Clark, *The Other Half* (1977) p. 40.

478 / 20   **operations:** *The Disciple and His Devil* p. 108.

478 / 26   **England:** Ibid., p. 109.

478 / 36   **exclusively:** Ibid.

478 / 38   **that way:** G.B.S. to Arthur Cox, 8 September 1947, *CL*4 p. 800.

479 / 2   **temperament:** *The Disciple and His Devil* p. 110.

479 / 4   **rights:** G.B.S. to Arthur Cox, 8 September 1947, *CL*4 p. 800.

479 / 10   **in mine:** G.B.S. to Gabriel Pascal, 18 June 1950, *CL*4 p. 869.

479 / 12   **luck:** *The Disciple and His Devil* p. 134.

479 / 15   **me:** Ibid., p. 136.

479 / 19   **sake:** Ibid., p. 197.

479 / 21   **to him:** Ibid., p. 142.

479 / 23   **oracle:** G.B.S. to Nancy Astor, 13 April 1945, *CL*4 p. 742.

479 / 24   **vacuum:** *The Disciple and His Devil* p. 145.

479 / 27   **EVERYBODY:** G.B.S. to Gabriel Pascal, 8 September 1947, *CL*4 p. 801.

479 / Ep.   **returns:** *CP*7 p. 306.

480 / 13   **careerists:** G.B.S. to Beatrice Webb, 26 November 1942, *CL*4 p. 650.

480 / 16   **leisure:** *EPWW* p. 351.

480 / 26   **liberty:** 'Shaw Says Hitler "Has Gone Limit"', *Sunday Referee* 12 June 1938, p. 9.

480 / 36   **practice:** *EPWW* p. 162.

480 / last   **to say:** G.B.S. to Eric Walter White, 2 July 1944 (privately owned).

481 / 16   **sins:** *EPWW* p. 78.

481 / 22   **world:** *New Republic* 26 April 1933.

481 / 24   **childhood:** *EPWW* p. 78.

481 / 28   **in it:** G.B.S. to Otto Kyllmann, 1 September 1944 (Cornell).

481 / 29   **finished too:** G.B.S. to Lillah McCarthy, 24 October 1942 (Texas).

481 / 32   *that can:* *EPWW* p. 366.

481 / last   **loathe war:** Ibid., pp. 144–5.

482 / 3   **line:** G.B.S. to U.S. Office of War Information, 27 August 1944 (Sotheby's Catalogue, 15 June 1975, item 211).

482 / 6   **Japan:** 'Shaw Calm over VE-Day', *New York Journal-American* 12 April 1945, p. 3.

482/ 9   **another:** 'What Does it Mean to You?', *News Chronicle* 16
        August 1945, p. 2.

482/19   **Buddhists:** 'The Atom Bomb', *Sunday Express* 12 August
        1945, p. 4.

482/19   **again:** 'Atomic Warfare', *The Times* 24 December 1949, p. 5.
        See *Bernard Shaw: Agitations: Letters to the Press 1875–1950* (ed.
        Dan H. Laurence and James Rambeau 1985) p. 352.

482/21   **coal-burning:** Ibid.

482/24   **dangerous:** 'Power from the Tides', *The Times* 14 February
        1947, p. 5.

482/26   **Prospero:** 'The Atomic Bomb', *The Times* 20 August 1945,
        p. 5. *Agitations* p. 337.

482/31   **war:** *The Tempest*, Act V Scene I.

482/34   **difficulties:** 'The Atomic Bomb', *The Times* 20 August 1945,
        p. 5. *Agitations* p. 337.

482/38   **pain:** Revelations XXI 4.

483/ 4   **peace:** '"The Catholic Herald" Makes a Christmas Appeal:
        Grant Amnesty to All War and Political Prisoners', *Catholic
        Herald* 20 December 1946, p. 1.

483/26   **them?:** 'Turn the Whole Lot Loose', *Daily Express* 3 October
        1946, p. 1.

483/29   **directions:** *Shaw the Villager and Human Being* p. 30.

483/33   **wrong:** *CP*7 p. 18.

483/35   **ourselves?:** 'Turn the Whole Lot Loose', *Daily Express* 3
        October 1946, p. 1.

483/38   **perfection:** G.B.S. to Mrs J. M. Fell, 18 June 1946 (Texas).

484/11   **party:** 'Reflections on the Elections', *Forward* 4 August 1945,
        p. 1.

484/21   **date:** G.B.S. to Nancy Astor, 10 February 1950 (Reading).

484/21   **Pioneer:** *Tribune* 14 May 1948.

484/25   **into fact:** *Tribune* 21 May and 4 June 1948.

484/27   **understood:** 'Rebuilding Babel', *The Times* 19 August 1948,
        p. 6. *Agitations* pp. 345–7.

484/32   **agony:** Ibid.

484/35   **fairy:** 'Shaw 40 Years Later – Eric Bentley Speaks His Mind
        on Eleven Neglected Plays: *Getting Married, Overruled, On the
        Rocks*, and others', *Shaw: The Neglected Plays* (ed. Alfred
        Turco, Jr); *Shaw: The Annual of Bernard Shaw Studies*, vol. 7
        (1987) p. 28.

484/37   **development:** G.B.S. to Claire Madden, 12 August 1946
        (privately owned).

484/last   **Westminster:** *CP*7 p. 208.

485/ 3   **woman:** Ibid., p. 209.

485/ 7   **numbers:** G.B.S. to Eirene Lloyd Jones, n.d. [c. 25 June 1945], *CL4* p. 745.

485/ 9   **for it:** G.B.S. to Claire Madden, 5 July 1946 (privately owned).

485/15   **achieved:** G.B.S. to Claire Madden, 12 August 1946 (privately owned).

485/17   **Idea:** *Wife and Citizen*, December 1948.

485/23   **London:** See R. F. Rattray, *Bernard Shaw: A Chronicle* (1951) p. 282.

485/26   **national theatre:** Raymond Mander and Joe Mitchenson, *Theatrical Companion to Shaw* (1954) p. 300.

485/last **miracle:** *CP7* pp. 307–10.

486/ 6   **next one:** Ibid., p. 311.

486/ 8   **thought:** *Picture Post* 30 July 1949.

486/12   **Manners:** *CP7* p. 303.

486/16   **manners:** Ibid., p. 375.

486/19   **us:** Ibid., p. 316.

486/31   **reconciled:** Ibid., p. 403.

486/39   **years:** Ibid., p. 382.

486/40   **fables:** Ibid., p. 383.

487/15   **forwards:** Ibid., p. 464.

487/20   **monster:** Charles A. Berst, *Bernard Shaw and the Art of Drama* (1973) p. xx.

487/21   **amateurs:** G.B.S. to Siegfried Trebitsch, 16 February 1949, Shaw/Trebitsch letters p. 453.

487/34   **floor:** *CP7* p. 489.

487/39   **in Shakespeare:** Ibid., p. 470.

488/ 1   **Shakespeare:** Sally Peters, 'Shaw's Double Dethroned', *Shaw: The Neglected Plays* (ed. Alfred Turco, Jr) pp. 301–16.

488/ 4   **myself:** *CP7* pp. 470–1.

488/10   **descended:** Hesketh Pearson, *Bernard Shaw* (1975 rev. edn) p. 11.

488/11   **playwrighting:** Archibald Henderson, *George Bernard Shaw: Man of the Century* (1956) p. 3.

488/19   **them:** *CP7* p. 469.

488/26   **the end:** Jakob Welti in an unsigned notice in *Zürcher Zeitung* 22 October 1948. See *Shaw: The Critical Heritage* (ed. T. F. Evans 1976) p. 376.

488/28   **greater:** 'Bernard Shaw Replies to "An Unprovoked Act"', *Tribune* no. 594, 28 May 1948, p. 1.

489/ 9   **myself:** Siegfried Trebitsch, *Chronicle of a Life* (1953) p. 390.

489/13   **prosperous:** G.B.S. to Trebitsch, 2 April 1941 and 25 August 1941, Shaw/Trebitsch letters pp. 402–3, 408.

489/17   **failed:** G.B.S. to Carl B. Mahler, 25 January 1943 (privately owned).

489/25   **ever:** G.B.S. to Trebitsch, 8 August 1942, Shaw/Trebitsch letters p. 412.

489/28   **times:** G.B.S. to Trebitsch, 22 February 1945, Shaw/Trebitsch letters, p. 420.

489/30   **again:** Ibid.

489/35   **Isles:** *Chronicle of a Life* p. 395.

489/40   **nonsense:** G.B.S. to Trebitsch, late March 1946, Shaw/Trebitsch letters p. 429

490/3   **90:** Ibid.

490/7   **as I was:** *Chronicle of a Life* p. 401.

490/9   **stick:** G.B.S. to Trebitsch, 28 September 1945, Shaw/Trebitsch letters p. 427.

490/11   **world:** *Chronicle of a Life* p. 394.

490/21   **help it:** G.B.S. to Trebitsch, 13 March 1946, Shaw/Trebitsch letters p. 428.

490/26   **you knew:** G.B.S. to Trebitsch, 8 September 1944, Shaw/Trebitsch letters p. 419.

490/28   **old age:** G.B.S. to Trebitsch, 17 August 1941, *CL*4 p. 612 (Shaw/Trebitsch letters p. 406).

490/last   **at all:** G.B.S. to Trebitsch, 28 September 1945, 13 July 1946, 28 July 1946, 23 October 1946, 23 May 1948, Shaw/Trebitsch letters pp. 427, 434, 435, 437, 444 (*CL*4 pp. 818–19).

491/5   **years:** G.B.S. to Trebitsch, 23 May 1948, *CL*4 p. 819 (Shaw/Trebitsch letters p. 445).

491/9   **again:** G.B.S. to Trebitsch, 13 March 1946, Shaw/Trebitsch letters p. 429.

491/11   **my life:** *Chronicle of a Life* p. 405.

491/14   **airy:** Ibid., p. 401.

491/16   **over 40:** G.B.S. to Trebitsch, 22 March 1949, Shaw/Trebitsch letters p. 455.

491/18   **imminent:** G.B.S. to Trebitsch, 29 November 1948, Shaw/Trebitsch letters p. 451.

491/19   **fortune:** *Chronicle of a Life* p. 391.

491/22   **my heart:** Ibid., p. 392.

491/26   **Shaw:** Ibid., p. 393.

491/27   **matters:** G.B.S. to Trebitsch, 29 May 1941, Shaw/Trebitsch letters p. 405.

491/35   **for you:** G.B.S. to Trebitsch, 16 February 1949 and 18 November 1949, Shaw/Trebitsch letters pp. 453, 459.

491/38   **business:** G.B.S. to Trebitsch, 23 November 1949 and 7 September 1950, Shaw/Trebitsch letters pp. 460, 470.

491/last   **my life:** Ernest Mandowsky, 'European Encounters', *Jerusalem Post* 10 November 1950. See Shaw/Trebitsch letters p. 427.

492/Ep. **of you:** 'Goodbye, Goodbye'. Shaw B.B.C. broadcast on his 90th birthday, 26 July 1946. See *Platform and Pulpit* (ed. and with an introduction by Dan H. Laurence 1962) p. 294.

492/ 5 **meditation:** G.B.S. to William Maxwell, 31 May 1946, *CL4* p. 769.

492/ 7 **anything:** 'G.B.S. is Ninety Today: My Birthday', *News Chronicle* 26 July 1946, p. 2.

492/11 **happily:** *Dear Mr Shaw* p. 211.

492/17 **others:** Ibid., p. 209.

492/28 **year:** *Bernard Shaw: A Bibliography* vol. 2, D17, p. 836.

492/29 **newsreelers:** G.B.S. to Denis Johnston, 28 June 1946 (copy privately owned).

492/last **over me:** G.B.S. to Mrs A. W. Tuke, 2 June 1946 (copy privately owned).

493/ 4 **fires:** *The Times* 26 July 1946.

493/10 **biographer:** Ibid.

493/27 **longer:** 'Goodbye, Goodbye'. See *Platform and Pulpit* p. 293.

493/35 **London:** G.B.S. to John Masefield, 26 July 1946, *CL4* p. 773.

494/ 3 **missionary:** G.B.S. to Sydney Cockerell, 29 September 1944, *CL4* p. 725.

494/ 7 **disgraced her:** G.B.S. to P. J. Heron, 10 February 1946, *CL4* p. 765.

494/11 **faces:** 'Shaw Speaks to his Native City', *New York Journal-American* 17 and 18 March 1946. See *The Matter with Ireland* (ed. and with introduction by Dan H. Laurence and David H. Greene 1962) p. 294.

493/13 **lethal:** G.B.S. to William Maxwell, 31 May 1946, *CL4* p. 770.

494/18 **of it:** G.B.S. to Herbert Samuel, 12 November 1946, *CL4* p. 784.

494/24 **off it:** G.B.S. to Patrick O'Reilly, n.d. [July 1946], *CL4* p. 772.

494/26 **world:** G.B.S. to Allan M. Laing, 8 February 1948 (North Carolina).

494/29 **to do:** *New York Times* 5 March 1936.

494/33 **reach:** G.B.S. to Sidney Webb, 26 March 1946 (Texas).

494/36 **we can:** G.B.S. to Sidney Webb, 29 April 1943, *CL4* p. 668.

494/last **a drunk:** G.B.S. to Sidney Webb, 26 October 1945, *CL4* p. 756.

495/ 1 **something:** *G.B.S. 90: Aspects of Bernard Shaw's Life and Work* (ed. Stephen Winsten 1946) p. 46.

495/ 5 **politics:** G.B.S. to Sidney Webb, 26 March 1946 (Texas).

495/ 9 **enterprise:** 'Election Prospects as I See Them', *Daily Mail* 5 November 1949, p. 4.

495/10 **driving licence:** 'Divorce Law Reform', *The Times* 14 July 1950, p. 7.

495/32   **U.S.S.R.:** 'Bernard Shaw on the Dock Strike', *Daily Worker* 30 June 1948, p. 2.

495/39   **pronounce:** G.B.S. to Dodd, Mead & Company, 12 July 1948, *CL4* p. 826.

496/ 6   **attend to:** *Bernard Shaw's Rhyming Picture Guide to Ayot Saint Lawrence* (1950) p. 30.

496/11   **people go:** Lilli Palmer, *Change Lobsters – and Dance: An Autobiography* (1976) pp. 191, 199.

496/18   **disturb them:** G.B.S. to Frances Day, 13 December 1949, *CL4* pp. 858–9.

496/25   **spoon:** Richard Stoddard Aldrich, *Gertrude Lawrence as Mrs A: an Intimate Biography of the Great Star by Her Husband* (1956) pp. 233–4.

496/26   **whistle now!:** Kingsley Martin, *Editor* (1968) p. 107.

496/31   **engaging:** James Lees-Milne, *Prophesying Peace* (1977) p. 20.

496/32   **beard:** William Saroyan, *New Republic* CXV, 22 July 1946.

497/ 2   **country:** R. da Costa, 'Pilgrimage to Bernard Shaw', *Palestine Post* 14 November 1947. See also *Shaw: Interviews and Recollections* (ed. A. M. Gibbs 1990) pp. 523–4.

497/ 4   **for him:** Tom Pocock, *Alan Moorehead* (1990) p. 230.

497/ 6   **walking:** John Mason Brown, 'Back to Methuselah: a Visit to an Elderly Gentleman in a World of Arms and the Man', *Saturday Review of Literature* 22 July 1944. See *Shaw: Interviews and Recollections* p. 521.

497/ 8   **the most:** Tom Pocock, *Alan Moorehead* p. 231.

497/11   **ever seen:** John Mason Brown, loc. cit.

497/14   **people:** St John Ervine, 'Bernard Shaw', *The Spectator* 10 November 1950. See *Shaw: Interviews and Recollections* p. 506.

497/15   **lonely:** G.B.S. to Ada Tyrrell, 14 July 1949, *CL4* p. 852.

497/20   **him up:** Margaret Wheeler to Roy Perrott, *Sunday Times* 31 July 1983.

497/25   **a time:** Margaret Wheeler to G.B.S., 22 January 1944 (privately owned).

497/27   **hobby:** G.B.S. to Margaret Wheeler, 29 January 1944 (privately owned).

497/35   **her up:** Margaret Wheeler to G.B.S., 2 February 1944 (privately owned).

497/38   **things:** Margaret Wheeler to G.B.S., 1 September 1944 (privately owned).

498/ 1   **possible:** G.B.S. to Margaret Wheeler, 25 March 1944, *CL4* p. 703.

498/ 6   **families:** G.B.S. to Margaret Wheeler, 10 July 1944 (*CL4* pp. 717–18); 12 April 1944 (privately owned); 28 June 1945 (*CL4* pp. 746–7). See also *CL4* p. 703.

498/ 7   **help you:** G.B.S. to Margaret Wheeler, 15 March 1944 (privately owned).

498/11   **consider:** Margaret Wheeler to G.B.S., 20 April 1944 (privately owned).

498/14   **to you:** Margaret Wheeler to G.B.S., 3 September 1947 (privately owned).

498/15   **at all:** G.B.S. to Margaret Wheeler, 22 March 1947 (privately owned).

498/18   **interested:** G.B.S. to Margaret Wheeler, 26 April 1944, 24 May 1946 (privately owned).

498/22   **practise on:** Margaret Wheeler to G.B.S., 26 July 1948 (privately owned).

498/24   **with you:** Margaret Wheeler to G.B.S., 2 May 1944 (privately owned).

498/29   **myself:** G.B.S. to Margaret Wheeler, 25 March 1944, *CL*4 p. 703.

498/31   **frightened:** Margaret Wheeler to G.B.S., 23 January 1947 (privately owned).

498/35   **to them:** Margaret Wheeler to G.B.S., 20 April 1944 (privately owned).

498/36   **charmer:** G.B.S. to Margaret Wheeler, 30 September 1944 (privately owned).

498/38   **at me:** Margaret Wheeler to G.B.S., 2 May 1944 (privately owned).

499/ 5   **alone:** Margaret Wheeler to G.B.S., 3 September 1947 (privately owned).

499/ 8   **must write:** *CP*7 p. 307.

499/ 9   **Meg:** G.B.S. to Margaret Wheeler, 6 January 1948, *CL*4 p. 809.

499/36   **results:** See Janet Dunbar, *Mrs G.B.S.: A Biographical Portrait of Charlotte Shaw* (1963) pp. 314–15.

500/ 7   **revenge:** *Irish Times* 21 August 1954.

500/14   **knife:** G.B.S. to W. L. Mulry, 22 March 1944, *CL*4 p. 702.

500/30   **best:** G.B.S. to John Wardrop, 22 December 1943, *CL*4 p. 687.

500/39   **Eire:** G.B.S. to Thomas Bodkin, 7 March 1944 (National Gallery of Ireland).

501/ 3   **career:** Clause 40 of Shaw's will. Vide supra p. 112, this volume.

501/ 9   **cranks:** 'A King's Spelling: Letters and Sounds', *The Times* 15 April 1941, p. 6.

501/12   **speech:** Preface to Richard Albert Wilson, *The Miraculous Birth of Language* (1941 edn) p. 26.

501/16   **sanity:** 'The Author as Manual Laborer', *The Author* LIV, Summer 1944, pp. 45–7.

501/19   **gung:** 'Orthography of the Bomb: Save as you Spell', *The Times* 27 December 1945, p. 2.

501/32   **impossible:** *CP2* p. 421.

501/37   **London:** *CP4* p. 671.

501/39   **alphabet:** G.B.S. to Matthew Forsyth, 3 November 1936, *CL4* p. 444.

502/ 2   **mountain:** 'Orthography of the Bomb: Save as you Spell', *The Times* 27 December 1945, p. 2.

502/ 9   **printing:** 'The Simplified Spelling Proposals', *The Times* 25 September 1906, p. 6.

502/11   **cranks:** G.B.S. to I. J. (Sir James) Pitman, 16 September 1941, *CL4* p. 619.

502/14   **risk:** Preface to *The Miraculous Birth of Language* pp. 32–3.

502/16   **damp:** 'The Simplified Spelling Proposals', *The Times* 25 September 1906, p. 6.

502/18   **speak it:** *CP4* p. 659.

502/21   **shorthand:** G.B.S. to Henry Drummond, 29 November 1927 (copy privately owned).

502/24   **language:** G.B.S. to Hannen Swaffer, 26 February 1938, *CL4* p. 495.

502/28   **money:** 'A King's Spelling: Letters and Sounds', *The Times* 15 April 1941, p. 6.

502/36   **good:** *Letter on Alphabet Reform* (Laurence, *Bernard Shaw: A Bibliography* A244). See also *The Author* (Summer 1944) and *George Bernard Shaw on Language* (ed. Abraham Tauber 1965 cdn) pp. 79–86.

502/38   **turn:** G.B.S. to James Pitman, 19 July 1944, BL Add. MS 50555 ff. 85–7.

502/last   **scheme:** loc. cit. (A244).

503/ 4   **concerned:** G.B.S. to James Pitman, 19 July 1944, BL Add. MS 50555 ff. 85–7.

503/12   **business:** Ibid.

503/32   **survive:** See *George Bernard Shaw on Language* p. 84.

504/ 3   **will win:** G.B.S. note for F. E. Loewenstein drafted to the President of the Linguaphone Institute, September 1948 (Texas).

504/15   **too old:** G.B.S. to James Pitman, 19 July 1944, BL Add. MS 50555 ff. 85–7; 16 December 1947 (copy privately owned).

504/18   **function?:** Hesketh Pearson, *Bernard Shaw* (1975 rev. edn) p. 465.

504/25   **nations:** *The Independent Shavian* (USA) vol. 1, no. 3, April 1963.

504/31   **sh:** Preface to Wilson, *The Miraculous Birth of Language* p. 21.

504/34   **and paper:** 'A King's Spelling: Letters and Sounds', *The Times*
          15 April 1941, p. 6.

504/39   **significance:** Hesketh Pearson, *Bernard Shaw* (1975 rev. edn)
          p. 465.

505/ 6   **command:** G.B.S. to R. J. Hayes, 6 December 1945, *CL4*
          p. 761.

505/10   **Trust?:** G.B.S. to Donald McLeod Matheson, 5 October 1943,
          CL4 pp. 681–2.

505/12   **beautiful:** James Lees-Milne, *Prophesying Peace* pp. 19–20.

505/16   **settled:** *Daily Herald* 3 November 1950.

506/13   **emergency:** G.B.S. to F. N. Hornsby, 16 February 1949, *CL4*
          pp. 839–40.

506/18   **I use:** G.B.S. to F. N. Hornsby, 17 May 1949 (Texas).

506/21   **Green:** G.B.S. to Blanche Patch, 23 May 1949, *CL4* p. 850.

506/37   **belongings:** G.B.S. to Nancy Astor, 27 June 1949 (Reading).

506/37   **beauty:** Ibid.

506/29   **shillings:** G.B.S. to Apsley Cherry-Garrard. See *Flyleaves* (ed.
          Dan H. Laurence and Daniel J. Leary 1977) p. 10.

507/ 2   **Harpagon:** Ibid., p. 9.

507/12   **name:** 'Man of the Half-Century?', *Leader Magazine* VII, 7
          January 1950, p. 8.

507/last **practice:** 'The Play of Ideas', *New Statesman* XXXIX, 6 May
          1950, pp. 510–11. Collected in *Shaw on Theatre* (ed. E. J.
          West 1958) pp. 289–94.

508/ 4   **of you:** *CP7* p. 675.

508/ 5   **the way:** Ibid., p. 677.

508/19   **thoughts:** *Shaw the Villager and Human Being* p. 27.

508/19   **luck!:** Hesketh Pearson, *Bernard Shaw* (1975 rev. edn) p. 498.

508/31   **cannot:** 'G.B.S. on the A-Bomb', *Reynolds News* 6 August
          1950, p. 4.

508/33   **spotting it:** *Shaw the Villager and Human Being* p. 30.

508/last **dead:** Ibid.

509/ 4   **acquaintance:** G.B.S. to George Cornwallis-West, 26
          February 1941, *CL4* p. 600.

509/13   **end it:** G.B.S. to Edward Esher, 8 May 1947, *Cavalcade* 22 July
          1950.

509/15   **wake again:** G.B.S. to the Very Rev. W. R. Inge, 28 May
          1948, *CL4* p. 820.

509/19   **great age:** G.B.S. to Maung Ohn, n.d. [c. 1 May 1950], *CL4*
          p. 863.

509/22   **lioness:** *Shaw the Villager and Human Being* p. 26.

509/25   **on you:** Ibid., p. 146.

509/29   **there:** Ibid., p. 33.

509/32   **see him:** Ibid., p. 49.

509/35   **or two:** *CP*7 p. 307.

509/38   **interest:** *Shaw the Villager and Human Being* p. 52.

510/ 4   **house:** Ibid., p. 49.

510/11   **stoical:** Ibid., p. 303.

510/17   **fairly comfortable:** *Manchester Guardian* 12 September 1950.

510/18   **very comfortable:** *Lancashire Evening Post* 12 September 1950.

510/19   **again:** *Daily Express* 13 September 1950.

510/20   **loose:** *Shaw the Villager and Human Being* p. 297.

510/31   **station:** See *CL*4 p. 879.

510/37   **mile:** *Daily Express* 14 September 1950.

511/ 2   **circumstances:** *Manchester Guardian* 22 September 1950.

511/ 5   **opposition:** *Shaw the Villager and Human Being* pp. 298–9.

511/29   **in peace:** Account written by Eleanor O'Connell for Hesketh
          Pearson (privately owned) and partially quoted in Hesketh
          Pearson, *Bernard Shaw* (1975 rev. edn) pp. 507–8.

511/31   **hundred:** *Shaw the Villager and Human Being* p. 302.

511/33   **prefaces:** *Daily Express* 18 September 1950.

511/36   **alive:** *CP*3 p. 237.

511/last **Bernard Shaw:** *Shaw the Villager and Human Being* p. 88.

512/ 6   **thank you:** *Manchester Guardian* 6 October 1950.

512/14   **again:** *Shaw the Villager and Human Being* p. 262.

512/15   **for me:** Ibid., p. 35.

512/21   **not you:** Ibid.

512/26   **outside?:** Valerie Pascal, *The Disciple and His Devil* (1971)
          pp. 203–4.

512/28   **clothes:** Esmé Percy, 'Memories of Bernard Shaw', *British
          Peace Committee News Letter*, March–April 1956, collected in
          Shaw: Interviews and Recollections p. 528.

512/30   **itself:** *Shaw the Villager and Human Being* p. 34.

512/39   **more:** *Daily Mail* 13 October 1950.

513/ 4   **with you:** Esmé Percy, 'Memories of Bernard Shaw'. See
          Shaw: Interviews and Recollections p. 529.

513/14   **Mrs Warren:** See *CL*4 p. 882.

513/18   **already:** Eileen O'Casey, *Sean* (ed. J. C. Trewin 1971) p. 210.
          See also Eileen O'Casey, *Cheerio, Titan: The Friendship
          between George Bernard Shaw and Eileen and Sean O'Casey*
          (1989) p. 128.

513/27   **atheist:** Thomas Mann, 'He was Mankind's Friend', *The
          Listener* 18 January 1951. Collected in *Shaw: The Critical
          Heritage* p. 402.

513/29   **individual:** See *CL*4 p. 883.

514/ 3   **face:** *Shaw the Villager and Human Being* p. 35.

514/ 4   **widow:** *Chips: The Diaries of Sir Henry Channon* (ed. Robert Rhodes James 1967) p. 448.

514/17   **of loss:** St John Ervine, *Bernard Shaw: His Life, Work and Friends* (1956) p. 594.

514/19   **now am:** G.B.S. to Ada Tyrrell, 8 June 1950, *CL*4 p. 867.

514/24   **socks off:** *Sunday Times* 31 July 1983.

514/25   **to me:** *Shaw the Villager and Human Being* p. 88.

515/ 3   **birds:** G.B.S. to Sydney Cockerell, n.d. [assigned to 3 May 1946], *CL*4 p. 767.

515/ 4   **ground:** Clause 1 of Charlotte Shaw's will. Vide supra p. 91, this volume.

515/last   **performance?:** Lilli Palmer, *Change Lobsters – and Dance* p. 200.

VOLUME FOUR
The Last Laugh

3/ 6   **alphabet:** *Lancashire Evening Post* 22 March 1951.

3/15   **figures:** See *George Bernard Shaw on Language* (ed. Abraham Tauber 1965 edn) p. 79.

4/ 7   **chaos:** Speech at Harvard University by George Marshall, United States Secretary of State, 5 June 1947. The total sum lent by the United States to Britain between April 1948 and December 1950 was $2,694,300,000.

4/36   **chose:** *Time and Tide* 22 December 1951.

5/13   **scale:** *The Times* 24 November 1951.

5/15   **appeal:** *Manchester Guardian* 24 November 1951.

5/24   **house:** *The Times* 24 November 1951.

5/31   **disapproval:** St John Ervine, *Bernard Shaw: His Life, Work and Friends* (1956) p. 598.

6/ 1   **place:** *Time and Tide* 15 December 1951.

6/ 3   **flop:** *Manchester Guardian* 10 August 1953.

6/17   **Shaw:** *The Star* 3 December 1951.

7/ 6   **right:** *Irish Times* 1 December 1951.

7/13   **say where:** *Manchester Guardian* 4 December 1951.

7/20   **nations:** *Irish Times* 1 December 1951.

7/24   **insults:** Ibid.

7/33   **subject:** *Irish Independent* 1 December 1951.

7/37   **parties:** *Manchester Guardian* and *Daily Telegraph* 4 December 1951.

8/ 2   **go there:** *Belfast News-Letter* 1 December 1951.

8/ 6   **intercourse:** *Irish Times* 1 December 1951.

8/12   **margin:** *Manchester Guardian* 4 December 1951.

8/15   **speculate:** Ibid.

8/18   **Mrs G.B.S.:** *The Bulletin and Scots Pictorial* 21 December 1951, *Daily Express* 17 December 1951.

8/24   **palaces:** *News Chronicle* 2 April 1952.

8/33   **£94,000?:** Ibid.

8/37   **year:** Ibid.

9/ 7   **bequest:** *Irish Independent* 19 August 1954.

9/19   **counties:** Letter from Aidan J. McGovern 14 June 1990.

9/22   **Trust:** Bank of Ireland to Michael Holroyd, 20 December 1990.

10/32   **1906:** G.B.S. to Public Trustee, 21 July 1910 (Public Trustee Office, London).

11/1   **duties:** *Evening News* 22 March 1951, *Manchester Guardian* 24 March 1951.

11/4   **assessment:** *Daily Telegraph* 17 July 1951.

11/24   **statement:** *The Times* 25 April 1956.

12/6   **Disciple:** *Manchester Guardian* 18 January 1957.

12/23   *Money:* Shaw to James Pitman, 7 August 1947 (privately owned).

13/23   **what?:** *The Times* 19 January 1957.

13/27   **heart:** Ibid.

14/2   **ago:** 'The £ s d of G.B.S.', *New Statesman and Nation* 23 February 1957.

14/35   **mix:** *Manchester Guardian* 18 January 1957.

15/29   **court:** Barbara Smoker to Lois Solomon, 10 March 1957 (North Carolina). *CP*4 p. 589.

16/32   **wootsum?:** *CP*4 p. 589. See also Alphabet Edition of *Androcles and the Lion* (Penguin 1962) pp. 30, 31.

17/32   **politics:** *The Times* and *Manchester Guardian* 21 February 1957.

18/25   **case:** G.B.S. to James Pitman, 19 July 1944, BL Add. MS 50553 ff. 85–7.

18/30   **limit:** G.B.S. to James Pitman, 7 August 1944, *CL*4 p. 721.

19/1   **seen:** Barbara Smoker to Michael Holroyd, 15 December 1990.

19/28   **character:** *The Times* 6 March 1957.

19/33   **report:** Parliamentary Debates (*Hansard*). House of Commons Official Report, Wednesday 8 May 1957, cols 935–46.

20/6   **good:** Barbara Smoker to Lois Solomon, 10 March 1957 (North Carolina).

20/9   **God:** *The Shavian* no. 11, December 1957, p. 8.

20/12   **encouraging:** *The Times* 31 August 1957.

20/15   **deserve it:** *The Shavian* no. 11, December 1957, p. 8.

20/23   **literature:** Barbara Smoker, 'G.B.S. and the A.B.C.' in *Shaw – 'The Chucker-Out'* by Allan Chappelow (1969) p. 428.

21/7   **pity:** *The Times* Law Report, 20 December 1957.

21/23   **progress:** *The Times* 20 December 1957.

21/33   **heart:** *The Shavian* May 1958.

22/24   **man:** *George Bernard Shaw on Language* pp. 193, 194, 183.

22/37   *day:* Ibid., p. 182.

23/5   **produced:** *The Times* 1 January 1960.

23/20   **going:** Ibid.

23/24   **way:** Barbara Smoker, 'G.B.S. and the A.B.C.', in *Shaw – 'The Chucker-Out'* p. 443.

23/31   **alphabets:** Ibid., p. 449.
23/34   **autumn:** *The Times* 15 February 1961.
24/ 6   **huff:** Barbara Smoker to Michael Holroyd, 15 December 1990.
24/ 9   **typeface:** *Daily Mail* 26 February 1982.
24/36   **them:** The Shaw Alphabet Edition of *Androcles and the Lion* p. 12.
25/ 2   **abbreviations:** Ibid., p. 13.
25/ 7   **add:** *George Bernard Shaw on Language* p. 188.
25/27   **wake?:** Barbara Smoker, 'G.B.S. and the A.B.C.', in *Shaw – 'The Chucker-Out'* p. 452.
25/34   **Britain:** Gordon Walsh to Peter MacCarthy, 15 September 1967 (Public Trustee Office, London).
25/36   **meeting:** *The Times* 24 September 1968.
26/ 1   **before:** *Sunday Times* 8 March 1970.
26/ 3   **busy:** Ibid.
26/ 9   **interest:** Barbara Smoker, 'Man of Letters', *The Genius of Shaw* (ed. Michael Holroyd 1979) p. 221.
26/Ep. **Symphony?:** G.B.S. to Edward Elgar, 29 June 1932 (Worcester Record Office) 970.5.445 BA 7495.
27/ 5   **library:** *The Times* 18 December 1959.
27/ 8   **offer:** *Sunday Times* 26 March 1962.
27/12   **3d:** *The Times* 27 January 1966.
27/16   **collections:** 'Objectives of the British Library', *The Independent* 9 April 1991.
27/20   **benefit:** *Sunday Times* 25 March 1962.
28/23   **RADA?:** *Sunday Times* 11 July 1965.
29/ 2   **adored:** Karin Fernald to Michael Holroyd, 20 February 1991.
29/20   **Street:** *Sunday Times* 11 July 1965.
29/33   **things:** Richard O'Donoghue to Michael Holroyd, 11 February 1991.
29/36   **unworkable:** Karin Fernald to Michael Holroyd, 20 February 1991.
30/38   **arts:** Parliamentary Debates (*Hansard*). House of Commons Official Report, 17 December 1959, col. 1749.
31/14   **available:** Ibid., cols 1752, 1753.
31/33   **Museum:** G.B.S. to Floryan Sobieniowski, 29 May 1924 (Dartmouth College Library, Hanover, New Hampshire).
31/last **acceptance:** G.B.S. to Edy Craig [1929], BL Add. MS 43800 ff. i–ii.
32/ 2   **Museum:** Clause 6 of Shaw will.
32/ 7   **fulfilled:** Parliamentary Debates (*Hansard*), 17 December 1959, cols 1754, 1756.
32/15   **Ireland:** Ibid., col. 1750.

32/18   pictures: *Sunday Times* 25 March 1962.

32/31   show: Raymond Keaveney to Nicole Paulissen, 16 February 1989 (Chatto & Windus).

33/ 5   smaller: *Sunday Press* 10 March 1991.

33/24   collection: Michael Wynne to Michael Holroyd, 22 February 1991.

33/28   benefactor: Michael Wynne to Michael Holroyd, 8 May 1991.

33/36   own: Ibid.

35/19   debts: G.B.S. to Charles Charrington, 8 November 1895, *CL*1 p. 569.

35/30   mortgages: G.B.S. to Ellen Terry, 13 September 1899, *CL*2 pp. 101–2 (*A Correspondence* p. 352).

36/ 1   date: *Carlow Nationalist* 1 April 1916.

36/ 4   roof: Quoted in G. B. Shaw Festival Brochure, Carlow, Ireland, 10–12 May 1991.

36/ 8   restricted: P. J. Griffin to G.B.S., 16 April 1915 (Carlow).

36/10   perpetuity: Ibid.

36/21   is: G.B.S. to P. J. Griffin, 24 April 1915, *CL*3 p. 293.

36/25   effect: G.B.S. to the Right Reverend Patrick Foley, Lord Bishop of Kildare and Leighlin, 15 February 1918 (Carlow).

36/33   on it: *EPWW* p. 105.

36/37   way: G.B.S. to William Fitzmaurice, 22 March 1916 (Carlow).

37/ 3   China: G.B.S. to William Fitzmaurice, 29 March 1917 (Carlow).

37/ 8   edifice: G.B.S. to William Fitzmaurice, 15 February 1918 (Carlow).

37/12   things: Quoted in G. B. Shaw Festival Brochure, Carlow, Ireland, 10–12 May 1991.

37/20   municipalized: *EPWW* p. 105.

37/27   country: G.B.S. to Éamon de Valera, 5 June 1945, *CL*4 p. 744.

37/35   town: G.B.S. to Éamon de Valera, 5 May 1945, *CL*4 p. 743.

38/19   money: G.B.S. to the Permanent Secretary of the Royal Swedish Academy, 18 November 1926, *CL*4 p. 34.

39/ 9   advertised: Memorandum on the Anglo-Swedish Literary Foundation by Terry Carlborn, Cultural Attaché, London, November 1980 (Swedish Embassy).

39/10   exhausted: G.B.S. note to F. E. Loewenstein, 12 March 1950 (Texas).

39/22   prizes: G.B.S. to Eaglefield Hall, 27 September 1918 (Hofstra).

39/last   sort: Stereotyped postcard, 1949, Dan H. Laurence, *Bernard Shaw: A Bibliography* (1983) vol. 2, D25, pp. 839–40.

39/ 5   benefits: Ibid.

40/ 7   **property:** Ibid.

40/23   **largest:** Introduction by Dan H. Laurence to *'So He Took His Hat Round', a facsimile of a manuscript by Bernard Shaw* (Washington University Libraries, St Louis, 1981).

40/26   **bequests:** St John Ervine, *Bernard Shaw: His Life, Work and Friends* (1956) p. 596.

40/last   **generation:** *'So He Took His Hat Round'.*

41/11   **greatness:** Sean O'Casey to National Trust, March 1951 (NT).

41/12   **with you:** Gabriel Pascal to National Trust, March 1951 (NT).

41/14   **upon it:** *The Times* 19 March 1951.

41/22   **staggered:** *News of the World* 18 March 1951.

41/29   **Ayot:** *Evening News* 30 March 1951.

42/ 3   **famous:** Ibid.

42/14   **earth:** *Daily Graphic* 2 April 1951.

42/26   **factotum:** G.B.S.'s inscription on F. E. Loewenstein's copy of *SSS* (privately owned).

42/35   **stands for:** F. E. Lowenstein to National Trust, 17 August 1944 (NT).

42/37   **guidance:** National Trust to Loewenstein, 18 August 1944 (copy, NT).

42/last   **back:** Ibid., 7 December 1944.

43/ 7   **study:** National Trust to G.B.S., 11 December 1944 (copy, NT).

43/15   **posted:** F. E. Loewenstein to James Lees-Milne at the National Trust, 14 December 1944 (NT).

43/21   **at most:** G.B.S. to James Lees-Milne, 19 December 1944 (NT).

43/25   **afraid:** James Lees-Milne to G.B.S., 21 December 1944 (copy, NT).

43/27   **agree:** James Lees-Milne to F. E. Loewenstein, 21 December 1944 (copy, NT).

43/28   **answer:** F. E. Loewenstein to James Lees-Milne, 24 December 1944 (NT).

44/ 2   **upkeep:** Memorandum by J. F. W. Rathbone, 8 November 1950 (NT).

44/ 8   **tenancy:** G.B.S. to Donald McLeod Matheson, 10 November 1943, *CL4* p. 685.

44/13   **bills:** Memorandum by Rathbone, 8 November 1950 (NT).

44/20   **chairs:** Ibid.

44/36   **particularly:** James Lees-Milne to F. E. Loewenstein, 15 January 1945 (copy, NT).

45/ 7   **memorial:** Loewenstein to National Trust, 20 November 1950 (NT).

45/17   **anybody:** Harold Nicolson to J. F. W. Rathbone, 28 November 1950 (NT).

45/20   **intensely:** Memorandum by J. F. W. Rathbone, 16 November 1950 (NT).

45/23   **necessary:** Harold Nicolson and James Lees-Milne to J. F. W. Rathbone, 11 December 1950 (NT).

45/25   **Trust:** J. F. W. Rathbone to Lord Crawford, 17 November 1950 (NT).

45/28   **envied:** See *CL4* p. 693.

46/ 6   **it well:** J. F. W. Rathbone to Lord Crawford, 17 November 1950 (NT).

46/10   **made up:** Ibid.

46/21   **problem:** Ibid.

46/37   **being:** Jack Rathbone to F. E. Loewenstein, 13 January 1951 (copy, NT).

47/ 8   **interest:** *Time and Tide* 29 December 1951.

47/ 9   **wonderfully:** *Shaw the Villager and Human Being: A Biographical Symposium* (ed. Allan Chappelow 1961) p. 35.

47/21   **with Shaw:** *Birmingham Post* 31 October 1951.

47/31   **reading:** *Manchester Guardian* 11 August 1953.

47/34   **with him:** *Evening Standard* 15 December 1951.

48/ 8   **self-denial:** *Time and Tide* 15 December 1951.

48/30   **loss:** Memorandum, 4 January 1954 (NT).

48/36   **competition:** *Birmingham Post* 31 October 1951.

49/ 6   **finance:** Jack Rathbone to Lord Crawford (copy, NT).

49/13   **neck:** C. J. Casserley to National Trust, 18 January 1957 (NT, Hughenden Manor).

50/11   **available:** Clause 46 of Shaw's will. Vide supra p. 114, this volume.

50/15   **to him:** Dan H. Laurence, *Bernard Shaw: A Bibliography* (1983) vol. 1, p. xii.

50/24   **engaged:** Agreement of 17 February 1950 (privately owned).

51/last   **commitment:** *Bernard Shaw: A Bibliography* vol. 1, p. xiii.

52/12   **wrong:** T. F. Evans, 'The First Quarter', *The Shavian* vol. 3, no. 5, Summer 1966 p. 11.

52/31   **ways:** Barbara Smoker to Michael Holroyd, 19 June 1990.

53/13   **secrecy:** 'Future Productions of "Pygmalion"', *The Times* 20 December 1956.

53/21   **avoided:** *The Times* 4 December 1956.

53/27   **affair:** Graham Greene to *The Times*, 3 December 1956, Graham Greene, *Yours etc.: Letters to the Press 1945–89* (selected and introduced by Christopher Hawtree 1989) pp. 53, 52.

54/Ep. **Shaw:** Brigid Brophy, 'I Never Eat Dead', *The Shavian* vol. 3, no. 6, Winter 1966–7, p. 7.

54/21 **mouse:** *Sunday Graphic* 4 October 1953.

54/29 **reputation:** *New York Times* 18 November 1952.

55/ 7 **into:** John Keates, *Howard Hughes* (1966) p. 248.

55/16 **meet:** *New York Times* 18 November 1952.

55/24 **picture:** Ibid.

55/27 **flop:** Valerie Pascal, *The Disciple and His Devil* (1970) p. 225.

55/30 **R.K.O.:** *The New Republic* 15 June 1953.

55/32 **life:** *The Disciple and His Devil*, pp. 245–6.

56/ 3 **men:** Ibid., p. 318.

56/15 **them:** Hesketh Pearson, 'A Shaw Musical', *The Shavian*, September 1958, p. 5.

56/16 **music:** Shaw letter 3 February 1948. See *Dear Mr Shaw: Selections from Bernard Shaw's postbag* (compiled and ed. Vivian Elliot 1987) p. 124.

56/18 **repeated:** G.B.S. to Siegfried Trebitsch, 23 July 1921, Shaw/Trebitsch letters p. 224.

56/26 **circumstances:** G.B.S. to Trebitsch, 28 April 1931, *CL*4 p. 236 (Shaw/Trebitsch letters p. 319).

56/31 **transaction:** G.B.S. to Trebitsch, 19 February 1942, *CL*4 p. 628 (Shaw/Trebitsch letters p. 411).

57/ 1 **outrage:** G.B.S. letter 3 February 1948. See *Dear Mr Shaw* p. 124.

57/ 5 **lifetime:** Siegfried Trebitsch to Archibald Henderson, June 1953. See Shaw/Trebitsch letters p. viii.

57/ 8 **pennyless:** Trebitsch to Archibald Henderson, July 1953. See Shaw/Trebitsch letters p. viii.

57/13 **attack:** Shaw/Trebitsch letters p. 471.

60/15 **experience:** Eric Bentley, *Bernard Shaw* (2nd British edn 1967) p. ix.

60/17 **Bentley:** Kenneth Muir, 'The Greatness of Shaw', *Essays in Criticism*, April 1957.

60/26 **again:** *English Drama (excluding Shakespeare)* ed. Stanley Wells (1975), no. 14: 'Shaw' p. 238.

61/34 **come:** *CP*6 pp. 839–40.

62/ 4 **police:** See Michael Holroyd, *Bernard Shaw* vol. 3 (1991) p. 175.

62/15 **sister:** G.B.S. to Frank Harris, 20 June 1930, *CL*4 p. 188.

62/18 **débâcle:** G.B.S. to Demetrius O'Bolger [February 1916], *CL*3 p. 369.

63/ 1 **cake:** Rex Harrison, *A Damned Serious Business* (1990) p. 156.

63/ 3 **business:** Charles Higham, *A Biography of Audrey Hepburn* (1985 edn) p. 132.

63/11   **Pygmalion:** David Shipman, *The Story of Cinema* vol. 2 (1984)
         p. 865.
63/29   **work:** Norman Sherry, *The Life of Graham Greene* vol. 1: *1904–
         1939* pp. 291, 206.
63/37   **innocence:** *New York Times* 17 February 1957.
64/ 2   **await her:** John Gielgud to Michael Holroyd, 11 April 1991.
64/18   **frailty:** *The Times* 12 May 1957.
64/23   **blame:** Otto Preminger, *An Autobiography* (1977) p. 153.
64/25   **later:** Typescript of Norman Sherry interview with Otto
         Preminger, 1978 (privately owned).
64/29   **killer:** Quentin Falk, *Travels in Greeneland: The Cinema of
         Graham Greene* (1984) p. 125.
64/32   **sandwich:** *Herald Tribune* 19 March 1958.
64/32   **pirates:** *Evening News* 19 June 1957.
64/33   **confidence:** National Theatre Programme (opening
         performance, London, 15 November 1983).
65/ 3   **verbal:** *New York Times* 17 February 1957.
65/17   **done:** *CP6* pp. 74–5.
65/23   **audiences:** *New Statesman* 14 September 1957, in Graham
         Greene, *Yours etc.* p. 62.
65/26   **interesting:** *Sight and Sound* Summer 1957 p. 38.
65/30   **author:** Graham Greene, *Reflections* (selected by Judith
         Adamson 1990) pp. 203–4.
65/36   **tone:** Graham Greene, *Yours etc.* p. 62.
66/ 8   **that:** Quoted in Quentin Falk, *Travels in Greeneland* p. 126.
66/10   **Bernard Shaw:** *CP3* p. 393.
66/16   **faithful:** Eric Batson, 'Shaw in Metrocolor', *The Shavian* June
         1959, p. 3.
66/23   **Pinter:** Dirk Bogarde to Michael Holroyd, 13 April 1991.
67/ 3   **daily:** Ibid.
67/26   **big:** Donald P. Costello, *The Serpent's Eye: Shaw and the Cinema*
         (1966) p. 149.
67/35   **better:** Kirk Douglas, *The Ragman's Son: An Autobiography*
         (1988) p. 291.
68/14   **screened:** *New York Times* 14 September 1958.
68/19   **dismissal:** Philip Kemp, *Lethal Innocence: The Cinema of
         Alexander Mackendrick* (1991) pp. 165, 167.
68/36   **film:** *Guardian* 5 September 1959.
69/ 5   **picture:** *New York Times* 14 September 1958.
69/ 8   **completely:** *The Ragman's Son* p. 291.
69/ 9   **continues:** *The Times* 25 April 1960.
69/23   **comic:** Michael Sellers, *P.S. I Love You: Peter Sellers 1925–1980*
         (1981) p. 67.

69/25   **Secombe:** R. J. Minney, *'Puffin' Asquith* (1973) p. 184.

69/30   **men:** A. E. Hotchner, *Sophia: Living and Loving* (1979) p. 117.

69/38   **baffling:** Peter John Dyer, *Sight and Sound* Autumn 1960, p. 152.

70/ 6   **work:** Quoted in R. J. Minney, *'Puffin' Asquith* p. 185.

70/12   **absurdity:** Ibid., p. 186.

70/17   **Shaw:** *The Shaw Review* (Pennsylvania) vol. IV, no. 2, May 1961, p. 36.

70/33   **zoo:** *Sight and Sound* Summer 1967, p. 155.

70/35   **made:** Hugh Leonard to Michael Holroyd, 18 February 1991.

71/ 9   **Greenaway:** Philip French to Michael Holroyd, 17 June 1991.

71/19.   **career:** Norman Wisdom to Michael Holroyd, 19 September 1991.

73/ 7   **surprise:** *The Times* 9 November 1956.

73/22   **vehicles:** *New Statesman* 25 May 1984.

74/16   **rodeo:** W. Stephen Gilbert, *Plays and Players* September 1976.

74/22   **mask:** Irving Wardle, 'The Plays', in *The Genius of Shaw* (ed. Michael Holroyd 1979) p. 143.

74/26   **revival:** *The Times* 31 December 1970.

74/30   **phase:** *The Times* 7 September 1965.

74/last   **ebb:** *The Times* 13 February 1973.

76/ 4   **sell:** Barry Morse, 'Niagara and I', *The Shavian*, Spring 1986, pp. 10–12. See also Brian Doherty, *Not Bloody Likely: The Shaw Festival 1962–1973* (Don Mills, Ontario, 1974).

76/34   **seen:** T. F. Evans to Michael Holroyd, 28 December 1990.

77/ 3   **point:** Christopher Newton to Michael Holroyd, 27 September 1991.

77/12   **continent:** *The Guardian* 30 June 1980.

77/14   **original:** Herbert Whittaker to Michael Holroyd, 4 December 1989.

77/26   **part:** G.B.S. to Ellen Terry, 6 September 1896, *CL*1 p. 647 (*A Correspondence* p. 46).

77/31   **wood:** G.B.S. to Laurentia McLachlan, 26 July 1946 (Stanbrook Abbey, Worcestershire).

77/32   **death:** G.B.S. to Herbert Samuel, 12 November 1946, *CL*4 p. 784.

77/last   **may be:** G.B.S. to Peter Watts, 3 October 1946, *CL*4 p. 780.

78/19   **similarities:** Margery M. Morgan, *The Shavian Playground* (1972) p. 3.

78/28   **abnormal:** *CP*1 p. 12.

78/37   **better:** *CP*1 p. 13.

79/ 8   **timely:** Sheridan Morley, *Review Copies: Plays and Players in London 1970–74* (1975) p. 182.

79/10   **future:** *Plays and Players*, December 1975.
79/16   **universe:** Leonard Woolf, *Beginning Again: An Autobiography of the Years 1911 to 1918* (1964) p. 120.
79/32   **future:** Eric Bentley on 'Shaw Dead', *Envoy*, February 1951. See *Shaw: The Critical Heritage* (ed. T. F. Evans 1976) p. 404.
80/ 5   **period:** *The Times* 11 August 1990.
81/36   **unreal:** *CP2* p. 919.
82/ 4   **love:** *Ellen Terry and Bernard Shaw: A Correspondence* (ed. Christopher St John 1931) pp. xlv–xlvi.
82/16   **discoverers:** *CP5* p. 331.
82/34   **prophecies:** *CP4* pp. 487, 479.
83/last **detachment:** Hugh Kingsmill, *The Progress of a Biographer* (1949) p. 14.

POSTSCRIPT

(The page/line numbers in brackets refer to the limited edition of Volume 4, *The Last Laugh*, published April 1992 in the UK only.)

85/14 (19)   **reigns:** *CP1* p. 253.
85/24 (29)   **writer:** *Evening Press* 20 July 1991.
86/ 2 (6)   **wreck:** *Irish Press* 28 May 1991.
86/ 3 (7)   **devastation:** *The Times* 17 August 1991.
86/ 8 (12)   **matters:** *Sunday Press* 20 July 1991.
86/11 (15)   **derisory:** Ibid.
87/ 5 (9)   **masters!:** *CP1* p. 225.
87/10 (14)   **date:** Ibid., p. 135.
87/34 (37)   **success:** *Sunday Telegraph* 24 November 1991.
87/35 (38)   **stuff:** *Guardian* 21 November 1991.
87/38 (88/2)   **play:** *The Times Literary Supplement* 24 November 1991.
88/ 2 (5)   **relations:** *The Spectator* 23 November 1991.
89/ 5 (9)   **changes:** *Independent* 17 May 1991.

ACKNOWLEDGEMENTS

My valiant team has stayed with me to the end: Sarah Johnson (who made my words legible), Margery Morgan (who helped to make them more accurate), Richard Bates (who transferred the corrected text on to disc) and Vivian Elliot who has switched her attention from quotations to notations. I am sincerely grateful to them all.

Alison Samuel at Chatto & Windus has continued steering a hazardous course between house style and my own way of doing things. Joe Fox at Random House in the United States has kept a distant eye on everything.

I would like to renew my thanks to all those individuals and institutions mentioned in the previous three volumes (*The Search for Love*, *The Pursuit of Power* and *The Lure of Fantasy*), and in particular to Bernard Dukore, T. F. Evans, David and Susannah Marcus, Richard O'Donoghue, Barbara Smokcr and Roma Woodnutt for their additional help with *The Last Laugh*. I also owe thanks to Sir Richard Attenborough, Sir Dirk Bogarde, K. Byrne, Karin Fernald, Mark Fisher, Philip French, Tom Geddes, Sir John Gielgud, Geoffrey C. Grant, Baroness Jeger, Helen Langdon, Mark Le Fanu, Hugh Leonard, Nora Lever, Donal McGahon, Aidan J. McGovern, Wolf Mankowitz, Michael Martin, Christopher Newton, Anthea Palmer, His Honour Judge David Pitman, Michael Purcell, Norman Sherry, Norman Wisdom, Michael Wynne.

I have also received assistance from a number of organizations: Academy of Motion Picture Arts and Sciences (California), Anglo–Swedish Literary Foundation, British Film Institute, Forás Éireann, International Shaw Summer School (Dublin), National Trust, Shaw Birthplace Museum Trust (Dublin), Shaw Festival Committee at Carlow, Shaw Society (Britain), Cultural Section of the Embassy of Sweden (London), Swedish English Literary Translators' Association, Trust and Custodial Services Bank of Ireland (Dublin).

CUMULATIVE INDEX

(Roman numerals I II III IV refer to Volumes I–IV; figures in brackets for Vol. IV refer to the single volume, entitled *The Last Laugh*, published as a limited edition in the UK in April 1992.)

Abbey Theatre, Dublin, II 82–3, 88, 89, 90, 96, 97, 228–9, 230–1, 379, 381, III 195, 196, 197, 199
Aberdeen, Lord, II 228
Aberdeen Daily Journal, I 381
Academy, The, II 205, 217, 226
Achurch, Janet (Mrs Charles Charrington):
  I. childhood, 255; marriages, 255; physical appearance, 255; first meeting with Shaw, 254; success as Nora in *A Doll's House*, 254; as inspiration for *The Cassone*, 278; Shaw writes to, 255–6; Australian tour with Charrington, 255, 256, 258; in revival of *A Doll's House*, 257, 258; mounts season of plays with Charrington, 257; his failure as her business manager, 257–9, 314, 370; addiction to alcohol and morphia, 258, 320–1, 371–2; her play as inspiration for *Mrs Warren's Profession*, 291, 292, 293; at first night of *Arms and the Man*, 302; and Florence Farr, 259, 307, 308; Shaw's 'spiritual intercourse' with, 310–11; and *Candida*, 314, 315–16, 318, 319, 320–5, 345, 370, 372, 378; Shaw on acting of, 345, 370, 374–5, 376, 377–8; in Wilkie Collins's *The New Magdalen*, 369–70; Ellen Terry on, 370, 377, 381, 382; illness, 371–2; Shaw's confidence diminishes in, 373, 375; pregnancy, 373–4; in *Little Eyolf*, 374–5, 376–7; replaced by Mrs Campbell, 376; Bertha Newcombe and, 428, 429; miscarriage, 377; as Cleopatra, 377; in *A Doll's House* again, 378; Shaw out of love with, 379, 380, 382, 383; in *Candida*, 381–3; plates 22A, 22B
  II. Charlotte Shaw's attitude to, 4; as Lady Cicely in *Captain Brassbound's Conversion*, 29, 292; Shaw turns his back on, 92; Shaw compares with Mrs Campbell, 295; death, 395
  III. Shaw compares Sybil Thorndike to, 79

mentioned: II 309, III 77, 128. *See also* Shaw to, *under* Shaw
Actors' Orphanage, II 102, 103, IV 40, 104 (108)
Actresses' Franchise League, III 183
Adam, Ronald, III 395
Adams, Elbridge, IV 88
Adam-Smith, Janet, IV viii
Adelphi Play Society, the, II 197
Adelphi Terrace, London, Shaw's flat in, II 9, 189, 280, 314, 368, III 27, 79, 119, 138, 446
Adler, Alfred, III 265
Adler, Friedrich, III 145; Shaw to, III 144
Admirable Bashville, The, see Shaw: *Works*
Adventures of the Black Girl in Her Search for God, The, see Shaw: *Works*
Agate, James, III 24, 58, 98, 415
Albert, Sidney P., IV 88
Alexander, King of Yugoslavia, III 181
Alexander Sir George, I 318–19, 337, 342, 343, 383, II 150, 236, 289, 294, 296, 324
Allan, Andrew, IV 75
Allen, Clifford, II 364
Allen, Grant, I 401; Shaw to, II 7
Allgood, Sara, II 402
Alma-Tadema, Lawrence, III 78
alphabetical reform: Shaw's battle for, III 444, 501–5; Shaw's will and, III 500, IV 3, 6, 10–21 *passim*, 22, 25, 110–12 (114–16); and competition for new 'alfabet', IV 21–3; *see also Androcles and the Lion* (translit.) *under* Shaw: *Works*
Altrincham, Lord, III 160
Amateur Musical Society, Lee's, I 24, 30, 42, 44, 45, 46, 47
American-Irish Historical Society, III 500
American Repertory Theatre, IV 90
American Theater Council, IV 20
American Vegetarian, The, III 364
American Women's Club, Dublin, IV 85 (86)
Ames, Captain Lionel G., III 447
Amrita Bazar Patrika, III 507

435

481

Michael Holroyd was born in 1935 and is half-Swedish and partly Irish. In 1968 his *Lytton Strachey* was hailed as a landmark in contemporary biography and, six years later, his *Augustus John* confirmed his place as one of the most influential modern biographers. The three volumes of his Life of Shaw, *The Search for Love*, *The Pursuit of Power* and *The Lure of Fantasy*, appeared to critical acclaim between 1988 and 1991.

Michael Holroyd is a past Chairman of the Society of Authors and past President of English PEN. He is a member of the Arts Council of Great Britain and Chairman of its Advisory Panel on Literature. He lives in London and is married to Margaret Drabble.

The title on page iii is set in
Caslon Old Face,
the design favoured by Bernard Shaw
when he was directing the manufacture
of his books at R. & R. Clark, Edinburgh.
The text is set in Linotron Ehrhardt,
a typeface derived from similar seventeenth-century
Dutch sources as Caslon Old Face.

𐑨𐑯𐑛𐑮𐑩𐑒𐑤𐑰𐑟 𐑯 𐑞 𐑤𐑲𐑩𐑯

𐑐𐑮𐑴𐑤𐑪𐑜

[𐑴𐑝𐑼𐑗𐑫𐑼: 𐑓𐑪𐑮𐑦𐑕𐑑 𐑕𐑬𐑯𐑛𐑟, 𐑮𐑹𐑦𐑙 𐑝 𐑤𐑲𐑩𐑯𐑟, 𐑒𐑮𐑦𐑕𐑗𐑩𐑯 𐑣𐑦𐑥 𐑓𐑱𐑯𐑑𐑤𐑦.

𐑩 𐑡𐑳𐑙𐑜𐑩𐑤 𐑐𐑭𐑔. 𐑩 𐑤𐑲𐑩𐑯𐑟 𐑮𐑹, 𐑩 𐑥𐑧𐑤𐑩𐑙𐑒𐑩𐑤𐑦 𐑕𐑳𐑓𐑼𐑦𐑙 𐑮𐑹, 𐑒𐑳𐑥𐑟 𐑓𐑮𐑪𐑥 𐑞 𐑡𐑳𐑙𐑜𐑩𐑤. 𐑦𐑑 𐑦𐑟 𐑮𐑦𐑐𐑰𐑑𐑩𐑛 𐑯𐑽𐑼. 𐑞 𐑤𐑲𐑩𐑯 𐑤𐑦𐑥𐑐𐑕 𐑓𐑮𐑪𐑥 𐑞 𐑡𐑳𐑙𐑜𐑩𐑤 𐑪𐑯 𐑔𐑮𐑰 𐑤𐑧𐑜𐑟, 𐑣𐑴𐑤𐑛𐑦𐑙 𐑳𐑐 𐑣𐑦𐑟 𐑮𐑲𐑑 𐑓𐑹𐑐𐑷, 𐑦𐑯 𐑢𐑦𐑗 𐑩 𐑣𐑿𐑡 𐑔𐑹𐑯 𐑕𐑑𐑦𐑒𐑕. 𐑣𐑰 𐑕𐑦𐑑𐑕 𐑛𐑬𐑯 𐑯 𐑒𐑪𐑯𐑑𐑩𐑥𐑐𐑤𐑱𐑑𐑕 𐑦𐑑. 𐑣𐑰 𐑤𐑦𐑒𐑕 𐑦𐑑. 𐑣𐑰 𐑖𐑱𐑒𐑕 𐑦𐑑. 𐑣𐑰 𐑑𐑮𐑲𐑟 𐑑 𐑦𐑒𐑕𐑑𐑮𐑨𐑒𐑑 𐑦𐑑 𐑚𐑲 𐑕𐑒𐑮𐑱𐑐𐑦𐑙 𐑦𐑑 𐑩𐑤𐑪𐑙 𐑞 𐑜𐑮𐑬𐑯𐑛, 𐑯 𐑣𐑻𐑑𐑕 𐑣𐑦𐑥𐑕𐑧𐑤𐑓 𐑢𐑻𐑕. 𐑣𐑰 𐑮𐑹𐑟 𐑐𐑦𐑑𐑦𐑩𐑕𐑤𐑦. 𐑣𐑰 𐑤𐑦𐑒𐑕 𐑦𐑑 𐑩𐑜𐑧𐑯. 𐑑𐑽𐑟 𐑛𐑮𐑪𐑐 𐑓𐑮𐑪𐑥 𐑣𐑦𐑟 𐑲𐑟. 𐑣𐑰 𐑤𐑦𐑥𐑐𐑕 𐑐𐑱𐑯𐑓𐑩𐑤𐑦 𐑪𐑓 𐑞 𐑐𐑭𐑔 𐑯 𐑤𐑲𐑟 𐑛𐑬𐑯 𐑳𐑯𐑛𐑼 𐑞 𐑑𐑮𐑰𐑟, 𐑦𐑜𐑟𐑹𐑕𐑑𐑩𐑛 𐑢𐑦𐑞 𐑐𐑱𐑯. 𐑣𐑰𐑝𐑦𐑙 𐑩 𐑤𐑪𐑙 𐑕𐑲, 𐑤𐑲𐑒 𐑢𐑦𐑯𐑛 𐑦𐑯 𐑩 𐑑𐑮𐑪𐑥𐑚𐑴𐑯, 𐑣𐑰 𐑜𐑴𐑟 𐑑 𐑕𐑤𐑰𐑐.

·𐑨𐑯𐑛𐑮𐑩𐑒𐑤𐑰𐑟 𐑯 𐑣𐑦𐑟 𐑢𐑲𐑓 ·𐑥𐑩𐑜𐑽𐑮𐑩 𐑒𐑳𐑥 𐑩𐑤𐑪𐑙 𐑞 𐑐𐑭𐑔. 𐑣𐑰 𐑦𐑟 𐑩 𐑕𐑥𐑷𐑤, 𐑔𐑦𐑯, 𐑮𐑦𐑛𐑦𐑒𐑿𐑤𐑩𐑕 𐑤𐑦𐑑𐑩𐑤 𐑥𐑨𐑯 𐑣𐑵 𐑥𐑲𐑑 𐑚𐑰 𐑧𐑯𐑦 𐑱𐑡 𐑓𐑮𐑪𐑥 𐑔𐑻𐑑𐑦 𐑑 𐑓𐑦𐑓𐑑𐑦-𐑓𐑲𐑝. 𐑣𐑰 𐑣𐑨𐑟 𐑕𐑨𐑯𐑛𐑦 𐑣𐑺, 𐑢𐑷𐑑𐑼𐑦 𐑒𐑩𐑥𐑐𐑨𐑖𐑩𐑯𐑩𐑑 𐑚𐑤𐑵 𐑲𐑟, 𐑕𐑧𐑯𐑕𐑦𐑑𐑦𐑝 𐑯𐑪𐑕𐑑𐑮𐑦𐑤𐑟, 𐑯 𐑩 𐑝𐑧𐑮𐑦 𐑐𐑮𐑦𐑟𐑧𐑯𐑑𐑩𐑚𐑩𐑤 𐑓𐑪𐑮𐑦𐑛; 𐑚𐑳𐑑 𐑣𐑦𐑟 𐑜𐑫𐑛 𐑐𐑶𐑯𐑑𐑕 𐑜𐑴 𐑯𐑴 𐑓𐑻𐑞𐑼: 𐑣𐑦𐑟 𐑸𐑥𐑟 𐑯 𐑤𐑧𐑜𐑟 𐑯 𐑚𐑨𐑒, 𐑞𐑴 𐑢𐑲𐑼𐑦 𐑝 𐑞𐑺 𐑒𐑲𐑯𐑛, 𐑤𐑫𐑒 𐑖𐑮𐑦𐑝𐑩𐑤𐑛 𐑯 𐑕𐑑𐑸𐑝𐑛. 𐑣𐑰 𐑒𐑨𐑮𐑦𐑟 𐑩 𐑚𐑦𐑜 𐑚𐑳𐑯𐑛𐑩𐑤, 𐑦𐑟 𐑝𐑧𐑮𐑦 𐑐𐑫𐑼𐑤𐑦 𐑒𐑤𐑨𐑛, 𐑯 𐑕𐑰𐑥𐑟 𐑑𐑲𐑼𐑛 𐑯 𐑣𐑳𐑙𐑜𐑮𐑦.

𐑣𐑦𐑟 𐑢𐑲𐑓 𐑦𐑟 𐑩 𐑮𐑭𐑞𐑼 𐑣𐑨𐑯𐑛𐑕𐑩𐑥 𐑐𐑨𐑥𐑐𐑼𐑛 𐑕𐑤𐑨𐑑𐑼𐑯, 𐑢𐑧𐑤 𐑓𐑧𐑛 𐑯 𐑦𐑯 𐑞 𐑐𐑮𐑲𐑥 𐑝 𐑤𐑲𐑓. 𐑖𐑰 𐑣𐑨𐑟 𐑯𐑳𐑔𐑦𐑙 𐑑 𐑒𐑨𐑮𐑦, 𐑯 𐑣𐑨𐑟 𐑩 𐑕𐑑𐑬𐑑 𐑕𐑑𐑦𐑒 𐑑 𐑣𐑧𐑤𐑐 𐑣𐑼 𐑩𐑤𐑪𐑙].